Edmund Venables, Johannes Friedrich Bleek, Adolf Hermann Heinrich Kamphausen, G. H Venables

An Introduction to the Old Testament

Vol. II

Edmund Venables, Johannes Friedrich Bleek, Adolf Hermann Heinrich Kamphausen, G. H. Venables

An Introduction to the Old Testament
Vol. II

ISBN/EAN: 9783744661317

Printed in Europe, USA, Canada, Australia, Japan

Cover: Foto ©Lupo / pixelio.de

More available books at **www.hansebooks.com**

INTRODUCTION

TO THE

OLD TESTAMENT.

VOL. II

AN INTRODUCTION

TO THE

OLD TESTAMENT.

BY
JOHANNES BLEEK.

EDITED BY
ADOLF KAMPHAUSEN.

Translated from the Second Edition (Berlin, 1865,) by
G. H..VENABLES, Esq.

EDITED BY
REV. EDMUND VENABLES, M.A.
Canon Residentiary of Lincoln.

IN TWO VOLUMES.

VOL. II.

LONDON: BELL AND DALDY, YORK STREET,
COVENT GARDEN.

1869.

LONDON: PRINTED BY WILLIAM CLOWES AND SONS, STAMFORD STREET
AND CHARING CROSS.

CONTENTS OF VOL. II.

FIRST DIVISION—*continued from Vol. I.*

THE PROPHETICAL BOOKS. § 176–269, p. 1–229.
GENERAL REMARKS UPON HEBREW PROPHETS AND PROPHECY.
§ 176–195, p. 1–40.

	PAGE
§ 176. General Aim, Nature, and Importance of Hebrew Prophecy ...	1
§ 177. Various Ideas as to Hebrew Prophecy	3
§ 178. Consideration of the Hebrew and Greek Names given to Hebrew Prophets, and the Ideas attached to them	4
§ 179. Other Names given to the Hebrew Prophets	7
§ 180. Nature of the Prophetic Office	9
§ 181. Hebrew Prophets—Their Mode of Life, Dress, &c.	11
§ 182. Their Origin	12
§ 183. Mode of Prophetical Inspiration	13
§ 184. Prophetical Inspiration by means of Visions	15
§ 185. Form and Mode of Delivery of Prophetical Utterances	16
§ 186. Symbolical Actions performed by Prophets	18
§ 187. Purport and Aim of the Prophetical Utterances	20
§ 188. References to the Future in the Prophetical Discourses	23
§ 189. Consideration of the various Opinions as to the Prophetical Predictions	24
§ 190. General Character of the Prophetic Discourses	27
§ 191. Messianic Predictions—Their Character	30
§ 192. Messianic Predictions—Special Details as to Time, Circumstances, &c.	32
§ 193. Messianic Predictions—Their Proper Interpretation	34
§ 194. Method of Fixing the Dates of the various Prophetical Writings	36
§ 195. The Authors of the Prophetical Scriptures	39

THE BOOK OF ISAIAH. § 196–205.

§ 196. Isaiah—His Name, Family, and Date of his Ministry	41
§ 197. Nature of Contents of the Book—Its three Sections	44
§ 198. Question as to Unity of Authorship	44

Contents.

		PAGE
§ 199.	Authorship of the third Section of the Book	47
§ 200.	Review of Contents—Chaps. i–xii.	50
§ 201.	,, ,, Chaps. xiii–xxiii.	53
§ 202.	,, ,, Chaps. xxiv–xxxv.	57
§ 203.	,, ,, The Historical Section	59
§ 204.	Date of the Compilation—Its Place in the Canon	60
§ 205.	Messianic Character of the Prophecies in the Book of Isaiah ...	61

THE BOOK OF JEREMIAH. § 206–219.

§ 206.	Jeremiah—His Name, Date, Parentage, and Circumstances ...	64
§ 207.	Prophecies belonging to the Reign of Josiah	67
§ 208.	,, belonging to the Reigns of Jehoiakim and Jehoiachin	69
§ 209.	,, belonging to the Reign of Zedekiah	74
§ 210.	,, in Zedekiah's Reign, and Historical Events connected therewith	77
§ 211.	Jeremiah's Imprisonment—Prophecies delivered during this Period	79
§ 212.	Prophecies uttered after the Capture of Jerusalem—Fate of Jeremiah	82
§ 213.	Different Arrangement of the Book in the Hebrew Text and in the LXX	84
§ 214.	Various opinions as to the respective Values of the Hebrew and Greek Recensions	87
§ 215.	Origin of the Greek Recension	89
§ 216.	Consideration of the Variations between the Hebrew and Greek Recensions	89
§ 217.	Cause of the Variations—Question as to the Priority of the two Recensions	92
§ 218.	Origin of the two Recensions	95
§ 219.	General Character of Jeremiah's Prophecies and Discourses ...	99

THE LAMENTATIONS. § 220.

§ 220.	Title—Position in the Canon—Date of Composition and Contents	101

THE BOOK OF EZEKIEL. § 221–228.

§ 221.	Name of the Prophet—His Family, Locality, and Period of Ministry	105
§ 222.	Review of Contents—Chaps. i–xxiv	106
§ 223.	,, ,, Chaps. xxv–xxxii.	108
§ 224.	,, ,, Chaps. xxxiii–xxxix.	110
§ 225.	,, ,, Chaps. xl–xlviii.	114
§ 226.	Reality of the Prophetic Visions	116
§ 227.	Written Record of the Prophecies—Their Compilation and Order of Succession	117
§ 228.	Language and Peculiarities of Style—Characteristics of his Prophetical Ministry	118

Contents.

THE TWELVE LESSER PROPHETS. § 229–253

	PAGE
§ 229. Their Collective Name—Compilation and Order of Succession	120

1.—THE BOOK OF HOSEA. § 230–233.

§ 230. Name of the Prophet—Period of his Prophetical Ministry ... 121
§ 231. Review of Contents—Chaps. i–iii.—Symbolical Actions ... 123
§ 232.   „   „   Chaps. iv–xiv.—Nature and Dates of the several Utterances 125
§ 233. General Character of the Prophecies—Their Style and Language 127

2.—THE BOOK OF JOEL. § 234–236.

§ 234. Name—General Purport—Mode of Interpretation 128
§ 235. Its Date 132
§ 236. Literary and Poetical Characteristics 136

3.—THE BOOK OF AMOS. § 237, 238.

§ 237. Name—Date and Period of his Ministry 137
§ 238. Divisions of the Prophecy 138

4.—THE BOOK OF OBADIAH. § 239.

§ 239. Name—Nature of the Contents—Date of the Prophecy ... 141

5.—THE BOOK OF MICAH. § 240.

§ 240. Name—Birthplace—Date—Purport of the Prophecies... ... 144

6.—THE BOOK OF NAHUM. § 241.

§ 241. Name—Birthplace—Date and Contents of Prophecy 148

7.—THE BOOK OF HABAKKUK. § 242.

§ 242. Name—Division of the Book—Date and Nature of the Prophecy 151

8.—THE BOOK OF ZEPHANIAH. § 243.

§ 243. Name—Descent—Nature of his Prophecy—Date 154

9.—THE BOOK OF HAGGAI. § 244.

§ 244. Name—Description—Nature of his Prophecy 157

10.—THE BOOK OF ZECHARIAH. § 245–249.

§ 245. Name—Division of the Book—The first Division 159
§ 246. The second Division of the Book—Opinions as to its Author ... 161
§ 247. Date of the Prophecies in the second Division of the Book—First Section 164

	PAGE
§ 248. Date of the Prophecies in the second Division of the Book—Second Section...	169
§ 249. Cause of the Union of the Older Prophecies with the Book of Zechariah	173

11.—THE BOOK OF MALACHI. § 250.

§ 250. Name and Person of the Prophet—Date and Contents of the Prophecy	175

12.—THE BOOK OF JONAH. § 251–253.

§ 251. Person of the Prophet—Contents of the Book	179
§ 252. Origin of the Book—Historical Value—Object	181
§ 253. Historical Foundation of the Book	186

THE BOOK OF DANIEL. § 254–269.

§ 254. Position in the Canon—Review of Contents	190
§ 255. Various Opinions as to the Origin of the Book	197
§ 256. Unity of Authorship	199
§ 257. Origin and Authorship	201
§ 258. External Arguments for an Earlier or Later Date	202
§ 259. Internal Arguments against Daniel's being the Author	205
§ 260. The Author's Aim in the second Division in the Book	209
§ 261. Difficulties arising from the passage Dan. ix. 2	210
§ 262. Date of the Narrative—Greek Names for Musical Instruments	212
§ 263. Historical Difficulties of the Narrative	213
§ 264. The real Object of the Historical Section of the Book	218
§ 265. Similarities in the Narrative to the Events of a Later Date	219
§ 266. Typical References to Antiochus Epiphanes	222
§ 267. Author's Aim in the two first Chapters	223
§ 268. Historical Existence of Daniel and his Companions	225
§ 269. Value of the Book	228

THE POETICAL BOOKS. § 270–291.

THE PSALMS. § 270–278.

§ 270. Title—Division into five Books	230
§ 271. Origin—Superscriptions	231
§ 272. The Authors of the various Psalms	234
§ 273. Anonymous Psalms—Latest Date of any of the Psalms	237
§ 274. Origin and Formation of the Collection	239
§ 275. Review of the various Classes of Psalms, and their Contents	241
§ 276. The Separations between the Single Psalms	246
§ 277. Integrity of the Individual Psalms	248
§ 278. Slight Alterations in the Ancient Text	250

THE WRITINGS OF SOLOMON. § 279–285.

§ 279. Works attributed to Solomon	252

Contents.

1.—THE PROVERBS OF SOLOMON. § 280, 281.

§ 280. Title of the Book—Review of its Contents 252
§ 281. Origin of the Compilation 256

2.—THE SONG OF SOLOMON. § 282–284.

§ 282. Title, &c. 257
§ 283. Subject of the Book—Various Interpretations of its Contents ... 258
§ 284. Authorship—Age of Composition 261

3.—ECCLESIASTES, OR THE PREACHER. § 285.

§ 285. Authorship and Tendency of the Book 263

THE BOOK OF JOB. § 286–291.

§ 286. Nature of the Book—Review of Contents 268
§ 287. As to the Historical Character of Job's Person and Life ... 272
§ 288. Ideas asserted as to the Aim of the Author 275
§ 289. The Prologue and Epilogue—Their Author 278
§ 290. Elihu's Discourses—Opinions as to their Originality, Nature, and Aim 280
§ 291. Question as to the Authorship and Date of the Book 284

SECOND DIVISION.

HISTORY OF THE CANON OF THE OLD TESTAMENT. § 292–321.

§. 292. Nature and Method of the Investigation 289

A.—HISTORY OF THE CANON OF THE OLD TESTAMENT AMONG THE JEWS. § 293–306.

§ 293. The Book of the Law 290
§ 294. Nature and Extent of Nehemiah's Collection of Books 291
§ 295. Books included in Nehemiah's Collection 293
§ 296. Union of the Torah with the other Books in the Collection ... 296
§ 297. Reception into the Canon of the Books not included in Nehemiah's Collection 297
§ 298. Books not included in Nehemiah's Collection—Their Position in the Canon 299
§ 299. Completion of the Canon—Comparative Authority of later Books 301
300. The Canon among the Hellenistic Jews—The Apocrypha ... 302
§ 301. Philo's References to the Canonical Books only 305
§ 302. References in the New Testament to the Canonical Books only ... 306
§ 303. Absolute Completion and Limitation of the Hebrew Canon ... 307
§ 304. General Adhesion of the Hellenistic Jews to the Hebrew Canon ... 309
§ 305. Views of the various Jewish Sects as to the Hebrew Canon ... 310
§ 306. Various erroneous Ideas as to the Formation of the Canon ... 312

VOL. II.

B.—HISTORY OF THE CANON OF THE OLD TESTAMENT IN THE
CHRISTIAN CHURCH. § 307–321.

	PAGE
§ 307. Reception of the Hebrew Canon in the Christian Church—Relative Authority of the Apocryphal Books	315
§ 308. Melito's Old-Testament Canon	317
§ 309. Origen's List of the Canonical Books	318
§ 310. Lists of the Old-Testament Canon—In the Greek Church	321
§ 311. „ „ „ In the Latin Church	327
§ 312. Opinions as to the Apocrypha in the Western Church	333
§ 313. „ „ „ in the Greek Church	336
§ 314. Position of the Apocrypha in the Protestant Church	336
§ 315. „ „ in the Romish Church	340
§ 316. Decision as to the Apocrypha in the Greek Church	342
§ 317. Modern Opinions in the Protestant Churches as to the Apocrypha	344
§ 318. Considerations as to the Apocrypha	346
§ 319. Position and Authority of the Old Testament in the Christian Church	349
§ 320. Difference in the Value and Authority of the several Books of the Old Testament	352
§ 321. Conclusions as to the Value and Authority of the Apocrypha	353

THIRD DIVISION.

HISTORY OF THE TEXT OF THE CANON, FROM ITS FORMATION DOWN
TO OUR OWN TIME. § 322–365.

§ 322. Various Opinions as to the Integrity and Purity of the Hebrew Text	358
§ 323. Criticism of the Hebrew Text—Houbigant—Kennicott—De Rossi	361
§ 324. Results of Criticism and Collation of Manuscripts	363

A.—HISTORY OF THE EXTERNAL FORM OF THE TEXT. § 325–334.

§ 325. The twofold Hebrew Character—The Phœnician Character	365
§ 326. Relation between the Phœnician and Babylonian Characters	367
§ 327. Partial and Temporary Retention of the Ancient Phœnician Character	370
§ 328. Origin of the Later or Babylonian Character	373
§ 329. Opinions as to the Antiquity of the Hebrew Vowel-Points and Accents	375
§ 330. Various Proofs of the Novelty of the Vowel-Signs and Accents	378
§ 331. Date and Origin of the Introduction of Vowel-Signs	381
§ 332. The Division of the Text into Words	384
§ 333. The Division into Verses	385
§ 334. Divisions into Sections and Chapters	387

B.—INTERNAL HISTORY OF THE TEXT. § 335–365.

	PAGE
§ 335. Proofs of Extreme Care in its Early Transmission	391
§ 336. Comparison of the Hebrew Text with the Samaritan Pentateuch	391
§ 337. The Septuagint—Traditions as to its Origin	395
§ 338. Conclusions as to the Real Origin of the Septuagint	399
§ 339. Completion of the Septuagint—Nature of the Text	404
§ 340. The Name given to the Greek Translation	408
§ 341. Authority of the Septuagint in the Jewish and Christian Churches	408
§ 342. The Greek Translations of Aquila, Theodotion, Symmachus, and others	412
§ 343. Origen's Hexapla and Tetrapla—Their Aim and Nature ...	416
§ 344. Other Recensions of the LXX—Variations in Manuscripts ...	421
§ 345. The four chief printed Editions of the LXX	425
§ 346. Ancient Greek Translations	430
§ 347. The Vulgate—Ancient Latin Translations	431
§ 348. Jerome's Latin Translations	434
§ 349. Acceptance of Jerome's Translation as the Vulgate	437
§ 350. Chaldee Paraphrases or Targums	439
§ 351. The Peshito—Its Origin and Character	443
§ 352. Other Syriac Versions	446
§ 353. Arabic Translations from the Hebrew Text	447
§ 354. Persian Translations from the Hebrew Text	449
§ 355. Our Hebrew Text the Basis of the Ancient Translations ...	450
§ 356. Ancient Quotations from the Hebrew Text ... .:. ...	450
§ 357. Proofs from the Talmud of the Care devoted to the Hebrew Text	451
§ 358. The Keri and Ketib	454
§ 359. Ancient Alterations by the Scribes	457
§ 360. The Masora and Masoretic Notes	460
§ 361. The Western and Eastern Readings	462
§ 362. Early Readings and Manuscripts	463
§ 363. The Masoretic Text	464
§ 364. Printed Editions of the Hebrew Old Testament—Polyglots ...	465
§ 365. Various Editions of the Hebrew Old Testament	471

THE PROPHETICAL BOOKS.

GENERAL REMARKS UPON HEBREW PROPHETS AND PROPHECY.[1]

§ 176.—*General Aim, Nature, and Importance of Hebrew Prophecy.*

IN the Introduction to the historical books, we have seen that many of the earlier historical works of the Hebrews, quoted in the existing Books of the Old Testament, are shown, by their titles, to have had prophets for their au-

[1] Chr. Aug. Crusius (Professor at Leipzig, d. 1775), *Hypomnemata ad theol. propheticam*, 3 Parts, Leipzig, 1764–78 : the first part contains general remarks ; the two others treat of the separate prophets ; the third, however, is confined to Isaiah.—Hengstenberg, *Christologie des A. T.* 1st edit. i. 1 (1829) pp. 293-332. "The Nature of Prophecy." Revised and essentially improved in the 2nd edit. iii. 2 (1857), pp. 158–217.—Hitzig, *Der Prophet Jesaja*, 1833. Introd. pp. xxii–xxxii; *Der Prophetismus.*—Knobel, *Der Prophetismus der Hebräer vollständig dargestellt.* 2nd Part, Breslau, 1837.—Fried. Burchh. Köster, *Die Propheten des A. u. N. T. nach ihrem Wesen und Wirken dargestellt*, Leipzig, 1838.—Redslob, *Der Begriff des Nabi oder der soy. Propheten bei den Hebr.*, Leipzig, 1839.—J. Chr. K. Hofmann (of Erlangen), *Weissagung u. Erfüllung im A. und im N. T. Ein Theol. Vers.* 1st half, Nördl. 1841 ; 2nd half, 1844.—Ewald, *Die Propheten d. A. B.*, 1 vol. (1840), pp. 1–64.—Delitzsch, *Die bibl.-proph. Theologie*, its continuation by Crusius, and its latest development after Hengstenberg's *Christologie*, Leipzig, 1845.—Fr. Düsterdieck, *De rei propheticæ in Vet. Test. quum universæ tum Messianæ natura ethica*, Göttingen, 1852.—Laur. Reinke (Professor at Münster), *Beiträge zur Erklärung d. A. T.* Vol. 2 (Münster, 1853), pp. 1–202 ; *Allg. Einl. in die Weissagungen*, &c.—Bunsen, *Gott in der Gesch.* Part 1 (Leipzig, 1857), pp. 221–256. *Die leitenden Ideen des Weltanschauung der Hebr. Proph.*—A. Tholuck, *Die Propheten und ihre Weissagungen: Eine apolog.-hermen. Studie*, Gotha, 1860.—Karl Köhler, *Der Prophetismus der Hebräer u. die Mantik der Griechen in ihrem gegenseitigen Verhältniss*, Darmstadt, 1860.—Gust. Baur, *Geschichte der Alttest. Weissagungen.* 1st Part : *Die Vorgeschichte der Alttest. Weissagungen*, Giessen, 1861.—G. F. Oehler, *Ueber das Verhält. der Alttest. Prophetie zur heidnischen Mantik.* Tübingen, 1861 ; also, by the same author in Herzog's *Real-Encyclop.*, articles "*Prophetenthum des A. T.*," and "*Weissagung.*"

VOL. II. B

thors. We may, therefore, infer that, at least for a considerable period, the prophets were the chief historians among the people. Although there is not one of the existing historical books of the Old Testament which can be certainly proved to have been composed by an author who, during his lifetime, was looked upon by his people as a prophet, still we cannot doubt that the above-named histories, composed as they were by prophets, formed the ground-work of the greater part of the historical books as we have them. There are, on the other hand, a series of other works written by prophets, which may be called κατ' ἐξοχήν, *prophetical;* these are the so-called *Prophetæ Posteriores*, forming the second sub-division of the נְבִיאִים, or second division of the Books of the Old-Testament Canon.

These works, like the historical books, tend to the confirmation and completion of the Jewish theocracy, but keep this object in view in a more direct way. The historical books depict the development of the theocracy as shown in the fortunes of the people of Israel, either in the events just occurring, or in those of past ages; they bring to our view how Jehovah chose this nation as his own possession, and added to the Covenant he made with them the most glorious promises with respect to its fulfilment; but that the people frustrated this fulfilment by their repeated transgressions, and brought upon themselves frequent and continued punishments. But the prophetical books (in the more limited sense of the term) have directly in view that special form and condition of the theocracy which was existing in the prophets' time. They presuppose the bygone history of the people and God's guidance of them, also their transgressions and their punishments, and closely connect all these facts with the present time by setting forth that a continued opposition to Jehovah's Will will certainly, as before, draw down upon them the Divine vengeance. They announced, also, what was required of the people for removing and averting the Divine chastisements, and for hastening on the time when Jehovah might accomplish for them all His promised blessings. The earlier promises which had been given to their fathers are in these books repeated and amplified in favour of the pious and God-fearing; but, for the rebellious, and those who are stubborn in their disobedience, the severest Divine corrections are again threatened.

These prophetical books, therefore, both from their character and purport, are well qualified to serve as sources of history. They introduce us into all the circumstances of the people of Israel as they existed at the time of the prophets, both foreign and domestic, and also into their religious and political relations; these subjects, too, are generally dealt with in a far deeper and more impressive way than in the proper historical books, as, in the latter, many periods are but very briefly handled, and these are the very periods in which the prophetical agency was most active. But to us they cannot fail to be of special importance, inasmuch as they are lively witnesses to the fact that God continued to guide this people by men raised up by Him, and to lead them on to the advent of the great salvation which was to arise among them, and from them was to spread over the whole world.

§ 177.—*Various Ideas as to Hebrew Prophecy.*

Very various ideas have been formed, especially in modern times, with regard to the special characteristics of the Hebrew prophets, and the real nature of their ministry, of which these prophetical works are the result. The cause for this difference of opinion is plain: these works are too often considered with a prejudiced mind, and with definite preconceived opinions, which are sometimes biassed by the somewhat similar phenomena which existed among other nations of antiquity.

In earlier times, the almost exclusive idea of a prophet was that of a man who predicted future events; and the only distinction drawn between such a prophet and the soothsayers and seers among other nations was, that in the case of the former, the result fully showed that he was inspired by the Spirit of the true God. In modern times, on the other hand, the Divine inspiration of these men has often been too much thrown into the background, and their utterances have altogether been considered as being nothing but the result of their natural intellect and of purely human information. They have often been compared to the demagogues and popular orators among the Greeks, and their influence over the people has been sometimes represented as actually injurious. Some have gone so far as to ascribe to them the troubles and ultimate ruin of the Jewish Commonwealth. By others they have been looked upon as men who, at all events, were distinguished among their contemporaries by their talents, learning, and acumen, and were thus enabled to form and lay down decisions as to measures necessary for the state, and not unfrequently were in a position to throw a correct glance into the future. Others have regarded them merely as poets, endowed with a rich poetical fancy, and therefore liable to be misled in their ideas as to the events that were impending. It has been sometimes thought that past events were the sole subjects of their effusions, and that these, by means of a poetical fiction, were made to refer to future times.

Almost all these opinions are based upon some measure of truth, and their erroneous character arises chiefly from the fact that this is brought forward in a one-sided way, to the exclusion of other points of view which are kept too much in the background. The only way in which we can attain to a comprehensive and correct idea on the subject is by impartially considering the prophets themselves, and duly weighing all the various points in which their ministry is set before us in the prophetical writings; also, by studying all that is said upon the point in the historical books, with which, however, certain declarations in the New Testament should be compared.

§ 178.—*Consideration of the Hebrew and Greek Names given to Prophets, and the Ideas attached to them.*

As regards the *name* and *idea* of the prophets among the Hebrew people, the most usual designation in the Old Testament is נָבִיא. The root of this word, נבא, does not occur in the Hebrew in Kal, but only in Niphal and Hithpael, and in significations which are only derived from that of the noun, as denominative from נָבִיא. The question however, arises as to the proper signification of the root itself, and also as to the original meaning of the word נָבִיא, derived from that root. The root is very probably connected with נָבַע = *ebullire, scaturire*, Hiph. to bubble forth, to pour out; in the Arabic ئبّ = *indicare, annunciare*,

Hebrew Prophets—Their Name. 5

c. accus pers. נָבִיא may, therefore, be explained in a two-fold way : (*a*) passively, as the name of him who is taught or apprised of anything, viz., by God. Köster accepts this; and the form of the word is certainly favourable to this interpretation, as קָטִיל is properly a passive form. But the derivation of this signification from the fundamental meaning is rather unnatural, especially as Redslob explains it, who likewise urges a passive form : *poured into* = *breathed into*, *i.e.*, by the Spirit of God.[1] (*b*) The form קָטִיל, when it comes from intransitive verbs, has not unfrequently an intransitive meaning, as, *e.g.*, נָגִיד, *prince* (from נגד, *in fronte esse*), פָּלִיט, *fugitive*, צָעִיר, *small*, עָתִיר. Now, נבא, in its fundamental meaning, is not improbably an intransitive = *scaturire*; and, the idea being transferred to the *pouring forth of words*, may be translated *to speak*. The noun may, therefore, have had a signification corresponding with this, and (as Gesenius and others think) may have been really equivalent to *speaker*, and, specially, a *spokesman* or *interpreter*. The weight of probability is in favour of this view. This word is used early in reference to God's relation to men in the designation of a man who acted as the medium, the speaker and interpreter, between God and man.

That this was, in fact, the real idea of the נָבִיא is especially shown in the passage (Exod. vii. 1) :

נְתַתִּיךָ אֱלֹהִים לְפַרְעֹה וְאַהֲרֹן אָחִיךָ יִהְיֶה נְבִיאֶךָ

"I have made thee a god to Pharaoh : and Aaron thy brother shall be thy *Nabi*;"—thou shalt be, as it were, the inspirer, to suggest to him what he shall say, and he shall be thy spokesman to lay before Pharaoh all that thou suggestest. The same idea is otherwise expressed (Exod. iv. 16) :

וְדִבֶּר־הוּא לְךָ אֶל־הָעָם וְהָיָה הוּא יִהְיֶה־לְּךָ לְפֶה וְאַתָּה תִּהְיֶה־לּוֹ לֵאלֹהִים

The Nabi appears in these passages as a medium between God and man, who is to announce God's words to man in an intelligible way, just as Aaron intervened between Moses and Pharaoh, in order to make known to the latter all that Moses charged him with, or suggested to him (cf. Deut. xviii. 18): "I will raise them up a Prophet from

---

[1] Hupfeld explains it as "he who has received something which is suggested (cf. נאם) or instilled into him," so that נָבִיא denotes the prophet as the recipient of the revelation.

among their brethren, like unto thee, and will put my words in his mouth; and he shall speak unto them all that I shall command him." Also, cf. Jer. xv. 19: "Thou shalt be my mouth," כְּפִי תִהְיֶה = my prophet.

The idea, therefore, of a Nabi is not limited to the functions of a seer and predicter of *future* events; neither does the term denote (as many in modern times suppose) every poet or teacher of the people. It conveys the notion of an interpreter between God and man—a confidant, as it were, of God—one to whom Jehovah manifests Himself in order to announce to men that which He desires they shall know: referring either to future events, or to the disclosure of Divine mysteries, or even to instruction in moral laws.

Thus Abraham is called a *Nabi*, Gen. xx. 7: "Now, therefore restore the man his wife, for he is a נָבִיא, and he shall pray for thee and thou shalt live." In Ps. cv. 15. the patriarchs generally are called Jehovah's prophets (נְבִיאָי).

Philo, *De Monarchia*, i. 9, fin. p. 820, Ed. Par.: ἑρμηνεῖς γάρ εἰσιν οἱ προφῆται θεοῦ καταχρωμένου τοῖς ἐκείνων ὀργάνοις πρὸς δήλωσιν ὧν ἂν ἐθελήσῃ. *De Præmiis et Pœnis*, § 9, p. 918: ἑρμηνεὺς γάρ ἐστιν ὁ προφήτης ἔνδοθεν ὑπηχοῦντος τὰ λεκτέα τοῦ θεοῦ. Cf. *De Vita Mosis*, ii. 7, p. 659. *Quis rer. divin. hæres?* § 52, p. 517; § 53, p. 518. *De Special. Legibus quæ referuntur ad octavum, &c.*, § 8, p. 343. Ed. Mang.

If this is the proper meaning of the word, the Greek term προφήτης, as used in the LXX, is the most suitable translation of it; for προφήτης among the Greeks did not originally signify a mere predicter of future events; it derives its sense from πρόφημι, not in the meaning of "predicting," but as "uttering," *palam proferre;* προφήτης, therefore, is properly a *speaker*, who, as such, intervenes between two individuals, and makes known to one the words or the will of the other person in an intelligible way. Thus Dionys. *Halic.* ii. 73, the priests are called προφῆται τῶν θείων, *interpretes cultus divini* = ἐξηγηταί, with which it is there combined. In Diod. *Sic.* i. 2, history is called προφῆτις τῆς ἀληθείας, the mouth, as it were, through which truth is made known. In Plato, *Phædr.* p. 262, poets are called Μουσῶν προφῆται. The word is also used of the interpreter of an author, Themistius, *Orat.* xxiii. p. 290, Ἀριστοτέλους προφήτην, *Aristotelis interpretem*. Aristoph. *Aves* 972: ἐπέων προφήτης, *carminum interpres.* The term

Hebrew Prophets—Their various designations. 7

προφήτης is, however, specially used for those who understood the broken and dark expressions of the μάντις when in a state of ecstasy, and explained them to others, and their occupation is called προφητεία. It is thus expressly defined in Plato, *Timæus*. Ed. Bip. ix. p. 391 *seq.* Ed. Bekker, P. iii. Vol. ii. p. 101 *seq.* (De Wette, § 202 *a*). Cf. Pindar, μαντεύεο, Μοῦσα, προφητεύσω δ' ἐγώ. At an earlier date among the Greeks this distinction between the μάντις and προφήτης was not always observed, and a seer in a state of ecstasy was sometimes called προφήτης; this is observed and blamed by Plato and others. The proper meaning of the term προφήτης, that, namely, which is in conformity with the general usage of the language, is that which we have stated, viz., *speaker, announcer,* or *interpreter,* and is therefore the most suitable equivalent for the Hebrew נָבִיא.[1]

Köster's opinion is unfounded, that the Hebrew word would have been more suitably rendered in the LXX by the term θεοπρόπος.

§ 179.—*Other Names given to the Hebrew Prophets.*

Elsewhere, the prophet is called " a man of God, (הָ)אֱלֹהִים אִישׁ. This is in itself a more general expression, which is, however, used more particularly of one in whom God confides, to whom also he manifests Himself in a direct way, and of whom he makes use to announce His will to others.

In Judges xiii. 6, we have this designation for supernatural beings sent from God to men; it is, however, usually used for men whom God makes use of in this way. Thus, 1 Sam. ii. 27; ix. 8, and frequently in the Books of Kings. There is nothing implied in this designation which would show that the gifts and employment of these men related exclusively or even principally to the prediction of future events; on the contrary, it simply points to a closer and more confidential relationship with the Godhead.

The names רֹאֶה and חֹזֶה, which are also often applied to prophets, are of a somewhat different kind.

The former often occurs as describing Samuel (1 Sam. ix. 9, ff.; 1 Chron. ix. 22; xxvi. 28); also for a prophet

---

[1] Cf. Bardili, *Significatus primitivus vocis* προφήτης, &c., Göttingen, 1786. A. Th. Hartmann, " Micah," newly translated, 1800. Gesenius, W. B. s. v. נָבִיא, and Schleusner, s. v. προφήτης, and the works quoted.

Hanani, in the time of Asa, King of Judah (2 Chron. xvi. 7, 10). This expression, also, has no definite relation to the future, as implying that it was laid open to these men; but it merely points out that their view penetrated into the Divine counsel and mysteries, and that thus they were in a position to explain them to others.

In 1 Sam. ix. 9, we find an intimation that the name רֹאֶה was the usual one in earlier times, and that the term נָבִיא was subsequently adopted: "Beforetime in Israel, when a man went to enquire of God, thus he spake, Come and let us go עַד־הָרֹאֶה, for לַנָּבִיא הַיּוֹם יִקָּרֵא לְפָנִים הָרֹאֶה." From this the term נָבִיא does not appear to have come into general use until a later time, most probably after the age of Samuel, when the prophets began to lead a more public life and to interfere more spontaneously in the course of public matters. For, up to the time of Samuel, this personal and direct illumination only from time to time fell to the lot of isolated individuals, who generally dwelt by themselves in a state of seclusion, and, unless they were asked for advice, lived an almost entirely contemplative life. The name רֹאֶה seems to point to these peculiarities, whilst the expression נָבִיא alludes to a more public course of life, and to an utterance of those sayings which were revealed and inspired by the Godhead; just as in מַטִּיף, which occurs in Micah ii. 11 for a prophet, and completely corresponds with נָבִיא in etymological signification.

חֹזֶה and רֹאֶה are quite synonymous. The former expression first occurs in 2 Sam. xxiv. 11, where Gad is called הַנָּבִיא חֹזֵה דָוִד. Elsewhere it is only met with in the Chronicles, and appears to have become usual in later times, in addition to the two other expressions.

In 1 Chron. xxix. 29, Samuel is designated as הָרֹאֶה, Nathan as הַנָּבִיא, and Gad as הַחֹזֶה, all one after the other. We must not, however, understand by this, that the author of the Chronicles distinctly intended these three words to represent three different or differently modified ideas; the cause for these designations, doubtless, arose from the accidental circumstance, that in the works cited by the author these various epithets were annexed to the writers' names.[1]

[1] In Knobel, i. § 9, various other names for the prophets are stated in addition to those quoted, such as (a) צֹפֶה, מְצַפֶּה, שֹׁמֵר, *spy, watch-*

§ 180.—Nature of the Prophetic Office.

Among that portion of mankind whose history is specially set forth in the Scriptures, prophets or men directly enlightened by God existed from the earliest ages. The most ancient historical books of the Old Testament are particularly devoted to relating how God manifested Himself to the pious and believing, and announced to them in a direct way His will and His counsel.

Noah, Abraham, Isaac, and Jacob, stand out the most prominently in this character; next, and above all, Moses, who is pointed out as a prophet that had none like him, either before or after him, who saw Jehovah face to face, and spoke to Him mouth to mouth. (Num. xii. 6–8; Deut. xxxiv. 10, ff.)

It was not, probably, till the age of Samuel, that the position of prophets among the Hebrew people was considered as an actual *munus*, so that they constituted a special class. Samuel appears to have formed certain institutions for the education of prophets, so far as human institutions could have any influence in the matter. Although it is nowhere expressly told of him, he is considered as the founder of the so-called "Schools of Prophets,"[1] and it is usually thought that the real prophetical age began with him.[2]

In Samuel's times we find the Nebiim assembled in companies; they wandered about in bands (1 Sam. x. 5, ff.), and dwelt together, with Samuel at their head, in Naioth (נָיוֹת; Ketib נְיוֹת); it is doubtful whether this is the name of a place near Ramah in Mount Ephraim, or a locality in the town itself (1 Sam. xix. 18, ff.), but the former idea is the more probable. There were perhaps a number of rural

---

man, inasmuch as they vigilantly watched over the affairs of the people of God, and the world generally, and sought by their warnings to avert evil from the people, &c.; (b) עֶבֶד יְהֹוָה, מַלְאַךְ יְהֹוָה. These, however, are not properly names, but only epithets or poetical expressions.

[1] Cf. Wilh. Rud. Kranichfeld, *De iis, quæ in testamento vetere commemorantur, prophetarum societatibus.* Berlin, 1861.

[2] Thus in Acts iii. 24, Samuel is spoken of as the first of the prophets; cf. Hebr. xi. 32. Likewise, in the *Talm. Hier. tr. Chaggiga*, fol. 77, he is called the teacher of all the prophets. The way in which Augustine, *De Civit. Dei*, xvii. 1, mentions Samuel should also be especially noticed.

habitations near this town. Just in the same way, in the time of Elijah and Elisha (850 B.C.), we find the prophets united in companies, and, at least, partially dwelling together.

2 Kings vi. 1, f. : " And the sons of the prophets said unto Elisha, Behold now, the place where we dwell with thee is too strait for us." Verse 2: "Let us go, we pray thee, unto Jordan, and take thence every man a beam, and let us make us a place there, where we may dwell." *Bethel* is mentioned as the place where they dwelt in 2 Kings ii. 3; Gilgal in ch. iv. 38; Jericho in ch. ii. 5.

The scholars who were being educated as prophets were called in this age בְּנֵי נְבִיאִים : *v.* 1 Kings xx. 35 ; 2 Kings ii. 3, 5, 7 (" fifty men of the sons of the prophets "), *v.* 15; iv. 1 ("a woman of the wives of the sons of the prophets"); *v.* 38 ; v. 22 ; vi. 1 ; ix. 1. Similarly, among the Persians, *filii Magorum*, scholars of the Magi. These " sons of the prophets," who were themselves often called prophets, must have been rather numerous, as may be gathered from the passages cited. *E.g.*, 2 Kings iv. 43 (100 men with Elisha), and 1 Kings xviii. 4, in the days of Ahab and Elijah, " when Jezebel cut off the prophets of the Lord, Obadiah took an hundred prophets, and hid them by fifty in a cave, and fed them with bread and water." Cf. also, 2 Kings vi. 1, ff. The sons of the prophets appear here to be all under the guidance of a superior ; as in former times they were under Samuel, in the same way afterwards they were under Elijah, and then under Elisha, whom Elijah himself, during his lifetime, had anointed, at Jehovah's command, to be a prophet in his stead, 1 Kings xix. 16.

At a later time we no longer find this living together, and union of the prophets in associations or schools, but see only single prophets appearing, and that till a little while after the conclusion of the Captivity. The last known prophet is Malachi, in the middle of the fifth century B.C. After that time prophetic inspiration ceased among the Israelitish people. They themselves had the feeling that the spirit of prophecy had departed from Israel, and they waited patiently for the time when a prophet should again arise who should proclaim Jehovah's words to the people through Jehovah's own revelation to him (cf. 1 Macc. ix.

27; iv. 46; xiv. 41). In the meantime the teachers of the people contented themselves with interpreting the utterances of earlier prophets.

With Christianity the spirit of independent prophecy again awoke. Among the gifts of the Holy Ghost which prevailed in the Christian Church in the apostolic age, was the χάρισμα προφητείας; the προφῆται are named as a particular class among those who, in the primitive Christian Church, were engaged in founding and building up the kingdom of God.

In addition to the prophets, we find *prophetesses* also occur; thus at the time of Josiah a prophetess, Huldah, was held in the greatest estimation, 2 Kings xxii. 14; 2 Chron. xxxiv. 22. At the time of Nehemiah, a prophetess, Noadiah, is mentioned by him (but not for good), Neh. vi. 14. So Miriam, the sister of Moses, is called a prophetess, Exod. xv. 20, and likewise Deborah, Judges iv. 4. Prophetesses are also spoken of in the New Testament (Acts xxi. 9, four daughters of Philip, and 1 Cor. xi. 5).

§ 181.—*Hebrew Prophets—Their Mode of Life, and Dress.*

As regards the *mode of life* of the Hebrew prophets, in some cases they might have lived by an acquired trade, but they mostly appear to have found their maintenance by the collection of vegetables and fruits, and sometimes by freewill gifts from pious Israelites, especially those who sought advice and help from them, who sometimes also would give them a hospitable reception (cf. 2 Kings iv. 8, ff., 38, ff., 42, ff.; 1 Kings xiv. 3, ff.; Amos vii. 14; cf. Jer. xl. 5). Their way of life was, on the whole, certainly very simple; yet we cannot exactly believe that every prophet, without exception, lived in great poverty.[1]

In their *clothing* they had something distinctive in the wide prophets-mantle, made of fur or of shaggy hair, particularly that of the camel.

Vide 1 Sam. xxviii. 14 (מְעִיל of Samuel); 1 Kings xix. 13, 19; 2 Kings ii. 13 (אַדֶּרֶת of Elijah); *ib.* ch. i. 8, where, doubtless in reference to his dress, Elijah is described as a hairy man, אִישׁ בַּעַל שֵׂעָר, ἀνὴρ δασύς. Cf. Zech. xiii. 4: "In

---
[1] We may instance Nathan and Isaiah. Cf. Jer. xxxii. 9, in which the prophet, although only in a symbolical way, buys a field for seven shekels (of gold) and ten pieces of silver.

that day the prophets shall be ashamed every one of his vision, when he hath prophesied; neither shall they wear a (*mantle of fur*) rough garment (אַדֶּרֶת שֵׂעָר) to deceive." Elijah is also described as being provided with a leathern girdle about his loins (2 Kings i. 8). Cf. Matt. iii. 4; Heb. xi. 37, περιῆλθον ἐν μηλωταῖς, ἐν αἰγείοις δέρμασιν.

§ 182.—*Hebrew Prophets—Their Origin.*

The Hebrew prophets did not belong to any particular tribe, nor to any particular region. Some prophets, indeed, belonged to the priesthood, as Jeremiah (i. 1), Ezekiel (i. 3), Zechariah, son of Jehoiadah (2 Chron. xxiv. 20). But these are only isolated cases, and the others belonged to different tribes, and during the division of the two kingdoms both to the kingdom of Israel, and to that of Judah. It may often have been the case, particularly so long as the schools of prophets were in existence, that the son of a prophet grew up as a prophet by the side of his father. We do not, however, find that those who were especially distinguished for prophetical activity had prophets for their fathers, but that they came forth without any such origin and without any previous training for their position, just as the Divine call fell upon them (cf., *e.g.*, Amos vii. 14). Their appearance, however, and their agency generally, were dependent on their being called by God, and being moved by His Spirit. Even in those on whom the Divine call to prophetical activity had once fallen, the inspiration was no lasting state of the mind, everywhere attending them, capable of being called forth by them at any moment in an arbitrary way, so that the prophet could everywhere and at every instant supply a solution to every difficulty from an inner light. On the contrary, he needed everytime a peculiar Divine revelation, as it is expressed, "the Spirit of God came upon him," or "the Spirit of God invested him" (לָבְשָׁה), or "covered him," or "the hand of Jehovah came upon him."[1]

Luther, *in Gen.* ch. xliv. (ed. Erlangen, x. 303 *sq.*) "usitato proverbio apud theologos dici solet; Spiritus Sanctus non semper tangit corda prophetarum. Illumina-

---

[1] Cf. as to this, *e.g.*, in Köster, p. 248, ff. We evidently see the same character belonging to the prophets of the New Covenant; cf. 1 Cor xiv. 30.

tiones propheticæ non sunt continuæ et perpetuæ, sicut Isaias non habuit continuas et assiduas revelationes de rebus maximis, sed per vices temporum . Idem testatur exemplum Elisæi, cum ait de Sunamitide: dimitte illam, anima enim ejus in amaritudine est, et Dominus celavit a me et non indicavit mihi (2 Kings iv. 27); ibi fatetur Deum non semper tangere corda prophetarum . Interdum etiam venit spiritus cum aut cithara aut psalterio luderent et psalmos quosdam et cantica spiritualia decantarent."

§ 183.—*Mode of Prophetical Inspiration.*

As regards the way in which the prophets received the Divine illumination, we find it often mentioned in the historical books, that God revealed Himself to them while they were asleep, in dreams.[1] But the usual condition of the prophets at the time of inspiration was a waking state. Consciousness and clearness of perception with regard to the outer world surrounding them is a characteristic attribute of this inspiration, by which alone the prophets were able to set forth to the people in an intelligible way the purport of the revelation received by them.

This attribute is particularly brought forward by the apostle Paul (1 Cor. xiv.) as a mark of the Christian prophets at that time. In this respect he places the inspiration of these prophets in contrast with the inspiration of those γλώσσαις λαλούντων. In the latter, the consciousness of the outer world was more or less lost, so that they spoke purely from an inner self-consciousness. They were not, therefore, usually able to act as their own interpreters or explainers of that which they had announced in inspired language whilst in a state of inspiration, since while in this state, they had no clear perception of the outer world surrounding them, and after its cessation, no distinct recollection of their thoughts and sensations during this condition, nor of what they had spoken about. Their inspiration was, in this respect, nearly allied with that of the Greek μάντις who needed the προφήτης as an interpreter and explainer of his utterances. Neither the Hebrew nor the New-Testament prophets needed any such aid.

It was not, therefore, necessary that the prophets should deliver forth the communications which they received at

[1] Cf. Knobel, i. 174, ff.

the moment they received them. They could quite as well deliver them subsequently, some time after the revelation; as during the state of prophetical inspiration, they possessed complete clearness and consciousness, and also had a full and distinct recollection of that which was revealed to them. The words, πνεύματα προφητῶν προφήταις ὑποτάσσεται, must refer to this, 1 Cor. xiv. 32.

The Fathers have justly noticed this characteristic of the clear consciousness of the prophets, and have perceived in it a distinguishing mark between them and the Greek soothsayers, as well as the Montanist fanatics.

E.g., Chrysostom, *Homil. ad* 1 *Cor.* xii. 2 : τοῦτο γὰρ μάντεως ἴδιον τὸ ἐξεστηκέναι, τὸ ἀνάγκην ὑπομένειν, τὸ ὠθεῖσθαι, τὸ ἕλκεσθαι, τὸ σύρεσθαι ὥσπερ μαινόμενον· Ὁ δὲ προφήτης οὐχ οὕτως, ἀλλὰ μετὰ διανοίας νηφούσης καὶ σωφρονούσης καταστάσεως, καὶ εἰδὼς ἃ φθέγγεται φησὶν ἅπαντα ὥστε καὶ πρὸ τῆς ἐκβάσεως κἀντευθεν γνώριζε τὸν μάντιν καὶ τὸν προφήτην. Epiphan. *Hær.* xlviii. 3. Hieronym. *Proœm in Jes.* : "neque vero, ut Montanus cum insanis feminis somniat, prophetæ in ecstasi sunt locuti, ut nescirent quid loquerentur, et, cum alios erudirent, ipsi ignorarent quid dicerent." Id. *in Ephes.* ch. iii. 5. Cf. Bleek's remarks, *Theol. Stud. und Krit.* 1829, i. pp. 57–61.

Hengstenberg (*Christol.* 1st Edit.) has incorrectly denied this characteristic of the Hebrew prophets, and considered, with Tertullian, *adv. Marc.* iv. 22, and the Montanists generally, that during their inspiration they were in an ecstatic state, as the μάντεις of the Greeks, and that in them also, the suppression of all human activity and intelligent consciousness was a consequence of the spirit of prophecy. This is absolutely opposed to all the phenomena and intimations which the Scriptures both of the Old and New Testament afford us as to the state of inspiration in the prophets. Without a great clearness of perception at the moment of inspiration, and a consequent distinct recollection, the prophets would not have been in a position to write down afterwards the very purport of the revelation received, which, at least with many of them, was certainly not done until after its verbal delivery, and the cessation of the inspired state.

§ 184.—*Prophetical Inspiration by means of Visions.*

We also find that revelations were often made to the prophets in *visions*, which came to them in a waking state, in which also subjects and circumstances of the external world were sometimes placed before them, as symbolical intimations of the circumstances and destinies of God's people and the world in general, sometimes also transcendental subjects under material forms. Thus, Is. vi; Amos vii. ff.; often in Ezekiel; also Zech. i–vi.

On this point, indeed, many modern interpreters have thought, and so, as it appears, even Köster (p. 274, ff.) that where the Hebrew prophets speak of such visions, it is only to be looked upon as rhetorical or poetical imagery, of which they availed themselves for the figurative representation of that which they wished to proclaim, without their having actually had any such vision. This may, of course, be partly the case, particularly with the prophets of a later time, who often copied the style of the earlier ones, and therefore sometimes made use of this device as a mere literary embellishment. This supposition gains force from the comparatively greater frequency with which this form of prophecy is found among the later prophets, and also from the fact that the visions related by them are sometimes very circumstantial and put together in such a way that the prophets, although the revelation was actually made to them in this way, have yet doubtless further amplified it. But, generally speaking, any such view is quite untenable. As a rule, the visions which the Old-Testament prophets announce, were as surely given to them as those seen by the apostles Peter and Paul, of which we read in the New Testament.

A vision is certainly always a kind of ecstatic state, in which, for the moment, the perception of external things is withdrawn, and the man is raised to a higher internal consciousness. Only, in the Hebrew prophets, this withdrawal of external perception cannot have existed, even during the vision, to such an extent that all connection between the circumstances of their inspired contemplation and the concerns of their life was entirely lost. For else, after the cessation of the state of rapture, they could have retained no clear recollection of what had been shown to them in the vision. They would have been unable to communicate these visions to others living in the outer world, either by proclaiming them to them intelligibly, or by writing them down.

Hengstenberg himself has, in his second edition, essentially modified and softened down his earlier opinions, and denies—particularly in reference to 1 Cor. xiv. (*vv.* 14, 15, 19, 32)—the *amentia*, the absence of intelligent consciousness, in the prophets; although even here he assumes an ecstatic state in them to too great a degree, and also holds that all the Old-Testament prophecies were communicated to the prophets in visions, even those prophecies about which we have no such intimation.

§ 185.—*Form and Mode of Delivery of Prophetical Utterances.*

As regards the *form* of the communication and *delivery* of the prophetical utterances, a difference is to be observed corresponding not only to the individuality of each prophet, but also to their various epochs, and we find a gradual change from poetry to prose, and from an oral delivery to written statements, similar to that found in the history of Greek literature in general. The utterances of the Nebiim were originally oral only. They declared by word of mouth what was suggested to them by the Spirit of God on every particular occasion; nor did they themselves, nor any one else, think of writing down the purport of their utterances for those that came after. Therefore, even during the properly prophetical age, from Samuel onwards, some centuries elapsed, during which no complete prophetical utterances have been preserved to us. The delivery of the prophets in the more ancient times was, however, certainly of a most lively character, and in lyrical and poetical language; and, like the delivery of lyrical poetry generally, accompanied by music.

Thus, in the age of Saul, the prophets appear marching along and holding their prophetic discourses to the sound of psalteries, tabrets, pipes, and harps, 1 Sam. x. 5, ff. Therefore the verb which properly designates prophetic language, נבא, is also used for an inspired delivery of songs accompanied by music; *e.g.*, 1 Chron. xxv. 1, "David and the captains of the host separated to the service of the sons of Asaph, and of Heman, and of Jeduthun, who should prophesy (הַנְּבִאִים) with harps, with psalteries, and with cymbals." So also, it is related of the prophet Elisha (2 Kings iii. 15), that when he wished to make known a prophetical judgment to the king Jehoram of Israel, and Jehoshaphat of Judah, he desired that a minstrel might be brought to accompany his discourse. We must hardly consider this as anything peculiar, or look for any particular intention in it, as, *e.g.*, to stir up the prophet's inspiration by the man's playing, or in a measure to curb and soften it down; but that it was, at the time, the not unusual mode of prophetical delivery, just as in the Greek' tragedies the declamation was accompanied by the playing of flutes, and a still more complete musical accompaniment entered into the chorus.

How soon the prophets generally began to write down their utterances, cannot be exactly decided. The earliest written prophecies which have been preserved to us in the collection of prophetical books, date about fifty years before the breaking up of the kingdom of Israel, shortly after 800 B.C. Their authors flourished as prophets contemporaneously, or shortly after one another, partly in Israel and partly in Judah; viz.: *Joel, Amos, Hosea;* then *Micah, Isaiah,* and *Nahum.*

The prophetic utterances of these prophets were, in general, originally delivered orally, and not written down until after they had been delivered; some of them, perhaps, very soon after, and some not until a later time; the prophet collecting in a written form the discourses which he had at different times delivered.

That the discourses were originally delivered orally appears very clearly in some of them (cf. Is. vii; Amos vii. 10, ff.).

The language of the above prohpets is poetical (except when they merely relate historical matter), and possesses the parallelism of members and other peculiarities of poetical diction. This is also the case with several prophets of a later time, up to and after the Captivity, but not to quite the same extent. In other prophets of the later time, on the contrary, the language is entirely prosaic, as partly in *Jeremiah,* and still more so in *Ezekiel, Zechariah, Haggai,* and *Malachi.*

It may be assumed with certainty, that the utterances

of many of these later prophets were first composed in a written form, without having been previously delivered orally, as, e.g., Ezekiel, particularly ch. xl–xlviii, also Is. xl. ff.; and even in the earlier prophets, the oracles as to foreign nations are in general of this sort; as it is not probable that these would have been orally delivered before they were written down, as they could not have been uttered in the hearing of those to whom they were addressed.

§ 186.—*Symbolical Actions performed by Prophets.*

Symbolical actions performed by the prophets also form a part of the prophetical mode of statement, and served as a more distinct way of setting forth that which they wished to make known.

We find this sort of action related in the historical books of some of the older prophets, before the time to which the prophetical Scriptures belong. The prophet Ahijah the Shilonite, when he wished to predict to Jeroboam, that he was to be the ruler of the kingdom of Israel, and that that kingdom should be torn asunder from the kingdom of Judah, took the new mantle which he wore and tore it into twelve pieces, and gave ten of them to Jeroboam: "take thee ten pieces: for thus saith Jehovah, the God of Israel, Behold, I will rend the kingdom out of the hand of Solomon, and will give ten tribes to thee." (1 Kings xi. 29, f.) There is another example, ch. xxii. 11, where a certain prophet, Zedekiah, made himself horns of iron, as signs that, as if with such horns, Jehoshaphat and Ahab, the united kings of Judah and Israel, should push at and destroy the Syrians. In the prophetical Scriptures preserved to us, we find such symbolical actions in Isaiah, Hosea, Jeremiah, and Ezekiel. This occurs in Isaiah only once (ch. xx), where he relates that he went about naked and barefoot, in order to warn the people against trusting in the help of Egypt and Æthiopia, as a sign that the Egyptians and Æthiopians should be taken away captive by the Assyrians in such a condition. This mode of statement occurs more frequently in Jeremiah, and repeatedly in Ezekiel.

We meet with the same difficulty here as in the visions of the prophets, viz., whether the prophets actually performed these symbolical actions or not. The Rabbinical interpreters assume that they did not: *e.g.*, Kimchi, Aben Esra, and particularly Moses Maimonides, who (*Moreh Nehochim*, part ii. ch. xlvi.) expresses himself fully about these matters, and declares his opinion that all the actions of this kind took place merely in visions. Hengstenberg also, among the modern expositors, adopts the same view. This opinion, however, is certainly groundless. Others consider them only as literary embellishments, which the prophets availed themselves of, but not based on any fact that had taken place. Stäudlin[1] may be specially mentioned as supporting this view. This, however, just as with the visions, can only be affirmed with any degree of probability, with reference to later times.

At a more ancient time, as long as the prophetic utterances were principally delivered orally, we cannot doubt that it actually was one of the customs of the Hebrew prophets to perform symbolical actions before the eyes of the people, in order to inculcate more distinctly and stringently that which they wished them to lay to heart, as the narratives quoted from the historical books clearly show. But subsequently, when the lively, oral delivery of the prophets was generally given up, and when they contented themselves with communicating their prophecies to the people in writing only, it is quite probable in itself that the symbolical actions which they relate were not previously actually performed by them, but that they only served as literary embellishments of their narrative; and in some of them, from the whole nature of the case, this may be affirmed with tolerable certainty. *E.g.*, in Jer. xiii. 1–7, where the prophet relates as a symbolical action, that he bought a girdle and placed it on his loins, and had gone to the Euphrates and there hidden it in a cleft of the rock, and when he afterwards came thither again he found the girdle marred (in reference to the destruction of Judah and Jerusalem). Ezek. xii. 1–7, in which the prophet on a certain day provided himself with a travelling equipage, and in the evening, digging a hole through the wall with his hand, and carrying his baggage, departed in the sight of the people (in reference to the king Zedekiah being led away into captivity through the broken down walls of Jerusa-

---

[1] *Neue Beitr. zur Erläuterung der Bibl. Propheten*, 1791. Pp. 123, 220, 240.

lem). So also Ezek. iv; Hosea i, ii. Such actions, *if actually performed*, would have quite failed of their aim.

§ 187.—*Purport and Aim of the Prophetical Utterances.*

If we now consider the essential *purport and aim of the prophetical discourses*, we shall find that they coincide with the special vocation of the prophets. They were Jehovah's ambassadors and mediators for the race of Abraham, which race had received the promise through their ancestors of a great salvation which should be theirs, and a great blessing which, from them, should be spread over all the nations of the earth. With them also Jehovah had, in the Mosaic legislation, renewed and strengthened the Covenant made with Abraham. The vocation of the prophets was altogether ethical; they were to keep the people chosen by Jehovah faithful to His Covenant, and to maintain them in it, both generally and particularly; and when they had gone out of the way, they were to bring them back again into the right path, and to keep alive all the theocratically founded relations between Jehovah and the people of Israel, in order to lead the people on to, and prepare them for, the predicted salvation and the destiny thus assigned to them. For this purpose, their first endeavour was to preserve the people in the worship of the one, true, living God, to maintain monotheism in all its purity, and to combat the idolatry, to which the people, up to the time of the Captivity, were so much disposed.

We find the prophets Elijah and Elisha very devotedly engaged in these efforts in the kingdom of Israel, then separated from the centre of the worship of Jehovah, and in conflict with the idolatrous kings. (Cf. Jeremiah, Deutero-Isaiah, &c.)

But the prophets' aim was not simply the furtherance of a mere *external* worship of Jehovah. They declaimed much against an adoration of Jehovah which satisfied itself with offering sacrifices, making long prayers and fasts, and with the observance of feast-days, but did not, before everything, study piety of the heart, and true obedience to God, which was preferable to all offerings. Thus they watched with all earnestness over the purity of the morals of the people, and as their leaders, fearlessly blamed their perversity and wickedness, chastised their thoughtlessness and arrogance in their good fortune, and their despondency and unbelief in their misfortunes, their debauchery, pride, corruptibility, hardness, &c.

Their ministry, however, was also often directed towards the *political relations* of the people, and in this respect also, they often appear as watchmen. They endeavoured, before everything, to excite and keep alive both in the people and in the princes the consciousness, that God the Lord was the true supreme king over Israel, and that, in all the affairs of the state, they were to show themselves submissive and obedient to Him, and that earthly princes were only to be considered as His vicegerents, and merely had to execute His will; but that the people should turn with confidence to their God before every one, when they were in danger or distress.

They exercised influence in multifarious ways in the arrangement of public matters. We see *Samuel* as the leader of the entire State. The prophet *Ahijah* the Shilonite, during Solomon's lifetime, made known to Jeroboam that he should be king over ten tribes. (1 Kings xi.) The prophet Elisha, at the time of the idolatrous king Jehoram, anointed Jehu to be king over Israel. (2 Kings ix.) At a later time in the kingdom of Judah, they often assisted the kings of the house of David with their advice and warnings. They particularly cautioned them, that in distress they were not to expect safety from the assistance of foreign and idolatrous nations and princes, to which, at that time, the great men of the people were very readily induced. Whenever they felt that they were afflicted and oppressed by any neighbouring powerful state, they were very ready to purchase the assistance of some other nation—a policy which must have made the enervated Judah still more the sport of their neighbours, and at last brought on the destruction of this kingdom, just as of the kingdom of Israel previously. The prophets, however, forewarn them against such idle confidence in the help of feeble and also idolatrous men, and rather counsel patience under the afflictions sent by God, and a believing confidence in Jehovah, their God, who would be ready with His help in His own good time.[1]

[1] Cf. Hupfeld, "The Policy of the Prophets of the Old Testament," in the *Neue Evangel. Kirchenzeitung*, 1862, No. 22.

As a result of these endeavours, of the love of truth regardless of consequences which animated them, and of the candour which they used towards great and small, princes and people, without distinction, the prophets could not fail to meet with opposition of every kind, and also to experience considerable persecution; sometimes on the part of the idolatrous kings, sometimes on the part of the judges and great men of the people, when they blamed their injustice, corruptibility and wickedness generally, or their unpatriotic and untheocratic inclinations; and sometimes on the part of the people, priests, and false prophets.

The Books of Kings tell us, how Ahab, the idolatrous king of Israel, under the influence of his wife the Sidonian princess Jezebel, raged against Jehovah's prophets, and put many of them to death, and repeatedly also attempted the life of Elijah, who once answered him, when the king asked him, " art thou he that troubleth Israel?" " Not I, but thou, and thy father's house, in that ye have forsaken the commandments of Jehovah, and thou hast followed Baalim." (1 Kings xviii. 17, 18). This same Ahab, caused another prophet, Micaiah, the son of Imlah, to be fed on bread and water, when he predicted an unhappy conclusion to his war with the Syrians, which prediction was confirmed by the result (1 Kings xxii); likewise Asa, king of Judah, persecuted Hanani the Seer (2 Chron. xvi. 7–10). Joash, king of Judah, caused Zechariah, son of Jehoiada, to be stoned in the court of the temple, when he, in prophetic inspiration, predicted destruction to the people, because they did not keep the commandments of their God (2 Chron. xxiv. 20). The prophet Isaiah was, according to an ancient tradition, sawn asunder in the time of Manasseh. Jeremiah experienced repeated ill-treatment.[1]

The opposition and ill-will of the princes and great men against the prophets, at the way in which the latter openly opposed them, might sometimes appear justifiable, if the prophets had come forward only from their own human impulse in expressing their opinions, advice, and blame.

But they everywhere act and speak in the consciousness that they are Jehovah's instruments, operating in His name, and urged on by His spirit, to execute His commands and to announce His words; in the consciousness that what

[1] Cf. Matt. v. 12, xxiii. 29, ff.; Luke vi. 23, xi. 47, ff.

they did, they dare not leave undone, without being guilty of the greatest disobedience towards their God.

§ 188.—*References to the Future in the Prophetical Discourses.*

It is a peculiarity of the discourses in the prophetical ministry, that their utterances have *a reference to the future,* and therefore assume an actually prophetical character. This is the case with those utterances which do not give advice on any particular occasion as to any prescribed line of conduct which was to be taken to be delivered out of affliction or to avert a danger or the like, but only generally warn the people to return to or persevere in the ways of Jehovah, or rebuke the prevailing depravity. This is the precise point where a great variety of opinions prevails, chiefly in modern times, based on a fundamental difference in the mode of interpreting these utterances. The difference between the opinions prevailing in ancient times and the more modern views, is generally this—that the former exaggerate the predictive character of the prophetical discourses, and the latter throw the Divine illumination of the prophets too much into the background. Eichhorn's view belongs to the latter class, and must be considered as a thoroughly defective conception. He considers almost all the utterances in our prophetical Scriptures, which have any references to the events of the near future, as poetical descriptions of events written *post eventum.*

E.g., in the various statements in the Book of Isaiah, in which the overthrow of the host of Sennacherib is predicted, Eichhorn thinks that this description of events as future, is a mere embellishment of a poet who must have lived at an epoch perhaps considerably later, and had no other aim in this mode of statement, except to glorify certain prodigies in this way. But if, in our prophetical Scriptures, certain utterances actually occur which have originated in this way, we cannot avoid considering them as interpolations; and even then it would be a mistaken opinion to regard the intention of their composition as merely an historical or poetical one. This idea arises in general from a complete misconception of these scriptures. This is at once evident, if we look at the narratives in the historical books referring to the age of the prophets. In them we find clearly, that the Hebrews

considered the prophets as men who were able by Divine
enlightenment to impart positive information with respect
to the future (*e.g.*, 1 Kings xxii; 2 Kings iii. 11–19). It is,
therefore, in the highest degree improbable, that all references to the future in their writings should bear the character
of predictions only under a false pretence; and should be in
truth nothing but poetical descriptions of past events. This
opinion appears still more untenable, if we consider the
writings of the prophets themselves, since it is by the
hypothesis of their predictive character that we can best
explain their present shape. The threatenings or promises
which appear sublime as regarding the future, would look
weak or unnatural as a representation of the past.

It is, however, at present pretty generally acknowledged
that this opinion and mode of treatment is absolutely mistaken, so that it is not necessary to further refute it.

§ 189.—*Consideration of the various Opinions as to the Prophetical Predictions.*

There are two other views which appear more plausible.
One of these regards the references to the future in the
discourses of the prophets, as the product of the human
wisdom of these men, of their experience and judgment in
the different circumstances of life, both of individuals and
of the people, which enabled them from a view of the past
and present to throw a correct glance into the future.
The *other*, however, finds in these discourses of the prophets nothing but purely human hopes and fears dictated
by their patriotism and poetic fancy, without any concern
whether they were fulfilled in futurity or not. The two
ideas are, perhaps, allied to another; yet they do not give
the full truth.

As regards the former, it certainly cannot be denied that
many of the prophets, as Samuel, Nathan, Isaiah, Jeremiah,
and others, were distinguished by great experience in
human affairs, and by a corresponding insight into dealing
with them. Their position in the State led to this, and
they were therefore often able, even when they were not
enlightened by any peculiar Divine revelation, to give very
wholesome advice for the judicious guidance of public
matters, both internal and external. But it would be,
nevertheless, quite wrong to consider the discourses of the

prophets relating to the future as the mere result of reflection and intellect.

There is abundant evidence that they very well knew how to distinguish between the results of their own human intellect and the suggestions of a higher illumination; since often, when they were asked as prophets for information as to the future, they owned that they were unable to give it until the Spirit of God had descended upon them, and God's hand had been laid upon them. The nature also of the prophecies now extant is such that we are by no means induced to consider them as the work of an intellect carefully taking account of external scenes; on the contrary, they were the result of a living faith and a Divine inspiration. Otherwise the prophets would hardly have clung with so firm a hold to the principle that, even in the most threatening dangers for the State, human help and power could avail nothing, and that confidence in Jehovah and His assistance was alone necessary, nor would they have dissuaded the people with such zeal from making treaties with foreign heathen nations, even when from them alone, according to the outward circumstances, prevention from destruction appeared to be in any way to be expected.

The *second* opinion finds support in the fact, that if we examine the prophecies as to the future which are preserved to us, we find many things in them, the exact fulfilment of which we cannot point out in the succeeding history, and much even which can be proved either certainly or with probability, *not to have been fulfilled* in the way in which it was predicted by them.

Ancient interpreters have often been led to adopt very forced explanations from the idea that the predictions must be fulfilled in every single feature, and have split up the predictions into their several parts, referring one part to quite different circumstances and times from another, although they are both closely connected together in the statement of the prophet. In doing this, they often leave the order and succession of the separate parts of the prophecy quite unnoticed, so that they refer to the earlier event the prediction which is the later in the prophetical delineation, and the later to the earlier; finally, in one and the same prophetical delineation, they arbitrarily take one feature of it quite literally and attach peculiar importance to the special literal fulfilment of it; whilst in another passage immediately connected with the former, they insist on a figurative interpretation, without any sufficient reason being shown from the contents and context of the prophecy itself for these different kinds of interpretation. The result of such a mode of interpretation is, that every detail perhaps is proved to have been fulfilled, but, at the same time, *not* the whole in the connection and relation in which it appears in the prophecy itself; for all the several widely-separated events and circumstances, to which, in this way, the separate features of one and the self-same prophecy are applied, do not when combined issue in a state of things at all corresponding to that to which the whole prophecy appears to us to point, if we look at it in its entire character, aim, and connection. Harmony of interpretation is entirely disregarded in this mode of treatment, and the reproach has not unjustly been made, that if we were to deal with the completely poetical delineations of heathen poets in the same way, just as literal a fulfilment could be shown as in the Biblical predictions.

If, however, we push this to such an extreme as to conclude that all particular fulfilments of the prophecies are merely accidental, such a conclusion is just as little to be accepted as the forced interpretations made of them particularly by the ancient interpreters; and for this reason, because such a view would not at all accord with what we know historically about the character of the prophets. From the fact that the contemporaries of the prophets often applied to them for information about the future, and consulted them as the mouth-piece of Jehovah, we perceive that a correct prevision and prediction of the future, and indeed of those separate future events of which they could have no foreknowledge by a judicious calculation of past circumstances, but only through some higher illumination, were regarded as requisites in a prophet. If then, that which the prophet predicted as to the future never came to pass, he was estimated as nothing but a false prophet—1 Kings xxii. Jer. xxviii. 9: "When the word of the prophet shall come to pass, then shall the prophet be known, that the Lord hath truly sent him." Deut. xviii. 20-22 even gives us a law [which, in this form, like the repetitions of the law in Deuteronomy generally, probably belongs to the prophetic age], according to which a false prophet is to be punished with death, and such a prophet is to be recognised by that which he announces in the name of Jehovah *not* taking place.

Added to this, there are many of the prophecies preserved to us, of the genuineness of which there can be no doubt, in which unconnected future events are predicted with great confidence, in such a way that it can be clearly seen that no doubt prevailed in the prophet's mind as to the certain and exact fulfilment of his prediction, and that he was led to this by a higher confidence than could be inspired by human judgment and forecast.

Of this sort, *e.g.*, are the prophecies in Isaiah as to the closely impending destruction of the kingdoms of Israel and Syria, which he predicted with great confidence at a time when the two kingdoms appeared particularly strong by their treaty with each other, and, as a testimony thereof, announced the birth of a boy (ch. vii); besides the repeated predictions as to the destruction of the mighty hosts of Sennacherib king of Assyria which besieged Jerusalem, and the deliverance of the state from the greatest distress. Among these predictions, those in ch. xxix. 1-8 appear to me particularly noteworthy, where he foretells that a long time hence Jerusalem should be besieged by a foreign host and pressed very hard, but that the latter, just as they believed they were getting possession of the city, should be scattered and annihilated; for this prediction, from its whole character, appears to have been uttered before any danger showed itself from this quarter. Further, the exact predictions in Jeremiah as to the return to their home of the people led away into exile, &c., and still more in Ezekiel. So we also find in the New Testament that those who are pointed out as prophets foresaw future events by means of the gift granted to them, as particularly Agabus (Acts xi. 28; xxi. 11).

§ 190.—*General Character of the Prophetic Discourses.*

I have before intimated (§ 178), and, in considering the different names for prophets in use in Hebrew, have particularly called attention to it, how little the oral ministry of the prophets must be looked upon as limited to the predic-

tion of future events spiritually seen by them. This clearly
results from 1 Cor. xiv, where Paul speaks circumstantially of the προφητεύειν in opposition to the γλώσσαις λαλεῖν;
but with regard to the former, he does not bring into any
prominence the gift of predicting the future, but rather
that of discerning and discovering the secrets of men's
hearts; which was also a gift of the Old-Testament prophets.
But even in those discourses of the prophets which contain
a reference to the future, the predictions of future events
are by no means always so exact as those in the single
examples previously quoted, and still less is foretelling
the future the sole or peculiar aim of their discourses.
For it was not their chief intention to make disclosures
as to the future in order to satisfy curiosity; but where
such disclosures are made, it was done to meet some particular necessity, to warn the people of some pernicious
counsel, or to comfort them in distress. It is by far most
commonly the case that their predictions as to the future
are bound up with further instructions, admonitions, warnings, or censures, and act only as a powerful motive for the
latter.

The chief ideas which they bring forward in this respect
are the same as those on which the Mosaic laws are based,
viz., that Jehovah had chosen the seed of Abraham as His
peculiar possession, as a race sanctified to Him, and destined
to become the salvation and blessing of the world: that
He made them find their reward in the fulfilment of His
commands, and their punishment in the disobedience
to His will, but that He would visibly show His grace
and compassion on those who turned to Him in sincere
penitence.

Thus, then, the prophets appeared everywhere in their
predictions as the announcers both of God's justice, and also
of His mercy and love to His people, sometimes the former
predominating, and sometimes the latter, according to the
different circumstances. When the people were in misery
and need, although by their own faults, if they only turned
again repenting to their God, the prophecies have chiefly a
comforting, supporting, encouraging character; when, on
the contrary, the people, induced by external security,
lived in arrogance and forgetfulness of God, the prophecies
are rebuking and threatening, and announce the Divine

judgments; yet even in these the threats are mostly followed by comforting promises.

The prophets, however, did not content themselves only with expressing these ideas in merely general terms, and we mostly find them more distinctly specified ; *e. g.*, it is stated what sort of punishment Jehovah had destined for the princes or the people who had hardened and blinded themselves against Him, and what foreign nation was to be called in for their chastisement, or what sort of happiness He would award to those who persevered in His ways, or turned again to Him. These descriptions are, however, often given in such a way that the exact fulfilment of their separate features cannot everywhere be shown, unless we resort to the very forced method employed by the ancient interpreters of examining the surface only, and giving interpretations which dislocate the connected portions of the prophecy. We must not, however, as has previously so often been done, leave unconsidered the *poetic element* which the prophets employed as the vehicle of their predictions. This involves the conclusion, that although their chief object was only to establish some general ideas, as, *e.g.*, that God would punish the wickedness of the people, and would deliver the steadfastly pious and faithful out of their danger and suffering, yet that they would individualize these thoughts in a poetical way by a more lively and graphic mode of statement, such as naming the prescribed kind of punishment and the exact way of rescue, without personally wishing to have any further importance laid on these special features, or considering that the truth of their prophecy would be dependent on the fulfilment of them.

As to this, it is very natural that the form of the special descriptions in these predictions should be, as a rule, settled by the then present historical circumstances by which the prophet was surrounded. We must mostly explain it psychologically, and as arising from the state of things existing at the time of the prediction, how the prophet was induced, *e.g.*, to threaten the Divine vengeance in this or that way exactly, or to announce the invasion of this or that foreign nation. It would, however, be wrong to assume as a rule that the prophets were wont to describe the details of their predictions exactly in the way in which it would be most probable that they would be individually fulfilled, from a judicious consideration of the political circumstances. They were wont rather to express them in the mode they thought best fitted to make the wholesome impression on the people which they had in view. Thus, *e.g.*, they do not threaten them with the invasion of those very nations which, at the time of the utterance, were hostile to and menacing the Israelites, and from whom, according to outward appearance, danger was the most readily to be feared; but often rather with those nations against whom they wished to warn the people or the king, when the latter was thinking of turning to them for help, or of forming a closer union with them.

§ 191.—*Messianic Predictions—Their Character.*

At this point we must particularly take into consideration the *Messianic predictions, or predictions of salvation.* These are, in the wider sense in which I provisionally use the word, all those predictions which refer to the realization of that salvation which was promised to the people of God in Abraham. And in this sense, almost all the predictions of the Hebrew prophets have properly a Messianic character. The longing after deliverance, and after the full appearance of the Divine salvation and the Divine rest, pervades the whole history of the Israelites, as they, with justice, cherished the feeling that all the promises given to Abraham were by no means fully realized by the taking possession of the land of Canaan (cf. also Heb. iv. 8); and this longing more or less prevails in the predictions of all the prophets, and forms the horizon to which every glance is directed.

But in details we find that this expectation shaped itself in different ways in different times and prophets:

First, (*a*) there are many predictions in which the great salvation which God had reserved for His people appears almost entirely or predominantly conceived and represented as of an external political character, as a victory over all outward enemies, and a glorious re-constitution of the Israelitish commonwealth, connected with a remarkable fruitfulness of the land and similar Divine blessings. There are others, on the contrary, in which the expectation has taken a purer and more spiritual shape, and principally expresses the promise of the blotting out of all misdeeds, and the cleansing from sin and the sanctification of men.

Next, (b) this longing *first* relates to the people of Israel, the seed of Abraham, Isaac, and Jacob, as the race chosen by Jehovah; and in many predictions these only, the natural descendants of the above patriarchs, are spoken of, as those to whom the deliverance and the salvation should be awarded. In others, however, the prophets' glance stretches further, and they predict that other nations also, even those who then stood hostilely opposed to Jehovah's people, should likewise have a share in Israel's salvation, and should be accepted into God's kingdom, which should spread itself over the whole world.

Finally, (c) as regards the bringing about of this salvation; in most of the predictions this is ascribed to Jehovah Himself, the Divine Defender of Israel, without distinct prominence being given to any human deliverer. There are *others* which express the hope that, under the Divine assistance, the triumph of the worship of the only true God should be completely or partly accomplished, and the glory and salvation assigned to the people of the Covenant should be made ready for them through some person then existing, e.g., the king sitting on the throne, or through a number of persons, as, e.g., the true servants of God generally; and *others*, also, in which the bringing about of this salvation is bound up with the appearance of some single future deliverer, particularly a ruler out of the family of David.

These latter predictions are those which, in the closer sense, are called Messianic. But the other predictions mentioned are also with justice likewise numbered among the Messianic ones, so far as the longing which is expressed in all of them, and the expectation on which they are all based, find their essential fulfilment only in the salvation proceeding from the Messiah, which came into the world with Christ.

But, as regards the various modifications with which this expectation is expressed in the prophecies, these must sometimes be looked at by regarding the *respective ages* to which the predictions belonged, and the *circumstances* among which the prophet ministered. Thus, e.g., in the prophetic utterances threatening the scattering of the people, or in those which were themselves composed at the time of the

Captivity, the promise of Messianic salvation is bound up immediately with that of the return of the people out of exile. These variations sometimes belong merely to the *individuality* of the several prophets; as in several prophets, as, *e.g.*, in Joel, Amos, Zephaniah, Obadiah, Nahum, Habakkuk, and Haggai, also Isaiah xl. ff., there is no distinct promise of any single future person as a Deliverer and Saviour. But even in one and the same prophet this promise is at times framed in different ways in different predictions, and sometimes one way and sometimes the other is made the more prominent.

§ 192.—*Messianic Predictions—Special Details as to Time, Circumstances, &c.*

In a certain way also, the different modifications in which the bringing about and form of the future great salvation is depicted in detail may be considered as the poetic side of the statement of the Messianic hope. But it cannot be overlooked, and must not be left unnoticed, that even this is connected with the incompleteness of the prophetic perception generally. All prophetic intuition, as we are acquainted with it in the Holy Scriptures of the Old Covenant, has something imperfect and limited about it; ἐκ μέρους προφητεύομεν, 1 Cor. xiii. 9.

This is usually acknowledged with regard to the *time*. In this respect the prophecies are usually so framed that they have a *perspective* character, great developments and catastrophes, occurring at considerable intervals of time, appearing to be brought close together, or to be quite intermixed.

When chronological statements occur in genuine, unaltered predictions, they are mostly of a general nature, employing round numbers of a somewhat sacred character —*seventy* being a favourite number—which cannot be intended literally by the prophets themselves, as may be proved pretty exactly from the details.

The limitation of the prophetical view, apart from the relations of time, is usually not less evident in the rest of their delineation of the future event, and of the nature and manner of its bringing about. This is particularly the case with the Messianic predictions. If we view these by themselves, and compare them not only with one another, but also with the nature of the actual salvation which appeared, we shall see plainly that it has not pleased Divine Providence to allow any one of the Hebrew prophets to conceive this future salvation, and the whole glory of Him by whom it was to be brought about, in such clearness as is granted to us now that it has come into the world. The prophets themselves belonged to the Old Covenant, and although their glance is always directed towards the new one, yet what was communicated to them by revelation as to the nature of it, has always more or less been perceived by them as through a veil, and not with that clearness in which it is now disclosed to us.

This is also intimated in 1 Peter i. 10, in which we see that the prophets themselves did not perceive, as clearly revealed, the time and circumstances to which the purport of their predictions referred. Therefore even the Saviour Himself speaks of the least in the kingdom of God as greater than John, whom he styles as the greatest of the prophets, *i.e.*, of the Old Covenant: Matt. xi. 11; Luke vii. 28. In 2 Peter i. 19, the prophetic word is appropriately compared to a light shining in a dark place; but this light is distinguished from and opposed to the brightness of the morning star, the light of day, which would not arise until its fulfilment.

This explains how it is that the purport of the Gospel in the New Testament is spoken of, especially by Paul, as something, on the one hand, revealed of old to the prophets, and also as a μυστήριον, which, kept in the counsel of God, had been hidden from all, and was not revealed until after the appearance of Christ, when it would be still more and more plainly revealed. It was disclosed that God intended, in His own good time, to cause a great salvation to appear; and this is expressed in every prophecy of those prophets who have intended, by means of their utterances on these points, to strengthen and confirm the people in faith and a steadfast fidelity to the worship of the true God, even in tribulation and grief, and to stir up and maintain in them the longing after the future salvation. But the exact mode in which this salvation was to be shaped was ever a μυστήριον, about which none of the Old-Testament prophets were able to give any distinct and clear information. The references to this in their utterances are to be taken as proceeding more from the human individuality of the several prophets; they express rather the particular way in which the various prophets conceived the Divine revelation of that great salvation by means of their human individuality. Thus there is a great variety in these ideas, and the separate features in the Messianic predictions are shaped in very different ways in different prophets.

§ 193.—*Messianic Predictions—Their proper Interpretation.*

Assuming the correctness of these remarks, we may gather from them how we ought to proceed in the *interpretation* of these predictions. On the one hand, we must always hold fast to the consciousness that Jesus Christ, and the kingdom of God founded by Him, is the aim of all these predictions, and that it is He in whom alone all the hopes and aspirations shown in these predictions were to find, and indeed could alone find, their complete satisfaction. On the other hand, we cannot expect that we shall be in a position to prove the exact fulfilment of all the separate details in these predictions in the person and history of Christ. It would be vain for us to attempt this. We must not, however, leave unconsidered all the various and special statements in the details of these predictions, since it is only by them we can discern in what way and with what modifications the hope of the Messiah shaped itself in the different prophets, and, historically, what course this hope had taken under the Divine guidance, from its first budding until it found its fulfilment in and with the appearance of Jesus Christ. This part of the question, indeed, which in former times has been frequently overlooked, should rather be the most prominent with us in the explanation of the details, as the chief importance of these Messianic predictions for us is that they bear testimony to the fact that God, before the appearance of Christianity, led on the Israelites in the old time by the eyes and lips of men raised up by Him until the time of the arrival of this salvation; whilst they can be of less service to us in teaching us the real essence and nature of this salvation itself; for this we must look rather to the history of its appearance.

It might however be, perhaps, regarded as difficult, or quite impossible, to determine in the prophecies generally whether any part was to be taken as a distinct special prediction, or only as serving to express a general thought. There are, of course, some cases in which there might be some doubt as to this at first; but, by an impartial and careful consideration of the context, and of the actual aim of the different prophecies, the means of decision is usually spontaneously afforded. Thus we may most certainly assume that any portion is to be taken as a special prediction, if the prophet states that the confirmation of his truth as a Divine ambassador is dependent on its fulfilment, as, *e.g.*, Is. vii. 14. Where, however, the case so stands that it is not easy to make a certain decision in this respect, no stress is to be laid upon it.

In forming our idea of the prophets, it is essential that no doubt should be entertained of their being men enlightened by God in a direct way, and that as such they could receive and communicate information as to various events of the future. But whether they made use of this gift in this or that case, is not very important to us in a religious, or even in an historical point of view, as these predictions were not given to us for historical investigation, any more than the Messianic predictions for instruction as to the being and person of the Saviour. But in general it is undeniable that cases of this kind of special predictions are comparatively seldom found in our prophetical Scriptures, and they were perhaps always only rare. What Nitzsch (*System der Christl. Lehre*, § 35) intimates is, therefore, very apposite—that the distinct gift of prediction must always be kept subordinate in revelation, and must show itself rarely and moderately, or else its whole relation to history would be destroyed. In our endeavours, therefore, to prove that certain special facts in a later age correspond with the separate details of this or that prophecy and are to be looked at as their fulfilment, we must not go further than we are led by an impartial consideration of the prophecy itself in its natural connection, and we must not generally lay too great a value on it in comparison with the rest of the purport of the prophetical utterances.[1]

At all events we have no reason for supposing that, in the prophecies of the Old-Testament prophets, any special predictions occur as to events happening after the com-

[1] The remarks of Nitzsch (*ut supra*, ed. 3, ff., against Hengstenberg) are appropriate.

mencement of the New Covenant. For the sum of all the predictions of the Old Covenant have their aim and end in the New, and are, for the most part, fulfilled by its institution. If it did not please the Divine wisdom to impart to any one of the prophets of the Old Covenant a thoroughly clear and lucid disclosure, either as to the commencement of this New Covenant or the appearance and person of the Saviour who founded it, it is still less probable that God would have caused them to have a clear perception of circumstances which occurred still later, in times which had been so entirely altered in comparison with any earlier epoch, by the intervention of that great event; as everything that occurred subsequently was necessarily connected with the mode in which this event had shaped itself. My meaning, however, is not that these prophecies were completely fulfilled in the first establishment of the Christian Church by the Saviour becoming flesh; for they certainly will not find their full accomplishment until the consummation of God's kingdom at the end of time. But the question here is only as to the predictions of certain special events; and among the Old-Testament prophecies we certainly cannot expect to find any which relate to events happening after Christ.

§ 194.—*Method of fixing the Dates of the various Prophetical Writings.*

We have still one point to consider briefly—*the dates of the prophecies.*[1] Most of the prophetical Scriptures of the Old Testament are provided with superscriptions, in which the age to wnich the prophets belonged is generally stated, according to the kings under whom they lived; and some part of them have special superscriptions or introductions fixing the time exactly at which, and the circumstances among which, the prophecy was issued. The prophecies of Haggai are distinguished the most exactly in this respect, according to the year, month, and day. There are, however, some of the prophetical Scriptures which do not contain any such statements, and in which we know nothing about the date and circumstances of the author from assured historical information derived from

[1] Cf. Bleek's work, "The Song of Moses, Deut. xxxii. 1-43," pp. 254-256.

other quarters, as, *e.g.*, Joel, Obadiah, Nahum, Habakkuk, Malachi. In other cases, the age to which the prophet belonged is stated generally, but nothing exact as to the times in which their different utterances took place; added to this, in many of the superscriptions of this kind it is doubtful whether they proceed from the prophets themselves, and to what extent they are authentic. It becomes a question, therefore, how to ascertain the dates of the different prophecies, where this is not made known by historical evidence, or at least not in a trustworthy way.

Of course a more exact study of the character of the language will help us in this as affording a proof of an earlier or later age. This criterion of the date always has, however, something very uncertain in it. The chief rule, therefore, which we shall use in this investigation is the result of our previous consideration of the nature of the Hebrew prophesying; viz., the two points—(*a*) that the aim of the Hebrew prophets in their utterances was throughout ethical, having in view the condition and necessities of their people; and (*b*), that during their inspiration they always retained a clear consciousness, and in their consciousness were never mentally isolated from the external circumstances surrounding them. From these points we at once gain the rule that, in the utterances presented to us, we should take notice of those circumstances with which the actual prophecy is bound up, which are presupposed in it as present and well-known; we can then look upon these as constituting the state of things surrounding the prophet, at the time of uttering or composing his prophecies. If these circumstances clearly point out and are characteristic of any particular age, or any particular date in preference to any other, we may thus ascertain the date of the composition.

Thus, *e.g.*, if we find prophecies in which the people of Judah are spoken of as having lived for a long time away from their homes among foreign idolatrous nations, and in which Jerusalem, together with the temple and the other cities of Judah are described as lying in ruins, in which, however, the people are comforted by the intimation of their liberation, return to their land, and re-institution of their state and temple, all closely impending according to the Divine counsel, we can then infer with certainty that the above are utterances of a prophet at the time of the Babylonian Captivity.

Yet even the employment of this rule will often fail to lead us to any very sure decision. *Firstly*, the circumstances then existing are not usually expressly stated in connection with the prophecy itself, but at the most are only hinted at, and, as a rule, merely inferred; they are therefore, often not easily to be discerned. *Secondly*, in the very deficient sources which are at our disposal as to the history of the people of Israel, there are only a small number of its epochs of which we have any knowledge sufficiently detailed and certain to enable us to draw a lively and distinct picture of the circumstances of the people at any particular age or date. Therefore, although some particular circumstances may be clearly prominent in a prophecy, yet we are not always in a position at the same time to state with certainty to what particular epoch these belong. In prophecies, therefore, which do not precisely state their date in the superscription or historical introduction, there frequently remains, in respect to this point, more or less uncertainty and indecision.

But still we must keep close to the above rule, and by its means follow out the investigation of the dates of the several prophets and their predictions, so far as is possible from a study of the then existing circumstances; and we must also make use of this rule in order to prove the correctness in this respect of the superscriptions of the different prophecies.

Among the opponents of the principles here developed, there are, among the modern interpreters, Hengstenberg, and others who followed him. Their opinion is (also in the 2nd edit. of the *Christol.*), (*a*) that the circumstances of the future were always represented to the prophets in the form of vision; and (*b*) that the prophet was transported by his vision into the various circumstances of a future, often far-removed, and prophesied prospectively from this stand-point, assumed by him as then present. Thus, for example, prophets who lived long before the Babylonian Captivity, were able to take their stand-point at this epoch, and from thence predict things impending still more remotely, treating nevertheless of the affairs of the Captivity as then present.

The assumption, however, is certainly erroneous, or at least not at all demonstrable, that the substance of their prophecy was always communicated to the prophets by way of vision. We have no right to assume that the communication was by actual eyesight, except where they themselves relate that visions were afforded them. In other prophecies we are not entitled to suppose, nor is it at all probable, that they were revealed to the prophets exactly in this form.

Even in the actual *visions* of the Old-Testament prophets, we do not find any such transference into the circumstances of another and much later epoch, but always a close relation to those of their own time and its wants. This is still more the case in the prophecies of another class. Although in these, the prophet sometimes appears to transport himself out of the circumstances then immediately existing, and to consider as present the facts revealed to him, which he really intends to predict as imminent, this was only for the moment, and the object was merely to depict the fact *poetically*, and in a more lively and graphic way. Moreover, whenever this took place, to those immediately round him and his contemporaries, to whom his discourse always referred in the first place, the matters treated of in it and the circumstances which were spoken of, were always perfectly clear. Besides, such a view as that of Hengstenberg and his followers, would preclude the possibility of ascertaining the dates of the several prophecies from their substance. The ethical character of the Hebrew prophesying would also be, in this way, as good as lost.

§ 195.—*The Authors of the Prophetical Scriptures.*

As regards the prophetical Scriptures in our Canon, the persons under whose names they have been preserved to us, are as follows. (*a*) in the second division of the Canon, Isaiah, Jeremiah, Ezekiel, and the twelve so-called Lesser Prophets, and (*b*) in the Hagiographa, the Lamentations of Jeremiah, and Daniel.

It has been seldom, if ever, questioned, that the greater part of these scriptures are, in general, the works of the men whose names they bear, viz., Jeremiah, Ezekiel, and the lesser prophets, with the exception of Jonah and Zechariah.

With regard to the Book of Jonah, amongst all the variety of opinions about it, it has been generally so far acknowledged, that it has been adopted into the collection of prophetical books, because the contents of it relate to the history of a prophet; and its name is assumed to refer not so much to the possible author, as to the chief person who appears in it. With regard to the Book of Daniel, the authenticity of the whole work and its origin have been, in modern times, the subject of continuous controversy; and it is questionable, whether the whole of the prophecies contained in the Books of Isaiah and Zechariah, belong to the prophets Isaiah and Zechariah, who are named in the superscriptions of the books as their authors, or whether some parts of them are not by other prophets of other times.

We shall treat of these books in general according to their order of succession in the Hebrew Canon; we shall, however, make our investigation of the Lamentations follow immediately after that of the prophecies of Jeremiah, and we shall consider the Book of Jonah the last of the lesser prophèts; and conclude with the investigation of the Book of Daniel.

THE BOOK OF ISAIAH.

§ 196.—*Isaiah—His Name, Family, and Date of his Ministry.*

The name of Isaiah, by which the first of the properly prophetical books is called, both in the printed editions of the Hebrew Old Testament and in the translation of Luther, is in Hebrew, יְשַׁעְיָהוּ, or in the abridged form in which it is written as the title of the book, יְשַׁעְיָה = *Jehovah's salvation;* in the Greek, 'Ησαίας, or more correctly, 'Ησαΐας, in the Latin, *Esaias*, also *Isaias*; Luther writes *Jesaia*.

Isaiah was the son of Amos, אָמוֹץ (ch. i. 1; 2 Kings xix. 2; xx. 1), otherwise unknown.[1] He appears to have had his regular residence in Judah, and indeed in Jerusalem, cf., as pointing to this fact, ch. vii. 3, ff., xxii. 1, ff. It follows from ch. vii. 3, viii. 3, 18, that he was married and had several sons; indeed from ch. vii. 14, ff., in comparison with *v.* 3, that probably he was twice married.

The age to which Isaiah belonged is stated in the superscription relating to the whole book (ch. i. 1), as the reigns of *Uzziah, Jotham, Ahaz,* and *Hezekiah,* kings of Judah. The first named died about 759 B.C., and Hezekiah reigned from 728 to 699 B.C. We possess clear evidence of the ministry of Isaiah in the reign of Ahaz and Hezekiah, partly given by express statements in his prophecies (and in regard to Hezekiah's reign, in the second Book of Kings) (ch. xix. ff.), and partly by the clear traces of date afforded by the contents of the various utterances.

We find Isaiah particularly active in the first year of the reign of the idolatrous king Ahaz, when Judah was assailed and hard pressed by the allied kings of Syria and Israel, Rezin and Pekah: and the king of Judah, in opposition to the warning of the prophet, had purchased the help of the Assyrian king, Tiglath-pileser. By his means, Judah was, indeed, delivered from the momentary distress, and

[1] Not to be confused with the prophet Amos (עָמוֹס), with whom many ecclesiastical authors identify him, because the two names are written in the same way in Greek and Latin ('Αμώς, *Amos*).

their enemies were humbled; but, at the same time, they became more and more oppressively dependent on the Assyrians, from whom they suffered much at the time of Hezekiah, after the kingdom of Israel had been completely broken up by the Assyrian king Shalmanezer, in the sixth year of the former king. Express statements show that the ministry of Isaiah was especially and very influentially directed to the relation of Judah with the Assyrians, and particularly to the distress arising from this nation under Sennacherib in the fourteenth year of Hezekiah.

King *Uzziah* is again named (besides the superscription) in ch. vi. 1; and the year of his death is mentioned as the time when the vision there related was vouchsafed to the prophet. This vision has quite the character of being an ordination of the prophet to his prophetic office, as if it commenced at this time. Yet, I think that it may be assumed with the greatest probability—particularly comparing an analogous indication of the time, ch. xiv. 28—that this vision is not intended to be " *before* the death of the king, in the year in which he afterwards died," as it is understood by the ancient expositors, but, " in the year in which he died;" so that it would have happened soon after Uzziah's death, at the beginning of Jotham's reign. Therefore the statement in the superscription ch. i. 1, as it now stands, proceeded doubtless not from the prophet himself, but from some later compiler, and must be considered as inaccurate, the days of Uzziah being therein named as a portion of the time in which Isaiah's prophecies were uttered.

Apart from this statement, ch. vi. 1, Jotham and his reign are not expressly mentioned in any of the prophecies of our book, nor is there in any of them internal evidence to lead us to suppose that they belonged to the succeeding years of this king. It may be, therefore, that the prophet did not commit to writing his prophetical deliveries made at that time, or that they are now lost to us.

The *latest* period at which we find any certain statements as to Isaiah's prophetical ministry is in the reign of Hezekiah, after the retiring of Sennacherib's host from Jerusalem, and after Hezekiah's illness and recovery; on the occasion of an embassy from the Babylonian king Merodach-baladan to the former, when Hezekiah, out of

Period of Isaiah's Ministry. 43

vanity, showed the ambassadors all his treasures. Then, it is related, Isaiah predicted to him the impending Babylonian bondage of the people of Judah, which ensued about 125 years after (2 Kings xx; Is. xxxviii. f.). This occurred in any case, some time after the 14th year of Hezekiah, (714 B.C.), therefore at least 46 years after Uzziah's death, at which time Isaiah received his calling as a prophet.

No further express statements are to be found as to Isaiah's ministry during the remaining part of Hezekiah's reign, embracing 15 years more. Yet we cannot doubt that he continued to exercise his prophetic office even till the reign of Manasseh. For we know that Isaiah wrote a history both of Uzziah and also of Hezekiah (cf. §§ 62, 63). The former is quoted 2 Chron. xxvi. 22, and the latter 2 Chron. xxxii. 32. We see from the words of this latter quotation, that what he had written concerning Hezekiah had been adopted into the great work of the "History of the Kings of Judah," and from the way in which it is mentioned as containing "the rest of the acts of Hezekiah, and his pious conduct," we cannot doubt that it was a very complete work, and not composed by Isaiah until after the death of the above king. An ancient tradition corresponds with the above, which tells us that Isaiah lived on until Manasseh's time, and died a martyr's death, being sawn asunder at the king's command.

[The same tradition occurs in the Talmud (*tr. Jebamoth*, f. 49, 2; *Sanhedr*. f. 103, 2), and in the Rabbis as well as in Justin Mart. (*Dial. c. Tryph.* p. 349); Tertull. (*de Patientia*, c. 14), and other Fathers, and in an apocryphal book ascribed to Isaiah, 'Αναβατικόν, in about the second century after Christ, which has been preserved in an Æthiopian version as well as partly in an ancient Latin translation (*v.* as to this, De Wette. § 214, Notes, and Lücke (*Introd. to the Apocal.* Edit. 2, § 16). Not improbably the ἐπρίσθησαν, Heb. xi. 37, refers to this.]

The fact itself, from the idolatrous and cruel character of Manasseh, is not at all unlikely, although it cannot be considered as certain. In our book, and in the Old Testament generally, there is no express evidence of any ministry of Isaiah in the reign of Manasseh. This, however, does not prove that it may not have lasted so long. At this time the prophet would have attained a very considerable age, as much as 80 years at least, but there is no improbability in this.

§ 197.—*Nature of Contents—Its three Sections.*

As regards the Old-Testament book preserved to us under the name of Isaiah, by far the greatest part of it consists of prophetical utterances, and there are only four chapters of historical narrative. It divides itself, at first sight, into three chief parts :

A. Chapters i–xxxv.—A collection of separate prophetic utterances, sometimes furnished with particular superscriptions and short historical introductions, and sometimes, without this, they are divided from each other by their substance, and show themselves to be different prophecies referring to different times, subjects, and circumstances.

B. Chapters xxxvi–xxxix.—An historical fragment of the history of Hezekiah, relating to the siege of Jerusalem by the Assyrians in the fourteenth year of this king, the deliverance of the city, the illness and recovery of Hezekiah, and the Babylonian embassy to him.

C. Chapters xl–lxvi.—Contains nothing but prophetic utterances, but more intimately connected with one another than the prophecies in the first part, by one joining on to the other, and all of them referring substantially to the same dates, viz., to the last period of the Babylonian Captivity of the Jews, and their deliverance therefrom.

§ 198.—*Question as to Unity of Authorship.*

All these elements of our book were formerly attributed to one and the same author, the prophet Isaiah, the son of Amos. Only Aben Esra[1] has given some slight intimations, which allow his opinion to gleam through, that the prophecies of the last part have for their author a later prophet, at the time of the Babylonian Captivity. No regard, however, has yet been paid to these hints. Quite independently of him, however, similar opinions in reference to these prophecies have been brought to bear by many Protestant divines of Germany, since the last twenty

---

[1] In his "Commentary on Isaiah," chaps. xl, xlix, liii; cf. Geiger, in the "Scientific Journal of Jewish Theology," edited by him, Vol. 2 (Frankf. 1836), pp. 553–557.

Unity of Authorship questioned.

years of the last century. They have denied Isaiah's authorship of various portions even of the first division, and have attributed them to other prophets and times. Other authors have, indeed, controverted this, and have earnestly endeavoured to vindicate the integrity of the book, and the unity of the authorship in all its divisions.[1] Yet, I believe that an unprejudiced consideration could not rest satisfied with these traditional opinions; particularly in reference to the *third division* (ch. xl–lxvi). Basing our investigation on the rule previously (§ 194) laid down, if we pay due regard to the circumstances presupposed, with which the actual prophecy is connected, we shall clearly see that these prophecies do not belong to Isaiah or to his age. We shall find circumstances alluded to quite at variance with the state of things in Isaiah's age, and corresponding to a condition of things that did not exist at all till towards the end of the Babylonian Captivity.

Although the external circumstances of the remote future were clearly unveiled to the prophet, there are in this division no predictions, as one would have expected in prophecies of the age of Isaiah, intimating that, as had happened with the kingdom of Israel, Judah should also be broken up, and the people carried away to Babylon, and that Jerusalem and the other cities of Judah should be destroyed. All this appears as if it had already taken place for some considerable time, Jerusalem and the other cities of Judah are lying in ruins, and the predictions declare that they should be again built up. The Jewish people are addressed as if they were in Babylon, rejected by their God on account of their sins, a prey to their enemies, and hemmed round by idolaters; and they are comforted by the prediction that Jehovah would yet again be moved to pity His own people, that He would deliver them, and bring them back again to their native land. It is not anywhere predicted, as from the stand-point of Isaiah might have been expected, that, in the course of time, the Babylonians

---

[1] Thus, keeping only to the German Protestant divines, Hengstenberg (*Christol.* Vol. 2); Kleinert ("On the Genuineness of the whole of the Prophecies in the Book of Isaiah," 1 vol. Berlin, 1829); Hävernick· Drechsler ("The Prophet Isaiah," 3 parts, 1845–57); Keil; Stier ("Isaiah not Pseudo-Isaiah," "Interpretation of Chapters xl–lxvi." Barmen, 1850, &c.

should get the dominion instead of the Assyrians, and that they should use their power for the enslaving of the Jews: but the Chaldeans appear as if already at the summit of power, although their destruction was now near, and it is merely predicted, that anon the Divine judgment would fall on them, especially on account of their cruelty towards the Jews. The Persian king Cyrus is here pointed out, and twice indeed even mentioned by name (ch. xliv. 28; xlv. 1), as the deliverer of the Jews out of the Babylonian slavery, and as the conqueror of the Babylonians; but it is nowhere predicted that, at some future time, a prince of the name of Cyrus should arise, and he appears as if already existing and well known to all, as distinguished by Jehovah by his former victories, and as a prince to whom the eyes of all were directed. All that is predicted of him is, that, impelled by Jehovah, and with His assistance, he should soon humble the might of the Chaldeans, destroy Babylon, dismiss the Jews to their homes, and again build up Jerusalem and the Temple.

This being the nature of the prophecies in Is. xl–lxvi, we are, in my judgment, perfectly entitled, if not compelled, to come to the decision that they cannot belong to the age of Isaiah, but to a considerably later time, the circumstances of which are so clearly presupposed as present; viz., to the last period of the Babylonian Captivity.

At that time, half a century had already elapsed since the breaking up of the state of Judah and the destruction of Jerusalem, during which the stock of the Jewish people were in exile in Babylon. Many Jews appear to have so settled themselves there that they had lost all longing to return to their desolated homes; and these had so closely connected themselves with the idolatrous people among whom they lived, as even in part to take to their worship, or at least to the adoration of images; some of these were indifferent spectators of the conflict of Cyrus with the Babylonians, while others sided with the latter.

Those Jews were far less numerous who, like the prophet, kept firmly faithful to Jehovah, even in exile, and who observed the law of their God, so far as it could be done without a temple and without the offering of sacrifices, particularly by hallowing the Sabbath, and by the particular observance of those fast-days which reminded them of the punishment decreed by Jehovah on their nation, and also by an abstinence from everything which had reference to idolatry. These cherished the longing after their native land, the re-institution of the temple, and the worship of Jehovah, and so much the more, the more they had to suffer persecution on the part both of their heathen tyrants and of the mass of their own fellow-countrymen. From the beginning, they followed the movements of Cyrus against Babylon with warm sympathy, and were the more inclined to recognise in him an instrument raised up by Jehovah for their liberation, as the religion of the Persians was much more nearly allied to the monotheism of the Jews than the religions of the other heathen nations, and they entertained the same detestation of the adoration of idols as the stricter observers of the law among the Jews.

Thus our prophet repeatedly praises Cyrus as a prince especially favoured by Jehovah, whom He had ordained to humble Babylon, to bring back to their homes the captive Jews, and restore again to them Jerusalem and the Temple. At the same time he repeatedly attacks idol and image-worship most energetically, and represents it in its vanity and folly with striking and almost sarcastic irony, pointing to Jehovah as the only living, almighty, all-seeing God, who aforetime had caused to be predicted what now was on the point of taking place,—the victory over heathenism, and the freeing of His people, whose deliverance would be delayed only by the continual sinfulness in the midst of them. Yet, that Jehovah would certainly bring this to pass; that He would atone for the sins of the people, and so make them fit to be partakers of the great salvation destined for them, which is here directly bound up with the return of the people out of Captivity, and, like this return itself, is gloriously depicted in poetical imagery.

§ 199.—*Authorship of the third Section of the Book.*

That all this series of prophecies have one and the same author may be inferred from the great similarity in the style and language which, in general, pervades the whole; this is also acknowledged by far the greatest part of those who deny Isaiah's authorship of this section; cf.

Knobel's *Jesaja*, p. 299, ff. Edit. 3. In this respect, however, we must remark as follows:

(1) We may assume with the highest probability of the section lvi. 9–lvii. 11 [as Ewald also thinks], that it was originally composed perhaps by Isaiah himself, as a prophetical utterance before the Captivity; probably not long before it, but at all events at a time when the kingdom of Judah still existed; as the purport and form of this portion can only be understood on this supposition.

The enemies of the people of Judah are therein summoned to approach and swallow them up, which would not be difficult for them to do, as the watchmen of the people, to whom their safety was confided, were asleep and quite blind to all danger, and unable to warn them against it.[1] This throughout presupposes the existence of the kingdom of Judah; likewise, in ch. lvii. 6–11, Jerusalem is spoken of and described as a harlot committing uncleanness with idols: *vide* also the same *v.* 3. Also the way in which, ch. lvii. 1–10, the unlawful offering of sacrifice is spoken of generally as a worship in high places, and *v.* 5, and also probably *v.* 9, as the (Ammonitish) worship of Moloch, agrees more with what we find in the prophets before the exile, especially just immediately before it, than the mode in which in the rest of this series of prophecies idolatry is represented in its ridiculous point of view. There is no sign, besides this, that the Israelites carried on the worship of Moloch at the time of the Captivity.[2]

It is, however, very probable, that this utterance was adopted by the author of the above series of prophecies (ch. xl–lxvi), and was inserted among his own discourses; perhaps, indeed, precisely on account of the earnest threaten-

[1] Cf. as to this, "Lectures on Isaiah," on this passage: "If this is the sense of ch. lvi. 9, ff., it appears to me that it is impossible it could have been written in one connection with what precedes. It is absolutely incredible, that the prophet, after the promises that no evil of any kind should again hurt the people (ch. lv), that the time of salvation was quite near, in which even the foreigners among the people should partake (ch. lvi. 1), should now suddenly summon up foreign nations to devour his people," &c.

[2] Cf. "Lectures on Isaiah": "From all this, since my first lecture on Isaiah, 1820–21, I have come to the conclusion that this section, which by its language is clearly distinguished from the prophecies near it, was originally written before the destruction of Jerusalem." Umbreit also confesses that the passage seems somewhat extraneous.

ings in it directed against the idolatry of the people, which in his time also was very prevalent, although carried on in a somewhat different form.

(2) As regards the author of this series of prophecies, we cannot doubt that he was *not* in Egypt at the time of its composition,[1] but on the whole in Babylon itself. The author, however, may have become acquainted with the circumstances of the land of Judah at that time by his own observation. Also, these prophecies were, in all probability, written by the author in the very order in which we have them, yet not quite all at one and the same time. The first part, at least to ch. xlvii. inclusive, was certainly written before the taking of Babylon by Cyrus, and perhaps much of what follows. It is not improbable that the latter part, on the contrary, was not composed until after the capture of the city of Babylon, when the hope of the speedy liberation and glorious restoration of the Jewish people had not been immediately realized. At a somewhat later time, after a part of the people, and the prophet among them, had already returned to Palestine, come perhaps the last chapters, from ch. lviii. onwards; more certainly, however, the four last chapters, lxiii–lxvi, which are generally more distinct from the preceding ones, as different prophetical utterances complete in themselves, but perhaps likewise by the same author.

(*a*) Ch. lxiii. 1–6.—A beautiful effusion, and complete in itself, announcing the Divine judgments on the heathen nations, and particularly on the Edomites. In it, verse 4, "For the day of vengeance is in mine heart, and the year of my redeemed is come," renders it very probable, that the composition occurred at a time when the people of the Covenant had been for a long time in oppression and captivity, and perhaps shortly before they were delivered out of it. A prediction against the enemies of the people would be very likely to take this particular form against the Edomites, as, at the breaking up of the state of Judah, the latter showed themselves peculiarly hostile and malicious against the Jews.

[1] This is the opinion of Ewald, who considers him as a descendant of those who went down to Egypt with Jeremiah, and also of Bunsen (*Gott in der Geschichte*, Part i.), who identifies him with Baruch, former minister of Jeremiah.

(*b*) Ch. lxiii. 7-lxv. *fin.*, first to lxiv. *fin.*—Confession of the sins of the people, and the prophet's intercession for them. In *v.* 10 of ch. lxiv. the destroyed temple is spoken of as that " in which *our fathers* praised thee," and yet there is no intimation that the author was in exile. This, very probably, belongs to a time, when, by the first of the returning exiles, a beginning, though only a feeble one, had been made in the rebuilding of Jerusalem. · Ch. lxv. is connected with this in which Jehovah answers these lamentations and entreaties. The substance of this likewise makes it most probable that the author, as is generally assumed, no longer lived in exile, but in Palestine, and that it was composed at a time when a part of the Jews had returned out of exile, and had united with the other part who were in the land; at a time, however, when the new state found itself still in continual need and distress, which the prophet considers as the just punishment of their continual sinfulness.

(*c*) Ch. lxvi. is of similar purport with ch. lxv.—Everything in it points to a prophet who lived in Palestine, in Jerusalem, or its neighbourhood, at a time when sacrifices were again offered there (*vv.* 3, 6, 20), namely, on the altar of burnt-offering, erected there by the returned exiles; and also, perhaps, at a time when the rebuilding of the temple had been begun.

§ 200.—*Review of Contents—Chapters* i–xii.

The *first principal division* of the book, ch. i–xxxv, contains, as we have already remarked, various separate utterances, and there are many among them which cannot belong to Isaiah and his age, because the circumstances of another time appear presupposed in them as present. As to the details, I will only here give a few short notes. This part may be most conveniently considered in three sub-divisions: ch. i–xii, xiii–xxiii, xxiv–xxxv.

I. Ch. i–xii.—This sub-division contains, according to the most probable view of it, eight different prophecies, separated from each other sometimes by particular superscriptions, and sometimes, without these, only by their contents. With the exception of a short fragment, ch. ii. 2–4, all this division contains nothing but the genuine words of Isaiah.

The different utterances are as follows:—

(1) Ch. i.—Threatening and warning discourses spoken to Judah and Jerusalem; after Jehovah had sent a heavy punishment on the land, most probably either at the time of Ahaz, after the inroad of the Syrians and Israelites into Judah, or still more likely, at the time of Hezekiah, in the fourteenth year of this king, after the departure of the Assyrians out of the land of Judah. The comparatively more general bearing of this utterance was, perhaps, the cause for placing it at the beginning of the whole book, as a sort of proem to it.

(2) Ch. ii–iv.—This, from the superscription, is also a discourse about Judah and Jerusalem, a threatening of the Divine judgment against the debauchery and idolatry prevalent in the land, with a conclusion, however, promising new blessings; most probably uttered in the reign of Ahaz, a considerable time after the inroad of the Israelites and Syrians into Judah, when this kingdom was again strengthened from without by the help of the Assyrians. The utterances of Isaiah, however, do not begin until ch. ii. 5. The preceding verses, 2–4, containing a Messianic promise in a wider sense, again occur, with almost verbal agreement, Micah iv. 1–3. How this is to be explained is very doubtful. I, however, think (*a*) that it may be assumed with tolerable certainty that the passage in Micah is the original one, as in his book it stands with a very suitable context, and (*b*) that it formed no part of the prophecy of Isaiah, either originally, nor as borrowed by the prophet from some one else; but that it was interpolated into the Book of Isaiah by some later reader or compiler; first, perhaps, it was placed in the margin, and thence, subsequently, got into the text.

(3) Ch. v.—Parable of the vineyard, in reference to Israel and Judah, joined with threatening discourses against the people, especially against the great men in Jerusalem, without any promise being added; probably at the later period of the reign of Ahaz.

(4) Ch. vi.—The vision, in which the prophet was initiated into his vocation, in the year of Uzziah's death, *i.e.*, at the commencement of Jotham's reign (*v.* above); the record in writing of this vision most probably did not take place until later, perhaps even in the reign of Ahaz.

(5) Ch. vii.—A discourse which is provided with an historical introduction, by which it appears to be of the time of the attack of the united kings of Syria and Israel upon Judah, at the time of Ahaz, and most probably at the beginning of his reign. The prophet predicts to the king the sure destruction of these enemies, and points out to him, as a testimony of the truth of his announcement, the birth of a boy from a עַלְמָה, probably the bride or young wife of the prophet himself; and then at the conclusion threatens the entire devastation of the land by the Egyptians and Assyrians. This threatening, vv. 17–25, is connected with what goes before in a very abrupt way, so that we may assume, perhaps with probability, that in the oral delivery, something else stood between them.

(6) Ch. viii. 1–ix. 6.—Likewise belonging to the reign of Ahaz, but one or two years later than the previous prediction. The prophet threatens the Israelites who were hostile to the house of David with devastation at the hands of the Assyrians, admonishes Judah and Israel to confidence in Jehovah, and concludes with a Messianic prediction, and with the promise of the deliverance of the people, especially of those tribes of the kingdom of Israel which had already been severely oppressed by the Assyrians, and also of the entire victory over their enemies, through some future glorious prince, who should reign for ever as a righteous ruler on the throne of David.

(7) Ch. ix. 7–x. 4.—An utterance against the kingdom of Israel, which Jehovah would punish with defeat and captivity, and by causing the members of the people to rage one against the other. This is probably some years later than the previous discourse, when the people had somewhat recovered themselves from the attacks of Tiglath-pileser.

(8) Ch. x. 5–xii. 6.—This discourse, from its purport, was given in Hezekiah's reign, after the breaking up of the kingdom of Israel, probably in the 14th year of Hezekiah, at the beginning of Sennacherib's campaign against Judah. The prophet threatens the Assyrians on account of their haughtiness and the oppression exercised upon his people, predicts to them the frustration of their enterprise against Jerusalem, and concludes with the promise of the birth of a Messiah from the stem of David, under whom general

peace should prevail on the earth, to whom even the heathen nations should gather themselves together, and with the promise also of the return of the scattered ones of the people of Israel to their native land. There is no reason for considering, with some interpreters, that the last part of this section, ch. xi. and xii, or, with Ewald, only ch. xii, are nothing but later additions.

§ 201.—*Review of Contents—Chapters* xiii–xxiii.

II. Ch. xiii–xxiii.—This sub-division contains, with the exception of ch. xxii, further prophecies against or about foreign nations, such as those in the other prophets. Jer. xlvi–li; Ezek. xxv–xxxii. Most of the discourses in this division are distinguished from the other prophecies of the Book by the word מַשָּׂא being used to describe them in the superscription. This may, perhaps, have been added by the compiler of this division; yet here also, all the several discourses are not divided from one another by superscriptions. This division most probably comprises fifteen different discourses, several of which cannot be by Isaiah.

(1) Ch. xiii. 1–xiv. 23.—Predicting the destruction of the city of Babylon and its king by the Medes, the deliverance of the Jews out of the hard bondage of the Babylonians, and their return to their native land. The contents decidedly show that this discourse belongs to the last period of the Babylonian exile, yet before the capture of the city of Babylon by Cyrus; and that it was composed by a prophet who himself lived in the Babylonian country, but not perhaps in the city itself.

(2) Ch. xiv. 24–27, relates to quite different circumstances from the preceding prophecy, and is, without doubt, just as the one after it, a genuine utterance of Isaiah; from its purport, it clearly relates to the invasion of the Assyrians into Judah at the time of Hezekiah, and predicts that Jehovah shall destroy them in His land. This discourse is perhaps a little later than that in ch. x. 5–xii. 6, and was given at a time when the Assyrians were already in the land.

(3) Ch. xiv. 28–32.—According to the superscription, "in the year of Ahaz' death," which without doubt means—for the substance of the prophecy shows it—after the death

of the king. This discourse is directed against the Philistines, and is intended, as it appears, to warn them not to exult too soon in the death of Ahaz, for in the person of his son and successor, a still more dangerous adversary should arise against them.

(4) Ch. xv., xvi, against the Moabites, a prediction of the impending desolation of their country, against which they would vainly turn for succour to their idols. The last verses of the section, ch. xvi. 13, 14, contain an epilogue, in which it is predicted, that the destruction of Moab, beforetime threatened by Jehovah in the preceding prophecies, would take place in exactly three years. Opinions differ very much as to the date of the composition of the prophecy itself, and as to its relation to the epilogue. It appears to me most probable that (a) the body of the prophecy is either by Isaiah, or at least in his age; composed at the time of the Assyrian king Tiglath-pileser, when the latter, in the first year of Ahaz, made his warlike invasion of these districts; (b) that the epilogue, however, although in the language it reminds one of Isaiah, was not added till a considerably later time, perhaps not until about the time of the Babylonian Captivity.

(5) Ch. xvii. 1–11.—According to the superscription is an utterance against Damascus. But from the purport of it, it is not against the Syrians of Damascus only, but also, and even more decidedly, against the kingdom of Ephraim, which, like Damascus, should be visited with desolation, as a righteous punishment for forgetting their God and attaching themselves to foreigners. This utterance is without doubt by Isaiah, in the reign of Ahaz, most probably composed when the Assyrians, sent for as succour by Ahaz, had already entered Syria.

(6) Ch. xvii. 12–14 forms, as it appears, a separate utterance; it is directed against hostile nations, most probably against the Assyrians in their attack on Jerusalem in the 14th year of Hezekiah.

(7) Ch. xviii.—A very obscure utterance, which, however, probably relates to the same period of time as the preceding one, and refers to the hostility of the Assyrians against Judah and Jerusalem at the time of Hezekiah, and to the annihilation of their hosts through the Æthiopians coming to the help of the Jews, of whom the prophet

predicts that they shall acknowledge Jehovah's power, and shall offer oblations to Him at Jerusalem.

The two discourses (6 and 7) are, without doubt, by Isaiah, and were composed at about the same time, most probably after the defeat and flight of the Assyrians.

(8) Ch. xix, as to Egypt, at first rebukes and threatens, and, after v. 18, conveys promises, stating that Jehovah should be acknowledged and worshipped even on the part of the Egyptians, and also on the part of the Assyrians, both of whom should join in a glorious alliance with Israel for the service of a common God, and all three should be acknowledged and blessed by Jehovah as His people. The origin and integrity of this prophecy is doubtful. But we may assume with the greatest probability, that the whole of it, as we have it, is a genuine utterance of Isaiah; it was probably given in the latest period of the ministry of the prophet, when the power of the Assyrians was already weakened, after the fourteenth year of Hezekiah, perhaps not until the reign of Manasseh.

(9) Ch. xx.—The narrative and interpretation of a symbolical action, which the prophet performed by command of Jehovah, in order to intimate that the Egyptians and Æthiopians should be carried away by the Assyrians with a scanty equipment. From the superscription, this belongs to the reign of Sargon, an Assyrian king, whose name does not elsewhere occur in the Old Testament; he must, however, either be the same as Shalmanezer, or else a king who reigned for a short time between Shalmanezer and Sennacherib. From verse 1, his army besieged Ashdod, a frontier fortification of the Philistines against Egypt. The Jews were perhaps, as well as the Philistines, much ill-treated and oppressed by the Assyrians, and hoped for deliverance through the Egyptians; the intention of the prophet, however, is to warn them, not to put their confidence in men who were also idolaters, but only in their God.

(10) Ch. xxi. 1–10.—As to the overthrow of Babylon by the Elamites and Medes, which the prophet predicts for the comfort of his oppressed and ill-treated people; this prophecy belongs, without doubt, to the last period of the Babylonian Captivity, and is, not improbably, by the same author as ch. xiii. 1–xiv. 23, only perhaps rather earlier.

(11) Ch. xxi. 11, 12.—An utterance against Dumah, an Ishmaelitish tribe in Arabia, and

(12) Ch. xxi. 13–17 against Arabia. Nothing certain can be ascertained from their purport as to the date of these two utterances; there is no peculiar reason for denying that they were written by Isaiah.

(13) Ch. xxii. 1–14.—A threatening prophecy against Jerusalem, of a hostile investment of the city, probably the siege by Sennacherib. The Jewish army had probably already fought with the enemy, and a part of them had been taken captive, and a part driven back. This was delivered perhaps rather later than that ch. x. 5, ff., perhaps also than that ch. xiv. 24–27.

(14) Ch. xxii. 15–25, against a certain Shebna, then *præfectus palatii*, governor of the palace; the threat is made to him, that Jehovah would punish him by removing him from his office and by a foreign banishment, and would raise up another man in his place, Eliakim, the son of Hilkiah. The latter filled this office at the time of the siege of Jerusalem by Sennacherib (ch. xxxvi. 3, 22; xxxvii. 2), so that this utterance must have taken place at an earlier time than that, before the fourteenth year of Hezekiah.

There is no question that both these two utterances in ch. xxii. belong to Isaiah.

(15) Ch. xxiii, as to the overthrow of Tyre.—The date of this prophecy is very doubtful. By the way, however, in which the Chaldeans are mentioned in *v.* 13, it is very probable, in my judgment, that it is not by Isaiah, to whom Gesenius, Umbreit, Knobel, and De Wette (Edit. 2, ff.), attribute it, but that it belongs to the time of the Chaldean dominion, and to the age of Jeremiah; from *v.* 18, however, it must have been composed before the destruction of Jerusalem and the Temple, perhaps during the reign of Jehoiakim. It has always seemed probable to me, that this is an utterance of Jeremiah's, and Movers also takes the same view (in the "Theolog. Quarterly Journal," 1837, pp. 506–537), and endeavours to prove it precisely, from its belonging to the fourth year of Jehoiakim.

§ 202.—*Review of Contents—Chapters* xxiv–xxxv.

III. Ch. xxiv–xxxv.—The prophecies comprised in this sub-division are of different purport and dates. They are best divided into three portions: ch. xxiv–xxvii; xxviii–xxxiii; xxxiv, xxxv.

(1) Ch. xxiv–xxvii.—These four chapters form, probably, one continuous prophecy. In its contents it presents considerable difficulty. Probably, however, it is not by Isaiah, but of a later time, and written by a prophet living in Judah or Jerusalem, after the destruction of the Assyrian kingdom, when the Jews had to suffer much from other hostile nations, probably from the Egyptians. The prophet considers this as the sign of a general judgment, which God would bring upon the earth on account of the sins of men, as to which the hope is expressed that Jehovah, the punishment being accomplished, will again accept His people, and, destroying their enemies, will make Jerusalem a meeting-place for all nations, and will dry up every tear, and annul death itself. The composition probably took place at the time of Josiah king of Judah, or immediately after.

(2) Ch. xxviii–xxxiii.—This section contains various separate prophecies, which are probably the purely genuine productions of Isaiah, and of the reign of Hezekiah.

(*a*) Ch. xxviii. 1–22.—An utterance which was made before the destruction of Samaria, but perhaps only a short time before, when ruin was approaching the city. He begins with a threatening discourse against it; its principal part, however, is directed against Judah and Jerusalem, particularly against the filthy, profligate, frivolous offenders among the people, including even the priests and prophets, whom Jehovah would unexpectedly destroy by the means of foreign nations, and that *those* only shall dwell quietly who trust in theocracy, the assured corner-stone laid in Zion by Jehovah.

(*b*) The remainder of the chapter (xxviii. 23–29) forms a separate utterance; it is really no prediction, but a Maschal, an instructive poem, which does not, as many interpreters imagine, seek to lay down the dealings of God with man, but much more unmistakeably relates to human actions, and, in the works of the husbandman, desires to illustrate the truth that everything has its proper time and way for doing it, and that man can neither do the same thing continually, nor all and everything in the same way.

Then follows, (c) in ch. xxix. 1–8, a prophetical utterance against Jerusalem (Ariel), spoken probably about a year before Sennacherib's attack against the city, the prophet predicting this distress to the city, as well as the repulse and annihilation of the besieger.

(d) Ch. xxix. 9–24, against the wicked among the (Jewish) people, whom Jehovah would strike with blindness, and within a short time would destroy by judgments in the midst of the people, which would serve to convert the latter, and bring them back to their God.

(e) Ch. xxx. and (f) xxxi. 1–xxxii. 8 relate to the same circumstances; the prophet blames the great men of the people, who, in the conflict with the Assyrians, instead of trusting in Jehovah, sent ambassadors to Egypt to purchase help from thence; also, generally, the obstinate are rebuked, who would not hear the prophets, except they prophesied according to their desire. He predicts that Jehovah Himself will protect the city and overthrow the Assyrians; and that then justice and righteousness should prevail in Israel, and that blindness should cease among men.

(g) Ch. xxxii. 9–20. — Penal and threatening language against the luxurious women in Jerusalem; a prediction of the desolation of the land and city, and then of the return of fruitfulness, and at the same time of peace and righteousness by the means of Jehovah's Spirit, and the destruction of the haughty (the enemy, perhaps the Assyrians).

(h) Ch. xxxiii. belongs probably to the time when the siege of Jerusalem by the host of Sennacherib had already begun, and predicts the annihilation of the enemy, which shall take place before the eyes of all, so that even the wicked in Jerusalem shall be amazed at it, and the pious shall dwell securely under Jehovah's protection; also that Jehovah will guard and defend His city.

(3) Ch. xxxiv. and xxxv.—Threatening of a judgment which Jehovah shall bring on the nations, particularly the Edomites, on account of the hostility which they had shown towards Zion; also an announcement of the return to Zion of the scattered members of Jehovah's people, and the blessings which would be there awarded them. The

purport leaves no doubt that this utterance belongs to a considerably later time than that of Isaiah; there is, however, no distinct reason for attributing it to the last period of the Babylonian Captivity, as ch. xl. ff. It may have been spoken in the first year of the time of the exile, shortly after the destruction of Jerusalem, or even before this event.

§ 203.—*Review of Contents—The Historical Section.*

So much as to the *first* principal division of our book. The two prophetical divisions of the book are divided by an historical section (ch. xxxvi–xxxix), narrating events in the reign of Hezekiah, from Sennacherib's campaign against Jerusalem in the fourteenth year of Hezekiah, to the illness and recovery of this king, and the Babylonian embassy to him. These events are also related 2 Kings xviii. 13–xx. 19; only that Hezekiah's song of thanksgiving (Is. xxxviii. 9–20) on his recovery is wanting. Excepting this, the two accounts agree completely, and mostly verbally, so that there can be no doubt that either one author took it from the other, or both from a common source. Now it can hardly be maintained, as many interpreters assume, that the author of the Books of Kings took this fragment out of Isaiah; because the composition of the Books of Kings took place earlier than the present form of the Book of Isaiah; added to which, where there are variations between the two texts, the form in the Books of Kings shows itself to be, in by far the most cases, the more original (*v.* as to this, Gesenius and Knobel). So it is in the highest measure probable that the indubitably genuine song of Hezekiah did not originally belong to the narrative, but was inserted in the already existing history, not, indeed, in a very skilful way, but so as to disturb the natural course of the narrative.

We have previously seen (p. 180, vol. i.) that according to 2 Chron. xxxii. 32, Isaiah had composed an historical work relating to Hezekiah, without doubt, however, a complete work, and not merely relating to these few events in the fourteenth year of his reign. This was adopted in the Book of the Kings of Judah and Israel, not, however, completely, but in an abridged or revised form. The author of the Books of Kings probably made use of this, and adopted the narratives referred to into his work; and from this it was probably received into our Book of Isaiah, by the last editor of the latter, and it is possible that at the same time the older work as to the history of the kings of Judah was also employed. The song of Hezekiah was in all probability, however, taken from quite another source, it may be from some collection of songs, or, perhaps, when circulating singly.

The cause that induced the compiler of Isaiah's prophecies to add this historical fragment was, doubtless, the leading part taken by Isaiah in the events recorded in it; and also that it contains a complete prophetical utterance of Isaiah (ch. xxxvii. 21–35).

The reason why he gave the fragment this particular position was, perhaps, because that which is recorded at the conclusion of it, how Isaiah predicted to Hezekiah the impending captivity of his people in Babylon, appeared to be a suitable introduction to the contents of the prophecies which follow relating to the circumstances of this Babylonian bondage.

§ 204.—*Date of the Compilation—Its place in the Canon.*

We may, however, conclude from what has gone before, that the compilation of this Book in its present form did not take place at a very early date, at any rate not until after the Babylonian Captivity, and a long time after the composition of the latest of the prophecies which is contained in it. In none of the prophecies in the book, which belong to a later time than that of Isaiah, is there any ground for supposing that the author intended to be taken for Isaiah, or that he wrote generally, as personating some more ancient prophet; but in every prophecy — both in ch. xl. ff., and also in those of the same sort in the first principal division—we cannot doubt from their whole nature that the author wrote and published them with the intention of their being looked upon as his own utterances, and belonging to his own time, and as revealed to him by Jehovah. It must, therefore, have been through an error in one of the later compilers that these prophecies, belonging to another and a later prophet, were united in *one* book with those of Isaiah.

That might easily have been done if the different prophecies were originally delivered singly, and not always with the prophet's name attached. Even if this were known to the first readers to whom the prophecies were committed, it might, in the course of time, easily be lost sight of, and, by some subsequent conjecture, an inexact or false opinion might be formed. It may be assumed, with the greatest probability, that Isaiah, like many other prophets, never formed any collection of his different utterances. What induced the compiler to attribute to him particularly so many prophecies belonging to a later time cannot be stated; but he was, perhaps, led to ascribe to him the prophecies specially relating to the Babylonian exile, by reading in the historical narrative (ch. xxxix. 6, ff.) that Isaiah had predicted the above Captivity. This, however, must always presuppose that the compilation was not made till a considerable time after the exile.

It has, perhaps, something to do with this, that this book, as it appears, originally had its place in the Hebrew Canon after Jeremiah and Ezekiel, although Isaiah lived considerably earlier than both of them, and was at all times held in much greater esteem by the Jews. (Cf. p. 36, vol. i.)

§ 205.—*Messianic Character of the Prophecies in the Book of Isaiah.*

The Book of Isaiah, and, indeed, both Isaiah's own utterances, and also the prophecies in it belonging to the other prophet, are, in a literary point of view, and as regards their form and language, among the most beautiful remnants of Hebrew literature. And the prophecies of this book have an eminent and special value from their religious and moral character, particularly in a Messianic respect.

We see a difference, however, between ch. xl. ff. and Isaiah's own prophecies. The last part of the book has, almost throughout, a Messianic character, and is a continuous series of Messianic predictions, all of them being devoted to the prediction of the near approach of the time when God would again accept His people, and bring them to salvation. First of all, they predict the nearly impending return of the people out of captivity, and with that is bound up the promise of an undisturbed peace, both within and without, together with the enjoyment of the greatest Divine blessings in the re-constituted State; not less, also, is it repeatedly brought forward how Jehovah would forgive His people their sins, in order to make them fit to be partakers of the salvation prepared for them. The fear of God, and the knowledge of God, are particularly named as the virtues by which the new race shall be distinguished; and it is, indeed, also predicted that, with them, other nations shall have a share both in these virtues and also in the salvation of the people of God. The bringing about of this salvation is, however, particularly attributed to the *Servant of God.* He is depicted as, up to that time, afflicted by his God with tribulation and misery of every kind, as in captivity, and even given over to death, and all this not so much on account of his own guilt, as for the transgressions of others; he is also to be endued with the Spirit of Jehovah, and destined to attain the highest glory, and to be the mediator of the Covenant between the people (of Israel) and Jehovah, and also a light to all (heathen) nations.

It is much questioned among interpreters how, according to the prophet's view, we must understand this idea of the *Servant of Jehovah.* If, however, we do not consider single passages by themselves, but take the whole course of prophecies pervaded by this idea, I feel convinced that the prophet does not exactly mean one single person, but that the pious and steadfast worshippers and servants of Jehovah in general are intended, Israel κατὰ πνεῦμα, the actual people of God, in opposition, not to heathen nations merely, but to the great mass of the people of Israel. And thus the prophecies have, in this respect, a somewhat general character, inasmuch as they do not precisely predict the appearance of any future single person as a Saviour and a Messiah. But the depicting of the character of the servant of God is quite ideal, and so drawn, that no single person, be he never so pious a servant of the true God, could correspond with it, only excepting the One, to whom the description applies in its most eminent sense, who, being the Son of God, is without sin. Through Him alone could the description of the servant of God, generally given in these prophecies, find essentially its complete fulfilment. (Cf. Bleek's *Vorlesungen über Jes.* lii. 13–liii. 12, in the *Theolog. Stud. und Krit.* 1861, pp. 177–218.)

Distinct Messianic Predictions.

There are some, on the contrary, among the prophecies of *Isaiah himself*, which distinctly predict the appearance of a single person as a Saviour. Thus, particularly, ch. ix. 6, 7, and ch. xi. 1. In both he is predicted as a prince of Israel, endued with Divine attributes, who shall sit on David's throne, and rule his people with righteousness and power. In the latter, however, it is at the same time more prominently brought forward, that, through him, peace and the fear of God shall be generally diffused in the land, and that other nations also shall assemble round him, and shall have a share in the salvation of the people of God.

THE BOOK OF JEREMIAH.

§ 206—*Jeremiah—His Name, Date, Parentage, and Circumstances.*

The name of Jeremiah occurs in Hebrew in the same two-fold form as that of Isaiah, יִרְמְיָה and יִרְמְיָהוּ, the former in the title of the book in the Hebrew manuscripts and editions, the latter usually in the book itself. We find, however, the probably later, shorter form יִרְמְיָה, *e.g.*, ch. xxvii. 1 (in a *not* genuine superscription), ch. xxviii. 5, 6, 10, 11, 12, 15, xxix. 1, also Dan. ix. 2. Etymologically, the name, which under both of its forms occurs in the Old Testament for different other persons, signifies from its construction from יִרְמֶה יְהוָה, *Jehovah casts, hurls, e.g.,* lightning. [Following the well-known interpretation of Origen, μετεωρισμὸς 'Ιαώ, Clericus (on Exod. iii. 15) goes back to רוּם, *altum esse,* as also Fürst explains, "Jah is the lofty one."] In the Greek it is 'Ιερεμίας, in Latin, *Jeremias* and *Hieremias*, in German, according to Luther, *Jeremia* (Ewald, *Jeremja*).

The ministry of this prophet occurred in the saddest and most tragical times of the Jewish State, during the reigns of the last kings of Judah, from the thirteenth year of Josiah down to the destruction of Jerusalem, and still later; it embraces therefore a period of more than forty years.

Since Jeremiah, during all this time, took a most active and effective part, both in the fate of his people and also in all the actions of the princes and great men, both in external and internal matters; and since the book bearing his name gives not only his prophetical utterances, but also very lively narratives of some of his struggles and adventures which were closely connected with those of his nation and state, it therefore affords us more matter than any other scripture of the Old Testament, even the historical books, for becoming acquainted in many respects with the circumstances and relations of the people at that time, in a more accurately distinct way.

Jeremiah was born at Anathoth (ch. i. 1; xxix. 27), a

Jeremiah—His Parentage, Residence, &c. 65

priestly town in the tribe of Benjamin, often mentioned in the Old Testament, lying north-east, and according to Josephus, about twenty *stadia* distant from Jerusalem.[1] He was of the priestly race, and son of Hilkiah, a priest.

Many think this was the high priest Hilkiah, by whom, in the eighteenth year of Josiah, the Book of the Law was found in the Temple; thus Clemens Alexand., Jerome, Jos. Kimchi, Abarbanel, and many others; also Von Bohlen (*Genesis, Einleit.* p. clxvi.), and Umbreit (*Jeremia, Einleit.* p. x. f.). But this is certainly incorrect, according to the way in which, ch. i. 1, the father of our prophet is designated, not as הַכֹּהֵן הַגָּדוֹל, or merely as הַכֹּהֵן, but only as "one of the priests that were at Anathoth." The high priest would hardly have had his dwelling-place with his family outside of Jerusalem. Therefore, Jeremiah's father was doubtless only a simple priest, who accidentally bore the same name as the then high priest, and, in order to be distinguished from the latter, is denoted in the way remarked; the name of Hilkiah was not generally rare, as it occurs, ch. xxix. 3, for some other person.

Jeremiah's family had landed possessions at Anathoth, as follows from ch. xxxii. 6, ff., where Jeremiah, as the nearest one belonging to it, purchases a portion of a field of one Hanameel, son of his uncle, for seventeen shekels, from which we gather that Jeremiah, even at this later period (he was in prison in the tenth year of Zedekiah), could not have been in needy circumstances. In the first period of his prophetical ministry, Jeremiah appears to have still dwelt at Anathoth (cf. ch. xi. 18-23), as the inhabitants of this place laid in wait to kill him on account of his prophecies. At a later time, however, he had his fixed residence in Jerusalem, till the time of the capture of the city by the Chaldeans.

From ch. xvi. 2, we may conclude that Jeremiah was not married then, nor had been lately a married man, this prophecy occurring probably at the time of Jehoiachin. Perhaps he was never at any time married, at least there is in his book no indication whatever that he had either wife or child; though there was no want of an opportunity of

---

[1] Doubtless the present Anata, a poor village on the ridge of a hill, 1¼ leagues north-east from Jerusalem (v. Robinson's "Palestine," ii. 319, f.; also Winer's *Realwörterb.* (under the word "Anathoth").

declaring the fact, in his circumstantial narratives about his own fortunes.

Jeremiah was tolerably young when he was called to be a prophet, as we may conclude both from the long duration of his ministry, and also from the account of his calling, in which (ch. i. 6, 7) he designates himself as נַעַר, and on this account considers himself unfit for public prophetical efficacy in the service of Jehovah.

That his calling and the beginning of his prophetical ministry took place in the thirteenth year of Josiah (about 628 B.C.), as stated in ch. i. 2, is also shown by ch. xxv. 3, where, in the fourth year of Jehoiakim, he says, that from the above-named thirteenth year of Josiah to that day, for twenty-three years, he had incessantly spoken to them in the name of Jehovah; therefore, since Josiah reigned thirty-one years altogether, there were in his time eighteen to nineteen years, under Jehoahaz three months, added to that the four first years of Jehoiakim, equal to twenty-three years. We gather therefrom that, even in this first period, he had been continually engaged in the delivery of prophetical discourses. A part only of these discourses have been preserved to us, and most of them, perhaps, were not generally written down.

In the reign of Josiah occurred the overthrow of the Assyrian monarchy by the Medes under Cyaxares and the Chaldeans under Nabopolassar, the latter of which nations particularly spread themselves over the west at a subsequent time.

We learn from Herodot. i. 15, 103–106, that the Scythians also in this age spread themselves in Asia, up to the coasts of the Mediterranean Sea, and, like the Medes and inhabitants of Asia Minor, overflowed Syria and Palestine generally, until the Egyptian king Psammetichus induced them to retire. Many of the modern interpreters, as Eichhorn, Hitzig, Ewald, Umbreit, Movers (*Zeitsch. für Philos. und kathol. Theolog.* Part 12, p. 98, f.) assume, that this occurred in the time of Jeremiah's prophetical ministry, and that the prophet, in some of his earliest utterances (particularly ch. iv-vi), where he threatens the people with a nation from the north, meant the Scythians. This certainly appears doubtful, inasmuch as in many utterances of Jeremiah, where also he speaks in general only of a nation

from the north, by means of whom Jehovah would chastise
His people, the Chaldeans are decidedly and confessedly
intended, and there is not any such essential difference in
the description and delineation in these other utterances,
as to distinctly justify us in assuming that he had an
entirely different nation in his mind. Added to this,
in the Old Testament historical books generally, there is
not the slightest intimation of any inroad of the Scythians,
and in the other scriptures of the Old Testament there is
nowhere any absolutely certain trace of it; for this reason,
we may well suppose, that even if Judah was visited by
them, she did not really suffer anything from them. Yet
one might very well imagine, when the Scythians were in
the neighbourhood of the land of Judah, that the prophet
might have threatened the stubborn people with a devastating inroad on their part, as a Divine punishment. [Cf.
Graf, *Der Prophet Jeremia*, p. 16, f.]

Josiah perished 611 B.C., in a battle against the Egyptian
Pharaoh-Necho at Megiddo. The king of Judah had gone
out against the Egyptians, when the latter were engaged in
a warlike expedition to the Euphrates. The people of
Judah then nominated as king Josiah's younger son, Jehoahaz.[1] After three months Necho captured Jehoahaz at
Riblah, on the northern boundary of Palestine, and brought
him away captive to Egypt, where he also died; and Necho
instituted as king of Judah, in his stead, his elder brother
Eliakim, who, as king, bore the name of Jehoiakim.

§ 207.—*Prophecies belonging to the Reign of Josiah.*

Of the prophecies in our book, besides ch. i, in which
the Divine calling of the prophet is told, only ch. iii. 6–
vi. 30 is expressly pointed out as having taken place in the
reign of Josiah.

The prophet reproves Judah for not having been warned
by the chastisement of Israel, and for transgressing still

---

[1] Jeremiah, ch. xxii. 11, calls him *Shallum*, perhaps on account of his
short reign, in allusion to the Ismelitish king Shallum, the murderer of
the king Zachariah, who reigned only one month (2 Kings xv. 13);
but perhaps he had actually borne the name of Shallum, and assumed
the name of Jehoahaz only when king.

1 Chron. iii. 15, where Shallum is spoken of as a different son of Josiah
from Jehoahaz, is in error.

more grievously in all kinds of idolatry, and threatens that Jehovah will bring for their punishment an ancient people from the far north, from the uttermost ends of the earth, with bows and javelins, whose language they shall not understand. Yet will He not utterly destroy them, promises being added for Israel's return, if they amend.

We may assume with great probability that the following also belong to the reign of Josiah: (a) the preceding prophecy, ch. ii. 1–iii. 5; (b) ch. vii. 1–ix. 25, and (c) ch. xi. 1–17.

(a) The prophecy ch. ii. 1–iii. 5, was probably uttered in the first period of Jeremiah's prophetical ministry, and at a time when Judah had a good understanding with Egypt. The prophet blames the disobedience, the idolatry, and the worship of Baal in high places, to which the people, together with their priests and prophets, had given themselves up, and predicts that their confidence in Egypt shall be to their disgrace, threatening them with destruction from the Egyptians themselves. This oracle is rightly interpreted when it is supposed that it was given at a time when the Scythians (cf. under, as to Zephaniah, § 243) made expeditions into these regions, and the Jews hoped to be defended against them by the Egyptians. Perhaps it likewise belongs to the thirteenth year of Josiah, and was spoken soon after the former prophecy in ch. iii. 6–vi. 30.

(b) Ch vii. 1–ix. 25, likewise blaming the criminality and idolatry even in the temple itself, and threatening that Jehovah, unless they became better, would do to their sanctuary as he had done at Shiloh, viz., desolate the land and scatter the people among nations who knew them not.

(c) Ch. xi. 1–17.—A summons to the Jews, to hear the words of the Covenant, which the prophet would make known in all the cities of the land; joined with the prediction that Jehovah, when they showed themselves disobedient, would cause to come upon them all the threatenings which were expressed in the Covenant, on account of their idolatry, &c.

There is the greatest probability that this oracle was given very soon after the discovery of the Book of the Law in the eighteenth year of Josiah; the preceding one, on the contrary, before this time, therefore between the thirteenth and eighteenth year of the above king.

There are, perhaps, still other portions of this book which belong to this reign; they cannot, however, be ascertained with any certainty.

§ 208.—*Prophecies belonging to the Reigns of Jehoiakim and Jehoiachin.*

The book does not again furnish us with expressly *dated* prophecies until the reign of Jehoiakim, who, coming to the throne at the age of twenty-five, reigned eleven years, 611–600 B.C., but who, according to the way in which Jeremiah (ch. xxii. 13–19) speaks of him (after his death), appears to have exercised an unjust, violent, and unpopular rule over his subjects. He appears to have maintained a good understanding with Pharaoh-Necho, who placed him on the throne.

Ch. xxvi, according to its express statement, belonged to the beginning of his reign. When Jeremiah again predicted in the court of the temple, that, if they would not hearken to Jehovah's words, that house should be made like unto Shiloh, and the city as a curse to all nations, he was seized by the priests, prophets, and people, and accused before the princes of Judah; but on this occasion was acquitted, Ahikam, the father of Gedaliah, being named as his protector. It is at the same time related how another prophet, Urijah, who prophesied to the same effect as Jeremiah, was persecuted by Jehoiakim, and although he had fled into Egypt, was brought back from thence by the royal command, and was put to death. This also points to a friendly relation between Jehoiakim and the king of Egypt.

The power of Egypt, however, was soon broken. In the fourth year of Jehoiakim, 607 B.C., Necho was slain in the battle at Carchemish, or Circesium, on the Euphrates, by the Chaldeans, under the leadership of Nebuchadnezzar, as commander in the place of his father who was incapacitated by age.

The utterance against the Egyptians, ch. xlvi. 2–12, relates to the above facts; its composition most probably took place immediately after the tidings had arrived about this battle.

Nebuchadnezzar came to the throne in the same year, according to Jer. xxv. 1, where (at least in the Hebrew text) the fourth year of Jehoiakim is pointed out as the first year of Nebuchadnezzar as king of Babylon. This is scarcely intended as some—Hitzig, Keil, F. R. Hasse (d. 1862)[1]—would have it, as the first year of his dominion at Jerusalem, when he made the Jews submissive to him, 2 Kings xxiv. 1; but as the first year of his rule over the kingdom of his father after the latter's death; agreeable to this is the statement of Berosus (Josephus, *Ant.* x. 11, 1), according to which Nebuchadnezzar was then (soon after the victory over the Egyptian ruler) induced to return to Babylon by the intelligence of his father's death.

In this year we must place the prophecy ch. xxv. 1–14, in which the people are warned of their disobedience, hitherto shown to the prophetical warnings. The prophet threatens, that Jehovah will cause a nation to come out of the north, against the land and all the surrounding peoples; and that the land shall be devastated and the inhabitants serve under the nations for seventy years (according to the LXX), after which that the above nations themselves shall be chastised. Then follows (in the Masoretic text) vv. 15–38, a prediction of the judgments that Jehovah would cause to come both on His people, and also on the foreign nations round, by means of the Chaldeans.

In this same fourth year of Jehoiakim, Jeremiah caused his servant Baruch to write out in a roll the whole of the prophecies which he had delivered to them since the time of Josiah, and to read these out to the assembled people in the temple, in the ninth month of the fifth year, on the occasion of a general fast. The matter came to the hearing of the king, who ordered the roll to be brought and read out, but cut it up and burnt it on a pan of coals. He ordered that Jeremiah and Baruch should be brought, who, however, concealed themselves, so as to escape his first wrath. Jeremiah then had the contents of the previous roll, together with many other utterances, written down in a fresh one. The wrath of the king was excited by the prediction that the king of Babylon would come and devastate the land (ch. xxxvi, cf. ch. xlv, a personal prediction to Baruch of the same time).

[1] In his *Programme, Dissertatio de prima Nebucadnezaris adversus Hierosolyma expeditione.* Bonn, 1856, pp. 7, 16.

From the emotion which this prediction of Jeremiah excited, it may be concluded with tolerable certainty, that up to this time, therefore up to the ninth month of the fifth year of Jehoiakim, the Chaldeans had not yet come to Jerusalem, which Hasse (*ut supra*, p. 16, f.) and others deny. There is nowhere any distinct and certain statement as to the time when they first occupied Judæa. As we read, 2 Kings xxiv. 1, that Jehoiakim became subject to Nebuchadnezzar, when the latter came up against him, for the period of three years, and that he afterwards revolted from him; and as Jehoiakim reigned eleven years in all, therefore Jehoiakim's submission, and the first entry of Nebuchadnezzar into Judah cannot have taken place later than the eighth year of Jehoiakim, nor earlier than the ninth month of the fifth year. It must, therefore, fall between the sixth and eighth year, and not as Hasse (*ut supra*) would have it, in the fourth year.

To this period belongs ch. xxxv, which is placed by the superscription in the reign of Jehoiakim, and from its purport pertains to the time of the first approach of the Chaldeans, when the Rechabites, a small wandering tribe on the borders of Palestine, retreated and took refuge in the fortified city of Jerusalem. These showed great fidelity in keeping to the precepts handed down to them by their ancestors, particularly in abstaining from all wine, so that Jeremiah held them up as an example to the Jews, with the threatening, that Jehovah, on account of their faithlessness and idolatry, would bring upon the latter every misfortune which he had predicted.

Whether the Chaldeans had then reached Jerusalem itself, or whether Jehoiakim had submitted himself to Nebuchadnezzar on the approach of his host, is not known. The latter is, perhaps, the more probable.

Several other prophecies of our book also, probably, belong to the time of his reign.

Thus particularly ch. xvi. 1–xvii. 18. Threatening the people, on account of their idolatry and transgression of the Divine law, with banishment to a land that they knew not, to a land of the north, &c.; also several other prophecies, as perhaps—

Ch. xvii. 19–27.—Admonitions to the kings of Judah and all the Jews, not to profane the Sabbath by work.

Ch. xiv, xv, at the time of a great dearth, when the prophet had been some time in his ministry and was well known.

Ch. xviii, which relates to ch. xiv, symbol of the vessel altered by the potter, in reference to Jehovah's different dealings with His people according to their behaviour.

Ch. xi. 18–xii. 17, as to the murderous plot of the Anathothites against the prophet, together with prophecies against the hostile neighbours of the Israelites.

When Jehoiakim, after paying tribute for three years, had revolted against Nebuchadnezzar, then, we read in 2 Kings xxiv. 1, Jehovah sent against him the hosts of the Chaldeans and other neighbouring nations, in order to destroy Judah. No further details are given us about the campaign; but after reference is made, in v. 5, as to the rest of the history of Jehoiakim, to the Book of the Chronicles of the kings of Judah, we read in v. 6, " and Jehoiakim slept with his fathers: and Jehoiachin his son reigned in his stead." On the contrary, it is related in 2 Chron. xxxvi. 6, that Nebuchadnezzar came up against him and bound him in fetters, to carry him away to Babylon.

Hasse is certainly wrong (*ut supra*, pp. 4, 10, 11) (*a*), in referring this to what is told in 2 Kings xxiv. 1, as to the first expedition of Nebuchadnezzar against Jerusalem, when Jehoiakim was subject to him for three years; it relates much more certainly to some later event in the last period of Jehoiakim's reign; and (*b*), when he believes (with Movers and Bertheau) that לְהוֹלִיכוֹ בָּבֶלָה is intended to express, that Jehoiakim was not actually carried away to Babylon. This certainly is not according to the meaning of the chronicler, as v. 7 also shows. But, of course, the statement of the carrying away of Jehoiakim to Babylon presents a difficulty.

From the way in which 2 Kings runs, we should be naturally led to the idea, that he died a natural death, and indeed at Jerusalem, perhaps before the army despatched against him had arrived at the city. Yet, Jer. xxii. 19, is opposed to this, where the prophet states, in an utterance in Zedekiah's time, that Jehovah had threatened Jehoiakim, that he should be buried as an ass is buried, drawn along and cast out outside the gates of Jerusalem (cf. ch. xxxvi. 30). As Jeremiah refers back to this threatening prophecy in a later utterance, it may be assumed with certainty that it was fulfilled; and therefore we may conclude that Jehoiakim was not carried away to Babylon, but that he did not die a natural death in Jerusalem; he had perhaps, gone out against the enemy, and so was slain outside Jerusalem.

His son Jehoiachin,[1] who after his father's death, ascended the throne at eighteen years of age, appears, from the way in which Jeremiah (ch. xxii. 24), expresses himself about him, to have awakened fair hopes; but these were realized only for three months and ten days; for the Chaldean army with Nebuchadnezzar himself, soon came before Jerusalem, when Jehoiachin went out and yielded himself to Nebuchadnezzar. He was carried away to Babylon with his mother, Nehusta, his wives, his officers, and the principal men, as well as the inhabitants who were fit for war,[2] among whom was the prophet Ezekiel. The royal palace and the temple was plundered by Nebuchadnezzar of their treasures and valuables, and an uncle of Jehoiachin was instituted by the former as king; he was the brother of Jehoiakim son of Josiah, named Mattaniah, but as king was called Zedekiah.

Perhaps ch. x. 17–25, belonged to the short reign of Jehoiachin, or to the last period of Jehoiakim's; in it, the prophet summons the Jews to collect their property out of the country, for Jehovah " will sling them out at this once," and will bring up a destroyer from the north, who will lay waste the cities of Judah; a prayer is added to Jehovah, to award the chastisement with equity, and to pour out his wrath against the nations who have devoured Jacob and laid waste his habitation.

Perhaps, also (ch. xiii), the symbolical action with the girdle, which the prophet took down to the Euphrates, and then found it again damaged, which action was applied to Judah and Jerusalem, with the threat to the king and queen (probably the queen-mother), that they should lose their crown, that the people out of the north should rule over

[1] In Jer. xxiv. 1, *Jechonjahu*, בְּנְיָהוּ; xxii. 24, 28; xxxvii. 1, *Chonjahu*, בניהו

[2] According to the 2 Kings xxiv. 16, 7000; according to Jer. lii. 28, 3023.

the land, and that the people should be scattered on account of their idolatry. By Ewald, Hitzig, and Umbreit, this is placed in the time of Jehoiachin, but may very well be of the time of Jehoiakim, since if the queen, mentioned with the king in *v.* 18, be the queen-mother, this might well refer to Zebudah, the mother of Jehoiakim, who was twenty-five years old at the beginning of his reign, therefore thirty-six at his death.

§ 209.—*Prophecies belonging to the Reign of Zedekiah.*

We find the most distinct accounts of the prophetical ministry of Jeremiah in the reign of Zedekiah. The vision in ch. xxiv. belongs to the first period of the reign of this king.

In it the prophet sees two baskets of good and bad figs: the former of which are referred to those who are carried away to Babylon, and the latter to Zedekiah and those remaining in Judah, and also the Jews dwelling in Egypt. The prophet predicts that Jehovah will extirpate the latter out of the land by the sword, famine, and pestilence, but that He will be favourable to the former, and will bring them back, and turn them to Himself.

This probably fell very soon after the carrying away of Jehoiachin, when the prophet himself still entertained some hope that the exiles would soon be brought back to their homes. It would, however, soon be clear to him that this was not in accordance with the will of God. He embraced the occasion of an embassy being sent by Zedekiah to Nebuchadnezzar at Babylon (Elasah and Gemariah) to write to the exiles in quite a different tenor (ch. xxix).

In this he admonishes them to settle themselves in Babylon and to pray for its welfare, and not to allow themselves to be deceived by the false prophets among them, particularly by one Ahab and by one Zedekiah, who flattered the wishes of the people, and disgraced them by their adulterous conduct; then that after seventy years Jehovah would again look upon them, would bring them home, and fulfil his gracious promises to them.

When Shemaiah, another false prophet in captivity, wrote to the priest Zephaniah at Jerusalem about this letter of Jeremiah, and reproached him that he allowed Jeremiah to do as he liked, Jeremiah wrote in threatening language against him (ch. xxix. 24–32).

The utterance (ch. x. 1–16) is also not improbably addressed to the exiles at that time.

The prophet depicts the folly of the heathen worship of the idols made by themselves, praises the power and greatness of Jehovah, and admonishes the Jews not to get accustomed to the ways of the heathen, nor to be dismayed at the signs in the heavens.

If we conceive that this was the occasion of its utterance, the whole form of this discourse admits of a very easy explanation, and also the circumstance that, in *v.* 11, it tells us in the *Chaldee language:* "Thus shall ye say unto them, The gods that have not made the heavens and the earth, they shall perish from the earth, and from under these heavens," without being compelled to pronounce against the genuineness of this verse, which is contained in the LXX, or, with Movers, De Wette, and Hitzig, to fix the date of the whole discourse after the destruction of Jerusalem, and to ascribe it to a prophet himself living in exile.

Chapters xxvii. and xxviii. also fall in the first year of Zedekiah's reign.

The prophet makes yokes and bonds for his neck, so as to intimate to the ambassadors of foreign nations who were in Jerusalem, as well as to Zedekiah himself, that Jehovah's will had subjected all these lands to the king of Babylon; and censures the false prophets, who predicted the immediate bringing back of the holy vessels carried away to Babylon. He then particularly rebukes a false prophet, Hananiah, who had taken the yoke from off his (Jeremiah's) neck, with the prediction that Jehovah would, within *two years*, break off the yoke of the king of Babylon from the necks of all the people, and would bring back all the Jewish captives, together with Jehoiachin and the temple utensils, out of Babylon. Jeremiah, on the contrary, predicted to him, that he, Hananiah, should die that very year, which also came to pass.

The superscription in the Masoretic text (ch. xxvii. 1), "in the beginning of the reign of Jehoiakim," can only proceed from a transposition of the writer (from ch. xxvi. 1), as the contents clearly show, that the utterance took place in Zedekiah's time. We must, therefore, read as in the Syriac, an Arabian translation, and some manuscripts, "in the beginning of the reign of Zedekiah," or, with the LXX, merely, οὕτως εἶπε κύριος, without any definition of the time.

In ch. xxviii. 1, the Masoretic text has, " in the *beginning of the reign* of Zedekiah king of Judah, in the fourth year, in the fifth month." The one part does not rightly suit with the other. We must either, with Ewald, consider the exact definition of the time as a later interpolation, or the former words "*in the beginning.*" These last words are wanting in the LXX, which has, on the other hand, the other statement of the date.

The great prophecy against Babylon (ch. l, li.) also took place in the fourth year of Zedekiah, according to the express statement (ch. li. 59).

The prophet predicts the overthrow of Babylon by nations from the north, particularly by the Medes and others, and at the same time the return home to Zion of both the Israelites and Jews, and their conversion to Jehovah, their God. We read in the epilogue to this prediction (ch. li. 59–64), that Jeremiah gave it to Seraiah, an officer of Zedekiah's, when the former went to Babylon in the above-named year,[1] with the charge that, on his arrival, he should read it, and then sink it in the Euphrates with a stone tied to it, as an intimation that Babylon should be thus sunk.

This prophecy has, from Eichhorn's days, been called in question by many interpreters; its authorship has been denied to Jeremiah, and the date of it has been transposed to the later time of the Captivity. This utterance, of course, presents some difficulty from its purport and the turn of mind shown in it, if we compare it what Jeremiah elsewhere expresses about the Chaldeans. But we must then assume, as Ewald supposes, that the author both composed this utterance in the name of an earlier prophet, Jeremiah, and then also added this epilogue to make it pass for a discourse of the latter prophet, which is not in itself probable. But we also find indications in the utterance itself that it was composed in Judæa during the existence of the

---

[1] According to the Hebrew text, Seraiah went *with* the Jewish king (אֵת), according to the more probable reading of the LXX, *on his behalf* (מֵאֵת), as his messenger.

Prophecies in Zedekiah's Reign. 77

Sanctuary at Zion (ch. l. 5; li. 50), and also of the city of Jerusalem (ch. li. 35). Also the words (ch. li. 51), "Strangers are come into the sanctuaries of Jehovah's house," suit well to Zedekiah's time, as stated, because then, after Jehoiachin had been carried away captive, Nebuchadnezzar had plundered the temple; but they would not suit a time when the temple was completely destroyed. Nor would the expression, "the vengeance for thy temple" (ch. l. 28; li. 11), according to the Masoretic reading, necessarily lead to the idea of its ruin; according to the LXX, however, probably the former passage is not genuine, and the latter originally stood, "vengeance for the people" (ἐκδίκησις λαοῦ αὐτοῦ ἐστίν).

Chapters xxii. 1–xxiii. 8, also belong to Zedekiah's reign, as their substance shows.

The prophet, pointing back to the three predecessors of Zedekiah and to what had been predicted about them, admonishes the king to rule righteously, if he, with his race, intended to look for happiness; he utters a complaint as to the shepherds who have scattered Jehovah's flocks, but then promises the return of those of the people of the Covenant that remained scattered, and their collection together under good shepherds, and under a righteous king from the house of David, whose name shall be *Jahveh Zidkenu*.

The prediction against false prophets (ch. xxiii. 9–40) likewise falls in Zedekiah's time.

§ 210.—*Prophecies in Zedekiah's Reign, and Historical Events connected therewith.*

The feeble king Zedekiah remained for a series of years subject to Nebuchadnezzar, who had placed him on the throne. He then allowed himself to be induced by his princes and counsellors to make himself independent of the Chaldeans, and to enter into an alliance with the Egyptian king (Ezek. xvii. 15), Pharaoh-hophra (חָפְרַע in Jer. xliv. 30),[1] who reigned about twenty years. This resulted in Nebuchadnezzar marching against Judah with his army, conquering the fortified cities, and besieging Jerusalem. The beginning of the siege of the city took place, according to Jer. xxxix. 1, in the ninth year of Zede-

[1] LXX, Οὐαφρῆ; Clemens Alex., Οὐάφρης; in Manetho, Οὐάφρις; in Herodot. and Diodor. Sic., Ἀπρίης. [Cf. Bunsen's *Egypt.* v. p. 414.]

kiah, in the tenth month; and, according to Jer. lii. 4 and Ezek. xxiv. 1, on the tenth day of this month.

Ch. xix. and xx. perhaps belong to the time of Zedekiah's revolt, before the Chaldean army had arrived in Judæa; they describe an emblematical action of Jeremiah's, and his being made a prisoner by Pashur.

At Jehovah's command, Jeremiah broke a bottle in the valley of Tophet, with the threat that Jehovah, on account of their horrible idolatry and their worship of Baal, Moloch, and the hosts of heaven, would make the city with their houses to be a mocking and an amazement, and would cause the inhabitants thereof to perish by the sword of the enemy, also by the hands of one another.

When the prophet afterwards repeated this prophecy to the people in the temple, he was struck and made captive by the priests and Pashur, the chief governor of the temple, the son of Immer. He was, however, set free on the following day, and then uttered threatening predictions both against Pashur and also against the whole of Judah, whom Jehovah would give into the hands of the king of Babylon, and would cause them to be carried away thither; adding lamentations as to the persecution which he, the prophet, had to endure in Jehovah's service; who, however, would help him, and overthrow his persecutors.

Later, in the first beginning of the blockade of Jerusalem, falls (*a*) ch. xxxiv. 1–7, when, except Jerusalem, only Lachish and Azekah were left of all the fenced cities of the land.

Jeremiah predicts to Zedekiah that Nebuchadnezzar would capture and burn Jerusalem, and that Zedekiah would fall into his power, and would be carried away to Babylon; however, that he should there die in peace, and be buried with royal honours.

(*b*) Chapter xxi. falls, perhaps, a little later, but still in the first beginning of the blockade of Jerusalem, when the Jewish army was still striving with the Chaldeans outside the city.

Zedekiah has Jeremiah asked by two deputies if Jehovah would not bring deliverance to them. The prophet, however, predicts that Jehovah would turn back the weapons of the Jews, and would slay the inhabitants of Jerusalem by famine, pestilence, and the sword; that he would give those

The Reign of Zedekiah. 79

that were left, together with their king, into the hands of Nebuchadnezzar and would destroy the city by fire, and that those only who went out to the Chaldeans should remain alive. At the same time he admonishes the royal house to exercise righteous judgments, and to interest themselves for the oppressed.

For a long time, indeed, matters seem to have gone favourably for the besieged. There was an army of their Egyptian allies approaching, and the Chaldeans were thus induced to march against them, and, for a while, to raise the siege of Jerusalem (ch. xxxvii. 5, 11). The Jews immediately gave themselves up again to their levity. In their distress they had solemnly laid themselves under an obligation in the temple to set free their native male and female bond-servants, but now nobody thought any more of this. Jeremiah blames them in the name of Jehovah for their perjury, and predicts to them that Jehovah would bring back the Chaldeans, and that they should again besiege the city, and that it should be captured and burnt, and that their king and princes should be given into their power (ch. xxxiv. 8–22). Jeremiah predicts the same thing at this time to the messengers whom Zedekiah sent to him to summon him to pray to Jehovah for them (ch. xxxvii. 3–10). The Chaldeans now actually returned and began the siege afresh, the Egyptians having marched back without having ventured on a battle.

§ 211.—*Jeremiah's Imprisonment—Prophecies delivered during this period.*

In the meantime, Jeremiah had lost his freedom. He had wished to go out from Jerusalem into the territory of his tribe Benjamin, but was arrested at the gate by Irijah, a captain of the ward, under the accusation that he intended to go over to the Chaldeans; he was brought before the princes, who smote him, and confined him in the house of one Jonathan, a scribe, which had been turned into a prison (ch. xxxvii. 11–15). From thence, after a long time, the king sent for him to come to him secretly, to inquire of him as to the word of Jehovah; and although Jeremiah predicted to him that he should fall into the hands of the king of Babylon, Zedekiah, in answer to his lamentations and entreaties, caused him to be brought into the court of the guard, perhaps a better and more respectable place of captivity, and as long as there was any bread in the city generally, he ordered that a loaf of bread should be delivered to him daily out of the bakers' street (ch. xxxvii. 16–21). Here he enjoyed a sort of freedom, and was not cut off from intercourse with the people.

It was here, at a time when the entrenchments of the besiegers were pushed up to the city, in the tenth year of Zedekiah, and the eighteenth year of Nebuchadnezzar, that Jeremiah bought of his uncle Hanameel a portion of a field, of which, as nearest relative, he had the right of redemption, for seventeen shekels, and carefully preserved the title-deeds, as an intimation of a future peaceable time, when houses and fields should again be bought in the land. At Jeremiah's prayer, Jehovah revealed to him that the city should surely for the present be given up as a prey to the king of Babylon by the sword, famine, and pestilence; but that afterwards Jehovah would collect the scattered ones out of all countries, and bring them back to that place, and would give them a pious heart and conclude an everlasting Covenant with them, so that they should again, in all the land, buy fields with perfect freedom and security, and should enter into contracts about them (ch. xxxii).

Thus also in ch. xxxiii, in the same place of confinement, he receives, at a time when the houses of the city and even the royal palace were pulled down to erect ramparts against the besiegers (v. 4), joyful promises as to the return of Judah and Israel from captivity, and the repeopling of the depopulated cities of Jerusalem, &c. (vv. 1–13).[1]

Chapters xxx. and xxxi. perhaps belong to this time, before the capture of Jerusalem; in these the prophet communicates the promises about Judah and Israel which were revealed to him by Jehovah. The first and largest portion of this utterance, up to ch. xxxi. 22, relates to the Ephraimites, whom Jehovah would redeem from the ruin sent upon them, and bring them back to Samaria, and maintain them in His worship at Zion under the royal house of David; and not less would Jehovah bring back the captivity of Judah, that every one should have their hearts' desire on the holy mount of Zion (ch. xxxi. 23–26);—that Jehvah would make the land of Judah and Israel fruitful

[1] Verses 14–26 are wanting in the LXX, and were perhaps added later.

for men and cattle; that He would henceforth cause each one to pay the penalty for his own sins only, and not for those of his fathers, and that He would make a new and everlasting Covenant with Israel and Judah, and rebuild and enlarge Jerusalem (*vv.* 27–40).

When, however, several of the chief men heard Jeremiah tell the people from his captivity, that Jehovah would give the city over as a prey to the Chaldean army, and that those only who went out to them should be preserved; but that those who remained in the city should perish by sword, famine, and pestilence, they urged the king to put him to death because he discouraged the army and the people. As the feeble king was not able to offer any opposition to them, they had Jeremiah let down by cords into a very muddy dungeon in the court of the prison. Then an eunuch of the king's court, Ebed-melech the Æthiopian, obtained, by his entreaties, permission from the king to have the prophet drawn up out of the dungeon, and the latter was again brought into the court of the prison, where he remained until the capture of the city (ch. xxxviii. 1–13, 28). All this took place perhaps in the last period of the siege, when want of bread prevailed in the city (*v.* 9).

To this time, also, belongs the short prophecy, ch. xxxix. 15–18, to Ebed-melech, to whom he promised, that in the misfortunes coming on the city, his life should be preserved.

The king again contrived a private interview with Jeremiah in order to ask advice of him. The prophet counselled him to give himself up to the Chaldean princes, as thus he would save his own and his sons' lives and also the city, but that if he did otherwise, he still would not escape the enemy, and would only bring about the burning of the city. The king, however, feared to follow the advice of the prophet, being most afraid of those Jews who had already gone over to the Chaldeans (ch. xxxviii. 14–28).

Soon after—on the ninth day of the fourth month of the eleventh year of Zedekiah, about one and a half years after the first beginning of the siege—were the walls of the city broken through by the besiegers. Zedekiah endeavoured to save himself with his army by a flight at night out of the gate of the city; the Chaldeans, however, pursued him, and overtaking him at Jericho, brought him to Nebuchadnezzar at Riblah in the land of Hamath. His sons and his princes were there put to death before his eyes; he himself was carried away to Babylon, blinded and in fetters, and died there in captivity. Soon after the Chaldean army under Nebuchadnezzar marched again to Jerusalem, where the temple, the royal palace, and other houses were burnt, the walls were broken down, and the principal inhabitants carried away to Babylon (according to Jer. lii. 29, 832 souls out of Jerusalem). The meaner people were left in the country, and fields and vineyards were given to them. This burning of the city took place on the seventh or tenth of the fifth month, according to 2 Kings xxv. 8; Jer. lii. 12.

According to Ezek. xxxiii. 21, one would be inclined to fix the date of this burning in the following year, therefore fully a year after the breaking down of the walls. But from the way in which, in Jer. and 2 Kings, the fifth month is named, without any statement as to the year, we cannot well doubt that the same year was meant as that of which the fourth month had just been named, therefore the eleventh year of Zedekiah; so that the burning of the city occurred only one month after its capture; this also is expressly confirmed in Ezekiel itself by the statement in ch. xl. 1. Cf. also Jer. i. 3, where the "carrying away captive" of Jerusalem is to be understood of this destruction of the city, and the fifth month of the eleventh year of Zedekiah is likewise stated for it.

§ 212.—*Prophecies uttered after the Capture of Jerusalem—Fate of Jeremiah.*

At the time of the first capture of Jerusalem, the princes of the king of Babylon, having heard of Jeremiah and his fate, through deserters or in some other way, allowed him to come out of the prison-court, in order that Gedaliah the son of Ahikam, should watch over him; and thus he at first remained in the city (ch. xxxix). When, afterwards, Nebuzar-adan had marched against Jerusalem and had burnt it, Jeremiah also was carried away in fetters along with the other Jews who were to be deported to Babylon; but he was only taken as far as the city of Ramah. Here Nebuzar-adan set him free, and gave him the choice either to go with him to Babylon or to remain in the land of Judah. On the prophet choosing the latter, Nebuzar-adan

Prophecies after the Capture of Jerusalem. 83

appointed him a fixed maintenance, giving him a present, and referred him to Gedaliah, who had taken the management of the land of Judah as vicegerent for the king of Babylon, and had taken up his residence at Mizpah. Many of those Jews soon returned who had at first fled away into the neighbouring countries through fear; Gedaliah, however, together with the Jews and Chaldeans with him, was soon after (in the seventh month) murdered at a banquet by Ishmael, the son of Nethaniah, of the race of the Jewish kings, and some other Jewish conspirators. The murderers were, indeed, pursued by the Jewish princes, but they could not get hold of them. The Jewish princes, from fear of the vengeance of the Chaldeans, now thought about escaping into Egypt. They, therefore, asked counsel of Jeremiah, who, after ten days, received a Divine revelation on the matter, according to which he decidedly dissuaded them from their design, and predicted to them, that if they remained in the land, Jehovah would protect them and defend them against the king of the Chaldeans; but that in Egypt they would be visited with destruction by the sword, famine, and pestilence (ch. xl–xlii). Jeremiah's advice, however, was not attended to by the Jewish princes, who, together with other Jews, both men and women, set out for Egypt, taking Jeremiah and Baruch with them. They came at first to Tah-panhes, *i.e.*, Daphne, near Pelusium (ch. xliii. 1–7).

Here Jeremiah spoke an oracle accompanied with a symbolical action (ch. xliii. 8–18), in which he predicted that Jehovah would cause the Egyptians to be conquered and their idol-temples burnt by Nebuchadnezzar.

The oracle, ch. xliv, was spoken still later, in the same country, to the Jews of the different cities among the Egyptians and of Pathros, who had assembled together, perhaps for the joint solemnization of a feast, or for some other reason.

The Jews, and, as it appears, the women still more zealously, had continued even in Egypt to take a share in the worship of idols, particularly of the queen of heaven. When Jeremiah reproached them with this, referring to the judgments executed on Jerusalem and the Jewish cities, on account of idolatry, they stubbornly declared that they would not relinquish it. The prophet, therefore, again predicted to them that all the Jews in Egypt should perish by the sword, famine, and pestilence, and that only a few of them should return into the land of Judah; and, as a pledge of the fulfilment of this judgment, he predicted that Jehovah would deliver Pharaoh-hophra into the hands of his enemies.

After this nothing else is known for certain as to Jeremiah's ministry and fate. At the time of the settling in Egypt he had been active as a prophet for over forty years, and was, therefore, sixty years old at least. It is asserted by some ecclesiastical writers, that he was stoned by the people (perhaps the Jews) at Daphne, on account of his prophecies.[1] Whether there is any truth in this cannot be ascertained; it is however probable, that, after settling in Egypt, he remained there until he died.

The idea has sometimes prevailed among the Jews that just as some other leading character of the Old Covenant, particularly Elijah and Moses, Jeremiah would also come back on earth, immediately before the appearance of the Messiah, to prepare the way for him by the preaching of repentance, cf. Matt. xvi. 14. According to another idea about him, which we find in 2 Macc. ii. 4, ff., Jeremiah, at the burning of the temple, saved the ark together with some other holy things, and hid them in a cave on Mount Horeb, from whence they shall again come to light in the days of the Messiah; cf. the expositors of Revelation ii. 19.

§ 213.—*Different arrangement of the Book in the Hebrew Text and the LXX.*

The book which we possess under the name of Jeremiah, contains some historical narratives besides its prophetical utterances. These narrate the circumstances that gave rise to certain prophecies, and their effect; also the fortunes of the prophet, and, connected therewith, the affairs of the Jewish people at the period after the burning of Jerusalem by the Chaldeans. It has been much questioned in modern times if, and how far, the whole contents of the book was written, or caused to be written, by Jeremiah himself; when this was done, and to what extent the text of the

---

[1] Tertull. *Scorpiace*, c. 8; Pseudo-Epiph. *De Vitis Proph.* Opp. ii. 239; Hieron. *adv. Jovin.* lib. ii. 19; Isidor. Hisp. *De Vita et Obitu Sanctor.* c. 38.

book has been preserved uncorrupted in its several parts. We have the more reason for uncertainty in this respect, from the fact that the book is extant in a two-fold, and in some respects very different, recension—the *Masoretic* in the Hebrew manuscripts and editions, and the *Alexandrine* in the translation of the LXX.

As the book exists in the Hebrew Canon it may be divided into the following elements:—

I. Ch. i-xxxix.—Prophetic utterances, sometimes with a narrative of their cause and effect, and almost entirely in reference to the people of the Covenant, from the first appearance of the prophet to the capture and destruction of Jerusalem by the Chaldeans.

II. Ch. xl-xlv.—Historical narrative with prophecies at the period after the destruction of Jerusalem, before and after the flight to Egypt; among which, however, ch. xlv, contains an utterance to Baruch in the fourth year of Jehoiakim.

III. Ch. xlvi-li.—Utterances as to various foreign nations. The superscription, ch. xlvi. 1, relates to this collection.

There are the following separate utterances :—

(1) Two against Egypt: (*a*) ch. xlvi. 2-12, in the fourth year of Jehoiakim, after the battle of Carchemish ; (*b*) ch. xlvi. 13-28, prediction that Jehovah would deliver the Egyptians into the power of Nebuchadnezzar ; perhaps, but not certainly, at the time of the sojourn of the prophet in Egypt.

(2) Ch. xlvii, against the Philistines, who are threatened with waters from the north (perhaps with the Chaldeans). The date runs in the Hebrew text, " before that Pharaoh smote Gaza," which is wanting in the LXX.

(3) Ch. xlviii, against Moab, partly from Is. xv, xvi.— We may conclude from *v.* 13, that this oracle falls before the breaking up of Judah, and perhaps at a time when Judah was not, for the moment, hard pressed (" Moab shall be ashamed of Chemosh, as the house of Israel was ashamed of Bethel their confidence ").

(4) Ch. xlix. 1-6.—Against the Ammonites, who are reproached with the possession of the territory of the Gadites, and on that account are threatened with destruction.

(5) Ch. xlix. 7-22.—Against the Edomites, who shall not remain unpunished (whilst those who had nothing to

do with it are forced to drink of the cup), notwithstanding their confidence in their wisdom and the natural strength of their land (cf. after, on Obadiah).

(6) Ch. xlix. 23–27.—" Concerning Damascus" (also Hamath and Arpad).

(7) Ch. xlix. 28–33.—" Concerning Kedar and the kingdoms of Hazor (חָצוֹר only in this passage) which Nebuchadnezzar, the king of Babylon, smote."

(8) Ch. xlix. 34–39.—About Elam, according to the superscription, at the beginning of Zedekiah's reign.

(9) Ch. l–li.—Against Babylon, in the fourth year of Zedekiah (v. p. 76).

IV. Ch. lxii.—An historical addition as to the capture of Jerusalem, the plundering and burning of the temple and city, and events connected with it, for twenty-six years after that catastrophe.

The LXX varies from the Hebrew Canon in the arrangement of the prophecies. The prophecies against foreign nations (ch. xlvi-li), stand in the LXX after ch. xxv. 13 to ch. xxxi, and in very different order of succession.[1] Then follows, as ch. xxxii, the prediction of the judgment which Jehovah would bring, both on Israel and also on foreign nations, which is, in the Hebrew, in ch. xxv. 15-38; to which in like order succeed the following sections, Hebrew, ch. xxvi-xliv = LXX, ch. xxxiii-li. (the last of the prophecies of this section, is the personal one to Baruch, Hebrew, ch. xlv; LXX, after ch. li). The historical addition, ch. lii, is also in the LXX at the conclusion of the whole book.

But, besides this different order of succession in the separate sections, the translation of the LXX presents very numerous variations from the Hebrew text. The LXX has very few additions, and these only single words or syllables; on the contrary, there are many omissions of words, sentences, verses, and whole passages (altogether about 2700 words are wanting, or the eighth part of the Masoretic text); also alterations of passages, sometimes not without influence on the sense.

Origen testifies to this relation of the two texts to each

[1] Namely, thus: (8) Elam, (1) a and b, Egypt, (9) Babylon, (2) Philistines, (5) Edom, (4) Ammonites, (7) Kedar, and the kingdom of Hazor, (6) Damascus, (3) Moab.

other, *Ep. ad Afric.* : πολλὰ δὲ τοιαῦτα καὶ ἐν τῷ Ἱερεμίᾳ κατενοήσαμεν, ἐν ᾧ τὴν πολλὴν μετάθεσιν καὶ ἐναλλαγὴν τῆς λέξεως τῶν προφητευομένων εὕρομεν.

§ 214.—*Various Opinions as to the respective Values of the Hebrew and Greek Recensions.*

As regards the origin of these variations, in earlier times the opinion prevailed, that the Hebrew text gave the book in the original and more ancient form, and that the variations in the LXX arose only through the negligence or arbitrariness, sometimes of the transcriber, and sometimes of the translator himself. This is the view of Jerome,[1] as well as by far the majority of those after him. De Wette also is inclined, in Edit. 4 of his *Introduction*, to refer all the variations to the arbitrariness of the translator.

Eichhorn, Bertholdt, and others, on the contrary, have supposed that the translator made use of a Hebrew recension differing from the Masoretic. Eichhorn supposes different versions executed by the prophet himself; and so also Dahler subsequently.[2] J. D. Michaelis[3] maintains the decided superiority of the Alexandrine Recension, but has not succeeded in pursuing this idea as closely as he intended. Movers[4] has applied great industry and much critical sagacity to the investigation of this matter.

In the first place, Movers supposes that many of the prophecies of our book have been considerably remodelled by some other author, particularly by Deutero-Isaiah, to whom he altogether attributes ch. x. 1–16 (as to this, however, see above, p. 75). He also supposes more than one version of the collected prophecies, one of which was made soon after the Captivity, by the redactor of the Book of Kings, which however, did not contain ch. xxvii–xxxi. and xxxiii ; also another more complete version by Nehemiah, in which the book received the form it has at present in the Hebrew

[1] *Proœm. ad Comment. in Jerem.*: Jeremiæ ordinem librariorum errore confusum (in the Greek and Latin translation); and *Præf. in Jerem.*: Præterea ordinem visionum, qui apud Græcos et Latinos omnino confusus est, correximus.

[2] *Jérémie traduit, accompagné des notes,* &c. Part 2. Strasb. 1825.

[3] "Notes on the New Testament for the Unlearned," Part 1 (1790), p. 285. Cf. Supplementa, s. v. שִׁעֵר.

[4] *De utriusque recensionis, vaticiniorum Jeremiæ, Græcæ Alexandrinæ et Hebraicæ Masorethicæ, indole et origine.* Hamb. 1837.

Canon. A little after, probably in the age of Alexander the Great, the Alexandrine Recension originated. Both the Masoretic and the Alexandrine Recensions are based upon an earlier one, common to both, which, however, had received manifold alterations from the original text of Jeremiah, from which alterations the Alexandrine Recension kept itself far more free than the Masoretic.

De Wette (edits. 5 and 6) has almost entirely followed Movers's inferences, only in a sceptical way. Hitzig also agrees with him in many points, particularly in giving a great preference to the Alexandrine text over the Masoretic.

Ewald's view is the same, but modified.

Ewald, indeed, as also many previously, denies Jeremiah's authorship of ch. 1–li, also lii, and attributes them to an author at the last period of the Babylonian Captivity, who also inserted some matter into ch. xxv; but in the variations of the two recensions, he gives an overwhelming preference to the Masoretic, and lays many of the variations in the LXX to the fickleness and arbitrariness of the translator. He, however, believes that not unfrequently [1] the original reading has been preserved in the LXX.

On the other hand, A. Küper [2] (Counsellor at Stettin), Hävernick, Joh. Wichelhaus [3] (of Halle, d. 1858), and Keil, have most decidedly pronounced for the integrity of the Masoretic text, and considered all the variations of the LXX as corruptions arising from the negligence or arbitrariness of the translator himself. But a careful, unprejudiced consideration of the phenomena presented to us, does not justify us in forming such a judgment. I cannot, however, here enter into an investigation of the details; I must content myself with stating, and shortly and suggestively proving, those principal points in general, which appear to me to be well founded; they are as follows :—

[1] That here and there this is the case, the modern interpreters of our book do not deny; on the other hand, Graf, who began the investigation with the most favourable intention in regard to the LXX, came to the conclusion, "that the form of the text presented by the Greek translator is one that has arisen at a much later time from the extant Hebrew text, and is both mutilated and spoilt."

[2] *Jeremias librorum sacrorum interpres atque vindex.* (Berlin, 1837), pp. 167–202.

[3] *De Jeremiæ versione Alexandrina.* Halle, 1847.

Variations between the two Recensions.   89

§ 215.—*Origin of the Greek Recension.*

(1) The LXX translation of this book is *in part* so verbally faithful to, and so closely follows, the Hebrew, that it is most improbable that the translator or translators should have permitted such arbitrary alterations and omissions in so many passages, as must have been the case if all the alterations proceeded from them, which their text presents in comparison with the Hebraico-Masoretic version. Neither is it at all probable that they are generally to be ascribed to later transcribers of the LXX. There would then exist in the different manuscripts of the LXX greater variations, and also greater coincidences with the Hebrew text, than is the case, and than *was* the case in Origen's time. In the first place, therefore, it must be held as certain that the Greek translators met with a Hebrew text of our book in a shape essentially agreeing with that of their translation. The book, therefore, at the time of the composition of the translation, must have had, in Hebrew manuscripts *in Egypt,* a form differing from the Masoretic Recension; as, on the other hand, we cannot doubt that, from the time when it was adopted into the collection of the prophetical books (by Nehemiah, *v.* § 294), the book always had *in Palestine* that shape which it now presents in the Masoretic Recension.

§ 216.—*Consideration of the Variations between the Hebrew and Greek Recensions.*

(2) If we impartially consider the several variations of the two texts, we shall come to the conclusion, with the highest degree of probability, in many cases from internal evidence, that the Alexandrine Recension affords us the original text, and the Masoretic presents one somewhat remodelled.

This, in the first place, applies to some larger passages which exist in the Masoretic text, but not in the LXX. In this case, it is everywhere much more probable that these passages are additions than that they were omitted by later transcribers or compilers, though originally belonging to the text.

Of this sort are the following passages :—

(*a*) Ch. xxix.—In Jeremiah's letter to those carried

away with the king. Jehoiachin. Here the Masoretic text has, in *vv.* 16–20, a threat of destruction against Zedekiah and those who remained at Jerusalem. This is wanting in the LXX, and most probably did not originally form a part of the letter, as Hitzig correctly decides. Unmistakeably the connection is now altogether interrupted, as Cappellus also thinks, whilst *v.* 21 follows on very suitably to *v.* 15 : *v.* 15, "Because ye have said, Jehovah hath raised us up prophets in Babylon ;" *v.* 21, " Thus saith the Lord of hosts, the God of Israel, of Ahab, &c., which prophesy a lie to you in my name; Behold, I will deliver them," &c.

(*b*) Ch. xxxix.—There is here wanting in the LXX the notice in the Masoretic text (*vv.* 4–13) concerning Zedekiah being taken captive, and the matters connected with it; also how Nebuchadnezzar particularly confided Jeremiah to Nebuzar-adan. This, however, is certainly, as Movers and Ewald rightly judge, a later interpolation very awkwardly disturbing the connection of the narrative, in which it causes great obscurity and inaccuracy; whilst *v.* 14 can be very properly connected with *v.* 3, where it is related that, after the capture of Jerusalem, the princes of the king of Babylon sat in the middle gate, and (in *v.* 14) from thence sent to fetch Jeremiah out of his confinement, and delivered him over to Gedaliah.

(*c*) In the historical addition, ch. lii, the Masoretic text has a list in *vv.* 28–30 of the Jews deported to Babylon at different times, which list is wanting in the LXX. This list has all the appearance of exactitude; yet we may assume with the greatest probability that originally it did not form a part of this narrative, as no reason at all can be discovered why it should have been subsequently omitted. Some later transcriber perhaps met with it, and inserted it here. If we assume the correctness of the Masoretic text in the remainder of the chapter, we may conclude that this list did not proceed from the author, because in *v.* 29 a deportation is dated as taking place in the eighteenth year of Nebuchadnezzar, which is, no doubt, intended for the one which took place at the time of the destruction of the city. This, in *v.* 12, according to another mode of reckoning the years of Nebuchadnezzar's reign, is fixed in the nineteenth year of this king, which statement, however, is also wanting in the LXX. Finally, it is in favour of this view that the purport of these verses is also wanting in the parallel passage, 2 Kings xxv.

(*d*) The promises in ch. xxxiii. only extend in the LXX to *v.* 13; but in the Masoretic text they are continued (*vv.* 14–26) in three different paragraphs, particularly in reference to the preservation and increase of the seed of David and the race of Levi. If this section were originally an element of the prophecy, it would be unintelligible, from the nature of its contents, how it could be either omitted or rejected by a later transcriber. Although the section, perhaps, may be actually a prophecy of Jeremiah, we must still assume that it was not originally written in immediate connection with what precedes, but as a separate utterance—perhaps not until after the destruction of Jerusalem—and that it was not discovered until after the rest of the book had been compiled, and that it was inserted here. Yet it is, perhaps, altogether an addition by another author, who, in the first verses, had in view Jeremiah's prophecy (ch. xxiii. 5, 6). It must be remarked that in ch. xxiii. "Jahveh Zidkenu" is pointed out as the name of the Messiah, the righteous seed of David, but that it appears here as the name of the restored Jerusalem.

There are short passages in the Masoretic text, wanting in the LXX, in which, in all probability, the circumstances are just the same as the above: as, *e.g.*, ch. viii. 10 *b*–12 (later interpolation from ch. vi. 13–15); ch. x. 6–8, 10; ch. xxvii. 19–22; ch. xvii. 1–4; ch. li. 44 *c*–49 *a*, &c.

There are additions of single sentences and words, or slight alterations, influencing, however, the sense; as *e.g.* as follows:—

Ch. xxx. 17 *b*, "Because they called thee an Outcast, (saying), This is *Zion*, whom no man seeketh after." *Zion* is wanting in the LXX, and is, doubtless, a later gloss, and indeed an incorrect one, arising from an improper reference of the passage to Judah and Jerusalem; this prophecy, from ch. xxx. 1–xxxi. 22, referring to the deliverance of the Israelites (the Ephraimites).

In the prophecy (ch. xxv. 15–38) as to the cup of fury which Jehovah would cause all nations to drink of, we are told in *v.* 26 *b*. after various other nations are named, "and the king of Sheshach (Babylon) shall drink after them." This sentence is wanting in the LXX, and here does not rightly suit the context; it is, without doubt, a later addition. Babylon is there called Sheshach *per Athbasch*,[1] a cabbalistic mode of naming which it is not at all likely that Jeremiah would have made use of.

The Athbasch occurs in our book again (*a*) in the same case (ch. li. 41), "How is Sheshach taken?" The word is here wanting in the LXX, and can well be left out; it is, doubtless, a later addition there also. (*b*) Ch. li. 1: יֹשְׁבֵי בְשִׂדִּים = יֹשְׁבֵי לֵב קָמַי, which latter, doubtless, originally stood here; the LXX has τοὺς κατοικοῦντας Χαλδαίους, the same words as *v*. 35 for יֹשְׁבֵי כַשְׂדִּים.

In the prophecy (ch. xxv. 1–14) the LXX presents many differences, but, on the whole, certainly has the original readings. Thus, in *v*. 9 and *v*. 12, neither Nebuchadnezzar nor Babylon are specially meant, which were inserted as a later gloss only (as likewise ch. xxi. 4, 7, &c.). In *v*. 11 it does not tell us "that *these nations*," but that "*Judah among the nations* shall serve the king of Babylon seven years."

There are also many other similar cases.

(3) On the other hand, there are cases where, in the variations of the two recensions, the Masoretic text is the more original, the text in the LXX, therefore, being presented in an altered, remodelled shape. This, however, is comparatively seldom.

Thus, *e.g.*, in the section (ch. xxix. 24–32) against the false prophet Shemaiah. Here, *v*. 26 appears in the LXX as words of Jeremiah; not as written words of Shemaiah to the priest Zephaniah, as in the Hebrew text, which, no doubt, is the genuine reading.

§ 217.—*Cause of the Variations—Question as to the Priority of the two Recensions.*

(4) The relation between the two recensions presented to us cannot be explained with any probability by the fact of two compilers at different places and quite independent of each other, collecting and editing Jeremiah's prophecies, which, up to that time, had circulated either singly or in small fragmentary collections; for we should then expect that the two recensions would show much

---

[1] According to the Athbasch (אתבש) instead of א a ת is put, instead of ב a ש, instead of ג a ר, &c.; instead of each letter the corresponding one in the inverted order of the alphabet.

more important variations in regard to their extent and purport than is actually the case. It could scarcely have failed to happen that many pieces would have escaped the notice of one compiler which would have fallen in the way of the other acting quite independently of the former. Both must at least have met with one larger collection containing ch. i–xlv. and ch. lii; for the sections contained in these chapters follow in a similar sequence in both recensions, and it is only the oracles against foreign nations which are inserted in different places, and follow on in a different order of succession. But it is altogether improbable that when a work as to the prophecies and fortunes of Jeremiah was compiled, so comprehensive as ch. i–xlv. and ch. lii. would be, the author of it, whoever he might be, should not have also adopted the oracles against the foreign nations.

We are, therefore, induced to assume that the relation between the Masoretic and Alexandrine recensions, even as regards the placing and order of succession of the oracles against foreign nations, is not that of two works originated independently of each other, but as between an earlier and more original one and a later one altered from it.

(5) As regards the question as to priority, it is usually assumed without dispute, even by Ewald, that the original position of these oracles is that in the Masoretic Recension. We cannot deny the possibility that the originator of the Alexandrine Recension, although he found the oracles in the place where they stand in the Hebrew Canon, might have been induced, by ch. xxv. 13, to continue them on from thence, and insert them at that place. But we may just as well imagine that if they originally had the above position, a later editor might think it right to place the oracle against foreign nations quite at the end of the collection. We are induced to imagine, by the result of our former considerations as to the relation between the two recensions with regard to the text of the separate prophecies, that the case actually is that the LXX gives the compilation in its more original shape.

A consideration of the respective order of succession of the separate oracles against foreign nations is also in favour of this view.

Supposing that the Masoretic Recension were the more

ancient of the two, it would be impossible to understand how the later Alexandrine editor, even though he gave these oracles in general a different position in the book to that in which he found them, should have come to so transpose them, as to place the oracle as to Elam first of all (the last but one in the Masoretic text), that about Babylon (the last in the Masoretic text) as the third, &c. We could far rather imagine, that if these oracles had at first the position and order assigned to them in the LXX, a later editor, moving them from thence to the end of the whole collection, might also have altered their successive order. For, looking at the fact that the immigration of the Jews with the prophet into Egypt had been just before related, with prophecies as to the destruction which should there befal them, and also about the conquest of the country by Nebuchadnezzar and the ruin of Pharaoh-hophra, he might easily have been induced to select from the oracles about foreign nations, the two about Egypt (which at first stood after that about Elam), and place them at the beginning; and he might also think it suitable to place the great oracle against the Chaldeans, the chief opponents of the people of the Covenant (originally following the one about Egypt), quite at the end.

In this way, therefore, the disarrangement of the positions of the whole of the oracles would be easily and almost spontaneously brought about.

Added to this, however, is the difference in the text of the two recensions in the passage, ch. xxv. 13. A more exact consideration of the relation between them on this point affords an important argument for the establishment of our opinion.

As ch. xxv. 13 runs in the Hebrew text, it is absolutely out of place, as in the preceding part of the book we find no threatenings at all against foreign nations. The matter, however, explains itself by comparison with the LXX. There it runs, "And I cause to come on this land (Judah) —what is written in this book." Then follows, ἃ ἐπροφήτευσεν Ἰερεμίας ἐπὶ τὰ ἔθνη, as a superscription to the prophecies, against various foreign nations which follow. The corresponding Hebrew words, אֲשֶׁר נִבָּא יִרְמְיָהוּ עַל־הַגּוֹיִם, were doubtless also so intended, that they appear only suitable when, as in the LXX, a series of utterances against foreign

Origin of the two Recensions. 95

nations immediately follows; but they are far less appropriate as a superscription of the separate prophecies following in the Hebrew Canon (ch. xxv. 15–38), although this utterance likewise threatens foreign nations. The originator of the Masoretic Recension, however, transplanting those other oracles against foreign nations from this place to the end of the book, has (as Movers justly remarks), mistakenly placed the words in question as part of the context of his prophecy, with the insertion of בְּ, and then also places a כִּי at the beginning of v. 14, as a link with what precedes, which also originally did not stand there, and is not expressed in the LXX.

§ 218.—*Origin of the two Recensions.*

(6) As regards the further question, as to the originators of the two recensions, we must first inquire, whether the collection, in the more ancient form in which essentially it is supplied to us in the LXX, was prepared and issued by Jeremiah himself, or by some other compiler. The former certainly cannot be very probable, if we look upon ch. lii. as an original element of the collection; for, as we have seen previously (p. 407, 1st vol.), its historical purport brings us to after the year 562 B.C., when Jeremiah must have been about ninety years old. This chapter, however, can very well be separated from the rest of the book, and we may easily imagine that it may have been added by a different person from the one who prepared the preceding collection. In order to narrow the decision of this question, the following points must be taken into consideration.

According to chapters xxxvi. and xlv, Jeremiah, in the fourth year of Jehoiakim, caused Baruch to write down the whole of the prophecies which Jehovah had revealed to him from the first period of his prophetical ministry up to that time, about the Jewish and other nations; these he also, in the fifth year, had read out publicly, and, when the king destroyed the roll, he caused them to be written again on a fresh roll, with other utterances added to them. Certainly, we can scarcely venture to infer from this, that Jeremiah had, up to that time, not yet written down any of his prophetic utterances during the twenty-two to twenty-three years of his ministry; we may rather, from the יִקְרָא in ch. xxxvi. 18, conclude, not indeed with certainty, but yet with some probability, that Jeremiah dictated his discourses to Baruch not from recollection merely, but that he read some of them out to him from earlier records, in order that he might then write them in *one* roll. Certainly, the collection cannot well have been preserved in our book in the shape in which it was then arranged, as there are prophecies long before ch. xxxvi. of a later date than the fifth year of Jehoiakim, as *e.g.*, ch. xxi. at the time of the siege of the city of Jerusalem under Zedekiah, &c. But, on the other hand, it is very probable, that those prophecies of our book, which are of an earlier date than the making of this roll, were preserved in it, therefore in a collection made in the fourth or fifth year of Jehoiakim.

This is particularly the case with the prophecy (ch. xxv. 1-13) according to the superscription, " in the fourth year of Jehoiakim." Referring to his previous prophetical admonitions during so long a period, to which admonitions they had continually shown themselves disobedient, the prophet here threatens them with the nations from the north, and with the seventy years' bondage; as to which it tells us, *v.* 13, " And I will bring upon that land all the words which I have pronounced against it, even all that is written in *this book* (cf. p. 93, ff.). These words, in which the LXX agrees with the Hebrew text, are considered spurious by most of the modern interpreters; they may, however, well be genuine, and originally a part of the text of the prophecy, if the "this book" be understood merely of the roll made by Baruch; which, indeed, the date of the prophecy renders necessary. This prophecy probably formed the conclusion of the utterances against the Israelitish people given here, and thereon perhaps joined some of the more ancient of the prophecies against foreign nations, which perhaps, at least in part, have been preserved in the collection of utterances relating thereto, contained in our book, which also, in the LXX, immediately follow the prophecy (ch. xxv. 1-13). At the head of this collection stood perhaps the prophecies (ch. ii-ix; ch. xi. 1-17); and it had as superscription exactly that which we now find (ch. i. 1, 2, without *v.* 3): " The words of Jeremiah, to whom the word of Jehovah came in the days of Josiah, in the thirteenth year of his reign."

After that, at a later time, we find in ch. xxx. 2, that

Jehovah commanded Jeremiah to write in a book all the words which He had spoken to him; this, however, perhaps relates to the prophecies immediately following (ch. xxx, xxxi). But from what is expressly told us about the earlier collection of his utterances and their being written down together in the fourth year of Jehoiakim, we must think it only probable that the prophet, in his later years, should have intended to place before the eyes of his contemporaries in *one* work his whole prophetical ministry, and a selection of the discourses delivered by him at an earlier time; and this may very well have been our book in the shape in which it has been preserved in the Alexandrine translation. We may then assume with certainty, that the prophet arranged this compilation in his later years during his sojourn in Egypt, and that he made use of Baruch's assistance in it, who (ch. xliii. 6) was taken down into Egypt with him. We may, however, well imagine, that Baruch himself made the compilation in a somewhat independent way, either during the lifetime of Jeremiah and prompted by the latter, or not until after his death. In the latter case he might have issued the fifty-second chapter together with the rest of the book, otherwise it would have been most likely, that it was subsequently added by Baruch.

The idea that the compilation of our book was either actually arranged by Jeremiah himself or by some one in close connection with him, who, like Baruch, was exactly acquainted both with his prophetical ministry and also with his fortunes, is much strengthened by the circumstance, that, among all the prophecies of the book, there is not one, according to my judgment, of which we have any reason for denying the authorship to Jeremiah; and likewise that the historical narratives bear a most distinct and graphic character, which a composition by a partaker in the events can alone rightly explain. But that, at any rate, Baruch took an active part in the compilation and editing the book, is made more probable by the prophecy relating to him personally; not so much the insertion of it, as pre-eminently its position.

It is of the fourth year of Jehoiakim, but stands in our book after the narrative about the flight and sojourn in Egypt; therefore in the Masoretic text in ch. xlv, before the prophecies against foreign nations; but in the LXX, and according to the more original arrangement, quite at the end, immediately before the historical appendix (ch. lii). If Baruch either superintended or wrote down this compilation, we should on this very account be inclined to think that he would place this prophecy, relating to him personally, quite at the end, although it belonged to a comparatively rather early time. Indeed, it is more probable that he should have placed it at the end of the work comprising Jeremiah's prophetical ministry, as it is in the LXX, than among the other prophetical sections, as is the case in the Masoretic text; so that there is herein another point in favour of the greater originality of the Alexandrine Recension, in preference to the Masoretic one.

Ch. i. 3 was probably inserted in the preparation of this collection as an addition to the superscription relating to the older compilation in the fourth year of Jehoiakim. The superscription was perhaps meant to relate to the whole book; the latter, indeed, refers to occurrences after the final time here named (the destruction of Jerusalem, in the fifth month of the eleventh year of Zedekiah), but not to much proportionately, so that we may well imagine that Jeremiah himself, or Baruch, might have fixed this fatal epoch, as the point to which his prophetical ministry extended itself, so far at least as the book presented it to us.

(7) The compilation and editing of the book without doubt took place in Egypt, and it appears to have been circulated there by means of manuscripts, in an essentially unaltered state, until the composition of the Greek translation. We may assume with great probability, however, that the book made its way from Egypt quite early, even during the exile, to the Jews who were at Babylon, for naturally it must have been of the greatest interest to them. It is not at all unlikely that the book there experienced the revision in which it is now presented to us in the Masoretic text, in which shape also, without doubt, it was from the very first admitted into the Hebrew collection of Canonical Scriptures, so that this revision took place, at any rate, at a time when it was still in circulation as a single book.

General Character of the Prophecies.

§ 219.—*General Character of Jeremiah's Prophecies and Discourses.*

The position, however, which the book assumed in the Old-Testament Canon, and its importance in an historical point of view, in introducing to us the history of the Jewish people at the time of the prophet and in placing before our eyes in so lively a manner both their external and internal affairs, are the natural results of the character of that which it imparts to us. In his personality, Jeremiah stands out as a genuine prophet, who frankly predicted, without fear or favour of man, all that was revealed to him as Jehovah's word and will; who undauntedly spent himself in the service of his God, thinking only how he could maintain the people in His Covenant and bring them back to His service, recommending them to that which could alone avail for their true happiness. He was opposed and persecuted both by the people and the princes, especially Jehoiakim; also by the chief men against whom the feeble-minded king Zedekiah was unable to protect him; by the priests and false prophets, who, just at his time, shaped their conduct to the ruin of the people, and endeavoured to excite the latter at a time when, unless they wished completely to perish, there was nothing to be done, except to keep themselves quiet, and in patient submission to await the Divine assistance.

We find Jeremiah repeatedly in conflict with the false prophets, whenever they appear to have pursued an immoral course of conduct. Ch. xxiii. 9—40 is specially directed against false prophets, who appear to have boasted of having received revelations from Jehovah in dreams; appeasing the Jews by false illusions, that no misfortunes should come upon them, without giving any care to the moral improvement of the people: v. also ch. xxviii. (Hananiah), ch. xxix. (Ahab, Zedekiah, Shemaiah); cf. also ch. ii. 8; xiv. 13, ff.; xviii. 18; xxvi. 7, f., 11, 16; xxvii. 14, ff.; xxxvii. 19.

We perceive from this book how strong was the tendency of the Jewish people to idolatry, to the adoration of the stars, and to the shameful worship of Moloch, even after the discovery of the Book of the Law and the reformation effected by the king Josiah; and not only in the country, on high places and in groves, but also in Jerusalem, in the streets and on the house-tops (ch. xi. 13; xix. 4, ff.; xxxii. 29), and even in the temple itself (ch. xxxii. 34). All this is censured by the prophet in the most emphatic way, and is pointed out by him as the cause of the Divine wrath and judgments on the people. He chiefly insists on the observance of the law, and appears, after the discovery of it in the eighteenth year of Josiah, to have been most zealously active in spreading and inculcating it (ch. xi. 1-17; cf. xvii. 19-27, warning against profaning the Sabbath by carrying burdens and other work). · Yet that it does not depend on a lifeless observance of the external precepts of the law, and in offering sacrifices to Jehovah, but in a willing obedience towards God (ch. vi. 20; vii. 22, f.). He stood forth against his adversaries in a vigorous and energetic way, and as he looked upon them as not merely his own personal enemies, but as the opponents of God and the destroyers of the people, he therefore summoned Jehovah as his helper (ch. xi. 20; xviii. 21-23; xx. 11, 12).

His prophecies have mostly a *threatening* import, predicting the ruin of the people on account of their sinfulness; yet, for the future, he is not wanting in joyful prophecies of a Messianic character.

Thus, *e.g.* (ch. iii. 14-18), prediction of the return home of the people out of exile, if they amend, both of Israel and Judah, who shall be united; promise of righteous shepherds for the people; Jerusalem will be called the throne of Jehovah, and to it shall all nations gather together in Jehovah's name, when there shall no longer be any question about the Old Covenant, which shall then be no longer thought of.

Ch. xxiii. 3-8, partly of a similar purport, together with the promise of a righteous offspring of David with the name of *Jehovah Zidkenu*, who shall reign as a righteous king, under whom Judah and Israel shall be blessed.

Ch. xxx, xxxi, and in them, especially ch. xxx. 8, f., that Israel (Ephraim) shall amend, and shall serve Jehovah and the king, David, whom He would set up, and ch. xxxi. 31-37 as to the New Covenant which Jehovah would conclude with Israel and Judah: ch. xxxii. 37-44, xxxiii.

Ch. xii. 14-17. — The prophet promises to the neighbouring nations also, that, if they would turn to Jehovah, He would take pity on them after their punishment, and would accept them among His people.

THE LAMENTATIONS.

§ 220.—*Title—Position in the Canon—Date of Composition and Contents.*

Besides the Book of Jeremiah which we have just considered, which has its place among the greater prophets, we have another shorter work, consisting of five chapters, forming the same number of elegiac songs; this work is likewise ascribed to Jeremiah.

In the superscription in the Hebrew manuscripts and editions, the *title* of the book is now איכה, taken from the first word of the first song (as also of the second and fourth), "*Ah how;*" which was thought appropriate to call attention to the tendency and character of these songs. In the Talmud and among the Rabbis it is usually called קינות, "*Songs of Mourning, Lamentations, Elegies;*" and so in the LXX, and in the Greek theological authors, θρῆνοι; in the Latin authors, as also in the Vulgate, *Lamentationes*, in others *Lamenta*, or *Threni*.

In the Hebrew Canon this book is placed among the *Ketubim*, as one of the Megilloth, between Ruth and Ecclesiastes; on the contrary, in the LXX and Vulgate, it stands after Jeremiah (cf. p. 35, 1st vol.). It is, however, very probable that at an earlier time it had its position here in the Hebrew Canon also (cf. §§ 295, 298). In the Hebrew Canon, the *composer* is not mentioned in the superscription, nor is it, in any express way, in the contents of the songs. The LXX and the Vulgate, on the contrary, have a superscription, in which these songs are placed in close connection with the preceding Book of Jeremiah, and are designated as the *Lamentations of Jeremiah* over Jerusalem, spoken after the carrying away of Israel into exile, and the destruction of the above city. Thus in the Talmud also, Jeremiah is named as the author of Lamentations (*v.* p. 408, 1st vol., notes); and Josephus presupposes the same thing, as, without doubt, he had our Lamentations in view when he says (*Ant.* x. 5, 1) that Jeremiah wrote a song of grief on the death of king Josiah, ὃ καὶ μέχρι νῦν διαμένει. At a later time, however, there have been doubts expressed by some as to Jeremiah's authorship of these songs, but only by few persons.

E.g., by Herm. von der Hardt in a *Programme*. Helmstadt, 1712, and subsequently by some others (*v*. Keil, in the continuation of Hävernick's "Introduction to the Old Testament,' iii. 517, f.). Ewald (*Gesch. Isr*. iv. 22, ff., cf. *Jahrb. f. bibl. W.*) considers it far more probable that one of Jeremiah's scholars in Egypt composed the book. Thenius (*Die Klagelieder* in the Sixteenth Part of the *Exeg. Handb*. 1855), ascribes ch. ii. and iv. to Jeremiah, the three other songs to a rather later poet. Bunsen (*Gott in der Geschichte*, i. 426) ascribes it to Baruch.

But the traditional view that Jeremiah was the author of these songs is much more generally considered to be well grounded, and it may be assumed as certain. In favour of this opinion we may note the agreement of the songs with Jeremiah's prophecies in their whole character and spirit, in their purport, and in the tone of disposition shown in them, as well as in the language (cf. De Wette, § 274); and also, particularly, that which the poet intimates about his own fortunes, ch. iii. 52, ff., cf. Jer. xxxviii. 6, ff.

As regards the *occasion* and *substance* of these songs, the two first and the two last relate to the misery which had been sent on the Jewish people, and particularly on Jerusalem; the middle one, however, ch. iii, chiefly refers to the personal sufferings of the author.

As regards the *date of their composition*, it cannot be doubted that they all belong to the period after the capture of Jerusalem by Nebuchadnezzar's army (in the eleventh year of Zedekiah, in the fourth month, on the ninth day). It is generally supposed that they were also preceded by the burning of the city and temple, which took place through Nebuzar-adan, in the same year indeed (*v*. p. 82), but still a month later, in the fifth month, on the tenth day. Yet, I believe, that we may assume, with great probability, that the songs were composed before this last catastrophe (*v*. however, ch. v. 18), therefore, in the interval between the surrender of the city and its destruction, during which time Jeremiah remained in Jerusalem (Jer. xxxix. 14).

We are led to this by the contents with tolerable certainty, at least in the songs of more general import (ch.

i, ii, iv, v). They all point clearly to a time when Jerusalem was captured by the enemy and partly desolated: when many of the Jews had either escaped or been carried away into captivity; when the king and chief men particularly were in bondage among the heathen (ch. ii. 9; iv. 20); when the temple had been profaned and plundered by the latter (ch. i. 10; ii. 6, f., 20), and no feasts were celebrated in the temple (ch. i. 4); but yet they also contain numerous hints, that the city and temple still existed (v. ch. i. 2, 4, 16, 19; ii. 6, ff., 10, ff., 19, ff.; iv. 1, 5, 18; v. 11, 14), and that fearful famine and want still prevailed in the city (ch. i. 11, 19, f.; ii. 19, 20; iv. 3–5, 9, 10), consequent on the lingering siege, so that they appear to have been written very soon after the capture of the place. The prophet also depicts the misery in so lifelike a way, that we may well suppose that he himself was present in the city; v. particularly ch. ii. 11, ff.

As regards ch. iii, in which the prophet pours out his complaints as to his personal calamities and persecutions, and indeed, as it appears, as to the scoffings and hostility which he had experienced from his fellow countrymen (vv. 14, 52, ff.), but at the same time mourns over the misfortunes of his people, as the punishment for their sins (v. 22, f., 42, ff., 45, ff., 48)—of course, this song, taken by itself, might perhaps have been written somewhat later, and after the destruction of the city. The contents, however, do not precisely point to this; indeed v. 51, where the prophet expresses his sorrow for the daughter of the city, makes it much more probable that the city still existed; and the way in which, in v. 52, ff., he speaks of the hostility and ill treatment he experienced makes it likely that it was written not long after the events described in Jer. xxxviii. 16, ff., which are probably those here meant, and therefore very soon after the surrender of the city. Added to this, we must note the position of this song among the others.

As regards the *form* of the Lamentations, the four first are alphabetical.

Ch. i, ii, and iv, consist of twenty-two verses, each verse commencing with a letter of the alphabet in regular succession and consisting of several divisions; ch. iii, on the contrary, contains in all sixty-six verses, three verses belonging to each letter; they are, however, shorter, each verse containing only one or two shorter divisions. Ch v. also consists of twenty-two verses, but without alphabetical arrangement.

It must be mentioned that in ch. ii, iii, and iv, פ stands before ע, which, occurring in all the three songs, cannot be accidental, although no satisfactory explanation has yet been given of it.

We must, however, consider the statement 2 Chron. xxxv. 25, that Jeremiah composed *Lamentations for Josiah* (וַיְקוֹנֵן יִרְמְיָהוּ עַל־יֹאשִׁיָּהוּ): "and all the singing men and all the singing women spake of Josiah in their lamentations to this day, and made them an ordinance in Israel: and, behold, they are written in the lamentations" (עַל־הַקִּינוֹת). We may perceive from this, that there was, at the time of the Chronicler a collection of elegiac songs by various authors, which contained lamentations on Josiah's death, and some, perhaps, by Jeremiah.

This passage has, perhaps, caused Josephus, *ut supra*, and Jerome (*Comm. ad Sach.* xii. 11), to refer these Lamentations of Jeremiah to the death of Josiah. This is quite untenable from the contents; nor is it at all probable that the chronicler was thinking of these songs, and should have incorrectly given them this reference. But the songs spoken of by him were some of Jeremiah's, which, like so many of the works quoted in the Chronicles, were not admitted into the Canon, and have therefore been lost.

THE BOOK OF EZEKIEL.

§ 221.—*Name of the Prophet—His Family, Locality, and Period of Ministry.*

The *name* of the prophet Ezekiel is in Hebrew, יְחֶזְקֵאל אֵל = "*God strengthens*" (ch. i. 3; xxiv. 24); in Greek, Ἰεζεκιήλ, and from that, in Latin and German, *Ezechiel* (in German also *Hesekiel*). The name occurs in the Hebrew in the same form, 1 Chron. xxiv. 16, for a priest at the time of David.

The prophet himself is not named in the Canonical Scriptures of the Old Testament, except in his own book. For his personal history we are entirely limited to his book, as in Ecclus. xlix. 8, f., he is praised only in reference to its contents.

Ezekiel was of the priestly family, the son of one *Buzi* (ch. i. 3), about whom nothing is otherwise known. He was a younger contemporary of Jeremiah, and like him, prophesied both before and after the destruction of the Jewish state by the Chaldeans, although he was in the land of the Captivity, and not with Jeremiah in Judæa and Egypt. He was one of the leading Jews at Jerusalem, who, together with the king Jehoiachin, were carried away by Nebuchadnezzar (599 B.C.). They took up their residence in the Chaldean kingdom in Mesopotamia, on the river *Chebar* (כְּבָר, ch. i. 3; iii. 15, 23; x. 15, 22).[1] Ezekiel appears to have always remained here; although not continually on the bank of the river, yet in the neighbourhood, at least during the whole time of his prophetic ministry; as he dates his prophecies according to the years of his exile, which coincide with the years of Zedekiah's reign. He received his prophetic call in a glorious vision (ch. i. 1, ff.), in the fifth year of Jehoiachin's being carried away captive.

There is also, in *v.* 1, another definition of the time, " in

---

[1] It is, perhaps, the same river as the *Chaboras* (חָבוֹר), to which—only to some other part of it—the Israelites of the ten tribes had been deported by the Assyrians (2 Kings xvii. 6, xviii. 11; 1 Chron. v. 26), which flows into the Euphrates at Circesium.

the thirtieth year" (in the fourth month, on the fifth day), which must be intended to refer to some publicly accepted era; it is, however, uncertain what it is, whether it is some Jewish or Babylonian one (that of Nabopolassar).

The prophet is earnestly warned to enter upon the office conferred upon him by Jehovah, as watchman over the Israelites, and to communicate to them the Divine admonitions, and not to shun doing this, or else he himself would grievously sin (ch. iii. 16, ff).

The latest date is stated in ch. xxix. 17, the twenty-seventh year of Jehoiachin's captivity (572 B.C.). From ch. xxiv. 18, we perceive that Ezekiel had been married, and that his wife died in the ninth year of his exile (590 B.C.); also from ch. iii. 24, viii. 1, that, in exile, he had a house of his own. About his subsequent fate nothing is known to us; he probably, however, died in exile, where he was held in considerable respect by his fellow-countrymen, the elders of whom often assembled themselves round him, to hear his prophetical counsel: *v.* ch. viii. 1; xiv. 1; xx. 1; cf. xxxiii. 30, ff.

No stress must be laid on that which is stated about him by Pseudo-Epiphan. (*De Vitis Prophetarum*, Opp. ii. 240), that he died as a martyr, being put to death by one of the chief men of the Jewish people, on account of the purport of his prophecies.

§ 222.—*Review of Contents—Chapters* i–xxiv.

The book, which we possess under the name of Ezekiel, contains the following elements :—

A.—Ch. i–xxiv.—This part contains about twenty-nine different utterances against the Israelites, particularly the inhabitants of Jerusalem. There is oftentimes a statement of the date when the prophet began a prophecy, giving year, month, and day, dated from his being carried away captive: ch. i. 1; viii. 1; xx. 1; xxiv. 1; and the fifth, sixth, seventh, and ninth years are named in chronological order; and besides, ch. iii. 16, is named as falling seven days later than that which proceeds. The rest of the intervening utterances are mostly joined on to what goes before by the words, "and the words of Jehovah came unto me;" but appear for the most part as separate utterances, to which the date next preceding has very little reference, except that they fall in the interval between the above date and the date following next. They were all composed before the breaking up of the kingdom of Judah; and, with the exception of the discourse against the Ammonites, ch. xxi. 33–37, they all refer to the Israelites, particularly Jerusalem.

They are repeatedly reproached with their sins, by which they have driven Jehovah from them, particularly the idolatry, the abominations, the sun-worship, &c., which was then carried on among them in Jerusalem, even by the elders of the people, among whom he particularly specifies one Jaazaniah, son of Shaphan (ch. viii. 11). He reproaches king Zedekiah with his alliance with Egypt, wherein he broke his covenant with the king of Babylon who placed him on the throne, and despised Jehovah's oath (ch. xvii. 15, ff.); not less does he speak against the false prophets, who only glossed over matters, and false prophetesses (ch. xiii). He threatens the Israelites, and especially the inhabitants of Jerusalem, that they,—not for their father's guilt, but for their own (ch. xviii),—shall be given up as a prey to certain ruin; that the king (Zedekiah) shall be dethroned (ch. xxi. 30, ff.), and shall be carried away to Babylon in the land of the Chaldeans (ch. xvii. 20), without, indeed, seeing the land (being blinded), and there shall he die (ch. xii. 12, ff.). That the people shall perish by the sword, famine, and pestilence; that Jerusalem and the other cities shall be burnt and destroyed, and those that escape the sword shall be scattered to the four winds; yet that Jehovah will leave a remnant of the pious of Jerusalem, who shall come to the (then) exiles, and mutually comfort themselves with Jehovah's righteous judgment. But those exiles, who persevere in their sinful intentions and desire to know nothing of Jehovah, but, like the heathen, practise abominable idolatry, will Jehovah carry away out of the nations and the countries in which they are scattered, not, however, to the land of Israel, but into the "wilderness of the people," and there hold judgment upon them (ch. xx. 30, ff.). Yet, that Jehovah had no pleasure in the death of a sinner, but much rather that he should turn from his wickedness, and live (ch. xviii. 23). And it is predicted, that the scattered ones of the people shall be brought to the knowledge of Jehovah (ch. vi. 9, f.; xxii. 16); that Jehovah

108   *Origin of the several Books—Ezekiel.*

shall collect the scattered ones out of all lands, and the land of Israel shall be given to them; and that there shall they root out every abomination, and that He will give them one heart and a new spirit, a heart of flesh instead of a heart of stone, so that they should walk in His statutes, and shall be His people, and He shall be their God (ch. xi. 16–20). That after their re-establishment, the whole house of Israel shall serve Him on the Holy Mount of Israel, in the righteous knowledge of God; and there will He accept their offerings (ch. xx. 40–44). Compare with this ch. xxi. 25, ff., where it is stated that after the overthrow of Zedekiah, the land shall be desolated, "until He come whose right it is" (עַד־בֹּא אֲשֶׁר־לוֹ הַמִּשְׁפָּט), perhaps in allusion to the Messianic passage Gen. xlix. 10); and ch. xvii. 22–24, where, following the image already made use of in reference to Jehoiachin and Zedekiah, after the announcement of the overthrow and destruction of the latter, Jehovah predicts that He will take a tender shoot from the top of the high cedar, and will plant it in the mountain of the height of Israel (Zion), where it shall grow prosperously to be a lordly cedar, in which birds of all kinds shall dwell, so that all the trees of the field shall know that Jehovah had done it.

§ 223.—*Review of Contents—Chapters* xxv–xxxii.

B.—Ch. xxv–xxxii.—This division contains further prophecies against foreign nations, like those we find in Isaiah and Jeremiah. In Ezekiel we find, firstly—short discourses against the *Ammonites, Moabites, Edomites,* and *Philistines,* in ch. xxv. without date, but according to the purport, soon after the capture and destruction of Jerusalem by the Chaldeans at the time of Zedekiah.

They are threatened on account of their hostility against Jerusalem, and their mischievous joy at the profanation of Jehovah's sanctuary and the carrying away of the house of Judah; that the Ammonites and Moabites should be given up as a prey to the children of the East, and that the Edomites should be chastised by the hand of the house of Israel, and that the Philistines should be rooted out by Jehovah.

Then follows, ch. xxvi–xxviii, a longer discourse with

several breaks, or separate discourses one joining on the other, against Tyre and its king, also against Sidon; the first of these, ch. xxvi. 1, is dated as in the eleventh year, on the first day of the month. It is not stated what month is meant but it must be one of the latter ones, either the eleventh or twelfth, as, according to *v.* 2, the capture and destruction of Jerusalem is presupposed.

Tyre had shown a very malicious joy at the fall of Jerusalem; on which account numerous nations should march against her, and Nebuchadnezzar should destroy her (ch. xxvi); she should sink ignominiously into the sea, and all her immense treasures should go to ruin (ch. xxvii, in which the extraordinary commercial business of the city is depicted in detail); the haughty king of the city, who considered himself wiser than Daniel, should be destroyed by foreign nations (ch. xxviii. 1–19). And not less should Sidon be punished by pestilence and the sword (xxviii. 20–23); after which the promise follows, that Israel should no longer as before be injured by the neighbouring nations, and that Jehovah should collect them from all nations among whom they were scattered, and should cause them to dwell peaceably in the land which he gave to his servant Jacob (*vv.* 24–28).

The four following chapters (xxix–xxxii), contain seven separate utterances against Pharaoh or against *Egypt*, with the exception of one, ch. xxx. 1–19, which is directed against Pathros and other neighbouring districts; they are all exactly dated, as falling in the tenth and the twenty-seventh years, two in the first month of the eleventh year, and two in the twelfth year.

They threatened Egypt, on which Israel leaned as on a staff, with destruction, mostly through Nebuchadnezzar the king of Babylon; that Egypt and her king should fall, just as Assur was overthrown; that the Egyptians should be scattered among the nations, to show Jehovah's might. Then would Jehovah cause the horn of the house of Israel to bud forth, and would open the mouth of the prophet (Ezekiel) among them, so that they should acknowledge Him as Jehovah (ch. xxix. 21). It is also promised in reference to the scattered Egyptians, that, after forty years, they shall be brought back to Pathros, the country of their origin, where, however, they shall form a mean kingdom only, in which Israel should be never again tempted to place a false confidence (ch. xxix. 13-16).¹

§ 224.—*Review of Contents—Chapters* xxxiii-xxxix.

C.—Ch. xxxiii-xxxix.—This division contains nine different utterances, of which (1), ch. xxxiii. 1–20, is, perhaps, the earliest, and previous to the prophet's receiving the news of the destruction of Jerusalem (cf. ch. xxiv. 26). It points out the duties of the prophet as watchman, viz., to warn the people of their ruin, or else their blood should be required of him (cf. ch. iii. 17, ff.); also, as to the justice of the ways of the Lord, who judges every one according to his conduct, and does not forbear from punishing the righteous, if they do wickedly while confiding in their righteousness, and allows the sinner to live, not remembering his sins, if he ceases from his wickedness.

The rest of the utterances fall later, and none of them until after the destruction of Jerusalem.

The *second* of these (ch. xxxiii. 21, 22) contains an exact date, which, however, occasions difficulty. It is named as the twelfth year, the tenth month, the fifth day, "of our captivity," and indeed as the day when one that had escaped from Jerusalem came to the prophet and announced to him that the city had been smitten (הֻכְּתָה הָעִיר). Now, however, as we have seen, p. 82, not only the capture but also the burning of Jerusalem occurred in the eleventh year, the latter in the fifth month of the same year, as also results from what Ezekiel himself says (ch. xl. 1), in which the same expression has the same reference. The prophet, therefore, could not have received the news of this catastrophe until nearly one and a half years after it happened, which is not likely. There may, therefore, perhaps, be an error in the text. The LXX has the *tenth* year, which naturally is quite unsuitable. Perhaps it should be read, "in the *eleventh* year (בְּעַשְׁתֵּי) instead of 'בִּשְׁתֵּי) with Syr., Döderlein, Ewald, and Hitzig.

¹ The nations, against whom the different utterances of this division (B) are directed, may be enumerated as seven: (1) Ammonites, (2) Moabites, (3) Edomites, (4) Philistines, (5) Tyre, (6) Sidon, (7) Egypt; but they do not at all appear as separate in this collection; still less that with regard to the total number, was it probable that the prophet placed any importance on the number *seven*, and purposely made use of it, as Ewald, Hitzig, and Keil think.

In the evening before the arrival of him that escaped, "the hand of Jehovah came upon the prophet," and he was thereby caused to break his long silence, and to speak until the arrival of him that had escaped. It is not stated what he then said; for what follows must be considered as a different utterance, as the *third*, ch. xxxiii. 23–33. ("And the word of Jehovah came unto me, saying"). Then follow, after the reception of the above intelligence, the words of Jehovah in reference to the (still remaining) inhabitants of the ruins in the land of Israel. Notice is taken of their (hitherto) illegal, idolatrous, vicious conduct, and it is threatened, that they shall be given over to ruin, and their land to complete desolation; at the same time the Israelites round the prophet are reproached, that they will indeed hearken to his speech, as to a lovely song, but that they will not heed his words.

(4) Ch. xxxiv.—Commences with a penal discourse against the shepherds of Israel, who, instead of faithfully tending their flocks, have been guilty of scattering and destroying them; that Jehovah will, on this account, punish them, and will no longer confide their flocks to them, but will Himself watch over their pasture with all carefulness, when He shall have collected them out of every place wherein they have been scattered, and brought them into their own land, where they shall not want for good pasture (*vv.* 1–16). The discourse next refers to the sheep themselves—that Jehovah will strengthen them, will restrain the fat from violently treating the feeble and sick (*vv.* 17–22); that Jehovah will set over them His own shepherd, His servant David, and will conclude a covenant of peace with them, and cause them to dwell on their land in full security, uninjured by other nations and by the wild beasts of the field, the land being blessed with rich fertility.

(5) Ch. xxxv. 1–xxxvi. 15, against the Edomites, on account of their hostility towards Israel, whose children they had put to the sword in the time of their calamity, during which they had reviled them and shown a malicious joy, and (after the destruction of the state of Judah) had endeavoured to appropriate their country (both of Israel and Judah), ch. xxxvi. 5; cf. xxxv. 10. They are threatened with the complete devastation of their land and the extirpation of the inhabitants thereof: but to the land of Israel, on the contrary, and the cities which had become the prey

and the derision of those that were left and the nations around, it is promised that Jehovah should again people them with the house of David, and should build up the ruins, and cause the cities to be again inhabited by numerous men and cattle.

(6) Ch. xxxvi. 16–38 likewise contains glorious promises for Israel, and was, without doubt, not composed until some time after the breaking up of the state of Judah. Israel, scattered among the nations on account of their unclean, idolatrous, and vicious conduct, continues to profane Jehovah's holy name. Jehovah, however, for His own sake, and the sake of His honour, will collect them again out of every country to their own land, will purify them from idolatry and all uncleanness by the sprinkling of pure water, and will give them a new heart of flesh instead of a heart of stone, and His spirit in their souls, and will cause them to walk in His statutes, and they shall be His people, and He shall be their God. The ruined cities shall be again rebuilt, and populously inhabited, and the land shall be blessed with fruitfulness, so that herein even the surrounding nations shall own Jehovah.

(7) Ch. xxxvii. 1–14.—A vision in which the prophet sees a field of dead bones which, at the prophet's word at the direction of Jehovah, were provided with sinews, flesh and skin, and then were quickened by the spirit. This is applied, in Jehovah's discourse, to the whole house of Israel, whom Jehovah, against all hope, would raise, as it were, out of the grave and bring into the land of Israel, in order that they shall know that He is Jehovah. The precise sense is, however, questionable. Usually, it is understood figuratively only, of the restoration of the community of Israel in their land. Hitzig, on the contrary, understands it literally, of a resuscitation and resurrection of dead Israelites, who should be reanimated at the restoration of the people, in order to have a share in the new community in the land of Israel. And thus, perhaps, it is intended by the prophet.

(8) Ch. xxxvii. 15–28.—Symbol of two sticks, which should become one stick in the hand of the prophet, in reference to the re-uniting of Israel (the tribes of the kingdom of Ephraim) and the Jews; that Jehovah should collect them all from out the nations among whom they

lived, and unite them as one people in the land of Israel, under one king and shepherd, David, the servant of Jehovah, under whose dominion they shall there dwell for ever, united and walking in Jehovah's statutes, who shall conclude an everlasting Covenant of peace with them, and will cause His sanctuary and His habitation to be for ever in the midst of them. This is, therefore, another prophecy with a comforting promise of a Messianic character.

(9) Ch. xxxviii. and xxxix.—A prophecy presenting much difficulty. It points to a last conflict, which Israel, the people of Jehovah, shall have to wage with heathen nations, and indeed after their restoration to their land; which, however, shall end with the utter destruction of these enemies, so that the people shall understand that it was on account of the misdeeds of the house of Israel, that Jehovah caused them previously to wander in captivity, and to perish by the sword of the enemy. *Gog, in the land of Magog*, is named as the leader of these nations in the extreme north (ch. xxxviii. 15; xxxix. 2), who shall be induced by Jehovah to come up in the latter days, with numerous nations from the north, west, and south, against the Israelites again dwelling in security in their land, where, however, they shall, one and all, meet with their destruction in fearful multitudes; their own land also shall be devastated by fire.

Ewald is, certainly, not correct in thinking that the prophet in all this intends the Chaldean monarchy and its overthrow. On the contrary, Hävernick (*Commentar über den Propheten Ezechiel*, 1843), and Hitzig (*Der Prophet Ezechiel*, 1847), explain it rightly. If the prophet had been thinking of the Chaldeans, he certainly would not have omitted to refer to the acts of violence previously committed by them against Israel; also the way in which the assembling of Gog's armies is depicted, in ch. xxxviii. 2, ff., does not at all induce us to suppose it was the above nation. We may see from ch. xxxviii. 17, 19, and xxxix. 8, that Ezekiel had some earlier prophecies before him, in which some such last decisive conflict of the heathen multitudes with God's people was spoken of; we cannot however ascertain how much of the details he has borrowed from them. The greatest part, however, belongs to him. The name of the land of *Magog* is perhaps derived from Gen. x. 2, where Magog is specified among the sons of Japhet, with other nations, several of which are mentioned here among the hostile armies. The name of the king *Gog*, is perhaps formed from Magog; it cannot however, be decided, whether this was done by the prophet, or whether he met with the name elsewhere. Gog, together with Magog, are mentioned in Revelations xx. 8, as nations whom Satan, after the termination of the kingdom of 1000 years, shall bring up from the uttermost parts of the earth for the last conflict against God's people. Ezekiel's prophecy, however, is based upon the same idea essentially.

§ 225.—*Review of Contents—Chapters* xl–xlviii.

D.—Ch. xl–xlviii, in the twenty-fifth year "of our captivity," fourteen years after the destruction of Jerusalem, a series of connected visions was afforded to the prophet, he being removed in these visions into the land of Israel. They all relate to the future circumstances of the people of the Covenant after the restoration.

Firstly, the arrangements and measurements of the building of the future sanctuary are stated, of the courts and doors of the temple, of the temple itself and its outbuildings, as they were shown and measured out to the prophet by an angel with measuring-rod and line in his hand (ch. xl–xlii). After that, the prophet saw how the glory of Jehovah made its entrance into the temple, which was to be no more profaned (ch. xliii. 1–12); the dimensions of the altar are stated, and precepts for offering sacrifices on it, also for priests and Levites (ch. xliii. 13–27; xliv.); next, directions for the division of the land, as to the share to be appropriated for Jehovah and the priests, for the Levites, the community, and the princes (ch. xlv. 1–8); also admonitions to the princes, to exercise justice, and not to oppress the people, and to have correct weights and measures (xlv. 9–12); further directions about the heave offerings which they, the princes, were to offer, and the oblations to be brought by them, and other things relating to the princes (xlv. 13–xlvi. 18); also as to the cooking of the offerings (xlvi. 19–24); then about the fountain springing up from the temple, full of fishes and fertilizing the land, whose waters flow into the Dead Sea (xlvii. 1–12); finally, as to the future boundaries of the land of the people of the Covenant, and its partition among the twelve tribes, the priests, the princes, and the citizens; and as to the twelve gates of the city, the name of which shall henceforth be יְהוָה שָׁמָּה (ch. xlvii. 13–xlviii. 35).

It is very doubtful what the prophet had in view in these visions. The descriptions contained in them differ very often from the arrangements of the time before the captivity.

Thus, as regards the arrangement of the sanctuary, the exterior extent of the temple and the buildings round it are much larger than that of Solomon's Temple, so as to be able to contain the new community, and it is represented as square and outside the city, which latter was also square. The internal arrangement of the temple, however, is more simple, and less gorgeous. The distinction between the Holy Place and the Holy of Holies is left out, inasmuch as the whole temple is the Holy of Holies; nor is any new ark spoken of, but only Cherubim, who take a place in the temple. No one of the priests is specified as the high priest; the priests generally, however, as before the high priest in particular, are laid under an obligation to keep away from all uncleanness. Among the sacrifices, the burnt offering is made most prominent, yet a daily evening offering is not spoken of, but the amount of morning offerings is stated as larger. Among the principal feasts, the Passover and the Feast of Tabernacles alone are named, but not Pentecost, nor the Great Day of Atonement, the omission of which is connected with the absence of any mention of the ark and the high priest. A new feast is instituted, on the first and seventh days of the first month of the year, when a solemn propitiation for the sanctuary was to take place, for the sake of those who have sinned through error or simplicity (ch. xlv. 18-20). In the division of the land among the twelve tribes, Joseph is named as one; he however is to receive two shares, but the others all alike; those indeed who, when on the other side Jordan, had their possession assigned to them by Moses in the land of Canaan, on this side Jordan. The strangers living among the Israelites were also to have a share with the various tribes in the division of the land, in the like manner as the Israelites (ch. xlvii. 22).

The prophet adverts in a peculiar way to the prince of the people in נָשִׂיא, for so he calls him, and not מֶלֶךְ (ch. xlv. 7, ff.; xlvi; xlviii. 21, f.). The prince is not merely to receive a separate share in the division of the land (that he should not oppress the people), but he also stands in a peculiarly near relation to the sanctuary, as if he were a superintending priest; and on him, as such, is to be imposed as a duty the offering up of all sacrifices, particularly on the feasts and sabbaths.

Exception has often been taken to the fact, that in the arrangements prescribed here both in political and ecclesiastical matters, no notice is taken of the return of the Jews to their native land, and of the restoration of the sanctuary; and thus a justification has been found for the opinion that all this matter in Ezekiel is to be explained as being merely symbolical and allegorical. This may sometimes be assumed, as, e.g. in the description of the fountain of the temple, ch. xlvii. 1, ff. &c., where it cannot well be imagined that the prophet could have expected a literal fulfilment of the prophecy; but this must not be carried too far. In most of the statements as to the future arrangements, it is evident that the prophet meant them in earnest, and in a literal sense. Not indeed as plainly binding precepts for the people in any future restoration, but as intimations of that which he would recommend for it, and thought worthiest and most suitable. It could not well be, that all these things should be carried out in the way stated here, because the return and restoration of the people never took place nearly so extensively or completely as is presupposed by the prophet.

§ 226.—*Reality of the Prophetic Visions.*

There is no adequate reason for asserting, that the *visions* forming the whole of the last part of the book, and indeed to be found elsewhere also in it, are *merely* literary embellishments, and that the visions related by him were never actually vouchsafed to the prophet, nor the objects presented to his sight. His human individuality must, nevertheless, have had an important influence in the shaping of these visions, and we may also imagine that the prophet would, in his written records of them, amplify

Symbolical Actions done by the Prophet. 117

them with further details, as, for example, is certainly the case in chapters xl–xlviii. We may, on the contrary, assume with tolerable certainty that, where the prophet speaks of *symbolical actions* he had performed, they were *not* actually done by him, but that this was merely a literary embellishment on his part. The whole character of nearly all of them clearly point out, that if they were actually outwardly performed, they could not have come to the knowledge of those for whom the prophecy was intended, cf. *e.g.* ch. iv. 4–6; v. 1–4; xii. 3, ff., &c.

§ 227.—*Written Record of the Prophecies—Their Compilation and Order of Succession.*

That Ezekiel sometimes exercised his prophetical vocation orally is clear from the passage (ch. xx. 1) as to his intercourse with the elders, who applied to him for counsel and instruction; *v.* also ch. xxiv. 19. We may, however, assume with great probability, with regard to the utterances which we read in his book, that they were not in general orally delivered before they were written out, but that, at any rate, they were read out to the people after they had previously been written. This applies specially to all those utterances which were intended for people not in the immediate neighbourhood of the prophet, as for the Jews in Jerusalem before the destruction of the State, and for foreign nations. The primary record of the several utterances followed, perhaps, not long after the revelation referring to them had been afforded to the prophet. Yet it is not improbable that he subsequently, here and there, somewhat remodelled them when preparing and issuing them in a collected form. It may, however, be considered as tolerably certain that Ezekiel himself prepared this compilation, and that therefore no utterances are admitted into it which are not Ezekiel's own.[1]

The prophecies relating to the people of Israel are doubtless all arranged here in chronological order, according to the date of their original conception; firstly, those of the

[1] The attacks of an English critic (1798) upon the prophecies against foreign nations have been disposed of, also those of Oeder and Vogel (1771) against ch. xl–xlviii, and those of Corrodi (1792) against ch. xxxviii–xl. Zunz (*Gottesdienstliche Vorträge der Juden*, 1832, p. 158, ff.) is inclined to fix the date of the whole book at some time in the Persian age, but on untenable grounds.

first part, ch. i–xxiv, as falling before the capture and destruction of the city, and next, those of the third part, ch. xxxiii–xxxix, which are all later than the former, and then the visions of the fourth part occurring still later. The reason that caused Ezekiel to place the prophecies against foreign nations between the first and third parts was, that at the conclusion of the former part (ch. xxiv. 26, ff.), it was disclosed to the prophet that "one that had escaped" should announce to him the fall of Jerusalem, and also, that the first of the utterances directed against foreign nations belongs without doubt to the time immediately after this catastrophe, and threatens the neighbouring nations on account of their hostility and malicious joy at the misfortunes of Jerusalem, and at the profanation of the Temple. This, then, has been the inducement to the prophet for placing the utterances against foreign nations in the position they fill. He would not, however, wish to conclude his book with these, but rather with promises as to Israel's future. Of this sort are (*a*) ch. xxxv. 1–xxxvi. 15, containing indeed a threatening discourse against the Edomites, and might, consequently, have been placed with ch. xxv. had it not contained in conclusion a promise as to the restoration of Israel; also (*b*) ch. xxxviii, xxxix, about Gog, &c. The visions in ch. xl–xlviii. form, apart from the date, a manifestly suitable conclusion to the whole collection.

§ 228.—*Language and Peculiarities of Style—Characteristics of his Prophetical Ministry.*

Ezekiel's language has not only much of a Chaldaic character, but presents generally a good deal that is peculiar, and, in a grammatical point of view, anomalous and incorrect, more so indeed than any other Old-Testament author. In his style he is very diffuse and redundant; and his thoughts are too much drawn out into particularities.

E.g., in the measurements and descriptions in the last part; in the recital of the wealth and commerce of Tyre (ch. xxvii); particularly also in the delineation of Jerusalem and Samaria as licentious women (ch. xvi, xxiii), in which the whole sketch is carried out in a way offensive to good taste, such as we do not find to this extent in any other of the Old-Testament prophets.

In moral earnestness, however, he stands inferior to none

Characteristics of his Ministry. 119

of the other prophets. He is, as a prophet, imbued with a solemn feeling of duty, that he must, as Jehovah's watchman, warn the people from false ways, and also by a consciousness of the guilt which he would incur in the neglect of this obligation (ch. iii. 17–21 : xxxiii. 7–9). He is thus worthy of his position among the other prophets, especially of ranking with his older contemporary, Jeremiah. The latter, at the time of Ezekiel's being carried away captive from Jerusalem, had been ministering there as prophet for about thirty years, and we can hardly doubt that Ezekiel knew him personally, and had often listened to him and read his discourses; perhaps some of them may have subsequently reached him in his exile, as Ewald and others have supposed with great probability that Ezekiel made use of Jeremiah's prophecies; *v.* De Wette, § 223, note *c*.

He shared with Jeremiah in his energetic opposition to the continual idolatry exercised in Judah and even in Jerusalem; in his insisting on the observance of the Sabbath, &c.; also in a political point of view, in his disapprobation of aid being sought in Egypt against the Chaldeans, which was held out to Zedekiah as a breach of faith with the king of Babylon, who had placed him on the throne. In these things, however, as compared with Jeremiah he shows much that is peculiar to himself.

The statement of Josephus (*Ant.* x. 5, 1), about "two books" of Ezekiel, is very obscure.[1]

[1] This can hardly be referred to Jeremiah, with Eichhorn, Bertholdt. Hävernick, and Movers (*de utriusque rec. Jer.* p. 47).

THE TWELVE LESSER PROPHETS.

§ 229.—*Their Collective Name—Compilation and Order of Succession.*

Ezekiel is followed in the Hebrew Canon by a collection of twelve shorter prophetical Scriptures, which, collectively, scarcely equal the extent of a single one of the three preceding greater prophets (Isaiah, Jeremiah, and Ezekiel).[1] They are always reckoned by the Jews as one book only, stating the number of the holy books as twenty-two (or twenty-four); Josephus has reckoned them in this way, also the Talmud and the Rabbis, as well as the ecclesiastical authors (*v.* §§ 303, 309–311). They are called *the twelve*, שְׁנֵים עָשָׂר, Chald. תְּרֵיסָר, οἱ δώδεκα (προφῆται), τὸ δωδεκαπρόφητον. That these writings were, in the second century B.C., already considered as one associated collection, is clearly shown by the unreasonably suspected passage, Ecclus. xlix. 10 (*v.* p. 33, vol. i.). The author of this collection is doubtless the same man who compiled the scriptures of the *Nebiim*, the second part of the Canon, therefore most probably Nehemiah (*v.* § 294, f.). The prophets by whom these works were severally written, or after whom they were named, belonged to various epochs from the time of Uzziah, about 800 B.C., up to the time of Nehemiah, about 450 B.C. Between these points are the earliest and latest that are preserved to us.

The order of succession of these works, as regards the six first, stands differently in the LXX and in the Hebrew Canon, as Jerome[2] remarks. Joel, in the LXX, not coming until after Micah, and Micah after Amos; therefore—

Hebr.—(1) Hosea, (2) Joel, (3) Amos, (4) Obadiah, (5) Jonah, (6) Micah.

LXX.—(1) Hosea, (2) Amos, (3) Micah, (4) Joel, (5) Obadiah, (6) Jonah.

---

[1] Cf. Hieron. *Proœm in Esaiam:* Cum Esaias duodecim prophetis juxta numerum versuum aut æqualis aut major sit.—Augustin. *De Civ. Dei*, xviii. 29: Qui propterea dicuntur minores, quia sermones eorum sunt breves in eorum comparatione, qui majores ideo vocantur, quia prolixa volumina condiderunt.

[2] *Præf. in XII Prophetas:* Non est idem ordo XII Prophetarum apud Hebræos, qui est apud nos.

Lesser Prophets—Order of Succession. 121

The six last are in the same order of succession in both: (7) Nahum, (8) Habakkuk, (9) Zephaniah, (10) Haggai, (11) Zechariah, (12) Malachi.

Which order of succession is the more original as regards the first half cannot be decided certainly, but probably that in the Hebrew Canon. We may assume, with the greatest probability, that the originator of this collection had a chronological order in view; but Jerome,[1] and others, and also Hävernick, Caspari (*Obadiah*, p. 37), and Hengstenberg, are decidedly wrong in attributing so much authority to the order in the Hebrew Canon, as to allow the sequence observed in it to determine their judgment as to the respective epochs of the several prophets.

We shall on the contrary see, without considering Jonah and the second part of Zechariah, that most probably, Joel is the most ancient of these prophets, and that Obadiah, on the other hand, chronologically considered, has too early a place, &c.

1.—THE BOOK OF HOSEA.

§ 230.—*Name of the Prophet—Period of his Prophetical Ministry.*

Name, in Hebrew, הוֹשֵׁעַ, = *salvation*, the same name which the last of the Israelitish kings bore, which also was the original name of Joshua (Num. xiii. 8, 16; cf. Deut. xxxii. 44); in the LXX and Vulg. 'Ωσηέ (also written 'Ωσηέ, Rom. ix. 25), and *Osee*. Jerome (*ad* i. 1) found another form, Αὐσή, *Ause*, in manuscripts, but rejects it. In German, in Luther, &c., it more follows the Hebrew form, *Hosea*.

This prophet is not named in the Old Testament, except in his book (in the title and ch. i. 1, 2). In the superscription, ch. i. 1, he is called the son of Beeri, about whom personally nothing further is known.

It is quite arbitrary in certain Rabbis to identify this man with Beerah (בְּאֵרָה), 1 Chron. v. 6. Little credence is likewise to be given to the statements of the later Jews and Fathers of the Church as to the place of birth of the

[1] *Ut supra:* in quibus autem (Prophetarum scriptis) tempus non præfertur in titulo, sub illis eos regibus prophetasse, sub quibus et ii, qui ante eos habent titulos, prophetaverunt.

prophet, especially as they do not agree among themselves about it.

The age to which Hosea belonged is stated in the superscription, ch. i. 1, to be in the reigns of (*a*) *Uzziah, Jotham, Ahaz, Hezekiah*, kings of Judah, exactly those who are named in Isaiah i. 1 ; and (*b*) of Jeroboam (II.), king of Israel, son of Joash. The two middle ones of these kings of Judah, Jotham and Ahaz, reigned each sixteen years, therefore the period from the year of Uzziah's death to the first year of Hezekiah would be thirty-two years. But the Israelitish king, Jeroboam, certainly died a considerable time before Uzziah, although how many years cannot with certainty be named from the various, and relatively incongruous, statements in the Books of Kings as to the relation between the reigns of the kings of Israel and Judah; at least as many as fourteen years (according to 2 Kings xv. 8); probably however about twenty-six years (by comparison of the corresponding statements, 2 Kings xiv. 2, 17, 23 ; 2 Chron. xxv. 1–25). The passages, 2 Kings xv. 1, xiv. 23, lead to a still longer period—of thirty-eight years. This much is certain, that according to the statement of the superscription, the ministry of the prophet must have begun some considerable time before the death of Uzziah, and must have been of long duration, at least fifty years, even if it began but a short time before the death of Jeroboam II. and extended only to the beginning of Hezekiah's reign. It depends, however, upon the question whether the superscription is authentic or not. There may be some doubt, whether, in its present shape, it was prefixed by the prophet himself. It is rather contrary to this idea, and indeed surprising, that four kings of Judah are named, and only one king of Israel, Jeroboam II., whose reign did not reach down to the death of even the first named of the kings of Judah; none of those kings being named—at least six in number—who reigned in Israel during the last part of Uzziah's time, and during the time of Jotham, Ahaz, and the first period of Hezekiah's.

We shall again return to this matter, and I will only remark here that the mention of the father of Hosea, nowhere else named, shows an acquaintance with the circumstances of the prophet's life, and is consequently in favour of the high antiquity of the superscription.

§ 231.—*Review of Contents* (*Ch.* i–iii.)—*Symbolical Actions.*

The Book of Hosea is divided into two principal parts, the *first* of which (ch. i–iii.) begins the prophecies with the narration and explanation of certain symbolical actions which were performed by the prophet at the command of Jehovah.

The prophet relates, in the first place, that at Jehovah's command he took as mistress a harlot named Gomer, daughter of Diblaim, and that she bore him several children (bastards) (ch. i. 2–9). The impurity of the woman points to the idolatry in the land, and the revolt from Jehovah (v. 2); the names of the three children have likewise a symbolical reference to Jehovah's relations to the people of the kingdom of Israel, as an intimation that Jehovah would scatter them, and that He would revenge on the house of Jehu the bloodshed through which he came to the throne; also that He would no longer favour the people of Israel, and would no more look upon them as His people, and that He would be no more their God, whilst, on the other hand, He would bless the house of Judah, and cause them to be saved.

The promise, however, immediately follows (ch. i. 10, 11) that Jehovah will again bless the people, and will acknowledge them as *His* people; also that He will make the Israelites very numerous, and will gather the children of Israel and Judah under one head, and will bring them up out of the land (perhaps to Jerusalem for worship).

Similar thoughts to those in ch. i. are repeated in ch. ii. 1–23, and mostly in similar imagery; in the first place, censure and threatening against the people of Israel on account of their whoredoms and their idolatry; and then, from v. 16, a promise that Jehovah will convert them through affliction, and renew His Covenant with them, and bless them with great happiness.

Ch. iii. contains another symbolical action. The prophet relates how at Jehovah's command he bought another mistress, who had previously committed adultery,[1] and made the condition with her that she should abstain for a long time from any sexual union whatever. It is thus

[1] From the mode in which it is expressed this is not meant, as *e.g.* Ewald would have it, for the *same* woman as that in ch. i.

intimated that the kingdom of Israel, as a punishment for their revolt, should be deprived for a long time of all their supports and leaders both from their rulers and from their worship, and that through this they should be induced to return again to Jehovah, their God, and to the house of David.

As regards the *symbolical actions* in ch. i. and ch. iii, there is no doubt that these are to be considered as mere literary embellishment,[1] and not as things actually done by the prophet. Without noticing the moral offence they would necessarily present, if they were to be looked upon as actual facts, they would be quite unsuitable, and would fail in their aim, because the actions, if performed, would run over a whole series of years, and the people would not easily have understood their signification.

Jerome's view of this matter is correct (cf. Lübkert, *Die symbolische Handlung Hosea's*, in *Theol. Stud. u. Krit.* (1835), vol. iii. pp. 647-656).

As regards the *date of composition*, it is evident from ch. i. 4, that the house of Jehu still ruled over Israel, for it is there threatened that Jehovah would within a short time punish the house of Jehu on account of their bloodshed, particularly, perhaps, on account of Jehu's own actions, and would exterminate them, and make an end of the kingship in Israel. Jehu, anointed by means of Elisha, had overthrown the Israelitish king Jehoram and usurped the throne, in all which he committed much cruelty (2 Kings ix-x). After him, there reigned of his posterity, one after the other, *Jehoahaz*, *Jehoash*, and *Jeroboam II.* (forty-one years), and then the latter's son *Zachariah*, who, however, after six months, was put to death by Shallum. This prophecy must have been composed before this event, probably in the latter part of the reign of the Jeroboam II. named in the superscription, so that the statement of the superscription, as regards the earliest point of time therein mentioned, is thus proved to be correct. Ch. iii. might also belong to the same time. This, however, perhaps, falls rather later in the unquiet and partly anarchical times which followed soon after the death of Jeroboam II. Verse 4 may intimate, although it is not cer-

[1] J. H. Kurtz thinks otherwise, "Marriage of the Prophet Hosea." Dorpat, 1859.

tain, that the prophet had then a state of things in view which was actually present.

§ 232.—*Review of Contents (Ch. iv–xiv.)—Nature and Dates of the several Utterances.*

There are no more symbolical actions in the *remaining portion* of the book (ch. iv–xiv). It consists of prophetical utterances, for the most part of a threatening import, directed against the kingdom of Israel.

The prophet censures the people, and particularly the priests, who are nourished by the sins of the people, and reject knowledge, and will on that account be rejected by Jehovah (*v.* chapters iv. 4–11[1]; v. 1; vi. 9); also the chief men on account of their revolt from Jehovah, and of the idolatry and the unlawful *cultus* generally which they zealously carried on on numerous altars and in groves, united with soothsaying (rhabdomancy particularly, ch. iv. 12), uncleanliness and adultery, wicked revelling, drunkenness, lies, perjury, violence, and bloodshed. The prophet, on this account, threatens them with destruction, which Jehovah will soon bring upon them. Vainly will they endeavour to propitiate Jehovah by oblations; also that Jehovah loves mercy and the true knowledge of God better than any sacrifice or burnt-offering (ch. vi. 6). In vain will they turn for assistance to foreign, idolatrous nations, particularly to Assyria and Egypt (ch. v. 13; vii. 11; viii. 9; xii. 2; xiv. 4). Jehovah will punish them by the means of those very nations in whom they

[1] Cf. "Lectures on Hosea," on ch. iv. 4: "According to the usual explanation of *v.* 4 *b*, it must be assumed that 'the striving with the priests' (cf. Deut. xvii. 8–13) had become an almost proverbial expression for designating a godless audacity worthy of death. Yet it cannot be denied that the expression, so understood, always has something characteristic about it, especially with this context; for the priests in Israel appear in this passage as equally godless as the people, and therefore 'the striving' with them could not serve to indicate a wicked opposition to Jehovah's commands. Hitzig's explanation is not so natural. J. D. Michaelis points it כְּמְרִיבַי : 'thy people, Oh priest, act as if they would strive against me,' a not unsuitable sense. The vocative thus standing at the end may, indeed, appear unnatural; what comes after is much against this mode of pointing. *V.* 6 is, in any case, addressed to the priests, without this fact being at all intimated; and the s cond person in *v.* 5 might also very suitably be referred to the priests so that the priests and false prophets of the kingdom are fittingly named together)."

put their trust, and will cause them to wander thither into exile (ch. vii. 16; viii. 13; ix. 3, 6; xi. 5; cf. v. 10, ff.).

The discourse of the prophet is here mostly directed against Israel and Ephraim, as in the first part, where, in ch. i. 7, the house of Judah, which Jehovah would bless and deliver, is named in express contrast to Israel. Thus here, in ch. iv. 15, Judah only is admonished not to imitate Israel in transgression by partaking in the idolatry at Gilgal and Bethaven.

But Judah is very often censured and threatened, together with Israel, as guilty of the same offences.

Thus, particularly in the section, ch. v. 8–vi. 3, which is directed against both kingdoms in common; also ch. vi. 4–11 a, and ch. xii, in which the same is the case, only that Ephraim stands forth to a greater extent; cf. ch. viii. 14; x. 11, where, in utterances otherwise entirely directed against Israel, Judah is only once named as sharing in the same guilt and the same punishment.

It is, however, evident that Hosea was chiefly concerned with the kingdom of Israel. He doubtless dwelt in it during his prophetical ministry, and perhaps also, as is the usual opinion, he belonged to it by birth, although it is not quite certain (cf., however, ch. vii. 5). He may, however, have subsequently visited Judah, and in it have made public his writings. This is, at least, not improbable, if the superscription, in which four kings of Judah are named first, was entirely prefixed by Hosea himself.

As regards this second part, however, various modern scholars have endeavoured to fix the dates to which the several utterances belong (v. in De Wette, § 227, note b). But this cannot well be accomplished with any certainty. Although we cannot doubt that this portion actually contains various utterances which were not all delivered at the same period, yet it cannot be decided everywhere with certainty where one begins and another leaves off, and still less the exact date for each of them. It is probable that Hosea himself subsequently selected some of those discourses which he had probably written down separately at an earlier time, and put them together in their present form. As to their dates, we can only determine with certainty that they all belong to a time when the kingdom of Israel still existed, therefore before the sixth year of Hezekiah, and the compilation and last editing of them probably also took place before the breaking up of the above kingdom. Besides, we are, in general, led to a time of anarchy such as ensued in Israel after the death of Jeroboam II. Nothing more exact than this can with certainty be determined about the date of any of the single utterances.

We may perceive, from the way in which, in various passages, the Assyrians and Egyptians are spoken of, that the Israelites were inclined to seek aid from one and the other nation alternately; and this renders it, at least, probable that the composition took place before the Assyrian king Tiglath-pileser had torn away a portion of its territory from the kingdom of Israel at the time of the Israelitish king Pekah (Ahaz being king of Judah): but perhaps hardly during the reign of the powerful king Jeroboam II. On the other hand, ch. x. 14, would lead us to a later time if the Shalman, there mentioned as devastating Betharbel, be Shalmanezer. This, however, is questionable, and the reference of this passage generally is very uncertain. The words (ch. x. 13) point to a time when the kingdom of Israel believed that it could still rely on the multitude of its warriors. Various passages, however, as particularly ch. vii. 7, viii. 4, apply to a time when the kings in Israel were rapidly changed, and were placed on the throne at the arbitrary will of the people.

It is possible that certain portions were not written until the beginning of the reign of Hezekiah; and the *superscription* of the book, ch. i. 1, might proceed entirely from the prophet himself. Perhaps *Uzziah* only of the kings of Judah was originally named, together with the Israelitish *Jeroboam*, son of Joash, when the superscription related only to two or three first chapters, and the three other kings of Judah were not added until the compilation and issuing of the whole book by Hosea himself.

§ 233.—*General Character of the Prophecies—Their Style and Language.*

As a whole, Hosea's prophecies have a *censuring* and *threatening* character; but yet they sometimes end with joyful promises of a Messianic kind.

In the last respect, it is predicted that, notwithstanding

the infidelity of the people, Jehovah would not withdraw His grace and mercy from them;—that the old relation between them should be again restored, and that the people should again faithfully be joined to Him, all which is here bound up with their return from the dispersion, also in the return of the *whole* people, both Israel and Judah, to the house of David, with which, also, a promise is united of the increased fertility of the land, and of undisturbed peace; *v.* chapters ii. 1–3, 16–25; iii. 5; xi. 8–11; xiv. 5–10.

As regards the literary character of the Book of Hosea, his symbolical actions are related in prosaic language; in the remainder his style of writing is poetico-rythmical, but is somewhat abrupt and harsh.

Cf. Jerome, *Præf. in XII Proph.*: "Osee commaticus est et quasi per sententias loquens." As regards the explanation of his details, he is one of the most difficult of the prophets and Old Testament writers generally.

2.—THE BOOK OF JOEL.

§ 234.—*Name—General Purport—Mode of Interpretation.*

Joel, the son of Pethuel, is named as the author of the second work in the collection of the lesser prophets, or rather he is, in fact, named as the person to whom "*the word of Jehovah came*," which is communicated in the book; he is, however, without doubt its author. The *name*, אֵל" = *Jehovah is God*, occurs in the Old Testament for different persons; the prophet himself, however, is not named in any other part of Scripture.

This much clearly appears from Joel's work, that he belonged to the kingdom of Judah, and, at the time of his utterances, dwelt in Jerusalem; *v.* particularly ch. i. 14, ii. 1; also ch. i. 9, 13, 16, ii. 9, 15, 17; besides ch. iv. 1, 16, ff., &c.[1] All interpreters are agreed as to the above, but not so as to the epoch of the prophet, nor, in many respects, as to the references of his prophecies, their occasion and purpose.

The general purport and train of thought are as follows. The prophets summons the inhabitants of the land to

[1] Bleek's references are to the Hebrew division, according to which ch ii. 28-32 (A V.) stands as ch. iii, and ch. iii. (A.V.) as ch. iv.—Tr.

The Plague of Insects.

mourn over a public calamity, which is denoted in ch. i. 4, as arising from various kinds of insects (cf. ch. ii. 25); a calamity more severe than almost any that had yet taken place, through which the whole land would be devastated, so that it would even be impossible to sacrifice meat and drink offerings to Jehovah; wherefore the priests are charged to ordain a general fast, and to call together the people to Zion. The plague is designated as the army and camp of Jehovah, as the executioners of His will, and as indications that the day of the Lord is come, or at hand (ch. i. 2–ii. 11). The prophet then calls on the people to turn now to Jehovah with their whole hearts, with fasts and public meetings for prayer, rending their hearts and not their garments; and then, perhaps, would He repent him in His grace and long-suffering, and anew pour out His blessings upon them, and restore the fruitfulness of the land, that they might again be able to bring to him meat and drink offerings (ch. ii. 12–17). That which the prophet here only ventures to hint at, he next expresses more confidently, viz., that Jehovah would remove the plague from them, which he designates as "the northern" (הַצְּפוֹנִי), and would overthrow it between two seas, and that he would bestow rain upon them at the right season, and a rich abundance of the produce of the earth, that he would show himself to be Israel's God, and that His people should never be put to shame (ch. ii. 18–27). After that, Jehovah further announces that He will pour out His Spirit upon all people, no longer on individuals only, but on all flesh (ch. iii. 1, 2), and will cause extraordinary appearances, both in heaven and earth, as forerunners of the fearful day of the Lord, in which, however, all who call on Jehovah's name shall find deliverance at Jerusalem and on Zion (ch. iii. 3–5); then will Jehovah bring back the captivity of Judah and Jerusalem, and will enter into judgment with all nations who shall have shown themselves hostile to His people, who have bought and sold them, scattered them into foreign countries, and plundered their treasures, among whom Tyre, Sidon, and the Philistines are specified by name; these Jehovah will requite, by means of the Jews, for all the evil they had done to the latter (ch. iv. 1–8). Then, however, the discourse is again directed against the surrounding nations generally, the heathen, who were hostile to God's people; they are summoned to prepare for a conflict with Jehovah (vv. 9-12); yet will they not escape a condemnatory judgment, which Jehovah will pass on them in the valley of judgment or decision, making His mighty voice resound from Zion during the darkening of the heavenly bodies, so that heaven and earth shall quake; He will be a protection and shield to His people Israel, making them know that He is their God, dwelling in Zion, at Jerusalem, which shall henceforth be holy, and no more profaned by strangers (vv. 13-17). Then follows yet again the promise, that Jehovah will bless His land with rich fruitfulness, and will water it with a stream proceeding out of the house of the Lord,—Egypt and Edom being laid desolate on account of the hostility exercised by them against the Jews. Judah and Jerusalem shall everlastingly be inhabited, and having cleansed them from the bloodshed that oppressed them, Jehovah shall dwell on Zion (vv. 18-21).

With respect to the calamity on the land, depicted in the two first chapters, it is a question among interpreters, (a), whether locusts and their devastations are actually spoken of, or whether it is to be taken figuratively for the invasion and ravages of hostile armies in the land of Judah; and, (b), whether the delineation is meant as of some then present plague, or as a prophecy of a future one.

Theodoret, and also many later interpreters, understand it as a prophecy; Luther, Calvin, and most of the modern expositors, as a description of something present. It is looked upon in a figurative sense, as referring to the *Chaldæans* by Jerome, Cyril (Alex.), Abarbanel, Luther, Grotius, Bertholdt, and others; on the contrary, Raschi, Aben Esra, David Kimchi (as also Jewish interpreters at the time of Jerome), and, following Bochart's example, most of the modern expositors understand it to refer to actual swarms of insects. Among the most modern expositors, however, Hengstenberg (*Christol.* Edit. 2) and Hävernick interpret it both figuratively and prophetically.

In favour of this description being understood as prophetical, the passages ch. i. 15, and ii. 1, ff., have been appealed to among others, under the idea that the misfortune of which the prophet speaks is there stated as closely impending, and therefore as still future. But the

Interpretation of the Prophecy. 131

day of Jehovah is also stated as being near, the day of the general Divine judgment; and the prophet looks upon the present plague as only the beginning of it, or as a sign that this day of decision is near at hand. The way in which the prophet speaks of the plague, just at the beginning of his discourse (ch. i. 2), really admits of no doubt that he refers to a plague that was present, and well known, without further question, to his first readers, and not to something in the future which was quite unknown to them; for, in the latter case, a more unnatural mode of statement could not well be imagined.

A similar sentence would also have to be pronounced, if the prophet had intended here to speak of hostile armies.

If this had been the case, the prophet certainly would not put it before everything that they had devastated the vines and fig-trees with lions' teeth, and had barked them, so that the branches became white (ch. i. 6, ff.; cf. *vv.* 12, 17–20); nor would he have pointed out the devastating host as being like to horses in appearance, and running as horsemen (ch. ii. 4), and as running *like* mighty men, and climbing walls *like* warriors (ch. ii. 7), and as entering into windows *like* to thieves (ch. ii. 9).

The whole imagery would be unnatural, artificial, and feeble, as applied to a hostile army, whilst, in reference to the devastations of such creatures as locusts, it would be just as distinct and striking. Only we must assume, as indeed results from the whole description, that this plague was of a particularly fearful character, not quickly passing away, nor confining itself to a small tract of the country, but pervading the whole of it for several years (ch. ii. 25, i. 4); joined also with great dearth and want of water. The prophecy must have been composed at the time of the sorest need.

The book was in former times sometimes divided into several separate, independent prophecies. This, however, is not admissible. The book, as we have it, forms without doubt, in a literary point of view, an undivided whole.

Ewald has put forward a peculiar opinion, which has been followed by E. Meier (*Der Prophet Joel*, Tübingen, 1841). They suppose that there are two different prophetical discourses in the book, the first of which, ch. i. 1– ii. 17, summoned the people to a penitential festival in the temple, whilst the other was spoken after this festival had been solemnly observed; and they regard ch. ii. 18, 19 a. as an historical parenthesis of the prophet connecting the two discourses, showing that Jehovah, in consequence of this festival, *had* again taken pity on the people, and now spoke what follows as a promise to them. This idea is very unnatural, and certainly incorrect. Without doubt, this passage forms a part of the continuous prophetical discourse, and is to be understood as a prophecy just beginning as a promise; and it is not opposed to this, that the verbs are in the imperfect with the *vau-consecutivum*, as in the prophetical discourses, this form of the verb is often elsewhere made use of as the perfect, to describe more vividly that which the prophet wished to predict. (Cf. 2 Chron. xv. 4.)

Yet, on the other hand, it is not altogether probable that Joel delivered orally the whole discourse, as we now have it, in one effusion. It is, perhaps, very probable, that during the long continuance of the visitation, the prophet repeatedly addressed the people, and that he collected in this work the essential purport of his discourses, so that the separate parts were not orally delivered in exactly the same form as that in which they are now presented to us.

§ 235.—*Date.*

The age to which Joel belonged is, however, very doubtful. The opinions of interpreters differ pretty widely as to this; varying from the middle of the tenth century down to the beginning of the sixth (B.C.). The most probable opinion, however, is, that, as a prophet, he was a contemporary of Amos, but somewhat his senior, and that he flourished like the latter in the reign of Uzziah.[1] A comparison of the two prophets favours this opinion in a two-fold point of view.

(*a*) Amos, in ch. iv. 6–9, points out to the Israelites, that Jehovah, in order to bring them back to Him, had brought on them famine, drought, and great dearth, also a destruction of the gardens and vineyards, the fig-trees and

---

[1] Thus Abarbanel, Vitringa (*Typus doctrinæ Proph.*, Appendix to *Hypotyposis Historiæ et Chronolog. Sacræ*), Eichhorn, Rosenmüller, Von Cölln (*de Joelis ætate.* Marburg, 1811), Knobel, De Wette, &c.

Date of the Prophecy. 133

olive-trees by means of locusts (palmer-worms); and for these destructive creatures the designation הַגָּזָם is made use of; the same term also occurs in Joel (ch. i. 4, ii. 25). amongst the names of the various kinds of devastating insects; a term which we do not find anywhere else. Apart, however, from this designation, the representation by Amos of the plague ravaging the land has, unmistakeably, a great similarity to Joel's description, so that it is most likely that Amos, in speaking of the plagues previously sent by God, refers to the same calamity which Joel had before his eyes. It is not opposed to this idea that Amos speaks of a plague befalling the kingdom of Israel, and Joel of one with which Judah was smitten.

In a plague of long duration, extending over several years, or again returning, it is exceedingly improbable that it should be limited to one small district. As to this, we must consider ch. ii. 20, where Joel calls the plague הַצְּפוֹנִי. This is, indeed explained in various ways, but, according to the derivation from צָפוֹן, it is most probably to be understood, in accordance with most modern interpreters, as *Septentrionale*, the *northern plague*, the *northern enemy*, as pouring itself over the land from the north. From this, therefore, it may be assumed that before Judah was visited with it, the plague had already raged in the territory of the kingdom of Israel.

(*b*) A comparison of Amos i. 6–10 with Joel iv. 4–6 points equally to a contemporary existence of the two prophets.

Joel, in the preceding verses (2, 3), threatens the nations in general with God's judgment, because they had scattered His people, the Israelites, had sold them as slaves, and had divided their land among them, and especially names the Tyrians, Sidonians, and Philistines, whom he reproaches with having plundered God's treasures, and made use of them in their own temples, and with having sold the children of Judah and Jerusalem to the Greeks (the Ionians, בְּנֵי הַיְּוָנִים), in order to remove them far from their home; wherefore they are threatened that the like shall also be done to them by the Jews. In Amos, however, besides, some other cities of the Philistines, Gaza, and Tyre as well, are specially threatened with the Divine punishment because they had carried away numerous captives (in which only Jews or Israelites can be intended), and had delivered them over to the Edomites.

Joel here naming the Greeks, and Amos the Edomites, as those to whom the Philistines had delivered over their captives, is not an essential difference, and cannot make it certain that they had a different point of time in view. The question is as to a trade in slaves, and it is natural, therefore, that those nations should have sold the captive Israelites and Jews in different quarters, just as it paid them best. In order, therefore, to show the harshness and cruelty of their conduct, the one prophet particularly names the Greeks, as a distant nation beyond seas; the other the Edomites, as a tribe allied indeed to the Israelites, but at different times showing hostility against them.

The similarity in the mode of threatening the foreign nations, and in the way in which their transgression against the people of the Covenant is described, is so great, that we may assume with the greatest probability, that the two prophets had the same historical events before their eyes. If we add to this the other coincidences (under (a)), we can, I believe, assume with the greatest probability, that Joel's prophecy falls somewhat earlier—several years, at most ten—than the prophecies of Amos, therefore in the *reign of Uzziah*, and perhaps *not quite in the last part of it*, about 800 B.C. (Cf. § 237.)

Most probably Zech. ix. also belongs to the same age, and we may conclude from v. 13, that "the sons of Javan" had kept some individuals of the people of the Covenant far from their home, which may very well refer to those who had been sold to them as slaves not long before by the Phœnicians and Philistines. Cf. *Theolog. Stud. und Krit.* 1852, p. 265, ff. I have there (p. 268) shown, that we may conclude from these passages, that not long before their composition, at the time of Uzziah, king of Judah, and Jeroboam II., king of Israel, the Philistines and Phœnicians had waged a successful war against the Israelitish people, indeed both Judah and Israel, and had sold captives from both kingdoms, particularly to the Greeks. There is nothing peculiar in the historical books of the Old Testament leaving these events unmentioned, as the latter treat of the protracted reigns of these two kings in so short and summary a way.

Date of the Prophecy. 135

The opinion here developed as to the age to which Joel belonged is not contradicted by the passage, ch. iv. 19.

In the promise as to the future great fertility of the land of Judah, it tells us in contrast to this, "Egypt shall be a desolation, and Edom shall be a desolate wilderness, for the violence against the children of Judah, because they have shed innocent blood in their land." Whether the latter part applies to the Egyptians also cannot be decided; if it did, we should only be forced to think that there were some invasions of the land of Judah, which might have taken place without the historical books mentioning anything about it. Besides, the Egyptians might be called the ancient enemies of Israel, although, just at the moment, no particular hostility had been practised by them. But with regard to the Edomites, of course we shall be compelled to assume that they must have shown hostility a short time before, although only by partial and very transient inroads into the land of Judah. That this took place at the time we suppose is shown clearly by Amos i. 11.

By far the greater number of expositors are agreed at present that the age to which Joel belonged was not *later* than that of Amos; but several entertain the incorrect view that he must be placed in a much earlier period.

Thus, Credner (*Der Prophet Joel,* Halle, 1831), Movers (*Chronik.* p. 119, f.), Hitzig, Ewald, Meier, Keil, and Davidson place him in the first period of the reign of Joash, king of Judah, before the Syrians of Damascus under Hazael had invaded Judah, whose departure Joash purchased by giving up the treasures of the temple (2 Kings xii. 18, 19; cf. 2 Chron. xxiv. 23, 24, from which latter passage it even appears as if the Syrians had captured Jerusalem itself), between 870 and 850 B.C. It is thought that if this event had previously happened, Joel would not have omitted to include the Syrians among those enemies of Israel who were to be punished, as Amos does in ch. i. 3, ff. But this idea could not be well founded unless this book were composed very soon after this inroad of the Syrians. But on our view of the date of composition, at least half a century must have elapsed since the invasion took place, during which time nothing is known to us of any further hostilities of the Syrians against the Jews. If, however, something of this sort had not happened just previously, like the attacks of the Phœnicians, Philistines, and Edomites, in the case of the Syrians there would have been the less inducement for expressly naming them, as their country did not lie quite close to that of the Jews, but was divided from it by the kingdom of Israel.

Bunsen (*Gott in der Geschichte*, i. 321. ff.) places Joel still further back, about fifteen or twenty-five years after the invasion of Judah by the Egyptian king Shishak, in the fifth year of Rehoboam, in which the temple and the royal treasury was plundered (1 Kings xiv. 25). And he thinks that Joel was induced by this event to utter the threats against Egypt in ch. iv. 19. As shown by our previous remarks, there is nothing to justify this opinion.

According to the opinion here developed as to the age to which Joel belonged, he is perhaps the earliest of the prophets, whose prophecies, written by themselves, have been handed down to us; only with regard to Zechariah, ch. ix, it may be doubtful if its composition did not take place somewhat earlier still.

§ 236.—*Joel—Literary and Poetical Characteristics.*

In a literary and *poetical* point of view Joel's prophecy is one of the most beautiful productions of Hebrew literature; in florid and vivid description it is surpassed by none. It is also important in a Prophetical and Messianic respect, although, of course, in this it is inferior to the prophecies of several other prophets.

In Joel the Messianic salvation is bound up with the existence of the then present state of the kingdom of Judah, with Jerusalem and Zion, and other nations are mentioned only as the enemies of Jehovah, and by no means as future partakers in the salvation of God's people. Also here, the idea of the Messiah is not defined as of any distinct human personality, but only in general Jehovah is specified as the author of salvation. We find here, however, the promise of the general pouring out of God's spirit (cf. Is. xxxii. 15; xliv. 3), which found its essential fulfilment in the Christian Church only, particularly in the first establishing of it, although, in the prophecy, it first related to the people of Judah. There are, however, at least hints that members of other nations should also partake of it, ch. iii. 2, 5.

3.—THE BOOK OF AMOS.

§ 237.—*Name—Date and Period of his Ministry.*

The name of the prophet, עָמוֹס, is not found in the Old Testament, except in this book (ch. i. 1, 7, 8, ff.; viii. 2), either in reference to the prophet himself, or any other person. The Fathers of the Church sometimes erroneously identify him with the father of Isaiah.

Amos was (according to ch. i. 1 ; vii. 14), a herdsman, in possession of a flock at Tekoa, a small city in the tribe of Judah, twelve Roman miles south of Jerusalem, near the wilderness of Tekoa, and named from it (2 Chron. xx. 20 ; 1 Macc. ix. 33), on the edge of the great Arabian desert. He was, as he says, ch. vii. 14, neither of a prophetical family nor prepared in any particular way, but only " a herdsman and a gatherer of sycamore fruit ;" but he willingly obeyed Jehovah's call, when His command came to him to stand forth as His prophet for Israel (the kingdom of the ten tribes); only for a short time, however, as may be concluded from ch. i. 1.

The *date* of the utterances of Amos is there specified as (*a*) the reign of Uzziah, king of Judah, and the Israelitish king Jeroboam, son of Joash, therefore the first period of Uzziah's and the latter period of Jeroboam II.'s reign (cf. ch. vii. 10, according to which, Jeroboam was then the king of Israel), and, (*b*), " two years before the earthquake."

There is nowhere any account of this earthquake in the historical books; but in a prophecy before the Captivity, of Jeremiah's age, it tells us, Zech. ch. xiv. 5, " Ye shall flee, like as ye fled from before the earthquake in the days of Uzziah king of Judah." We cannot ascertain more nearly the year in which this earthquake took place. The statement, however, in the superscription of our book limits the utterances contained in it to the one year (two years before the earthquake), and probably his public prophetical ministry had no longer duration than this. When the Divine summons came to him, Amos must have left his home and the land of Judah generally, and have sojourned in the kingdom of Israel, and probably he must subsequently have returned from thence to his home. He was, as it appears (ch. vii. 13), ministering more particularly at Bethel, in the kingdom of Israel, a chief place for the Israelitish cultus, where, perhaps, the king of Israel was peculiarly wont to perform his worship; there was also a royal residence there, where the king had a palace, in which he resided from time to time, although his actual court was then at Samaria.

It was at Bethel that Amos was particularly opposed by *Amaziah*, the high priest of the sanctuary at that place. This man accused him to the king of conspiring in the land by means of his prophecies, by predicting that the king would perish by the sword, and that the people would be carried away captives out of the land. Amaziah charged Amos to return to Judah, and there eat bread and prophesy, but not at Bethel; against which Amos referred to the Divine call which he had received (ch. vii. 10, ff.). But, as already intimated, Amos could not have continued his prophetical ministry there for more than one year, at most.

§ 238.—*Divisions of the Prophecy.*

The book, as presented to us, is divided by the form of statement into two distinctive parts.

A.—Ch. i-vi.—Simple prophetical utterances of a threatening nature.

These are, firstly, ch. i. 2-ii. 5, penal discourses against various neighbouring nations : (*a*) Damascus; the Syrians of Damascus, ch. i. 2-5; (*b*) the chief cities of the Philistines (*vv.* 6-8); (*c*) Tyrus (*vv.* 9, 10); (*d*) Edom and its chief cities (*vv.* 11, 12); (*e*) the Ammonites (*vv.* 13-15); (*f*) Moab (ii. 1-3). These foreign nations are reproached with various crimes, especially cruelty against the Israelites, and they are threatened with desolation. Then follows (*g*) an utterance against Judah, which had despised Jehovah's law, and had allowed themselves to be led away by lying idols, on which account the fire of Jehovah should be sent upon them, and the palaces of Jerusalem should be consumed (ch. ii. 4, 5).

These short discourses form only a kind of introduction, and the last one against Judah is the transition to

Nature of the Prophecies. 139

the prophecies that follow on to ch. vi. 14, all directed against Israel (only in ch. vi. 1 are the careless in Zion mentioned, as well as those who trusted in the mountain of Samaria, although just afterwards the prophet appears to have again had the Israelites alone in view). The prophet does not censure political errors, but earnestly rebukes the heavy moral and religious crimes prevailing among the people, especially among the great; the idolatry (at Bethel, Gilgal, and Beersheba, actually belonging to Judah), the cruel harshness of the rich and important men (as well as of the women also, ch. iv. 1–3) against the humble and poor; the injustice and corruption of the judges, the frivolity, revelling and unchastity. He censures also a merely outward service of Jehovah, and requires justice and righteousness (ch. v. 21, ff.). He energetically admonishes them to turn to Jehovah, and threatens them with heavy Divine punishment—with the overthrow of Samaria and the other cities of Israel, and a removal out of the land to Hermon[1] (ch. iv. 2), beyond Damascus (ch. v. 27 ; cf. vi. 7–14).

B.—Ch. vii-ix.—This part contains various visions, succeeded by their interpretation and other prophetical utterances.

(1) Ch. vii. 1–9.—Vision, in which the overthrow of Israel and Jeroboam's house is, successively, represented under the figures of grasshoppers, of fire, and of a plumb-line.

(2) Ch. vii. 10–17.—Narrative of the hostility shown by the priest Amaziah, at Bethel, against Amos, and the prophetical threatening by the prophet against him and his house, together with the menace of Israel's being carried away out of the land.

[1] Cf. *Vorl. über Amos*, on ch. iv. 3 : " השלכתנה must be, with the ancient translators, unhesitatingly pointed as Hophal, as it is in a Cod. of Rossi, since the הֽ in ההרמונה, at least according to the accents, is paragogic, and is doubtless indeed the local ה. If we do not consider the difficult word ההרמונה us the name of an entirely unknown place, it would most probably refer to Hermon. Vater also would read הַהֶרְמוֹנָה, and indeed in some Codd. of Rossi, ח stands instead of ה. It might, however, very well be imagined that Amos would have written the name of this mount with a ה. The Israelites must have passed by Hermon when they were removed to Assyria or Syria. Cf. Ps. xlii, xliii, probably the lamentation of a Jewish priest living in captivity at Hermon, at the source of the Jordan."

(3) Ch. viii. 1-3.—Vision of a basket of fruit, as an intimation that Israel was ripe for destruction, to which follows, in *vv.* 4-14, a discourse threatening punishment on those particularly who oppressed and devoured the poor and carried on a disgraceful traffic in corn; also against those who gave themselves over to idolatry; that Jehovah will bring upon them great affliction and mourning, also hunger and thirst, all according to the Word of God (through the mouth of the prophet).

(4) Ch. ix.—A new vision, in which the prophet saw the Lord standing on the altar, ordaining a destruction from which no one shall be able to escape (*vv.* 1-4). The threatening of the Divine judgment then goes still further,—that Jehovah would blot out the sinful kingdom, and that all the sinners in the people should certainly perish by the sword, and that the House of Israel should be sifted among all nations; but yet that the house of Jacob should not be entirely blotted out, and that in the sifting no grain of corn should fall to the ground (*vv.* 5-10). Then follows the further promise, that Jehovah would again reinstate the fallen tabernacle of David in its former security and splendour, and that Israel shall take possession of the remnant of Edom, and of all the nations that are called by Jehovah's name; that the land should be blessed with the richest plenty and fruitfulness, that the scattered ones of the people should again be brought back, that the overthrown cities should be built up, and that they themselves should be firmly planted in the land (*vv.* 11-15).

The book concludes with these *Messianic* prophecies; a book, the remainder of whose purport is of so *penal* and *threatening* a character, that Luther says (W. A. vi. 2438), "this prophet employs almost the whole of his book in mere censure, and in preaching the threats and terrors of the impending Divine judgment. That it appears as if he were therefore called *Amos*, that is, a *burden*, as being a heavy, rough, and burdensome preacher."

The book, as we have it, with the superscription, ch. i. 1 (which, from its exact statement of the date, doubtless proceeds from the prophet himself), cannot have been written until after the earthquake therein mentioned, and consequently, at all events, some years later than the time of Amos's prophetical ministry in Israel; whether during

Jeroboam's lifetime, or not till after his death, cannot be ascertained. We must, perhaps, consider the book as a record of his prophetical ministry in the kingdom of Israel, composed by the prophet himself at a subsequent time. The well-arranged order of the different parts of the book is in favour of this idea, and also the Messianic promise forming the conclusion to the whole of it.

As regards the *literary character* of the Book of Amos, its language is poetical, even in the narrative of the visions; it is, however, on the whole very simple, quiet, and measured. His Hebrew is in general pure.

Jerome (*Proæm. in Amos*) designates him as "imperitum sermone, sed non scientia." The former opinion, however, is too strongly expressed, looking at the nature of his writing, and can only be applied to some variations from the usual orthography (*v.* De Wette, § 234, note b; Ewald, *Die Propheten*, i. p. 84).

4.—THE BOOK OF OBADIAH.

§ 239.—*Name—Nature of the Contents—Date of the Prophecy.*

Under the name of Obadiah, we have a prophecy with the superscription, חֲזוֹן עֹבַדְיָה. There can be no doubt that here עֹבַדְיָה = the servant of Jehovah, is not, as Augusti supposes, appellative "*the prophecy of some pious man*" (this construction nowhere thus occurs, and the mode of designation would be strange and against all analogy), but that it is a proper name, as it often occurs for different persons at different times. LXX, Cod. Vat., &c., Ὀβδίας, Cod. Al. and in the Alexandrine ecclesiastical authors, Ἀβδίας (from another form, עַבְדְיָה, or עֲבַדְיָה), and so in the Latin, *Abdias*. In Luther, according to the Masoretic text, *Obadja*.

Obadiah's work is directed against the Edomites, beginning with the words, "Thus saith the Lord Jehovah concerning לֶאֱדוֹם."

This nation, which by its descent from Esau was allied with the Jews and was adjacent to them, had shown themselves to be full of malicious joy and hostile to the highest degree, when the Jewish army was vanquished by foreign enemies and carried away captive, when Jerusalem itself was captured, so that lots were cast over it, and its inhabitants had fled. For this, the prophet threatens this perfidious brother-people; he compares the house of Jacob and Joseph (Judah and Israel) to the fire and the flame, and the house of Esau to the stubble, which shall be entirely consumed by the flame; that the day of the Lord was near upon all the heathen, and then would Edom with its wise men and its mighty men be blotted out, notwithstanding the natural strength of the land, whilst the house of Jacob shall again receive its possessions, and shall find deliverance on the holy Mount Zion, and the kingdom shall be Jehovah's.

In ascertaining the date of the composition, we must fix in the first place, on the particular misfortune of the Jews which is intended, at which the Edomites showed such malicious joy. It has been pretty generally considered to have been the destruction of Jerusalem by Nebuchadnezzar; and this is certainly correct. The composition, therefore, cannot have taken place until after this event.

Jahn thinks it was the capture of the city at the time of Jehoiachin, 599 B.C., in which the king himself with a considerable number of Jews was carried away captive. As the Chaldeans are not expressly named, but only generally, נָכְרִים זָרִים, v. 11, as the enemies who had vanquished the Jewish army and captured Jerusalem, we might just as well suppose that they were the Egyptians who slew Josiah at Megiddo, 611 B.C. and, three months after, came to Jerusalem, and took away Jehoahaz to Egypt. But the whole description of the destruction of Jerusalem and the Jews (vv. 11–14, 16; cf. vv. 17, 20, f.), leaves but little doubt that the prophet refers to the above-named great catastrophe.

It is quite a mistake, when Hävernick, Caspari (*Der Prophet Obadja*, 1842), and Hengstenberg (*Die Geschichte Bileams*, p. 253, f. Notes), although acknowledging the reference assumed by us, understand the description as prophetic, and fix the composition of it in the age of Uzziah, on account of its position in the Canon. Hitzig is equally wrong in postponing the date of the composition until after Alexander, and as taking place in Egypt. There is in the contents no adequate cause whatever for such an opinion, and it is untenable, because the compilation of the twelve minor prophets, and that of the Nebiim generally was arranged, without doubt, long before Alexander's time.

A special question arises as to the relation of this prophecy to Jer. xlix. 7–22. The two agree occasionally surprisingly, even verbally, so that we cannot help assuming that one prophet must have borrowed of the other.[1] It is very doubtful which of the two is the more original. (Cf. Graf's *Jeremia*, p. 559.) If our previous remarks as to the date of Obadiah be correct, we cannot doubt that Jeremiah is the more original, as his prophecy, in all probability, took place before the destruction of Jerusalem, perhaps in the reign of Jehoiakim. It is in favour of this view, that there is no intimation in Jeremiah of hostilities, or of a hostile disposition on the part of the Edomites, against Israel and Judah.

At all events, Obadiah's work, chronologically considered, has an improper place in the Canon. This is caused in all probability, as Schnurrer correctly remarks (*Dissertat. philol. in Obadiam.* Tübing. 1787; in his *Dissertatt. philol. crit.* Gotha et Amst. 1790, p. 383, ff.), by the conclusion of the Book of Amos, ch. ix. 12. There Obadiah's work appears as a further description of that which Amos only cursorily hinted at, and thus the originator of the compilation of the lesser prophets has allowed it to follow Amos.

Nothing is known to us about this prophet, beyond that which we gather from his work, according to which he was a Jew at the time of the Babylonian Captivity, and had lived to see the overthrow of his people and their chief city, and, from *v*. 20, was perhaps himself among the captives.

[1] Ewald's opinion is but little probable, that both passages were based on an older prophecy, which both Jeremiah and Obadiah had made use of. [G. F. Jäger shows in his "Programme" ("On the Age of Obadiah," Tübingen, 1837), that Obadiah did not borrow of Jeremiah, but is wrong in making our present Book of Obadiah precede Jeremiah; the position of the former book in the Canon is, in the opinion of Augusti, Ewald, Graf, and others, sufficiently explained.]

5.—THE BOOK OF MICAH.

§ 240.—*Name—Birthplace—Date—Purport of the Prophecies.*

The *name*, מִיכָה, occurs in the Old Testament for several persons, sometimes with this form and sometimes the longer ones מִיכָיְהוּ, מִיכָיָה.

The latter forms must be considered as the more original, etymologically signifying "*who is like Jehovah?*" (cf. Michael), and מִיכָה only as proceeding from the former by contraction. The prophet is named by the shorter form both in the title and superscription of his book, ch. i. 1; and also Jer. xxvi. 18, in the Keri; the Chetib, on the contrary, has מִיכָיָה in this passage. LXX, Μιχαίας; Vulgate, *Michæas;* and Luther, *Micha.*

Micah is designated both in his book and also in Jer. xxvi. 18, as the *Morasthite*, הַמֹּרַשְׁתִּי; doubtless from the place of his birth, Moreshet, about which Jerome (*Prolog. in Mich.*), says, calling it Morasthi, that it was still existing in his time as a not very considerable village in the neighbourhood of Eleutheropolis (westward from Jerusalem). Most probably this place is intended in ch. i. 14, by the name מוֹרֶשֶׁת גַּת, so called perhaps, because it formed a part of the territory of Gath.

Luther, &c., are incorrect in deriving the designation Morasthite from Maresa, מָרֵשָׁה, a town in the plain of the tribe of Judah, the name of which often occurs, and is mentioned by Micah (ch. i. 15).

The prophet is distinguished by his designation as a Morasthite, from another older prophet Micah (Micaiah), son of Imlah, a contemporary of Elijah, at the time of Jehoshaphat, king of Judah, and Ahab of Israel, 1 Kings xxii. 8, ff. The ecclesiastical authors look upon both as the same men, and the author of the Books of Kings appears to have done the same, as, in *v.* 28, he puts into the mouth of the son of Imlah, the very words which form the beginning of our Book (ch. i. 2), שִׁמְעוּ עַמִּים כֻּלָּם. This, however, certainly only arises from the above author, who

Date and Contents.

belonged to the time of the Captivity, mistaking the one for the other.

The *age* to which this prophet belonged is stated in the superscription (ch. i. 1) as the reigns of Jotham, Ahaz, and Hezekiah, kings of Judah, according to which he was a contemporary of Isaiah, and perhaps somewhat later than Joel, Amos, and Hosea; about the time of the breaking up of the kingdom of Ephraim. There is another ancient testimony, in Jer. xxvi. 18, as to the age to which Micah belonged, and as to a prophecy contained in his book actually being uttered in Hezekiah's reign.

Jeremiah here relates, that the accusations against him were referred by the elders of the people to the former conduct of Micah the Morasthite, as one who had likewise prophesied in Hezekiah's time the complete destruction of Jerusalem and the Temple (and the passage, Micah iii. 12, is literally quoted) without being put to death by the king and the people, as was threatened to Jeremiah. At the same time they point out how Micah had induced Jehovah by his piety and his prayers, not to bring on the predicted misfortune (cf. Micah vii. 7, ff.).

The subject of this book is specified in the superscription as prophecies concerning Samaria and Jerusalem. The first section, ch. i. 1–16, is expressly against the two kingdoms or their chief towns, and chiefly against Samaria, which is threatened with complete devastation, which, however, would reach Judah and even Jerusalem. In what follows, however, no further reference to Samaria is made distinctly prominent. Sometimes the utterances may be referred to both kingdoms in common, as ch. ii, iii. 1–8; but in other places Judah, and particularly Jerusalem, expressly stand forth as the objects of the prediction,—as ch. iii. 9, ff.; iv. 9, ff.; and vi. 9, ff.;—and it is probable that the prophet in his threatening discourses everywhere, from chapter ii. onwards, speaks of this latter kingdom only, to which he belonged by birth, and where he doubtless resided; even where he mentions Jacob and Israel in general, as ch. iii. 1, 8, 9. This is most easily explained by the supposition that the first utterance took place *before* the breaking up of the kingdom of Israel, and the following ones *after* this catastrophe, when the kingdom of Judah was alone remaining, and the members of this kingdom would therefore be meant by the general designations of Jacob and Israel. These prophecies, then, would all fall in the reign of Hezekiah, as is stated in Jer. *ut supra;* and the first section also belongs to this reign, only to the earlier period of it. According to this the statement of the superscription appears to be inexact; but it probably refers to the whole period of Micah's prophetical activity generally, and not exclusively to the time to which the utterances of the book belong.

As regards the separate parts of the book, we cannot but observe that, apart from the first section chiefly relating to Samaria, it is not a single continuous prophetical utterance with various sections; but that there are various utterances which were not perhaps originally all issued at the same time. But it cannot always be ascertained with certainty where they severally begin and end; and still less can we state anything at all exact as to their respective dates. It is perhaps probable, that the prophet himself subsequently collected some of the utterances of his prophetical ministry, which he had previously written out separately, and combined them together into the form in which we now have them, perhaps without attending to the retention of their chronological order.

As regards the *tendency* of Micah's prophetical ministry, as it strikes us in his book, his utterances do not take notice of the *political* transgressions and errors of the leaders of the commonwealth,—as if often the case with Jeremiah and Isaiah particularly,—but only, like Amos, of the religious and especially the moral condition both of the people and princes.

The prophet censures the idolatry in the land (ch. i. 5, 7; vi. 16); he specially rebukes the princes and important men for their violent and rapacious conduct towards others, particularly against women and children, wherewith they flay and devour the people; for their bloodshed which they load themselves with, and for their corruption as judges. He rebukes the false prophets, who, for love of gold, prophesy in favour of those who pay them, and nevertheless think that they may rely on Jehovah; he rebukes the people generally for their fickleness, for their lying, deceitful conduct in their daily business (false measures and weights), for their want of trust in their nearest friends

Purport of the Prophecies. 147

and relations, and for the discord existing even among members of the same family (ch. vii. 6); he laments that there are scarcely any pious and just men in the land (ch. vii. 1, f.). The prophet, therefore, threatens the people and the princes with the Divine judgments, and with devastation of the land (ch. i. 9, ff.; ii. 3, ff.; vii. 13), particularly with the destruction of Jerusalem and the Temple (ch. iii. 12; vi. 13, ff.), with the expulsion and captivity of the inhabitants (ch. ii. 10), also specially with a removal to Babylon (ch. iv. 10); that they will cry in vain to Jehovah, for He will not hear (ch. iii. 4). He admonishes them to become better, and brings to their recollection, how gracious Jehovah had ever been to His people, and that they were not to make oblations to Him of various kinds, but rather to do justly, to love mercy, and walk humbly with their God (ch. vi. 1–8). Then, however, the prophet predicts the return of the Divine mercy and blessing, with a pardon for their offences; from the exile whither Jehovah had caused them to wander, will He again send them deliverance. He will again gather the remnant of Israel into a numerous flock, under a new ruler, who shall proceed from Bethlehem from the ancient family (as David), and shall tend Jehovah's people with power, and cause them to dwell safe from all attacks of their enemies. Then shall the mount of the Temple be splendidly glorious, and numerous foreign nations shall turn to Zion, in order to seek there for Divine instruction, acknowledging Jehovah as their Lord and Arbitrator, and that henceforth there shall be no more war among them (ch. ii. 12, 13; iv. 1–8; v. 1–8; cf. vii. 7–20).

Micah's *style of writing* is throughout poetical; it is for the most part similar to that of Isaiah, and, in some respects, to that of Hosea; it is sometimes quite as difficult and abrupt as the latter. He loves eccentricities and plays upon words, with which the section, ch. i. 10–15, is too much loaded.

6.—THE BOOK OF NAHUM.

§ 241.—*Name—Birthplace—Date and Contents of Prophecy.*

The *name* נחום = *consolation* (in Greek Ναούμ; Vulg. and with us, Nahum and Naum), occurs both on a Phœnician and Greek inscription (נחם, Νάουμος, the latter for a man of Aradus), but is not found in the Old Testament, except in our book.

Nahum is designated in the superscription as the Elkoshite, which, doubtless, is to be understood as a *nomen gentile*, from Elkosh, the place of his birth. It is so understood by Eusebius in the *Chronicon*, and Jerome (*in Prœm. Nahum*), the latter of whom points out Helkesaei, a small, and, at that time, almost ruined village in Galilee, which appears to have been shown him as the birthplace of Nahum.

Up to the beginning of the last century it was usual to look upon the Galilean Helkesaei as the prophet's birthplace. After this time, however, a place in Assyria has been sometimes decided upon for it—a place called Alkosch, or Elkosch, on the eastern bank of the Tigris, not far from the city of Mosul and the ancient Nineveh, where the pretended grave of Nahum is shown; among others who have thought this, are J. D. Michaelis, Eichhorn, Ewald, &c.; *v.* also Ritter, "Geography," ix. 742, ff. It is thought, therefore, that Nahum was born here of Israelitish ancestors, who were in exile in Assyria. This opinion, however, has very little in its favour. Even if the prophet were born there, it would not necessarily result that he should have died there. According to Layard, Nahum's pretended grave is not even very ancient, and is, without doubt, of Christian origin. Probably at a tolerably late time people were induced by the perhaps accidental similarity of the name of the Assyrian place to Nahum's designation as the Elkoshite, to derive this designation from the above place, and to look upon some monument which they found there as the tomb of this prophet, whose work is directed against Nineveh.

Contents and Date of the Prophecy. 149

The purport of Nahum's prophecy corresponds with the superscription, "The burden of Nineveh. The book of the vision of Nahum the Elkoshite."

It does not matter whether the book is divided into two discourses, the second beginning with ch. iii. 1; or whether it is considered as only one; at any rate, the whole of it relates to the same circumstances, and was written at the same time. It is all directed against Nineveh, the chief city of the Assyrian kingdom, and its king; both being threatened with complete destruction because of their hostile proceedings against Jehovah, His people, and their chief city.

The *date of composition* is variously stated. As to this, I remark as follows:

(a) There can be no doubt that Nineveh still existed as the chief city of the Assyrian kingdom. The Assyrian monarchy was overthrown and Nineveh taken by storm by the Medes under Cyaraxes in alliance with the Chaldeans under Nabopolassar, Nebuchadnezzar's father, a little before the year 600 B.C. This work must, therefore, have been composed before this time.

(b) It may, besides, be assumed with probability that the composition took place some time after the defeat and retreat of Sennacherib's army from Jerusalem, but still before the death of this king, who was murdered by his two sons in a temple at Nineveh.

Judah and Jerusalem must unmistakeably have suffered much from Nineveh and the Assyrian king not long before, as was particularly the case after the breaking up of the kingdom of Israel at the time of Hezekiah, and especially in the fourteenth year of his reign, at the time of Sennacherib. It may be supposed with the greatest probability that the prophet meant this prince and his expedition against Jerusalem, when he says (ch. i. 11): "There is one come out of thee (Nineveh), that imagineth evil against the Lord, a wicked counsellor." This opinion is generally entertained, even by Ewald. Ewald is, however, wrong in thinking that this prince is here spoken of as if he had been dead a long time, and the circumstances were then quite different. The prophet certainly has the same prince in view in ch. i. 14, in the threat that Jehovah would blot out his race, that He would cut off out of his idol-house his carved and molten images, and that He would make his grave for that he was vile.[1]

(c) The passage (ch. iii. 8) also agrees with this, according to which the city of No-Amon (Thebes) in Egypt must, not long before, have been conquered by a hostile nation, and the inhabitants have been carried into captivity.

We have no exact historical accounts as to this event; but it is not improbable that it agrees with Isaiah xx, and took place through the Assyrians before the fourteenth year of Hezekiah; and thus the reference to this event can be easily understood if our opinion be followed as to the age to which Nahum belonged, but not if Nahum flourished considerably later, as, *e.g.*, Ewald and Hitzig suppose.

I must also notice that Ewald thinks that the prophet must have been in the neighbourhood of Nineveh when he composed this threatening discourse. But this in no way follows from the mode of statement in the book; it is much more probable, particularly from ch. i. 12, ff., that he was living at Jerusalem, or at least near it.

In a literary point of view, Nahum is very eminent; his diction is original, very poetical and vivid, without any redundance.

This work presents no Messianic matter except in a general sense, as in the threatening of the destruction of the opponents of the people of God, in the prediction that Jehovah would henceforth no more humble Jerusalem, and that He would no more lay waste Judah; but that He would give them cause for feasts of joy, and that He would again set up the greatness of Jacob (Judah) and Israel (ch. ii. 1, ff.).

---

[1] Cf. *Vorles. über Nahum*, on this passage: קָלוֹת is perhaps best to be understood "thou art cursed." The *Kal*, indeed, does not otherwise occur with this signification, the *Piel*, however, does in the active meaning, *to revile, to curse*, and thence the noun קְלָלָה.

7.—THE BOOK OF HABAKKUK.

§ 242.—*Name—Division of the Book—Date and Nature of the Prophecy.*

The *name* of this prophet, which only occurs in the Old Testament, as applied to him, and, in his book only in the superscriptions, ch. i. 1, and ch. iii. 1, runs in the Hebrew חֲבַקּוּק = *embracing, clasping round;* in the Greek, the LXX, and in the Greek ecclesiastical writers, 'Αμβακούμ, the first syllable of which has, perhaps, proceeded from חֲבַקְקוּ ; the transformation, however, of the ק in the last syllable into μ is without analogy, and it must remain undecided whether it was done by the Greek translator himself, or whether it arose through some *very ancient* corruption. In Latin and German, *Habacuc, Habakuk.*

In the superscription, ch. i. 1 ; iii. 1, Habakkuk is merely designated as הַנָּבִיא, but nothing else is stated about him, not even the age to which he belonged; for ascertaining this we are confined to his book only.

In the Greek additions to the Book of Daniel, in the account of the Dragon at Babylon (*v.* 33, ff.), Habakkuk is mentioned as the man who was brought from Judæa to Babylon by an angel of the Lord, in order to feed Daniel in the den of lions; according to that he would have lived at the time of the Babylonian exile, or after it, at the time of Cyrus. As, however, the whole of this narrative has altogether the character of a fabulous composition, not the least attention should be paid to it in fixing the time of the prophet, and just as little also both to the statement of Pseudo-Epiphan. (*De Vitis Prophetarum*) and other ecclesiastical authors, and also to that of the Rabbis, none of whom agree very much with one another; *v.* De Wette, § 242, note *a,* and Delitzsch (*De Habac. Prophet., Vita et Ætate,* Leipzig, 1842).

The book itself is divided into two parts, (1) ch. i. 2, with the superscription, "The burden which Habakkuk the prophet did see;" (2) ch. iii, with the superscription, "A Prayer of Habakkuk the prophet," עַל שִׁגְיֹנוֹת.

Both parts refer essentially to the same circumstances,

treated of, however, in different ways, viz., to the judgment which Jehovah either threatens or executes on His people by means of a foreign nation, namely, the Chaldeans, who are mentioned by name (ch. i. 6). A portion of the *first part* of the prophecy is framed in the shape of a dialogue between Jehovah and the prophet.

The prophet is deeply grieved at the internal corruption of his people, the deeds of violence in the land, the injustice, the oppression of the righteous by the wicked, and the relaxation of the law (to this without doubt refers ch. i. 2–4; query whether also ch. i. 13?). To these lamentations of the prophet, Jehovah answers by an intimation of the punishment which He will prepare, through the Chaldeans, who are accurately depicted as a fearful nation, extending their conquering march over the whole earth with great swiftness and success (ch. i. 5–11). The prophet acknowledges therein the righteous judgment of Jehovah, who is too pure to behold iniquity, but relies on the living, never-dying[1] God, that He will not allow the destroyer to have his will without cessation (ch. i. 12–17). In ch. ii. it is then predicted more exactly, and is stated as certain to ensue in due time, that this haughty, destructive, insatiable people shall also experience that which they dealt out to other nations, that they should become an object of contempt and derision, and that their idols should be unable to help them; also that this judgment should cause that the earth should be filled with the knowledge of the glory of Jehovah (*v.* 14); but "the just (among God's people) shall live by faith" (*v.* 4).

Opinions are very various as to the *date of the composition* of this prophecy, and also as to the age generally to which Habakkuk belonged. This much follows clearly from the contents, (*a*) that the Chaldeans had already extended their march of conquest and destruction to the west, and (*b*), on the other hand, that this march had only very shortly begun, and that they had not yet arrived at Judah and Jerusalem, so that they were as yet little known there. This clearly results from the way in which they are spoken

---

· Cf. *Vorles. über Habak.* on ch. i. 12: "Ewald correctly reads תָּמוּת instead of נָמוּת; the latter has come into the text by Tikkun Sopherim (cf. § 359). Cf. *Theol. Stud. und Krit.* 1858, p. 352."

The Prophet's Prayer or Song. 153

of in ch. i. 6, ff. We shall, therefore, fix upon the reign of Jehoiakim as the most probable.

We think it decidedly erroneous to fix, with some, the time after the destruction of Jerusalem by the Chaldeans; it is likewise inadmissible when others have desired to put it forward into the Assyrian age.

Chapter iii. shows, in its whole character and tone, as well as by its separate superscription, that it is a distinct poem from ch. i. and ii; Bertholdt and Justi (*Habakuk*, 1821) erroneously deny this. It is a psalm-like song, which might have found a place in our collection of Psalms. That it was made use of for public musical delivery is shown both by the superscription (cf. Ps. vii. 1) and by the postscript, as also by the expression *selah* occurring three times (vv. 3, 9, 13).

The prophet here depicts in a sublime manner that which he had learned in the spirit by Divine revelation—how Jehovah would appear for the assistance of His people and of His anointed, and to pronounce judgment on the adversaries oppressing His people (doubtless the Chaldeans); he beseeches that Jehovah, in the course of years, would execute this judgment, and in His wrath against His people for their misdeeds, would yet turn in mercy to them. Fear and hope alternate in the prophet's mind; joyful confidence, however, retains the mastery.

This chapter belongs, in general, to the same age as the first part, but is perhaps a little later; at a time when the Chaldeans had come closer, and had to some extent oppressed and attacked Judah itself.

Habakkuk's book is confessedly one of the most beautiful remains of Hebrew literature, notwithstanding the somewhat late age of its composition. He is excelled in sublimity of description by none of the Old-Testament authors, either poetical or prophetical; the song, ch. iii, is peculiarly beautiful and sublime. He is also distinguished by purity of *language*.

8.—THE BOOK OF ZEPHANIAH.

§ 243.—*Name—Descent—Nature of his Prophecy—Date.*

Name, Hebr. צְפַנְיָה = *Jehovah covers or protects* (a name often occurring in the Old Testament); LXX, Σοφονίας: Vulg. *Sophonia* (from the form צָפְנְיָה, as particip.); Luther, *Zephanja*.

Zephaniah's descent is stated in the superscription, ch. i. 1, from the fourth generation, *i.e.*, from his great-great-grandfather Hizkiah. Many persons have thought that it was Hezekiah,[1] king of Judah, and it is not improbable. If this were so, it might however be expected he would be expressly styled "the king of Judah;" but the very circumstance that the family of the prophet is traced so far back makes it probable, both that his family was no unimportant one, and also that the man as far as whom it is carried back was a peculiarly well known and eminent person. According to the relations of time, such a connection between this prophet and the king Hezekiah is by no means impossible.

We have only a short work by him, which consists of one continuous utterance, with various pauses in it, which however was certainly not written at different times.

The prophet is deeply moved at the idolatry which was practised in Jerusalem and Judah together with the external worship of Jehovah, and predicts a general Divine judgment, which was close impending, and would, in a dreadful way, extirpate every one (ch. i); he admonishes his people to gather themselves together, ere the fire of Jehovah's wrath should come upon them, which should be poured out on the nations, among whom he names the Philistines, the Moabites, the Ammonites, the Æthiopians, and especially the Assyrians with their chief town Nineveh (ch. ii). His threatening then turns again against Jerusalem, which is profaned by the injustice of its princes and judges, and the practices of its prophets and priests; Jehovah had

---

[1] Thus Aben Esra, and also Eichhorn, Hitzig, Fr. Ad Strauss (*Vaticinia Zeph. comment. illustr.* Berlin, 1843), Hävernick, Keil, &c.

Nature and Date of the Prophecy. 155

in vain admonished them to repent; but that now the day of judgment was near when Jehovah would assemble the nations, in order to pour out His fury on the wicked among His people (ch. iii. 1-8).[1] That He will then awaken these nations, that they shall call upon His name, and shall serve Him with one consent; and that, after the extirpation of the wicked and stubborn, there shall be left remaining in Judah an humble and afflicted people, who shall live in righteousness and trust in Jehovah; then also will Jehovah make Jerusalem glorious, will annihilate her oppressors, bringing back all the scattered ones of His people, and that henceforth they shall see evil no more (ch. iii. 9-20).

The *age* to which Zephaniah belonged is stated in the superscription to be the reign of Josiah, king of Judah (642-611 B.C.); and this also agrees throughout with the purport of the prophecy and the circumstances presupposed in it.

It follows from the threatening against Assyria and Nineveh (ch. ii. 13-15), that this oracle must have been composed before the destruction of this city and the overthrow of the Assyrian monarch by the Medes and Babylonians, therefore by no means later than Josiah's reign. We also find a similar state of things as to the Jewish people, such as different kinds of idolatry, false prophets, and the like, as we notice in Jeremiah's prophecies, likewise uttered during this reign.

It may be assumed with probability that the composition took place before the discovery of the Book of the Law in the eighteenth year of Josiah—there is, at least, no intimation whatever of any such reform as to idolatry, as Josiah then instituted in the whole land—unless the composition took place a very considerable time after that event, which, on account of the prophecy against Nineveh (ch. ii. 13-15) is not very probable.

Certain passages are certainly *not* in opposition to the above opinion, although they have sometimes been considered so.

(*a*) In ch. i. 8, the king's sons are named together with the princes, as partakers in foreign heathen customs. It

[1] In ch. iii. 8, the suff. in עֲלֵיהֶם does not relate to the nations, as Ewald, Hitzig, Strauss, &c., would have it, but to the wicked Jews.

has been thought that this could not have been the case before the eighteenth year of Josiah, as the latter was only eight years old at his coming to the throne. But it is not necessary to refer this expression to the king's *sons* only; as it might be intended to refer to his brothers and other descendants of the house of David.

(*b*) It has been thought that it might be inferred from the words "the remnant of Baal," in ch. i. 4, that Josiah's reformation in this respect must already have begun. But even if this were correct, the composition might still have taken place before the eighteenth year of Josiah, as this prince, according to 2 Chron. xxxiv. 3, began to purge Judah and Jerusalem from idolatry, from the twelfth year of his reign onwards. Thus the composition is fixed by Jahn, v. Cölln (*Spicileg. Observat. Exeget. Crit. in Zeph.* Breslau, 1818), Hitzig, and Keil, between the twelfth and eighteenth year of Josiah. This may be correct, although the above passage does not render this idea necessary, as the words may be simply understood, with Ewald and others, as "the Baal-worship up to the last remnant."

(*c*) Still less is it to be inferred from ch. iii. 4, "her priests have polluted the sanctuary, they have done violence to the law," that this must have been written after the eighteenth year of Josiah, as previously to this Jehovah's law could not have been quite an unknown thing, and its infringement by wicked priests might very well have been spoken of before this time (cf. Jer. ii. 8; viii. 8), which prophecies likewise occurred before the discovery of the Book of the Law. (Cf. also p. 334, 1st vol.)

It is also most probable that the composition took place at the time when the Scythians made their devastating march into Asia, and extended it to Palestine.

It may be inferred from the prophecy that the prophet, at least at the time of its composition, must have been dwelling in Judah and at Jerusalem. Nothing further is known as to his personal circumstances.

This work is worthy of attention in a *prophetical* point of view, particularly on account of the prediction of the conversion of heathen nations, even those who carried out the judgments on Israel, to the worship of Jehovah, and even before the conversion of Israel. Zephaniah has no promise as to the person of the Messiah.

We must mention, that there was extant in the ancient Christian Church an apocryphal work in Zephaniah's name (ἀνάληψις, or προφητεία τοῦ Σοφονίου προφήτου), out of which Clemens Alex. (*Strom.* v. p. 585), and Pseudo-Epiphan. (*De Vitis Prophetarum*), quote passages. In the *Synopsis Scripturæ Sacræ*, and in Nicephorus, *Stichometria*, No. 9, it is added among the Apocryphal Books of the Old Testament, and its extent is stated as 600 verses.

9.—THE BOOK OF HAGGAI.

§ 244.—*Name, &c.*

Name, חַגַּי = *festivus*; LXX, Ἀγγαῖος; Vulg. *Aggæus*; in German, *Haggäi*; the name occurs only in reference to this prophet, it is, however, really equivalent to חַגִּי, Gen. xlvi. 16; Num. xxvi. 15.

We find Haggai named, in addition to the repeated mentions of him in his book, in Ezra v. 1, vi. 14. He was a contemporary of Zerubbabel, with whom perhaps he may have been brought out of exile to Jerusalem, where he subsequently resided, and, together with Zechariah, endeavoured by his prophesyings to urge on the renewed undertaking of the rebuilding of the temple, which had indeed been begun at the time of Cyrus, but was soon put a stop to. From Hagg. ii. 3, Ewald conjectures, and it is, of course, not improbable, Hävernick and Keil being also of the same opinion, that Haggai was among those who had beheld the first temple. According to this, he must have been of a very great age at the erection of the new one, and at the time of his prophetical ministry, as almost seventy years must have elapsed since the burning down of the ancient temple.

Jerome (*Commentar. ad Agg.* i. 13) mentions that some persons entertained the opinion that Haggai, John the Baptist, and Malachi, were really angels, and possessed bodies in appearance only. In Haggai's case this rests on the statement in his book, ch. i. 13, " then spake Haggai מַלְאַךְ יְהוָה ;" added to which, that his father's name is never mentioned in connection with his own, from which it may be concluded that the latter was not a person of well-

158   *Origin of the several Books—Haggai.*

known importance. Cyril Alex. regards the above view as absurd.

The Book of Haggai, which was, without doubt, both composed and issued in its present shape by the prophet whose name it bears, contains four short prophetical utterances, made in the first place to Zerubbabel and Joshua, and exactly dated according to year, month, and day; they all took place in the second year of Darius Hystaspis, in the sixth, seventh, and the two last in the ninth month (on the same day); the first also has an historical addition as to the effect of the utterance. They all relate to the rebuilding of the temple.

The prophet admonishes his fellow countrymen, who themselves dwelt in ceiled houses, that they should not allow the house of God to lie waste; and that for this cause Jehovah would punish them with the failure of their crops, and with unfruitfulness in the land, both for man and beast (ch. i. 1–11). The result of this prophetical warning was, that after three weeks the building of the temple, which had ceased since the time of Cyrus, was again formally begun, as is related ch. i. 12–15. Soon after, in the following month, the prophet is induced to appease his countrymen, those particularly who had seen the former temple in all its glory, on account of the new temple being so very inferior to the old in extent; he admonishes them to continue actively at work, and promises that in a short time the glory of the new house shall be greater than that of the old, that Jehovah will cause the riches of all nations to flow into it, and that He will bring peace and salvation upon that place (ch. ii. 1–9).[1] Of the two last utterances, both of which fall upon the same day, the former particularly sets forth, that the curse still continually remains on the people on account of their uncleanness, but that Jehovah will from that day bless them with richer fruitfulness (ch. ii. 10–19); the second (*vv.* 20–23), that Jehovah will bring about a universal revolution and

---

[1] In *v.* 7, Luther has translated חֶמְדַּת כָּל־הַגּוֹיִם, "*aller Heiden Trost*" (A. V., "the desire of all nations"); also Jerome, "desideratus cunctis gentibus." It is, however, intended to mean the treasures of the nations, which they shall bring into the temple (cf. 1 Sam. ix. 20), and is perhaps to be read חֶמְדֹת, since the predicate בָּאוּ stands in the plural.

Zechariah—Name—Divisions of the Book. 159

will overthrow both thrones and kingdoms; but that He will take Zerubbabel, whom He has chosen, under His especial protection.

Zerubbabel, as a scion of the house of David, may be here looked upon as a type of Christ; there being no distinct promise in Haggai as to the future appearance of any other personal Saviour; but the promise as to the future glory of God's new house is Messianic in a wider sense (ch. ii. 6-9); so also is the prediction as to the future shaking of heaven and earth and all the kingdoms of the world (ch. ii. 21, f.).

10.—THE BOOK OF ZECHARIAH.

§ 245.—*Name—Division of the Book—The first Division.*

This book consists of two divisions—(A.) ch. i–viii; (B.) ch. ix–xiv.—each of which contains several separate utterances. It is, however, a matter of dispute whether the utterances in the second division belong to the same author as the first, or to one or several other prophets. There are superscriptions in the first part (ch. i. 1, 7; vii. 1) which mention Zechariah as the prophet to whom the word of the Lord came, and name the time as the reign of the king Darjavesch (Darius Hystaspis) in his second and fourth year. There is no question whatever that the whole of the utterances in the first part belong to the above prophet.

The name in Hebrew, זְכַרְיָה, frequently occurs in the Old Testament for different persons; LXX and Vulg., Ζαχαρίας, *Zacharias*; Luther, *Sacharja*.

This prophet was, according to the above statement, a contemporary of Zerubbabel and the high priest Joshua, and also of the prophet Haggai, with all of whom he is named in Ezra v. 1; vi. 14; yet he is there designated as the son of *Iddo*, but in our book, on the contrary, he is called בֶּן־בֶּרֶכְיָה (בֶּרֶכְיָהוּ) בֶּן־עִדּוֹ.

Ancient interpreters, as Jerome and Cyril, take this to be *filium Berechjæ, filium Iddonis*, and then endeavour to explain in what sense the prophet could be styled at the same time the son both of Berechiah and Iddo. But, as it runs in the passage, it can only mean the son of Berechiah, who was the son of Iddo, so that he is really styled the grandson of the latter, whilst in the Book of Ezra he is called his son. The latter may, perhaps, be explained by the assumption that Berechiah, the father, had died very early, or had been much less known than the grandfather Iddo. It might thus happen that Zechariah might often be looked upon and styled as the son of his actual grandfather Iddo, with the omission of his real father; yet the matter was, perhaps, differently circumstanced (v. as to which, § 249).

I must here mention that a certain Iddo is named in Neh. xii. 4, as among the chief priests who returned with Zerubbabel and Joshua out of exile, and also in v. 16 a certain Zechariah is named as his immediate successor. It is not improbable that these two are the very Zechariah and Iddo of whom we are speaking, whether the latter were the father or grandfather of the former. It would result from this that Zechariah belonged to the priestly race, and that he officiated as priest, or as one of the principal priests, under the high priest Joiakim (ib. v. 12), the son and successor of Joshua. It agrees well with this that in ch. ii. 4, he speaks of himself as a young man (נַעַר); therefore, at the time of this utterance, in the second year of Darius Hystaspis, and at the time of the high priest Joshua, he must have been still tolerably young.

There is, therefore, no question but that the prophecies in the *first* part of the book (ch. i–viii.) belong to this Zechariah. They were delivered, according to the statement (ch. i. 1, 7; vii. 1), at the time of the re-commenced building of the temple, before the completion of the building, in the second year of Darius Hystaspis.

The prophet here exhorts his fellow countrymen to turn earnestly to Jehovah, their God, to whom their fathers were so often disobedient, and to apply themselves with zeal to righteousness and piety; and that then Jehovah would bless them, and increase them numerously; and that their days of penitence and fasting, which they had been wont to observe since the exile, would then be turned into days of joy and feasting.

These utterances in reference to his people have a general character of promise and consolation. The threatenings are directed only against the enemies of the people of the Covenant, whom they had for so long time oppressed. Like Haggai, he praises by name Zerubbabel and Joshua, the builders-up of the temple, and promises to them Divine blessings. He puts upon Joshua two crowns as symbols of the priestly and royal power, both of which shall one day be united in the *branch* (צֶמַח, following Jeremiah) who shall come and reign.

The object of almost all these prophecies is clothed in symbolical imagery, which the prophet sees in visions. These images, however, often have some obscurity about them, and do not indicate their purpose distinctly. The whole purport of the prophecy is too general in its conception, and is not unfrequently wanting in force and vivacity.

§ 246.—*The second Division of the Book—Opinions as to its Author.*

Although the composition of the *first* part of the book is undisputedly ascribed to Zechariah, a prophet after the Captivity, it has been a subject of question in modern times how the matter stands with regard to the second part (ch. ix–xiv); whether the prophecies contained in it belong to the above-named prophet, or to one or several other prophets of an earlier time.

The first cause for doubt was given by the passage (Matt. xxvii. 9, 10), inasmuch as in this a prophetical utterance is quoted under the name of Jeremiah, which can be nowhere found in the writings of this prophet, while it bears considerable resemblance to Zech. xi. 12, 13, so that it may be assumed with great probability that the Evangelist had this passage in view. This caused Mede (d. 1638) to ascribe ch. ix–xi. of Zechariah to Jeremiah, and in this idea Whiston (1722) and others of his countrymen have followed him, as also Döderlein (1787), who extended it to the whole of the last six chapters. Subsequently, to establish the view that these chapters do not belong to the same prophet as the eight first, less reliance has been placed on the quotation in the New Testament than on internal evidence. In the more exact investigation and proof of this point, B. G. Flügge (Preacher in Hamburg, d. 1792) took the lead in a work appearing anonymously (*Die Weissagungen welche den Schriften des Proph. Zach.*

beigebogen sind, Hamburg, 1788). Most of the other critical divines of the German Protestant Church have declared themselves in favour of the same opinion: as, among others. G. L. Bauer, Augusti, Bertholdt, Eichhorn (4th ed.), Rosenmüller (*Schol.* 2nd ed.), De Wette (1st to 3rd ed.), Hitzig, Ewald, Maurer, Knobel (*Prophetismus*), Bunsen (*Gott in der Geschichte*, i. 449, ff.), Bleek (upon the age of Zech. ix–xiv, together with occasional contributions towards the explanation of these utterances, in the *Theol. Stud. u. Krit.* 1852, vol. ii. pp. 247–332), v. Ortenberg (*Die Bestandtheile des Buches Sach.* Gotha, 1859), and others. Others, however, in modern times have pronounced quite a contrary opinion, as particularly Fried. B. Köster (*Meletemata critica et exegetica in Zachariæ prophetæ partem posteriorem*, cap. 9–14, Gött. 1818); Hengstenberg (*Authentie des Daniel und Integrität des Sacharjā*, 1831. pp. 361–388); De Wette (4th to 6th edits.); Umbreit, Hävernick, J. D. Fr. Burger (*Etudes exég. et crit. sur le prophéte Zacharie*, Strasb. 1841, p. 118, ff.); Stähelin (*Die Messianischen Weissagungen des A. T.*, Berlin, 1847, p. 125, ff., pp. 173–177); Keil [Köhler, Professor at Jena], and others.[1]

Most of those scholars, however, who deny that Zechariah (the composer of the first part) is the author of these last prophecies, agree also in thinking that they belong to an earlier time, before the Captivity, although they differ from one another in exact definition of the time. Rosenmüller and Hitzig place the whole in Uzziah's age. Bertholdt, on the contrary, assumes at least two different authors, the first of whom (ch. ix–xi.) must have written in the age of Ahaz, the second (ch. xii–xiv.) shortly before the Babylonian Captivity, at the time of Jehoiakim (or Jehoiachin). Likewise Knobel, Bunsen, v. Ortenberg, and, in general, Ewald also, and Hitzig (2nd ed. of "The Twelve Minor Prophets," 1852). I am decidedly of opinion that this view is correct in its main outlines, viz., that (*a*) the prophecies of this second part, as a whole, are not to be ascribed to the prophet Zechariah, who lived after the Captivity, but that they were composed at an earlier time, and before the Captivity; and (*b*) that ch. ix–xi. belong to an earlier time than ch. xii–xiv; the former to the age

[1] As to the writings on this question, cf. also Köster, *ut supra*, p. 10, ff., and Ortenberg, pp. 1–13.

of the very earliest prophets whose writings have been preserved to us, viz., to the age of Uzziah and Ahaz; the latter to the age of Jeremiah; and therefore that these two sections must have been written by different prophets.

I do not place any particular importance on the quotation in St. Matthew.

We may, perhaps, regard it as certain that the Evangelist, although quoting this passage as an utterance of Jeremiah's, only followed the tradition as to its origin which was generally accepted among the Jews since the compilation of the prophetical Scriptures, and that the mention of the name of Jeremiah proceeds only from an accidental mistaking of one for the other on the part of the Evangelist, or to an error either in memory or writing down ;· for it follows from the nature of the quotation that this passage must have been floating in his memory in a rather dim way.

There are, however, decisive internal reasons which compel us to deny the authorship of the prophecies of this part to Zechariah, a prophet living after the Captivity. These reasons are similar to those which induced us to deny Isaiah's authorship of Is. xl–lxvi, and of some other prophecies in his book, namely, because the historical circumstances which are presupposed, and with which the prophecies are connected, are quite different from those existing in the age of Darius Hystaspis, to which age the first part of the book belongs.

De Wette (4th to 6th edits.) cannot deny this, and has therefore thrown out the very improbable opinion that the later prophet (Zechariah) had purposely adopted a prophetic scheme of an archaic character in order to throw over his prophecies a veil of mystery. When, however, De Wette says that the purport of these chapters is, in part, enigmatical, it is certainly very true if we proceed on the supposition that they were composed in the Persian age, for then the purport is, for the most part, incomprehensible; but, although some few difficulties may still remain, the general perplexity vanishes, if we place the actual composition at the time to which we are led by the historical circumstances intimated in the contents. For this purpose we must briefly consider the details.

§ 247.—*Date of the Prophecies in the second Division of the Book—First Section.*

I.—Chapters ix–xi.—This first section of the second division of the Book embraces four different utterances: (1) ch. ix; (2) ch. x; (3) ch. xi. 1–3; (4) ch. xi. 4–17.

(1) Chapter ix.—This utterance is directed against various foreign nations, particularly those that were neighbours of the Israelitish people, who are threatened with destruction; but it is predicted, in reference to the Philistines, that idolatry shall be rooted out from among them, and that they shall henceforth become Jehovah's possession, and shall dwell in the midst of Judah like the Jebusites (*vv.* 1–7). It is promised to Jehovah's people that their God shall in future protect His house, and will no more give it as a prey to the oppressor. Jerusalem is called upon to rejoice, because its king shall come to it just and victorious, meek, and riding on the foal of an ass, on which account he is styled the Prince of Peace; that he shall do away with all war; that he shall possess the rule over the land of Israel to the fullest extent; and it is also promised that Jehovah shall deliver the Jews languishing in prisons, and shall bring them to a safe place (*vv.* 8–12). Then follows the further prediction that Jehovah shall protect and strengthen His people in a contest against their enemies, the Greeks (the children of Javan), and that they shall increase gloriously in the land (*vv.* 13–17).

That this utterance does not belong to the Persian age, but to a much earlier one, namely, that of King *Uzziah*, is clearly pointed out to us by the shape and way in which both the children of the Covenant, and in opposition to them, also various foreign idolatrous nations, are spoken of.

As regards the former, it clearly follows from *v.* 10, "And I will cut off the chariot from Ephraim, and the horse from Jerusalem, and the battle bow shall be cut off," that the kingdom of Israel was still existing as an independent state, as well as Judah and Jerusalem; cf. also *v.* 13.

As the enemies of Jehovah's people the following are named quite in the beginning.

(*a*) The *land Hadrach*, or, more probably, *the land of Hadrach* (חַדְרָךְ) and *Damascus*. From the way in which

Consideration of Contents of the second Division 165

both are named together in v. 1, it may be concluded, that Damascus was the chief city of that land; and it is most natural to understand Hadrach as the name of its prince (v. Stud. und Krit. 1852, p. 257). The country in question, then, was Syria, belonging to Damascus: and we must presuppose that this then formed an independent kingdom, with a prince of its own; also from the way in which the second half of this verse is connected with the first, we may assume, that it had, at that time, shown itself particularly hostile to the people of the Covenant. Now, the Syrian kingdom of Damascus was broken up in the earlier period of the reign of Ahaz, king of Judah, by the Assyrian king Tiglath-pileser, 2 Kings xvi. 9; Rezin, the last king, was then slain by the Assyrians. After that time Damascus remained subject to the Assyrians, afterwards to the Chaldeans, and then to the Persians; but it never afterwards formed an independent kingdom. We shall, therefore, be justified in fixing the date of the composition at some time before the breaking up of the kingdom of Damascus, and before Rezin, therefore also before Ahaz. Hadrach was, perhaps, Rezin's immediate predecessor, and we shall then be brought to the reign of Jotham or Uzziah.

(b) *Hamath* (v. 2). This kingdom was conquered and subjected by the Assyrians shortly before the time of Hezekiah (v. Is. x. 9; xxxvi. 19; xxxvii. 12, f.) As it is mentioned here, we are induced to suppose that it still formed an independent state, which permits us to fix the age of Isaiah as the very latest.

(c) *Tyre* and *Sidon* (vv. 2–4). From the mention of these places nothing decisive can be concluded as to the date of composition.

(d) *The Philistines* (vv. 5–7). The same four towns are mentioned here as their chief cities, as in Amos i. 6–8, and afterwards Zeph. ii. 4; Jer. xxv. 20. We must particularly note the statement in v. 5, that the king shall perish out of Gaza, from which it would appear but natural that this city was then the seat of an independent king, which certainly was not the case in the days of Darius Hystaspis.

It is quite in accordance with the inference to be drawn from these passages that in v. 13 the sons of Javan are named as those against whom Jehovah will stir up and arm the Jews and Israelites, and, as indeed appears evident from the joining of this verse to v. 12, because they had taken captive some of the people of the Covenant and kept them far from their homes. We may recollect that in Joel iv. 6, it appears that in the age of this prophet—at the time of Uzziah—Phœnicians and Philistines had sold Jews as slaves to the (Insular) Greeks (v. p. 134, f.). If, in addition to the evidence derived from the other passages, we consider the way in which the Greeks are here spoken of, we shall be justified in concluding that the prophecy was uttered at a time when the selling and carrying away to Greece of captive Jews had taken place not long before, so that the minds of the Jews were vividly affected by it; therefore that the composition of these prophecies was nearly contemporary with that of *Joel*.

(2) Chapter x.—This chapter forms a distinct prophecy. The prophet admonishes the people not to direct their prayers (for the fruitfulness of the land) to the *Teraphim* and soothsayers, but to Jehovah, whose wrath, even out of love for His people, shall be inflamed against their shepherds, but that He shall glorify Judah, and shall grant victory to the house of Joseph (Ephraim). That He would indeed scatter the Ephraimites among the nations, but that those who should think upon Him when afar off should be brought back out of Egypt and Assyria into the land of Gilead and Lebanon, that He would multiply and strengthen them, but that He would, on the contrary, humble Assyria and Egypt.

The purport of this prophecy leads us to the reign of *Ahaz*, soon after his war with Pekah and Rezin. From this, the composition would fall somewhat later than that of ch. ix, but not so very much later, that both might not have proceeded from the same author.

From the contents, it follows:—

(*a*) In the first place (from *v*. 11), that at the time of the composition, Assyria and Egypt both existed as powerful independent states, which had shown themselves hostile to Jehovah's people, and from which danger was almost continually threatened; this, however, does not lead us to the Persian age, but in general to that of Isaiah. To this we are also led by the circumstance that Assyria and Egypt are here (*v*. 10) prominently mentioned as the two countries

Contents of the second Division. 167

out of which the scattered Israelites should be brought back (cf. Is. xi. 11; xxvii. 13; Hosea xi. 10, f.).

(b) That the kingdom of Israel particularly had suffered very much, and that many of its inhabitants were in exile (vv. 6, 9, ff.).

(c) But that the breaking up of this kingdom by Shalmanezer had not yet ensued; for then we should expect the whole of Israel or Samaria would have been named as the land to which the scattered ones should be brought home, and not, as in v. 10, the land of Gilead and Lebanon, the most northern portion of the kingdom of the ten tribes. This can be easily explained, if we assume that the composition took place during the reign of Ahaz, soon after the war waged by Pekah and Rezin against Judah, after, and in consequence of which, the Assyrians under Tiglathpileser summoned by Ahaz, both destroyed the Syrian kingdom at Damascus and took away from Israel the northeastern districts, and carried away their inhabitants to Assyria (2 Kings xv. 29; 1 Chron. v. 6, 26).

(3) Chapter xi. 1–3.—These three verses are not immediately connected with what precedes, as Hofmann (*Weissagung u. Erfüllung*, i. p. 316) would have it, nor with what comes after, as Hengstenberg, Hitzig, Ewald, and most expositors are of opinion. They appear to form a distinct utterance by themselves, as is thought by Flügge, Rosenmüller, De Wette, and Knobel. Mention is made in them of a destruction of the pride of Jordan, the cedars of Lebanon, and the oaks of Bashan. This is for the most part taken only figuratively, as of the destruction of mighty heroes, or the like. But in this case, the mode of description would be somewhat unnatural.

By comparison with other passages such as Is. xxxvii. 24 (2 Kings xix. 23), Hab. ii. 17, Is. xiv. 8, these verses are simply to be understood as a lamentation on account of some northern king having deprived Lebanon and Jordan of their pride; perhaps by a needless devastation which he had committed in mere wantonness, just as, according to the above passages, both the Assyrians and subsequently the Chaldeans seem to have done. We are induced to think that an Assyrian king is here meant, for there is no reason for placing this utterance in any other or later age than either the two preceding ones, or the one that follows, and least of all in the Persian age, in the time of Darius Hystaspis.

(4) Chapter xi. 4-17.—A figurative passage presenting much difficulty and obscurity, which, however, can only be explained by the hypothesis of a composition in about the same age as that to which ch. ix. and x. are ascribed.

The object of the passage manifestly is, to set forth as a Divine decree, that Jehovah would Himself give over the people of the Covenant to punishment, as they would not show themselves to be obedient to the leading of their God, nor estimate it at its true value; that Jehovah would neither any longer concern Himself to preserve peace between the two kingdoms, Judah and Israel, nor would He keep off foreign nations from injuring His people; that He would set over them godless shepherds and rulers, who would only consume them, but that these shall not escape a just retribution.

It clearly follows from the whole of it that this utterance belongs to a time when the two kingdoms of Judah and Israel both existed close to one another as portions of the people of the Covenant; for the way in which, in *v.* 14, the destruction of the brotherhood between Judah and Israel is spoken of, could scarcely be understood, if one of these kingdoms no longer existed. It results clearly from *v.* 6, that the people were still under the government of their own king, and the whole statement points to a time when they were ruled over by bad kings, who took no care for their welfare. Verse 8 is particularly to be noticed, by which we are led to the anarchical period in Israel, after the death of Jeroboam II.

The prophet here relates in symbolical style, that he had put to death three shepherds in one month. This is certainly not intended, as many ancient and modern interpreters have understood it, to mean three different classes of leaders of the people, but as pointing out three individuals, three distinct historical personages, whom the prophet could presuppose were well known to his readers, and that they would understand whom he meant by this designation; three persons indeed who stood out before the people as princes and rulers. This passage then leads us to some very anarchical, stormy period, when the rulers of the kingdom followed one another in quick succession;

and we may assume with great probability that it relates to the state of the kingdom of Israel after the death of Jeroboam II., when king Uzziah reigned in Judah. In two of the three shepherds the prophet perhaps figured Zachariah, son of Jeroboam II., who reigned only six months, and his murderer Shallum, who, according to 2 Kings xv. 10, 13, f., usurped the kingdom, but after one month was himself slain by Menahem; and in the third shepherd, some other usurper, who, at this time,—either before the murder of Zachariah or after that of Shallum—may have placed himself at the head of the kingdom, but only maintained his place for a very short time, whose name is not mentioned in our historical books, these being generally very brief and incomplete in their accounts of the circumstances of the kingdom of Israel at this time.

We are induced by all this to suppose that the composition of this prophecy took place during the reign of the Israelitish king *Menahem*, and the latter part of that of *Uzziah*, king of Judah, therefore in general, in the same age as ch. ix, although rather later. There is, however, no reason for naming as its author any other prophet than the author of ch. ix, and perhaps also of the two utterances standing between them.

§ 248.—*Date of the Prophecies in the second Division of the Book—Second Section.*

II.—Chapters xii–xiv.—These chapters contain the following prophecies, which, however, are differently circumstanced from those we have just considered. The purport of these last utterances leads us to place them in an earlier age than that of Zechariah, living after the Captivity, in a later age, however, than ch. ix–xi.

(1) Ch. xii. 1–xiii. 6, with the superscription, "the burden of the word of Jehovah for Israel," similarly to ch. ix. It is a joyful promise for Judah and Jerusalem presenting much difficulty in its expressions.

In it mention is made of a future attack on Jerusalem on the part of the other nations of the earth, in which attack Jehovah will show Himself to be the deliverer of His people and His city, and will blot out the hostile nations through the princes of Judah, in such a way that the latter shall understand that all their strength and succour come from

Jehovah. That Jehovah would pour out on the house of David and the inhabitants of Jerusalem a spirit of grace and deep repentance for their past misdeeds, and would open a fountain for them to purify them from all sin and uncleanness; that He would root out all idolatry in the land, as well as all soothsayers and false prophets, and would take away from every one the desire of coming forth as a prophet.

That this utterance belongs to a later time than ch. ix-xi. may be inferred from ch. xii. 11, for in this passage it may be assumed with the greatest probability, that by "the mourning of Hadadrimmon in the valley of Megiddon" is meant the lamentation over the death of king Josiah; see 2 Kings xxiii. 29, f.; 2 Chron. xxxv. 22-25. That the breaking up of the kingdom of Israel had then taken place some considerable time before, is proved by the fact that the prophecy is concerned with Judah and Jerusalem only, and that these are dealt with as if they comprised the whole people of God, although in the superscription it is designated as "a burden for Israel." On the other hand, we are pointed to a time before the destruction of the kingdom of Judah and Jerusalem.

From the very beginning, and all through the discourse, Jerusalem appears as the chief city of an independent kingdom, as the object of warlike attacks by other nations, and ruled over by the house of David. The prophet speaks of the house of David as most of all in need of penitence and purification (ch. xii. 10, 12; xiii. 1); and in ch. xii. 7, in the promise of Divine safety for his people, he prominently sets forth, that Jehovah would first help the tents of Judah (before Jerusalem), in order that the house of David and the dwellers at Jerusalem should not magnify themselves against (what was left of) Judah. It is very improbable that Zechariah, living after the exile, would have expressed himself just in this way. In the days of the Persian governor Zerubbabel, himself belonging to the house of David, the prophet would have been more likely to have commended and exalted him in every way; see ch. iv; cf. Haggai ii. 23.

The foregoing considerations lead us to fix upon the latter period of the Jewish kings, after Josiah; *i.e.*, *the last years of Jehoiakim's reign, or Jehoiachin's, or Zedekiah's*. With this age, being that of Jeremiah's, Zech. xiii. 2-6 is quite in harmony.

(a) According to ch. xiii. 2 a, idolatry appears to have been not yet blotted out of the land, in conflict with which idolatry we find both Jeremiah, Zephaniah and Ezekiel; whilst it does not appear to have existed among the Jews who returned out of exile with Zerubbabel, for we do not find any denunciation of it either in the former part of our book, nor in the Books of Haggai, Malachi, Ezra, and Nehemiah.—(b) According to ch. xiii. 2 b–6, many false prophets and soothsayers must have been carrying on their calling in the land of Judah, with whom also we continually find Jeremiah in conflict.¹

(2) Ch. xiii. 7–xiv. 21.—This section forms a separate prophecy. Ewald and Ortenberg are quite wrong in separating ch. xiii. 7–9 from it, and looking upon this passage as the close of the prophecy in ch. xi. The essential purport of this prophecy may be condensed as follows: that Jehovah, after the purifying punishment decreed on His people, in which He gives Jerusalem as a prey to her enemies, and causes her king to perish, and a great part of her people to be delivered to captivity and spoiling, would again accept His people, and would punish the foreign nations, their enemies, destroying a portion of them, and converting a portion to Himself, so that, in common with His people, they should worship Him; and that then everything should be holy unto Jehovah amid God's people, in Judah and Jerusalem, and that henceforth nothing unholy or unclean should be found therein. These ideas are ex-

¹ The interpretation and reference of the passage ch. xii. 10, is difficult. אֵלַי is probably to be read here instead of אֵלָי; "they shall look upon *him* whom they have pierced, and mourn for him," &c.; cf. John xix. 37; Rev. i. 7, where the passage is quoted and made use of in reference to the Saviour; but it more probably refers originally to some historical matter of fact which the prophet had in view, and might suppose to be familiar to his readers; to the person of some martyr, perhaps, who shortly before had been slain in the service of the true God; and therefore, in its reference to the death of Christ, it must be considered as a type and not as a prediction. Bunsen, *ut supra*, p. 451, f., refers it to the prophet himself, namely, to *Urijah*, son of Shemaiah, who was killed by Jehoiakim (Jer. xxvi. 20-23). But if this were the correct reference, Urijah himself could not very well be the author, for the murder is here supposed to have taken place.

pressed here very poetically, but some of them rather too diffusely, and the mode of expression presents a good deal of difficulty in the immediate reference of the details.

The following data are to be considered in ascertaining the *date of the composition* of this prophecy.

(*a*) It may be inferred, from ch. xiv. 5, that it was not composed until some long time after Uzziah's death; for it there refers to the terror at the fearful earthquake in the days of this king (Amos i. 1), and in a way in which the prophet would not have expressed it, if it had not been some long period of time since it took place.

(*b*) It falls *after* the destruction of the kingdom of the ten tribes, on the contrary,

(*c*) before that of the kingdom of Judah.

(*d*) In ch. xiv. 10 *a*, according to the correct interpretation, the territory of the people of God is pointed out as "the plain from Geba to Rimmon south of Jerusalem." Now, Geba was the most northerly border town of the kingdom of Judah, so that no notice seems to be taken of the territory of the ten tribes, which leads us to conclude that this kingdom no longer existed.

(*e*) That, on the contrary, the kingdom of Judah still existed cannot be doubted from the nature of the beginning of the prophecy. It begins (ch. xii. 7) with a summons of Jehovah to his sword, to slay his shepherds and fellows, in order that the sheep may be scattered. We cannot doubt that by these shepherds and fellows of Jehovah the prophet here means the then reigning native king of the people, who, as he was, before all, a partaker in the sinning of the people, so must, before all, suffer in their punishment. By this, therefore, we are pointed to a time before the breaking up of the state of Judah, when it still had its own independent native king. Cf. ch. xiv. 10, where the king's wine-presses are spoken of.[1] The passages (ch. xiii. 8, f.; xiv. 1, f.) also tell against a composition in the time of Darius Hystaspis, for in that case we should expect that the prophet, in threatening the punishment coming on Judah and Jerusalem through foreign nations, would

[1] According to *Theol. Stud. und Krit.*, 1852, p. 302, Bleek lays no particular weight on this, "since this name might have been retained as a topographical designation of some particular place in Jerusalem at an earlier time, even after the rebuilding of the city."

have made some reference to the fact that the city and people had already, and not very long before, been visited with a chastisement of this kind, and had been only very scantily restored from the effects of it. We find, however, nothing of this kind.

(*f*) In ch. xiv. 18, f., it appears presupposed, that, although at the time of salvation, the heathen shall be brought to Jerusalem, in order there to take a part in the worship of Jehovah, the Egyptians should for the most part strive against it, and to their own destruction. From this we may conclude with probability, that the Egyptians at that time were showing themselves peculiarly hostile against the people of the Covenant. And if we put this together with the other indications, as well as with the position of this utterance after that which precedes, we shall be led with the greatest probability to place the composition in the days of Josiah or Jehoiakim.

This prophecy, therefore, falls somewhat earlier than the one before it, but there are no grounds for doubting that they both belong to the same prophet, who lived in the age of Jeremiah and composed them both, at any rate before the destruction of Jerusalem; on the contrary, the four prophecies of the first half of this division (ch. ix. 11) belong to a considerably earlier time, probably the period from Uzziah to Ahaz, and all the four are not improbably by the same prophet.

§ 249.—*Cause of the Union of the older Prophecies with the Book of Zechariah.*

We find, therefore, that these prophecies by different prophets at different times were united in one book with those of Zechariah, living after the Captivity. This union can only have taken place, as in the like case in the Book of Isaiah, by some error on the part of the later compiler of the prophetical Scriptures.

It has been sometimes thought, and this is Hengstenberg's view, that in the case of Zechariah, it was the less likely that extraneous fragments should be joined on to his prophecies, as he lived in the same age with the compilers of the Canon, and that, therefore, the latter would have known what belonged properly to him. But this was not the case. The compilation of the *Nebiim*, and also of the twelve lesser prophets, was, as we shall see, most probably made by Nehemiah, somewhere about eighty years after Darius Hystaspis, in whose time Zechariah prophesied, and therefore at a time when this prophet was certainly not alive. We may, therefore, very well imagine that the compiler attributed to Zechariah not only his own prophecies, but also, in error, some which belonged to another prophet and another age. As long as the prophecies of any prophet were in circulation singly, and not yet collected together in a completed form with canonical authority, it might well happen that, even within a short period after they were written, discourses by different composers, at different times, should be written down together, and should afterwards be considered to be writings of one and the same author, if these discourses, as at least was often the case, were issued singly and without any express mention of the author's name, and were not subsequently collected together by the author himself.

In the present case the fact might be still easier explained, if, perhaps, the real author of these prophecies had also borne the name of Zechariah, a name which so frequently occurs in the Old Testament.[1] The supposition of Bertholdt, as regards the *first section* of this older prophecy (ch. ix-xi), approved of also by Gesenius (*Jesaia*, i. 327, ff.), Knobel, and Bunsen, has something rather striking about it; it is that this section had as its author *Zechariah*, the son of *Jeberechjahu (Jeberechiah)*, who is mentioned in Isaiah viii. 2 (in the first year of Ahaz' reign). Since this man is spoken of in *v*. 16 as a disciple of Jehovah, it may very well be supposed that he might also have been efficient and well known as a prophet. The name Jeberechjahu is avowedly the same name as Berechjahu and Berechja (Berechiah) which occurs in Zech. i. 1, 7, as the name of the father of the Zechariah after the exile. This former Zechariah not only then bore the same name as the later prophet, but their fathers also bore the same name. Under these circumstances it might have been all the easier, for any written prophecies belonging to the former to have

---

[1] Thus, *c.g.*, in 2 Chron. xxiv. 20, f., an older prophet, Zechariah, son of Jehoiada, who died as a martyr at the time of Joash, king of Judah, the grandfather of Uzziah; and *ib.* xxvi. 5, another prophet Zechariah in the beginning of Uzziah's reign.

Malachi—Name, &c. 175

been attributed to the latter, as being better known to the compiler. But perhaps the case was somewhat different to this. We have before seen that the Zechariah living after the exile is called the son of Iddo in Ezra v. 1; vi. 14 (cf. also Neh. xii. 16). Now it might have been possible, and Knobel and Ortenberg look at the matter in this way, that in reality he was a son and not a grandson of Iddo, and that originally he was thus designated in the superscription (Zech. i. 1, 7), and that the בֶּן־בֶּרֶכְיָהוּ going before was first added by some compiler who subsequently took it out of the superscription to the prophecies of the similarly named contemporary of Isaiah. This certainly can be regarded only as a supposition, and cannot claim the same degree of certainty as the decision as to the *age* to which these prophecies belong.

As regards the *second section* (ch. xii–xiv), it may not be improbable that, as Bertholdt thinks, the two prophecies contained in it were joined in the manuscript with ch. ix–xi, previously to their being placed in connection with ch. i–viii. by the compiler of the Nebiim.

It must remain uncertain, whether the prophet Urijah, son of Shemaiah, was the author of this second half, as Bunsen thinks (Jer. xxvi. 20-23).

11.—THE BOOK OF MALACHI.

§ 250.—*Name and Person of the Prophet—Date and Contents of the Prophecy.*

The work of Malachi takes the last place in the collection of the lesser prophets and the Nebiim generally, and is also, without doubt, the latest also in point of time.

Name of the author, in Hebrew, מַלְאָכִי, in the title of the book, and in the superscription ch. i. 1; LXX, in title, Μαλαχίας; in Latin, *Malachias*; in Luther, *Maleachi*, according to the Hebrew. The Hebrew name is most probably to be explained as derived from מַלְאָכִיָה, *Jehovah's messenger*, through abbreviation; to which the Greek and Latin forms also point. The name does not occur elsewhere in the Old Testament. It is, however, a question whether it be really a proper name here or only a symbolical designation for the author as a divine ambassador, from the signification, "Jehovah's messenger," or "my messenger." The LXX has, in the superscription belonging to the book, ἐν χειρὶ ἀγγέλου αὐτοῦ, for בְּיַד מַלְאָכִי. From this, some have entertained the same idea about the author of this book as about Haggai, as we perceive from Jerome (*ad Agg.* i. 13, and *Proœm. in Malach.*), and Cyrill. Alex. (*Proœm. in Malach.*); others have so understood it, that at least the human author was pointed out by it in a symbolical way only. Thus the Jewish writers at the time of Jerome, as *Targ. Jonath. ad* i. 1 (who think that Ezra was the author, which Jerome appears to approve of); thus also, Vitringa (*Obervatt. Sacræ*, tom. ii. p. 338, ff.), Simonis (*Onomasticon*, p. 298), and, latterly, Hengstenberg (*Christol.* iii. p. 583, ff.). Yet the form of the term induces us far rather to look upon it as an actual name, in which also most expositors agree.

As to the person of the prophet, nothing is known except from his book. It is the general opinion, that he belonged to the period after the Captivity, and flourished considerably later than Haggai and Zechariah; and from the contents of his book, there can be no doubt as to this. The temple then stood completed (ch. i. 10; iii. 1-10). Most interpreters place him decidedly in the age of Nehemiah, and many of them at the period of the latter's second presence in Judæa, therefore not before the thirty-second year of Artaxerxes Longimanus (433 B.C.).[1] This view is based on the fact, that Malachi sometimes denounces the same faults and violations of the law as those Nehemiah strove against, especially (according to Neh. xiii), after the latter had returned to the Persian Court, and from thence had gone back again to Judæa, in the thirty-second year of the reign of Artaxerxes, twelve years after his first arrival in Judæa. Among these faults we may specify neglect of the payment of the legal tithes for the maintenance of the priesthood and Levites (Mal. iii. 8–10; Neh. xiii. 10–12); also the marriages of the Jews, especially of the priests, with foreign wives (Mal. ii. 10, 11; Neh. xiii. 23–30). The agreement in these two points, however, is scarcely sufficient to induce us to recognize this period as that of the composition of our book.

[1] Thus Vitringa, *ut supra*, p. 333, ff., Jahn, Rosenmüller, Bertholdt, Hengstenberg, Hävernick, and Keil.

Date and Contents of the Book.

Hitzig has correctly remarked, that the way in which the governor of Judæa is mentioned in ch. i. 8, renders it improbable that the book was composed at the time of Nehemiah's governorship. The prophet there reproaches the Jews for bringing unclean, defective beasts as offerings, and demands of them, if they would dare to bring the like to the governor. Now, it is much more probable, that the governor of Judæa at this time was a Persian, who preceded Nehemiah, from the way in which the latter (in Neh. v. 14) boasts, that from the beginning of his governorship he had not troubled the people for bread, wine, and money, as former governors had done. From this it is more likely, as also Maurer, Herbst, Ewald, and Reinke[1] assume, that this book was composed at a time when some Persian, a predecessor of Nehemiah, governed Judæa. As in all probability Nehemiah arranged the compilation of the prophets, this book could not, at any rate, have been composed *after* his time; and from its reception into the collection it is much more probable that it was composed rather before.

The prophet besides shows himself to have entertained essentially the same sentiments about the law, as those Ezra and Nehemiah acted on.

Much discontent and murmuring prevailed among the Jews in Judæa on account of their miserable and depressed condition. They excused themselves for not properly paying the tithes to the temple, on account of the meagre produce of the fields; and the priests appear to have allowed them to intercept many better beasts, which they had received as offerings, and to substitute for them inferior, defective animals; other unseemly things also took place, such as oppression of the poor, and various evil deeds. For these reasons the prophet threatens the people with Divine judgment.

Malachi's work embraces several utterances, which are not, however, divided from one another by any separate superscriptions, but only by their purport. They were doubtless written and issued at the same time, and in the same order in which we now possess them, so that they must be considered as one prophecy with different divisions.

[1] *Der Prophet Maleachi.* Giessen, 1856, pp. 29-32.

The separate utterances or sections are as follows :—

(1) Chapters i. 2—ii. 9.—The prophet endeavours, in the first place, to show to the Jews, by a comparison of Israel with Edom (which latter must then have been waste and desert), how unfounded was their idea that Jehovah no longer loved them, and also adds a sharp censure on the Jews, and particularly on the priests, who did not hesitate to bring inferior cattle as offerings to Jehovah. The prophet calls the attention of the tribe of Levi to their original duty, and threatens them that, if the priests would not fulfil their obligations, Jehovah also would cancel his treaty with them, and would punish them with failure of crops, and would make them contemptible before all people.

(2) Ch. ii. 10–16.—A denunciation of those who (a) married foreign heathen wives, and (b) separated themselves from their former (Israelitish) wives. Perhaps the prophet had before him an example, where some one had put away his Jewish spouse, and had married a foreign one.

(3) Ch. ii. 17–iii. 6.—Against those who fancied, because everything did not yet go well with the people, that piety was of no avail in pleasing Jehovah, and that God would never appear for righteous judgment. The prophet predicts to them that Jehovah will send His messenger to prepare His way before Him, and that the Lord whom they had longed for should suddenly come into His temple; but would then purify the people, and especially the sons of Levi, and would execute judgment on all sinners and wicked men. And that then the offerings of Judah and Jerusalem should again be pleasant to Jehovah, as in the days of old.

(4) Ch. iii. 7–12.—A censure against the irregular offerings of the tithes, which is characterized as a robbery of Jehovah, and as a cause why Jehovah had afflicted the land with unfruitfulness, but that, if in future they showed themselves to be more conscientious in offering the tithes, Jehovah would bless their land to overflowing.

(5) Ch. iii. 13—iv. 6.—Another censure on those who said that it was in vain that they served Jehovah and kept His commandments, for that the proud and wicked appeared to be better off; but that this was not the case, as would be experienced in the day of Jehovah, who would then destroy the wicked, but that to those who worshipped Jehovah, and kept the law of Moses, would He give a glorious

reward; and that before the coming of this day Jehovah would send the prophet Elijah, to "turn the heart of the fathers unto the children, and the heart of the children to their fathers, lest I come and smite the earth with a curse."

As a *Messianic* prophecy in this book, ch. iii. 1 deserves particular attention; yet this is not, as has been frequently understood, a prediction of an appearance of any human personality as a Messiah and Saviour; but the word Lord is to be understood of Jehovah, who shall again take up His abode among God's people, as beforetime on the Ark of Covenant, and shall there hold his separating and purifying judgment; and to prepare the hearts of the people for this, He would send beforehand a prophet like Elijah; as to which, see also ch. iv. 5, 6.

12.—THE BOOK OF JONAH.

§ 251.—*Person of the Prophet—Contents of the Book.*

The Book of Jonah is distinguished from the rest of the Scriptures of the Lesser Prophets in being purely narrative. It can only have been received into this collection, because the principal person in the narrative was a prophet, whose conduct as a prophet is therein set forth. This is one *Jonah* (יוֹנָה), son of Amittai, ch. i. 1. Neither of the names occur elsewhere in the Old Testament, except in similar connection—2 Kings xiv. 25, where we read that the Israelitish king Jeroboam II. " restored the coast of Israel from the entering of Hamath unto the sea of the plain" (*i.e.* up to the Dead Sea), " according to the word of the Lord God of Israel, which he spake by the hand of his servant Jonah the son of Amittai, the prophet, which was of Gath-hepher " (a town in the tribe of Zebulon). We must, doubtless, consider that this was the Jonah who appears as the principal character in this book. From him, therefore, prophecies must have proceeded of a similar purport to those intimated in the above passage, either handed down in writing or only by oral tradition, probably the former. At all events none of them have been preserved.[1] Jonah probably lived at the time of the Israelitish king Jeroboam II., certainly not later, and consequently not later than the most ancient prophets whose writings have been preserved. The scene of his prophetic ministrations was perhaps the kingdom of Israel, where also he was born.

Of this prophet the book which bears his name gives the following account. The command of Jehovah came to him to go to the city of Nineveh, and to cry against it, that its wickedness had come up before God; the prophet had no desire to comply with this command, the reason being as appears from ch. iv. 2, because he feared that the Ninevites might repent at his preaching, and that Jehovah would be thereby induced to have mercy on the city. In order to get out of the reach of the power of Jehovah, the God of Israel, he left the latter country, and embarked in a ship at Joppa to go to Tarshish. But Jehovah stirred up a violent storm on the sea, and the sailors, in order to find out on whose account it was sent, cast lots, and the lot fell on Jonah, who had, however, himself acknowledged that he was guilty, and had summoned them to throw him into the sea; this they then did, with prayer to God, and the sea was immediately still; but the fear of Jehovah fell upon the ship's company, and they made sacrifices and vows to Him (ch. i. 1–16). Jehovah then prepared a great fish, which swallowed up Jonah, and the prophet remained in its belly three days and three nights (ch. i. 17). In these circumstances he addressed to Jehovah a prayer of thanksgiving on account of the deliverance which he had experienced from great peril to life (ch. ii. 1–9). The fish then vomited him up on to the dry land at the command of Jehovah (ch. ii. 10). The prophet complied without delay with the renewed command to go and preach at Nineveh. He predicted to the city, that within forty days it should be entirely destroyed. The Ninevites immediately, without exception, believed the prediction, and proclaimed a fast, and put on mourning; the king himself arose from his throne, covered himself with sackcloth and ashes, and

[1] Hitzig's opinion is quite untenable (*Des Proph. Jonas Orak. über Moab*, Heidelberg, 1831; and *Der Prophet Jesaja*, 1833), that the prophecy there mentioned is the oracle against Moab,—Isaiah, ch. xv. and xvi.

issued a decree that neither men nor beasts should taste anything, and that all, both men and beasts, should put on sackcloth, and that they should fervently cry to God, and turn, every one of them, from their wicked ways, and that perhaps God would repent him of his anger and avert the destruction from them (ch. iii. 1–9). This earnest penitence moved God to spare the city (ch. iii. 10.) Jonah was most displeased at Jehovah's mercy, but Jehovah replied to him merely, "Doest thou well to be angry?" (ch. iv. 1–4). Jonah then made himself a tent outside the city, to see what became of the place; here he forgot his anger in his satisfaction at the shade afforded him by a plant¹ which the Lord God had provided for him (vv. 4–6). But when God caused the plant to be smitten in the night by means of a worm, so that it withered up, and a sultry east wind being also sent, the sun beat upon the head of Jonah, the latter fainted and wished for death; and when inquired of by Jehovah, said that he had good grounds for being displeased at the destruction of the plant (ch. iv. 7–9). Jehovah then showed him how wrong he was to allow himself to be so much grieved on account of a tree for which he had taken no trouble, which came up in a night and perished in a night, and yet blamed Jehovah for showing pity to such a city as Nineveh, with "more than six score thousand persons that cannot discern between their right hand and their left hand, and also much cattle." This speech of Jehovah to Jonah concludes the book.

§ 252.—*Origin of the Book—Historical Value—Object.*

Opinions have much varied, especially in modern times, as to the origin of this book, its historical value, and its aim.² In former times the general opinion was, that the book contained a purely historical account of some events in Jonah's prophetical ministry, and that it was composed by this prophet himself. This same opinion, in both

¹ קִיקָיוֹן only here; Luther, from the LXX, *Kürbis* (gourd). It is most probably (with Syr. and Jerome) the *Ricinus*, or so-called *Palma Christi*.

² Cf. Friedrichsen ("Critical Review of the Various Opinions as to the Book of Jonah"), 2nd edit., Leipzig, 1841). G. F. Jäger ("On the Moral and Religious Aim of the Book of Jonah," &c. Tübing. 1840.

respects, has been asserted in modern days, also, by several scholars.[1] This book, therefore, according to 2 Kings xiv. 25, would be at least contemporary with the most ancient of the prophetical Scriptures which have been handed down to us, and probably the most ancient of all. There are, however, no particular grounds for the opinion that Jonah himself wrote the book. Not only is Jonah always spoken of in the third person, but there is not the least intimation anywhere that the author wished to be considered as the prophet himself. Others, therefore, without taking any notice as to the author or date of composition, have pronounced in favour of the purely historical character of the book.[2] Still the contents of the book, considered in this light, present no inconsiderable difficulties.

The chief difficulty in my eyes consists in the improbability, which must necessarily appear to any unprejudiced reader, that the whole of the inhabitants of so enormous a city as Nineveh is represented to be should have immediately felt such remorse at the exhortation to repentance of a foreigner of a strange nation, and that they should have been turned to such sincere contrition as is here described, from the king downwards to the very meanest of the people; added to which, that in the history of this nation not the slightest trace of this event and its results is at all alluded to. If the fact had occurred, as it is here related, we should certainly expect that some permanent results would have remained, and that the king and at least a portion of the people would have been led to the knowledge and the confession of the one, true, living God; and also that the prophet, after he had seen his error, would have taken the trouble to assist somewhat further this knowledge among the people. But there is no intimation of this, either in our book, nor any trace of it in the following history of the Assyrians. They appear continuously as idolaters, trusting only in the power of their idols, and

[1] Thus, particularly, Hävernick (in the E.K.Z., 1834, No. 27, ff., and "Introduction to the Old Testament."); also Delitzsch (in Rudelbach's and Guerike's *Zeitschr. für Luth. Theolog.* 1840, Part 2); M. Baumgarten (*ib.* 1841, Part 2); Keil.

[2] Thus Sack (*Christ. Apolog.*, Edit. 2, p. 345, f.); Welte (in Herbst's *Introduction*, ii. 2, pp. 125-142), which section is entirely by the editor. [Franz Kaulen, *Librum Jonæ prophetæ exposuit. Morguntiæ.* 1862.]

as despisers of Jehovah and the gods of all other nations generally ; as, *e.g.*, appears clearly from Isaiah xxxvii. 10 ; cf. v. 23, f. ; x. 10, ff. Apart from all this, a comparison with the later prophets who 'predicted against Assyria and Nineveh, such as Isaiah, Nahum, and Zephaniah, tends to confirm our views. Had these men been at all acquainted with the fact, that an older Israelitish prophet had been ministering there in so powerful, and for the moment so successful, a way, we should surely expect that they would have referred to it in some way in their prophecies; but this is not the case in the remotest degree. Ezekiel iii. 5, 6, is certainly not a reference to this event, as Hävernick (p. 344) affirms.

It also appears surprising, on the hypothesis of the historical character of the book, that the name of the Assyrian king in whose time all this took place, who also was converted with such earnest repentance to the confession of the true God, is not once mentioned in it, nor anything else stated as to him personally, which in an historical event would certainly have been of great interest. The narrative also presents some other instances of want of precision in things where we should expect more exact statements in an account of a purely historical character, and especially in a record made of it by an eye-witness and principal sharer in the events : *e.g.*, in what place Jonah again came to land, and what became of him subsequently, particularly (as is before remarked) as to the further relation he stood in to the Ninevites after the Divine communication made to him.

To the above must be added some other circumstances in the narrative itself which occasion no slight difficulty; of these I will only particularize one,—that Jonah not only remained three days and three nights in a fish's belly, and was vomited out from it in a living state, but that he also, under these circumstances, while still in the fish's belly, should have composed a psalm. It may be supposed that a human being might live for a period of time in the stomach of a marine animal, and we will also allow that by Divine assistance this period might be extended to thrice twenty-four hours, still, we can hardly suppose that this state of things was attended with a full clear consciousness, and that the prophet would have found himself in a position to compose psalms. Least of all could this position of the prophet be felt to be a state of complete deliverance, as would appear from the song ch. ii. 2–9; which song, however, does not appear at all suitable to his circumstances, as it is not a prayer for deliverance, but rather a thanksgiving for salvation experienced. It is quite contrary to the tenor of the narrative to suppose, as many have thought, that the thanksgiving song of the prophet was composed and sung after the fish had vomited him up; for we are expressly told, in v. 1, that Jonah made this prayer out of the belly of the fish, and this, as his swallowing up and preservation are spoken of immediately before, can only be intended to refer to the time during which he was in the stomach of the creature; and it is not related until after the communication of the psalm, that the fish, at Jehovah's command, vomited Jonah up on to the dry land.

The aim of the book is, however, in no way historical, but purely didactic.

If the book had really had any historical aim or tendency, we must necessarily have supposed that the narrative was not written down till some later time, from some inaccurate and partly distorted tradition as to the actual course of the facts. And it has been thus understood by many interpreters, as by Bunsen (*Gott in der Geschichte*, i. 349, ff.), some of whom have taken the trouble to distinguish the actual facts contained in the book, and to separate them from the embellishments and additions. But even if the general tendency of the book were historical, we should be compelled to relinquish this attempt, as means would be wanting for effecting such a separation with any degree of certainty. But some of the same grounds which are brought to bear against a purely historical view of the narrative, also make it improbable that the author should have had an historical tendency generally; for then it would necessarily be expected that he would have given more precise details of many of the circumstances, and particularly would have further followed out Jonah's relations to the Ninevites, and not have broken off at a point giving so poor a conclusion, and so unsatisfactory for the history. On the contrary, all this would find a satisfactory explanation if we assume that the aim of the author was purely *didactic*, and that he wished to bring under the attention of his people certain moral and

Aim of the Book. 185

religious truths: for then he would have no need to continue the narrative any further than the prominence of these truths required. In this case Jehovah's address to Jonah (ch. iv. 9, ff.) forms a very proper conclusion, for therein a very essential truth is prominently brought forward in an impressive manner.

Among the Jewish interpreters, the didactic aim of the book has been asserted by Kimchi, ad i. 1 (cf. De Wette, § 236 h). Among Christian expositors, Semler (*Apparatus ad liberal. Vet. Test. interpret.* p. 271) was the first to bring specially forward this point of view, by considering the whole as a didactico-moral poem. He has been followed by J. D. Michaelis, Herder, and many others; also Hengstenberg (*Christologie*, Edit. 2, i. pp. 467-474).

Let us now inquire rather more *closely* into the author's aim, and ascertain what were the chief truths which he wished principally to assert. This is indeed decided in different ways, but in general there can be no doubt, that he proposed to offer some opposition to the narrow-minded, religious bigotry which prevailed among the mass of the Jews, and to their idea that Jehovah, the one true God, worshipped by them, was their God only, and had His habitation only in their land, and that He embraced with His fatherly love their people alone, and that it was right to entertain hostile feelings towards all other nations, simply as foreigners, and to wish for their destruction instead of their conversion.[1] Jonah, the Israelitish prophet, appears here as the representative of these feelings and this way of looking at things. The author brings these forward: (*a*) in the first refusal of Jonah to go to Nineveh as a preacher of repentance, the reasons for which the prophet states, ch. iv. 2; (*b*) in the delusion of the prophet (and it is certainly little likely that one of God's prophets would have actually entertained it in such a shape) that he, if he left the land of Israel and went beyond the sea, could get out of reach of Jehovah's power; and (*c*) in his displeasure

[1] Among various opinions Riehm's views (*Stud. und Kritik.* 1862, p. 413, f.) may find a place. "The practical aim of this little book is, to afford guidance in the proper treatment of the prophetical threatenings; that which the prophet predicts against his will is to be considered as the work of God; but man may be able to avert its fulfilment by means of repentance, and if this be done, objections must not be made that God's word is not fulfilled."

at the recalling (on account of their conversion) of the punishment ordained by God on the Ninevites, and the ultimate preservation of the city. In contrast to the above, our narrative shows how Jehovah knew how to find out the obstinate in every place, and that His power and control were not limited to the land of Israel; and, chiefly, that He manifested Himself as a merciful God, not merely towards the people of Israel alone, but towards other nations also, if they repented of their sins, and turned to Him in penitence. In a beautiful and striking way is this great truth brought forward at the conclusion of the book (ch. iv. 4, 9–11). It might well be said that the all-embracing fatherly love of God, which has no respect for person or nation, but is moved to mercy on all who turn to Him, is brought into view in no book of the Old Testament, in a way so impressive and so nearly approaching the Christian religion, as it is in this book.

§ 253.—*Historical Foundation of the Book.*

As regards any historical foundation of the narrative, it is of course possible, that, by means of tradition, the author had met with something of the sort which he partly followed. It is at least an historical personage, one of the ancient prophets, whom he introduces as filling the chief place. What it was, however, which led him to fix upon Jonah—whether there was any distinct inducement for it in the traditionary account of him, or in any of his prophecies which were extant, we cannot ascertain, as nothing whatever has been handed down as to the life and actions of this prophet, except in this book, besides the short notice of him in 2 Kings xiv. 25, which gives no information on these points.

The passage, Tobit xiv. 4, where, according to the Greek revision of the book, but not according to the Latin, Tobit says, " I believe that which the prophet Jonah spake as to Nineveh, that it should be destroyed," relates, without doubt, merely to the contents of our book, although in an improper way, and is doubtless to be attributed only to the Greek reviser of the Book of Tobit.

As regards Jonah's sojourn and preservation in the fish's belly, after he had embarked on the sea at Joppa, many modern interpreters, as Gesenius, De Wette, Rosenmüller, Friedrichsen, and others, have quoted two Greek myths as being parallels to them, and have supposed a connection between them and our narrative; they are as follows:—

(a) The myth of Hercules, who freed Hesione, daughter of the Trojan king Laomedon, when bound to a rock in order to serve as a prey to a sea-monster (κῆτος) which devastated the land, which was killed by Hercules. The myth runs thus in Diod. Sic. iv. 42; Apollod. ii. 5, §§ 9–12; Ovid. *Metamorph.* xi. 217; and in this shape offers no points of comparison with our narrative. Only in some later authors,—such as in Lycophron's *Cassandra*, 33, ff., which work, however (according to Niebuhr) most probably is of the second century A.D.—it is stated that Hercules himself was swallowed by a sea-monster, or had jumped down his throat; and it was some still later Christian authors who first relate that he remained three days in the bowels of the creature. But neither the one thing nor the other originally belonged to the Greek myth, and were both later additions to it; both perhaps, certainly the latter, having arisen from this very narrative of Jonah.

(b) The myth of Perseus, who rescued Andromeda, when bound to a rock on the coast near Joppa, in order to be made the prey of a sea-monster (κῆτος) which devastated the land, and which was killed by Perseus with the aid of Medusa's head. This latter myth has a great resemblance with that of Hercules, and is, perhaps, only a variation of it. But it has very little in common with our narrative, except the locality being placed near Joppa.

Consequently there is not the slightest probability that what is told in our book about Jonah's sojourn in the fish's belly could have been derived, either directly or indirectly, from this Greek myth. Least of all have we any reason to think, as many scholars have done, that a foreign myth would have taken such a shape in the mouth of the Israelitish people, as we read in this book; in this case we should be led to expect that it would have been done in a way which was more conformable to the prevailing dispositions and ideas of the people, than is the case in the whole contents of this book. Although the matter—the historical *substratum*—of this book may really have been partly derived from some other source, it must be supposed, that the author remodelled what he met with in an unfettered way, conformably to his didactic aim.

We must consider as entirely mistaken, and in the highest degree unnatural, the opinion of F. v. Baur ("The Prophet Jonah, an Assyrico-Babylonian Symbol," 1837, pp. 88-134), which derives the substance of the narrative from popular tradition, and compares thereto a Babylonian myth of the monster Oannes, and the mourning festival of Adonis; v. on the contrary, Jäger, *ut supra*, p. 86, ff.

It is, however, very probable that the author found some moving cause in the circumstances around him for giving prominence to those truths which he asserts in his book. But nothing more definite can be ascertained with any certainty, nor again as to the *date* of the composition. The Chaldaizing character of the language of the book points to a somewhat late date. Also, it cannot be doubted that it was not written until some considerable time after the prophet's death, as he is spoken of in it in so poetic a manner; perhaps, also, a considerable time after the destruction of Nineveh. For this city is spoken of as one known in ancient history, and not as one then in existence (ch. iii. 3). Consequently we get, at least, to the Chaldaic age. Perhaps it was somewhat later, in the *beginning of the Persian age*, and then it might be possible that the author, as Jäger thinks, intended by Nineveh to mean Babylon, and desired to bring before his fellow-countrymen a reason for the fact that this hostile city also was not immediately destroyed at its capture by Cyrus. It seems more probable, however, to me, that it was composed in Judæa than, as Jäger thinks, in Babylonia.

Ewald fixes the composition somewhat later still, in the fifth century B.C. He also considers the aim of the book didactical, but in a very general way; and that it intimates (*a*) in the foreign sailors, (*b*) in Jonah, (*c*) in Nineveh, that only true fear and repentance can bring salvation from Jehovah.

Hitzig's opinion is decidedly wrong and entirely mistaken, which makes out that both this book and Obadiah's prophecy were composed in Egypt, at the time of Ptolemy Lagus (sæc. 4, fin.), with the intention of vindicating God on account of the non-fulfilment of Obadiah's oracles against the (heathen) Edomites, also to exculpate the prophet on this account, and to put to silence the displeasure of the Jews about it.

I also consider the opinion of Bunsen as untenable. He considers the song, in ch. ii. 2-9, to be a genuine song of the prophet Jonah, who composed it on the occasion of his deliverance from the dangers of the sea, and believes that this song, through an error, has given cause for the history of Jonah being composed in the way in which we have it, and endeavours to restore the actual matter of fact on the basis of this song. The didactic character of the book, which is unmistakeably its main point, is scarcely at all put forward by him.

THE BOOK OF DANIEL.

§ 254.—*Position in the Canon—Review of Contents.*

This book stands in the Hebrew Canon among the *Ketubim*, between Esther and Ezra; in the LXX and Vulgate, as well as in Luther, as the fourth of the greater prophets, after Ezekiel. It consists of twelve chapters, partly in the Hebrew, partly in the Chaldee language, the first six of which relate matters of fact of a substantive character, the last six contain various visions afforded to Daniel. The first half of the book is again divided into several separate sections, which are only loosely joined on to one another without any formula of transition, and indeed, form complete narratives by themselves, but still so that the former ones are presupposed in the latter.

Their substance is as follows:—

(1) Ch. i. (Hebrew).—In the third year of the reign of Jehoiakim, at the capture of Jerusalem by Nebuchadnezzar,—in which the Jewish king came into his power, and a portion of the holy vessels of the temple were carried away into the land of Shinar—Daniel and three other Israelitish youths of noble families, Hananiah, Mishael, and Azariah, were brought to Babylon; and there, in the king's palace for three years, they were taught the language and learning of the Chaldeans, and were educated for the service of the king. They desired, however, during this time to keep from any kind of defilement, through partaking of the meat and drink of the king, and therefore lived upon bread and water. They also made distinguished progress in their learning, so that the king found at the expiration of the time that they excelled all the wise men of his kingdom in judgment, and Daniel "had understanding in all visions and dreams." Verse 21 concludes the chapter—"and Daniel continued (יְהִי) unto the first year of king Koresch (Cyrus);" this probably means, that he remained in Babylon up to the date named, when the Jewish exiles generally received permission to return home.

(2) Ch. ii.—Nebuchadnezzar, in the second year (?) of

his reign, had a disquieting dream. He caused all the magicians, sorcerers, astrologers, and Chaldeans, to come before him, and demanded of them, not only the interpretation of his dream, but also that they should tell him the purport thereof; none of them were able to do it, the king therefore gave command that they should all be slain, and for this purpose Daniel also was sought for. To the latter, both the dream and its interpretation was revealed in a vision at night, and he made them known to the king, who was thus convinced of the might and omniscience of Daniel's God. He fell on his knees before Daniel, made oblations to him, and nominated him chief governor over all the wise men of Babylon, and also, at his request, made over the management of the province of Babylon (which had been intended for Daniel), to his three companions, whilst he himself remained in the king's palace. The dream itself related to a great image which the king saw, the head of which was of gold, the breast and arms were of silver, the belly and thighs of brass, and the feet partly of iron and partly of clay; a stone, dug out without hands, struck against the feet of the statue and broke all the parts of it in pieces. Daniel interpreted this of several successive kingdoms; to the then existing kingdom of Nebuchadnezzar (the head of gold), an inferior kingdom should follow, and then a third of brass, ruling over the whole earth, and a fourth, strong as iron, breaking in pieces and subduing all things; next a divided kingdom, partly of iron and partly of clay, *i.e.*, partly strong, and partly fragile, in which they (the several portions or rulers) shall be mixed in races, without cleaving to one another; but that in the days of this king (of the divided kingdom), God would Himself set up a kingdom upon earth, which should destroy all kingdoms, but which should itself endure for ever, and that it should be made over to no other peoples.

The narrative is completely finished at the end of the chapter. It begins in Hebrew *vv.* 1-3; but in *v.* 4, the Chaldean wise men are represented as speaking in the Chaldee language, and this dialect continues in what follows, for the narrative itself: and the succeeding narratives of the first portion of the book, are also entirely written in Chaldee.

(3) Ch. iii. 1–30.—Another narrative complete in itself, which is not connected even by a ꝩ with what goes before, although the contents of ch. i. are presupposed. It states that Nebuchadnezzar set up in the neighbourhood of Babylon a monstrous golden statue, sixty cubits high, and six cubits in breadth, and collected together for its dedication all the high officials of his kingdom, and ordered them, under penalty of being cast into a burning fiery furnace, to fall down before the image and worship it. Daniel's three companions—of Daniel himself no mention is made—neglected to do this, and on being denounced on this account to the king by certain Chaldeans, they still persistently refused to do it; they were, therefore, by the king's command, cast into a most fiercely burning furnace, in which, by God's help, they were wonderfully preserved, so that Nebuchadnezzar, full of wonder, acknowledged the power of their God; he issued a command in which any one was threatened with death who should dare to blaspheme the God of these men, and to the men themselves he entrusted high positions in the land of Babylon.

(4) Ch. iv. 1–*fin.*—This section also is complete in itself, without being joined on to what precedes by any transitional formula or words of connection; here again, also, the contents of ch. i. are presupposed as being well known. It is a letter of king Nebuchadnezzar, addressed to all the nations of the whole earth, in which he relates that Daniel had interpreted to him a dream, which all the magicians, astrologers, Chaldeans, and soothsayers, were unable to explain. That this dream was fulfilled with regard to himself twelve months afterwards; that, as a punishment for his pride, he had been afflicted with madness, and had lived in this state seven *times* (years) in the open fields with the cattle, and like them, feeding on grass; that then his reason had returned to him, and he had praised the power and greatness of the Most High; that he was again established in his kingdom, and his might was increased; so that he now praised and honoured the King of Heaven before all the world. In ch. iv. 28–33, the epistolary form is dropped, and the king is spoken of in the third person, but from *v.* 34 to the end, he again speaks in the first person.

(5) Ch. v. 1–*fin.*—This narrative, also, is not connected with what precedes it by any connecting formula, although

the purport of the narrations that go before, particularly ch. i, ii, and iv, is presupposed in it as well known. A king Belshazzar of Babylon, who is spoken of as a son of Nebuchadnezzar (vv. 11, 13, 18, 22). caused, in his arrogance, the holy vessels to be brought, which his father Nebuchadnezzar had carried away out of the Temple at Jerusalem, and drank out of them, with his princes and concubines, singing songs of praise to their idols. Suddenly the king perceived a hand, which wrote on the wall of the dining-hall. After all the wise men of Babylon had in vain attempted to read it, at the queen's suggestion, Daniel was sent for, who read and explained the writing, to the effect that, on account of his profanation of the holy vessels, and his wicked contempt for the Lord of Heaven, the king Belshazzar should lose his kingdom, and that it should be given to the Medes and Persians. The king caused Daniel to be invested—as he had promised to the man who should explain the writing—with scarlet and a golden neck-chain, and proclaimed him as the third ruler in the kingdom; the king himself was, however, slain that same night, and Darius (Darjavesch), the Median, took the kingdom.

(6) Ch. vi. 1-*fin.*—This narrative, also, is complete in itself. King Darius set over the whole kingdom 120 governors, and over these, three princes; as one of these latter, Daniel was appointed, who had so distinguished himself, that the king thought to put him over the *whole* land. Whereupon, the other princes and the governors sought for an opportunity to ruin Daniel. They, therefore, persuaded the king to issue a decree, according to the law of the Medes and Persians, which altereth not, forbidding every one, for thirty days, to ask a petition of any god or man, except of the king. Daniel, however, did not refrain from his custom of praying to his God three times a day in his house, with his windows open towards Jerusalem. He was, on this account, denounced by those who envied him, and the king found himself compelled by the law—although it was very painful to him—to order Daniel to be thrown into the den of lions. When, next morning, he found him still unharmed, he was overjoyed and had him drawn out, and ordered that his accusers should be thrown into the den, where they were immediately torn to pieces by the lions. The king then wrote a decree to all

194   Origin of the several Books—Daniel.

the nations on the whole earth, that every one throughout all his dominions should reverence the God of Daniel, who had shown himself as the everlasting and almighty Ruler, and Doer of wonders. The narrative concludes, v. 29, "So this Daniel prospered in the reign of Darius (Darjavesch), and in the reign of Cyrus (Koresch), the Persian.

The second division of the book may be divided into four sections, setting forth the same number of visions occurring to Daniel at different times.

(1) Ch. vii.—A vision in a dream of Daniel, which he saw and wrote down in the first year of Belshazzar, king of Babylon. He saw four great beasts come up out of the sea: (a) one a lion with eagle's wings, which received the appearance and heart of a man; (b) a second beast like a bear, with three ribs in his mouth, which is told to devour much flesh; (c) a third beast like a leopard with four fowl's-wings and four heads, to which beast dominion was given; (d) a fourth beast with great iron teeth, devouring and smashing all things, and with ten horns; among these another little horn rose up, which spoke proud things, and before which three of the other horns were rooted out. Then appeared the Ancient of days in judgment; the beast is slain on account of the proud words spoken by the horn, and is thrown into the burning flame, and the dominion was taken away from the rest of the beasts for a certain time. Then one appeared like the Son of Man with the clouds of Heaven, and to him was given glory and dominion over all nations, and an everlasting kingdom. This vision is then interpreted to Daniel, at first in general, as referring to four kings, i.e., kingdoms or dynasties, which shall arise out of the earth, but that afterwards the saints of the Most High (the people of God), shall possess the kingdom for ever and ever. It is then explained specially in respect to the fourth beast and its horns; the fourth kingdom symbolized in this way is styled "diverse from all kingdoms," and as devouring, treading down, and breaking in pieces the earth; the ten horns are ten kings arising in it, after whom another king shall appear, diverse from the others. The latter shall subdue three kings, shall utter blasphemies against the Most High, and make war upon His saints, and shall think to alter the (feast) times and laws; they shall be given into his hand for

three and a half *times* (years), until judgment shall sit and make an end of his dominion, and then shall the kingdom and dominion over all the nations of the earth be given for ever to the people of the saints of the Most High.

This dream-vision of Daniel has, unmistakeably, a great similarity to that of Nebuchadnezzar, in ch. ii, and in both we are induced to explain the consecutive kingdoms in the same way. This section is also written in Chaldee. What follows, however, is again entirely in the Hebrew language.

(2) Ch. viii.—A vision of Daniel in the third year of Belshazzar, in which Daniel was (perhaps only in a vision) in the palace of Shushan in Elam by the river Ulai. He saw a ram with two horns, and the higher of the two came up last; the ram pushed mightily towards the west, north, and south, until a he-goat, spreading over the whole earth, with a notable horn, came from the west, and pushed the ram to the ground, breaking both his horns; then the he-goat broke his great horn, and in its place four came out towards the four quarters of the world; out of one of these came forth a little horn, which increased very much toward the south, and the east, and toward Judæa, and it waxed great even to the host of heaven, and the prince of the host, whose habitation it threw down, and took away from him the daily sacrifice. Daniel then heard the vision explained by the angel Gabriel; that the ram with the two horns signified the kings of Media and Persia, the he-goat the king of Greece (the Grecian monarchy), his notable horn the first king (Alexander), the four horns coming up in its place are four kingdoms which shall stand up out of the nation, but not in the power of the first king (this, perhaps, is only meant for four kingdoms arising out of that of Alexander); the little horn, however, is a bolder and more crafty king, who shall arise at last, and shall ruin many of the people of the saints, and shall stand up against the prince of princes, but shall be finally destroyed without the agency of the hand of man. Daniel had been previously told that the transgression of the destroyer and the hindrance of the daily sacrifice should last for 2300 evenings and mornings (עֶרֶב בֹּקֶר = so many times when the daily sacrifices in the evening and morning were to be offered =

1150 days = 3½ *times*, ch. vii). He is finally commanded to seal up the vision, which shall last for a long time (according to *v.* 17 at the time of the end). He was for sometime sick through his amazement at the vision, which neither he (nor any one) could understand. It appears, however, to be clearly evident that the little horn is here intended to signify the same as in ch. vii.—a heathen prince in one of the kingdoms which proceeded out of that of Alexander, who violently oppressed the Jewish nation and stopped the regular offering of sacrifice in the temple.

(3) Ch. ix.—A vision of Daniel in the first year of Darius (Darjavesch), son of Ahasuerus (Xerxes?), of the seed of the Medes, who was made king over the realm of the Chaldeans. Daniel reflected on the number of seventy years, which Jeremiah prophesied should be accomplished in the desolations of Jerusalem, and implored Jehovah with fasting, and sackcloth and ashes, to put aside the sins of the people and avert the Divine wrath from Jerusalem and Zion. Then the angel Gabriel appeared to him and revealed to him the explanation of the prophecy of the seventy years; that it would be seventy weeks (weeks of years = Septennia), until the guilt of the people should be entirely atoned for, and the prediction of the prophet find its fulfilment, and the Most Holy be anointed. This entire period is again divided into three smaller ones, 7 + 62 + 1 ; viz., (*a*) seven weeks from the going forth of the commandment as to the restoration of Jerusalem, up to the time of an anointed prince (Cyrus); (*b*) within the next following sixty-two weeks (therefore, during the time of this anointed prince to the sixty-ninth week of years) will the city be rebuilt, yet in troublous times; (*c*) after the expiration of these sixty-two weeks (therefore of the sixty-ninth week of years), will an anointed one be cut off, and the people of a prince that shall come will destroy both city and sanctuary; he shall enter into a covenant with many, and during the (last) half of a week (during one-half of this week of years) he shall cause the sacrifice and oblation to cease, until destruction shall be poured out on the desolater.

We are here induced to consider that this destroyer is the same prince as is intended by the little horn in ch. vii. and viii. But it appears to be intimated here, that with the overthrow of this prince, the whole of the period had elapsed intended by Jeremiah up to the full appearance of the salvation, which Jehovah had intended for His people.

(4) Ch. x–xii.—A vision of Daniel, in the third year of the Persian king Cyrus (Koresch), by the Tigris (Hiddekel). After Daniel had mourned and fasted for three weeks an angel appeared to him, who referred to the contest which he had had to carry on with the guardian angels of Persia and Greece, in which he had been assisted only by Michael, the guardian angel of the Jews; he then gives him a revelation as to the future, from ch. xi. 2 on. Beginning with the Persian kings succeeding Cyrus, he goes on to Alexander and his successors, and describes in detail the relations and conflicts of the kings of the north and of the south (Syria and Egypt) with each other. But he dwells most particularly on the description of one of the kings of the north, viz., of Antiochus Epiphanes, as to whom there can be no doubt from the whole mode of statement, both as to his conflicts with Egypt and in his attempts and violent acts against the Jews, and all his insolent, cold, God-despising nature, down to v. 45, where his end is spoken of, which he shall meet without any to help him. The angel then, in ch. xii. 1–3. concludes the prediction, that in a time of trouble to an extent before unheard of, all the elect of Daniel's people shall find salvation, and many of those in the sleep of death shall awake, some to everlasting life, and some to everlasting contempt. In v. 4, Daniel is again commanded by the angel to shut up these words, and to seal up the book, until the time of the end. Then Daniel heard the period stated from the time of the taking away of the daily sacrifice, as 1290 days (v. 11), and in v. 12, that he is called blessed who shall wait and come to the 1335 days.

§ 255.—*Various Opinions as to the Origin of the Book.*

Opinions vary much both as to the *origin* of the book and as to its *aim* and *value*. As regards the first point, Daniel has been considered as its author both by Jewish tradition and the entire ancient Christian Church, connected with which is the fact, that the contents of the book have been looked upon as purely historical: the first part as a purely historical narrative of events which took place in the lifetime of Daniel, the second part as an historical account of visions and revelations which were actually afforded to Daniel. To the latter particularly, considerable importance has been ascribed, on account of the great exactness—surpassing all the other prophets—in the prediction of future events, and their chronological relation to one another; thus Josephus, *Ant.* x. 11, 7; Theodoret, *Præf. in Dan.*, &c. The book experienced, tolerably early, an attack on its genuineness, but this came from an opponent of all revealed religion generally, Porphyrius, the Neo-Platonist (d. 304).

Out of his fifteen books against Christianity, the whole twelfth book is taken up with an attack on the Book of Daniel. He maintained that it was fabricated by a Jew who lived at the time of Antiochus Epiphanes, and that it was rather an account of things that had taken place, than a prophecy of the future; and that, therefore, he appears to predict truly in everything before this date, and falsely in everything that goes beyond it. In order to prove his assertions he made a most exact study of the Syrian history particularly. There are fragments of his argument in Jerome's "Commentary on Daniel," in which he is frequently opposed, as also by other ecclesiastical authors, whom Jerome mentions (Methodius, Apollinaris of Laodicea, and Eusebius of Cæsarea).

In modern times, however, the opinion in favour of Daniel's authorship of the book has also met with manifold opposition in the Christian Church, particularly among the Protestant German divines, since the end of the last century.

Thus: Corrodi (*Freimüthige Versuche über verschiedene in Theol. u. bibl. Kritik einschlagende Gegenstände*, 1783, p. 1, ff.; *Versuch einer Beleuchtung der Gesch. des Bibelkanons*, 1792, i. p. 75, ff.).—Eichhorn, then Bertholdt (*Daniel neu übersetzt u. erklärt*, Part 2, 1806–1808, and *Einleitung in d. A. u. N. T.*), Augusti, De Wette, and others. I have given a more exact consideration to this subject, in *Abhandlung über Verfassung u. Zweck d. Buches Daniel; Revision der neuerem darüber angestellten Untersuchung*, in Schleiermacher, De Wette, and Lücke's *Theol. Zeitschrift*, Part 3 (Berlin, 1822), pp. 171–294, in which I also have decided for the later composition of the book. Partly in reference to this treatise, other divines have again endeavoured to vindicate Daniel's authorship of the book. Thus, amongst others, Sack (*Christl. Apologetik.* 1 edit., 1829); —Hengstenberg (*Die Authent. des Daniels und die Integr. des Sacharjah*, 1831); —Hävernick ((*a*) *Commentar über das Buch Daniel*, Hamburg, 1832, (*b*) *Neue krit. Untersuchung über das Buch Daniel*, Hamburg, 1838, (*c*) *Einleitung in das A. T.*); —Herbst, Keil, Auberlen (*Der Prophet Daniel u. die Offenbarung Johannis*, Basle, 1854, 2nd edit. 1857); —Delitzsch (in Herzog's *Real-Encyclop.*, Art. "*Daniel*"), and others. The following have decided in favour of the later composition, and endeavoured to prove it :—Kirmss (*Commentat. hist. crit. exhibens descriptionem et censuram recentiorum de Dan. libro opiniorum*, Jena, 1828); —Redepenning (*Theol. Stud. u. Krit.* 1833. Part 3, 1835); —Von Lengerke (*Das Buch Daniel verdeutscht u. ausgelegt*, Königsberg, 1835); —Ewald, Hitzig (*Das Buch Daniel erklärt*, Leipzig, 1850); —Bunsen (*Gott in der Geschichte*, i. pp. 514–540); —Lücke (*Versuch einer vollständigen Einleitung in die Offenbarung Johannis*, 2nd edit. p. 41, ff.); —Bleek (*Die Messianischen Weissagungen im Buche Daniel, mit besonderer Beziehung auf Auberlen's* (d. 2nd May, 1864) *Schrift;* in the *Jahrbuch für deutsche Theologie*, 1860, i. pp. 45–101).[1]

§ 256.—*Unity of Authorship.*

The unity of authorship has been also questioned, although incorrectly.

Among the modern defenders of the authenticity of the prophecies of the book, Sack, Herbst, and Davidson attribute to Daniel himself only the second portion of the book, and consider that ch. i.-vi. were written by some Israelite at a later time as an introduction to the visions. Among those scholars who place the date of the book generally at a later time, Eichhorn (edits. 3 and 4) assumes that there were two authors, (*a*) for ch. ii. 4 to ch. vi. *fin.*, and (*b*) for ch. vii-xii. and ch. i. 1-ii. 3; and Bertholdt, followed by Augusti, assumes different authors for the separate sections of the book, in all nine different authors at somewhat different times. Some other modern scholars, on the contrary,

[1] David Zündel has lately entered the lists in favour of the orthodox opinion (*Krit. Untersuchungen über die Abfassungszeit des Buches Daniel.* Basle, 1861). Cf., on the contrary, Rudolf Baxmann, *Ueber das Buch Daniel*, in the *Theol. Stud. u. Krit* 1863, Part 3.

who deny Daniel's authorship of the book, attribute the whole to one and the same author, and this may be assumed as certain. The changes in the dialect can in no way be decisive on this point, as in ch. ii. it can be explained in a natural way, and the Chaldee elements could in no case have formed by themselves an independent work. But Bertholdt's opinion as to the multiplicity of authors is entirely untenable and is now generally given up. What he alleges in favour of this idea, is either quite unfounded and incorrect, or valueless as a proof. Thus, he appeals to the different historical contradictions in the various sections, particularly ch. i. 21 with x. 1; ch. i. 1, 5 with ii. 1; ch. ii. 48, 49 with v. 11–14. Some of these, however, are by no means certain, and all of them of such a nature that the circumstances can be explained even under the supposition of the same author, at least, if he were a late author, and not Daniel. Bertholdt himself is compelled to allow that the authors of the later sections must almost always have been acquainted with the former ones, and must have followed them as continuators, also that they must have imitated them in the whole mode of statement, as well as in the use of certain words and expressions; and that this must have been done in such a way as is scarcely imaginable. In favour of the unity of authorship of the first division of the book, there is also the fact, that in ch. i. and ii. there are hints which seem to refer to the contents of the following chapters. Thus, in ch. i, Daniel's skill in the interpretation of dreams, is certainly so prominently brought forward in reference to the narrative in ch. ii; also in ch. i. Daniel's three companions being named with him, and in ch. ii. 49 its being told that the king made over to them the management of the province of Babylon, are both in reference to ch. iii, in which they appear in the condition of officials of the land; and the mention in ch. i. 2 of the carrying away by Nebuchadnezzar of the holy vessels of the Temple has doubtless been made in reference to ch. v. Also, the assumption that the first division of the book was composed by a different author from that of the second, and that it was, at a later date, intended by him as an introduction to this latter, appears altogether improbable if we observe the great similarity which they both offer to each other in respect to their whole spirit, ideas, literary style, and language, which similarity is of that nature that it could only be looked for in one and the same author. Cf. Bleek's treatise in the *Theol. Zeitschrift*, p. 241, ff., p. 255, ff.; De Wette, § 256.

§ 257.—*Origin and Authorship.*

As regards the question as to the origin and author of the book, the controversy still is, whether it was composed by Daniel, who must have lived, according to our book, during the whole time of the Babylonian exile, up to the third year of Cyrus, or by some Jewish author living about three and a half centuries later, in the age of Antiochus Epiphanes. We certainly must not conceal from ourselves that the question involved here is of another kind from that as to Isaiah xl. ff., and Zech. ix. ff.; for in this latter case, there is really no question at all as to the genuineness or non-genuineness of these portions, but only as to their authors and ages, as the authors themselves nowhere mention their own names, and make no claim in any way to be looked upon as Isaiah and Zechariah. But with regard to the Book of Daniel it is a somewhat different matter. The historical sections, chapters i–vi, make no express claim to being composed by Daniel himself; for Daniel is everywhere spoken of in them in the third person, as also his three companions. But in the second division of the book, it is expressly mentioned in ch. vii. 1, as to the first vision, that Daniel himself wrote it out, and in all these visions Daniel is regularly spoken of in the first person, so that he appears as the narrator: " I saw," " a vision appeared to me, Daniel," &c. It appears, therefore, from this, that this part at least, and—by its connection with the first part—the whole book lays claim to be considered as a work of Daniel; and if the date is fixed at a later age, it must be assumed that a similar state of things exists, as, *e.g.*, with regard to the Deuteronomic law-giving, or Jacob's blessing, or Ecclesiastes, viz., that the introduction of Daniel as the writer or relator of his visions is only an embellishment of the author, for some moral or didactic end, which is for us to ascertain. We are necessitated by overpowering reasons, as I think, to pronounce in favour of this opinion, partly from external, and partly from internal evidence.[1]

§ 258.—*External Arguments for an earlier or later Date.*

As regards the external evidence, the champions for Daniel's authorship appeal to the following as proof that it was extant before the age of Antiochus Epiphanes, namely:

(*a*) To 1 Macc. ii. 59, 60, where the dying priest Mattathias refers his son to the deliverance which God afforded to Hananiah, Azariah, and Mishael, and also to Daniel, and does it in that way, that most probably there is a reference to the narrative in chaps. iii. and vi. of our book. But Hävernick himself (*Einl.* ii. p. 459) acknowledges that this speech of Mattathias is an arbitrary composition of the author, and thus only affords a proof that the Book of Daniel was extant at the time of the composition of the first book of Maccabees, which would be about the year 100 B.C., therefore sixty to seventy years after the death of Antiochus Epiphanes. This passage, therefore, can prove nothing.

(*b*) To the narrative of Josephus (*Ant.* xi. 8, 5), that when Alexander the Great, in his conquering march, came to Jerusalem, the Book of Daniel was there shown to him; and that he took to himself the prophecy in it, that a Greek should destroy the Persian empire, and was much pleased at it. But Josephus' whole narrative, with its concomitant circumstances, has something in it so improbable, and sometimes manifestly fabulous, that certainly not the slightest importance can be attributed to it in reference to the above circumstance: *v. Theol. Zeitschrift*, pp. 183–187.

On the other hand, we meet with many things which cause us to conclude with the greatest probability that the book and its contents could not have been known until a considerably later time than the age of Daniel. Among these are as follows:

(*a*) The position of the book in the Hebrew Canon, that is, its being placed among the Ketubim and not among the Nebiim, and as one of the last of the former. This can scarcely be explained, except by the supposition, that the

---

[1] I can only bring forward here the chief points, referring sometimes to the further explanation in the *Theol. Zeitschrift* (and in the *Jahrb. für deutsche Theologie*).

book was not known at the time when the compilation of the Nebiim was made, which was most probably by Nehemiah, about 450 B.C., therefore at least 100 years after the age of Daniel.

The position of the book in the LXX has been occasionally appealed to, in which it is placed after Ezekiel. But in this case there can be no doubt, and it is now generally acknowledged, that this was not its original place in the Canon; if it were, it would be difficult to understand how it got to be shifted to the place which it occupies in the Hebrew Canon, whilst, on the other hand, it might very easily be explained how it got to be transplanted into the list of prophets from its original place in the Canon. Others have thought that the compilers of the Canon considered that Daniel was differently circumstanced to the other actual prophets, whose writings form the second class; *e.g.*, that he was not an actual נָבִיא, but only a חֹזֶה (thus Hävernick), or that he was a prophet by his gifts only, and not by his office, and that his ministry lay in a foreign land and at the court of a heathen king, and not among his own people; whilst in the second class of the Canon, the writings of those only were included who were prophets by office (thus Hengstenberg). There is nothing tenable, however, in this. If the visions were afforded to Daniel which are related in our book, he might just as well have been included in the list of Nebiim, as, *e.g.*, Amos, Ezekiel, and Zechariah, who also received a great part of their revelations in visions; and just as well, also, as the Book of Jonah, which sets Jonah before us in his prophetic ministry among a foreign nation only, and not among the people of Israel. This peculiarity cannot well be explained, except under the supposition that the compiler of the books of the second part of the Canon, which, from their contents, could not well have been collected before Nehemiah's age, was not acquainted with the Book of Daniel. This, again, cannot easily be understood, if the book, or even only the visions in it, were written by Daniel himself, therefore about 100 years before.

(*b*) The silence of Jesus, the son of Sirach, as to Daniel, in Ecclus. xlix, where we should be entitled to expect an express mention of him.

He devotes ch. xliv–l. altogether to praising the worthies

of his nation, who were distinguished as rulers, or by their
wisdom as lawgivers, prophets, &c. Thus he himself, in
ch. xliv. 1-15, announces his purpose; and, firstly, in
ch. xliv, he treats in succession of the patriarchs, Enoch,
Noah, Abraham, Isaac, Jacob; then, in ch. xlv, of Moses,
Aaron, Phineas; in ch. xlvi, of Joshua, Caleb, the Judges,
Samuel; in ch. xlvii, of Nathan, David, Solomon;
ch. xlviii, of Elijah, Elisha, Hezekiah, Isaiah; ch. xlix,
of Josiah, Jeremiah, Ezekiel, the twelve lesser prophets, of
Zerubbabel, Joshua, and Nehemiah, and, in ch. l, he concludes with praise of the high priest Simon. The passage
where the twelve minor prophets are mentioned, is declared by Hengstenberg, Hävernick, Keil, and Davidson
(also by Bretschneider) to be not genuine, but without
satisfactory reasons. As these twelve minor prophets are
mentioned and put together as one body, it is most surprising that Daniel is not also mentioned; one would
expect to find him close to Jeremiah and Ezekiel, and it is
difficult to explain how Jesus Sirach came to omit naming
him with the others, if he had been known to him as a
prophet who had seen such visions and performed such
deeds, as we read of in the book extant in his name. This,
too, cannot well be explained, except by the supposition
that our book was not known to Jesus Sirach (about 200 to
180 B.C.), and, at any rate, that it was not then acknowledged as canonical. Hengstenberg has, indeed, brought forward with some plausibility that Ezra and Mordecai are not
named. But there is a marked distinction here, for Daniel,
as he appears in his book as a prophet and doer of wonders,
stands out quite differently from Ezra, who was neither the
one nor the other, but only a certainly not undistinguished
priest and scribe, who, however, was made much more of
by the later Jewish tradition than appears from his book;
although, perhaps, he even would not have been omitted if
the book extant in his name had been an element of the
Canon at the time of Jesus Sirach. The omission of Mordecai can still less be compared with that of Daniel,
without mentioning that the Book of Esther, in which he
is signalised, was, at the time of Jesus Sirach, not yet
perhaps existing, and certainly not of acknowledged authority. It is, then, in the highest degree improbable that
the Book of Daniel was known and acknowledged by the

son of Sirach, who lived more than 300 years after the Captivity. But it is very difficult to explain how it could then be unknown to him, except under the supposition that at that time it was not yet in existence.

(c) There is still another point that must not be lost sight of. If the Book of Daniel had been composed in the age of Cyrus, and therefore existed ever since, and was also well known to the Jews, we should certainly expect that traces of some use having been made of it would be found in the prophets flourishing after the Captivity, Haggai, Malachi, and particularly in Zechariah, ch. i-viii, and that it would, in particular, have exercised some influence on the shaping and modification of the Messianic ideas in these later prophets. But this is not anywhere the case.

As regards Zechariah particularly, the Messianic prophecies of Jeremiah have exercised influence over him in shaping out his idea of a Messiah; but this is not the case with the visions of Daniel, not even the prediction of a ruler like unto the Son of Man coming in the clouds: Dan. vii. The same thing holds good with regard to the Angelology, in which it cannot easily be mistaken, that the accounts in our book bear a later and much more finished character than those in Zech. i-viii, which at the most can only be compared with the former.

§ 259.—*Internal Arguments against Daniel's being the Author.*

The internal features of the book, under the supposition of its authorship by Daniel, present equal difficulty as regards both the purport and nature of its prophecies, and also its historical elements. We will first consider the former. As regards this point, under a supposition of its composition by Daniel, the prophecies would have something about them at all events altogether peculiar and distinguishing them from those of the other prophets of the Old Testament. There is in them a distinctness of prediction of even special events in a tolerably distant future, such as we meet with in no other prophet to a like extent. This especially applies to the last sections, ch. x-xii, in which are depicted the several conflicts of the Ptolemies and Seleucidæ, the two ruling dynasties over kingdoms, which in Daniel's time did not yet exist, but which proceeded considerably later out of another great kingdom, likewise not existing in

Daniel's time; and this is sometimes done so exactly and with such detail that one would imagine it an historical narrative, rather than a prophecy. Not less surprising are the chronological definitions for certain future events, which are sometimes given even in days, as ch. viii. 14, xii. 11, 12; this, too, is contrary to the usual analogy of the Hebrew prophets, who, in general, very seldom fix the dates of future events, and (if we except the certainly interpolated passage, Is. vii. 8) state them in round and holy numbers. Added to this, the fact is particularly important, that the special distinctness of the prediction extends only to the time of Antiochus Epiphanes, when this Syrian prince exercised his tyranny against the Jewish people, and endeavoured in every way to suppress the worship of Jehovah, and for this purpose sought to introduce the Greek *cultus* itself into the Temple at Jerusalem; whilst the prophecies either break off with the destruction of this prince, or immediately annex to it the prediction of the deliverance of God's people from all distresses, and of the Messianic salvation and kingdom, and even the resurrection of the dead.

In several of the sections it is indeed a question if the matter stands quite in this way, many interpreters referring the purport of these visions to other events.[1] But, in the first place, with regard to the last section, it is at the present day generally acknowledged, and cannot be doubted, that in ch. xi. 21-45, the reign of Antiochus Epiphanes is spoken of, his wicked conduct and proceedings, and particularly his enterprises against the Jewish people and the worship of Jehovah, up to his overthrow. The promise, however, is immediately joined on to this, that at the same time all the elect of the Jewish people should find salvation, and that many of those who slept in death should be awakened; so that evidently the hope is expressed that this would ensue immediately after the overthrow of the tyrant. This is also clearly confirmed by the way in which, afterwards, the time of the oppression exercised by him, and the duration of the abolition of the worship of Jehovah in the temple, enforced by him, are stated (ch. xii. 7, 11).

[1] For what follows, cf. *Jahrb. für deutsche Theologie, ut supra*, in which, purely from an exegetical stand-point, the untenableness is shown of the orthodox interpretation of these visions.

It is just as indubitable and generally acknowledged, that the king, symbolized in ch. viii. by "the little horn,"—of whom it is told that he would arise out of one of the four kingdoms which would be formed out of the Grecian monarchy after the death of its first king—is Antiochus Epiphanes; for the prophecy breaks off with the destruction of this prince (v. 25) after his insolent conduct had been previously most particularly depicted, which he would pursue both against God's people, and also against Heaven and the Lord of Heaven himself, whose daily offering he would hinder.

If, however, this is correct, it cannot well be doubted, as already (p. 197) remarked, although this is less generally acknowledged, that the same prince is intended:

(a) In ch. vii, by the little notable horn, which is there expressly explained of a king who would utter blasphemies against the Most High, would make war upon the saints, and think to alter (feast) times and laws. The description of this prince is so similar to that of Antiochus Epiphanes (ch. viii. 9, ff., 23, ff.; xi. 21, ff.), that it would not be permissible to refer it to any other personality than the one meant in these latter passages.[1] Here, also, to the destruction of this prince is immediately joined on the promise of a general Divine judgment, the appearance of the Messiah, and the establishment of His kingdom.

(b) In ch. ix, by the prince of whom it is told, in v. 27, that he would, for a half-week of years ($3\frac{1}{2}$ years), hinder the sacrifices and oblations; and this is also stated of Antiochus Epiphanes in the other visions.[2] Here, also, the prophecy breaks off with the death of the prince, and with the intimation that then the whole period would be elapsed which should elapse, conformably to Jeremiah's prophecy and according to Divine counsel, until the sins of the people should be atoned for, and the salvation destined for them should appear. There is, also, the phenomenon in all these visions, that the events and catastrophes in them are predicted with a surprising distinctness, and

[1] Delitzsch also acknowledges this, ut supra, p. 280.
[2] Now, even many of the defenders of the authenticity of the book partly allow that the reference is to Antiochus Epiphanes, thus Hofmann (Weissagung u. Erfüllung, i. 296, ff., Delitzsch, Reichel (Die 70 Jahreswochen Dan. ix. 24-27, in Theol. Stud. u. Krit. 1858).

that this is especially the case as to the time of the Ptolemies and Seleucidæ, and eminently so as to the period of the dominion of Antiochus Epiphanes, up to his death; but that after that time it is different, and that the prophecy either breaks off with his death, or assumes a more indistinct and more general character, the promise of the Messianic salvation for Jehovah's people being immediately annexed.

Under the supposition of Daniel's authorship of these visions, the above circumstances have a very extraordinary and perplexing air. Having to do with a seer who actually lived and wrote at the time of the Babylonian Captivity, as Daniel is here represented, we should expect that he would be much more likely to direct his prophetic glance to the liberation of his people from the then existing Babylonian slavery, than to their deliverance from the oppression of Antiochus Epiphanes, who belonged to a dynasty which did not come into power until centuries afterwards; and also that his Messianic hope and his prediction of Messianic salvation for his people should have been closely bound up with their return into the land of their fathers, as, e.g., in Jeremiah, Ezekiel, and Isaiah xl–lxvi. But nothing of this is mentioned in the visions of Daniel. This phenomenon, which is repeated in all the prophecies of the second part, presents the greatest difficulties, under a supposition of their genuineness, and cannot easily be explained in a natural way. The very same phenomenon leads us to fix the date of the composition of these visions in the age of the Maccabees, and, more exactly, at the time of Antiochus Epiphanes; for then, when Jehovah's people were suffering so grievously under the hand of this despotic prince, who sought in every way to hinder the worship of Jehovah, it was very natural that the pious should await with especial longing for the appearance of the salvation promised to their fathers by the mouth of the prophets; and it may easily be imagined that they would give way to the hope that their heavy oppression would soon come to an end, and that then the Messianic salvation would immediately appear. Thus, then, the way in which the Messianic hope is framed in these visions, and the connection into which it is brought with the preceding events and catastrophes, cannot be explained in a natural

Aim of the Author.

way, except by the supposition that they were composed in the age of Antiochus Epiphanes; not *before* the time when the Jewish people were still groaning under his tyranny, and the worship of Jehovah in the Temple was stopped by him, nor *after* a period immediately following his death.

At any long interval after this, the Messianic hope would no longer have retained this shape. It is, therefore, certainly wrong, when Bertholdt places the date of the last section in the middle of the age of the Maccabees.

§ 260.—*The Author's Aim in the second Division of the Book.*

The aim of the author is only to comfort and support his oppressed nation by an intimation of the nearness of deliverance, and of the salvation destined for them by God. His speaking in the person of Daniel is to be considered only as an appropriation on the part of the author, just as in Deuteronomy or in Ecclesiastes. An appropriation of this kind was by no means unfrequent in this age, both among the Greeks and Jews; where an author, who was convinced that he was in the possession of certain salutary truths, and yet that he did not enjoy a personal authority adequate to procure them the hearing he wished for, placed them in the mouth of some other wise men or prophets. This adoption of a name in our case is connected with the fact, that in the age of the Maccabees the spirit of independent prophecy had long departed from Israel, and the consciousness of this prevailed among the people (1 Macc. ix. 27; cf. ch. iv. 46, xiv. 41). The appropriation of the special name selected by this author brought with it the result that he is carried back with his prophecies to the Babylonian exile, in which he places Daniel, and takes his starting-point from thence; and it is thus very conceivable how he touches but cursorily on the times immediately following this point, and dwells far more in detail on those circumstances by which he himself was directly affected, those, namely, which were existing at the time of the composition, and those immediately preceding it.

An analogy can be found in Jewish literature of the same age, in the still extant so-called *Sibylline Oracles.* Among these there is no inconsiderable portion, viz., almost the whole of the third book, which may be shown in the most evident way (v. my *Abhandlung*, in Schleiermacher's, &c., *Theol. Zeitschrift*. Part 1, 2), to have been composed by a Jew, an Alexandrine, indeed, and also in the age of Antiochus Epiphanes, probably about 170–168 B.C. The overthrow of the then most considerable heathen monarchy is therein predicted, and Antiochus Epiphanes himself is threatened with destruction, from which prince the Egyptians were suffering much by his repeated invasions of their country, as also the Jews who were in it. A general upsetting of the then existing system of the world is spoken of as closely impending; and that God's people will then immediately extend their dominion over the whole earth for ever, under a king sent by God Himself; and idolatry, together with the ungodly, will be blotted out, and the true God will be everywhere worshipped, and that the quiet and happiness of men shall never more come to an end. These predictions, partly threatening, and partly containing promises of Messianic salvation, as they were, perhaps, at first intended for the Greeks round him, were by the Jewish composer placed in the mouth of the sibyls who were esteemed among them as prophetesses, and in conformity with this dressing up, descriptions of former kingdoms and events were brought forward as predicted by the sibyls.

There are other works with a similar assumption of Jewish or Judaico-Christian authors,—the Books of the *Sibylline Oracles*, written for the most part by Christian authors, the so-called *Fourth Book of Ezra*, the *Book of Enoch*, the *Ascensio Jesaiœ*, the *Testament of the Twelve Patriarchs*, &c. All these may be considered as more or less analogous to the visions of Daniel.

§ 261.—*Difficulties arising from Dan. ix. 2.*

I will mention one single passage (ch. ix. 2) in this second part, which also is not without difficulty, under the supposition of Daniel's authorship of it.

We are there told, that Daniel "understood by books" (בַּסְּפָרִים) the seventy years which, according to Jeremiah's prophecy, should be accomplished in the desolations of Jerusalem. The expression הספרים, as it here stands, can mean only a compilation, κατ' ἐξοχήν, of sacred books of canonical authority, and it is supposed that the prophecies of Jeremiah were already to be found in such a collection. This, however, cannot well have been at the time stated in the superscription of the vision, viz., in the first year of Darius the Mede, who, at any rate, must be placed before Cyrus. For at that time, the prophetical Scriptures were certainly not yet brought together into one collection, and still less were they united with the Pentateuch. For this very reason, also, we are led to fix a considerably later time for the composition.

It is also not very probable, that so early as the time indicated, doubt could exist in any of the Jews as to the actual sense of Jeremiah's seventy years, as Daniel intimates he felt; as, at that time, not even seventy single years had elapsed since the exile, and particularly after the destruction of Jerusalem, and until after the expiration of this period no one would readily entertain a doubt, that the number of years should be considered as anything more than so many common years. Not until the full expiration of seventy years and upwards since the utterance of the prophecy (Jer. xxv. 11, ff.; xxix. 10) and the destruction of the city, had a great part of the people returned to their homes, but the people then found themselves in so distressed a condition, that the feeling must have pervaded them, that the salvation, promised by God through the prophets, and so also by Jeremiah, had not yet appeared, and that therefore the prophecy had not yet been fulfilled according to its essential purport; not until then, could further thoughts as to the said seventy years have originated among the pious of the people, whether they were not to be understood in some other than the literal way, and by some mode of reckoning different from the usual one. Thus we may very easily imagine, that in the age of Antiochus Epiphanes, when Jehovah's people again fell into such grievous distress, their attention would be directed both to the predictions of other prophets, and also to Jeremiah's utterances as to the seventy years, and they would inquire whether they would not allow of an interpretation by which a correct, speedy, and complete fulfilment of the Divine promises contained in them might be hoped for. It is such an explanation as this, which is here placed in the mouth of the angel in the communication to Daniel, that the seventy years were at the point of expiring just at that very time, viz., the time of Antiochus Epiphanes, so that the last part of it would be taken to be the period during which the Jewish people and the sanctuary at Jerusalem were given up to the above foreign king, by which means the hope is intimated, that, at the expiration of the half week of years of Antiochus' tyranny, the time would arrive, when Jehovah would fulfil all His great promises to His people.

§ 262.—*Date of the Narrative—Greek names of Musical Instruments.*

If, however, the visions in the second division of the book were composed at the time assumed by us, the later composition of the narrative portion of the first half of the book follows also as a matter of course, for, as we have seen before (p. 200), both divisions had one and the same author. The nature of these sections make it very improbable, when considered by themselves, that they were composed by Daniel or any contemporary author. Against the idea of a contemporary authorship is the fact, that the names for the various musical instruments, which are repeatedly named in ch. iii, are almost entirely Greek, and at least many of them are such that it cannot well be assumed that the Babylonians and Greeks got them from a common source, or that the Greeks got them from the Babylonians; but there can be no doubt that they became known to the author through the Greeks either directly or indirectly.

Thus particularly סוּמְפֹּנְיָה (vv. 5, 15), or according to another reading, סִיפֹנְיָא (v. 10). Both are quite clearly the Greek συμφωνία, about the Greek origin of which there can be no doubt, for it is evidently composed of the Greek words σύν and φωνεῖν. It seems very strange when Hengstenberg, to prove that the word is not of Greek origin, appeals to the fact that the Chaldee corresponds to the Syriac ܩܣܕܒܐ, *tibia;* for there can be no doubt that the Syriac word also is derived from the Greek, as is the case in so many Syriac words. Also פְּסַנְתֵּרִין, ψαλτήριον, from ψάλλειν, ψάειν; קַתְרֹס, κίθαρις (from κίθαρος, *breast*); also סַבְּכָא = σαμβύκη.[1]

[1] The weakness and untenableness of these arguments derived from the names of musical instruments is exposed by Dr. Pusey, "Daniel the Prophet," pp. 24–30.—Tr.

It is but little likely, that the musical instruments of the Greeks with Greek names should have been in customary use at Nebuchadnezzar's court. For although some intercourse already existed at that age between the inhabitants of Upper Asia, and the Ionians in Asia Minor, the influence exercised on the former by the Greeks would not probably be of that nature, which such a fact would presuppose. It is likewise improbable, that Daniel or any other Jew of Palestine, of his age, should have become so familiar with the Greek instruments and their Greek names from any other source, that he would, as a matter of course, have employed those names instead of the names actually in use. We can far more easily conceive this being done by some Jewish author, in the age of Alexander's Hellenic successors, when Judæa was under the alternate dominion of the Ptolemies and Seleucidæ.

§ 263.—*Historical difficulties of the Narrative.*

Added to all this, there are many other *historical difficulties* presented by these sections, the purport of which we must consider as purely historical, if they were composed by Daniel. There is, generally, a very great difficulty in the circumstance, that the Chaldean and Median kings should not only have *themselves* acknowledged the Omnipotence of the God worshipped by the Jews, the God of Daniel and his companions, as the God who alone had power to deliver, and to work signs in heaven and earth, but that they should also have issued a royal edict to all the inhabitants of their vast empire, in which they commanded, as Nebuchadnezzar did, that no one should dare to utter a blasphemy against this God, and indeed went so far as to decree, as Darius did, that every one should fear and worship the God of Daniel.

The same difficulty appears here, as in the Book of Jonah, the contents of which, historically considered, involve the circumstances, that the Ninevites were *all of them* converted to the true God. Here also, in the succeeding history of these nations not the slightest trace of such an event can be discovered. An edict like this, especially from one of the Median kings, which, according to ch. vi. 9, could not be repealed even by the king himself, must have had some important results, either that it would be obeyed, or, as is certainly more to be expected, that it met with opposition; nothing, however, is known either of one state of things or the other, and even in the narrative itself there is not the least further intimation, as might well be expected.

Added to which, there are many things, which occasion difficulty in an historical respect, making it at least altogether improbable, that the narratives were composed as an historical account by an eye-witness and partaker in the events.

I will only mention some of them here:—

(1) In ch. i. 1, we are told that Nebuchadnezzar as king of Babylon captured Jerusalem[1] in the third year of Jehoiakim. But it can be shown, from Jeremiah and 2 Kings, that Nebuchadnezzar did not come to the throne until the fourth year of Jehoiakim (cf. p. 71, f.), and as the main point (from Jer. xxxvi. 9–29), that the Chaldeans themselves, in the ninth month of the fifth year of Jehoiakim, had not yet arrived at Jerusalem. It can also be shown, at least with probability, although less certainty, that, during the reign of Jehoiakim, they had neither captured the city generally nor carried away the sacred vessels of the temple, but that the first capture of the city by the Chaldeans did not take place until the reign of Jehoiachin (v. *Theol. Zeitschrift*, p. 280, ff.).

(2) From ch. ii. according to v. 1, Nebuchadnezzar must have had his dream in the second year of his reign. This does not agree with ch. i, in which Nebuchadnezzar is mentioned as king when the Jewish youths were carried away, but according to v. 5, these youths were educated for three years at the court of the king, and that during their stay there, the king discerned their great wisdom; but the interpretation of the dream in ch. ii, cannot, from the nature of the narratives, have occurred before the expiration of the period of education; and thus, the statement in ch. ii, if considered historically, produces great difficulty. It is, besides, almost incredible, that Nebuchadnezzar should

[1] This is a mis-statement on Bleek's part. It is not asserted, Dan. i. 1, that the king of Babylon *took* Jerusalem in the third year of Jehoiakim, but that he *besieged* it, and that the king and part of the sacred vessels —nothing is said about the city—were given into his hands. "The mention that, not Jerusalem, but Jehoiakim, fell into the hands of Nebuchadnezzar rather implies that the city was not taken then."— Pusey, *ut supra*, p. 397.—Tr.

have sent such a summons, as is here described, to all the wise men of his land of various classes, not only to explain to him his dream, but also previously to state to him the purport of the same, and that he should have punished them *all* with death for their inability to comply with his demand, and not *those* merely whose peculiar vocation it was to interpret dreams. It is also difficult to imagine, that so zealous a worshipper of Jehovah, as Daniel appears to have been, should have undertaken the office of chief governor over the wise men and magi (ch. ii. 48)[1]; for their institutions were certainly bound up with the Babylonian idolatry. *Chaldeans*, also, who are here mentioned among others as a peculiar class of wise men, according to *Herodot.* i. 181, 183, and Diodor. *Sic.* i. 24, 29, was the name of the most important priests of the land; none therefore could easily hold such an office as that of chief governor of the wise men and magi, without being an entire partaker in the idolatry of the land.

(3) Ch. iii. 1–30.—In this passage, it seems very improbable, that so monstrous a *golden* image of sixty cubits long, should have been set up in the open plain. It is also surprising, that nothing at all is mentioned in it as to what became of Daniel on the occasion of the dedication of the image, for the chief governor of the establishment of magi, especially from his connection with the priesthood, certainly could not have been absent on such an occasion.

(4) Chapter iv. 1–*fin.*—Nebuchadnezzar's seven years' madness. An event like this must have brought with it considerable change and complication in the Babylonian empire; and it could not well have been omitted to be mentioned by historians, although they may have abridged the account of the reign of this prince. Nevertheless, except in this book, no one says anything about it. Berosus, the Chaldean historian, can have mentioned nothing whatever about it, as may be clearly observed from what Josephus has taken from him. Josephus himself relates the matter, only following the Book of Daniel; and Origen and Jerome, notwithstanding all the trouble they

---

[1] See Pusey, *ut supra*, pp. 421–424. Daniel " is not called Rab-mag, chief of the Magi; but is simply said to have been *head of the sayans* (*or governors*) *over all the wise men of Babylon*, perhaps a sort of minister of public instruction."—Tr.

took, could find nothing in any historian which pointed to such an event. The idea that Nebuchadnezzar's letter, addressed to all nations, in which the whole occurrence is set forth as a narrative, was not actually written by him, is corroborated by the circumstance that, in the middle of it, the epistolary form is relinquished for a time, and Nebuchadnezzar is spoken of in the third person (*vv.* 28–33), but both before and after it in the first person. This could hardly have happened to Nebuchadnezzar himself, as the writer of the letter, but easily to some one else writing such a letter in his name.[1]

(5) Chapter v.—This narrative, if taken as purely historical, presents considerable difficulty, because in it so many things are crowded together into one night, that it is scarcely credible that they should have followed one after the other within so short a period. First, the banquet, which appears to have lasted some little time before the king ordered the sacred vessels of the Jews to be fetched, and a still longer time before the hand showed itself writing on the wall. Then the summons to all the wise men, astrologers, Chaldeans, and soothsayers, and their consultations as to the purport of the writing, in the investigation of which they must certainly have consumed a considerable time before they acknowledged their ignorance; next the summons to Daniel, which took place at the queen's advice—as to which it is difficult to understand why he, as chief governor over all the wise men, had not been sent for at first. Then Daniel's interpretation of the writing; and immediately on this, notwithstanding the interpretation predicted such misfortunes for the king, and the latter could not yet tell whether it was correct or not, follows Daniel's clothing with purple and a chain, and the proclamation of the latter as the third ruler in the kingdom; and, finally, Belshazzar's death, according to the express statement, in that same night. It is also not without difficulty that Darius, a king of the Median race, follows Belshazzar as king; which Darius is (ch. ix. 1; xi. 1) designated as a Mede, and in ch. ix. 1, as son of Ahasuerus, *i.e.*, Xerxes. He is, therefore, a prince of another (the Median) dynasty, and it appears to be represented that this dynasty commenced after the destruction

[1] *See* Pusey, *ut supra*, pp. 425-433, 437-439.—Tr.

of the Chaldæo-Babylonian dominion generally. There is, indeed, always a question on this point, whether, after the overthrow of the Chaldean dominion, Babylon fell to the Median dynasty first, or immediately to the Persian. In favour of the former opinion, beside some others, is Xenoph., *Cyrop.* i. 5, 2, and also Josephus, *Ant.* x. 11, 4, according to whom Cyrus conquered Babylon for his father-in-law, Cyaxares II., son of Astyages, and attained to an independent rule only after his death. We must, therefore, look upon Darius, the Median, as being this Cyaxares; and the author of our book has certainly considered that, after the overthrow of the Babylonian monarchy, first a Median and then a Persian dominion flourished. But, not only *Herodot.* i. 130, and Ktesias, but also Isaiah xl. ff., lead to the idea that Cyrus conquered Babylon as an independent prince, the supremacy being at that time made over by the Medians to the Persians (as to this v. Lengerke, *Einleitung*, on ch. v).

(6) Chapter vi.—There is a peculiar difficulty occasioned here, besides that arising from the contents of Darius's edict, *v.* 25, ff., to all nations of the earth (*v.* p. 213), by the circumstance that the princes and satraps of the Babylonian empire all appear as if living for a considerable time in the city of Babylon, indeed, with their families (according to *v.* 24). It is, however, scarcely credible that king Darius should have issued an edict like this to all his subjects, as is previously related, forbidding them, under pain of death, for a whole month to offer prayer to any man or god. There is also something very surprising in the way in which the den of lions is here spoken of; the author appears to have imagined the same as a hollowed-out receptacle, which was under the ground, coming to a point at the top, which might be closed up with a stone (*v.* 18). In reality, the lions' den could not have been like this; in such subterranean pits, without air and light, the lions could not have lived long.[1]

---

[1] Such a paltry argument as this is unworthy of our author, generally so fair and judicious. In our complete ignorance of the construction of the den, such an objection weakens instead of strengthening his case. See Pusey, *ut supra*, pp. 415–417.—Tr.

§ 264.—*The real Object of the Historical Section of the Book.*

The nature of the first division, considered by itself, shows, therefore, that these narratives could not well have been composed by Daniel or any contemporary author, and very slightly opposes the assumption to which we were led by their similarity to the second division, that they were written by the same author as the visions—not, therefore, until the time of Antiochus Epiphanes. If we take this view, the question arises as to the *end* the author had in view in this part of his work. As to this, we might consider that an historical tendency is intended: that the author sought to collect together, as an historical introduction to the visions which follow it, all that he could ascertain, either from other works or through oral tradition, as to the history of Daniel, in whose mouth he wished to place his prophetical hopes in the visions. But yet, in this case, he would have had no inducement to relate the history of Daniel's three companions, when it was not closely connected with that of Daniel himself; but in *one* section, ch. iii. they alone are spoken of, without Daniel being at all mentioned. Added to this, if the author had intended these narratives to be really historical, we must necessarily expect that he would have placed the separate narratives in some sort of connection with one another, by forms of transition at least, and would have somehow knit them together in an historical whole. This, however, is by no means the case. If they are historically intended, we should also expect, (*a*) that the author would have given some intimation in ch. iii. how it happened that, when Nebuchadnezzar commanded all the officials of his empire to assemble together at the dedication and setting up of the golden image, Daniel had nothing to do with it, who was, however, at the king's court; and (*b*) that, at the end of ch. vi, he would have given some intimation as to the subsequent destinies of Daniel, and as to his death.

If we are now induced to seek out some other aim in these narratives than a really historical one, we shall find that this, as regards the four last sections (ch. iii–vi), can have been at first only an *hortatory* one; and we are entitled to assume this by the whole character of these narratives, particularly by the existing conclusion of them;

and the aim which we assume, is indeed one which bears an exact and special reference to the circumstances of the time at which these narratives were composed. If we consider these circumstances, we can have no doubt that the author had in view, by setting forth the examples of Daniel and his three companions, on the one hand, and Nebuchadnezzar and Belshazzar, on the other, to exhort his fellow-countrymen and contemporaries to imitate their inflexible, courageous faith, shown in the open, daring confession of their fathers' God, and to point out that this only true, almighty God will, in due time, know how to humble and overthrow those who, like Antiochus Epiphanes, have opposed Him in their presumptuous arrogance, and have endeavoured to render His people faithless to His worship, and also, on the other hand, to afford to His own true, steadfast worshippers the final victory. Thus, essentially the same aim prevails in these narrative sections, as in the visions which follow them. By the assumption of an aim like this, to which the purport of these narratives is so unmistakeably adapted, the disconnection and individual completeness of the several narratives does not appear at all surprising; for his hortatory aim does not depend upon showing any connection between the separate histories, as without that, each taken separately would be able to make clearly prominent (as is, in fact, the case) those truths which the author had in view to make manifest.

§ 265.—*Similarities in the Narrative to Events of a later Date.*

Even allowing this hortatory intention in these narratives (ch. iii–vi), it certainly may still be the case that they are historical at least as regards their essence. But, on the other hand, we have before ascertained how difficult it is to consider them as historical as regards their chief points; and by this we are in some measure entitled to presume that the author freely handled the traditionary materials he met with according to the subject-matter, as best suited his hortatory aim. We are confirmed in this opinion by perceiving to how great an extent the events set forth in these narratives as belonging to the time of the Babylonian Captivity, correspond sometimes, even in detail, with the events and circumstances which took place in the land of Judæa under Antiochus Epiphanes' oppression. If we transport ourselves into the spirit and circumstances of these days, particularly by reading the Books of Maccabees, we shall find that the author, in his descriptions in ch. iii–vi, has had before his eyes, almost everywhere, both as a whole and in details, these very circumstances of his time and country, and has set them before his readers in a mode which, though disguised, could be easily understood by them.

Thus the narrative, ch. iii. 1–30, reminds us of the attempt of Antiochus Epiphanes to force the Greek *cultus* on the Jews: 1 Macc. i. 43, ff.

He dedicated the Temple at Jerusalem to Jupiter Olympius (2 Macc. vi. 2), and caused the altar of burnt offering there to be prepared as a heathen altar, and built on it a smaller idol-altar in the year 145 ær., Seleuc., 167 B.C. (1 Macc. i. 54), in doing which he no doubt caused a statue to be erected of the God to whom the Temple was dedicated (cf. Dan xii. 11; xi. 31; ix. 27). After that, he used every exertion to compel the Jews to observe this Greek cultus, and those who were obstinate he tortured and put to death, sometimes by means of fire: *v.* 1 Macc. i. 29–63; 2 Macc. vi, vii; Dan. xi. 33. The first readers of our book, particularly of ch. iii, must have been induced almost spontaneously to think of the events then taking place round them, and it may be assumed with the greatest probability, that the author composed this narrative as a parabolic representation, intended to set forth to his fellow-countrymen the example which they should follow in the steadfast rejection of all participation in idolatry, and also to stir up in them the hope that, if they maintained themselves constantly faithful, and preferred to bear patiently all that could be done to them, rather than show even an outward veneration for the idols to whom their temple was dedicated, Jehovah would at last deliver them, and so visibly afford them His assistance, that even their despisers, who persecuted them on account of their faith, would be compelled to acknowledge His power; cf. *vv.* 17, 18, 28, 29, where this hortatory and also prophetic tendency is most clearly shown.

If this reference of the narratives in Daniel is the correct one, they must probably have been written not long after the dedication of the altar of burnt offering in the Temple at Jerusalem to the worship of Jupiter. In this way also are the Greek names for the musical instruments in our narrative best explained.

It is not probable that these instruments and their Greek names should have been in common use among the Jews themselves, so that the Jewish author could have derived them from this source. There is, on the contrary, every probability that they were in use at the court and in the army of the Seleucidæ, particularly of Antiochus Epiphanes, who followed Greek customs in all his arrangements. And it may be, perhaps, supposed that the dedication of the Temple of Jerusalem to the worship of Jupiter took place in a solemn manner, with processions and music, just as the subsequent re-dedication of the temple was performed by Judas Maccabæus with singing and music, with citherns, harps, and cymbals (1 Macc. iv. 54), and we may thus conjecture that at the former solemnity just such Grecian instruments were used, and that our author got their names in this way.

In ch. vi. also the case is similar. It certainly is, as already remarked, scarcely credible that a prince should have allowed himself to be persuaded into making so foolish and impracticable an enactment as is here told of Darius the Median, a king who is otherwise altogether unknown to us, at least under this name. But the first readers of the narrative, at the time of Antiochus Epiphanes, would certainly be led, without further question, to attribute it to the latter prince, of whom we read that, after he had captured Jerusalem by surprise, he issued an edict to the whole of his empire, to the effect that they should all be one people, and that every one should give up their νόμιμα; who also endeavoured to compel the Jews to relinquish their ancestral law, and no longer to appeal to Jehovah, the God of their fathers (1 Macc. i. 41 ; 2 Macc. vi. 1–9). We may well imagine that the author, in order the better to show forth the perversity and wickedness of such an attempt, might have represented in a parabolic narrative, as is done here, that it was an attempt on the part of the king to direct to his own person only all worship and prayer.

But the tendency of the narrative is here again both

hortatory and, at the same time, prophetical. The author seeks, by Daniel's example, to encourage his countrymen to give themselves up to the most evident danger of death rather than become unfaithful to the worship of their fathers' God, or even only conceal this worship. For this purpose he brings forward prominently how, notwithstanding the rigorous edict of the king, Daniel did not omit to make his prayer punctually to his God, and did it without any concealment at the open window, whilst he might have been able to avoid the threatened danger if he had prayed in secret (cf. the corresponding conduct of the aged Eleazar at the time of Antiochus Epiphanes, 2 Macc. vi. 18–31). But, at the same time, the author also strives, in the course of his narrative, to confirm the faithful in the confidence, that if they held steadfast to the acknowledgment of their God, without denying or even concealing their faith, He would not forsake them, and would make the worship of His name victorious, and acknowledged even by His opponents.

§ 266.—*Typical References to Antiochus Epiphanes.*

These narratives have, therefore, essentially the same aim as the visions in the second division of the book. The same remark applies to the two narratives between, in ch. iv–v, only that they have more of a threatening character as regards the unbelieving who, in their insolent haughtiness, oppose the only true, almighty God.

Both in Nebuchadnezzar, in ch. iv. and in Belshazzar, in ch. v, the author has, doubtless, had Antiochus Epiphanes distinctly in view. This is peculiarly manifest in the latter narrative, in ch. v. In this, the reader at the time of Antiochus Epiphanes would be naturally led to imagine that this prince was being depicted, of whom it is told as something most wicked, that he broke into the Temple at Jerusalem and with unclean hands carried away the golden basins, cups, goblets, and other sacred vessels (1 Macc. i. 21, ff.; 2 Macc. v. 15, ff.). The author, doubtless, intended to point out the wickedness of this profanation of holy things, and by Belshazzar's fate to represent to the Syrian prince the Divine judgment which threatened him for such impiety. This reference would be still clearer if it had happened—which is not expressly told, but still is not in itself improbable—that the holy vessels had been used by Antiochus Epiphanes or his servants at common entertainments, or the sacrificial feasts in honour of the Greek divinities.

In the composition, also, of Nebuchadnezzar's letter in ch. iv. the author's aim, doubtless, is to show to Antiochus Epiphanes, as in a mirror, by the fate of that mighty Chaldean prince who had destroyed Jerusalem and the Temple, whither his haughty presumption against the Most High, the King of Kings, was leading him, and how necessary it was for him to acknowledge with penitence His power and sublimity if he wished to escape the heaviest Divine punishment (v. ch. iv. 14, 22–24, 29, 31, f., 34).

This exact reference of these narratives to the circumstances surrounding the author must, however, make it more and more improbable that they were founded on actual matters of fact occurring at the time of the Babylonian exile. Nevertheless, it might have been the case that certain events in the history of the Chaldean and Median monarchy may have floated across the author's mind, but they could have been nothing but isolated matters which he, perhaps, followed; and we must still assume that everything that he met with was made use of by him in a perfectly arbitrary way suitably to his aim and end, and that he absolutely had no actual historical purpose. We cannot, therefore, make use of these narratives to increase and correct our knowledge of the Babylonian and Median empires, and to introduce us to the spirit and circumstances of those days which they *appear* to treat of. They may, however, well assist in giving us a vivid picture of the state of things among the Jews at the time of Antiochus Epiphanes, and especially of the courageous faith which the more pious of the people then showed, and of the hopes which they entertained.

§ 267.—*Author's Aim in the two first Chapters.*

We have now still to consider the *two first* chapters, and, in the first place, ch. ii. The author's point in view in this is certainly not to do honour to Daniel for his skill in the interpretation of dreams, for this is only a secondary consideration in the story. The chief point is evidently the purport of Nebuchadnezzar's dream, and its reference to the future. The end of it is the everlasting kingdom to be established by God, the Messianic kingdom, before which all other kingdoms shall disappear. This is symbolized by a stone cut out without human instrumentality. The establishment of the kingdom is here also bound up with the same circumstances as those in the visions in ch. vii, ff.

It has been already remarked that this dream of Nebuchadnezzar's in ch. ii. offers a great similarity to that of Daniel's in ch. vii, and that, without doubt, the consecutive kingdoms in both of them are to be interpreted in a corresponding way. If, therefore, according to our preceding remarks, as to ch. vii, Antiochus Epiphanes is, without doubt, to be considered as the little notable horn, then the fourth beast, devouring and breaking in pieces the whole earth, having ten horns, between which this lesser horn stood up, can be intended only for Alexander the Great's empire and the empires of his successors proceeding out of it; and this leaves no doubt that in ch. ii. also we must look upon the fourth kingdom corresponding to the iron thighs, which, like iron, breaks everything to pieces, as the empire of Alexander the Great; also in its feet and toes, partly iron and partly clay, which is explained by the divided kingdoms, partly weak and partly strong, among Alexander's successors.[1] The establishment of the Messianic kingdom is then subjoined to these empires, of which we are told that they shall mix with one another in race (by affinity), but shall never be united. In this it was most natural for the Jews to refer it to the Ptolemies and Seleucidæ, under whose dominion they were alternately subject.

For the same reasons which were brought forward in regard to the visions of Daniel (ch. vii–xii), we may now assume that this framing of the dream belongs to the age of the Ptolemies and Seleucidæ, and if we consider what has gone before, we shall be warranted in attributing its form to the author of the book. So also we may assume that the whole narrative was not related by him as he received it from tradition, but was arbitrarily shaped out to suit his hortatory aim, so as to comfort and maintain his

[1] Delitzsch even allows this. Besides, cf. *Jahrbuch für deutsche Theol.* p. 57, ff. [See, in opposition to this, Pusey, *ut supra*, § ii.]

people in the time of their affliction by the statement of his prophetical hope of the near approach of deliverance, and of the appearance of the kingdom of the Messiah.

Finally, as regards the first chapter, the chief aim is, at all events, to serve as an introduction to what follows, both to the remaining sections of the narrative and also to Daniel's visions. Here also, however, a certain hortatory aim may be perceived which relates distinctly to the circumstances which existed at the time of the composition. When the author brings so prominently forward, how Daniel and his companions kept themselves, even at the court of a heathen king, free from all uncleanness as regards meat and drink, and for this purpose partook of no flesh-meat and wine, but only vegetable food, pulse and water, and that God had turned this to their peculiar blessing, he certainly had in view to exhort his fellow-countrymen under similar circumstances, when they were in danger of being defiled by the enjoyment of meat and wine, to observe a like conduct, and to be willing to entirely abstain from them. There was a peculiar inducement for an admonition like this in the land of Judæa during the dominion of Antiochus Epiphanes, when sacrifices were offered to the Grecian divinities all over the land and even in the Temple at Jerusalem, and when the Jewish inhabitants might easily have happened to eat and drink the flesh and wine which had been made use of in the offerings and libations to idols; for we also read that at this time zealous worshippers of Jehovah, such as Judas Maccabæus and others, carefully guarded themselves from pollution by means of food, and, that they might not incur the danger of being defiled, subsisted constantly on vegetables. (2 Macc. v. 27 ; cf. 1 Macc. i. 62, ff.)

§ 268.—*Historical Existence of Daniel and his Companions.*

It would of course be quite in accordance with all that has gone before, that Daniel and his three companions should have been historical personages, Jewish exiles, who were distinguished in Babylon by their piety and wisdom, and had even attained to favour and esteem with the rulers of the country; and this is assumed by most of those scholars who date the composition of the book in a later age, and look upon the details of it as unhistorical. It is, however, questionable if there be any adequate sanction for this assumption. A special proof of the actual existence of Daniel is found in Ezekiel xiv. 14, 20, and xxviii. 3, where this prophet makes mention of a Daniel in a very laudatory way. But the way in which this is done is not without difficulty. In both passages Ezekiel's principal aim is not to praise and magnify Daniel particularly, but it is clear that he mentions him, because, like Noah and Job, between whom he is named in ch. xiv. 14, 20, he might be supposed to be well known to his readers and to the king of Tyre himself as a man distinguished by his wisdom and righteousness. But, by the way in which he is mentioned, we are not induced to look upon him as a man who was living at the same time as Ezekiel in the Babylonian exile and at the time of Ezekiel's utterances, could not have been of very mature years, but far rather as some long well-known personage of past ages; he may, therefore, have been some historical person, who had been influential in the history of the Israelitish people, or, like Job, more of a poetical character. which is perhaps more probable, as we know nothing of him from any other source. From the way in which Ezekiel mentions him, it is scarcely credible that he should have been a Jewish exile contemporary with Ezekiel, as the Daniel of our book appears to have been.[1]

But, on the other hand, we are induced by the way in which Ezekiel mentions Daniel on account of his righteousness and wisdom, to consider that he was speaking of a man equally as distinguished for virtue and wisdom, as Daniel appears in the book we are discussing, and also to conjecture that there must have been some connection between the character appearing in this book, and the man whom Ezekiel had in view. It may, perhaps, be assumed with probability, that Ezekiel was acquainted with some older work which treated of one Daniel as a man distinguished both by his legal piety, and his profound wisdom, but yet afforded no precise details as to the age in which he flourished. This book, however, was perhaps early lost, during

[1] I have pointed this out in the *Theol. Zeitschrift*, p. 283, ff.; and I do not believe that the things I there brought forward have been at all set aside by the opposing remarks of Hengstenberg, *ut supra*, p. 70, ff., and Hävernick, *Einleit.* ii. 2, p. 455.

the Babylonian Captivity, or soon after it; at any rate, it was not extant at the time of the composition of our book; and thus, nothing more distinct was known about Daniel to the author of the book and his contemporaries than could be deduced from these passages in Ezekiel. He might thus use the utmost freedom in dealing with his history in his parabolic narratives, just as best agreed with his hortatory aim.

His chief reason, perhaps, for placing his narratives at the time of the Babylonian Captivity, was, that at this time, when the Jewish nation were in a foreign land, without a temple or sacrificial service, and, living surrounded by heathen, were so easily induced to partake in their idolatry, the greatest similarity was offered to his own age, and the best opportunity was given him for making Daniel and his companions appear and show their faith under circumstances similar to those in which the pious Jews were placed in the days of Antiochus Epiphanes. Something else, however, may very feasibly have had its influence on Daniel being placed in the Babylonian exile, viz., the person mentioned by Ezekiel being confounded with some later Daniel, who was one of the Jews in exile.

An exile named Daniel actually occurs, but as a contemporary of Ezra and Nehemiah,—a priest of the family of Ithamar. He was one of the exiles who returned with Ezra from Babylon to Judæa (Ezra viii. 2), and is subsequently mentioned as one of the priests who, at the reading out of the Mosaical law by Ezra, solemnly pledged themselves to observe the same, by signing their names (Neh. x. 7). It is curious that there are also named, as contemporaries of this Daniel, a *Mishael, Hananiah*, and *Azariah;* the two latter, the same as Daniel, as among the priests and chief men who pledged themselves to the maintenance of the law (Neh. x. 3, 24), and Mishael, as one of those who stood by the side of Ezra while he was reading out the law (*ib.* viii. 4). This coincidence of names with those of the heroes of the faith appearing in our book may have been accidental, but still it is remarkable that it occurs in reference to *all four*, and Daniel and Mishael are names which are seldom met with. Of course the age of these four contemporaries of Ezra and Nehemiah is a later one than that of Daniel and his friends in our book, as the period from the third year of Jehoiakim to Ezra's reading out the Book of the Law would be about 160 years. But, nevertheless, the supposition is a reasonable one, that the author of the Book of Daniel derived the names of his heroes from these four men. Whether he was further acquainted with any particulars of their history and adventures in Babylon, we know not. But at all events, we may perhaps assume that, when he makes Daniel so distinguished both for his piety, and also especially for his wisdom, he must have had floating across his mind some idea of that Daniel previously mentioned by Ezekiel in so laudatory a manner.

There is, however, something very improbable and unfounded in the suppositions of Ewald, (a) that the Daniel spoken of by Ezekiel was perhaps a descendant from the kingdom of the ten tribes, who lived at the heathen court of Nineveh (similarly also Bunsen, *Gott in der Geschichte*, i. 514, ff.); and (b) that the author of our book was acquainted with and made use of a work of Alexander's age or of the time succeeding him, wherein prophetical utterances as to the kingdoms of the world were placed in the mouth of the above Daniel referred to by Ezekiel and living in exile in Assyria. The explanation as to the origin of our book is in no way facilitated by an assumption of this sort, but is, on the contrary, rendered more difficult.

Hitzig's opinion is also quite unjustifiable,—that the book was written in Egypt, by the high priest Onias IV., who also wrote Isaiah xix. 16-25.

§ 269.—*Value of the Book.*

If, however, the opinion as to the Book of Daniel here developed were generally acknowledged, it would of course lose something of the position which it filled, owing to the accepted idea of its composition by Daniel, in the history of Old-Testament prophecy. But it would still retain no slight significance in the Canon of the Old Testament. Not only does it teach us to realize in an eminently distinct way the spirit of the age to which it belongs, and also the courageous faith and trust in God of the pious, amid the severest afflictions and persecutions, but it is also of no slight importance in a Messianic point of view, for it shows us how the Messianic hope was still clung to, after the conclusion of the actually prophetic age, and the shape that it took, at an epoch of which on this point at least we have no further information in any other part of the Old-Testament Canon. And thus, even after this book had doubtless fulfilled its immediate purpose of strengthening and confirming the faithful ones among the Jewish people at the time of the tyranny of Antiochus Epiphanes, it has also had no inconsiderable influence in after ages, not only in the maintenance, but also in the wider development of the Messianic idea, as we may also see particularly in the New Testament.

THE POETICAL BOOKS.

THE PSALMS.

§ 270.—*Title—Division into five Books.*

THIS book forms a collection of 150 songs of various purport, all of them, however, coinciding in their prevailingly religious character. This collection may be compared with our hymn-books, and we must consider that its aim is similar to that of the latter, and that the originators of the collection intended to provide a book of religious songs, suitable for use both in song and prayer, both by the community generally and also by single persons in all the various circumstances of life: for edification, for confirmation in faith and trust in God, for penitence, and for praise.

The title of this book is in the Hebrew Canon, תְּהִלִּים, a plural-form, not used elsewhere, from תְּהִלָּה, *praise*, therefore *a song of praise to God, Hymnus* (thus in the superscription to Ps. cxlv); also in the contracted form תִּלִּים, or תִּלִּין. This designation of *songs of praise* is selected *à parte potiore*; as is the case with the designation, תְּפִלּוֹת דָּוִד, in the conclusion of Psalm lxxii. The usual Greek name ψαλμοί, is a more suitable one, which designates them as lyric poems which were sung with the accompaniment of music. To the Greek ψαλμοί corresponds the term מִזְמוֹר, which occurs in the superscription of a considerable number of psalms. In some other of their superscriptions we find the general designation שִׁיר, *song*, which is often joined with מִזְמוֹר; and there are various other names for different psalms. The term ψαλτήριον, *Psalterium*, occurs in Greek and Latin.

The whole collection is divided into five books (סֵפֶר): (1) i–xli; (2) xlii–lxxii; (3) lxxiii–lxxxix; (4) xc–cvi; (5) cvii–cl. At the end of each of the four first books there is a doxology of one or two verses, which, in the numbering of the verses, belongs to the Psalm preceding— the last of each book—but still does not form a part of it, and only serves to conclude the book in a way worthy of its contents, and to separate it from what follows, e.g., Ps. xli. 14: "Blessed be Jehovah the God of Israel from everlasting, and to everlasting. Amen, Amen," and similarly at the conclusion of the second, third, and fourth books. These doxologies are found in the LXX and all ancient translations, which speaks for the antiquity of this division into books, which is probably of the same age as the entire collection in its present extent, and perhaps as Epiphanius (*De Mens. et Pond.* c. 5) thinks, was chosen as an imitation of the fivefold division of the Torah.

§ 271.—*Origin—Superscriptions.*

As regards the *origin* of the book, the two first books are, as already remarked, styled *Prayers of David* at the end of the second book, after the doxology. Many persons have considered all the songs, not only of the two first books, but of the whole collection, to be songs of David, an idea of which Clauss[1] was the latest advocate, but which scarcely needs refutation, as the superscriptions of no inconsiderable number of these songs name other persons as their authors. About two-thirds of the Psalms are provided with superscriptions referring to their authors, and the author is most generally indicated in them by the prefix ל, e.g., לְדָוִד, or מִזְמוֹר לְדָוִד, or לְ־מִזְמוֹר, and the like. In some cases the ל, has another signification, e.g., certainly in Ps. xxxix. 1, where יְדוּתוּן indicates the choir to whom the song was assigned for musical performance. In two instances it perhaps points out the person for whom the song was originally composed, e.g., probably Ps. lxxii, perhaps also Ps. xx, xxi, cx. In these latter cases, however, it is not quite certain it was thus intended by the author. At any rate, these are only isolated exceptions, and in by far most cases there can be no doubt that it is intended to point out the composer.

But it is more questionable what authority is due to the superscriptions. Theodorus of Mopsuestia[2] considered them to be of later origin; many modern interpreters,[3] also, not

[1] *Beiträge zur Kritik u. Exegese der Psalmen.* Berlin, 1831.
[2] In Leontius Byzantin., *Contra Nestor. et Eutych.* lib. iii. n. 15.
[3] Thus particularly, De Wette (*Commentar über die Pss.* 1811, Edit. 5, by G. Baur, 1856; and *Einleitung*); Hitzig (*Die Pss.* 2 vols. 1835-36); Ewald, J. Olshausen (*Die Psalmen*, 1853).

only look upon them as not genuine, and not prefixed by the authors themselves, but attribute to them no authority at all. It cannot be denied that, in many Psalms the statements in the superscriptions as to the author or the accounts that are given in some as to the occasion for the song, do not at all agree with the contents, so that in these cases they must be unmistakeably incorrect, and could not have proceeded from the authors themselves, e.g., Ps. lix, cxxii, cxliv, &c. In these cases the superscriptions may, of course, have been prefixed by later transcribers or compilers from some incorrect tradition or hypothesis; and it is certainly a mistake, when some modern scholars[1] assume the correctness of all the superscriptions, which sometimes causes a necessity for most unnatural explanations. But, on the other hand, I believe that it is going too far, to think that on this account they must all be rejected in a mass, without further question. In many of the superscriptions we may conclude from their whole character, that they are of very high antiquity, because events and circumstances are therein referred to and presupposed as well known, which in our Old-Testament Books are either not mentioned generally, or told in a somewhat different way.

Thus, Psalm vii. is called in the superscription a song, which David sang in reference to a Benjamite named Cush, who was probably one of David's opponents at the court of Saul, who, however, is not named anywhere else in the Old Testament. This circumstance is a direct assurance of the high antiquity, and also of the correctness of the statement.

Psalm lx, according to the superscription, falls in the time of David's wars (2 Sam. viii; 1 Chron. xviii), but the Psalm affords several variations from the statements in these historical books; easy enough to explain, but serving as proof that the author of the superscription did not have these books before his eyes, and therefore as an evidence of high antiquity.

There is nothing improbable in the circumstance that the Hebrew composers themselves, when writing or delivering their songs, should have given their names or the

[1] Thus Hengstenberg (*Commentar über die Psalmen.* 4 vols. 1842-1847, 2nd Edit. 1849-1852); Tholuck (*Uebersetzung und Auslegg. der Psalmen*, 1843), Keil.

occasions for which they were composed, as this is quite usual among the Arabian poets, and was at least often the case among the Hebrew prophets.

Among compositions of another kind, *Hezekiah's Song of Praise* (Is. xxxviii), must particularly be considered. This has a superscription in v. 9, which is so abrupt and so little worked into the narrative itself, that in no way could it have been prefixed by the author of Is. xxxvi–xxxix, but must have been found by him already annexed to the song, which serves to prove that it must have been prefixed either by Hezekiah himself, or at least at a very early date, soon after the composition of the song.

Even when the superscriptions were not prefixed by the authors themselves, we may in general venture to suppose that it was done subsequently, not on a purely arbitrary hypothesis, but in conformity with some well considered tradition.

In some cases the songs were in circulation singly, before they came into this collection; and then it was natural that some tradition as to their author and occasion should accompany their use, and thus this statement was prefixed by some reader, copier, or compiler. The songs of the various composers were, however, frequently brought together previously in separate collections, and these were perhaps arranged by the composers themselves; there was, for instance, a collection of David's songs, of Asaph's, &c. From these the separate songs were adopted into this mixed collection, and the author's statement, which stood at the beginning of each separate collection, was prefixed to the several songs, perhaps in exactly the same words. Even then the superscriptions must have no small weight with us, although, in their present form and in their present positions, they may not have proceeded from the authors themselves.

Although it cannot be asserted of any of the superscriptions that, in and by themselves, they afford any adequate security for their correctness, still we have good cause to attribute some weight to their statements; and if a consideration of the contents and character of the Psalm does not discover anything which is in contradiction to the superscription, we have no reason to be so sceptical as to their statements as many expositors have been.

234   *Origin of the several Books—The Psalms.*

§ 272.—*The Authors of the various Psalms.*

The most ancient of those who are named in the superscriptions, as the authors of certain psalms, is *Moses*, to whom Ps. xc. is attributed. There is no adequate reason for denying to the lawgiver the authorship of this Psalm, and, at all events, it bears the stamp of very great antiquity.

Many of the Psalms, seventy-three in all, are designated as *of David*, mostly in the two first books, only eighteen of them being in the following ones. In some of them, the לְדָוִד may perhaps mean, *for David, in reference to him* (xx, xxi, cx). Among the rest there are several, which very probably,—as partly shown by their contents and historical relations, and partly by their language and other characteristics,—may belong to some other composer, as certainly Ps. xiv, liii, cviii, cxxii, cxxiv, cxliv; also, perhaps, iv, xxiii, xxv, xxvi, xxviii, xxix, xxxi, xxxviv, xxxvii, xl, lviii, lix, lxxxvi, ciii, cxxxi, cxxxiii, cxxxix, cxliii, cxlv. The character of many is such, that there is nothing in them decidedly opposing the statement of the superscription, nor anything peculiarly to confirm it. But no inconsiderable number, most probably, belong to David, and especially, we cannot doubt from all that we are told of him as a poet in the historical books, that he distinguished himself by the composition of such songs as our Psalms, and we may therefore suppose, with all probability, that many of his songs have been preserved in our collection, as may be asserted of several with tolerable certainty, as Ps. iii, vii, xv, xviii, xxxii, li, lv, lx, lxi, lxiii, &c.

Solomon is twice named in the superscriptions, in Ps. lxxii, cxxvii. In Ps. lxxii, לִשְׁלֹמֹה is perhaps intended to signify *ad Salamonem.* the song, however, was probably not composed for Solomon, but for one of his later successors; and with a still greater probability, the Ps. cxxvii. belongs to a considerably later date, and in this case the superscription is wanting in the LXX.

There are, besides, twelve Psalms imputed to *Asaph*— Ps. l, lxxiii–lxxxiii. Asaph is often mentioned in the Chronicles as a Levitical singer at the time of David, who was appointed, together with Heman and Ethan, for conducting the singing in the House of God at Jerusalem. In 2 Chron. xxix. 30, he is called *the Seer* (הַחֹזֶה), and it may be inferred from this passage that he was famous as a *poet*, and that religious songs must have been in existence composed by him, which, from the statement in the Chronicles, were used in Hezekiah's time in Divine worship, together with those of David. Nothing, however, in the purport of any of these songs, which in the superscriptions of our collections are designated as *of Asaph*, point very distinctly to the age of David; they more probably belong to a poet in the kingdom of Israel (lxxx, lxxxi, lxxxiii, perhaps also lxxxii); others belong to a poet of Judah, but at a later time, about the date of the exile, as particularly lxxiv, lxxv, lxxvi, lxxix, and perhaps also the remainder of them. These, perhaps, belong to a poet living at that time who likewise bore the name of Asaph, perhaps as the head of the family of singers springing from the Asaph at the time of David, and named after him, which we meet with in later times under the name בְּנֵי אָסָף; or else they are songs which were composed by various members of this family, and were previously brought together in a separate collection, and from this were adopted into the compilation we are discussing.

It is still more probable that the case is the same with the eleven songs *for the sons of Korah*; these are entitled לִבְנֵי קֹרַח, Ps. xlii. (forming one song with Ps. xliii), xliv–xlix, lxxxiv, lxxxv, lxxxvii, lxxxviii.

The sons of Korah are often named in Chronicles as a family of singers and servants of the Sanctuary, and twice as being appointed by David to be door-keepers to the same; in 2 Chron. xx. 19, they are mentioned as Jehovah's singers in the army of Jehoshaphat, king of Judah, so that this superscription affords no distinct proof as to the age of these songs. It is rather questionable, whether this superscription relates to the author, as Eichhorn and Bertholdt will have it, or to the body of singers to whom the song was made over for musical performance. But in most of them, the arrangements of the words, as compared with other superscriptions, clearly shows that they must point to the author, particularly so Ps. xlv, lxxxiv, lxxxvii.

The plural form, *sons of Korah*, which would not be easy to understand, if these superscriptions were originally selected for these songs singly, can be explained without difficulty by the assumption, that there was previously a separate collection of songs which was in general designated *of* (or *for*) *the sons of Korah*, because it contained songs by various members of this family of singers. These would be adopted singly into our collection of Psalms, and the above superscription would be prefixed to each, which was, in fact, suitable only for them collectively.

Thus it may be explained, that in Psalm lxxxviii, two superscriptions are joined together, the first of which styles the Psalm *for the sons of Korah*; the other attributes it to *Heman the Ezrahite*. According to 1 Chron. vi. 33, Heman was a descendant of Korah at the time of David, and thus this Psalm may have been specified in the separate collection of songs of the sons of Korah, as a song of Heman, and this intimation was subsequently united with the more general statement as to its author.

In 1 Kings iv. 31; 1 Chron. vi. 33, ff.; xv. 17 (cf. 2 Chron. xxxv. 15), one *Ethan the Ezrahite* is named, together with Heman, as among the wise men and singers in the days of David. He is named in the superscription of the Psalm following the above (Ps. lxxxix); the contents, however, of both Psalms, particularly Ps. lxxxix, render it probable that they belong to a later time than that of David; and the same remark applies to the rest of the songs of the sons of Korah, although many of them are amongst the most beautiful in the collection. It is perhaps the case, that Ps. xlii–xlix, lxxxiv, all belong to the same composer, a Jewish priest in the Assyrian age, in the days of Ahaz and Hezekiah,[1] and Ps. lxxxvii. to the Chaldean age, and Ps. lxxxv. to the first period after the return out of exile.

[1] In confirmation of this idea, cf. the following out of *Die Vorl. über die Psalmen* :—" The song, Ps. xlii, xliii. bears much resemblance to the likewise Korahite Psalm lxxxiv. Both express the longing of a pious man after Jehovah's Sanctuary, from which he was living far away, which also is presupposed as still existing : it may be assumed from Ps. xlii, xliii : (*a*) that the author was in the region by Hermon, and that his sojourn there was not temporary (Ewald), but of long duration ; (*b*) from Ps. xlii. 5, that he was a Levite or priest, perhaps one of the high priests, by which his calling himself an *anointed* (Ps. lxxxiv. 9) can be well explained. As regards the cause of the poet's exile, we may consider that he was perhaps captured by the Assyrians in Hezekiah's time, and carried away to the above district, which was then subject to them, or that he was taken prisoner at the time of Ahaz.

§ 273.—*Anonymous Psalms—Latest date of any of the Psalms.*

As regards those anonymous, and, as it were, unfathered Psalms, which present no statement as to their author (יְתוֹמִים), it is but very seldom possible, from a consideration of their (chiefly) general purport, to ascertain the authors with any probability. Many among them may well have been by David, but which they are is difficult to make out. Likewise with regard to those Psalms, in which we have good cause for doubting or rejecting the statements in the superscriptions as to their authors, it is not easy to specify

or somewhat earlier, by the Syrians of Damascus, who at that time still formed an independent nation, in one of the wars of the latter with the Jews. Nothing more exact can be determined with any certainty.— Ps. xliv. might not improbably belong to the same age. This Psalm throughout does not give the impression of a time, such as that of the Babylonian exile, when both nation and state were entirely broken up. Verse 12 is to be understood as speaking, at any rate, of a *partial* scattering only, which long previously had happened to the Jews, after defeats in which captives had been taken and carried away.—In Ps. xlv. according to v. 15, a king is intended, several of whose ancestors had filled the throne with glory. It may, besides, be supposed, from the relations of this song with the one preceding it, that it belongs to a somewhat later time than that of Solomon, to whom, however, it is referred by Hupfeld [also Colenso ("The Pentateuch," &c., ii. p. 279), who finds the name of the Bride in 1 Kings xiv. 21, and compares it with 2 Sam. x. 2, xvii. 27]. It, therefore, probably refers to a successor of Solomon, or to some Ismelitish king, several of whose forefathers had filled the throne, as perhaps Jeroboam II. (Ewald).—Ps. xlvi. presupposes that violent and exterminating wars had raged between neighbouring nations, in which Judæa, and Jerusalem especially, appear to have been threatened. A comparison with the other Korahite Psalms induces us perhaps to conclude that this also belongs to the age of Isaiah; and I might, indeed, with Hitzig, place it in the time of Ahaz, after the defeat of Pekah and Rezin; it may though, perhaps, have been somewhat earlier. Hitzig expressly attributes it to Isaiah; but this must remain undecided, though there is much in it that reminds us of this prophet.—Ps. xlvii. also very probably belongs to the same age as the other Korahite Psalms. It appears as if composed at a time when the Jewish people had been engaged in a successful war; cf. particularly verse 4, which we cannot venture to refer to the future, but to the continuation of what had gone before.—Ps. xlviii. is now mostly referred to the deliverance of Jerusalem from the hosts of Sennacherib; and this is not untenable, yet the mention, in v. 4, of kings banded together against Jerusalem, makes it seem more probable that it refers to the attacks on the city by the Israelites under Pekah and the Syrians under Rezin, when the Jews were at the same time oppressed by the Edomites and Philistines" (2 Kings xvi; 2 Chron. xxviii.)

the real authors; we mostly find some *indicia* of their approximate age, yet in this respect opinions vary very much. It is also in general doubtful at how late a date any of the Psalms in this collection are to be placed. Various early interpreters have dated certain Psalms in the Maccabean age; but Hitzig, Von Lengerke, and J. Olshausen go the furthest in this respect.

Hitzig (*Begriff der Kritik*, 1831, but more particularly in *Commentar über die Pss.*) ascribes but very few of these songs to David and the most flourishing period of Hebrew literature, on the contrary, he places the whole of the three last books (Ps. lxxiii–cl.) together with Ps. i, ii. in the Maccabean age, and some of them in quite the latter part of it.—Olshausen (*Die Psalmen*, 1853) does not place a single song of the Psalter in the age of David and Solomon, and by far the most of them in the Maccabean age, down to the time of John Hyrcanus.—Von Lengerke (*Die fünf Bücher der Psalmen*, Königsberg, 1847).

But this is decidedly wrong,[1] because beyond doubt the collection was existing in its present shape long before this time; and, from 2 Macc. ii. 13, it is probable that it was united with the Nebiim by Nehemiah, and then received its present extent (*v.* § 294). It may also be shown, by comparing 1 Chron. xvi. 36 with the concluding doxology of the fourth book (Ps. cvi. 48), that our *collection* of Psalms, with the concluding doxologies, existed even before the composition of Chronicles.[2] In fact there is no song in our Psalter, which, from any well founded reason, should be

---

[1] Ewald's remarks against the Maccabean Psalms are very good (*Ueber das Suchen und Finden sog. Makk. Psalmen*, in the *Jahrb. der bibl. Wiss.*, vi. pp. 20–32.

[2] *Vide Vorl. über die Psalmen*, Ps. cvi:—" This Doxology was doubtless not added until the completion of the collection of Psalms and its arrangement in five books. In 1 Chron. xvi. 36, in a song professing to be by David, made up from Ps. cv. and cvi, this verse is adopted in connection with the preceding one. This proves that the compiler of this song, who was probably the author of Chronicles, had met with this verse at the conclusion of the Psalm, and that, therefore, he must have become acquainted with the latter after it was adopted into the collection of Psalms as it now exists. *Vide Theol. Stud. und Krit.* 1858, ii. p. 371, f., and Ewald, *ut supra*, pp. 22-24. We must also note the following considerations: Among the pretended Maccabean Psalms there are some which the superscriptions expressly attribute to ancient authors, to David, and others, and even to Moses. In every instance

Date of the latest Psalms.

placed later than in Nehemiah's age, therefore about 300 years before that of the Maccabees; and there are but few which we should be induced to date even so late as the above. It may be assumed with probability that many Psalms belong to the *prophetic age*, and were the work of *prophets*, particularly those in which some pious servant of Jehovah bewails over persecutions and ill-treatment which he had undergone on account of his zeal for his God. Likewise the historical references in many of the Psalms lead to the belief that they belong to the time of the Captivity and the return from it.

Psalms cii, cxxxvii. were clearly composed during the Captivity; probably also cxix, cxxiii, cxxiv, and perhaps several others. Certainly after the partial return of the exiles and the restoration of the commonwealth, Psalms cvii, cxxi, cxxii, cxxvi, cxlvii, probably also lxxxv, xcvi-xcviii, ciii, civ, cxiii, cxvi, cxxv, cxxvii–cxxix, cxxxv, cxxxvi, cxliv, cxlvi, cxlviii–cl).

Certainly, however, these later Psalms are not in the preponderating number, which not only Hitzig, but also Ewald, Köster,[1] J. Olshausen, and others assume, and they are to be found in the second half of the collection especially, whilst by far the larger part of those, which are pointed out in the superscription to be *by David*, are contained in the first half.

§ 274.—*Origin and Formation of the Collection.*

As regards the *formation of the collection* itself, it may be assumed with the greatest probability that it was brought to a conclusion by Nehemiah, by whom also it

---

these songs seem to express vividly the feelings of the author, and are sometimes caused by special historical circumstances by which he was then surrounded. In no case can it be assumed that the composer himself intentionally fathered these songs on more ancient authors, and composed them in their names; there was not the slightest inducement for this procedure. These superscriptions could not then have been added until a still later time, either through false tradition or some wrong notion of the copier or compiler; yet this assumption must be a very questionable one, because these statements are found in the LXX likewise, which translation of the Psalms was composed probably earlier, but certainly not later than the Maccabean age.

[1] *Die Psalmen nach ihrer stroph. Anordnung übersetzt.* Königsberg 1837.

was united with the Nebiim, but also that it was not begun by him. The entire nature of the collection leaves no room for doubt, that it was formed and added to *gradually;* this is incorrectly denied by Hengstenberg.

Had it all been formed at one time, the songs would certainly have been arranged differently from the present mode, either according to their authors, or according to the similarity of their purport, or some other intelligible design; for in our present collection, although a number of Psalms sometimes follow one another which are ascribed by the superscriptions to the same author, or by their contents seem to be allied to one another, frequently, also, those that belong together in this way are quite separated from each other.

The gradual formation of the collection is also proved by the concluding formula at the end of the second book (Ps. lxxii. 20).: "The prayers of David the son of Jesse are ended." This conclusion cannot have proceeded from the originator of the whole collection, or from any copier who had the whole collection before him; because in the two first books, to which the concluding formula relates, there are several Psalms (seventeen) which, in some cases, have no author named, and in others are attributed to other composers (such as the sons of Korah, Asaph, and Solomon), and also because among the Psalms in the books which follow, there are many (eighteen) which are described to be David's. Just in the same way, for the former reason, it is not probable that the above concluding formula should have proceeded from a person who compiled the two first books, and *only these.* The expression כלו seems, too, to intimate that there were other songs by other authors to follow. This phenomenon is most readily explained by assuming that the seventy-two first psalms previously formed a separate collection, arranged for the purpose of Divine worship, and that some one who subsequently continued the collection, placed this formula as a division between the compilation he had met with and the following portion added by himself, and that he attributed the former *à potiori* to David. But he could only have done this under the idea of appending no more Psalms of David, but those of other authors only. Perhaps he only added the eleven Psalms immediately following, which are designated in the super-

Formation of the Collection.

scription as *of Asaph*, for we find an intimation in 2 Chron. xxix. 30, that at a tolerably early time the Psalms of Asaph were made use of together with those of David for the purposes of Divine worship. Thus the Psalms of the two first books would have originally formed a collection by themselves, and Psalms lxxiii–lxxxiii. were the first added, and subsequently the rest of the Psalms in the third book, as well as the whole of the fourth and fifth books. The number of compilers engaged in this cannot easily be ascertained. But, as I believe, it may be assumed with some probability, that the compilation of the two first books took place before the Babylonian Captivity.

§ 275.—*Review of the various Classes of Psalms, and their Contents.*

The contents of these songs vary very much according to the causes which prompted them. They may be primarily divided into those which are of more *general* purport, without any special historical motive, and into *historical* songs, which are based on some individual historical motive, the influence of which is reflected in the composer's feelings. This separation, however, cannot be very strictly carried out, and the distinction is generally only a relative one. It may in general be assumed that most of the songs in our collection have been prompted by some individual historical motive, particularly the older ones. Except among those of a later time, we do not find many songs in which the author entirely fails to regard the peculiar historical circumstances around him,—which were composed from beginning to end for future use, either for himself or for others, *e.g.*, for public Divine worship; thus we scarcely meet with the latter class, except in the last part of our collection, where there are many Psalms, which appear to have been composed entirely with a view to the worship in the Temple, as *e.g.*, Ps. cv, cxxxiv–cxxxvi, cxlviii, cl, &c. ; but they are less frequent among the earlier ones, *e.g.*, Ps. lxvii. But even among those Psalms which have originated in the vivid expression of the author's feelings at any particular time, there are a good many in which either the prompting cause was of so very general a kind, or the special matter pointing out the latter and expressing the feelings awakened by it is kept so much in the background, that they are almost entirely taken out of the class of *historical* Psalms, and must take a place among the songs of more *general* purport. The intention of the collection required, that in general those songs should be excluded, in which the special historical references stood out too strongly, so that they did not generally admit of being readily used for the edification of others or of the whole community in public Divine worship; this is the case, *e.g.*, with David's beautiful elegy on the death of Saul and Jonathan (2 Sam. i.) and others.

The songs in our collection of more general purport are again of different kinds.

(1) *Didactic Poems,—Maschals* on religious and moral subjects; *e.g.*, Ps. 1.—on the right way in which to worship God, as opposed to a wicked hypocrisy and a merely outward service; Ps. lxxviii.—exhortation to keep the Divine commands; Ps. cxxviii.—happiness of the pious man who puts his trust in Jehovah; Ps. xv.—description of the attributes of the pious who shall dwell in Jehovah's tabernacle on His holy hill; Ps. cxxxiii.—praise of unity among brethren. Some of them are taken up with considering the lot of the righteous and the wicked, and have intrinsically the character of a *theodice, e.g.*, Ps. xxxvii, xlix, lxxiii, sometimes, however, they bear reference principally to the destinies of the Israelitish nation.

(2) *Hymns,*—songs of praise to Jehovah. These praise Him, either (*a*) as the Creator and Lord of nature (*e.g.*, Ps. viii, xix, 1–7, xxix, civ, likewise lxv.) (with prayer for rain added); or (*b*) more in His relation to mankind, particularly to the pious, as their Protector, Sustainer, and Father full of love and forbearance (*e. g.*, Ps. ciii, cvii, cxiii, cxvii, cxxvii, cxlv), particularly also as the protecting God of the Israelites by his favour and help shown to them at all times, by His Covenant and Law imparted to them, the preference thus given to them, and the like (cf. Psalms xcix, c, cv, cxi, cxiv, cxxix, cxlvi, cxlvii, cxlix); or (*c*) as contrasted with other gods, as superior to them, and as the only almighty Lord and Judge of nations (Ps. xcvii, cxv). In connection with this the people are urgently required to be obedient to their God (*e.g.*, Ps. xcv), to wait patiently for Him (Ps. cxxxi), to keep His feasts (Ps. lxxxi.) and the like.

(3) The *historical* Psalms in a stricter sense relate either (1) to purely *personal* circumstances affecting the author himself, or, (2) to *national* affairs. The middle place between these two classes is taken by those songs in which the individual to whom they refer is, by his position the representative of many others, or of the whole people ; *e.g.*, when a king thanks Jehovah for victory over enemies (*e.g.* Ps. xviii), or when the composer expresses himself in prayers, wishes, &c., for a prince ; this kind may be perhaps called *royal-psalms* ; thus Ps. ii, xx, xxi, xlv, lxxii, cx. In the greater part of these, and most of all in Ps. ii, xlv, lxxii, cx, it has always been a question, whether they refer to the king ruling Israel at the time or to some future monarch,—the Messiah.[1] A decision as to this is the province of exegesis. I will only remark here, that in my opinion, the contents of all these songs induce us to look upon the prince reigning at the time as their *immediate* object, but yet nevertheless they present Messianic elements of more or less importance, partly typical and partly prophetical.

There are other Psalms, which refer first of all to the personal condition of the composer, which was of that nature, that many others were similarly circumstanced, either the whole people or at least a very considerable part of it, *e.g.*, all the pious and faithful worshippers of Jehovah (*e.g.*, Ps. xiv, liii, lviii). Others, however, have the circumstances of the whole people more distinctly and actually as their object ; these either express *thanks* to Jehovah for safety afforded to the people for deliverance out of affliction, for victories won and the like (*e.g.*, Ps. xlvii, xlviii, lxvi, lxxvi, xcviii, cxviii, cxxiv, cxxvi) ; of this sort also are some songs on the entry of the ark into the sanctuary after the return from a war (*e.g.*, Ps. xxiv, xlvii, lxviii, perhaps also xv),—or they are *prayers for the Divine assistance* in times of trouble (Ps. x, xliv, lix, lxxvii, lxxx, lxxxix, xc, cvi, cxlii), especially in wars with foreign nations (*e.g.* Ps. lx, lxxiv, lxxv, lxxix, lxxxiii, cviii), or in the time of

---

[1] A Messianic interpretation of Ps. xlv. is given in the *Utrechter Doctorschrift*, by H. F. Kohlbrügge, Amstelod, 1829), whose son-in-law. Edward Böhl (*Zwölf Messianische Psalmen erklärt, nebst einer grundlegenden christologischen Einleitung.* Basle. 1862, propounds strange views.

captivity of the people (*e.g.*, Ps. cii, cxxxvii, probably cxxii, and others).

Among the Psalms which have arisen purely out of personal relations, there are also some *songs of thanksgiving* for deliverances experienced (as Psalms xxx, xxxii, xl. 2–12; cxvi). But by far the greater part of them are *Psalms of Lamentation*, and express the complaints of the author at his unhappy fate, and at the wrongs and afflictions with which he is visited, joined with prayers for Divine assistance. In most of them the wrongs consist in persecutions by adversaries, either heathens, or, as appears to be much more frequently the case, on the part of his own fellow-countrymen; in several, however, it is unmistakeable, that there must have been some severe disease, as leprosy or something similar, in addition to the external distresses, by which disease even the friends of the author were driven away from him, and he was all the more given over to the revilings of his adversaries (thus particularly Ps. vi, xxxviii, xxxix, xli, lxxxviii). Many of these songs express also the consciousness of guilt in the most vivid manner, the pious author looking upon the misfortunes befalling him as the just punishment for his sins, and praying, before everything, that these might be forgiven him, and that power might be granted to him for his moral improvement (these penitential Psalms are Ps. xix. 8–15; xxv, xxxviii, xxxix, li); others simply express the quiet and certain confidence which the pious sufferer places in his God in all that may befall him (*e.g.*, Ps. xvi, xxiii, xxvi, xxvii, xxxvi, lii, lvi, lxii).

There are also many of these Psalms of Lamentation, which ancient and sometimes also modern interpreters have considered as immediately Messianic; so that they do not regard the author himself as speaking in them, but the suffering Messiah, in whose name they were composed through prophetic inspiration; thus particularly Ps. xvi, xxii, xl, &c. We shall, however, be compelled by the contents of these songs, to decide that they were without doubt originally composed by the author in reference to himself and his own sufferings, but still, like many others of the Psalms, that they have Messianic elements, inasmuch as the pious author, both in the cause of his sufferings and also in the way in which he endures them in faith and hope, appears as a type of the Redeemer, and sometimes even expresses hopes, which can find their essential fulfilment in Him and His kingdom only. On the other hand, De Wette (in Daub and Creuzer's *Studien*, vol. iii. P. 2, p. 252, ff., and in his *Commentar über die Psalmen*) has endeavoured to prove that by far the greater part of these Psalms of Lamentation are of a national character, and composed in the name of the Israelitish people in reference to the hostilities of other nations; so also Rosenmüller (*Scholia in Pss.* Ed. 2). De Wette has retracted this in reference to many of them in the 4th Edition of his Commentary, but yet has held to his opinion as to some, an unprejudiced consideration of which will, I believe, render it in the highest degree probable that originally they only had the person of the author himself as their object, in reference to the sufferings inflicted on him by his fellow-countrymen; thus particularly Ps. vi, xiii, xvii, xxv, xxvii, xxxi, xxxvi, xxxviii, lii, liv, lxiv, lxix, lxxi, cix, cxx, cxl, &c. On the other hand, there certainly can be no doubt, that *originally personal* Psalms of Lamentation of this sort were frequently applied in later times to general *national* circumstances, just as subsequently in the *Christian* Church they were, and are still, made use of in reference to the tribulations of the community or of individual believers. This is sometimes quite admissible from the spirit and purport of many of these songs. But we must not venture to think, with many ancient Christian interpreters, that they were originally composed in reference to these later circumstances, and that the author had these distinctly in view. All we can say is, that in his suffering and the emotions awakened by it, he stands forth as a type to other sufferers in after times, both in the Old and New Covenants, of the resignation and trust in God, by which they may evade or endure such afflictions. But in making use of these songs for the edification of the Christian community, it should not be done without some caution, and not without paying attention to the fact, that in the Old Covenant that spirit could not yet prevail, which, in all its fulness and clearness first came into the world through Christ, which, in the sermon on the mount and elsewhere, appears to form a contrast between the moral spirit of the Old and New Covenants. As in the Old Testament gene-

rally, so also in the Psalms, there is expressed, generally
most prominently, the confidence of the pious in the providence of the only God, who would never forsake those
who patiently wait for Him. But we find in these songs,
that their hopes were confined to *this present* life, as if the
pious and believing, after their death, were no longer in
God's hand, and could no longer glorify Him; and it is
only in isolated Psalms that there is any hint as to a future
life. The Psalms express in a peculiarly forcible and energetic way the abhorrence of sin, and many add an acknowledgment of individual guilt, and continual sinfulness;
e.g., Ps. xix. 13; xxv, xxxii, xxxviii, xxxix, li; cvi. 6, f.;
cxxx, cxliii. (no man is righteous before God). But this
genuine Christian humility does not pervade them all in
an equal measure; there is in some of them more of a
haughty self-confidence in personal innocence, and an
appeal to individual righteousness, cf. Ps. vii, xi; xviii.
21, ff.; xxvi, lix, 4, 5; lxvi. 18, and some others. There
are likewise several Psalms, in which we miss the spirit of
love which the Gospel enjoins its professors to manifest
even towards their enemies, and not only towards personal
offenders, but even against the adversaries of the Lord. A
spirit of vindictiveness and vehement hostility is particularly shown in Ps. cix, cxxxvii. But after the revelation
of the New Covenant and the Christian spirit, we must
no longer venture to consider songs of this kind as fitted
to be adopted into hymn-books for Christian communities
without some alteration and softening down, although this
has not unfrequently been done, especially in the Reformed
Church, by an identification of the spirit of the Old and
New Testaments. On this point we ought rather to
acknowledge, that through Christianity, something higher
and holier has come into the world, by which the Old
Covenant and the Scriptures of the Old Testament could
not, at that time, have been completely imbued.

§ 276.—*The Separations between the single Psalms.*

We have still two points to bring under consideration:
(*a*) the *division of the single Psalms from one another*; and,
(*b*) the *integrity* of these songs generally, in the form in
which we now have them in our collection. As regards
the former point, those of the songs which are provided

Separation of the single Psalms. 247

with a superscription as to their authors, the occasion of composition, &c., are by this means naturally divided from the Psalm before them. This, however, is not the case with those which have no such superscription. As at the origin and completion of the collection, the single Psalms were not perhaps sufficiently indicated by ciphers, and thus divided from one another, the beginning of a fresh Psalm being perhaps marked merely by a small intervening space, or by new lines, it would thus be very easy for mistakes in copying to arise in the course of time. Thus in the LXX, and in consequence also in the Vulgate, they are in many cases not divided in the same way as in the present Hebrew text.

They have thus (a) joined together Ps. ix. and x. as one song; (b), likewise Ps. cxiv. and cxv; on the contrary (c) Ps. cxvi. is divided into two songs, vv. 1–9 and vv. 10–19; and likewise (d) Ps. cxlvii. into two songs, vv. 1–11 and 12–20. There is, therefore, in the LXX and Vulgate, as in the Greek and Latin Fathers, a different numbering to that in the Hebrew Canon, viz.:—

Hebrew Text.	LXX and Vulgate.
Psalm ix, x.	Psalm ix.
xi–cxiii.	x–cxii.
cxiv, cxv.	cxiii.
cxvi.	cxiv, cxv.
cxvii–cxlvi.	cxvi–cxlv.
cxlvii.	cxlvi, cxlvii.
cxlviii–cl.	cxlviii–cl.

In the three last of these four cases the division in the Hebrew text is the correct one, according to my judgment; on the other hand, it is very probable that Ps. ix. and x, in the form in which we now have them, form one song, with an alphabetical arrangement, although this is not quite carried out. There are, besides, several cases in which—although both texts agree in the division made—it may be assumed with more or less probability that they are not rightly divided.

It is most certain that Ps. xlii. and xliii. originally formed only one song, with three strophes concluding with the same recurring verse. Perhaps also, Ps. cxiii. and cxiv. belong together as one song, and Ps. cxvii. (only two verses) with Ps. cxviii.

On the other hand, the following Psalms probably contain each two originally separate songs:—

(1) Ps. xxiv.—(a) vv. 1–6, who may dwell in Jehovah's sanctuary; (b) vv. 7–10, on the entry of the ark into the sanctuary.

(2) Ps. xxvii.—(a) vv. 1–6, trust in God; (b) vv. 7–14, suppliant cries for help.

(3) Ps. xxxii, perhaps—(a) vv. 1–7, happiness of the forgiveness of sins and open confession; (b) vv. 8–11, exhortation to willing obedience to God.

§ 277.—*Integrity of the individual Psalms.*

As regards the *integrity* of the separate Psalms, we find distinct signs that, at least many of them, between the time of their first composition and of their being received in a fixed shape into canonical estimation, have experienced in many ways greater or less alteration in the text, both with and without influence on the sense.[1] A wide popular currency of these songs at an early period, when they circulated singly, and were often copied, read, learned, and applied to individual circumstances, would render this adaptation all the more easy. In this way it was, perhaps, often the case, that these songs, by means of additions, omissions, and slight alterations, received a shape in which they became more fit to be applied to circumstances of a later period, which were somewhat similar, but yet not quite parallel.

Ps. li. is an example of the kind. The superscription styles it a Psalm of David's, composed by him after his adultery with Bathsheba. This was, no doubt, the prompting cause of the song, and its purport quite coincides with this, with the exception of the two last verses, 20, 21. These manifestly point to a date, when Jerusalem and the Temple were destroyed, so that, for a time, the legal sacrifices could not be offered; these circumstances, too, are presupposed as then existing, whilst in all the rest of the song there is no trace of them, nor any intimation whatever,

[1] Of this sort is the religious awe—which is far rather to be laid to the compiler than the author—having for its result the exclusive or prevailing use of the term Elohim, in Ps. xlii–lxxxiv; cf. Ps. liii. with xiv, also xliii. 4; xlv. 8; l. 7; also lvii. 10, with cviii 4; as well as lxviii. 8, 9, with Judges v. 4, 5, &c., and *vide* Hupfeld's *Psalmen*, iv. p. 461.

Integrity of the single Psalms. 249

that it has any reference to the general affairs of the people. It may be assumed with the greatest probability, that the present conclusion of the Psalm was subsequently added at the time of the Captivity, when this Psalm of David's was made use of as a penitential Psalm in reference to the Jewish people and their condition at the time.

A similar case occurs in Ps. lxix. (vv 35, 36), and in Ps. xxv (v. 22), perhaps also in Ps. cxxxi. (v. 3).

In some places the application of ancient Psalms to other and later circumstances has led to alterations in the body of the Psalm, which are more closely blended with it, so that they cannot be so easily recognized. Such a case is brought under our notice by comparing Ps. xiv. and liii, which for the most part agree even verbally, but yet differ in one passage in a way which can be only explained under the supposition that the Psalm, which has, perhaps, been preserved in its original state in Ps. xiv, was subsequently applied to other circumstances, and was thus brought into the shape which Ps. liii. presents. Yet if we only possessed Ps. liii, we should not be in a position to ascertain and restore the original form of the song.

In other places, a portion only of some more ancient and larger song has been appropriated at a later time, perhaps for liturgical use, as Ps. lxx. = Ps. xl. 14–18; or two songs or parts of several songs have been united in one. Thus Ps. cviii. is made up from Ps. lvii. 8–12, and Ps. lx. 7–14; and the song in 1 Chron. xvi. 8–36, from Ps. cv, xcvi, and cvi. 1, 47, 48. Ps. xix. contains two portions of quite different natures, which, both in purport and form, are quite distinct from each other: (a) vv. 1–7, a hymn to God as Creator, at the end dwelling upon a consideration of the glory of the sun; (b) vv. 8–15, praise of the purity and rectitude of Jehovah's law, with acknowledgment of individual moral weakness, and entreaty for deliverance from its tyranny. The two parts were not, perhaps, originally written in connection with each other, but as two separate songs which were subsequently, and perhaps intentionally, united in one. Ps. ix. and x. are also to be looked upon as *one* song, but worked up together out of three more ancient ones: (a) Ps. ix. 2–13, originally a thanksgiving song for the conquest of enemies; (b) Ps. ix. 14–21, a prayer for deliverance from enemies; (c) Ps. x. a song both of supplication and lamentation. These three songs were afterwards worked up together into one, with some alterations and additions, and with an alphabetical arrangement, which, however, is not carried out.

Many, therefore, of the ancient Hebrew songs have been dealt with in a similar way to numerous songs of ancient Christian poets, which had been composed for some particular occasion, and were revised, abridged, enlarged, or otherwise altered by later authors, perhaps with a view to their adoption into a book of hymns, so as to render them more fitted for public use, or for immediate application to a state of things different from that in reference to which they were originally composed. It is certainly often the case, as regards our Psalter, that we have the Psalms in it in a later and revised shape; for the compilers of the collection—just as the arrangers of our hymn books—felt no very great critical or literary interest in the matter, and for their purpose, handing down the songs in the original shape in which they came from the hand of David, Asaph, &c. was of much less importance, than issuing them in the form in which they would be best fitted for application to various circumstances in the life of the people and of individuals, and for general use in Divine worship. This certainly produces a peculiar difficulty in their historical explanation, and the effect of it is, that we are no longer able to look upon many of the songs, in the shape in which we now have them, as entirely the work of their various original authors, but more generally as productions of the Israelitish people and the theocratical spirit of the Old Testament. Another circumstance connected with the above is, that in some of these songs, as in those we have just considered, we do not meet with that connection and that agreement of the various parts, nor that individuality of the disposition of mind shown in them, which would be the case in the absolutely independent and unaltered productions of one author.

§ 278.—*Slight Alterations in the Ancient Text.*

But besides these alterations purposely made to fit them for later use, the Psalms, until they had received a fixed shape as elements of our collection and had attained canonical authority, must have occasionally experienced many slight alterations in their text—just as our ancient sacred songs have done—as regards orthography and language; forms and expressions, which were more regular and more in use at a later time, being sometimes substituted for those which were obsolete, unusual, or anomalous; sometimes, also, alterations were made by the copiers, either through error or wilfully. Thus it might happen, that in the course of time different recensions of the same song might exist, each varying more or less, although the song itself had not experienced any very great or intentional alterations.

We have an example of this in David's song of victory, Ps. xviii, which also occurs in 2 Sam. xxii. There are slight variations between the two copies in almost every verse, but almost entirely unimportant, and with little or no influence on the sense. There are none of those variations, which would be caused by a later revision of the song to fit it for Divine worship or some other special use; still less is it at all probable that the author himself should have issued the song at different times in these different recensions. But these are variations which would easily be formed in the course of time in a song which was so much read and copied, partly through quite accidental errors, either of the reader or writer, and partly through attempts to amend the text. In this case, the recension in 2 Sam. xxii, gives the original readings,[1] not everywhere, but very usually; and we may assume with great probability, that the compiler of the Psalms derived it from the Book of Samuel, but that the song subsequently experienced various alterations, both in the Book of Samuel and in the collection of Psalms, and that the alterations were rather more important and numerous in the latter, than in the historical book.

This example leads us to suppose, that other songs in our collection may also have experienced alterations more or less in this way. This has been the case with the Psalms, perhaps to a greater extent than in the historical and prophetical Scriptures, because the former were more frequently read and copied.

[1] The opinions of many modern interpreters are just the reverse, as De Wette, Hitzig, Ewald, Olshausen, and Hupfeld.

THE WRITINGS OF SOLOMON.

§ 279.—*Works attributed to Solomon.*

We learn from 1 Kings iv. 29–34, that Solomon had acquired a distinguished name, both for his wisdom and also as a poet. But of his numerous poetical productions, pointed out in this passage, but very few are preserved to us.

Besides the Book of *Wisdom*, which stands in the name of this king among the Apocryphal Books of the Old Testament, we possess in the Canon the following works ascribed to Solomon:—(1) Two Psalms (Ps. lxxii. and cxxvii. (*v.* p. 234), and (2) three independent works; (*a*) The Proverbs or Sayings, (*b*) the so-called Song of Solomon, and (*c*) The Preacher (Ecclesiastes). But it is doubtful how far these works are actually the composition of Solomon himself.

1.—THE PROVERBS OF SOLOMON.

§ 280.—*Title of the Book—Review of its Contents.*

The *title* of this work is מִשְׁלֵי שְׁלֹמֹה. The word מָשָׁל, really signifies *likeness;* thence *simile*, *parable*, and, as the Arabic, مثل, very often occurs for,

(*a*) Short maxims, sentences, or Gnomes, which among the Orientals consisted often in comparisons; a thought of a religious or moral nature being brought out more distinctly by a reference to circumstances of the external world. The Orientals were generally very fond of such sentences as these, which frequently became quite proverbial (thence the title of our book in the LXX, παροιμίαι, Vulg. *Proverbia;* among us frequently *Proverbs*, more suitably, as in Luther, *Sprüche Salomo's*); cf. Jerome, *ad Matt.* xviii. 23 : " Familiare est Syris et maxime Palæstinis, ad omnem sermonem suum parabolas jungere, ut, quod per simplex præceptum teneri ab auditoribus non potest, per similitudinem exemplaque teneatur." This mode of teaching is also peculiarly popular among the Arabians, whose oral law, the *Sunna*, is full of such sentences. There are also certain collections of these Sayings arranged by various Arabian poets, among others, one by a grammarian, Al Meidani (d. 1141), who endeavours to investigate the historical origin of them. In this he thus expresses himself as to the high value of aphoristic wisdom:—" The knowledge of aphorisms graces with its beauties all classes of society, and is an ornament to the inhabitants both of cities and the desert; it gives brilliancy to the contents of books, and, by its allusions, sweetens the words both of preachers and teachers. And why should it not do so? For the word of God, the Koran, is itself imbued with it, the language of the prophets is enriched by it, and the most excellent scholars, who have traced out the courses of the most abstruse knowledge, have chosen it as their auxiliary." "Aphorisms," he says somewhere else, "are to the mind what a mirror is to the eyes."

(*b*) (Longer or shorter) connected didactic poems, so far as these contain separate sentences joined on to one another. Many of the didactic poems among the Psalms are of this nature; and in the book we are discussing, ch. i–ix, praise of wisdom; and ch. xxxi. 10–31, praise of a virtuous woman; also ch. xxii. 17–xxiv. 22. But the greater part of the book is made up of separate short moral sentences. There is a similar collection in the Book of Jesus Sirach in the Apocrypha.

The passage in 1 Kings iv. 29–34 clearly proves that Solomon was very famous as a composer of proverbs; and from this passage we may also suppose, with probability, that at least many of his sayings have been preserved in the book named after him. The whole of it, however, as we now have it, cannot have been his composition, but various authors must have had a share in it, as is clearly proved by express statements in the book itself, and by several superscriptions prefixed to the several parts.

The book consists of the following portions:—

(1) Ch. i–ix.—A connected Maschal, in which wisdom is praised, and the young are called upon to apply themselves to it, and are warned to beware of enticements to evil, and particularly of the seductions to impurity and adultery; to these vices and their evil results the author repeatedly

reverts, so that it is easily seen that in the circumstances and persons surrounding him, he had some particular prompting cause for bringing them forward so prominently. To ch. i. 1–6, is prefixed a superscription and introduction, in which what follows is styled " The *Proverbs of Solomon*, the Son of David, king of Israel," and their aim is stated to be, to teach wisdom and instruction, so as to understand the words of the wise and their dark sayings.

(2) Ch. x–xxii. 16.—With the superscription, " *Proverbs of Solomon*," a collection of separate sayings and various maxims of an ethical and politic nature, which are but loosely connected with one another; the connection is mostly confined to each single verse, which is followed by fresh ideas, without any close union with what precedes.

(3) Ch. xxii. 17–xxiv. 22, is a Maschal of a more connected character, with precepts of justice and prudence, unmistakeably constituting a *whole* to some extent; which, however, has no separate title, but yet has a special introduction, ch. xxii. 17–22, consisting of a summons to hearken to (the following) instruction, and to the words of the wise.

(4) Ch. xxiv 23–34.—With the superscription גַּם־אֵלֶּה לַחֲכָמִים, which may be understood, " This also is *for* the wise," but is more probably intended for " This also is *of* (or *by*) the wise;" this section is also formed of unconnected Maschals, which by this superscription are described to be maxims of various unknown wise men, and are an addition to what precedes them.

(5) Ch. xxv–xxix.—With the superscription, " These are also the *proverbs of Solomon*, which the men of Hezekiah, king of Judah, collected " (הֶעְתִּיקוּ, *compiled*, *re-wrote*). This also is a collection of single Maschals joined on to one another.

(6) Ch. xxx.—Likewise a small collection of single didactic and sometimes paradoxical thoughts, with the superscription, " *The words of Agur, the son of Jakeh, a, prophecy, speech of the man unto Ithiel, even unto Ithiel and Ucal.*" As to the persons named here, and their age, we know absolutely nothing. Jerome and other interpreters, both Christian and Jewish, look upon Agur as merely a symbolical name for Solomon, just as Koheleth, and meant to be in the sense of *compiler*. This designation, however, would be a very unsuitable one for Solomon, and likewise his being

called the son of Jakeh. There is quite as little probability about other modes of explanation, which understand it as a merely symbolical mode of designation in reference to the origin of the collection. In all probability, Agur is the real name of some otherwise unknown Israelitish sage, who composed the Maschals which follow. Jakeh is the name of his father. Ithiel and Ucal were, perhaps, his sons or scholars. Ewald,[1] indeed, is of opinion that the latter name is, perhaps, arbitrarily formed, and used by the composer for his purpose, and explains it, " *With me is God,*" and " *I am strong*" (likewise Keil). This, however, from the actual nature of the name, is at least improbable.

(7) Ch. xxxi. 1–9.—Wise instruction for kings, with the superscription, " *The words of Lemuel* (לְמוּאֵל, which in v. 4 is pointed לְמוֹאֵל), *the king, the prophecy that his mother taught him.* Nothing is known as to this Lemuel. Some ancient interpreters, and also Ewald and Keil, consider this as merely a symbolical name for Solomon, equivalent, according to Ewald, to *to God—he who is turned to God—devoted to God.* This, however, is not very probable, because Solomon is elsewhere named in this book by his own name. It is also improbable that, as Grotius thinks, it should be a designation for Hezekiah, as if a remodelling of his name, from לְבִיא, according to the Arabic = *iniecta manu cepit,* as חִזְקִיָּה, from חָזַק. It ought rather to be considered, with Eichhorn, Jahn, and Bertholdt, as a name arbitrarily formed ; and that the *sayings* are the work of some Israelitish sage—of Agur, as Jahn thinks, whom Ewald also takes to be the author. But it may be the case, that Lemuel was the real name of some prince in the neighbourhood of Judæa, some Arabian or Edomite prince, from whom the wise maxims proceeded, and were only copied or translated by an Israelitish compiler.[2]

[1] *Theolog. Stud. und Krit.* 1828, ii, p. 343, f., and in *Comment. zu d. Spr.;* cf. *Jahrbuch,* i. p. 109, f. Others, by means of altered punctuation and alteration of the division of the words, consider the two words as an independent sentence, with which the series of these sayings is opened.

[2] Hitzig discovers in the מַשָּׂא ch. xxx. 1, and xxxi. 1, a kingdom of Massah, in Arabia, formed by the emigrant Simeonites (1 Chron. iv. 38–41; Gen. xxv. 14; 1 Chron. i. 30), from which these two chapters proceed ; in doing this he very much alters the pointing and division of words. Cf. the acute arguments in favour of this opinion in *Das*

(8) Ch. xxxi. 10–31, an alphabetically arranged didactic poem in praise of a virtuous woman, without any special superscription, but distinct in purport and form from what precedes it.

§ 281.— *Origin of the Compilation.*

With regard to the origin of the *compilation*, we may in general assume as follows:—It is made manifest by the superscription, ch. xxv. 1 ("These are also proverbs of Solomon," &q.), that the proverbs immediately following were brought together at the time of Hezekiah, and perhaps at his instance; they passed for sayings of Solomon, but up to that time had been chiefly in oral circulation among the people. It may be inferred from this superscription, that the collection following was arranged as an addition to the one already existing in the preceding part of the book. In all probability, the series in ch. x. 1–xxii. 16, formed the most ancient collection, and was the original portion of our book; but in this shape it hardly proceeded from Solomon, although without doubt it contains many genuine proverbs of Solomon. The passages ch. xxii. 17–xxiv. 22, and ch xxiv. 23–34, were then added, the latter of which sections has the superscription, "*These things, also, are from the wise.*" It cannot well·be ascertained as to these, whether they were added by the servants of Hezekiah, the same as in ch. xxv. ff., or whether these already formed a part of the original collection; they could not anyhow have been added later than the time of Hezekiah. It cannot be ascertained when the last portions (ch. xxx–xxxi.) were added, perhaps, also, by the learned men at the court of Hezekiah; more probably, however, at a later time; and thus, also, perhaps, ch. i–ix. This connected Maschal was, at least probably, composed by the last editor of the book, as a kind of introduction to the Proverbs of Solomon, which follow; and ch. i. 1–6, is intended by him as a superscription and declaration of its

---

Königreich Massa, in Zeller's *Theol. Jahrb.* 1844, pp. 269–305, and *Die Sprüche Sal.* 1858. Bertheau essentially agrees with this (*Die Sprüche Sal.* in the 7th part of the *Exeget. Handbuch,* 1847); cf. also Hahn (in Reuter's *Repert.* N. Folge, xiv.), and Bunsen (*Bibelwerk, Einl.* p. clxxviii. ff.).

purpose, in reference rather to the whole book and the Proverbs of Solomon in it especially, than as applying to his own special Maschal.

2.—THE SONG OF SOLOMON.

§ 282.—Title, &c.

This work is called in ch. i. 1, שִׁיר הַשִּׁירִים אֲשֶׁר לִשְׁלֹמֹה, and in the title, שִׁיר הַשִּׁירִים. This combination is not to be understood, with Aben Esra, Kimchi, &c., as "*A Song of the Songs (of Solomon)*," and certainly not as Velthusen and Paulus (in Eichhorn's *Repert.* xvii., p. 109, f.) have explained it, by using the שִׁיר the first time in a sense quite different to the last, as "*a chain (series) of songs*" (according to the Chald. and Arab. שִׁיר, سُوَرٌ); but the proper explanation is, "*The song of songs*" = the most beautiful, the most valuable of songs; as a paraphrase of an idea of the superlative, as *e.g.*, 1 Kings viii. 27, שְׁמֵי הַשָּׁמַיִם, *heaven of heavens*—Ezek. xvi. 7, עֲדִי עֲדָיִים, *ornament of ornaments*, &c. Luther expresses this idea, and calls it "*Das Hohelied Salomonis.*" In the LXX and the Greek ecclesiastical authors, the title runs ᾆσμα ᾀσμάτων, a literal translation of the Hebrew, also ᾆσμα merely (Cod. Vat. in title); in Latin, *canticum* (also *cantica*), *canticorum*. The לְ in לִשְׁלֹמֹה must doubtless point to the author, as in the superscription of so many Psalms. The אֲשֶׁר prefixed is peculiar. This relative is not perhaps intended to refer, as a singular, to the whole idea, as "song of songs, *which is* Solomon's," but as plural to the genitive הַשִּׁירִים, as "song of songs, *which are* Solomon's;" so that it is thus placed in comparison with other songs of Solomon. Thus Ewald, *Poetische Bücher*, i. p. 184. We may assume, with the greatest probability, whatever we may decide as to the origin of the book itself, that this designation of it did not proceed from Solomon. It may be concluded, although not with certainty, that it was not prefixed by the same person who composed the book, from the use of אֲשֶׁר, as everywhere else in the book שׁ only is used as a relative.

§ 283.—*Subject of the Book—Various Interpretations of its Contents.*

The subject of the book is in general the love and mutual relations of two lovers. It contains, for the most part, sometimes the separate speeches, and sometimes the conversational speeches, of two lovers, who praise each other, express their longing for one another, and the like. There is, in the first place, a question as to what kind of love it is which is treated of in this book, and who the lover and the loved one were who appear in it. The explanation as to these points, which was very popular in earlier times, is, that it is only spiritual love which is spoken of, and that the lover was either God (Jehovah), or the Messiah (Christ), and the object of love was either God's people generally, or the individual souls of believers; but both ideas are quite untenable.

Solomon's Song is understood in this allegorical way both by Jewish interpreters, and by most of the ancient Christian ones, from Origen downwards. In the first place, the explanation of the lover as personifying the person of Christ, put forward by Hengstenberg (*Das Hohelied Sal.*, Berlin, 1853, and *Christol. d. A. T.*, 2nd ed. i., pp. 177-179), is altogether unnatural. In this case, the purport of the whole book would have to be taken as prophetical, and as referring to persons and circumstances which, from the stand-point of the author, were entirely future, not the slightest intimation of this being given in the book, but rather everything to lead us to believe that the persons and circumstances brought forward in it were present to the author. It may be assumed with tolerable certainty, that Christ and the apostles did not understand the contents of the book in the above way; for it would thus have afforded them so many things which they might have made use of and referred to, when they spoke of the communion of the Lord with His people or with individual believers; but in no single passage in the New Testament is the book either made use of or quoted. Hengstenberg (*Hohelied,* p. 253, ff.) quotes a multitude of passages out of the New Testament, particularly from Jesus' words, in which Solomon's Song is referred to; but not a single one of these references has even the slightest probability about it, and with regard to all of

Various Interpretations. 259

them without exception, it is inconceivable how any one can really think that an intentional allusion or reference has been made to the Old-Testament passages (cf. Bunsen's *Gott in der Geschichte*, i. pp. 467–476).

The explanation of the lover as God, Jehovah, and of the loved one as the people of God, is found in the Chaldee paraphrasers, and in modern times it has been again brought forward with many modifications. By Rosenmüller (in Keil and Tzschirner's *Analekten*, i. p. 138, ff.; but otherwise in the *Scholiasts*); Hengstenberg (*Evang. K. Ztg.* No. 27, ff., 1837); Keil (in Hävernick's *Einl.* and in his own *Einl.*). In later times, the aim of Solomon's Song has been pointed out to be a delineation of the communion between the Lord and His chosen people, which, through the faithlessness of Israel, was often interrupted, but was again reinstated on the latter returning to their true Covenant-God, through God's unchangeable love. This mode of interpretation, however, is also, from the nature of the book, quite unnatural, and still more so, if Solomon, the lover appearing in the book, is considered as the author of it, as by Hengstenberg and Keil. It is not, indeed, unusual among the Hebrew prophets to depict the relation of the Jewish people to Jehovah under the image of a marriage, and Jehovah as the lawful consort of His people. But when the Hebrew prophets and poets avail themselves of this allegorical mode of representation, they do not readily omit to apply it to the matter that is thereby symbolized, or to point out distinctly the reference to it, so that it shall be clear to the reader. But throughout this book, there is no such application of the mode of delineation to the relations between God and men, nor any intimation that it at all refers to it; in the whole book the name of God does not, once occur, except in ch. viii. 6, in the combination שַׁלְהֶבֶתְיָה (the flames of love are flames of fire, a flame of *Jah*). The section (ch. iii. 6–11) contains a song on Solomon's nuptials. It would be in the highest degree unnatural to consider this as a delineation of the union of Jehovah with His people, so that, without the least intimation of it in the song itself, Solomon would stand directly for Jehovah, particularly if Solomon were the author, or even if he were not. So also in the other sections of the book, if their sense and aim is to be understood in this way, the whole mode of statement—especially of Jehovah as a lover—is carried out most unnaturally, indeed in a way both repulsive and also most painful to good taste.

Some explanations of another kind, which have been attempted for Solomon's Song, are, however, quite as unnatural.

Thus, *e.g.*, Rosenmüller in his *Scholiasts* refers it to the intercourse of Solomon with Wisdom, taking the loved one (Sulamith, ch. vii. 1) to be wisdom; Hug (*Das Hohelied in einer noch unversuchten Deutung*) understands the lover and loved one to be Hezekiah and the people of the ten tribes who were still remaining in the land after the breaking up of the kingdom of Israel, which latter expressed their longing to come under Hezekiah's rule, as of a second Solomon, and that this prince also entertained the same wish, but was opposed by the citizens of Judah, represented by the brothers of Sulamith. H. A. Hahn (*Das Hohelied von Salomon*, Breslau, 1852) refers it to the relation of the Israelitish king to heathen nations, and of the missionary duty of the former towards heathenism; and other interpreters have explained it in various other ways.

All these allegorical explanations, however variously they may be modified, are unnatural from the nature of the work itself, and can only be carried out in a very forced way; and none of them are suggested by the contents of the book itself. By impartially reading it, we are, on the contrary, led to the belief that the book contains songs of an erotic character, referring to the love between two persons of different sexes.

An interpretation of this sort was brought forward by Theodorus of Mopsuestia (d. about 425), to whom, however, it was imputed as heresy, as, long after his death, the fifth Œcumenical Council of Constantinople, A.D. 553, pronounced a general anathema on him. Subsequently also, for the same reasons, the Reformist divine Seb. Castellio, who wished, under this conception of the book, to remove it out of the Canon, was impeached before the Senate at Geneva, and was expelled the city (1544; d. 1563, as Professor of Greek at Basle). Other interpreters, who understood at least the immediate sense of the book in this way, are H. Grotius, Simon Episcopius, Clericus, &c., and, later, J. D. Michaelis, Herder, &c. By the ingenious way in which the book is dealt with by the latter (*Lieder der Liebe, die ältesten und schönsten aus dem Morgenlande*, Leipzig, 1778), the above ideas as to it have been circulated in a wider sphere, at least in the German Protestant Church, and have been acknowledged to be correct by most of the scholars of this Church; as also by Delitzsch (*Das Hohelied untersucht u. ausgelegt*, Leipzig, 1851).

This opinion would doubtless have prevailed more generally and at an earlier time, if it had not been for the fact that the book was included in the Canon of Holy Scripture. It is certainly probable, as we shall see in the history of the Canon, that the book first attained to general acknowledgment as a canonical scripture in the Jewish Church itself, only because it was considered to admit of an allegorical explanation. We see, however, from this very fact, that this interpretation was not the usual and prevailing one at the time of the formation of the Old-Testament Canon, but that then and up to that time it had been referred to sexual love. We have, however, in the Old-Testament Canon itself at least one song, although a shorter one, which may be considered as a parallel to our song in this sense, viz., Ps. xlv, which was without doubt composed as a nuptial song, or congratulation at the marriage of some Jewish or Israelitish king, and does not admit of any allegorical interpretation without much forcing.

§ 284.—*Authorship—Age of Composition.*

Those expositors, however, who agree in the opinion which we have here expressed, still differ very much on other points, viz., as to the *author* and *age* of composition; whether it was composed by Solomon, to whom the superscription attributes it, and if not, whether in the age of Solomon or later; whether by one or several authors, and, in the former case, if it is the work of one author, whether the whole of it was composed as one work or at least in reference to one and the same circumstance, so that the lover and the loved one are the same persons throughout, or whether there are not various songs unconnected with one another in reference to different circumstances and persons. On these points I will content myself here with making the following remarks:

(*a*) In the first place it may be assumed with the greatest probability, that the book had but one author; this is pointed out by the similarity of character, literary style and language, and the recurrence of so many individual references.

(*b*) Some passages clearly relate to Solomon and the circumstances of his time, so that there can be scarcely a doubt that they were written in the age and neighbourhood of this prince; thus especially the nuptial song, ch. iii. 6–11; also ch. i. 5; viii. 11, ff.

Many persons incorrectly fix the date of the book considerably later, at the time of the Captivity or in the Persian age, thus Eichhorn, Bertholdt, Umbreit (*Lieder der Liebe*, &c., 1820, second edit. 1828), Rosenmüller (Hupfeld) and others; Ewald (*Gesch. Isr.* iii. 458, ff.) places it in the first century after Solomon, in the kingdom of Israel.

(*c*) The very same passages however make it in the highest degree probable that Solomon himself was not the author, but some other poet at the time and in the vicinity of Solomon; cf. also ch. i. 4, 12.

(*d*) Finally, as regards the *composition* of the book, several modern interpreters[1] have endeavoured in various ways to prove its *unity* as a continuous dramatical representation of one and the same circumstance. But none of these attempts at explanation are satisfactory, not even the one carried out by Delitzsch in so ingenious a way.

He refers the whole, as composed by Solomon, to the circumstances affecting one maiden from the first falling in love of the lovers up to their wedding, and divides the whole into six acts and each of these into two scenes:— (1) Ch. i. 1–ii. 7: the commencement of mutual love. (2) Ch. ii. 8–iii. 5: their mutual seeking for and finding each other. (3) Ch. iii. 6–v. 1: the going to meet the bride and the nuptials. (4) Ch. v. 2–vi. 9: the rejected but afterwards regained love. (5) Ch. vi. 10–viii. 4: how Sulamith, who is ravishingly beautiful, shows herself to be as a princess both simple and modest. (6) Ch. viii. 5–14: visit of Solomon and Sulamith to the home of the latter and confirmation of their covenant of love. This conception of it presents, however, much that is difficult and improbable, as to which I will only mention as follows. The section, ch. iii. 1–5 and ch. v. 2–7, Delitzsch would con-

[1] Thus, *e.g.*, Umbreit, Ewald (*Das Hohelied Sal.* Göttingen, 1826, and *Die Poetischen Bücher d. A. B.* i. p. 41, ff.), Delitzsch, &c.

sider as a dream of Sulamith, only because they could not be understood as statements of actual events in the history of the love of Solomon and Sulamith; but the account in the book itself offers no suggestion at all to consider these passages as a dream. In ch. i, the passages v. 7, f., v. 12, ff., also v. 17, are altogether unfavourable to the idea that Solomon himself was the lover; the latter manifestly appears, on the contrary, to have been a shepherd, and a different person to the king; in the same way he appears as a herdsman, ch. ii. 16. also ch. vi. 8, 9, where the speaker and lover contrasts the *one* object of his love to the numerous queens and concubines of the king. Solomon's wedding-song, ch. iii. 6–11, appears clearly to have been composed by some other poet than Solomon himself; and in the same way we cannot imagine that Solomon would have praised himself in so extraordinary a way, as that in which the lover is spoken of in ch. v. 9–16. Thus these views of Delitzsch can hardly be considered as correct, and some other ideas, which look upon the book in this way as a *unity*, are just as untenable.

The more probability we find for the belief that the whole book was composed by one author, and in the age of Solomon, the more, I think, we are compelled to assume that it includes various erotic songs, which bear reference to various circumstances and various persons, and only partly to Solomon; on the contrary, they mostly relate to the circumstances of persons in a pastoral condition and in the country; and there must of course exist a doubt, whether they were actual matters of fact which the author had in view, or merely ideal circumstances.

3.—ECCLESIASTES, OR THE PREACHER.

§ 285.—*Authorship and Tendency of the Book.*

This book, like Proverbs, is one of the class of didactic compositions, or Maschals; it does not, however, consist of a number of maxims loosely strung together, but forms the continuous soliloquy of a wise man on the vanity of all human affairs. These remarks are placed in the mouth of a man who is called (ch. i. 1, 2, 12; vii. 27; xii. 8, 9. 10) קֹהֶלֶת, and is designated as the son of David, and king in

264   *Origin of the several Books—Ecclesiastes.*

Jerusalem (ch. i. 1, 12). There can, therefore, be no doubt that they are intended to be considered as spoken by king Solomon, and that קֹהֶלֶת is therefore a designation of Solomon, and is a term framed by the author himself in reference to the way in which the king appears in the book. The most ancient, the most usual, and also the most probable explanation is, that it proceeds from קהל, *to gather together* (the people), and therefore signifies the *assembler*, and thence the *orator before the assembly* of the people or wise men.

In the same way Ἐκκλησιαστής, as the LXX expresses the word, from ἐκκαλεῖν. Cf. Jerome, *ad Eccles.* i. 1—" ἐκ-κλησιαστής Græco sermone appellatur, qui coetum, id est ecclesiam, congregat; quem nos nuncupare possumus concionatorem, eo quod loquatur ad populum et eius sermo non specialiter ad unum, sed ad universos generaliter dirigatur." In Luther, *Prediger*.

The feminine form here occasions some difficulty, as the form קֹהֵל would have been more looked for. In opposition to this, it has been remarked that in proper names the gender is often not suitable to the sex of the person indicated, and that many names of men occur, particularly in later times, with the termination ת ָ־, as סֹפֶרֶת and פֹּכֶרֶת. Ezra ii. 54, 57; Neh. vii. 57, 59. But this explanation is not sufficient, because קֹהֶלֶת is no actual proper name, but only an appellative designation for Solomon, selected by the author. Ewald and Köster (*Das B. Hiob u. d. Pred. Sal.* &c. Schleswig, 1831), interpret it as actually expressing— *the thing preaching* (wisdom), and that this was, by the author, treated as a proper name. Essentially, it amounts to the same thing, when Knobel and others (*Comment. über d. B. Koheleth*, Leipzig, 1836), give it an abstract signification as a neuter. But it must not be lost sight of that it is intended here as a designation of Solomon, and is therefore treated as masculine; *v.* ch. i. 2, xii. 8, 9, 10. In one passage, ch. vii. 27, in the Masoretic text indeed, we read אָמְרָה קֹהֶלֶת; yet there, without doubt, we should follow earlier interpreters, and join ה to the following word, אָמַר הַקֹּהֶלֶת, just as it is in ch. xii. 8 even in the Masoretic text.[1]

[1] Cf. *Das Berliner Gymnasialprogramm*, von C. Kleinert; *Der Prediger Salomo: Uebersetzung, sprachliche Bemerkungen und Erörterungen zum Verständniss*, 1864.

As regards the origin of the book, the universal opinion in ancient times was that it was written by Solomon; which is the view of Welte and Ludwig von Essen (Rector of the Progym. at Juliers)[1] among modern writers. But Grotius and Herm. von der Hardt[2] (1714) have pronounced a contrary opinion, and it is at present almost generally acknowledged that the author's assumption of Solomon's name, for the person speaking, is nothing but a literary embellishment. The composer might very easily be induced to do this, inasmuch as he could not readily have found a more suitable person to testify to the vanity of all earthly things, than this king who had so thoroughly given himself up to the enjoyment of them. That there is an assumption of Solomon's name is clearly shown by several passages.

Among these are not only the conclusion, ch. xii. 9–14, in which the author appears speaking in his own person as distinct from Koheleth,[3] but also several passages in the rest of the book, in which the character of the person assumed has not been strictly carried out, as ch. i. 12— "I, Koheleth, was (הָיִיתִי) king in Jerusalem over Israel;" ch. i. 16, "I have gotten more wisdom than all *that have been before me in Jerusalem;*" and ch. ii. 9, "I increased more than all *that were before me in Jerusalem,*"—all which does not appear very natural as coming from the son of David, who first captured Jerusalem.

As to the date of the composition of the book, it may be assumed with certainty that it took place at a period after the Captivity.

(*a*) It was written at a time when the temple and the service in it existed. This is shown by passages such as ch. v. 1, ch. ix. 2. (*b*) Yet certainly not before the Captivity but some considerable time after it; this is pointed out by the whole nature of the language and the prosaic character of the composition. It is also full of Chaldaisms,[4] such as

---

[1] *Der Pred. Salomo.* Schaffhausen, 1856.
[2] *Vide Introd.* ii. p. 204, ff., by Carpzov.
[3] This concluding speech is indeed pronounced by many interpreters, as Döderlein *Scholia in libros V. T. poeticos*, 1779, and *Salomo's Pred. u. hohes Lied.* 1784, J. E. C. Schmidt (*Salomo's Pred.* 1794), Bertholdt and Knobel, to be not genuine, but, as I believe, for insufficient reasons.
[4] The *Dissertatio de Aramaismis libri Koheleth*, in which Ed. Bohl (Erlangen, 1860) endeavours to claim the authorship for Solomon, is unsatisfactory. Also Heinr. Aug. Hahn, in his commentary on our

we scarcely meet with in any other of the Hebrew books of the Old Testament. (c) In favour of its composition at a later age, is the complaint as to much book-making, ch. xii. 12. (d) It may be inferred from various passages that the Jewish people were then under kings who gave much occasion for complaint, and to whom they paid but an unwilling obedience, and that these were foreign kings, and not hereditary monarchs of their own race (cf. ch. iv. 13–16; v. 8; viii. 1, ff., 9; x. 4, 16, f., 20).

We cannot ascertain anything more exact on this point. The composition may have perhaps taken place in the latter period of the Persian dominion, as Ewald and others assume; perhaps, however, still later, at the time of the Syrian rule over Judæa.

The passage, ch. iv. 13, ff., appears to refer to some distinct historical fact, when some personage not sprung from the royal race had come to the throne out of a prison. But to whom this may refer cannot be ascertained.

As regards the *prompting cause for*, and *aim* of the book—it represents to us the internal struggle which the author felt in the contemplation of earthly human matters, and of the vanity of human efforts in the constantly recurring periodical course of events. He repeatedly recommends as true worldly wisdom the enjoyment of the good things and pleasures of life (ch. ii. 24–26; iii. 12, f., 22; v. 17–19; vii. 14; viii. 15; ix. 7, 10; xi. 7–xii. 7). But these remarks manifest no atheistical epicureanism in the author.

Not only does the book conclude (ch. xii. 13, f.), as summing up the whole matter, with the summons to fear God and keep His commandments, for "God will bring every work into judgment, with every secret thing, whether it be good or whether it be evil," but the whole course of the argument is based everywhere upon the consciousness, expressed in the most distinct way, that God is the Almighty, from whom everything proceeds, who gives life, wisdom, and all good things to men, whose working is for everlasting, who makes everything beautiful and watches over

---

book (Leipzig, 1860), as well as Hengstenberg and Keil, express themselves in favour of Solomon being the author, and think that it tends to the disgrace of orthodox divinity, that the rationalistic opinion as to Ecclesiastes has been so willingly given way to.

all (ch. ii. 26; iii. 10, f.; v. 1, 7, 17–19; viii. 14; ix. 1–3); that in His own good time He will bring everything to judgment, and that He will finally bless those who fear Him, but not so the wicked (ch. viii. 12, f.; iii. 17; xi. 9); that mere man cannot understand the works of God, and that they are unintelligible to him (ch. iii. 11; viii. 16, f.), and that man must not venture to strive with God, who only tries him (ch. iii. 18; vi. 10), but that he must fear God (ch. iii. 14; v. 1; vii. 18). Koheleth, therefore, recommends the enjoyment of the good things of life, inasmuch as they are given us by God (ch. iii. 12, f., 22; v. 17), and places this in opposition to those who are unsatisfied with their lot and complain about present things, as if former times had been better (ch. vii. 10), and also to those who only strive after riches without taking pleasure in the enjoyment of them (ch. v. 11, ff.; vi. 2, ff.), also to those who, in their proud self-conceit, consider that they alone are wise, and aspire to the fame of an austere righteousness (ch. vi. 16–18), as there is no man on earth who is just and without sin (ch. vii. 20).

Certainly the book affords no just satisfaction for any religious want. In it, as Oehler[1] justly remarks, "the contrast between the Divine perfection and the vanity of the world is represented as irreconcileable the latter as an undeniable experience, the former as a religious postulate." But it is both moving and elevating to see how this latter belief is held fast to amid every doubt, and how the author everywhere recurs to it.

The book, too, is frequently deficient in a well-arranged train of thought, and the author gives himself up freely to the course of his own feelings, adopting foreign matter and appropriate aphorisms, just as they occurred to him, although they were but distantly connected with the leading idea of the book, and could be joined on but very loosely to the matter preceding them.

[1] *Prolegomena zur Theol. des A. T.* Stuttg. 1846, p. 90.

THE BOOK OF JOB.

§ 286.—*Nature of the Book—Review of Contents.*

This book is a long and continuous didactic composition in an interlocutory form. For the chief matter of the book, and by far the larger portion as to extent (ch. iii–xlii. 6) consists of long discourses, the speakers being partly Job and his friends, and partly Jehovah Himself. An introduction or prologue in the form of a narrative (ch. i. and ii.) precedes these, and in the same way they are followed by a concluding narrative or epilogue (ch. xlii. 7–17).

In the prologue Job is at once represented as the chief person (איוב),—a pious, righteous man in the land of Uz, blessed with many good things. Uz was probably situate in the desert of Arabia, north of Idumæa, and east of Judæa, not however immediately adjacent to the latter land. On the occasion of an assembling of the sons of God, among whom was Satan, the latter raised wicked doubts as to the disinterested sincere piety of Job, who was then given up to him by Jehovah, so that Satan received power to bring upon Job whatever evil he wished, but was forbidden to lay his hand upon his person; and that thus Job's piety would have an opportunity of showing itself. In consequence of this, great misfortunes came upon Job; in one day he lost his flocks, his servants, and all his children; but he still bent in pious submission to the will of Jehovah who had given and also taken away. But when, nevertheless, Satan persevered in his doubts to Jehovah, Job was given up to him for bodily chastisement, only his life was to be spared; Satan therefore brought a leprosy of the sorest kind upon Job, who, however, by all this, was not induced to sin against God. Three of his friends, Eliphaz the Temanite, Bildad the Shuhite, and Zophar the Naamathite, heard of all the misfortune, which, in this shape, had come upon Job, and came to him by common agreement, but found him so disfigured that they could not recognize him; silent and full of grief they sat round him for seven days and nights.

Thus much we find in the prologue. Next follow the long discourses, firstly between Job and his three friends, ch. iii–xxvi. This section may be divided into three *acts*, so to speak, the three friends answering Job's complaints and discourses three separate times, one after the other: First, Eliphaz, next Bildad, then Zophar, only that the third time, the two former alone speak; Zophar, as it appears, not venturing to interfere again. The essential point aimed at in the discourses of the friends is, from the very first, that no innocent person suffers; this rule they always distinctly apply to Job, arguing that he also must have merited his sufferings by his sins, and urging him to turn to God in full confidence, and to be converted to the Almighty, Most High, and Holy God, who punishes only in conformity with justice. Job perfectly acknowledges the greatness of God, before whom all must bow; but he maintains that God destroys the innocent as well as the wicked, indeed that the wicked who care nothing about God are seldom visited with destruction, but that, on the contrary, they enjoy lasting and flourishing good fortune. He repeatedly pours forth vehement lamentations as to the intolerable nature of the misery brought on him, and complains that his friends insidiously utter accusations against him, which they are not able to prove. Even if he had sinned, God, to whom no injury would arise from it, should rather forgive him, than allow him to perish in his misery; still he is conscious of no injustice, and protests his innocence, often expressing the hope that God Himself would undertake his justification. After Job had thus reduced to silence his three friends, he still goes on speaking (ch. xxvii–xxxi), at first addressing himself to his friends (ch. xxvii–xxviii), then in what follows (ch. xxix–xxxi), without paying any attention to them. His discourse begins again with another decided protestation of his innocence; but he then adds the expression of the idea that the lot of the wicked would be certainly hopeless, and that sudden destruction should fall upon him, whilst God's protection should be afforded to the pious and righteous, (ch. xxvii); to this is joined a consideration of the value and profundity of wisdom, which man, though he may penetrate the depths of the earth, cannot fathom, and only God can understand; who sets before men, as the only wisdom,—to fear God and to avoid evil (ch. xxviii). Next follows a sorrowful consideration of his former prosperity, and of the misery and ignominy into which God had now plunged him, although he feels conscious that by his former conduct he had not deserved it (ch. xxix. 1–xxxi. 34): he then expresses the wish that God might hear him, and that for his justification He would set before him, in what he had sinned, and that he would boldly confront Him, concluding with an imprecation upon himself, if he had been guilty of any injustice (ch. xxxi. 35–39). The chapter concludes with the *postscriptum*, תַּמּוּ דִבְרֵי אִיּוֹב.

It goes on to relate, how another man, not hitherto named, Elihu, the son of Barachel, the Buzite, of the race of Ram, took up the discourse, full of indignation against Job, because he justified himself before God, and not less angry with the three friends,—before whom, he, as the younger, had kept silence,—because they knew not how to answer Job's discourses (ch. xxxii. 1–6). Elihu's discourses extend to the end of ch. xxxvii, in different portions, which are also sometimes specially introduced (ch. xxxiv. 1, xxxv. 1, xxxvi. 1). His discourses, by their style, give the impression of a diffuse, vain character; they are not, however, otherwise inferior in their value to those of the previous speakers. The essential ideas contained in them are these: that Job acted very wrongly in maintaining that he was pure, and thinking that he suffered innocently and God had brought these misfortunes on him through enmity, and that man was no better off through his piety, than if he sinned; but that, on the contrary, God requited every one only according to his conduct, and punished without partiality, and with equal severity, both the highest and the meanest; that this is done to warn men and make them better, if they sin against Him, but that He will bless for ever those who feel remorse, and will give up to shameful sufferings those who harden themselves and are exasperated at their visitation; that the suffering ones must wait with patient submission; that God is generally too lofty for man to venture to call Him to account for His dealings; and that a human being must not dare to accuse God of injustice, who in His works in nature shows Himself so sublime and unsearchable, whom also, we are not able to find out, but only have to fear.

Now, however, Jehovah Himself condescends to speak, answering Job out of the whirlwind; the latter having challenged Him to set forth his guilt (ch. xxxi. 35, ff.; cf. ch. xiii. 22). Summoning Job to prepare for the conflict, He proposes to him, one after the other, a series of questions as to the wonderful phenomena of nature, both animate and inanimate, both of earth and heaven, so as to induce in him a vivid consciousness of the imperfection of the human intellect and human knowledge, as opposed to Divine wisdom and omnipotence (ch. xxxviii, xxxix). He calls upon Job to answer it,—him who had presumed to dispute with the Almighty (ch. xl. 1, 2). Job, however, now acknowledges himself humbled, and that he is too mean to be able to answer anything, and that he will no longer speak against God (vv. 3–5). But Jehovah repeatedly calls upon Job, to prepare himself to declare to him his questions; he asks, whether, in order to justify himself he would be really willing to condemn Him, and whether he can rule the thunder with Divine power and majesty, and bow down the proud and annihilate the wicked; for that then He would praise him (vv. 6–14). Then Jehovah describes still more in detail as to their nature and doings, two wonders of the animal world,—the hippopotamus and the crocodile, which were especially well fitted to show to men their own weakness and the creative power of God (ch. xl. 15–xli); in this description Jehovah also (ch. xli. 11) asks the question,—who hath surpassed Him, that He should repay him? but that everything on the earth was His. Job now confesses more decidedly his acknowledgment of the Divine omnipotence, and is full of repentance for his wrong and foolish behaviour in calling God to account, for which his only excuse was his previous imperfect acquaintance with God (ch. xlii. 1–6).

The epilogue (ch. xlii. 7–14), then tells us that Jehovah· reproved Job's three friends—of Elihu, nothing is said— on account of the purport of their discourses, in which they had not spoken rightly of God, as Job had done, and they are enjoined to offer up a burnt offering for themselves and to induce Job to intercede for them; and that for his

272   *Origin of the several Books—Job.*

sake only, Jehovah would not punish them for their perversity. This demand they then complied with. After that, Jehovah restored to Job the double of all the good things which he had lost, and gave him also seven sons and three daughters, the most beautiful in the land, to whom their father gave possessions; and Job lived (after this) 140 years, and saw his descendants to the fourth generation, and then died, old and full of days.

§ 287.—*As to the Historical Character of Job's Person and Life.*

In the first place, it is a question if this book gives, and intends to give, a *history based on facts*, or merely an imaginary composition. Most of the ancient interpreters adopt the former view. They not only take Job to be an historical person, but also consider the entire contents of the book as historical. Ezekiel xiv. 14-20, mentions Job, naming him between Noah and Daniel, as the only men whom Jehovah would deliver, in their own persons, an account of their righteousness, when he gave over their whole country to destruction on account of its sinfulness. It may, however, be assumed with probability, that this mention of Job took place merely in reference to the way in which he appears in the book we are discussing; and that we cannot infer from it, that Ezekiel was acquainted with anything else as to the existence and history of Job. No authority, however, can be given to the statements of the LXX, and of later authors, especially of the Arabians.

The latter go so far as to relate all kind of things about Job, as to his family, his age, his disease, &c.; his grave is also shown, but in *six* different places, from which it can be sufficiently inferred, how little value is to be put on these later statements. V. Flügel, in Ersch and Gruber's *Allgem. Encycl.*, Art. "*Hiob*" (Sect. ii. vol. viii. p. 298, f.); d'Herbelot, *Orient. Bibl.*, under "Ajub" (i. p. 235, ff.) The LXX have some additions at the end of the book, which are indeed ancient, but still of only Christian origin; they mostly contain genealogical statements as to Job and his friends, in which, among other things, we are told that his name was previously Jobab, who is mentioned in Gen. xxxvi. 33, as an Edomite king; this is, however, manifestly an entirely arbitrary combination, to which a certain similarity between the names אִיּוֹב and יוֹבָב, particularly in the Greek, form 'Ιὼβ, 'Ιωβάβ, has given rise. Josephus mentions nothing about Job.[1]

Therefore for deciding the question as to the historical character of Job's person and the narrative about him, we are exclusively directed to the book itself. But from its whole nature, it may be asserted with certainty, that the book has no historical tendency.

In the Talmud the contents are pronounced by a Rabbi Resch Lakisch[2], to be a purely parabolic composition; *Baba Bathra*, fol. 15, 1—" Jobus nunquam exstitit neque creatus est, sed parabola est." The verdict of Moses Maimonides is the same (*More Neboch*. iii. 22), as well as that of the ecclesiastical author Junilius (*De Partibus Legis. Div.*). lib. i., of Theodorus of Mopsuestia, and, at a later time. of Clericus and others. In modern times it is pretty generally assumed, that the book neither is, nor is intended to be, of an historical nature.

From its whole contents it can in no way be considered as purely historical; on the contrary, its composition is, without doubt, generally poetical.

In particular, the consultations and resolutions at the assemblage of the heavenly hosts could not well be a subject for human narrative. The kind of matter, therefore, which our book gives in the prologue, even if the rest of the book were historical, could only be deduced from the result, namely, from the whole course of the events occurring on the earth; and the statements in this part of the work must be considered as a poetical embellishment. It is, besides, absolutely incredible that in the condition in which Job was when the hand of God was so heavily laid upon him, such long and ingeniously-composed discourses should

---

[1] Cf. on this point "Lectures on Job:" "It cannot be decided that Josephus did *not* consider Job to be an historical person; he might have omitted to mention him, because, according to our book, he does not appear either as an Israelite or as one of the ancestors of the Israelitish people, nor is he included in any part of their history. That Josephus, on the contrary, considered our book as actually historical, may be concluded from the passage *Cont. Apion*, i. 8, where, in the enumeration of the Sacred Books, he must have included Job among the thirteen, in which the prophets living after Moses down to the time of Artaxerxes (Longimanus) τὰ κατὰ αὐτοὺς πραχθέντα συνέγραψαν.'

[2] Others incorrectly ascribe this to the Rabbi Samuel bar Nachmanja, who, on the contrary, attacks R. Resch Lakisch. It is correct in Magnus (*Commentar zum Buche Hiob*, i. (Halle, 1851), p. 298).

have been actually maintained between him and his friends as we here read of (as Luther says, "There is not so much talk in trouble;" *Tischreden* [W. A. xxii. 2082]); and it is just as little credible that, even if these conversations were really held, they could have been subsequently exactly repeated by any author, even an ear and eye-witness, indeed not even by Job himself. We must, therefore, in any case, consider that the discourses which manifestly form the principal part of the book are, in their present form and extent, the literary work of the author. But even in that portion which tells about Job's external circumstances the poetic hand is readily to be discerned if we notice the parallel which exists, according to the epilogue, between the things which were given to Job after his sufferings and those which he previously possessed—the same number of sons and daughters, the exactly doubled number of his herds of cattle, &c.

It might possibly be the case that the author did not originate all his matter spontaneously and independently, but that he followed something that he met with, either in tradition or in some earlier work.

Thus it is, at least, not improbable that he did not form the name of Job on purpose for his work; for in that case we should expect that the name would present, in its etymology, some clearly prominent reference to the part that Job was to play in it, which, however, is not the case. It is, therefore, at least not improbable that the author met with the name of Job in connection with either a written or oral tradition as to the heavy trials of some man bearing this name in former times, with, perhaps, also the land of Uz mentioned as his dwelling-place. How much besides he may have met with cannot, from the nature of the case, be ascertained with any certainty or even probability.

This, however, is certain, that the portion of the book which is, perhaps, historical, was not related by the author with any historical aim, but was made use of by him only as a foundation for his composition, and to suit his purpose, and that the discourses in the book especially were composed in an arbitrary way just as the didactic aim of the author suggested.

§ 288.—*Aim of the Author —Ideas asserted.*

The author's[1] *aim* is differently understood even by those who look upon the whole as a didactic composition. Many ancient interpreters have conceived its chief aim to be, to set forth Job's behaviour as an example of patience for the imitation of all sufferers. But for this purpose Job appears in the book as too little in action, and is also by no means represented as so perseveringly patient and resigned without hesitation to the will of God. Among modern interpreters Schlottmann[2] particularly has sought to establish that the aim of the book is to represent the conflict and victory of the pious in the heaviest troubles. But this is certainly not the correct idea. On the contrary, the author, doubtless, seeks to impart instruction as to the procedure and counsel of God in reference to the relation of evil to the moral conduct of men ; for the subject to which all the discourses in the book relate is the heavy afflictions which were brought upon Job by Divine dispensation or permission, and the Divine intention in this visitation.

According to the idea prevalent among the Hebrews, in the spirit of strict retribution inherent in the Mosaic law, the worldly fate of men, both in general and in detail, was considered to be settled by their conduct according to either their piety or sinfulness ; therefore when a man was visited by great affliction it was thought that he had offended God by some act of peculiar guilt, and they were also inclined to look upon continuous worldly prosperity as the reward of eminent piety. Thus the unfortunate who were visited with severe and long-continued afflictions must have often found that they were considered as the peculiar objects of the Divine wrath and displeasure, and that it was thought that their afflictions were brought upon them on account of their sins—sins perhaps hidden from the eye of man—and that for this reason, harsh, injurious judgments were passed upon them by their pious fellow-countrymen, indeed by their closest friends, although they

[1] A peculiar revival of the allegorical comprehension of the book is given by the Archidiaconus Seinecke (*Der Grundgedanke des Buches Hiob*, Clausthal, 1863), who understands by Job the servant of God, in Is. xl-lxvi. or the pious nucleus of the people.
[2] *Das B. Hiob verdeutscht u. erläutert.* Berlin, 1851.

themselves might be conscious that they had not knowingly wandered from God's paths. Now, the author of our book may have felt these bitter experiences either in his own person or in that of another. Many of the songs in the Psalter—the so-called Penitential Psalms—relate to circumstances of this sort in which pious sufferers heavily visited with evil of various kinds, and on this account exposed to the insults of men, pour out their lamentations to God, and implore His help. Some Psalms are devoted to considering the lot of the pious and ungodly, in reference to the Divine justice, and with giving instruction on the point, as Psalms xxxvii, xlix, lxxiii. This, then, may be considered as the theme also of the Book of Job. The usual opinions of the Hebrews are represented in it by the speeches of Job's friends, Eliphaz, Bildad, and Zophar, also partly of Elihu. Proceeding on the idea that every misfortune happening to men is well deserved, and that the godless only can be continuously unfortunate, they believe they are justified in supposing that Job also had merited his sufferings by his sins. They express this to him sometimes insiduously, sometimes candidly, but always with great harshness, and call upon him to turn to God. Many truths occur in their discourses, but the leading idea from which they proceed is unmistakeably intended by the author to be pointed out as erroneous, as evidently appears from the prologue and epilogue: from the prologue, inasmuch as in it the whole of Job's misfortune and sufferings are pointed out as brought upon an altogether pious man, who was earnestly intent on walking in God's ways, and on keeping himself and his house pure from sin, whom also God recognized as His faithful servant, in whom He had a peculiar pleasure; in the epilogue, inasmuch as we are here expressly told that Jehovah admonished Eliphaz and his two friends, and imposed upon them an atoning sacrifice, because they had not spoken rightly of God, as Job had done.

It now becomes a question what idea the author himself entertained as to the cause for such afflictions. This is understood by modern interpreters in various ways; yet, by an impartial consideration of the whole book, we shall, I think, be induced to consider that the leading idea and essential truths which it seeks to assert are as follows:—

(a) That even a pious man may be visited by God with heavy and manifold afflictions without its being necessary to consider these as punishments for any peculiar sinfulness, or as signs of peculiar Divine displeasure; that it was reprehensible to reproach such a one with his sufferings as if they were caused by God's displeasure, but that, on the contrary, they were decreed or permitted by God, so that the piety, faith, and virtue of the sufferer might be proved, and might find a suitable opportunity of showing themselves (for this is expressly pointed out in the prologue as the aim of the misfortunes happening to Job).

(b) That it is foolish presumption on the part of men to be angry with God on account of the misfortunes befalling them, and to wish to call Him to judgment on account of them. That no man is in a position to fathom the wisdom and the counsel of God, and that true wisdom for men must be set down as this—to fear God, and to avoid evil.

(c) But that Jehovah will at last certainly pity the pious sufferer if only he persevere in his piety and hold fast to God, or, in case he has transgressed in his depression, if he repents, and will bless and glorify Him.

In the first place, ancient interpreters are wrong in understanding the author's idea to be (as, *e.g.*, J. D. Michaelis, *Einleitung in die göttl. Schriften des A. B.* p. 23) that Divine justice will not show itself until in a future world, after the resurrection, in the rewards and punishments which will then be decreed for men according to their piety or ungodliness. This opinion is gathered from an explanation of Job's speech (ch. xix. 25–27), which was formerly very popular—followed even in the Vulgate and Luther's translation—in which these passages are referred to the resurrection, and the justification to be expected after it. In modern times also this interpretation has sometimes been brought forward, in reference at least to a future life after death, and the justification to be then expected, *e.g.*, by Ewald, Schlottmann particularly, and others. But this, according to the words, is decidedly wrong,[1] as in the whole book generally there is no conception of a resurrection, or of a retribution after death; but, on the contrary,

---

[1] Cf. also the work of Seinecke, and my remarks in the *Theol. Stud. und Krit.*, 1863, p. 811, f.; also the treatise by J. F. Räbiger, Professor at Breslau, *De libri Jobi sententia primaria*, 1860.

as in many of the Psalms, there are various expressions which decidedly indicate the opposite idea (v. ch. vii. 7–10; x. 20-22; xiv. 7–12; xvii. 13–16).

On the other hand, the author's view cannot have been, as has been supposed sometimes in modern times (*e.g.*, by Bernstein in Keil and Tzschirner's *Analekten*, Bd. i. [1812], Part 3), to oppose the doctrine of retribution altogether and absolutely, and to attack the idea of any connection existing between the worldly fate of a man and his morality. In Job's discourses it is indeed repeatedly asserted that the wicked who despise God are the very ones to enjoy a continuous, flourishing good fortune; thus particularly ch. xxi. and xxiv. But we certainly cannot consider this as an idea, the assertion of which was the author's aim. These expressions can only be the utterances of a depression of mind, into which the best of men might fall if they were in the condition in which Job then was, and spoken in opposition to the speeches which his friends made against him. But after the latter were put to silence the author makes Job himself—before the appearance of Jehovah, in ch. xxvii. 8, ff.—express his own conviction that the lot of the wicked was a hopeless one, and his wealth of short duration, and that sudden destruction should strike him. But, finally, in the epilogue, Job's piety finds its reward after he had humbled himself before God, and had acknowledged with repentance how wrong and foolish his conduct had been when he called God to account. He is eminently restored to his former prosperity; he is blessed by children in his house, and attains to a good old age.

From the foregoing it also appears to be wrong when many interpreters, as Knobel (*De carminis Jobi argumento fine ac dispositione*. Breslau, 1835), Heiligstedt (*Comment. in Jobum*. Leipzig, 1847), and Hupfeld (*Deutsche Zeitschrift für Christl. Wissenschaft*, &c., 1850. Nos. 35–37), consider the aim of the author to be exclusively or principally to point out that men cannot penetrate into the Divine counsel, and must therefore submit, in believing resignation, to everything that the latter decrees for them.

§ 289.—*The Prologue and Epilogue—Their Author.*

If the idea here developed as to the didactic aim of the book be correct, it follows that the *prologue* and *epilogue*

Prologue and Epilogue. 279

form a most necessary part of it, and that the view entertained by many that they did not originally form a part of the book is decidedly erroneous. Some of the reasons which have been brought forward for this view are manifestly wrong, and some are irrelevant.

Carpzov thinks, that although the whole of the discourses were written by Job himself (before Moses), the prologue and epilogue were subsequently added (by Samuel); and many later interpreters have also considered that they were added subsequently, among others, Stuhlmann (*Hiob; Ein religiöses Gedicht*, &c., Hamb., 1804), Bernstein, also earlier, De Wette, and finally Knobel (*ut supr.* and *Theol. Stud. u. Krit.* 1842, ii. pp. 485–495). Considerable importance has also been laid on the circumstance, that in the prologue and epilogue God is usually called Jehovah, but in the discourses this designation is avoided. But the cause for this is that the composer himself was a Hebrew, and he does not make either Job or his friends appear as Israelites, but as pious men of some other race, and, indeed, in patriarchal times. For this reason, in their discourses he makes them abstain from the use of that name, which had prevailed among the Israelites from the time of Moses for the only true God, whilst he himself, the Israelitish author, usually makes use of it, not only in his narrations in the prologue and epilogue, but also wherever, in his introductory words to God's speeches, he is compelled to name Him, ch. xxxviii. 1; xl. 1, 3, 6; xlii. 1. Even in the prologue, when Job and his wife speak, they call God Elohim and not Jehovah, ch. i. 5; ii. 9. It is otherwise, indeed, in ch. i. 21, where Job says Jehovah more than once; this, however, must be considered as a mere inconsistency, which we might have well expected to find in an Hebrew author. The term Jehovah also occurs in Job's speech, ch. xii. 9, and, according to the original reading, most probably also in ch. xxviii. 28, likewise the result of a certain inaccuracy in the language. Therefore, from the existing data, we may absolutely conclude that there is no variety of authors. There may be a greater appearance of difficulty in the contradiction which exists between ch. i. 19, where all Job's children are made to perish, and ch. xix. 17, where, in Job's discourse in his time of suffering, his children are presupposed to be existing. It is not probable that in the latter passage the children spoken of are intended for grandchildren, as Ewald, Hirzel (*Hiob*, 1839, 2nd edit. 1852), and others will have it; it should rather be acknowledged as another inaccuracy of statement. But it is not at all to be wondered at, if, in the purely poetical treatment of his matter in a comparatively voluminous work, the author should have, as it were, forgotten himself in the flow of his language : and this can all the less feasibly serve as a proof of a variety of authors, as in ch. viii. 4, xxix. 5, the account in the prologue of the destruction of Job's children is evidently presupposed.

Without the prologue, the whole book would not be easily intelligible. It is only in the prologue that it is distinctly made clear to the reader—what neither Job nor his friends make known in their discourses—how Job's sufferings are really to be understood, viz., that they were sent on him that his piety might find an opportunity of showing itself. That this is actually the author's intention cannot well be doubted from the tendency of the discourses themselves; yet in the latter, even in Job's last speech and in Jehovah's, it is not made distinctly prominent, which would certainly have been done if the author had not previously laid it before his readers.

For the same reasons, Heiligstedt's opinion is untenable, who, indeed, looks upon the prologue generally as original, but excepts the account of the transactions in Heaven, between Jehovah and Satan, ch. i. 6–12, ii. 1–7; for it is in these very verses that the idea is intimated of the reason for Job's sufferings. The epilogue, too, must necessarily form part of the book, the contents of which, without the former, would be evidently insufficient for the reader, especially for the Hebrews.

§ 290.—*Elihu's Discourses—Opinions as to their Originality, Nature, and Aim.*

Another opinion, however, must be passed as to the *discourses of Elihu* (chapters xxxii–xxxvii). By many modern critics these are looked upon as a later interpolation.[1] On the other hand, others have pronounced decidedly for

[1] Thus Stuhlmann, Bernstein, De Wette, Eichhorn (Edit. 4), Ewald, Hirzel, Knobel, Heiligstedt [Delitzsch], and others. Cf. Bleek, *Theol. Stud. und Krit.* 1858, ii. p. 368, ff.

Elihu's Discourses.

their originality.[1] But the greater probability is in favour of the former opinion.

The principal reasons are as follows :

(a) These discourses are unmistakeably inserted with a very disturbing effect on the rest of the contents of the book.

Thus, when we are told in ch. xxxviii. 1: " Then Jehovah answered Job out of the whirlwind and said," we should certainly expect that *Job's* discourses immediately preceded, to which this admonition of Jehovah referred. Everything here would fit in beautifully if we looked upon Jehovah's admonition as being in immediate connection with Job's last discourse preceding the questionable section, in which last discourse, just before its conclusion, ch. xxxi. 35–37, he expresses, with bold confidence, his earnest longing that God Himself would answer his complaints, and would acquaint him how he had sinned against Him. God's appearance follows on to this in a very suitable way, which leaves nothing to be suggested, whilst the intervention of Elihu's reproofs, divided into four long discourses, form a very disturbing element.

(b) It is very surprising that, in the rest of the book, not the slightest notice is taken of Elihu and his discourses.

He appears without his coming being spoken of, whilst we should expect that this would have been mentioned just in the same way as that of Job's other three friends (ch. ii. 11. ff.), especially as he evidently shows himself to have listened to all the previous discourses, and must, therefore, have been present from the first. It is still more surprising that afterwards, when he had delivered his discourses, he is no more spoken of at all. Neither does Job answer *his* discourses, as he did all the preceding ones, nor is he named in the epilogue, in which it is told that the other three friends were reproved by Jehovah on account of their harsh speeches against Job.

Among the defenders of the originality of Elihu's dis-

[1] Thus Jahn, Bertholdt, Rosenmüller, Stäudlin (*Beiträge zur Philos. u. Gesch. der Relig. und Sittenlehre*, ii. p. 132, ff.), Umbreit, Köster (*Das B. Hiob u. d. Pred. Salomon*, 1831 , and particularly Stickel (*Das B. Hiob*, Leipzig, 1842 ; also Herbst. Welte (*Das Buch Hiob*, Freiburg, 1849 , Hävernick, Hahn (*Comm. über d. B. Hiob*. Berlin, 1850), Schlottmann, Keil, and, in a certain sense, Bunsen who considers that these discourses were supplementarily added by the same author).

courses there are two directly opposite opinions as to their *aim* and *character*. Many, as Umbreit, Köster (and formerly Eichhorn), and others, are of opinion that the author wished to represent Elihu as a superficial babbler, who spoke very diffusely, without being able to adduce anything of a striking nature, who, therefore, was tacitly despised by Job, and was not considered by Jehovah as worthy of any special notice. But, then, we should necessarily expect that Elihu's discourses would be in themselves entirely vain and worthless, and that they would contain nothing but trivial or false assertions, so that the author would presuppose that their emptiness and objectionable character would be recognised by the reader as a matter of course; but this, as we have before remarked, is in no way the case. Others—and among them Stäudlin, Rosenmüller, Stickel, Hävernick, Schlottmann, and Bunsen —take the opposite view, considering that the poet has already in these discourses sought to give the solution of the question, and thus to prepare for the appearance of Jehovah. This opinion, from the didactic character of the discourses, is, at any rate, more natural than the former. The author unmistakeably seeks to vindicate as religious truths those thoughts which he attributes to Elihu as his own. But then we should quite expect that something would be told us of their effect, and the impression which they made on Job and his three friends, and that, in the epilogue, Jehovah would have expressed his approbation of this champion, as he did his disapprobation of the three others, and that the author would have in some way intimated what relation he intended Elihu and his discourses to bear to the rest of the book and its aim.

The explanation given by Hahn is quite insufficient; he thinks that Elihu filled the part of arbitrator between Job and his three friends, and that on this account he was not further noticed. But he does not at all appear as an arbitrator, but, just like the three others, as an opponent to Job; and even if he were an arbitrator, no motive is shown for Jehovah's silence about him, notwithstanding that, according to Hahn's own opinion, Elihu's discourses must have proceeded from the same point of view as those of the three other friends.

(*c*) There is something very surprising about these discourses as regards their style, in the pomposity and boastful tone which prevails in them ; cf. ch. xxxii. 8, ff. ; xxxvi. 3, &c. If we compare them with the other discourses in the book, we might readily form the supposition that the author intentionally planned to represent Elihu as a vain, ostentatious fool. But as this opinion would be inadmissible on account of the didactic contents of the discourses, this peculiarity of form can be caused only by the literary character and individual taste of the author himself; so that this also would be a ground for thinking that they were composed by a different author from that of the rest of the book, who shows, in this respect, a much simpler feeling, and sounder taste.

Many other differences may also be brought forward, which, although not decisive in themselves, may yet seem to corroborate the above.

Among these, *e.g.*, is the fact that Elihu alone addresses Job by name (ch. xxxiii. 1, 31 ; xxxvii. 14 ; cf. ch. xxxii. 12 ; xxxiv. 5, 7, 35, 36 ; xxxv. 16), and that he at the outset expressly recapitulates the point in dispute, to which his discourse is to refer (ch. xxxiii. 8–10 ; xxxiv. 5, 6 ; xxxv. 3): also that these discourses present often recurring peculiarities in the language, and, in particular, more Chaldaisms than the rest of the book.

The author's aim is again only a didactic one ; to assert the truths which he makes Elihu utter as to God's relation to men, and as to the way in which men should look upon the sufferings sent by God, and how they should comfort themselves with regard to God's dealing with them. These truths may not have appeared to him to be set forth sufficiently and expressly enough in the book as he found it, and he perhaps feared that the way in which, in the epilogue, Job is justified by God, and Job's three friends are reproved, might work prejudicially, if he did not meet Job's assertions, so liable to give offence, in some other way than either by means of the three friends, or by Jehovah's appearance.

He sought, therefore, to explain in these discourses how, in his opinion, such expressions of displeasure were to be met. It may be assumed, with great probability, that the words, at the conclusion of ch. xxxi, " the words of Job are ended," were added at the time of the insertion of Elihu's discourses, and by the same author, in order to separate the long discourses of Job which precede from Elihu's discourses, which were here inserted.

Various expositors have endeavoured to prove that some other passages in the book are also later additions; thus (*a*), Bernstein, the fragment ch. xxvii. 7–xxviii. 28, in Job's speech; (*b*) Stuhlmann, Bernstein, and De Wette, the description of the crocodile, ch. xli. 4–26, Ewald (in Zeller's *Theolog. Jahrbb.* 1843, No. 4, pp. 740–751), the description of the crocodile, and the hippopotamus, *i.e.*, the whole section, ch. xl. 15–xli. 26 ; but all alike, as I believe, without sufficient grounds.

§ 291.—*Question as to the Authorship and Date of the Book.*

With regard to the *origin* of the book, there can be, in the first place, no doubt that it is the work of an Israelitish, *i.e.*, Hebrew author.

But very few have entertained a different opinion to this, as *e.g.*, Herder (*Geist der Hebr. Poesie.* Vol. i.), and Ilgen (*Jobi antiquissimi carminis Hebraici natura atque virtutes.* Leipzig, 1789), who consider that the author was an Idumæan. This, however, must be considered as an antiquated idea, for the Israelitish origin of the book is at present generally acknowledged; as to this, *v.*—particularly—Bernstein, *ut supra*, and De Wette, § 291, Note (*a*). There is likewise very little foundation for its being considered by others as a translation from a foreign original, either from the Arabic and Syriac. For the latter opinion, the addition at the end in the LXX is especially relied upon; οὗτος ἑρμηνεύεται ἐκ τῆς Συριακῆς βίβλου. Most probably, however, it is the existing Hebrew book which is there incorrectly styled Syriac; otherwise no importance at all can be placed on this statement, which is to be considered decidedly false.

There is more difficulty as to the age of the composition. The date of it falls, on the one hand, later than the days of David and Solomon, and on the other hand, before the Babylonian Captivity—probably between the Assyrian and Babylonian exiles.

The Talmud ascribes the book to Moses (*v.* p. 192, vol. i.), likewise also other Rabbis, the author of a commentary extant under Origen's name (as to this, *v.* Carpzov, *Introd.* ii.

Date of the Composition. 285

52), Ephraem Syrus, and various later Christian scholars, especially J. D. Michaelis. Others go so far as to assume a pre-Mosaic age, as Carpzov, Eichhorn, Jahn, Stuhlmann, and Bertholdt. The chief reason for fixing this early age is, that, in the book itself, there is not thought to be any reference to the Mosaical law and institutions, and to the Israelitish history. But this, so far as it is correct, is caused by the literary disguise assumed by the author, making Job and his opponents to appear as pious men of some adjacent nation, and not as Israelites, for which reason also, he makes him abstain from the usual term—Jehovah. But as the author, in the discourses here given, does not, as we have seen, follow out the abnegation of his religion and his nation with full consistency, neither does he completely exclude the circumstances of his age, by which he was surrounded. Thus, when in ch. xii. 17, in a discourse of Job, we are told that "God leads away captive councillors and priests, places kings in fetters, and renders impotent the noble and mighty," we may assume with the greatest probability that the author had had experience of such proofs of the Divine power in his own people. And when, in ch. xv. 18, Eliphaz says that he will show that which "wise men have told from their fathers, unto whom alone the earth was given, and no stranger passed among them," we may suppose that at the date of the composition, the author's native country was repeatedly overrun by enemies, and partly occupied by them. (Cf. also ch. ix. 24.) Passages also, such as ch. xiii. 26, xxxi 35, lead us to a later time than at least the Mosaic age, since it appears from them that, at the time of the author, it was customary to bring written complaints before tribunals. Moreover, our book appears so much the product of varied, continuous reflection, that we are necessarily led to presuppose that a more comprehensive and multiform system of literary art prevailed among the people than can be assumed with any degree of probability to have existed among the Israelites in the Mosaic age or still earlier.[1] These con-

---
Cf. *Vorl. über Hiob:* "There are ideas in them, which, framed in this way, do not occur at least in the older Scriptures of the Old Testament, and in all probability were not generally adopted by the Hebrews until a later time, as particularly that about Satan. Also, the whole language of the book has unmistakeably a greater similarity to the later than to the earlier Scriptures of the Old-Testament Canon."

siderations decidedly lead us to bring down the composition to a later age than that of Solomon or David, in which it has been placed by Luther, Döderlein (*Scholia in libros Vet. Test. poet.* Halle, 1779), Stäudlin, Rosenmüller, Welte, Hävernick, Hahn, Schlottmann, Keil, and others.

On the other hand, it is inadmissible to date the composition at the time of the Babylonian Captivity, or in the Persian age, as some of the Rabbis named in the Talmud, as well as H. von der Hardt, Clericus, Bernstein, Gesenius, (*Gesch. der Hebr. Spr. u. Schrift*, § 11), Umbreit, Bunsen, Seinecke, and also De Wette (*Einl.* edits. 1 to 4), and Vatke (*Bibl. Theologie.* i. p. 563), have done. For it may be assumed with great probability that Ezekiel was acquainted with this book (Ezek. xiv. 14-20 ; cf., above, p. 226), and not less so, that Jeremiah had it in view and repeatedly imitated it, thus particularly in Jer. xx. 14, ff. (cf. Job iii. 3, ff.), and in some other passages. Thus, also, the last editor of the Book of Proverbs—the author of ch. i-ix.—appears to have imitated several passages (*v.* in Rosenmüller, *Schol.* p. 35, f. ; Heiligstedt, p. xxiii). We shall, therefore, be led to a time at all events before the Babylonian exile, and probably between the Assyrian and Babylonian captivities; among modern expositors, Ewald, Hirzel, De Wette (edits. 5 and 6), Stickel, Heiligstedt, and others, generally agree in this.

The composition of Elihu's discourses consequently falls later, probably after the Babylonian Captivity, which, perhaps, the author had in view in ch. xxxvi. 8.[1]

As regards the *place of composition*, it may be assumed with great probability, that the Israelitish author lived and wrote in Palestine, but perhaps not in Jerusalem or its neighbourhood—(for in that case we should expect that some allusions to this centre of the worship of the true living God would have unconsciously escaped him)—but more on the borders of the land, in a region, where not only the life in cities, but also that of the wandering

[1] Cf. *Vorl. über Hiob:* "The frequent occurrence of Chaldaisms, and the general linguistic character of these discourses also lead us to a later age than the rest of the book does; likewise, with great probability, certain things among the dogmatic conceptions, as particularly ch. xxxiii. 22, f., the idea of death-bringers (destroyers) as a *distinct* class of angels, which certainly did not belong to the time before the exile, as also the idea of angels who minister by instruction.'

tribes was presented to his perception, in a region also repeatedly attacked and beset by hostile armies; and perhaps situate, as Stickel thinks, in the south-east of Palestine, on the borders of the Edomites and Arabians. The author appears, at least, to be well acquainted with the customs and ideas of the people of the East, and also not without some knowledge of Egypt. At least his description of the hippopotamus and the crocodile, although not quite exact as regards natural history, makes it not improbable that he had at some time lived near the native country of these animals.

It must not, however, be concluded from this that the book was written in Egypt (as Hitzig, without proof, alleges, *Der Prophet Jesaja*, p. 285), and still less, as Hirzel assumes, that it was the work of a Jewish exile in Egypt, or as Bunsen decides it, of *Baruch*. On the contrary, the particular way in which he expatiates on the description of these two creatures, as extraordinary natural wonders, in which more than anything else the power and wisdom of God are shown, makes it probable that he had not known them from his earliest youth, but that he had found an opportunity of becoming acquainted with them in his later years, and for a comparatively short time.

As regards the more approximate motive for the composition, several interpreters, as Bernstein, De Wette, and others, look for it in national circumstances. They are of opinion that the author had in view the unhappy condition of the Israelitish people, in their relations to other heathen nations, and that in the course of the book he intimated that the people, if they only maintained a firm faith in Jehovah and His worship, would finally be brought by their God to a state of prosperity and to greater glory than they had previously possessed. But there are in the book no distinct intimations which justify such an opinion, any more than in the greater number of the Psalms of Lamentation. It is, on the contrary, much more probable that the author was first incited to the composition of his work by the circumstances which were presented to him in the domestic affairs of his people; by the contemplation of the severe and continuous sufferings which the most pious servants of Jehovah specially underwent, which, too, he himself perhaps had sometimes experienced, so that in his composition, he strove both to ward off the unjust, hard-hearted opinions formed by others, as to the reasons for such sufferings, and also to admonish those who were suffering not to dispute with God as to their afflictions, but to consider them as only a trial coming from Him, and to wait patiently in humble faith and obedience, sure that then He would at last certainly again bless and glorify them.

SECOND DIVISION.

HISTORY OF THE CANON OF THE OLD TESTAMENT.[1]

§ 292.—*Nature and Method of the Investigation.*

THE whole of the books which we have been considering are united in one complete collection of writings, which we call the Canon of the Old Testament, *i.e.*, the aggregate of those books which are of authority as authentic sources of knowledge for revealing the Old Covenant, and as a code of rules (κανών) for determining the faith and course of life of those who are in relation to the ancient Book. The second part of our task is to show how this collection of books was formed and how it has fared with it, as regards both its actual extent and also its authority, from its first formation up to the present time, firstly in the Jewish and then also in the Christian Church. As regards the formation of the Canon, we find ourselves in much the same position as when we considered the origin of so many of the separate books—viz., that any distinct express statements on the point which we have at our command are of a date at which they could no longer be considered as authentic tradition, and they are also of that nature, that much that is unmistakeably false is mixed up with matter which is to some extent true. In this consideration we are constantly driven to suppositions, and to combinations of separate matters of fact; and in doing this we must lay down as our basis, on the one hand, the earliest possible statements as to the collection of the Sacred Books, and, on the other, the results of our previous investigations into the origin of these scriptures separately. I can only give here some short notices on these points.

[1] Cf. A. Dillmann: *Ueber die Bildung d. Sammlung heil. Schriften A. T.*, in the *Jahrbb. für deutsche Theolog.* iii. (1858) 3, pp. 419–491.

A.—HISTORY OF THE CANON OF THE OLD TESTAMENT AMONG THE JEWS.

§ 293.—*The Book of the Law.*

The *Torah*—*the Mosaic Law*—confessedly forms the groundwork of the Canon of the Old Testament. We have before seen that a considerable number of laws were not only promulgated by Moses himself, but were also written down by him, and that these were, perhaps quite early, united in collections and were, at least from the age of Saul and David, adopted as integral elements of historical works which contained the history of the people of Israel at the time of Moses, as well as of the preceding and subsequent periods up to the taking possession of the land of Canaan. The Mosaic law, although it was often disregarded and infringed, had, of course, at all times prescriptive and canonical authority for the Israelites. Still it cannot be shown, indeed it is altogether improbable, that at any time before the completion of the Pentateuch and the composition of Deuteronomy, any such authority was ascribed to any single work containing these laws. This authority was doubtless first ascribed to our present Pentateuch, after Deuteronomy was added, but not before its discovery in the Temple in the eighteenth year of Josiah, thirty-six years before the destruction of Jerusalem, although its composition in its present extent may have taken place fifty to eighty years earlier. We may perhaps assume that then and afterwards it was considered that this work contained the Mosaic law in its authentic shape, and the work thus received as a Scripture a prescriptive canonical authority. During the Captivity, however, which so soon followed, when the Temple was destroyed and the people were living far from the Holy Land, the law could have been but little observed as regards its ceremonial precepts. The Book of the Law was then perhaps read by few; as we see in Isaiah xl. ff., that a great part of the people were at that time partakers of the idolatry, or at least of the image-worship of heathen nations. But it is indubitable that since then the Pentateuch has remained unaltered as the Book of the Law, and that the Jews brought it back out of their Captivity in the same state as that in which they took it thither. According to Neh. viii–x, it was solemnly acknowledged by the people at Jerusalem in the days of Ezra and Nehemiah, nearly 100 years after the return of the first exiles.

We read (Neh. iii. 9, x. 2) that Ezra, at a time when Nehemiah was governor of the land of Judæa, therefore about 444 B.C., read out the Book of the Law to the people assembled in Jerusalem for several days from morning to mid-day, and that afterwards the people pledged themselves to it in a solemn manner, all the princes of the people, and the Levites and priests (who are particularly mentioned), binding themselves to its observance by formal subscription, the rest of the people following them by taking an oath, and swearing that they would be willing to comply with the Divine Law given by Moses.

Ezra now, doubtless, took care to make the Book of the Law more accessible to the people by means of copies, since he is styled as הַסֹּפֵר throughout the Books of Ezra and Nehemiah, and this is often done in express reference to the Mosaical law; v. Ezra vii. 6: וְהוּא־סוֹפֵר מָהִיר בְּתוֹרַת מֹשֶׁה, and vv. 12, 21, in the letters of Artaxerxes: סְפַר דָּתָא דִּי־אֱלָהּ שְׁמַיָּא גְּמִיר. We may assume with probability, as before remarked (p. 366, vol. i.), that if the Book of Joshua had remained up to that time united with the Book of the Law, and was not separated from it at Josiah's time, the separation must have been made in Ezra's time, and perhaps by him. Thus much is certain, that since that time our Pentateuch in its present extent has been continually acknowledged by the Jews as the authentic Book of the Law, and has maintained as a Scripture a prescriptive canonical authority.

§ 294.—*Nature and Extent of Nehemiah's Collection of Books.*

There can be no doubt that in this age, and perhaps by Ezra and Nehemiah, *other writings* also of peculiar national and religious interest were collected together, both historical, prophetical, and poetical. Many of these writings were already invested with authority, but they had not been combined in any fixed collection, and had not been divided from others of the same nature.

This applies, *e.g.*, to the prophecies of the earlier prophets, so far as they were extant in a written form. We find that the later prophets sometimes appealed to the earlier ones; cf. Jer. xxvi. 17, f. Thus the author of Isaiah xl. ff. appeals to the earlier prophecies, in which Jehovah predicted the things which were just then on the point of happening; thus also Zechariah refers (ch. i. 4, vii. 7, 12) to the warnings which Jehovah had given to his people through the prophets before the Captivity (הַנְּבִיאִים הָרִאשֹׁנִים). But there was no one *collection* formed of these older prophetical writings, to which any peculiar authority had been attributed beyond any others then extant. And in the same way we cannot doubt that even before the Captivity, and both during it and also after the return of the exiles, the lyric songs of ancient poets, particularly David's, were made use of for public worship, as well as for private edification; cf. 2 Chron. xxix. 30, where we are told that Hezekiah caused the Levites to sing praises to Jehovah in David's and Asaph's words. Doubtless even before the Captivity, collections of songs were made for the same purpose as our hymn-books, but not perhaps with fixed limits and exclusive authority. This was also the case with the many historical works which were in existence as to the earlier history of the people of Israel or of certain distinguished men among them.

There is an express statement on this point in the 2 Macc. ii. 13: "The same things also were reported in the writings and commentaries of Neemias (ἐξηγοῦντο δὲ καὶ ἐν ταῖς ἀναγραφαῖς καὶ ἐν τοῖς ὑπομνηματισμοῖς τοῖς κατὰ τὸν Νεεμίαν τὰ αὐτά); and how he established a library (καὶ ὡς καταβαλλόμενος βιβλιοθήκην), and collected (ἐπισυνήγαγε) τὰ περὶ τῶν βασιλέων καὶ προφητῶν (βιβλία) καὶ τὰ τοῦ Δαυὶδ καὶ ἐπιστολὰς βασιλέων περὶ ἀναθεμάτων."

This passage is found in the certainly unauthentic letter of the Jews of Palestine to those of Alexandria, in which they summon the latter to take part in the festival of the consecration of the temple. The author, however, quotes and, as may be easily seen, reports accurately, the above statements out of some other work, which he styles Nehemiah's writings and commentaries. This is not our Book of Nehemiah, but some Apocryphal work, perhaps that of which a part has been preserved under the name of the Greek Ezra, or the Third Book of Ezra, also ὁ ἱερεύς. Touching the

Nehemiah's Compilation.

statement itself, as it stands, we have certainly no reason for doubting its correctness. This tells us that Nehemiah arranged a public collection of books, doubtless such as had some peculiar interest for the people, but which had not been before collected together.[1] We have perhaps a right to suppose that the above statement is not quite complete and exact. It shows us however of what kind these scriptures were generally.

There are named here, firstly (1) τὰ περὶ τῶν βασιλέων καὶ προφητῶν. By the former expression we may doubtless understand historical writings as to the reigns of the kings of Israel and Judah ; the latter expression, however, which is perhaps joined to the former somewhat incorrectly, we must suppose to mean prophetical writings, which contained the predictions of prophets. And if we notice how, in the Hebrew Canon, the prophetical Scriptures follow immediately after the Scriptures relating the histories of the kings of Israel and Judah, we shall be led to the view that these are the very books which Nehemiah caused to be collected, and to which he gave their present combination and order of succession.[2] This is corroborated by the fact that there is also named (2) τὰ τοῦ Δαυΐδ, by which our Book of Samuel is certainly not intended, as Bertholdt thinks, but David's writings, doubtless the Psalms, which, in the Hebrew Canon, now immediately follow the prophetical Scriptures.

§ 295.—*Books included in Nehemiah's Collection.*

If now we compare the present contents of the Canon of the Old Testament with the result of our previous investigations into the origin of the several books, we may, with probability, make the following assumptions:—

(*a*) That the collection of Psalms either had at that time

---

[1] According to Dillmann (*ut supra*, p. 447, ff. , the books named here were a part of a larger collection of books arranged by Nehemiah, which, however, contained many works not become canonical. The full completion of the second division of the Canon falls, on the contrary, in the fourth century B.C.

[2] It is decidedly wrong, when Movers (*Loci quidam historia canonis Vet. Test. illustrati.* Breslau, 1842, p. 15, understands the whole expression, τὰ περὶ τῶν βασιλέων καὶ προφητῶν, as designating our Books of Chronicles, which could in no case have been thus styled.

or then received its present extent; probably, also, it was then brought to a conclusion, and divided into five books, after the manner of the Pentateuch.

(*b*) That the collection of the prophets then formed contained all the prophetical Scriptures which now exist in the second division of the Canon, and in the shape they are therein found—the Books of Isaiah, Jeremiah, Ezekiel, and the Twelve Minor Prophets. Not improbably several of these books, as particularly Isaiah and Zechariah, then first received their present shape, in which the prophecies of some other prophets of either a later or earlier date were united with those of the above-named prophets.

(*c*) That the works (τὰ περὶ τῶν βασιλέων καὶ προφητῶν) mentioned first and before the prophetical ones were intended for the Books of *Samuel* and *Kings*, which, at any rate in the Hebrew Canon, precede the prophets and, as we have seen, are so closely connected with one another, and also have been constantly considered by the Hellenistic Jews as one work, the *Books of Kings*. But we may also suppose that some works treating of the history of the people of Israel previous to the Books of Samuel were adopted into this collection; and that they were the very books which now exist in the Canon, therefore the Book of *Judges*, and also perhaps the Book of *Joshua*, if this latter had been then separated from the Pentateuch, as was highly probable. The point Nehemiah had in view in this collection as regards the historical books was, in all probability, to include those which contained a continuous history of the people of Israel, from the point at which the already generally acknowledged Pentateuch left off down to the Babylonian Captivity.

(*d*) It may be assumed with probability that this collection was not arranged until after the solemn renewal of the people's obligation to the Torah, and also that while Ezra lived, he also took a personal share in the arrangement of it. But on this point nothing more certain can well be ascertained. It is not, however, improbable that on this occasion the historical books underwent some alterations at the beginnings and conclusions, so as to connect them more closely one to another, as we now find them. Yet anything of this sort which then took place was not very important, nor such as to warrant either Ezra or the then compiler being styled the author of the books (as Bertheau says, *v. above*, p. 388, vol. i.)

(*e*) It may be assumed with probability that the Book of *Ruth* was then adopted into the series of historical books, after the Book of Judges; and its acceptance must have appeared to be justified, inasmuch as it supplied information about the early history of the forefathers of David, the ancestor of the kings of Judah.

The Book of Ruth not only follows Judges in the LXX and Vulgate, but it also appears to have had the same position in the first century after Christ among the Hebrew Jews, and to have been numbered with the Book of Judges as one work, as we may conclude from the statements of Josephus, Melito, Origen, Jerome, and others, as to the Hebrew Canon (cf. §§ 303-308, ff.). But this is most easily explained, if it received its position at the first collection of these books.

(*f*) Similar reasons lead us to assume, with regard to the *Lamentations*, that they also were adopted into this collection, and had their place after the prophecies of Jeremiah, which they have continually retained in the LXX.

(*g*) It cannot be decided whether any other of the poetical books, which are now in the third division of the Hebrew Canon, were then adopted into Nehemiah's collection.

Evidently, this could be the case with those only which were then existing, and this can be assumed with certainty only of the Book of Job, Solomon's Proverbs, and Solomon's Song. It is possible that these were then adopted, and have, since then, remained combined with the others; but it is also possible, and indeed more probable, that they were not joined to the rest until later.

(*h*) In 2 Macc. ii. 13, after the τὰ τοῦ Δαυὶδ are named as having been adopted into Nehemiah's collection, there is also mentioned ἐπιστολαὶ βασιλέων περὶ ἀναθεμάτων. By these, doubtless, are intended, as Grotius rightly understands it, letters of foreign princes, and particularly of the Persian kings, as to the plans and donations for founding the newly-instituted Temple at Jerusalem, and certainly not, as Hengstenberg thinks (*Beiträge*, i. 243, f.), merely the letters of the Persian kings contained in our Books of Ezra and Nehemiah, but some other letters, which, from their purport, must have been of considerable interest for the Jews at that time.[1]

(i) We are not told in the passage, 2 Macc. ii. 13, nor is it very probable in itself, that Nehemiah then combined these books with the Book of the Mosaical Law in *one whole*. On the contrary, we must doubtless think that he made a collection of them separately from the Book of the Law, and that in this he combined, out of the writings of his own time and those that were extant of a more ancient date, just those books, which, as well as the Book of the Law, were of peculiar interest for his people, partly as evidences through history and prophecy of the continual Divine guidance and revelation, and partly for liturgical and didactic use. In all probability this collection remained separate from the Torah for some time longer, and enjoyed from the very first an authority which, although not similar to that of the Torah, was of no inconsiderable importance, and greater than that of other ancient writings which were then extant, but had not been adopted into this collection, although sometimes of similar contents; as particularly many historical books with which we become acquainted from the quotations in the Chronicles.

§ 296.—*Union of the Torah with the other Books in the Collection.*

The authority of Nehemiah's collection of books perhaps increased in course of time. How long a time elapsed before it was united with the Torah into one whole cannot be ascertained with any exactitude. The passage, Dan. ix. 2, shows that, in the beginning of the Maccabean age, the collection of scriptures, in which the prophecies of Jeremiah were found, were designated as the Scriptures, κατ' ἐξοχήν (הַסְּפָרִים), by which only Holy Scriptures with prescriptive, canonical authority can be intended; this, however, makes it most probable that these books were then united into *one* whole with the Pentateuch, and were, indeed, considered as one.

In this combination the several books of Nehemiah's collection were, doubtless, arranged in the order in which they stood when they formed a separate collection, which

[1] Movers is quite incorrect (*ut supra*, p. 15), in thinking that by this expression our Book of Ezra is meant.

also is pointed out in 2 Macc., viz., in essentially the same order in which they are now found in the Hebrew Canon; the historical books, from Joshua to Kings, following the Pentateuch (only that probably the Book of Ruth came in after Judges); next, the actually prophetical Scriptures, the greater prophets—and among these probably Lamentations came after Jeremiah—the twelve minor Prophets, and then followed the Psalms, with any other of the poetical Scriptures which then might form elements of the collection.

"The Epistles of the Kings concerning the holy gifts," the last named in 2 Macc. ii. 13, were omitted; this was done when Nehemiah combined his collection with the Book of the Law, if not earlier; doubtless because it was felt that these letters, although interesting in their contents, were, notwithstanding, unsuitable to remain as independent works in a collection of books, which were looked upon as Sacred Books with a specific, canonical authority.

§ 297.—*Reception into the Canon of the Books not included in Nehemiah's Collection.*

As regards those books of our Hagiographa which Nehemiah did not then include in his collection, and indeed in some cases could not have done because they were not composed till a later time, we cannot ascertain, as to most of them, whether they were added to Nehemiah's collection before the combination of the latter with the Book of the Law, or not until after this event.[1] This applies, to the Book of Job, and also to the three writings of Solomon, and the Books of Esther, Ezra, Nehemiah, and Chronicles. As to these latter historical books, it is not altogether improbable that the authors themselves united them with, and annexed them to, the other books of the collection; either the collection of Nehemiah separately, or that and the Pentateuch combined. They soon obtained currency, perhaps in reference to their contents:—the Chronicles, because it both contained interesting, and sometimes not unimportant, additions to the books already in the

[1] According to Ewald, Ezra (and Nehemiah) were added at the beginning of the Grecian dominion, and the rest of the Ketubim in the Maccabean age, in the re-arrangement of the canonical compilation by Judas Maccabæus, mentioned 2 Macc. ii. 14; v. *Geschichte Isr.* vii. pp. 403–470; *Gesch. d. Sammlung heil. Schriften,* p. 131, ff.

collection, and in it matters relating to the institutions of Divine worship have special prominence ;—the Books of Ezra and Nehemiah, because they contained a history of the people of God during a period after the return from exile, which is not dealt with in the rest of the books—a history specially referring to the civil and religious institution of the re-established Jewish commonwealth ;—the Book of Esther, because it gave an explanation as to the origin of the Feast of Purim, which had begun to be observed as particularly sacred. We find, however, in *Talm. Hieros. tr. Megilloth*, 70, 4 [*v.* above, p. 449, 1st vol. and cf. Bertheau's *Erklärung des B. Ester*, p. 283] a statement that the introduction of this feast met with opposition from some Jews of importance, from which we may conclude that the Book of Esther itself must also have been much questioned before it met with general recognition.

It is also unknown at what date the *writings of Solomon* were adopted into the collection, and met with general recognition. The reception of the Book of Proverbs can be readily explained, both from a consideration of its moral value, and also from the name of its author, after whom the book is named, and to whom, perhaps, the whole was attributed. The reception of the two other books was, perhaps, chiefly caused by a respect for Solomon, after whom they were named, and to whom their composition was, perhaps, attributed; yet it is not improbable that they had then already begun to explain Solomon's Song mystically and allegorically. There are also express intimations among the later Jews, that all the three works of Solomon, and particularly Ecclesiastes and Solomon's Song, met with opposition at a later time from those who opposed their acceptance among the number of the Sacred Books, and that this opposition only disappeared because they began to be differently explained than they were previously—the Song of Solomon doubtless allegorically.

Thus we read, *Capitula*, R. Nathan, c. i, at the beginning : " At the beginning, there were some who said that the Proverbs, Solomon's Song, and the Preacher, were apocryphal (גנוזים); alleging that they are מְשָׁלוֹת, and not among the number of the Ketubim ; and thus they opposed and concealed them (withdrew them from public use, and pronounced them to be *apocryphal*), until the men of the

Great Synagogue came and explained them."—In the *Mischna*, tr. *Jadaim*, iii. 5, there are statements as to the disputations of certain Jewish scholars of importance concerning the Song of Solomon and Koheleth, whether they were to be reckoned among the Sacred Books or not in which a different decision as to Koheleth is spoken of as being given by the scholars of Hillel and those of Schammai (*v.* Movers, *ut supra*, p. 25, f.).—*Vajjikra Rabba*, sect. 28, fol. 161, col. 2: "Voluerunt sapientes ἀποκρύπτειν librum Coheleth, quod deprehenderent in eo verba, quæ ad ἀνομίαν (improbitatem s. hæresin) vergunt."—*Tr. Schabbath*, f. 30, c. 2: "Sapientes quærebant ἀποκρύπτειν librum Coheleth, eo quod verba ejus se mutuo everterent;" but that it was not expunged (גנז), in consequence of its beginning (ch. i. 3), and its conclusion (ch. xii. 13, f.), both of which were words of the law. Agreeable to this is the statement of Jerome, *ad Coheleth*, xii. 13, in which he mentions that it was declared by the Hebrews, that although the Preacher appeared to be excluded, together with other works not adopted into the Canon, on account of its contents giving offence, still that it was placed among the number of the Holy Scriptures in reference to its conclusion (ch. xii. 13, f.), which sets forth, as the sum of the whole matter, to fear God and keep His commandments.

The Book of Daniel appears, from the result of our investigations, to be the latest of the Books of the Canon of the Old Testament. We may suppose, with the greatest probability, that this book at its appearance met with considerable recognition and no opposition among the pious and law-observing Jews, and that it was very soon inserted in the collection of Canonical Books.

§ 298.—*Books not included in Nehemiah's Collection—Their Position in the Canon.*

Of all the books which were composed after the age of Ezra and Nehemiah, as is certainly the case with the Book of Daniel, as well as with Esther, Ezra, Nehemiah, and Chronicles, not one has a position in the Hebrew Canon among the historical and prophetical Scriptures collected by Nehemiah; although, from their contents, they might well have been among the former, they are all placed after the Psalms and the other poetical books. We may gather from this that the Scriptures collected by Nehemiah must have attained to so much authority among the Jews of Palestine, and must have also so maintained this authority after their being combined with the Torah, that they did not venture to insert any other work in this series, but were contented with placing them at the end of the whole collection. Thus, the Hebrew Canon is so shaped that the historical and prophetical books collected by Nehemiah follow first after the Torah, next come the Psalms and other poetical books, and then some later historical and prophetical Scriptures.

The name for the historical and prophetical books collected by Nehemiah, which was usual at least in the second century B.C., was *the Prophets*, נְבִיאִים, whilst it was some time afterwards before any established designation was in use for the rest of the Scriptures, beginning with the Psalms. We may gather this from the preface, prefixed about 130 B.C., by the Greek translator of the Book of Ecclesiasticus, in which preface the books standing in canonical authority among the Jews are mentioned according to the three divisions into which the collection is still separated, and these are designated—the first as ὁ νόμος, the second as οἱ προφῆται (twice; once as αἱ προφητεῖαι), the third as τὰ ἄλλα πάτρια βίβλια, and τὰ λοιπὰ τῶν βιβλίων, cf., at the beginning of the preface, τῶν ἄλλων τῶν κατ' αὐτοὺς ἠκολουθηκότων (perhaps masc.).

Connected with the above are the various *public uses* made of these books, viz., that, after they had begun to read out in the Jewish synagogues some of the other books of the Canon as well as the Pentateuch, passages of the Nebiim only were made use of for the regular course on the Sabbaths; the Psalms, however, were employed for common liturgical use as before, both in the temple and in the synagogue; whilst, on the contrary, no regular public use of the rest of the Ketubim was made in the synagogue generally. The custom that some of them, the so-called Megilloth, should be read out on prescribed feast-days, was perhaps not introduced till later. Then, also, but not until a long time after the destruction of the second Temple, perhaps because they were to be made use of in the same way, the Books of *Ruth* and *Lamentations* were taken out of their original place in the second division, and placed among the books of the third division, with the three other Megilloth.

§ 299.—*Completion of the Canon—Comparative Authority of later Books.*

From our previous observations as to the writings of Solomon and the Book of Esther, it may be inferred that some books of the Canon were for a long time subject to the question whether they should be looked upon as Holy Canonical Scriptures; and we must assume that it was but gradually that they attained to more general recognition. It is likewise connected with this, that it was some considerable time before the Canon was considered as fully completed as regards this third division of it, and as no longer susceptible of any further enlargement and alteration. Of course this view became so far established, at least among the Jews of Palestine, that some centuries before Christ, they entertained a feeling and consciousness that the Spirit of God no longer prevailed among the people in such a way as to produce works deserving to be considered as actual Holy Scriptures, and to be placed by the side of the Torah and the Prophets. Thus, among the Jews of Palestine, no work was received into the Canon which was known to have been composed later than about 100 years after the Captivity.

Thus, *e.g.*, the Book of Ecclesiasticus (written probably about 210-180 B.C.) was not accepted into the Canon, because its late origin was known; the book itself making no claim to high antiquity, and the Greek translator, the grandson of the author, expressly distinguishing this, his grandfather's book, from the Canonical Scriptures.

(*a*) But, in the first place, with regard to historical or didactic works, the age of which was unknown, or which, by means of the appropriation of some name as author, laid claim to be the work of ancient prophets or wise men,—if this assumption found belief, a disposition must have arisen to attribute to any such work the authority of a prophetical and Holy Scripture. Thus, as we have already remarked, Ecclesiastes and the Book of Daniel were certainly received into the Canon and also recognized as Canonical Scriptures only because they were regarded as writings of Solomon and Daniel. Although other works, which were similarly circumstanced as regards their origin and assumption of an author, were never adopted into the series of Scriptures of the Hebrew Canon, yet we cannot doubt that even the Hebrew Jews, taking for granted the genuineness of these works, placed them in a position more or less similar to the Canonical Scriptures in authority and sanctity.

(b) But with regard to some other writings of a later time, the contents of which were of peculiar interest, as, e.g., the Books of the *Maccabees*, which relate the struggles of the Jewish people for their faith and worship against the oppression of Antiochus Epiphanes, we may well imagine that they attained a certain authority as authentic historical evidence as to a period not unimportant in the maintenance of Theocracy, and, although they were not adopted into the series of Scriptures of the Hebrew Canon, they nevertheless closely approached in authority to several of the books in the third division, such as the Books of Esther, Ezra, and Nehemiah.

§ 300.—*The Canon among the Hellenistic Jews—The Apocrypha.*

(c) It is more probable that among the *Hellenistic Jews*, the Canon remained unsettled for a longer time, and no marked distinction was made as regarded their authority between the books which had been admitted into the Hebrew Canon and several others of a somewhat later date. The question has been frequently propounded, whether the Jews of Alexandria and Palestine had a different Canon. This is answered in the affirmative by some,[1] but, on the contrary, has been denied by most of the Protestant divines (also De Wette, § 17 b). But it may be held as certain that among the Jews of Alexandria, even at the time of Christ, the limits of the Canon of Scripture had not been exactly fixed. The Greek translation of the LXX was almost entirely used among them in reading the Books of Holy Scripture. In this translation not only had several of the Books of the Hebrew Canon received considerable additions, which did not exist and never had existed in

[1] Semler, Corrodi (*Beleucht. des Jüd. und Christl. Bibelkan.* i. 155, ff.); Münscher (*Dogmengesch.* i. 257, f.); Augusti (*Die Fortbildung des Christenth. zur Weltrelig.* i. 130,), and others.

the Hebrew text, such as the additions to Job, and especially to Esther and Daniel, which were certainly looked at by the Hellenistic Jews in just the same light as the portions of the books which were in the Hebrew, but there were also several books not in the Hebrew Canon, such as Jes. Sir., 1st and 2nd Macc., Wisdom, and others which stood among the Canonical Books, and it may be assumed with probability that these still existed in the manuscripts of the LXX at the time of Christ and the apostles. It may thus be easily imagined that most of those Jews who read the Old Testament in this translation, which at the time of Christ was much circulated in Palestine, would not be in a position to make any precise distinction between those books which occur only in the translation and not in the Hebrew Canon, and the books which form the latter. The former books are called by us in the Protestant Church, by way of distinction, the *Apocrypha of the Old Testament.*

This name is often met with in the ancient Church, but not always in the same sense. The word is, at any rate, derived from ἀποκρύπτειν, and = *abscondita.* Augustine (*De Civ. D.* xv. 23) explains it as pointing out those writings, the origin of which was obscure, " *eo quod earum occulta origo non claruit Patribus.*" Others, as Hottinger, Bertholdt, Hug, and Herbst, look upon it as a translation of the Hebrew. It is often used in the Talmud and by the Rabbis for certain works as contrasted with the Canonical Scriptures, as particip. pass. from גנז = *abscondere, i.e.,* to withdraw from public use. This word often occurs among the later Jews, sometimes in reference to manuscripts of the Holy Scriptures, which, because they were obscure, faulty, or deficient, were to be withdrawn from public use ; and sometimes in reference to certain books, which likewise were withdrawn from public use, *i.e.,* were separated from the number of orthodox canonical books prescribed for that purpose. It is, however, very probable that this use of the terms גנז, גנב by the Jews, for designating certain writings as ἀπόκρυφα, had not much influence on the ecclesiastical writers, at least originally. Among these, the use of this word originally proceeded from an idea of *secret and mysterious matters,* and indeed first came into vogue among heretical sects, particularly the Gnostics. These possessed various books, to which they attributed a peculiar sanctity, the greater part of which bore the names of holy personages, either of the Old or New Covenant; they asserted that they had obtained these by means of a certain secret tradition, and for this reason called them ἀπόκρυφα. In the main body of the Church, not only was the genuineness of these works repudiated, but they were looked upon with all the greater distrust in proportion as more importance was laid upon them by the heretics. Ecclesiastical authors retained for these works the designation ἀπόκρυφα, partly borrowed from the heretics in reference to these works, but joined with it generally an idea of something not genuine and heretical. There were, however, some teachers of the Church who did not use the name in so decidedly bad a sense, but applied it generally to certain works most of which were made some use of in the Church, in addition to the really Canonical Scriptures; although they would not wish to see an equal authority ascribed to the former as to the latter, because it was at any rate uncertain what their origin was. Thus Augustine (*ut supr.*) used and explained the word; thus also Jerome, in the *Prologus Galeatus in libr. Reg.*, where he places in contrast the Canonical Scriptures and the apocryphal, speaking of the latter as books which, as he expresses it in the *Præf. in libros Salom.* were indeed read in the Church, ad *ædificationem plebis*, but not ad *auctoritatem ecclesiasticorum dogmatum confirmandam*. And in this sense the term Apocrypha has become usual in the Protestant, particularly the Lutheran, Church, as a *terminus technicus* for a certain number of works, those, namely, which, although not in the Hebrew Canon, exist in the LXX and Vulgate in close conjunction with the elements of the Canon, and are placed in Luther's translation as an appendix. There are, besides, some other books bearing the names of patriarchs, prophets, or wise men of the Old Testament, which do not form a portion of the above apocryphal writings in the LXX, such as the Fourth Book of Ezra, the Book of Enoch, the Ascensio Jesaiæ, &c., which have been called, perhaps as a distinction from the Apocrypha, the *Pseudepigrapha* of the Old Testament. [Cf. Herzog's *Real-Encyclop.* xii. p. 300, ff.]. Cf. J. A. Fabricius, *Codex pseudepigraphus Vet. Test. castig. et illustr.* Ed. 2, Hamburg, 1722–23.

§ 301.—*Philo's References to the Canonical Books only.*

The fact that none of our Old-Testament Apocrypha are quoted in Philo and the New Testament is often appealed to as a proof that not only the Jews of Palestine, or Hebrew Jews, but also the Jews of Alexandria and the Hellenistic Jews generally, looked upon the Canon as strictly defined and concluded after the adoption in it of the latest of our Old-Testament Books, and that they attributed to no other works an authority similar to that possessed by those in the Hebrew Canon. But from the New Testament, at least, we may rather deduce proofs of a directly contrary opinion, and Philo affords none that are valid. Philo certainly does not quote expressly any one of our Old-Testament Apocrypha; but there are many of our Canonical Books which he also does not cite.

His work is principally devoted to the interpretation of the Pentateuch, considering, as he does, Moses to be the ἀρχιπροφήτης, and the other sacred authors only as Μωυσέως ἑταίρους. Out of the Pentateuch he quotes innumerable passages, as well as about twenty utterances out of the Psalms, but only a few out of the other scriptures; *e.g.*, he does not quote anything from Ezekiel, Daniel, Lamentations, Ecclesiastes, Solomon's Song, Esther, Ruth, Joel, Amos, Obadiah, Micah, Nahum, Habakkuk, Zephaniah, Haggai, and Malachi; out of Job only once, and out of Isaiah and Jeremiah very few times. Thus, from the fact that he does not expressly quote any of our Apocrypha, it cannot be concluded with any certainty that he did not place them in a similar category with the prophetical and hagiographical Scriptures of the Old Testament. It may be readily supposed that he does not draw any very nice distinction between them, because he extends very widely his idea of inspiration, and even attributes it to himself, so that, excepting those of Moses, he allows no difference, or at least only a very slight one, between the rest of the books and his own writings; *v. De Cherubim*, § 9, p. 112, Ed. Par.; *De Migratione Abraami*, § 7, p. 393; cf. Gfrörer, *Philo*, i. p. 57, ff. And in the passage, *De Præm. et Pænis*, § 19, p. 927, he quotes an expression which does not exist in our Old-Testament Books, but must have been found in some work which is lost, mentioning it just as if it were a statement of a θεσπίζων, exactly as elsewhere he quotes canonical passages of the prophets; and he even brings forward with it a passage of the Psalms, as being of the same nature.

§ 302.—*References in the New Testament to the Canonical Books only.*

In the *New Testament*, none of our Old-Testament Apocrypha are expressly quoted. But (*a*) the influence of many of these books—as of Sirach, the Wisdom of Solomon, and the Books of Maccabees—is unmistakeably shown in the tone of thought observable in the New-Testament authors; numerous reminiscences of them are also found in their writings.

Thus, particularly in the Epistle of St James, and also in other books; and in the Epistle to the Hebrews, in ch. xi, the examples brought forward in the Books of Maccabees of persevering faith at the time of Antiochus Epiphanes are alluded to and glorified in exactly the same way as those heroes of the faith who are described in the Canonical Books. Cf. my remarks, *Theol. Stud. u. Krit.* (1853) ii. pp. 337–349.

(*b*) In the New Testament we find a use made of the pseudepigraphical and other non-canonical works of Hebrew literature, most of which have been lost; and this use is similar to that made of the Books of the Hebrew Canon.

Thus, St. Jude (*v*. 14) expressly quotes a passage from the Book of Enoch, as a prophecy of Enoch; and (in *v*. 9) makes use (without express quotation) of the purport of a passage in another pseudepigraphical book (ἀνάληψις Μωϋσέως) quite as if it were a genuine scripture. In James iv. 5, a sentence, otherwise quite unknown to us, out of some lost work in all probability belonging to later Jewish literature, is quoted with the form of citation (ἡ γραφὴ λέγει) usually employed for the Sacred Canonical Books. In the 1 Cor. ii. 9, a passage is cited (καθὼς γέγραπται) which certainly is not, as has been supposed, Is. lxiv. 4, but is taken out of some lost Jewish work, according to Origen and others, an Apocryphum of Elias. So, most probably, the words quoted by the Saviour, John vii. 38, as statements of Scripture (καθὼς εἶπεν ἡ γραφή) are derived from a work since lost; and also in Luke xi. 49, the expression in the discourse of our Lord—ἡ σοφία τοῦ θεοῦ εἶπεν—is to be considered as introducing a quotation, and that, as in the former case, from some work of later Jewish literature which is now no longer extant : v. *Stud. u. Krit.*, *ut supra*, 326–335.

(c) On the other hand, several of our Canonical Books, as Obadiah, Nahum, Esther, Ezra and Nehemiah, the Song of Solomon and Ecclesiastes, are not mentioned at all in the New Testament, and we find no traces of any influence being exercised by them or any use being made of them. We must not indeed conclude from this that the authors of the New Testament were unacquainted with these books as forming elements of the Old-Testament Canon. But, in conjunction with other things, it shows that the use made in the New Testament of the Hebrew Canonical Scriptures was of a freer and more eclectic character, and that no marked distinction was drawn between them and the uncanonical works of ancient Jewish literature. And since we may assume, that in the quotation of Scripture generally, Christ and the New-Testament authors followed the course usual among their nation, we may, therefore, conclude that at that time there was still a somewhat lax and not strictly defined idea of the Canonical Holy Scriptures, and that no strict distinction was made, at least by all, between the books in the third division of the Canon—the Ketubim—and many other works of the later Jewish literature, such as our Apocrypha and Pseudepigrapha.

§ 303.—*Absolute Completion and Limitation of the Hebrew Canon.*

On the other hand, it may be assumed with the greatest probability, that except those that are now in it, no other books have ever been received into the *Hebrew* Canon, and inserted in the manuscripts of it. At least there is nowhere any intimation of the kind. Thus, it might be the case, that the Hebrew Jews considered the Canon as absolutely concluded with this number of books, and that this opinion was increasingly prevalent among them.

We find that this is the case pretty certainly, in a passage of Josephus, *c. Apion*, i. 8.

He there says, that they—the Jews—have not among them myriads of books, disagreeing with one another, but only twenty-two which are justly held to be Divine, extending down to the reign of Artaxerxes Longimanus; and that since the time of Artaxerxes down to his own time, sundry books (ἕκαστα) had indeed been written; but that they were not considered equally worthy of belief with the earlier ones, διὰ τὸ μὴ γενέσθαι τὴν τῶν προφητῶν ἀκριβῆ διαδοχήν. And that it was in fact clear what faith they, the Jews, entertained towards their scriptures, for, although so long a time had elapsed, no one had ventured either to take anything away from, or add anything to them. In these assertions there is much that is exaggerated, and merely the result of Josephus' opinion. Thus, in his statement that the time of Artaxerxes Longimanus was the latest date of the composition of any of the Canonical Books, he certainly does not rely on any tradition, but it is merely an inference in which he thought himself justified by the contents of the Canonical Books themselves; as he proceeds on the supposition that all the books in the Canon were written by those whose names are given in the titles, or, at any rate, by contemporaries of the events related in them. Thus, he considers the Book of Esther to be the latest, and fixes the date of its composition at the time of the Persian king Ahasuerus, who appears in it, whom, as appears from *Antiq.* xi. 6, 13,[1] he incorrectly takes to be Artaxerxes. But this much may be clearly seen, that he at that time considered the Canon as completed, and that this was not an idea peculiar to him only, but that a similar opinion must have prevailed among the Jews of the period, at least in part.

He states the whole number of the Sacred Books as twenty-two (corresponding with the number of letters in the Hebrew alphabet), and it may be assumed as in the highest degree probable, that this number is intended for the whole of the present Canonical Books of the Old Testament, as we find further statements as to this mode of numbering in the ecclesiastical writers. Josephus indicates more precisely the books he intended, thus: (*a*) Five books of Moses (No. i–v).—(*b*) Thirteen books of Prophets after Moses (No. vi–xviii). These latter he most probably reckoned as follows:—(1) Joshua, (2) Judges and Ruth, (3) Samuel, (4) Kings, (5) Chronicles, (6) Ezra and Nehemiah, (7) Esther, (8) Isaiah, (9) Jeremiah and Lamentations, (10) Ezekiel, (11) Daniel, (12) the Twelve Minor Prophets, (13) Job.—(*c*) Four books of Hymns and Moral

[1] Ἔγραψε δὲ Μαρδοχαῖος τοῖς ἐν τῇ Ἀρταξέρξου βασιλέως ζώσιν Ἰουδαίοις, ταύτας παραφυλάσσειν τὰς ἡμέρας, καὶ ἑορτὴν ἄγειν αὐτὰς, κ.τ.λ.

Josephus' Testimony. 309

Rules, by which doubtless the Psalms and the three books of Solomon are meant. With the exception of the three books of Solomon and Job, Josephus, in his writings, makes use of and quotes all the above books.

Nevertheless, Josephus' view as to the absolute limitation and closing up of the Canon is not always so decided as in the above passage.

In another place, namely, in the *Archæology*, he expresses himself so as to appear to have included among the *Holy Scriptures* which he made use for the historical contents of his work, some other writings besides our Canonical Books, in which writings the history was further continued. Thus, for the history after the Captivity down to Artaxerxes, he appears to have made a particular use of the apocryphal Greek Ezra, instead of availing himself of the Canonical Book of the same name. *V.* Movers, *ut supra*, p. 14 f., 29, f.

Among the Jewish evidences on the point, the Talmud follows Josephus, and not only speaks of *all* our Old-Testament Books as canonical, but *those* only. Here, also, the collection appears as absolutely concluded, and indeed expressly divided into the three parts : the Torah, the Nebiim, and Ketubim.

Cf. tr. Baba Bathra, fol. xiv. 2.—After the Torah the rest of the books are thus enumerated :—

סדרן של נביאים יהושע ושופטים שמואל ומלכים ירמיה ויחזקאל ישעיה ושנים עשר--- סדרן של כתובים רות תהלים ואיוב ומישלי קהלת שיר השירים וקינות דניאל ומגילת אסתר עזרא ודברי הימים

Ruth and Lamentations are here reckoned with the Ketubim and as separate books, and the whole number of books is therefore stated as twenty-four. But Ruth and Lamentations, as already remarked (§ 298), were probably not so placed until after the destruction of the second temple, in reference to the use that was then made of them for reading out on certain feast days, and probably just at the very time when our present Haphtharoth were fixed.

§ 304.—*General Adhesion of the Hellenistic Jews to the Hebrew Canon.*

If we now take a glance back at our previous considerations, we are bound to confess that, in the history of the

Canon, particularly as regards its fixed completion, much obscurity remains. Yet, from all the intimations we have, it may be assumed with the greatest probability, that the Canon first obtained its entirely settled form [1] and completion from the scribes of Palestine, whose schools flourished both before and after the destruction of Jerusalem. By them, perhaps, the canonicity of several of the books of our Hagiographa would be first decided, which indeed had already found a place in the collection, but had not yet received general acknowledgment, such as the Book of Esther, Ecclesiastes, and the Song of Solomon; and, on the other hand, a decision would be given as to the exclusion of other books, which, without having been adopted into the Hebrew collection of Sacred Books, still, up to that time had been made use of in much the same way as those Holy Scriptures that were contained in this collection; in the Greek translation, some of the former were found in among the Canonical Books, and were therefore made use of by the Hellenistic Jews who adopted this translation, and read indiscriminately with the Books of the Hebrew Canon. But the authority and the influence which these schools of the Hebrew Jews gained over the whole of their fellow-countrymen, particularly after the destruction of the second temple, soon brought about a complete identity of views as regards the Canon among the Jews in different countries, even those speaking Greek; from this it resulted that even these latter more and more relinquished the use of the Alexandrine translation of the Sacred Books, and acknowledged them only to the extent and in the shape which they were found in the Hebrew Canon.

§ 305.—*Views of the various Jewish Sects as to the Hebrew Canon.*

It is a matter of dispute whether the Jewish sects, which we meet with at the time of Christ, entertained different opinions as to the Canon. Thus, especially, as regards the Sadducees. Many fathers, as Tertullian, *Præscr. Hæret.* 45, Origen, *c. Cels.* i. 11, § 1, Jerome, *ad Matth.* xxii. 31, f., distinctly assert that the Sadducees accepted only the five books of Moses, and rejected the prophets.

[1] Cf. Oehler. in Herzog's *Real-Encyclop.* vii. p. 231, f.; also Holtzmann, *Kanon und Tradition*, p. 157, ff.

This, however, is now usually regarded as an error, caused by the fact of the Sadducees acknowledging as legal precepts the written law of Moses only, and not the later traditions of the Pharisees. Josephus says nothing further about them in an express way (*Ant.* xiii. 10, 6; xviii. 1, 4), and even in the above passage as to the Canon, he does not in the least intimate that the Sadducees differed in that respect from the Pharisees. Other reasons also seem to favour the idea that the Sadducees did *not* reject all the rest of the books except the Pentateuch; *v.* particularly Winer, *Real-W. B.*, under the word "Sadducee" (ii. p. 353). But yet, on the other hand, it is not altogether probable that they attributed canonical authority to the whole of the books of the Old Testament, for they would be unable to reconcile such passages as Dan. xii. 2, with their denial of the resurrection and immortality generally.

The most probable view is that the Sadducees acknowledged as a lawgiver Moses only, and the Pentateuch as the only authentic source for the knowledge of the Divine law. They in no way rejected the rest of the historical, prophetical, and poetical books, but yet did not allow to them any actual prescriptive canonical authority in the establishment of their faith and views of life.

As to the *Essenes* and *Therapeutæ*, from the accounts which we have of them in Josephus and Philo, we may assume that they accepted the Canonical Scriptures of their people, but that they possessed as well various writings of a prophetical and lyrical kind, which were held in authority among them; cf. Hävernick, i. 1, p. 75 (2nd ed. p. 85, f.).

The Samaritans, on the contrary, decidedly acknowledged as Sacred and Canonical Scripture, the Pentateuch only; rejecting all the other prophetical and poetical books. At the time when this people constituted themselves as a separate religious and ecclesiastical community, after the Jews who had returned out of exile had refused to allow them to partake in their worship at Jerusalem, they then accepted the completed Pentateuch as a book of the law and as a rule of faith, this alone of all the scriptures having real canonical authority among the Jews at that time. The Samaritans, however, stopt there, and have not adopted any one of the other books which subsequently received prescriptive canonical authority among the Jews. Most of these books were extant before this time, but some were not composed until later; the Samaritans acknowledged none of the later prophets; but Moses alone is their prophet for all time, the friend of God and the son of his house.

They indeed possess a Book of Joshua, but it differs much from the Hebrew Book of Joshua, although it is founded on the latter[1]; it carries the history to a period long after Joshua's time down to the days of the emperors Constantine and Constantius. It never obtained canonical authority among the Samaritans; as to this book, *v.* De Wette, § 171.

§ 306.—*Various erroneous Ideas as to the Formation of the Canon.*

In the history of the Canon here given, I have taken no notice of those accounts of it of later date, which, partly from the sources in which they are found, and partly from their own nature, clearly appear to be decidedly untrustworthy or entirely fabulous. [Cf. Oehler, in Herzog's *Real-Encyclop.* vii. p. 245, ff.]

Among these are:—

(*a*) The statement that is found in some of the Fathers, as in Tertullian, *De Habitu Muliebri*, c. 3, Iren. *adv. Hæres.* iii. 25, Clemens Al. *Strom.* lib. i. pp. 329–342, Theodoret, *Præf. Comment. in Cant.*, Chrysostom, *Homil.* viii. *in Epist. ad Hebr.*, Pseudo-August. *De Mirabilibus Scrip.* s. ii. 33, that, after the original copies of the Holy Scriptures which, as it was thought, were deposited in the temple, were burnt together with the latter, Ezra restored them by inspiration, both the Law and the Prophets. The Fathers, doubtless, derived these statements from some Judaico-Apocryphal source, and not improbably from the Fourth Book of Ezra, ch. xiv; in this passage, however it is not quite clear what the author really meant, and, besides, the reading is not certain. Cf. Lücke, *Einl. in die Offenb. Joh.* p. 183.

(*b*) The statement which is found in the Jewish Rabbis, but only the very late ones, as particularly Elias Levita, which has been also followed by several Christian divines,

[1] It is known to us by means of one codex, which formerly belonged to Scaliger, in the Arabic language, with Samaritan writing, and from that, now edited complete with a Latin translation, by W. J. Juynboll, Lugd. B. 1848; as to this, *vide* Rödiger's Recension in the *Hall. Allg. L. Z.* 1848. No. 217, ff., who is of opinion that it was originally written in Arabic, perhaps not until the thirteenth century.

Statements as to its Formation. 313

that the Canon was formed by the so-called *Great Synagogue*, בְּנֶסֶת הַגְּדוֹלָה. A college thus named is mentioned in the Mishna, which Ezra is said to have instituted at the restoration of the Jewish Church and State; the number of its members is stated to be 120 (cf. Stähelin's *Specielle Einleitung*, p. 10), and among them, the Jews place all the men of note who lived in their country down to *Simon the Just*. Bertholdt and Hävernick ascribe to this college an important share in the arrangement of the Canon. Hävernick in the completion of it, Bertholdt in the first formation of it, viz., the union of the Pentateuch with some of the prophets. But hardly any weight is to be given to the accounts in this shape. It may certainly be assumed that Ezra and Nehemiah, in their endeavours for the restoration and strengthening of the institutions in church and state, were supported by associates, and so also in what they did in the collection of the Holy Scriptures of their people. But that there was a formal college of the kind stated in the Mishna and the Talmud is very problematical, and J. Eberh. Rau (Prof. of Div. at Herborn, d. 1770), *De Synagoga Magna*, Utrecht, 1726. P. ii. p. 66, ff., Jahn, De Wette, and others have justly pronounced against its existence, and designated it as a fabrication of the later Jews, who by this means sought to show the continuous connection of tradition; neither in the Books of Ezra and Nehemiah, nor in Josephus and Philo, nor generally before the Mishna, is the slightest trace of it to be found. Bertholdt has wrongly considered the συναγωγὴ γραμματέων, 1 Macc. vii. 12,[1] to be a particular division of this college which had to do with the formation of the Canon; but a distinct authoritative body, a separate college of scribes is not at all the thing here spoken of. Certainly, in the Talmud (*tr. Baba Bathra*, f. 15, 1), it is said of this college that its members *wrote* (בָּתְבוּ) Ezekiel, the twelve (minor) prophets, and the Books of Daniel and Esther. But this is decidedly not intended to describe their introduction into the Canon, as Bertholdt and Hävernick think, but that they first actually wrote them down: v. de Wette, § 14, note c. A collection of the books in the Canon was first attributed to the Great

[1] Leop. Löwe, Chief Rabbi at Szegedin, in his *Monatsschrift Ben-Chananja* (1858, p. 102, ff., particularly p. 194, ff.) discovers the Great Synagogue also in 1 Macc. xiv. 28.

Synagogue, as already named, by Elias Levita in the sixteenth century, to whose testimony not the slightest weight could be given, even if the existence of the college itself was made much more certain than is the case.

(c) Another idea very prevalent in early times fixes the formation of the Canon at a date long before the Captivity. It is assumed that from the time of Moses the several books of the Old Testament, as they appeared and were acknowledged as Divine, were united with the Book of the Law, and immediately received a prescriptive canonical value, and that authentic copies of them were deposited in the sanctuary. Thus, *e.g.* Hävernick, who ascribes the completion of the Canon to those to whom he attributes the composition of the latest of the books, namely, to Ezra and Nehemiah. But this is quite unhistorical. There are certainly signs which lead us to think it was not unusual among the Hebrews, as among other ancient nations, to preserve in the sanctuary any peculiarly important documents (cf. Deut. xxxi. 26 ; 1 Sam. x. 25, and the account of the finding the Book of the Law in the Temple at the time of Josiah). But yet it is in itself altogether improbable that this should have been the case with the historical, prophetical, poetical, and didactic writings in the Canon ; for in that case the same thing would have happened with several other prophetical and historical works composed by prophets, which we know through quotations in our books, which works would then have been likewise considered as canonical before the Captivity; but this was certainly not the case, for then they would have been existing after the Captivity. But it is shown by the account of the discovery of the Book of the Law itself in the time of Josiah, and therefore in the really prophetical age, that it was not distinctly expected that it was in the temple, and still less that there was any idea that a depôt of sacred writings was to be found there in particular. Such an opinion, however, appears quite untenable, if we consider the way in which, according to the result of our previous investigations, so many of our Canonical Books received their present form in the Canon after manifold revisions and compilations.

(d) Finally, I mention the opinion of Bertholdt and De Wette, who think that some little time after the second division of our collection was completed and united with

Opinions as to its Formation. 315

the Pentateuch, the formation of the third division of the Canon was next begun. In this opinion no notice is taken of the statement, bearing throughout the appearance of truth, in 2 Macc. ii. 13, that a collection of prophetical books and the Psalms was arranged by Nehemiah. If our opinion as to the sense and credibility of this passage be well founded, it cannot be doubted that the Psalms were united with the Pentateuch in this collection of Nehemiah at the same time as the prophetical Scriptures. And it is also altogether improbable that when they began to place other scriptures, historical and prophetical, by the side of Moses' Books of the Law, and to combine them together in one whole, they would not also at the same time have adopted the religious songs of David and other poets of the old time; for we have certain signs that even before the Captivity, these songs were made use of liturgically in Divine service.

B.—HISTORY OF THE CANON OF THE OLD TESTAMENT IN THE CHRISTIAN CHURCH.

§ 307.—*Reception of the Hebrew Canon in the Christian Church —Relative Authority of the Apocryphal Books.*

As in the Jewish Synagogue, so also in the Christian Church, excepting some anti-Judaizing heretical factions, the Books of the Old Testament were employed both for public use in congregations, and also for private use, for edification and instruction. At first these alone were used as Scriptures; but, afterwards, when Christian Scriptures had been composed by the apostles and other teachers in the apostolic age and had attained to some authority, both kinds of scripture, the latter together with the former, were made use of in a similar way. Thus the Christian authors continually more or less avail themselves of the Books of the Old-Testament Canon as Holy Scriptures of canonical authority and as the Word of God, both with and without formal quotation. It was but seldom, however, that the Christian ecclesiastical authors were acquainted with the original language of the Old Testament, and by far the most of them were taught from the Greek translation, and knew the Holy Scriptures of the Old Testament in that shape only in which they existed in Greek. It might, therefore, easily happen that even after the apostolic age, at a time when among the Jews the conception of the Canon became more and more firmly settled and more and more definitely limited to the books that were then contained in the Hebrew Canon, Christian authors might make use, as Sacred and Canonical Books, of Jewish writings which had no place in the Hebrew Canon, and might quote passages out of them as utterances of Scripture, of the Holy Spirit, and the like, just as if they were portions of the Canonical Books. This was the case *sometimes* with our *Apocrypha*, both with the independent books, such as Ecclesiasticus, the Wisdom of Solomon, the Books of the Maccabees, and also with the apocryphal additions in the LXX to some of the Canonical Books of the Old Testament, for instance, to the Book of Daniel ; and *sometimes* with several other pseudepigraphical books.

Thus we find that the apocryphal additions to the Book of Daniel (*Bel and the Dragon and Susannah*) were used by Irenæus and Cyprian in a similar way to the Scriptures of the Hebrew Canon ; the *Book of Baruch* and the *Wisdom of Solomon* by Irenæus, Clemens Alex., Tertullian, and Cyprian ; *Jesus Sirach* by Clemens Alex. and Tertullian ; the Books of *Tobit* and *Judith* by Clemens Alex. and Cyprian ; the *Books of Maccabees*, and the *Third Book of Ezra*, by Cyprian. Clemens Alex. makes a peculiarly frequent use of these apocryphal books, mostly of Ecclesiasticus, whose language he often quotes just in the same way as passages out of the Scriptures of the Hebrew Canon ; likewise, only less frequently, he quotes passages out of *Wisdom, Baruch*, &c. (*v.* Welte in Herbst's *Einleit.* i. p. 24, ff.). Among other pseudepigraphical works, the *Fourth Book of Ezra* is quoted in the epistles of Barnabas and Clemens Alex. ; the Book of *Enoch* by Tertullian and Origen. Tertullian speaks expressly on the point, *De Habitu Muliebri*, c. 3 ; it was not unknown to him that the book had not been received by the Jews into their Canon ("in armarium Judaicum non refertur"), and he gives as a reason for this, that it prophesied of Christ; this exclusion did not prevent him from ascribing canonical authority to it, as he considered it genuine, and that it had the testimony of Jude in its favour.

§ 308.—*Melito's Old-Testament Canon.*

A need soon arose among Christian divines, perhaps owing to the disputes with the Jews, for introducing some more exact knowledge as to the real extent of the Sacred Books of the Old Testament, and for forming a more definite view about them. We first see this in Melito, Bishop of Sardis, about 172 A.D., in his letter to a Christian brother Onesimus (Euseb. *Hist. Eccl.* iv. 26), who wished to have more accurate information as to the number and arrangement of the Books of the Old Testament, to whom Melito communicates the result of his inquiries on the point made in a journey to the East and Palestine. He quotes in this the Books of the Hebrew Canon only, and none of the Apocrypha or Pseudepigrapha, but he does not quote them in the order of the Hebrew Canon, but more according to the order of the LXX, and under the Greek names, *e.g.*, βασιλειῶν τέσσαρα, &c.

'Εν ταῖς γραφείσαις αὐτῷ ἐκλογαῖς (Μελίτων) τῶν ὁμολογουμένων τῆς παλαιᾶς διαθήκης γραφῶν ποιεῖται κατάλογον· — "Μελίτων 'Οιησίμῳ τῷ ἀδελφῷ χαίρειν. Ἐπειδὴ πολλάκις ἠξίωσας σπουδῇ τῇ πρὸς τὸν λόγον χρώμενος γενέσθαι σοι ἐκλογὰς ἔκ τε τοῦ νόμου καὶ τῶν προφητῶν περὶ τοῦ σωτῆρος καὶ πάσης τῆς πίστεως ἡμῶν· ἔτι δὲ καὶ μαθεῖν τὴν τῶν παλαιῶν βιβλίων ἐβουλήθης ἀκρίβειαν, πόσα τὸν ἀριθμὸν καὶ ὁποῖα τὴν τάξιν εἶεν, ἐσπούδασα τὸ τοιοῦτο πρᾶξαι, ἐπιστάμενός σου τὸ σπουδαῖον περὶ τὴν πίστιν καὶ φιλομαθὲς περὶ τὸν λόγον· ὅτι τε μάλιστα πάντων πόθῳ τῷ πρὸς θεὸν ταῦτα προκρίνεις, περὶ τῆς αἰωνίου σωτηρίας ἀγωνιζόμενος. Ἀνελθὼν οὖν εἰς τὴν ἀνατολὴν, καὶ ἕως τοῦ τόπου γενομένος ἔνθα ἐκηρύχθη καὶ ἐπράχθη, καὶ ἀκριβῶς μαθὼν τὰ τῆς παλαιᾶς διαθήκης βιβλία, ὑποτάξας ἔπεμψά σοι· ὧν ἐστὶ τὰ ὀνόματα· Μωυσέως πέντε· Γένεσις, Ἔξοδος, Λευιτικὸν, Ἀριθμοὶ, Δευτερονόμιον· Ἰησοῦς Ναυῆ, Κριταὶ, Ῥοὺθ, βασιλειῶν τέσσαρα, Παραλειπομένων δύο· Ψαλμῶν Δαβὶδ, Σολομῶνος παροιμίαι, ἡ καὶ Σοφία, Ἐκκλησιαστὴς, Ἆσμα ᾀσμάτων, Ἰώβ· Προφητῶν, Ἡσαΐου, Ἰερεμίου, τῶν δώδεκα ἐν μονοβίβλῳ, Δανιὴλ, Ἰεζεκιὴλ, Ἔσδρας· ἐξ ὧν καὶ τὰς ἐκλογὰς ἐποιησάμην, εἰς ἓξ βιβλία διελών."

Ezra is placed after the prophets, quite at the end, perhaps in reference to its contents. *Nehemiah* and *Esther* are not mentioned; Nehemiah is doubtless included with Ezra, as indeed the Jews numbered the two as one book (cf. § 157). It is, however, altogether improbable, that the same is the

318   History of the Canon—In the Christian Church.

case with Esther, as Eichhorn, Hävernick, and Keerl think (*Die Apocryphen des A. T.* 1852, p. 122, note). We may, on the contrary, rather assume, that this book was not communicated to Melito by the Christians of Palestine, as being one of the Canonical Scriptures, since, as we shall see, in some later lists it was not included among the Canonical Books, being either omitted in silence, or mentioned as doubtful, as one of the books of the second class. Even in the Jewish Church, there were probably, at that time, various opinions prevailing as to the value of this book, and this helped to bring about that, in the Christian Church also, attention was drawn to the spirit ruling in the book, and for a long time it was questionable whether the book should be received into a collection which was to enjoy authority in the Christian Church, as Holy Canonical Scriptures. The *Lamentations* are not separately named above, but are doubtless included with Jeremiah, after whose prophecies they were *originally* placed in the Hebrew Canon, and are so placed constantly in the LXX ; the Book of *Ruth* he names separately after Judges. As already remarked, he mentions none of our Apocrypha. It is remarkable, his saying : Σολομῶνος παροιμίαι, ἡ καὶ Σοφία. [It must not be inferred from this that there is a confusion of the Canonical Proverbs with the apocryphal book, the Wisdom of Solomon, as the former is frequently called by the later Jews, ספר חכמה, and by the Fathers, Σοφία; cf. Bertheau's *Comment. on Proverbs. Introd.* § 1].

§ 309.—*Origen's List of the Canonical Books.*

Origen is the next Father from whom we possess a list of the Sacred Books of the Old Testament. He gave it in his interpretation of the first Psalm, from which Eusebius supplies it (*Hist. Eccl.* vi. 25). In this he specifies the books, as he himself says, according to the tradition of the Hebrews, as twenty-two in number; his list contains the whole of the Books of the Hebrew Canon, in the way in which the Jews numbered them :

Τὸν μέν τοιγε πρῶτον ἐξηγούμενος Ψαλμὸν, ἔκθεσιν πεποίηται (Ὠριγένης) τοῦ τῶν ἱερῶν γραφῶν τῆς παλαιᾶς διαθήκης καταλόγου, ὦδέ πως γράφων κατὰ λέξιν. "Οὐκ ἀγνοητέον δ' εἶναι τὰς ἐνδιαθήκους βίβλους, ὡς Ἑβραῖοι παραδιδόασιν, δύο καὶ εἴκοσι, ὅσος ὁ ἀριθμὸς τῶν παρ' αὐτοῖς στοιχείων ἐστίν." Εἶτα

μετά τινα ἐπιφέρει λέγων· "Εἰσὶ δὲ αἱ εἴκοσι δύο βίβλοι καθ'
Ἑβραίους αἵδε· ἡ παρ' ἡμῖν Γένεσις ἐπιγεγραμμένη, παρὰ δὲ
Ἑβραίοις ἀπὸ τῆς ἀρχῆς τῆς βίβλου Βρησὶθ, ὅπερ ἐστιν ἐν
ἀρχῇ· Ἔξοδος, Οὐαλεσμώθ, ὅπερ ἐστι ταῦτα τὰ ὀνόματα·
Δευιτικὸν Οὐϊκρά, καὶ ἐκάλεσεν· Ἀριθμοί, Ἀμμεσφεκωδεὶμ·
Δευτερονόμιον, Ἔλλε αδδεβαρὶμ, οὗτοι οἱ λόγοι· Ἰησοῦς υἱὸς
Ναυὴ, Ἰωσοῦε βὲν Νοῦν· Κριταὶ, Ῥοὺθ, παρ' αὐτοῖς ἐν ἑνὶ
Σωφετίμ· Βασιλειῶν πρώτη, δευτέρα, παρ' αὐτοῖς ἐν Σαμουὴλ,
ὁ θεόκλητος· Βασιλείων τρίτη, τετάρτη, ἐν ἑνὶ Οὐαμμέλεχ
Δαβὶδ, ὅπερ ἐστὶ βασιλεία Δαβίδ· Παραλειπομένων πρῶτον,
δεύτερον, ἐν ἑνὶ Διβρῆ Ἀϊαμὶμ, ὅπερ ἐστὶ λόγοι ἡμερῶν·
Ἐσδρας πρῶτος καὶ δεύτερος (Nehemiah), ἐν ἑνὶ Ἐζρᾶ, ὅ ἐστι
βοηθός· Βίβλος Ψαλμῶν, Σέφερ Θιλλὶμ Σολομῶντος Παροι-
μίαι, Μισλώθ· Ἐκκλησιαστὴς, Κωέλεθ. Αἴσμα ᾀσμάτων,
Σὶρ ἀσσιρίμ· Ἡσαΐας, Ἰεσαΐα· Ἰερεμίας σὺν θρήνοις καὶ τῇ
ἐπιστολῇ, ἐν ἑνὶ Ἱερεμία· Δανιὴλ, Δανιήλ, Ἰεζεκιὴλ,
Ἰεεζκήλ· Ἰώβ, Ἰώβ· Ἐσθὴρ Ἐσθήρ. Ἔξω δὲ τούτων ἐστὶ τὰ
Μακκαβαϊκά, ἅπερ ἐπιγέγραπται Σαρβὴθ, Σαρβανὲ ἔλ."

The Epistle of Jeremiah is a pretented letter of Jeremiah to the Babylonian exiles, against idolatry, which, in
Luther and the Vulgate. stands at the end of the Book of
Baruch (as ch. vi), but in ancient manuscripts of the LXX,
after Lamentations. Origen must have met with it in the
latter place, which was doubtless its original position in
the LXX. The letter is decidedly spurious, and without
doubt, was originally written in Greek. It is possible that
there was a Hebrew translation of it, and that at the time
of Origen it existed in this form in some manuscripts of
a Hebrew codex. But it is more probable, that Origen
was acquainted with it only in the LXX, and that he was
induced to mention it, as he did, in the Hebrew Canon, only
because he had been accustomed to read it after the Canonical Scriptures of Jeremiah. The twelve lesser prophets
are not mentioned by Eusebius, which can only proceed
from some accidental oversight, either of Eusebius himself
in giving the passage from Origen, or of some copier of
Eusebius; and this may be inferred from the circumstance,
that although Origen expressly states the number of the books
as twenty-two, without the twelve lesser prophets. there are
only twenty-one enumerated in this list. They were probably named between Solomon's Song and Isaiah, as they
are in Rufinus's translation. Daniel is named between Jere-

miah and Ezekiel. After Ezekiel comes Job, and next, *Esther*, the latter, therefore, not among the historical books; and this may perhaps be explained by the fact that no complete unanimity prevailed either in the Christian or Jewish Church, as to the historical character and perhaps even as to the canonical authority of this book.

Of our Apocrypha, besides the *Epistle of Jeremiah*, Origen also mentions τὰ Μακκαβαϊκά, which he not only names quite at the end, but divides them from what precedes by ἔξω δὲ τούτων ἐστὶ τὰ Μακκαβαϊκά, by which he appears to specify them as not belonging to the number of the books of the Canon, as they would amount to the number of twenty-two, if the minor prophets are reckoned with them. The other Apocrypha he does not mention at all, and thus tacitly excludes them from the Hebrew Canon. He acts in quite a different way in some of his other works, where he has not especially in view to set forth the Canon according to Hebrew tradition. In this latter case, just as Clemens Alex., he makes use of our Apocrypha and Scriptures of the Hebrew Canon in a similar way, and repeatedly cites passages out of the former as utterances of Scripture, and the like.

Thus he often quotes these books as *Ecclesiasticus* and the *Wisdom of Solomon*, c. *Cels*. iii. 72; viii. 50, as θεῖος λόγος, although he expresses himself in *Prolog. in Cant.* as follows: "We do not find this in the Canonical Scriptures, but only in the Book of Wisdom, which is attributed to Solomon, but does not enjoy authority with all;" he also quotes from *Baruch*, and from the Books of the *Maccabees* (which, in *De Princip.* ii. 1, and likewise in other passages, he quotes as *Scripturarum auctoritas*). As showing Origen's opinion, the *Epistola ad Africanum* is peculiarly important. Africanus had pointed out, that in the Books of Daniel and Esther several passages which occurred in the LXX, were wanting in the Hebrew; Origen acknowledges this as well as the general relation between the Hebrew Canon and the LXX, but he does not think that the passages occurring in the LXX are to be rejected on this account; he particularly makes it his business to defend the history of Susannah, as to which, he thinks, that it had been first excluded from the Canon by the Jewish teachers. Thus he remarks, in reference to the Books of Judith and Tobit, that the Jews

Lists of the Old-Testament Canon. 321

made no use of them, and that they did not possess them in their Apocrypha written in the Hebrew language ; nevertheless, he makes no objection to the Christian community availing themselves of them.

Thus, therefore, Origen appears to have shown some vacillation, but to have agreed with Tertullian so far that, in deciding what books and passages of books in the præ-Christian Jewish literature should have value attributed to them in the Church, he does not depend alone on the extent of the Hebrew Canon, and on the opinion of the Jewish scribes at the time.

§ 310.—*Lists of the Old-Testament Canon—In the Greek Church.*

The *list of the Hebrew Canon*, given by Origen, exercised, as it appears, in aftertime no unimportant influence over the opinion of other religious writers of the Greek, and, partly also, of the Latin Church. In this list, Origen quoted in general those books only which were contained in the Hebrew Canon ; he also in other places called attention to the fact, that many elements of the LXX (in which alone the Old Testament was read in the Greek Church), were not contained in the Hebrew Canon. To this very point the Christian teachers were continually referred by the Jewish scholars in their disputes with the former. We, therefore, find, that in the list of Canonical Books of the Greek religious authors in the fourth century and the succeeding period, only the elements of the Hebrew Canon are in general quoted, and not the independent works which are found in the LXX only.

The lists are as follows : (*a*) that of the *Council of Laodicea* (c. 360); (*b*) that in the *Canones Apostolorum;* (*c*) of *Cyril of Jerusalem* (d. 386); (*d*) of *Gregory of Nazianzus* (d. 389); (*e*) in that of the *Iambi ad Seleucum*, in the same age ; (*f*) of *Athanasius*, Bishop of Alexandria (326-373); (*g*) in the Σύνοψις τῆς θείας γραφῆς, also perhaps of the Alexandrian Church, after the time of Athanasius (on the contrary, according to Credner, *Zur Gesch. des Kanons*, p. 127, ff., of the ninth century at the earliest, on the ground of an imperfect manuscript of the *Stichometria* of Nicephorus); (*h*) of *Epiphanius* (d. c. 402). All these keep in general to the Hebrew Canon, and represent books which are not in this as not canonical, with the exception only of the *Epistle of*

VOL. II. Y

Jeremiah, which Origen also names with Jeremiah and the Book of *Baruch* ; these are expressly mentioned with Jeremiah, just as the Lamentations, in the lists of the Council Laod., of Cyril Jerus., and of Athanasius. In the other lists—Canones Apost., Gregory Naz., Iambi ad Seleuc. —they are not indeed expressly named, but neither are the *Lamentations*, so that it may be perhaps assumed, that like the latter, the two former works are included in Jeremiah. This is the case in a list of Epiphanius, *De Mens. et Pond.* c. 23 ; so *ib.* c. 4; although he remarks, in cap. 5, that the " Epistles of Baruch," οὐ κεῖνται παρ' Ἑβραίοις . In another list, *Hæres.* viii. 6 (Opp. i. 19), we are told by Epiphanius, without further question, "Τὸν προφήτην Ἱερεμίαν μετὰ τῶν θρήνων καὶ ἐπιστολῶν αὐτοῦ τε καὶ τοῦ Βαρούχ." The Book of Baruch and the Epistle of Jeremiah appear to have attained pretty general recognition in the Greek Church in this age. In the *Can. Apost.* only, *three books of the Maccabees* are mentioned among the Canonical Books, and (edit. Coteler), the Book of *Judith* also; but both are in this series only and in none of the other lists. In some of them, however, several of our Apocryphal Books are specified as profitable for reading, especially for catechumens and the young. The Council of Laodicea indeed, decreed (Can. 59), that none whatever of the non-Canonical Books should be read, but only the canonical ones of the Old and New Testament; Cyril of Jerusalem expressly cautions against the reading of the non-Canonical Books, and desires that the books which are not read and generally acknowledged by the Church should not be read even at home. But Athanasius, who was induced to put forth his list on account of some persons having presumed to invent apocryphal books and mix them up with the inspired Scriptures, admits a middle-class between the Canonical and the Apocryphal Books, *i.e.*, those devised and forged by heretics ; this class consisted of *reading books*, ἀναγινωσκόμενα, which had been prescribed by their forefathers to be read by catechumens; and in this class he—and following him, the *Synopsis*—places the *Wisdom of Solomon, Jesus Sirach, Judith, Tobit* ; the Synopsis adds the *four books of Maccabees* and the *History of Susannah*, which Athanasius does not name. The Canones Apostolici expressly separate Ecclesiasticus from the Canonical Books, but speak of it as a work, which the young were to learn. And Epiphanius who, in *Hæres.* 8, styles *Ecclus.* and *Solomon's Wisdom* as books which are held to be doubtful, says in a later passage that they are profitable. It is remarkable that in another passage, *Hæres.* 76, where he first points out in general the Books of the Old Testament, and then mentions those of the New Testament, he names *Solomon's Wisdom* and *Sirach* in an uninterrupted series after the Apocalypse, and then unites them altogether under the designation of " Divine Scriptures;" although, in another place, he had expressly severed them from the Books of the Old-Testament Canon. Epiphanius appeals to both works, particularly *Wisdom*, in various other passages, just as if they were utterances of Scripture; Athanasius does the same, and so also does Cyril of Jerusalem (*v.* Herbst, *Einleitung.* i. 35, f.), so that even he is not always so strict in his separation of these works from the Canonical Scriptures, as he claims to be in the above list.

(*a*) *Council of Laodic.* Can. 59, in Mansi *Sacrorum Concill. nova et ampliss. collectio*, tom. ii. (Florence, 1759), p. 574: Ὅτι οὐ δεῖ ἰδιωτικοὺς ψαλμοὺς λέγεσθαι ἐν τῇ ἐκκλησίᾳ, οὐδὲ ἀκανόνιστα βιβλία, ἀλλὰ μόνα τὰ κανονικὰ τῆς καινῆς καὶ παλαιᾶς διαθήκης. Next follows, in Can. 60 (on the genuineness, however, of which a doubt is thrown by Credner, *Geschichte d. Neutest. Kanon*, p. 219), a list of the Canonical Scriptures (Ὅσα δεῖ βιβλία ἀναγινώσκεσθαι τῆς παλαιᾶς διαθήκης), which contains the same books, and in the same order, as that of Cyril (only Job is after Solomon's Song). "Ἰερεμίας καὶ Βαροὺχ, θρῆνοι καὶ ἐπιστολαί."

(*b*) *Canones Apostolici* (*Patrum Apost. Opera*, ed. Cotelerius, i. 448), in 76 (al. 85) Canon: Ἔστω πᾶσιν ὑμῖν κληρικοῖς καὶ λαϊκοῖς βιβλία σεβάσμια καὶ ἅγια, τῆς μὲν παλαιᾶς διαθήκης Μωυσέως πέντε. —— Ἰησοῦ τοῦ Ναυῆ ἕν, τῶν κριτῶν ἕν, τῆς Ῥοὺθ ἕν, Βασιλειῶν τέσσαρα, Παραλειπομένων τοῦ βιβλίου τῶν ἡμερῶν δύο, Ἔσδρα δύο, Ἐσθὴρ ἕν, Ἰουδεὶθ ἕν (wanting in many Codd.), Μαχαβαϊκῶν τρία, Ἰὼβ ἕν, ψαλμοὶ ἑκατὸν πεντήκοντα, Σολομῶντος τρία. —— Προφῆται δεκαέξ. Ἔξωθεν δὲ προσιστορείσθω ὑμῖν, μανθάνειν ὑμῶν τοὺς νέους τὴν σοφίαν τοῦ πολυμαθοῦς Σειράχ. Ἡμέτερα δέ, τ. ε., τῆς καινῆς διαθήκης· Εὐαγγ. τέσσαρα. —— Παύλου ἐπιστολαὶ δεκατέσσαρες, Πέτρου ἐπ. δύο, Ἰωάννου τρεῖς, Ἰακώβου μία, Ἰούδα μία, Κλήμεντος ἐπιστολαὶ δύο καὶ αἱ διαταγαὶ ὑμῖν τοῖς ἐπισκόποις δι' ἐμοῦ Κλήμεντος ἐν ὀκτὼ βιβλίοις προσπεφωνημέναι (ἃς οὐ δεῖ δημοσιεύειν ἐπὶ πάντων, διὰ τὰ ἐν αὐταῖς μυστικὰ) καὶ αἱ πράξεις ἡμῶν τῶν Ἀποστόλων.

(c) *Cyril of Jerusalem* in the 4th Catechesis : Φιλομαθῶς ἐπίγνωθι παρὰ τῆς ἐκκλησίας, ποῖαι μέν εἰσιν αἱ τῆς παλαιᾶς διαθήκης βίβλοι, ποῖαι δὲ τῆς καίνης, καί μοι μηδὲν τῶν ἀποκρύφων ἀναγίνωσκε. Ὁ γὰρ τὰ παρὰ πᾶσιν ὁμολογούμενα μὴ εἰδὼς, τί περὶ τὰ ἀμφιβαλλόμενα ταλαιπωρεῖς μάτην; Ἀναγίνωσκε τὰς θείας γραφὰς, τὰς εἴκοσι δύο βίβλους τῆς παλαιᾶς διαθήκης, τὰς ὑπὸ τῶν ἑβδομήκοντα δύο ἑρμηνευτῶν ἑρμηνευθείσας. — — — Οὐ γὰρ εὑρεσιλογία καὶ κατασκευὴ σοφισμάτων ἀνθρωπίνων ἦν τὸ γινόμενον, ἀλλ' ἐκ πνεύματος ἁγίου ἡ τῶν ἁγίῳ πνεύματι λαληθείσων θείων γραφῶν ἑρμηνεία συνετελεῖτο. Τούτων τὰς εἴκοσι δύο βίβλους ἀναγίνωσκε, πρὸς δὲ τὰ ἀπόκρυφα μηδὲν ἔχε κοινόν. Τοῦ νόμου μὲν γάρ εἰσιν αἱ Μωυσέως πρῶται πέντε βίβλοι. — — ἑξῆς δὲ, Ἰησοῦς υἱὸς Ναυῆ, καὶ τῶν Κριτῶν μετὰ τῆς Ῥοὺθ βιβλίον ἕβδομον ἀριθμούμενον. Τῶν δὲ λοιπῶν ἱστορικῶν βιβλίων, πρώτη καὶ δευτέρα τῶν Βασιλειῶν μία παρ' Ἑβραίοις ἐστὶ βίβλος· μία δὲ καὶ ἡ τρίτη καὶ ἡ τετάρτη· ὁμοίως δὲ παρ' αὐτοῖς καὶ τῶν Παραλειπομένων ἡ πρώτη καὶ ἡ δευτέρα μία τυγχάνει βίβλος, καὶ τοῦ Ἔσδρα ἡ πρώτη καὶ ἡ δευτέρα μία λελόγισται· δωδεκάτη βίβλος ἡ Ἐσθήρ. Καὶ τὰ μὲν ἱ σ τ ο ρ ι κ ὰ ταῦτα. Τὰ δὲ στιχηρὰ τυγχάνει πέντε· Ἰώβ, καὶ βίβλος Ψαλμῶν, καὶ Παροιμίαι καὶ Ἐκκλησιαστής, καὶ Ἄισμα ᾀσμάτων, ἑπτακαιδέκατον βιβλίον. Ἐπὶ δὲ τούτοις τὰ προφητικὰ πέντε· τῶν δώδεκα Προφητῶν μία βίβλος, καὶ Ἡσαΐου μία, καὶ Ἱερεμίου μία μετὰ Βαροὺχ καὶ θρήνων καὶ ἐπιστολῆς· εἶτα Ἰεζεκιὴλ· καὶ ἡ τοῦ Δανιὴλ εἰκοστηδευτέρα βίβλος τῆς παλ. διαθ. Τῆς δὲ καίνης διαθ., τὰ τέσσαρα Εὐαγγ. τὰ δὲ λοιπὰ Ψ ε υ δ ε π ί γ ρ α φ α καὶ βλαβερὰ τυγχάνει. Ἔγραψαν καὶ Μανιχαῖοι κατὰ Θωμᾶν εὐαγγέλιον, ὅπερ ὥσπερ εὐωδίᾳ τῆς εὐαγγελικῆς προσωνομίας διαφθείρει τὰς ψυχὰς τῶν ἀπλουστέρων. Δέχου δὲ καὶ τὰς πράξεις τῶν δώδεκα Ἀποστόλων· πρὸς τούτοις δὲ καὶ τὰς ἑ π τ ὰ Ἰακώβου καὶ Πέτρου, Ἰωάννου καὶ Ἰούδα κ α θ ο λ ι κ ὰ ς ἐ π ι σ τ ο λ ά ς. Ἐπισφράγισμα δὲ τῶν πάντων καὶ μαθητῶν τὸ τελευταῖον, τὰς Παύλου δεκατέσσερας ἐπιστολάς. Τὰ δὲ λοιπὰ πάντα ἔξω κείσθω ἐν δευτέρῳ. Καὶ ὅσα μὲν ἐν ἐκκλησίαις μὴ ἀναγινώσκεται, ταῦτα μηδὲ κατὰ σαυτὸν ἀναγίνωσκε.

(*d*) *Gregory Nazianzen, Carmen de veris Scripturæ libris,* Opp. ed. Caillau (Paris, 1840), ii. 259, *sq.* : Ὄφρα δὲ μὴ ξείνῃσι νόον κλέπτοιο βίβλοισιν· πολλαὶ γὰρ τελέθουσι παρέγγραπτοι κακότητες· δέχνυσο τοῦτον ἐμοῖο τὸν ἔγκριτον ἀριθμόν. Ἱστορικαὶ δυοκαίδεκα (as Cyril, the Book of Ruth being

Lists of the Old-Testament Canon. 325

separately numbered instead of the deficient Book of Esther)
.... στιχηραὶ πέντε ... προφῆται πέντε.
(e) *Iambi ad Seleucum*, in Gregorii Naz. Opp. ed. Caillau, ii. 1102, *sq.*

(ƒ) *Athanasius*, in a fragment of an *Epistola Paschalis*, Opera ed. Colon. (1686), ii. 38, *sq.*: Ἐπειδὴ—φοβοῦμαι, μή πως ὀλίγοι τῶν ἀκεραίων ἀπὸ τῆς ἁπλότητος καὶ τῆς ἁγνότητος πλανηθῶσιν ἀπὸ τῆς πανουργίας τινῶν ἀνθρώπων, καὶ λοιπὸν ἐντυγχάνειν ἑτέροις ἄρξωνται τοῖς λεγομένοις ἀποκρύφοις, ἀπατώμενοι τῇ ὁμωνυμίᾳ τῶν ἀληθινῶν βιβλίων· παρακαλῶ ἀνέχεσθαι, εἰ περὶ ὧν ἐπίστασθε, περὶ τούτων κἀγὼ μνημονεύειν γράφω, διά τε τὴν ἀνάγκην καὶ τὸ χρήσιμον τῆς ἐκκλησίας. Μέλλων δὲ τούτων μνημονεύειν, χρήσομαι πρὸς σύστασιν τῆς ἐμαυτοῦ τόλμης τῷ τύπῳ τοῦ Εὐαγγελιστοῦ Λουκᾶ, λέγων καὶ αὐτός· Ἐπειδήπερ τινὲς ἐπεχείρησαν ἀνατάξασθαι ἑαυτοῖς τὰ λεγόμενα ἀπόκρυφα, καὶ ἐπιμίξαι ταῦτα τῇ θεοπνεύστῳ γραφῇ, περὶ ἧς ἐπληροφορήθημεν, καθὼς παρέδοσαν τοῖς πατράσιν οἱ ἀπ' ἀρχῆς αὐτόπται καὶ ὑπηρέται γενόμενοι τοῦ λόγου· ἔδοξε κἀμοὶ, προτραπέντι παρὰ γνησίων ἀδελφῶν καὶ μαθόντι ἄνωθεν, ἑξῆς ἐκθέσθαι τὰ κανονιζόμενα καὶ παραδοθέντα, πιστευθέντα τε θεῖα εἶναι βιβλία, ἵνα ἕκαστος, εἰ μὲν ἠπατήθη, καταγνῷ τῶν πλανησάντων ὁ δὲ καθαρὸς διαμείνας χαίρῃ πάλιν ὑπομιμνησκόμενος. Ἔστι τοίνυν τῆς μὲν παλαιᾶς διαθήκης βιβλία τῷ ἀριθμῷ τὰ πάντα εἰκοσιδύο· τοσαῦτα γὰρ, ὡς ἤκουσα, καὶ τὰ στοιχεῖα τὰ παρ' Ἑβραίοις εἶναι παραδέδοται. Τῇ δὲ τάξει καὶ τῷ ὀνόματί ἐστιν ἕκαστον οὕτως ..... (the historical and poetical books, as Gregory, " Ἰερεμίας καὶ σὺν αὐτῷ Βαροὺχ, θρῆνοι καὶ ἐπιστολή"). Τὰ δὲ τῆς καίνης πάλιν οὐκ ὀκνητέον εἰπεῖν· ἔστι δὲ ταῦτα (as Cyril).... καὶ πάλιν Ἰωάννου ἀποκάλυψις. Ταῦτα πηγαὶ τοῦ σωτηρίου .... ἐν τούτοις μόνοις τὸ τῆς εὐσεβείας διδασκαλεῖον εὐαγγελίζεται. Μηδεὶς τούτοις ἐπιβαλλέτω, μηδὲ τούτων ἀφαιρείσθω τι .... Ἀλλ' ἕνεκά γε πλείονος ἀκριβείας προστίθημι καὶ τοῦτο, γράφων ἀναγκαίως, ὡς ἔστι καὶ ἕτερα βιβλία τούτων ἔξωθεν, οὐ κανονιζόμενα μὲν, τετυπωμένα δὲ παρὰ τῶν πατέρων ἀναγινώσκεσθαι τοῖς ἄρτι προσερχομένοις καὶ βουλομένοις κατηχεῖσθαι τὸν τῆς εὐσεβείας λόγον· σοφία Σολομῶντος καὶ σοφία Σιρὰχ, καὶ Ἐσθὴρ, καὶ Ἰουδὶθ, καὶ Τωβίας, καὶ Διδαχὴ καλουμένη τῶν Ἀποστόλων, καὶ ὁ Ποιμήν· καὶ ὅμως, ἀγαπητοί, κἀκείνων ἀναγινωσκομένων καὶ τούτων κανονιζομένων, οὐδαμοῦ τῶν ἀποκρύφων μνήμη· ἀλλὰ αἱρετικῶν ἐστιν ἐπινοία, γραφόντων μὲν ὅτε θέλουσιν αὐτά· χαριζομένων δὲ καὶ προστιθέντων αὐτοῖς χρόνους, ἵνα ὡς παλαιὰ προφέροντες πρόφασιν ἔχωσιν ἀπατᾶν ἐκ τούτων τοὺς ἀκεραίους.

(g) Σύνοψις τῆς θείας γραφῆς, in Athanasii Opp. ed. Colon. ii. 55, sq.: Τινὲς μέν τοι τῶν παλαιῶν εἰρήκασι κανονίζεσθαι παρ' Ἑβραίοις καὶ τὴν Ἐσθήρ· καὶ τὴν μὲν Ῥοὺθ, μετὰ τῶν Κριτῶν ἐνουμένην, εἰς ἓν βιβλίον ἀριθμεῖσθαι, τὴν δὲ Ἐσθὴρ εἰς ἕτερον ἕν· καὶ οὕτω πάλιν εἰς εἴκοσι δύο συμπληροῦσθαι τὸν ἀριθμὸν τῶν κανονιζομένων παρ' αὐτοῖς βιβλίων.

(h) *Epiphanius*—in several passages of his writings, in every case in a peculiar order; 1 and 2 Ezra and Esther are always at the end, after the prophets. He reckons sometimes 22, sometimes 27 books (*e.g. de Mensur. et Pond.* 23), taking Ruth, 2 Chronicles, 2 and 4 Βασιλειῶν and 2 Ezra separately.—*Hæres.* viii. 6: . . . . Καὶ αὗταί εἰσιν αἱ εἴκοσι ἑπτὰ βίβλοι αἱ ἐκ θεοῦ δοθεῖσαι τοῖς Ἰουδαίοις . . . . . Εἰσὶ δὲ καὶ ἄλλαι δύο βίβλοι παρ' αὐτοῖς ἐν ἀμφιλέκτῳ, ἡ Σοφία τοῦ Σιρὰχ καὶ ἡ τοῦ Σολομῶντος, χωρὶς ἄλλων τινων ἐναποκρύφων. —*Hæres.* 76: Εἰ γὰρ ἦς ἐξ ἁγίου πνεύματος γεγεννημένος, καὶ προφήταις καὶ ἀποστόλοις μεμαθητευμένος, ἔδει σε διελθόντα ἀπ' ἀρχῆς γενέσεως κόσμου ἄχρι τῶν τῆς Αἰσθὴρ χρόνων, ἐν εἴκοσι καὶ ἑπτὰ βιβλίος παλαίας διαθήκης, εἴκοσι δύο ἀριθμουμένος, τέταρσι δὲ ἁγίοις εὐαγγελίοις, καὶ ἐν τεσσαρεσκαιδέκα ἐπιστολαῖς τοῦ ἁγίου ἀποστόλου Παύλου, καὶ ἐν ταῖς πρὸ τούτων καὶ σὺν ταῖς ἐν τοῖς αὐτῶν χρόνοις πράξεσι τῶν ἀποστόλων, καθολικαῖς ἐπιστολαῖς Ἰακώβου καὶ Πέτρου, καὶ Ἰωάννου καὶ Ἰούδα, καὶ ἐν τῇ τοῦ Ἰωάννου ἀποκαλύψει, ἔν τε ταῖς σοφίαις Σολομῶντος τέ φημι καὶ υἱοῦ Σιρὰχ καὶ πάσαις ἁπλῶς γραφαῖς ἁγίαις, καὶ ἑαυτοῦ καταγνῶναι, ὅτι κ.τ.λ.—*De Mensur. et Pond.* 4: Ἐπληρώθησαν οὖν αἱ εἰκοσιδύο βίβλοι . . . . Αἱ γὰρ στιχήρεις δύο βίβλοι, ἥτε τοῦ Σολομῶντος ἡ Πανάρετος λεγομένη καὶ ἡ τοῦ Ἰησοῦ τοῦ υἱοῦ Σιφὰχ . . . . . καὶ αὗταὶ χρήσιμοι μέν εἰσι καὶ ὠφέλιμοι, ἀλλ' εἰς ἀριθμὸν ῥητῶν οὐκ ἀναφέρονται.—*Ibid.* 23, we are told, after the enumeration of the 27 BB.: Ἔστι δὲ καὶ ἄλλη μικρὰ βίβλος, ἣ καλεῖται Κινὼθ, ἥτις ἑρμηνεύεται θρῆνος Ἰερεμίου, αὕτη δὲ τῷ Ἰερεμίᾳ συνάπτεται, ἥτις ἐστὶ περισσὴ τοῦ ἀριθμοῦ καὶ τῷ Ἰερεμίᾳ συναπτομένη.

We must also consider the position of the Greek Church in this age as regards the Book of *Esther.* Not only at the time of Melito and Origen (*v.* above, § 308, f.), but also after the middle of the fourth century, when, in the Jewish Church, this book had certainly become generally acknowledged, doubts appear to have been entertained whether it should be reckoned among the Holy Scriptures of full canonical authority; and this was doubtless in reference to the spirit which is shown in it, which harmonizes so little with that of Christianity.

The lists of the Council of Laod., the Can. Apostolici, Cyril of Jerus., and Epiphanius mention it among the Canonical Books without question. On the other hand, in that of Gregory Naz., it is entirely wanting, and certainly not through an accidental error; for in the *Synopsis*, he expressly tells us that some of the ancients declared that this book was held as canonical by the Hebrews—a proof that, at that time in the Church so far as the author was acquainted with it, and at least in the Alexandrian Church, it was not generally looked upon in this way. *Athanasius* also agrees with this, who mentions it only in the series of ἀναγινωσκομένα, and not among the Canonical Books. It is not mentioned among the latter, in the list in the *Iambi*; it is named only at the end: τούτοις προσεγκρίνουσι τὴν 'Εσθήρ τινες.

§ 311.—*Lists of the Old-Testament Canon—In the Latin Church.*

We find, however, traces of doubt in regard to the Book of Esther in the Greek Church only, and not in the *Latin*, where it appears to have been adopted with the rest of the Books of the Canon without any opposition. In this Church, however, our Apocrypha came into acknowledged canonical authority in this age, together with the Scriptures of the Hebrew Canon. Nevertheless, we find lists of the Canonical Scriptures from the middle of the fourth to the beginning of the fifth century, in which the two classes are expressly divided, and canonical authority is awarded only to the elements of the Hebrew Canon. We possess lists by three men, who in their theological and exegetical studies were much devoted to the Greek Fathers, particularly to *Origen*, and who also follow him in their Canon of the Old Testament;—*Hilarius, Rufinus,* and *Jerome.*

(1) Hilarius Pictavensis (d. 368), in his revision of the Psalms, *Prolog.* p. 8, mentions the Canonical Books of the Old Testament as twenty-two in number, from Genesis to Esther, exactly in the same order as Origen (*v.* § 309), whose list he manifestly had before his eyes; with Jeremiah he mentions the *Epistle* together with Lamentations:

"Hieremias cum lamentationibus et epistola . . . . . .
Quibusdam autem visum est, additis *Tobia* et *Judith* viginti
quatuor libros secundum numerum Græcarum literarum
connumerare."

(2) Rufinus, Presbyter of Aquileia (d. c. 411), in his
Expositio Symboli Apostolici. In this he seeks to specify, according to the tradition of the Church, the Scriptures inspired by the Holy Ghost, and, in the Old Testament, names the whole of the Books in the Hebrew Canon, not mentioning Lamentations but doubtless including it with Jeremiah, and in the same way most probably the *Epistle of Jeremiah*. [Spiritus S. est, qui in V. T. legem et prophetas, in Novo vero evangelia et apostolos inspiravit
. . . . . . Et ideo, quæ sunt Novi ac Vet. Instrumenti volumina, quæ secundum magnorum traditionem per ipsum Spiritum Sanctum inspirata creduntur et ecclesiis Christi tradita, competens videtur in hoc loco evidenti numero, sicut ex patrum monumentis accepimus, designare.]—(Then follow the books of the Old and New Testaments.)—In reference to these Scriptures, he says : " Hæc sunt, quæ patres intra Canonem concluserunt, ex quibus fidei nostræ assertiones constare voluerunt." Then, however, he mentions a second class of books, which he calls *ecclesiastici*, corresponding to the *reading book* of Athanasius, and again distinguishes from the latter the *Scripturas apocryphas*:
[Sciendum tamen est, quod et alii libri sunt, qui non canonici, sed *ecclesiastici* a majoribus appellati sunt : ut est *Sapientia Salomonis*, et alia sapientia, quæ dicitur *filii Sirach*, qui liber apud Latinos generali vocabulo Ecclesiasticus appellatur, quo vocabulo non auctor libelli, sed scripturæ qualitas cognominata est . Ejusdem ordinis est *libellus Tobiæ* et *Judith* et *Macc*. libri . In Novo vero Test. libellus, qui dicitur *Pastoris* s. Hermatis, qui appellatur duæ viæ, vel judicium Petri : *quæ omnia legi quidem in ecclesiis voluerunt, non tamen proferri ad auctoritatem ex his fidei confirmandam* . Ceteras vero Scripturas, *apocryphas* nominarunt, quas in ecclesiis legi noluerunt].

(3) Jerome (d. 420) gives, in the *Prolog. Galeatus in libros Regum*, a list of the Old-Testament Books, twenty-two in number, according to the division into Law, Prophets, and Hagiographa, Ruth being expressly reckoned with the Judges as one book, and the Lamentations, tacitly,

with Jeremiah; and he remarks that some persons place Ruth and Lamentations among the Hagiographa as separate books, and thus make twenty-four books (the Epistle of Jeremiah not being noticed). He then asserts: "quicquid extra hos est, inter Apocrypha esse ponendum." He forms his idea of the Apocrypha in a more comprehensive and milder sense than, e.g., Rufinus, thinking that the *libri ecclesiastici* should be included with it (cf. *Præf. in libros Salom.*, and above, § 200). As books of this sort, he mentions in the *Prol. Galeat.* the *Wisdom of Solomon, Jesus Sirach, Judith, Tobit,* and the *Pastor,* subsequently also the two Books of *Maccabees.* It is doubtful what book is meant by Jerome as the *Pastor.* Augusti (§ 54) and Bertholdt (iii. 1006), are of opinion that it is the third Book of Ezra (*i.e.*, the Greek Ezra), which has the title of ἱερεύς, of which, as is thought, *Pastor* is the translation; but it seems more probable to me that, as is usually supposed, the so-called *Pastor of Hermas* is intended, which Rufinus and Athanasius mention among the Libri Apostolici, ἀναγινωσκόμενα.

In the *Bibliotheca Divina,* and in the *Epistola ad Paulinum* (*v.* Christ. Fried. Schmidt, *Historia antiqua et vindicatio Canonis*), Jerome brings forward the twenty-two books of the Hebrew Canon, without indeed mentioning the Apocrypha, in the same way as in the *Prolog. Galeat.*

[*Prolog. Galeat.*: " Viginti et duas literas esse apud Hebræos, Syrorum quoque lingua et Chaldæorum testatur .... Porro quinque literæ duplices apud Hebræos sunt, Caph, Mem, Nun, Pe, Sade. Unde et quinque a plerisque libri duplices existimantur, Samuel, Melachim, Dibre Hajamim, Esdras, Jeremias cum Kinoth, *i.e.*, Lamentationibus suis . Quomodo igitur xxii elementa sunt .... ita xxii *volumina* supputantur . Primus apud eos liber vocatur *Beresith*, quem nos Genesim dicimus : secundus *Veelle Semoth*, qui Exodus appellatur : tertius *Vajikra, i.e.* Leviticus : quartus *Vajedabber,* quem Numeros vocamus : quintus *Elle haddebarim*, qui Deuteronomium prænotatur . Ili sunt quinque libri Mosis, quos proprie *Torah, i.e.,* Legem appellant . Secundum Prophetarum ordinem faciunt, et incipiunt at *Jesu filio Nave*, qui apud illos, *Josue ben Nun* dicitur . Deinde subtexunt *Sophetim, i.e.,* Judicum librum : et in eundem compingunt *Ruth*, quia in diebus Judicum facta ejus narratur historia : tertius sequitur *Samuel*, quem

"Hieremias cum lamentationibus et epistola . . . . . .
Quibusdam autem visum est, additis *Tobia* et *Judith* viginti
quatuor libros secundum numerum Græcarum literarum
connumerare."

(2) Rufinus, Presbyter of Aquileia (d. c. 411), in his
Expositio Symboli Apostolici. In this he seeks to specify, according to the tradition of the Church, the Scriptures
inspired by the Holy Ghost, and, in the Old Testament,
names the whole of the Books in the Hebrew Canon, not
mentioning Lamentations but doubtless including it with
Jeremiah, and in the same way most probably the *Epistle
of Jeremiah.* [Spiritus S. est, qui in V. T. legem et prophetas, in Novo vero evangelia et apostolos inspiravit
. . . . . . Et ideo, quæ sunt Novi ac Vet. Instrumenti
volumina, quæ secundum magnorum traditionem per ipsum
Spiritum Sanctum inspirata creduntur et ecclesiis Christi
tradita, competens videtur in hoc loco evidenti numero,
sicut ex patrum monumentis accepimus, designare.]—(Then
follow the books of the Old and New Testaments.)—In
reference to these Scriptures, he says : " Hæc sunt, quæ
patres intra Canonem concluserunt, ex quibus fidei nostræ
assertiones constare voluerunt." Then, however, he mentions a second class of books, which he calls *ecclesiastici*,
corresponding to the *reading book* of Athanasius, and again
distinguishes from the latter the *Scripturas apocryphas :*
[Sciendum tamen est, quod et alii libri sunt, qui non
canonici, sed *ecclesiastici* a majoribus appellati sunt : ut est
Sapientia Salomonis, et alia sapientia, quæ dicitur *filii Sirach*,
qui liber apud Latinos generali vocabulo Ecclesiasticus
appellatur, quo vocabulo non auctor libelli, sed scripturæ
qualitas cognominata est . Ejusdem ordinis est *libellus
Tobiæ* et *Judith* et *Macc.* libri . In Novo vero Test. libellus,
qui dicitur *Pastoris* s. Hermatis, qui appellatur duæ viæ,
vel judicium Petri : *quæ omnia legi quidem in ecclesiis voluerunt, non tamen proferri ad auctoritatem ex his fidei confirmandam* . Ceteras vero Scripturas. apocryphas nominarunt,
quas in ecclesiis legi noluerunt].

(3) Jerome (d. 420) gives, in the *Prolog. Galeatus in
libros Regum*, a list of the Old-Testament Books, twenty-two in number, according to the division into Law, Prophets, and Hagiographa, Ruth being expressly reckoned
with the Judges as one book, and the Lamentations, tacitly,

with Jeremiah; and he remarks that some persons place Ruth and Lamentations among the Hagiographa as separate books, and thus make twenty-four books (the Epistle of Jeremiah not being noticed). He then asserts: "quicquid extra hos est, inter Apocrypha esse ponendum." He forms his idea of the Apocrypha in a more comprehensive and milder sense than, e.g., Rufinus, thinking that the *libri ecclesiastici* should be included with it (cf. *Præf. in libros Salom.*, and above, § 200). As books of this sort, he mentions in the *Prol. Galeat.* the *Wisdom of Solomon, Jesus Sirach, Judith, Tobit,* and the *Pastor,* subsequently also the two Books of *Maccabees.* It is doubtful what book is meant by Jerome as the *Pastor.* Augusti (§ 54) and Bertholdt (iii. 1006), are of opinion that it is the third Book of Ezra (*i.e.,* the Greek Ezra), which has the title of ἱερεύς, of which, as is thought, *Pastor* is the translation; but it seems more probable to me that, as is usually supposed, the so-called *Pastor of Hermas* is intended, which Rufinus and Athanasius mention among the Libri Apostolici, ἀναγινωσκόμενα.

In the *Bibliotheca Divina,* and in the *Epistola ad Paulinum* (*v.* Christ. Fried. Schmidt, *Historia antiqua et vindicatio Canonis*), Jerome brings forward the twenty-two books of the Hebrew Canon, without indeed mentioning the Apocrypha, in the same way as in the *Prolog. Galeat.*

[*Prolog. Galeat.* : " Viginti et duas literas esse apud Hebræos, Syrorum quoque lingua et Chaldæorum testatur .... Porro quinque literæ duplices apud Hebræos sunt, Caph, Mem, Nun, Pe, Sade. Unde et quinque a plerisque libri duplices existimantur, Samuel, Melachim, Dibre Hajamim, Esdras, Jeremias cum Kinoth, *i.e.,* Lamentationibus suis . Quomodo igitur xxii elementa sunt .... ita xxii *volumina* supputantur . Primus apud eos liber vocatur *Beresith*, quem nos Genesim dicimus : secundus *Veelle Semoth*, qui Exodus appellatur : tertius *Vajikra*, *i.e.* Leviticus : quartus *Vajedabber*, quem Numeros vocamus : quintus *Elle haddebarim*, qui Deuteronomium prænotatur . Hi sunt quinque libri Mosis, quos proprie *Torah, i.e.,* Legem appellant . Secundum Prophetarum ordinem faciunt, et incipiunt at *Jesu filio Nave*, qui apud illos, *Josue ben Nun* dicitur . Deinde subtexunt *Sophetim, i.e.,* Judicum librum : et in eundem compingunt *Ruth*, quia in diebus Judicum facta ejus narratur historia : tertius sequitur *Samuel*, quem nos *Regum* i et ii dicimus : quartus *Melachim*, *i.e.*, Regum, qui iii et iv *Regum* volumine continetur . . . . . Quintus est *Esaias* : sextus *Jeremias* : septimus *Ezechiel* : octavus liber *duodecim Prophetarum*, qui apud illos vocatur *Thereasar*. Tertius ordo Hagiographa possidet . Et primus liber incipit a *Job* : secundus a *David*, quem quinque incisionibus et uno Psalmorum volumine comprehendunt : tertius est *Salomon* tres libros habens, *Proverbia*, quæ illi *Misle*, *i.e.*, Parabolas appellant : quartus *Ecclesiastes*, *i.e.*, *Coheleth* : quintus *Canticum Canticorum*, quem titulo *Sir Hassirim* prænotant : sextus est *Daniel* : septimus *Dibre Hajamim*, *i.e.*, *Verba dierum*, quod significantius Chronicon totius Divinæ historiæ possumus appellare, qui apud nos *Paralipomenon* i. et ii inscribitur ; octavus *Esdras*, qui et ipse similiter apud Græcos et Latinos in duos libros divisus est : nonus *Esther*. Atque ita fiunt pariter Veteris Legis libri xxii, *i.e.*, Mosis v et Prophetarum viii, Hagiographorum ix . Quanquam nonnulli *Ruth* et *Kinoth* inter Hagiographa scriptitent et hos libros in suo putent numero supputandos ac per hoc priscæ legis libros viginti quatuor . . . . . Hic prologus scripturarum quasi galeatum principium omnibus libris, quos de Hebræo vertimus in Latinum, convenire potest, ut scire valeamus, quicquid extra hos est, *inter Apocrypha esse ponendum* . Igitur *Sapientia*, quæ vulgo Salomonis inscribitur, et *Jesu* filii *Sirach* liber et *Judith* et *Tobias* et *Pastor* non sunt in Canone . Maccabæorum primum librum Hebraicum reperi, secundus Græcus est, quod ex ipsa quoque phrasi probari potest."—*Præf. in libros Salomonis :* Fertur et πανάρετος Jesu filii Sirach liber et alius Ψευδεπίγραφος, qui Sapientia Salomonis inscribitur . Quorum priorem Hebraicum reperi . . . . . secundus apud Hebræos nusquam est . . . . . Sicut ergo Judith et Tobi et Maccabæorum libros legit quidem Ecclesia, sed inter canonicas Scripturas non recipit, sic et hæc duo volumina legat ad ædificationem plebis, non *ad auctoritatem ecclesiasticorum dogmatum confirmandam.*—More strongly against the Apocrypha, *e.g.*, *Epist.* 107, *ad Lætam :* Caveat omnia apocrypha ; et si quando ea non ad dogmatum veritatem, sed ad signorum reverentiam legere voluerit, sciat non eorum esse, quorum titulis prænotantur ; multaque his admixta vitiosa, et grandis esse prudentiæ aurum in luto quærere.]

But Jerome himself, elsewhere in his works, particularly

in the later ones, unhesitatingly quotes passages out of the various apocryphal books, just in the same way as passages out of the Books of the Hebrew Canon, and intermingled with them, as utterances of Scripture and the like.¹ Perhaps, the decrees of the *African Synods* taking place in the meantime may have been of influence; in which decrees the adoption of these works was formally sanctioned.

Thus, firstly, at the Council at Hippo Regius in Numidia, A.D. 393, in the thirty-sixth Canon. In this our Apocrypha were named among the Canonical Books in the Old Testament; viz., the *Wisdom of Solomon*, and *Jesus Sirach* (which, with the Proverbs, Ecclesiastes, and Solomon's Song, are without question put together as *Salomonis libri quinque*), the Books of *Tobit* and *Judith*, and two Books of *Maccabees*.

This decree was repeated and confirmed in the third Carthaginian Synod, A.D. 397 (Can. 47 in Mansi, iii. 891). Augustine, presbyter, and after 395, Bishop of Hippo Regius, being present at both synods, was particularly active, and of great influence. It is evident from his expressions, especially in his work written soon after the above synod, *De Doctrina Christiana*, ii. 8, on what principles the determination of the Canon was managed. In forming an opinion as to this, he desires that the authority of as many Catholic communities as possible should be followed, and therefore that the pre-eminence should be given, first to the generally acknowledged Scriptures, *i.e.* to those works which have been accepted by the most numerous and important communities. He then states the several books of the Canon, first those of the Old-Testament Canon,—exactly those named by the above-named synods; he also justifies the *Wisdom of Solomon* and *Jesus Sirach* (Ecclesiasticus) being numbered among the Canonical Books, as deserving such authority, although it was not unknown to him that they were not composed by Solomon, and had only been named "of Solomon," on account of a certain similarity to his writings. Just in the same way he is in favour *(contra Gaudent.* i. 31) of the Church accepting the Books of *Maccabees*, notwithstanding the Jews had not done so.

The decree of the two above-named African Synods was once more repeated in that of Carthage, A.D. 419, in which Augustine likewise took a part, and it was then deter-

¹ *Vide* Herbst, *Einl.* i. p. 36, f., and Welte's notes on it.

mined to apply for the confirmation to it of the Bishop of Rome, and other bishops, which doubtless did not fail to be given. Somewhat earlier, in 405, *Innocent* I., Bishop of Rome, had given in a letter (in Mansi, iii. 1040) to *Exsuperius*, Bishop of Toulouse, at his wish, a list of the books adopted in the Canon, which entirely agrees with the decrees of both the two before-named synods; and, in the same way, a list by Gelasius I., Bishop of Rome, which is said to have been made at a synod at Rome (in Mansi, viii. 146; Credner, *Zur Gesch. des Kanons*, pp. 151–290).

The decree of the Council of Hippo has been preserved only in an abridgement, "in quo quædam diligentius constituta videntur," in the acts of the above Carthaginian Synod (in Mansi, iii. 924): " Ut præter scripturas canonicas nihil in Ecclesia legatur sub nomine Divinarum Scripturarum . Sunt autem Canon. Scripturæ: Gen., Exod., Levit., Numb., Deuteron., Jesu Nave, Judicum, Ruth, Regnorum libri quatuor, Paralipom. libri duo, Job, Psalterium Davidicum, *Salamonis libri quinque*, duodecim libri Prophetarum. Esaias, Jerem., Dan., Ezech., *Tobias, Judith*, Hester, Hesdræ libri duo, *Machabæorum* libri duo . Novi autem Test. Evangeliorum libri quatuor, Actus Apostol. liber unus, Pauli Apost. epistolæ tredecim, ejusdem ad Hebræos una, Petri duæ, Joannis tres, Jacobi una, Judæ una, Apocalypsis Joannis. Ita ut de confirmando isto Canone transmarina Ecclesia consulatur. Liceat etiam legi passiones martyrum, cum anniversarii dies eorum celebrentur."—Augustine, *De Doctrina Christiana*, ii. 8 : " In canonicis scripturis ecclesiarum catholicarum quamplurium auctoritatem sequatur, inter quas sane illæ sint, quæ apostolicas sedes habere et epistolas accipere meruerunt. Tenebit igitur hunc modum in Scripturis Canonicis, ut eas, quæ ab omnibus accipiuntur ecclesiis catholicis, præponat eis, quas quidam non accipiunt; in eis vero, quæ non accipiuntur ab omnibus, præponat eas, quas plures gravioresque accipiunt, eis, quas pauciores minorisque auctoritatis ecclesiæ tenent. Si autem alias invenerit a pluribus, alias a gravioribus haberi, quamquam hoc facile inveniri non possit, æqualis tamen auctoritatis eas habendas puto." In the list of the Biblical Books which follows, he says: " Illi duo libri, unus, qui Sapientia, et alius, qui Ecclesiasticus inscribitur, *de quadam similitudine Salamonis esse dicuntur:*

nam *Jesus Sirach* eos conscripsisse constantissime perhibetur, qui tamen, quoniam *in auctoritatem recipi* meruerunt, inter propheticos numerandi sunt."—*Contra Gaudent.* i. 31 : "Hanc quidem scripturam, quæ appellatur Maccabæorum, non habent Judæi, sicut legem et Prophetas et Psalmos, quibus Dominus testimonium perhibet, tanquam testibus suis Luc. xxiv. 44, sed *recepta* est ab Ecclesia non inutiliter, si sobrie *legatur* vel audiatur."

§ 312.—*Opinions as to the Apocrypha in the Western Church.*

Thus, therefore, in the Western Church the insertion of our Apocrypha into the Old-Testament Canon (which was chiefly brought about by Augustine) and the equalization of it with the elements of the Hebrew Canon, were sanctioned by authoritative decrees, and the use of it was thus naturally very much promoted, so that these books found a place in the ancient Latin translation made from the LXX—the so-called *Itala*—as also in the LXX itself, among the elements of the Hebrew Canon. But yet even in the West itself there was a counterpoise formed against this by the lists of Hilarius, Rufinus, and Jerome, so esteemed on account of his erudition. Thus, during the next century, even in the West, the Apocrypha was prevented from attaining *generally* acknowledged canonical authority, so that although by most readers it was made use of equally with the Scriptures of the Jewish Canon, yet, among the more learned authors of the Church who read the works of the older Fathers, and even among those who (as was the case with almost all), from ignorance of Hebrew, could not read the Old Testament in the original language, the consciousness was maintained of a distinction between the Apocrypha and the elements of the Hebrew Canon.

Thus we find that Cassiodorus, *De Institutione Divin. Script.* cap. xii. f., places together the enumerations of the Old-Testament Books made by both Jerome and Augustine, and that Gregory the Great (590–604) thinks that he must apologize for introducing a proof out of 1 Macc., it being *not a canonical* book (*Moral. in Job*, xix. 17 : " Non inordinate agimus, si ex libris non canonicis, sed tamen ad ædificationem editis testimonium proferamus "). We also find, somewhat later, however, that many of the most distinguished divines of the Western Church in the middle ages, down to the Reformation, looked upon the Apocrypha in the same way as Jerome, either numbering only twenty-two books of the Old Testament, or expressly specifying the other books as indeed profitable for reading, but as not being in the Canon; that they also pointed out the distinction between them and the Canonical Books, or would not allow the proofs derived from the former to be valid.[1]

Thus, *e.g.*, in the eighth century, the Venerable Bede [*in Apocal.* 4: "Alæ senæ quatuor animalium, quæ sunt 24, totidem Vet. Instrument. libros insinuant." Cf. *De sex ætatibus mundi* (ad a. 3496): "Hucusque (Div. Script.) temporum seriem continet . Quæ autem post hæc apud Judæos sunt digesta, de libro *Maccabæorum* et Josephi atque Africani scriptis exhibentur"].—Alcuin [*adv. Elipantum*, Tolet. lib. i. on Jesus Sirach: "Quem librum Beatus Hieronymus atque Isidorus (?) inter Apocryphas, *i.e.*, dubias Scripturas deputatum esse absque dubitatione testantur"].—Rabanus Maurus, d. 856, *De Instit. Clericorum*, c. liv.

Notker, Abbot of St. Gall, d. 912 [in his *Notatio* of the most distinguished interpreters of Scripture, says, as to the Wisdom of Solomon: "Ab Hebræis penitus respuitur et apud nostros quasi incertus habetur; tamen quia priores nostri cum propter utilitatem doctrinæ legere consueverunt, et Judæi eundem non habent, *Ecclesiasticus* etiam apud nos appellatur . Quod de hoc, id etiam de libro Jesu filii Sirach sentias oportet, nisi quod is ab Hebræis et habetur et legitur . . . . De libro Judith et Esther et Paralipomenon quid dicam, a quibus et qualiter exponantur, quum etiam ipsa in eis litera non pro auctoritate, sed tantum pro memoria et admiratione habeatur? Idem de libris Machabæorum suspicari poteris."]

In the twelfth century, Peter of Cluny, *Epist. contra Petrobrusianos*. Hugo of St. Victor [counts twenty-two books of the Old Testament, and, in the preface to lib. ii. *de Sacram.*, calls the Apocrypha *libros controversos*, which were indeed read, but were not *in corpore textus vel in Canone auctoritatis*. Cf. *de Scriptura*. cap. 6].—Richard of St. Victor, *Excerpt.* ii. 9 (in Hugo of St. Victor, Opp. ed. Migne, iii. 208, sq.).—Rupert von Deuz, *in Gen.* iii. 23.—

[1] For what follows, *vide* Joh. Gerhard, *Loci Theol.* tom. ii. loc. 1. c. 6. §§ 9-96 [Hody, *De Bibliorum textibus original.* p. 654, ff.], and Keerl, *Die Apokryphen des A. T.* 1852, pp. 140-144.

John of Salisbury [*Epist.* 143 (al. 172), ed. Migne: "Quia de numero librorum diversas et multiplices patrum lego sententias, Catholicæ ecclesiæ Doctorem Jeronimum sequens . . . . 22 libros V. Test. in 3 distinctos ordinibus indubitanter credo . . . . Liber vero *Sap.* et *Ecclesiasticus*, *Judith*, *Tobias* et *Pastor* non reputantur in Canone, sed neque Machabæorum liber, qui in 2 vol. scinditur."]

Hugo Carensis (thirteenth century), *Prolog. in Jos.*: "Restant Apocrypha: Jesus, Sapientia, Pastor, et Machabæorum libri, Judith atque Tobias. Hi quia sunt dubii, sub Canone non numerantur; sed quia vera canunt, ecclesia suscipit illos."—Nicolaus Lyranus (fourteenth century), in a treatise, *De libris Biblie canonicis et non canonicis*, preceding his *Postillæ perpetua in Biblia*, complains that no distinction is made between the Apocryphal and Canonical Books, enumerating the latter according to Jerome, and stating their relation to the former in the same way as the above Father and Rufin: "Nam Canonici sunt confecti Spiritu Sancto dictante, noncanonici autem sive apocryphi nescitur quo tempore quibusve auctoribus sint editi," &c.; *v.* Gieseler, *K. Gesch.* ii. 3, p. 238; 2nd edit. p. 270.

Antoninus, Archbishop of Florence (fifteenth century) [*Chron.* Pars i. tit. 3, cap. 9, § 12: "Ecclesia etiam Apocrypha recipit ut vera, et ut utilia et moralia veneratur, etsi in contentionem eorum quæ sunt fidei, non urgentia ad arguendum." Cf. *ib.* cap. 4, and *Summ. Theol.*, part 3, tit. 18, c. 6, § 2: "Unde forte habent auctoritatem talem qualem habent dicta sanctorum Doctorum approbata ab Ecclesia."]

In the sixteenth century, Cardinal Francis Ximenes, *Præf. Bibl. Complut.*; Johannes Pico of Mirandola; Faber Stapulensis. Cardinal Cajetan, in the dedication to Clement VII. of his "Commentary on the Old Testament" (1532), praises the great merits of Jerome: "Propter discretos ab eodem libros canonicos a non canonicis;" and at the conclusion of his "Commentary on Esther," he demands: "Ad Hieronymi limam reducenda sunt tam verba Conciliorum quam Doctorum." Santes Pagninus, at the end of his Latin translation of the Old Testament, 1528.

I must also remark, that subsequently, in the Roman Catholic Church, for the canonical value of the Apocrypha they appealed to the Florentine Council (1439), which gave, in its seventh decree, a list of the Biblical Books, and mention in it the Apocrypha as Canonical Books. It becomes, however, very probable, from external grounds, that this seventh decree, which no one was acquainted with before the Tridentine Council, is not genuine, but was interpolated at a later date to favour the Apocrypha; v. Keerl, *ut supra*, p. 150, f.

The inference from what has preceded is, therefore, this, that although in the West, after the fourth century, the Apocrypha was often made use of just in the same way as the elements of the Hebrew Canon, yet the opinion about it remained unfettered, and no general, valid, binding authority was attributed to the conclusions of the African Synods, and the determinations of the Bishop of Rome in the fifth century.

§ 313.—*Opinions as to the Apocrypha in the Greek Church.*

In the Greek Church during this period, the decrees of the Council of Laodicea and the Fathers of the fourth century remained unaltered. This remained the case up to the time of the Reformation, when the above church came to a more exact decision, to acknowledge as canonical the books of the Hebrew Canon only.

Johannes Damascenus (c. 720), *de fide Orthod.* iv. p. 18, mentions as the Scriptures of the Old Testament, the twenty-two books of the Hebrew Canon only, and goes on to say of the Wisdom of Solomon and Sirach, that they were indeed admirable and beautiful (ἐνάρεται καὶ καλαί), but were not to be included with the others. And a list, at the end of the Chronographia of Nicephorus, Patriarch of Constantinople (d. 828), which, however, he had perhaps met with somewhere, mentions only the twenty-two books of the Hebrew Canon as the Divine, Canonical Scriptures accepted by the Church; naming, however, *Baruch* instead of Esther, and styling our Apocrypha including Esther, a second class—*Antilegomena*—which were not accepted by the Church,

§ 314.—*Position of the Apocrypha in the Protestant Church.*

In the Protestant Church, the Apocrypha—the works and passages contained in the LXX and Vulgate, and not in the Hebrew Canon—has from the very first had a separate position.

Andreas Bodenstein (Karlstadt) in his work, *De Canonicis Scripturis Libellus*, Wittenb. 1520 (printed by Credner, *Zur Gesch. des Kanons*, 1847, p. 291, ff.), referring to Jerome's list and comparing it with that of Augustine, directs attention to the difference between them, and designates as Apocryphal the works and passages which are not contained in the Hebrew Canon. But even among these works he makes a distinction, specifying the Books of *Wisdom, Jesus Sirach, Judith, Tobit*, and the two Books of *Maccabees*, as Apocrypha simply, as being "extra canonem Hebræorum, tamen hagiographi;" on the other hand, the third and fourth *Book of Ezra, Baruch*, the *Prayer of Manasseh*, and the *additions to the Book of Daniel*, he designates as "*plane apocryphos.*" This work of Karlstadt, however, has not exercised any great influence on the opinion of Protestants generally.

Luther himself originally translated the Apocrypha (only *not* the third and fourth books of Ezra) singly, just as the Hebrew books. In the first Protestant editions of the whole German Bible (Zürich, Worms, and Strasburg, 1529–30), these books occur according to the translation of *Leo Judæ*, and are designated as the books which were not enumerated by the ancients among the Biblical Scripture, and were not found in the Hebrew Canon. The same title, with the prefix of the name *Apocrypha*, is given to these books in the Frankfort edition of 1534, in which those of them which had already been translated by Luther separately were adopted according to his translation, and the others were retained according to that of Leo Judæ. In the same year there appeared at Wittenberg the first German Bible, executed by Luther himself, which contained the whole of these books and passages according to Luther's own translation (namely, Judith, Wisdom, Tobit, Sirach, Baruch, 1 and 2 Macc., the Greek additions to Esther and Daniel, and the Prayer of Manasseh) after the Books of the Hebrew Canon, and with the title: "Apocrypha: These are books which are not considered equal to the Holy Scripture, yet are profitable and good to be read." Luther has not expressed himself further as to these works and passages as a whole, but only as to each singly in the separate preface to each (W. A. Part xiv). His opinion as to their value is given differently as regards each; what he says, however, shows how very far he was from denying to them any value at all in the Christian Church; how inclined he is, indeed, almost to put some of them on a par with the Canonical Books of the Old Testament, and how he estimates them more than, *e.g.*, the Book of Esther; although he separates them from the Canonical Books, and in general gives them an inferior rank.

He speaks peculiarly favourably of 1 *Macc*. "This book is one of those which is not reckoned in the Hebrew Bible. Nevertheless in its style, in language and words, it closely resembles the rest of the Books of Holy Scripture, and would not be unworthy to be enumerated with them, because it is a very necessary and useful book by which to understand the eleventh chapter of the prophet Daniel." He speaks much more unfavourably, though, and justly so, of the 2 *Macc*. "Summa: just as rightly as the first book should be accepted into the number of the Holy Scriptures, so the second book should be rejected from them, although there may be something good about it. Let it be, however, committed and brought home to the pious reader to judge and decide." As to the Book of *Judith*, he is in favour of the opinion that it is not a history, but a poem, perhaps intended for public dramatic representation; it is, however, he says, "a spiritual and beautiful poem, by a holy and clever man, who desired to depict and typify in it the good fortune of the whole Jewish people, and their victory against all their enemies;" also that it is a "graceful, good, holy, useful book, *well for us Christians to read*." He expresses his opinion in a like manner about the *Book of Tobit*: "If it is a history, it is an elegant and holy history. If, however, it is fiction, it truly is a thoroughly beautiful, salutary, and profitable fiction, and the composition of a clever poet. Judith presents a good, earnest, vigorous tragedy; and Tobit a polished, lovely, godly comedy. This book, therefore, is good and profitable for us Christians to read, as an elegant Hebrew poem, which deals with worthy and not frivolous facts, and in the main is managed and described in a Christian spirit." His opinion as to the Book of *Baruch* is much more unfavourable. "This book is very mean, whoever the good Baruch may be. For it is not credible that the servant of St. Jeremiah, who also was called Baruch (to whom this epistle is attributed), should not have been more eminent and richer in talent than this Baruch is. Besides, the number of the years does not agree with the history. I wish that I had put it aside with the third and fourth books of Ezra. For these two books of Ezra we have been simply unwilling to translate into German, because there is nothing at all in them which could not be met with better in Æsop, or even some more trifling work. We have allowed Baruch to remain among this collection, because he wrote so severely against idolatry, and stands up for the law of Moses." In the preface " to the *portions* of *Esther and Daniel*," he says: "here follow certain passages which we have not wished to translate in the prophet Daniel and in the Book of Esther. We have, therefore, plucked up these *corn-flowers, because they do not exist in the Hebrew Daniel and Esther*, yet still have placed them in a separate garden or bed, because nevertheless much that is good is found in them;" in addition to which he remarks, that the text of *Susannah*, and of *Bel, Habakkuk*, and the *Dragon*, are beautiful and spiritual compositions, just as Judith and Tobias. Of *Jesus Sirach* he says: that it was "not reckoned by the ancient fathers in the number of the Sacred Books, but merely as an excellent and beautiful work by a wise man, and thus we let it remain;" that "in this book none of the passages are well adapted to one another, as the work of a master, but it is extracted from sundry authors and books, confusedly mixed up together, as a bee extracts the juices from various flowers, and mingles them with one another;" that it is "a profitable book for ordinary men; for all its endeavour is to make a citizen or the father of a family godly, religious, and prudent .... that it might well be named a book as to domestic discipline or as to the virtues of a pious master of a house, which is, and is to be called, true religious discipline." Cf. also, *De servo arbitrio*, in Erasmus (1526) (W. A. xviii. p. 2188, f.) where, in reference to a quotation made by Erasmus out of Jesus Sirach, he says: " Although I might reject this book, *as not being in the Canon*, I shall, however, adopt it, because we thus do not lose time, and come at once to the question, what does or does not stand in the Jewish Canon." Finally, as to the Book of Wisdom, he says, among other things, that for a long time "it was a matter of dispute whether it should be reckoned among the Books of the Holy Scriptures of the Old Testament, or not;" he is of opinion that the ancients looked upon Philo as the author of this book "*not without great cause;*" but that there are "many good things in it, and well worthy of being read. Particularly should it be read by great men who storm against their dependents, and rave against the innocent on account of God's Word. And it pleases me in it that he for the most part commends the Word of God so highly, and ascribes to the Word all the wonders which God had wrought against His enemies and for His saints." Also, that the book is a correct interpretation and example of the first commandment, "for it is to be seen in it that he throughout teaches men to fear God and trust in Him; and terrifies with the Divine wrath those who have no fear of, or reverence for, God; on the other hand, he encourages with instances of Divine favour those who believe and trust in Him; and all this is nothing else but a right understanding of the first commandment."

In the *other Protestant translations* of the Bible, these books received the same position—after the Books of the Hebrew Canon—as in Luther's translation; and this was the case not only in the Lutheran, but also in the Reformist, the Germano-Swiss, the Dutch, and the English translations.

§ 315.—*Position of the Apocrypha in the Romish Church.*

In opposition to the system of separation and distinction adopted by the Protestants—who, agreeing as to the position of the Apocrypha in their translations of the Bible, certainly considered these books as profitable and edifying for Christian perusal, but yet, like Jerome, Athanasius, and others, excluded them from the Canon, and did not award to them any authority in the proof of doctrinal matters—in the *Romish Church* they began to concur more decidedly in Augustine's opinion, and, conformably to the decrees of the African Synods and the prescriptions of the Romish bishop, to equalize in authority the Apocrypha and the elements of the Hebrew Canon; and they were also the more induced to do this on account of these books being placed among the latter, both in the authentic translation of the Bible—the Vulgate—and also in the LXX. Thus, in a synod (usually called the *Synod of Sens*) held at Paris in 1528, in opposition to Luther and his adherents, in their fourth decree, the Apocrypha is classed with the Canon; this Council, however, could lay no claim to general authority. It was otherwise, however, with the *Tridentine Council*, which is considered by the Romish Church as a *general* one, and in which the teaching of the Romish Church, as opposed to that allowed by Protestants, was in general decided upon and fixed. At first various opinions were broached. Some of those present proposed that two classes of Scriptures should be admitted into the Bible, and that in the first, those books only should be adopted which had always remained uncontested, and that in the second, those books should be placed which had in former times been rejected or doubted. But the views of these parties did not prevail, and the opinion of those triumphed who advised that the Sacred Books should be arranged without distinction in one series. The fourth sitting (on the 8th April, 1546) settled a nominal list of all the Books of Scripture of the Old and New Testaments; in this the books styled as Apocrypha by Jerome, and not found in the Hebrew Canon, were included among the Scriptures of the Old Testament. An anathema was pronounced against those not adopting the whole of these books as sacred and canonical, in all their parts, as they were wont to be read in the Catholic Church and as they stood in the Vulgate (including, therefore, the apocryphal additions to the Books of Esther and Daniel).

In conformity with this decree, the Romish Church has *since*, as regards the Old Testament, acknowledged as canonical, in addition to the Books of the Hebrew Canon: (1) The Book of Baruch, with the Epistle of Jeremiah; (2) Jesus Sirach; (3) The Wisdom of Solomon; (4) The Book of Tobit; (5) The Book of Judith; (6) Two Books of Maccabees; (7) The additions to the Book of Esther, ch. x. 4–xvi. 24; (8) The additions to the Book of Daniel, viz., (*a*) The Prayer of Azariah, and the Song of the three men—Daniel's companions—in the furnace, Vulg. Dan. iii. 24–90; (*b*) The Story of Susannah, Dan. xiii; (*c*) The narrative of Bel and the Dragon at Babylon, Dan. ch. xiv. There are, besides, usually annexed in the Vulgate (*a*) The

§ 317.—*Modern Opinions in the Protestant Churches as to the Apocrypha.*

In the *Protestant Church*, however, in opposition to the Catholic Church as regards the Apocrypha, a much more strictly exclusive opinion was subsequently asserted than existed at first and was prevalent generally in the first century after the Reformation. Among Protestant confessions, those of the *Lutheran* Church neither give lists of the Canonical Books of Holy Scripture, nor in any way express an opinion as to the relation of the Apocrypha to the Canon. In the "Apology of the Augsb. Conf." there are two passages quoted out of these books (out of Tobit and the second Maccabees), and they are not distinctly rejected.[1] The later orthodox Lutheran dogmatists have held fast to the distinction between the Apocrypha and the Scriptures of the Hebrew Canon laid down in Luther's Bible, and attribute to the former no independent authority in proof of matters of faith, yet without denying them a certain value in the instruction and edification of Christian people. The Reformed dogmatists make use of them in general in the same way. The Episcopal Church of England has also selected lessons out of the Apocrypha for use in Divine service on week-days. Several of the Reformist confessions of faith express themselves definitely on the subject, giving lists of the Books of the Bible, and, in the Old Testament, separating the Apocrypha from the elements of the Hebrew Canon ; also insisting that no independent authority was to be attributed to the former, stating, however, that they were useful, and were to be read in churches for the edification of the people.

Thus, the strict Calvinist *Confessio Gallicana*, 1559, the Thirty-nine Articles, 1562, the second Helvetic Confession of 1564, the Belgic Confession (which was subsequently confirmed by the Synod of Dort), the Declaration of Thorn, 1645 ; *v. Theolog. Stud. u. Krit.* 1853, p. 278, f.

The Confession of the Westminster Assembly of Puritans or Presbyterians in the year 1648 (approved of also by the Scotch Church), expresses itself more strongly against the Apocrypha, without distinctly allowing its usefulness or indeed any difference between it and other non-Biblical

[1] *Vide* Bleek's remarks, *Theol. Stud. und Krit.* 1853, ii p. 280.

books.[1] These stricter views have in modern times often been asserted, and have become prevalent in the Protestant Church; thus, firstly, in the Presbyterian Churches of Scotland and England, and also in the so-called evangelical party in the Anglican Church, they have sometimes prevailed to the extent that it was considered not merely as a doubtful matter, but as decidedly dangerous and pernicious, to outwardly combine the Apocrypha with the Canonical Books of Scripture in the language of the country. Since 1825, the English and Scotch Bible Societies have most emphatically protested against the circulation of Bibles containing the Apocrypha. This at first occasioned many controversies with the Bible Societies of Germany and other Protestant countries. Very latterly, however, the same strict exclusive judgment has found more favour even in Germany.

In the year 1851, various Protestant divines pronounced the same opinion in small pamphlets; as Ebrard (*Zeugnisse gegen die Apokr.* Basle, 1851; a very frivolous and superficially written work, with incorrect historical assertions, which are scarcely to be excused), and others. Next, the committee of management for the Home Mission in the Grand Duchy of Baden, in a meeting, July 1851, looked upon the Augsburg Confession in the same strict way on the occasion of a presentation of prizes; of the nineteen works entering for it, two were successful: (*a*) Fried. Keerl (Minister in Baden), *Die Apokryphen des A. T., ein Zeugniss wider dieselben auf Grund des Wortes Gottes.* Leipzig, 1852; (*b*) Ed. Klage (Minister in Silesia), *Die Stellung und Bedeutung der Apokryphen; zwei Gespräche*, Frankfort, 1852. The latter work is considered the more popular, and discusses the subject in a tolerably temperate manner; the first is more learned, and contains much that is instructive, but entirely proceeds from the bitter, absolute point of view which the proposers of the question demanded. Some later works have appeared by Keerl to the same effect; the

---

[1] After quoting severally the Canonical Books of the Old and New Testament, it tells us c. i. § 3 : Libri apocryphi vulgo dicti, quum non fuerint divinitus inspirati, canonem Scripturæ Sacræ nullatenus constituunt proindeque nullam 'aliam auctoritatem obtinere debent in Ecclesia Dei, *nec aliter quam alia humana scripta sunt aut approbandi aut adhibendi*.

last, *Die Apokryphenfrage mit Berücksichtigung der darauf
bezüglichen Schriften Stier's und Hengstenberg's aufs neue
beleuchtet. Mit einem Anhange: Philo im N. T.* Leipzig,
1855. Another work of the same purport, induced by this
award of prizes, although not successful, is that of Oschwald
(Minister in the Canton of Zürich), *Die Apokr. in der Bibel.*
Zürich, 1853. The Bible Society of Berg, on the 2nd of
December, 1853, pronounced for the exclusion of the
Apocrypha by a resolution to the effect, that it should only
be supplied at the express desire of the purchasers of
Bibles; and likewise the Conference of the 14th of September, 1853, at the Sandhof at Frankfort, expressed the
opinion, that it was an obligation on evangelical Christendom
to strive against the Apocrypha being printed and bound
up with the Canonical Books.

The principal Bible Society at Berlin has, however,
pronounced a different opinion, and continues, just as before,
to circulate the Bible with the Apocrypha; the Wupperthal
Bible Society (formed in 1854) did the same thing; and
Hengstenberg (*Evangel. Kirchenzeitung*, 1853, No. 54, ff.,
1854, No. 29, ff.), and Stier (*Die Apocryphen, Vertheidigung
ihres althergebrachten Anschlusses an die Bibel.* Brunsw.
1853), have endeavoured to defend their course of action;
and the Evangelical Consistorium at Münster have expressed themselves to the same effect. I have fully stated
how I look at the matter in a treatise, *Ueber die Stellung
der Apocryphen des A. T. im Christl. Kanon*, in *Theol. Stud. u.
Krit.* 1853, pp. 267–354, to which I now refer, confining
myself here to a few short remarks.

§ 318.—*Considerations as to the Apocrypha.*

Among those who wish to see the Apocrypha entirely
excluded from Bibles intended for popular use, and are
unwilling to allow it even a separate and subordinate place,
some allege and endeavour to prove, that these books not
only deserve but little credit, but also contain much that
is opposed to the doctrine and spirit of the Canonical
Books, and many errors dangerous to the soul. Others urge
more general considerations—that they are purely human
productions, which were never acknowledged by the Jews
as canonical and Divine, nor had in their favour the testimony of Christ and the Apostles, as was the case with the

Books of the Hebrew Canon, and that it is, therefore, inadmissible to join them with the Canonical Books of the Old and New Testaments as Divinely-inspired Scriptures, containing the Word of God. But these assertions are exaggerated in their severity, and are not tenable, as partially follows from the results of our previous considerations. The formation of a correct judgment on the whole question chiefly depends on this—in what way we conceive the idea, first, as to the Canon and what belongs to it generally; next, as to the relation of the Word of God to Holy Scripture, and of the Old Testament to the Christian Canon. The opponents of the Apocrypha proceed on the principle that a similar dignity belongs to all the Books of the Bible, as canonical, Divine, and inspired Scriptures; and that the same authority is to be ascribed (even for the Christian Church) to the Old-Testament Scriptures, both as a whole and in detail, as to the New Testament. In such a mode of looking at it, of course it must appear warrantable that these books should be considered absolutely and finally as a completed collection, and that no other books should be placed in that state of union with them, in which, in the Protestant Church, the Apocrypha formerly stood as regards the Books of the Hebrew Canon in the Bibles intended for popular use; and I do not believe that those divines are right, who, as Hengstenberg and Stier, proceeding from the above point of view, are nevertheless of opinion that the previous practice in the Protestant Church can be vindicated. But I believe that the whole way of looking at it in this harsh, absolute, peremptory manner is indefensible, and cannot well be justified by means of the New Testament, by the personal procedure of Christ and the Apostolical authors. In the "Introduction to the New Testament," I point out that the different component parts of the New Testament are to be considered as canonical in different degrees, and some of them only very subordinately: also that this fact has been recognized, both by the ancient Fathers and also by Luther and many old Lutheran divines, and is evident even in Luther's translation of the Bible by the position of certain books in it, and by Luther's prefaces to them.[1] This applies still more

[1] *Vide* the "Epistle to the Hebrews," i. pp. 437–479, and *Theol. Stud. und Krit.*, ut supra, pp. 283–298.

in reference to the Old-Testament Scriptures. As regards the relation of the Old Testament to the New Testament and to the Christian Canon, there have been various opinions, especially in modern times: sometimes violently opposed to one another, the one side attributing scarcely any authority at all to the Old Testament in the Christian Church, as Schleiermacher especially among the distinguished divines of modern times; the other side not only considering the Old Testament as an integral constituent of the Christian Canon, but attributing to the Old-Testament Scriptures exactly the same canonical dignity and authority as to the New Testament. But neither of these opinions, in this shape, can be recognized as the correct one. As regards the former, it is indubitably agreeable to the doctrine of the New Testament, and most unmistakeably based on the language of Christ and the Apostles, that the Old Testament contains a Divine revelation to the people of the Covenant—communications of the Spirit and the Word of God; this is too little acknowledged by Schleiermacher and others. But, on the other hand, we must also acknowledge that the Old-Testament revelation, in its relation to the New Testament, has only a preparative character, with the defined purpose of educating the people of Israel, and leading them on to the salvation which was to appear in the world through Christ, as παιδαγωγὸς εἰς Χριστόν (Gal. iii. 24). It results from this, that the Old-Testament revelation has a more imperfect character than that of the New Testament; and also further, that, after the absolute, complete revelation through Christ and the salvation in and through Him had been made manifest, to which the Old Testament was to lead on, the latter no longer had, for those who recognized the former, the like prescriptive signification as for the faithful of the Old Covenant itself; and that it could no longer afford a system of regulations for the faith and life of Christians similar to that made known *through* Christ and *in* Him. The Old-Testament revelations are all of the nature which St. Paul (Gal. iv. 3, 9; Col. ii. 8, 20) designates as elementary (rudimentary), as "the elements of the world," which, when they had accomplished their prescribed purpose of leading on to Christ, after the time was fulfilled and Christ appeared, must necessarily lose their previous significance. The

Authority of the Old Testament for Christians. 349

relation between the two covenants is in general similar to that between Christ and the Baptist, as described by the latter (John iii. 30), " He must increase, but I must decrease." And this equally applies both to the legal and prophetical constituents of the Old Testament, and also to its whole moral and religious tone.

§ 319.—*Position and Authority of the Old Testament in the Christian Church.*

The Old-Testament law was given for the people of Israel, and in the form in which it is laid down in the Pentateuch could find its application among this nation only, bearing, as it does, both an ecclesiastical and a national, civil character. This law still retained its national validity for the Jew even after his conversion to Christ so long as he did not renounce his nation, and so long as the Jewish State and Church, so closely interwoven together, still remained in existence. Since the foundation of the Christian community this law has no longer had any religious value for Christians, especially now that the Israelitish State has been so long destroyed, and the Christian Church has been so long and so fully separated from the Jewish. This abrogation of the Jewish law as regards the members of the New Covenant is in conformity with the express teaching of the New Testament, and is asserted with peculiar emphasis by St. Paul, and also by the author of the Epistle to the Hebrews in reference to the Levitical institutions. The Old-Testament law, therefore, can no longer have for us the same prescriptive authority which it had, and was meant to have, for the Israelites before the appearance of Christ. The Old-Testament law certainly contains also elements of permanent significance and value. For us, however, these have no continued validity merely as elements of the Old-Testament law laid down for the people of Israel, but only so far as they are acknowledged and adopted in the Gospel. For in the law these elements are confusedly mixed up with its other component parts even in the Decalogue, *e.g.*, the law as to the Sabbath in the shape in which it there stands; and the law itself affords no guidance in separating the two elements, representing, on the contrary, *all* its precepts as inviolable (Deut. xxvii. 26; cf.

Gal. iii. 10); so that from the law itself we cannot ascertain what those commandments are which are of universal authority, and can only learn them from the teaching of Christ, as Matt. xxii. 37–40; Mark xii. 29–31.

The prophetical elements of the Old Testament are essentially similarly circumstanced, even those which, in a narrower or wider sense, may be considered as Messianic. These show us that, from the very beginning, pious men, filled and enlightened with the Spirit of God, have pointed to the salvation which the Lord God had destined for the people of the Covenant and mankind in general. They are not only of extraordinary interest to us for purely historical considerations, but they may also in many ways contribute to stir up and strengthen the faith of the Christian reader. But, on the other hand, owing to the nature of these predictions, as previously considered in connection with the character of prophecy generally, they are not in themselves, either separately or as a whole, fitted to warrant any dogmatic conclusions as to the real nature of the Saviour and the character of His kingdom. and cannot lay down rules for the guidance of our ideas as to Christ and His salvation. We are, therefore, in preference directed to a consideration of the actual historical appearance of Christ as depicted in the New Testament, and by this means only are able to discern and judge what is the essential and Divine part in these Old-Testament prophecies, and what is due to human infirmity.

But as regards the *moral and religious tone* of the Old Testament in general, in this respect also it may serve to edify (cf. Riehm's *Vortrag über die besondere Bedeutung des A. T. für die Gemeinde.* Halle, 1864), as faith in the one, true, living God as the Almighty Creator and Ruler and righteous Judge of the world pervades the whole of it, so that all human circumstances are considered in reference to Him, and from Him only all safety is expected; also the consciousness is expressed that sin removes us from Him, and renders us unworthy of His blessing. This is the characteristic common to and shared by all the Books of the Old Testament, with very slight exception, and constituting the common ground both of the Old and New Testaments. But still there is on this point a not unessential difference, and even a partial antagonism, between the two Testaments. Christ himself points this out in his Sermon on the Mount (Matt. v. 21, ff.), where He shows His disciples, that He requires from them quite another kind of fulfilment of the law than that set forth under the old system. He there represents the Jewish moral law — not the law, as often understood, according to the conception and handling which it met with from the later pharisaical scribes, but even in the shape in which it was made known to the people by Moses himself—as no longer in harmony with the stand-point of the kingdom of God; indeed that the two stand-points,—that of the old law and that of God's kingdom,—form in a certain measure a contrast to each other as regards their entire spirit. This contrast between the two is especially evident in the narrative Luke ix. 52–56, where the conduct which Elijah, the great prophet of the Old Covenant, pursued towards his enemies, with an appeal indeed to his Divine mission (2 Kings i. 9, ff.), is characterized by the Saviour as being contrary to the spirit of the kingdom of God, by which spirit His disciples were to be pervaded and allow themselves to be guided. In like manner would the Saviour certainly have judged as regards, for instance, Samuel's command for the extirpation of the Amalekites and the killing of Agag (1 Sam. xv). although this course of action was quite in harmony with the stand-point of the Old Testament. Therefore, from the very language of Christ himself, we are not warranted in considering the moral law of the Old Testament, and the corresponding mode of action of men of God named therein as forming rules for us; but in order to understand what and how much is therein contained which forms a model for and is obligatory on us, we must always take the stand-point of the Gospel in forming our judgment.

The above also holds good in forming a judgment as to the moral and religious spirit of the *Scriptures* of the Old Testament in general, *e.g.*, as to the *Psalms*. Notwithstanding these songs have continually afforded such copious matter for teaching and admonishing Christians, and for building up and strengthening their faith, there is still much in them which is not compatible with the doctrine and spirit of Christianity. Of this nature is the fact, that in them the faith and hopes of the pious appear to be limited to this present life, and that in many of the songs a certain proud reliance is shown on individual innocence and an appealing to individual righteousness; that in other places there is manifest a spirit of passionate enmity and revenge against adversaries, and the spirit of love is very much wanting which Christians are commanded to exercise towards their enemies, and not only towards personal offenders, but even towards those who stand forth as opponents of the Lord (cf. § 275). This is bound up with the peculiar spirit of the Israelitish law and the Old Testament in general, by which even the most pious servants of Jehovah were actuated, which, too, pervades most of the Scriptures of the Old Testament. Nowhere, however, is this disposition shown in a way more bitter and more opposed to the spirit of the Gospel than in the Book of *Esther*, as to which Luther expressed himself so severely (v. § 173). There are, indeed, some of the Scriptures and utterances of the Old Testament which show a spirit which is more comprehensive and more approaching to that of the Gospel; and in this the Book of *Jonah* is distinguished above all. But, in general, as regards its moral and religious tone, there is not the same prescriptive authority due to the Old Testament as to the New, and even to those Scriptures of the latter, which can only be looked upon as belonging to the second or third class of Canonical Books.

§ 320.—*Difference in the Value and Authority of the several Books of the Old Testament.*

It follows from what precedes that the several Old-Testament Scriptures, and passages of Scripture, have not all the same enduring value for us. The prophetical Scriptures in the stricter sense, and the prophetical elements which pervade the whole of the Old Testament, will in general always have a greater significance for us than the historical part; and the various books and portions are so much the more valuable just as they correspond with or approach the ruling spirit in the Gospel. The participation of the Holy Spirit in the composition of these Scriptures, or the inspiration of their authors, is in general only to be considered as the impletion and guiding of the latter by the theocratical spirit of the Old Testament, in such a way, however, that the personality and independence of the authors was not annihilated or withdrawn; so that in some of them the legal and individual stand-point might show itself more forcibly, whilst in others it might be mixed up with prophetical and universal elements, and thus some portions of the Old Testament may, in their whole tone, approach nearer to the New Testament than others do. But, besides this difference as regards the whole moral and religious tone, the participation of the Spirit of God in the composition of Scripture is of a different nature in those books in which the revelations given relating to any general or special matter were actually written down by those who received them, as in the laws written down by Moses personally, and the prophecies recorded by the prophets themselves; and, again, of a different nature in those books in which men, moved by the theocratic spirit, expressed their personal feelings or reflections, as in the Psalms, the Book of Job, and Koheleth; again, also, of a different nature in the historical books, which deal with the history of past times which the authors relate with a peculiar regard to the theocracy and what relates to it, as they discovered it, and arrived at it from verbal or written tradition.

§ 321.—*Conclusions as to the Value and Authority of the Apocrypha.*

If the preceding remarks are acknowledged to be correct, we cannot well help allowing (*a*), that there may be certain portions of our Old-Testament Scriptures which, from their origin and internal nature, stand on the boundary, as it were, so that they are almost entirely removed out of the sphere of Divine revelation and of the impulse and guidance of the theocratic spirit, and thus present no particular points affecting the history of the development of the Old-Testament theocracy as preparing for Christ, and educating for Him; and (*b*) that, in works written before the time of Christ, in Jewish or Israelitish literature, we are not entitled to limit the participation of the Holy Spirit to those in the Hebrew Canon, and to deny that other works, such as our Apocryphal Books, or some of them, may to a certain extent have shared in it.

The Jews indeed, as we have previously seen, had the consciousness, and certainly with reason, that after the age of Malachi and Nehemiah, the spirit of independent prophecy had departed from Israel. But nevertheless, the composition of works—both historical, and also didactic and poetical—had not come to an end, the authors of which were actuated and guided by the theocratical spirit, which works had their influence in the development of the latter up to the time of Christ. From the result of our previous investigations, several of the books in the third division of the Hebrew Canon, appear to be of this kind, as especially the Book of Daniel, so important in a theocratic point of view, the composition of which certainly took place at the beginning of the Maccabean age, but nevertheless, at a time which is inferior to few periods in the ancient history of the Israelitish nation in the true theocratic inspiration of the real essence of the people, and, therefore, was well fitted to produce works of abiding significance in the history and development of theocracy. Therefore, although the whole of the Apocrypha was not composed until after the age of Malachi and Nehemiah, it does not follow, as a matter of course, that an absolute distinction exists between it and the elements of the Hebrew Canon, and that it is altogether inadmissible to consider that in the former, at least in part and to a certain extent, evidences of the Divine Spirit leading on to Christ may be found; especially as, from the matters we have previously brought forward, it follows: (a) that at the time of Christ, some of these works had a certain authority among the Jews as Holy Scripture, and that the Canon was not considered by them as absolutely closed, although then containing all its present Hebrew elements; and (b) that Christ and the authors of the New Testament made no specific difference between the present elements of the Hebrew Canon, and other works dealing with holy things in previous Jewish literature; that most of the Books of our Apocrypha are often made use of and noticed in the New Testament,[1] and also that manifold and clear

---

[1] The author seems to have forgotten his previous statements on this subject *supra*, p. 306. He has there correctly stated that though the influence of some of them is evident in the New-Testament Scriptures, no express quotations by our Lord and His Apostles from the Books of the Apocrypha can be pointed out. Bleek is inclined to state the case too favourably for the Apocrypha. It is a question whether one clear, indisputable reference to the Apocrypha in the New Testament can be brought forward.—Tr.

Conclusions as to the Value of the Apocrypha. 355

traces are shown of their influence on the ideas, the literary style, and the language of the New Testament.

If our Apocrypha is impartially considered, it cannot well be denied that some of the books in it appear pervaded with the theocratical spirit in a higher measure than certain books in the Hebrew Canon, and have been of influence in the development of the doctrine of salvation, and in the history of theocracy up to the time of Christ. This especially applies to the First Book of Maccabees, to Ecclesiasticus, and the Wisdom of Solomon, which works have been duly honoured by Luther (cf. § 314).

The *First Book of Maccabees* gives an account, credible in all essential points, of the history of the ancient people of the Covenant in their heroic struggles for their faith and for the service of the true God, during a period of forty years, in the course of which the composition of the Book of Daniel occurred. The former book is written decidedly far more in the spirit of theocracy, than the Book of Esther; Luther also expresses his opinion that this book deserves to be admitted into the number of the Sacred Books just as much as Esther deserves to be excluded from the same. *Ecclesiasticus* was originally written in Hebrew or Aramaic, and indeed earlier than Daniel, and we may compare it, as also the *Wisdom of Solomon*, with Solomon's Proverbs and Ecclesiastes in the Hebrew Canon; and I believe that we may well say of them, that they are not in general inferior to the above-named Canonical Books in importance in the development of the Old-Testament theology and ethics up to the time of Christ, and that they stand higher in this respect, than *e.g.*, Solomon's Song, although the latter contains so much that is beautiful.

Nevertheless, we cannot approve of what the Catholic Church has done in placing not only the Books of the Apocrypha themselves, but also the Apocryphal additions to the Books of the Hebrew Canon indiscriminately among the Canonical Scriptures of the Old Testament, without giving any intimation of any difference between them, nor of the fact that they were never acknowledged or adopted as canonical by the great body of the Jewish Church, from whom we received the Canon of the Old Testament. The Protestant Church has acted judiciously in pointing out the difference between the two series of books, by giving them a separate position in the editions of Bibles arranged for popular use.[1] On the other hand, we cannot lay down the rule that Bibles intended for popular use *must necessarily* all of them contain the Apocrypha. Since many editions are published containing only the New Testament in the language of the country, and others containing the New Testament with the Psalms, it must certainly be considered allowable to circulate editions containing the New Testament, together with the Canonical Books of the Old Testament, but without the Apocrypha. But the exclusion of the latter, as a matter of principle, cannot be justified; we have no right to withhold entirely from Christian people the various though more sporadical matter which these books afford for discerning the development of the doctrines of salvation and ascertaining the history of the people of the Covenant after the age of Ezra and Nehemiah; which matter also contributes to the comprehension of the New Testament. This inflexible adhesion to the principle of the exclusion of the Apocrypha has, in modern times, not a little contributed to impede the introduction of Bibles in the vernacular tongue among the Christians both of the Roman Catholic and Greek churches; for the superior ecclesiastics of these churches are only too glad to use the fact of this exclusion as a pretext for an accusation of mutilating the Holy Scriptures. For this reason, also, it would be advisable either to adhere to the former practise of the Evangelical Church, both the Lutheran and the Reformed, or to return to it, and to permit the Apocrypha to find a place in the complete Bibles intended for popular use, as an addition to the Canonical Books of the Old Testament. No dogmatic scruple against this old Protestant line of action can arise, if the principle be recognized, which, as 1 think, is not only a matter for scientific acceptance, but must more and more come home to the consciousness of Christians, that in the Christian Church generally, canonical prescriptive authority is not due to the Scriptures of the Old Testament in an absolute sense, but subordinately only as compared with those of the New Testament; and that it is indeed due in different measures to different

[1] Ewald proposes us a title. *Zwischenbücher minder guten Werthes*, "Intermediate Books of Less Material Value."

books, according to their respective significance in the development of the doctrine of salvation, and for the history of theocracy down to the time of Christ, and also according to their respective agreement with the spirit and doctrine of the Gospel. Where this principle is recognised, it will also be acknowledged that, in bringing out this significance of the Old Testament, the Apocrypha, too, has a share, greater or less, which a Christian people is well qualified to appreciate, and we have no right to withhold from them.

THIRD DIVISION.

HISTORY OF THE TEXT OF THE CANON, FROM ITS FORMATION DOWN TO OUR OWN TIME.

§ 322.—*Various Opinions as to the Integrity and Purity of the Hebrew Text.*

IN this division it will be our duty to answer the question whether, since the time when the Old-Testament Books in the shape and extent in which we have them in the Jewish Canon received canonical authority from the Jews, the text of these books has experienced any and what kind of alterations, or whether they have been subsequently preserved to us without change? The latter idea has been often asserted, and sometimes indeed to the extent of embracing the whole external form of the text, the characters, the vocalisation, &c., and even of supposing that, in the period between the first composition of the Books and their collection in the Canon, the text had likewise experienced no alterations. On the other hand, it has often been asserted that the Hebrew text had been corrupted, not so much from pure criticism as in some dogmatic interest, so as to favour some translation accepted in the Church, particularly the LXX or Vulgate. Thus, in respect to the variations existing between the LXX and the Hebrew Text, the Fathers frequently reproached the Jews with falsifying their books with the view of getting rid of the expressions which bore testimony against the Jews and in favour of the Christians. Origen and Jerome, however, do not generally agree in these charges.[1] At a subsequent period, after the Hebrew text was printed, the supposition arose among Protestant divines, in connection with their strict notion as to the absolute canonical dignity of the Books even of the Old Testament, that the text of the latter had proceeded from the hands of the authors themselves in the very shape in

---

[1] *Vide* Jerome, *in Jes.* c. 6; in De Wette, § 84, note *a*.

which it appeared in the printed editions, and that it had been preserved altogether ungarbled. Luther, however, particularly, formed a more unfettered judgment in this matter. The Catholic divines were also less rigid in this respect, as the Vulgate stood in greater authority with them than the original Hebrew text. During the sixteenth century, however, they did nothing as to pronouncing the Hebrew text to be corrupt, in opposition to the Protestants or the Jews. A vehement dispute on this subject broke out about the middle of the seventeenth century; it was first set on foot by the French divines, the Catholic Joh. Morinus and the Reformist Ludw. Cappellus (*v.* §§. 5, 53).

Joh. Morinus was born (at Blois, 1591) of Reformist ancestors, but went over to the Catholic Church, and became a zealous opponent of Protestantism. He became priest of the Oratory at Paris; d. 1659. In previous works he had allowed to the Samaritan Recension of the Pentateuch a decided preference over the Masoretic, and endeavoured to prove the modern date of the vowel-points. But his principal work in Biblical criticism consists of his *Exercitationum Biblicarum de Hebræi Græcique textus sinceritate, Libri duo*, which are distinguished by great erudition and many valuable collections, and investigations. The former part appeared first at Paris, 1633; the whole, however, was not published until after Morinus' death, Paris, 1669. He took pains to show that the original text of the Bible had been so distorted and garbled by the copiers, not exactly with malicious intent, but through negligence, that it could no longer be made use of by us with any certainty; also that, as regards the Old Testament the LXX must be adhered to, and as regards both the Old and New Testaments the Vulgate, as the authentic ecclesiastical translation. His work is really directed against the Protestants, since he endeavours to establish in opposition to them, that the Holy Scriptures, which were acknowledged by them as the only source of the truth of their creed, were but uncertain and unreliable in themselves, unless the authority of the Church was submitted to in making use of the same. Among other things, he made the assertion that writing Hebrew without vowel-points proceeded from God Himself, who intended by this means to make men submit themselves to the judgment of the Church in the interpretation of Holy Scripture.

Louis Cappelle (Ref. Minist. and Prof. at Saumur, d. 1658). After having in his previous works endeavoured to prove the modern date of the Hebrew vowel-points, he attacked, in his *Critica Sacra*, the integrity and absolute correctness of the Hebrew text of the Old Testament generally. He laboured at his work thirty-eight years, and after its completion he could not find any one who would undertake to print it, on account of its contents being at variance with the views generally entertained, especially by Protestants. At last, through the mediation of his son, Joh. Cappelle, who had gone over to the Catholic Church, he obtained permission from the French king to have it printed in the royal printing-office; but in doing this, he was compelled to submit his work to the censorship of the Catholic divines, who were permitted to alter much in it against the author's will; among them Morinus was prominent, who from his zeal against the Protestant Church was very active in editing the work. It appeared at Paris, 1650 (a new edition by Vogel and Scharfenberg, Halle, 1775-83. 3 Parts). The aim of the work is to prove that the Hebrew text of the Old Testament is no longer absolutely correct, but corrupted by copyists in many passages and in various ways, but not intentionally or in points so essential as to influence the doctrines of faith and morals in it, or to afford any justification for regarding the records of revelation as dubious. He seeks to derive his proofs of this partial corruption of the text from the variations which parallel passages present when compared with one another (*e.g.* Ps. xviii. and 2 Sam xxii, &c), from the quotations in the New Testament, from the Keri and Ketjb, and from the Samaritan Recension of the Pentateuch. He takes no notice of Hebrew manuscripts.

The correctness of the Hebrew text of the Old Testament was also assailed by Isaak Vossius (*de LXX interpp.* Hague, 1661, and *Append. ad librr. de LXX interpp.* 1663), from a still more one-sided stand-point, viz., an over estimation of the LXX.

There was, however, no want of other scholars of various confessions, who pronounced decidedly against these opinions from the very first. Among them we must particularly mention Joh. Buxtorf, the younger, whose *Anticritica s. vindiciæ veritatis Hebr.* (Basle, 1653) contains a complete criticism on the work of Cappellus, in which he minutely investigates and endeavours to refute not only his first principles, but also his examples in detail. Buxtorf was much superior to Cappellus in a well-grounded, grammatical knowledge of Hebrew, and thus well knew how to discover the weak points in his work. Yet even he was wanting in impartial judgment in determining what was correct, for he proceeded entirely on the principle of maintaining the originality of the present Hebrew text throughout, and that it was handed down unfalsified from the time of the composition of the books; and he even did this in reference to the vowels and other diacritical marks. R. Simon (1678) acted more circumspectly and more impartially; he neither considered our Masoretic text to be faultless, nor yet made it unconditionally subordinate to any evidences leading to another shaping of the text. Carpzov, on the contrary, in his *Critica Sacra V. T.* (1728) maintains the complete integrity of our Masoretic text, that it proceeded from the authors of the different books entirely in its present shape, with the vowels and accents, the present form of character, and the division into verses. In the third part of his work he endeavoured to prove this, in opposition to William Whiston, an Englishman, who, in an "Essay towards restoring the true Text of the Old Testament," gave a decided preference to the Samaritan Recension of the Pentateuch over the Judæo-Masoretic version, and sought to prove that the Jews, in the controversy with the Christians in the second century after Christ, had falsified the manuscripts both of the Hebrew text and also of the LXX. Carpzov, indeed, could not deny that the existing Hebrew manuscripts presented variations; but he felt warranted in denying that any passage in *all* the manuscripts extant had been corrupted, so that the true reading must always have been preserved in certain manuscripts.

§ 323.—*Criticism of the Hebrew Text—Houbigant—Kennicott —De Rossi.*

Subsequently, criticism of the Hebrew text was again aroused by Carl Fried. Houbigant (Priest of the Oratory at Paris, b. 1686, d. 1783).

In his edition of the Hebrew Bible, and the *Prolegomena in Scripturam Sacram*, printed separately from it, Paris, 1746, he propounds the opinion that the Hebrew manuscripts, from which the text in the printed editions of the Old Testament is derived, are extraordinarily faulty through the negligence and ignorance of the copyists, and he believes that in the restoration of the text he is justified in not only venturing to employ a collation with other Hebrew manuscripts, both of the ancient translations and of the Samaritan Recension of the Pentateuch, but also frequently in using mere conjectural criticisms on the point. He has thus brought forward numerous conjectures as to the restoration of the text, many of which are certainly but poorly justified, and altogether too arbitrary; but he is not wanting in sagacity, and some of his conjectures are, as I believe, worthy of more notice than they have met with. He found an opponent superior to himself, in a grammatico-philological respect, in Sebaldus Rau, who in his *Exercitationes philologicæ ad Houbigantii Prolegomena*, &c. L.B., 1785, followed him step for step, and endeavoured to confute him, mostly in a well-grounded way.

In the same age certain collations of various extant Hebrew manuscripts were instituted, more comprehensive than any of a previous date, particularly by Benj. Kennicott (Div. Prof. at Oxford, d. 1783), and Joh. Bernh. de Rossi, Prof. of Orient. Languages at Parma [died in March, 1831].

Kennicott first published two works on the nature of the Hebrew text, Oxford, 1753-59, translated into Latin by Wilh. Abr. Teller: *Kennicotti Dissertatio* (now *Diss. Secunda*) *super ratione textus Hebraici Vet. Test.* Leips. 1756-65. In the first work, among other things, he furnishes observations on seventy Hebrew manuscripts, with an abstract of the variations in them, which he examines to prove their value; in the second, among other things, he gives a list of the Hebrew manuscripts known at that time, and a history of the Hebrew text, divided into six periods, together with directions for the correct use of the *data* extant for the emendation of the text. He manifests a great predilection for the Samaritan Recension of the Pentateuch in comparison to the Masoretic. In the same year in which the second *Dissertatio* appeared (1759), he announced a much greater undertaking, viz., to collate, and cause to be collated, as many Hebrew manuscripts as possible. For this purpose he obtained in England ample pecuniary means by subscriptions, in all about £9000. He thus found himself in a position to devote himself exclusively to the collation of manuscripts, and to cause those manuscripts to be collated which were out of England, particularly by Paul Jac. Bruns (born at Preez in Holstein, previously Prof. of Hist. and Librarian at Helmstadt, afterwards Prof. at Halle, d. 1814); altogether over 600 manuscripts were collated, and their readings—only however as regarded the consonants— he fully made known in his edition of the Old Testament, Oxford, 1776-80. At the beginning of the second volume stands a *Dissertatio generalis in V. T. Hebraicum* (published separately by Bruns, Brunswick, 1783), in which he vindicates his undertaking, and seeks to prove that the Hebrew text of the Old Testament had, from the most ancient times, continuously throughout the various periods, actually experienced many kinds of alteration, and describes the manuscripts collated, &c. The number of readings was considerably increased by De Rossi: *Variæ lectiones V. T.*, &c. 1784-88 (with a supp. vol., 1798). In the *Prolegomena* prefixed, he sought to give a history of the Hebrew text, besides critical canons for forming a judgment as to the readings, and a description of the various manuscripts and editions collated. In giving the readings themselves, he sometimes brings forward variations in reference to the vowel-marks. The whole number of manuscripts collated by Kennicott and De Rossi amounted to 1346.

§ 324.—*Results of Criticism and Collation of Manuscripts.*

However meritorious these arduous undertakings, carried out with so much industry, may have been, yet in their results they did not answer the expectations that had been formed of them. It was expected by some, that in the Hebrew manuscripts, proofs would be found of more important corruptions of the Hebrew text as it stood in the printed editions, and of important variations, such as, *e.g.* the LXX presents in several books, and also traces of alterations which the Old-Testament Books had experienced in their shape soon after their composition. But these expectations were not verified; and from the nature of the circumstances, some of which, however, were only first brought to light through this collation, it could not have been otherwise.

In the first place, the Hebrew manuscripts of the Old Testament, all revert to that form of the text of the books which they had at the time when they received canonical authority among the Hebrew Jews. Before the actual canonical acceptance of these books, various manuscripts of them existed, which presented greater or less variations; thus after their acknowledgment as of canonical authority, and their union in a collection bearing this authority, they would no longer be written and circulated in the shape they had hitherto taken in the single manuscripts, but would follow the manuscripts of the whole Canon or at least of complete parts of the latter, and consequently in the shape in which they exist in the Canon (cf. under § 362, f.). Added to this, the Hebrew manuscripts of the Old Testament are all of a comparatively rather modern date, none of them being anything like so old as the most ancient manuscripts of the New Testament and the LXX; nor can any with certainty be placed at an earlier date than the eleventh century, and only a few so far back as this.[1] The reason for this may, perhaps, partly be found in a Talmudical law, which commanded that manuscripts which were faulty, being torn or spoiled through age, should be destroyed. Still fewer ancient Hebrew manuscripts have come down to us from Christian sources, since Christian divines in the middle ages scarcely studied the Old Testament in the original tongue at all. Naturally, therefore, the Hebrew manuscripts which are extant give the text only in the form which was the usual one at a proportionately late time, and indeed they all give it in a comparatively very similar shape. The various manuscripts all indeed present readings differing more or less, but these variations are comparatively unimportant, affecting for the most part only single letters; the widest

---

[1] The collection of Hebrew manuscripts purchased by the Emperor of Russia from the Karaite teacher, Abraham Firkowitsch of Eupatoria, must contain several still more ancient manuscripts; cf. the communications of Edw. v. Muralt in Heidenheim's *Deutscher Vierteljahrsschrift*, No. 6, p. 186, ff.; of Jul. Fürst in the *Bibliotheca Judaica*, iii. p. lx. f.; also the *Protestantische Kirchenzeitung*, 1863, p. 195.

Results of Criticism. 365

differences in them even are not so important, as, *e.g.*, the variations which the most ancient manuscripts of the New Testament afford mutually and in comparison with the most modern ones.

The collation, therefore, of so great a number of Hebrew manuscripts furnishes us really only with a proof that, since the time to which the oldest of them belong, the Hebrew manuscripts have been preserved unaltered *generally*, and this in a measure of which we find no second example in other works which have been multiplied and circulated by numerous manuscripts. But we have every reason for assuming, and shall indeed find it distinctly proved, that the Jewish scribes (through whom we receive the Hebrew Canon of the Old Testament), in earlier times preceding the most ancient of our Hebrew manuscripts, had taken care, as much as possible, to preserve and propagate the text in an uncorrupted state, since the date when the books first received canonical authority.[1] As to this point, however, we must distinguish between the *external* form of the text and its *internal* nature. For in the former respect, the text, in the course of time, has of course experienced many kinds of not unimportant alterations, namely, as regards the *form of writing*, and its accessories.

A.—HISTORY OF THE EXTERNAL FORM OF THE TEXT.

§ 325.—*The twofold Hebrew Character—The Phœnician Character.*

(1) In the more ancient books of the Old Testament—the whole of those written *before the Captivity*— the whole *character of the writing* has been altered; a different form of letter from that now existing in the manuscripts and editions of the Hebrew Old Testament having been employed

[1] In spite of the high antiquity of the documentary groundwork of the present Hebrew text, we possess it actually in one recension only; and the various readings are wanting which we have in the New Testament. It is a matter of fact (cf. *e.g.*, 2 Sam. xxii. with Ps. xviii), that the transcribers wrote more unfetteredly before canonical authority kept a stricter watch over the characters, *i e.*, at a time which in general lies beyond the reach of our critical apparatus. Thus, however, is the necessity for merely conjectural criticism shown to be undeniable (*vide above*, § 323); cf. Olshausen's *Vorrede zum Psalmen Commentar*, Hupfeld's *Psalmen*, i. p. 235, notes, &c.

by the author originally. The true state of the case is, however, still a matter of controversy, and we think it necessary to consider the subject somewhat accurately.

We find that the monuments which are preserved in the Hebrew, or more generally the Canaanitish language, are written in a twofold *character*, the *Babylonian* and the *Phœnician*. The form of character in which the Hebrew of the Old Testament is at present usually printed and written is allied to the Babylonian.

Among the later Jews it is called the *Quadrate-character* (כְּתָב מְרֻבָּע), from the quadrangular shape of many of the letters; also the *Assyrian character* (אַשּׁוּרִית, כְּתָב אַשּׁוּרִי) is called by the (later) Samaritans *Ezra's character* (*v.* Eichhorn's *Repert.* xiii. 273).

The Phœnician character is found (*a*) on Maccabean coins, (*b*) in Samaritan manuscripts, and (*c*) on Phœnico-Punic inscriptions.

(*a*) On Jewish coins of the Maccabean age, struck off by Maccabean princes after the middle of the second century, B.C.; some by Jonathan; others, and the greatest part, by Simon; others by Alexander, Antigonus, and Jannæus (the last d. 78 B.C.). On these coins most of the letters are found, but not ן, ם, or ס.

(*b*) In the manuscripts of the Pentateuch written by the Samaritans, which are of the thirteenth to sixteenth century. The same form of character, only with small letters, is made use of by the Samaritans in other works, both in the Samaritan and Arabic languages. This character, usual among the Samaritans, is called in the Talmud (*tr. Sanhedr.* 21, f.) Hebrew writing, כְּתָב עִבְרִי.

(*c*) On Phœnico-Punic coins and stone monuments (cf. § 30).

The shape of the letters on these various monuments very often varied in details, but yet so that they are clearly and unequivocally based on the same form, both in the Phœnico-Punic monuments as compared with one another, and also with the Jewish coins and the Samaritan character. As regards the latter, as we see it in manuscripts, even those of the Samaritan Pentateuch, it differs more from the character on the Jewish coins and on the Phœnico-Punic monuments than it doubtless did in earlier ages, the characters we now find being not those originally used, having gradually assumed their present shape by means of curtailment, and especially of ornamentation of the forms. In one case we have express evidence on this point. Jerome, *in Ezek.* ix. 4, says, that in the characters which the Samaritans even then made use of, the last letter, *Thau*, had the shape of a cross. Now this is not the case as regards the *Thau* in the later Samaritan character, neither in the manuscripts of the Hebrew Pentateuch, nor in other works; but it is the case in the characters on the Jewish coins, and in the Phœnico-Punic monuments. From this case, we may conclude in others that the Samaritan character, down to the fifth century, was more similar in details to that on the Jewish coins and on the Phœnico-Punic monuments than it is in the Samaritan manuscripts which are preserved of a later date.

§ 326.—*Relation between the Phœnician and Babylonian Characters.*

As regards the relation which the Phœnician character bears in general to the Babylonian (in our Quadrate character), it is acknowledged that the two were not formed altogether independently of one another.

In certain letters they present great similarities, *e.g.*, in *Shin*, in which it is evident, in both forms of character, that the figure corresponding to the word שׁן (*i.e., tooth*), is grounded upon the shape of a row of teeth; in *Koph*, *Beth*, and *Daleth*; also in others the letters do not differ so much, but that the various shaping may not be derived from the same original form.

But the closer historical relation of the two kinds of character to each other is a matter of question, both in general and also as to their use among the Hebrews. As regards the latter, it is at present acknowledged that the two written characters were not, as formerly Buxtorf and many other scholars were of opinion, always in common use among the Hebrews, the one as a sacred and the other as a profane character for writing; and also that the Phœnician character did not, as others have formerly thought,[1] gradually result (through tachygraphy) from the Quadrate, the latter being the more ancient form among the Hebrews; but that, on the contrary, the Phœnician character was the

[1] Steph. Morinus, *De Lingua Primæva*, p. 271; Löscher, *De Causis Ling. Hebr.* p. 207, f.

one most commonly in use among the Hebrews at an earlier date, and the Quadrate character did not come into use among them until subsequently. The only question is, when this change of character took place among them, and how it was brought about. On this point, I believe that the right idea in general is, that, down to the time of the Babylonian exile, the Israelites had both the same language and the same written characters as the Phœnicians and Canaanites generally—viz. the Phœnician; but that in the Captivity they appropriated both the Chaldean language and the *Babylonian character*, and that after the return from exile, the ancient Sacred Books which had been written in the Phœnician, were re-written in the Babylonian character, and that this was probably done at the time of Ezra and Nehemiah. The express statements of Origen and Jerome, and those in the Talmud, are all equally in favour of this view.

Origen, *Hexapla*, ed. Montfaucon, tom. i. p. 86, expressly specifies two different kinds of writing Hebrew: the one as the more ancient and previously usual, the other as in use at that time, which also, as has been said, Ezra employed after the Captivity; and *ad Ezek.* ix. 4, he says that in the ancient character the *Thau* has the figure of a cross, which proves that he considered the Phœnician as the more ancient. And Jerome, *Prolog. Galeat. ad libr. Reg.*, states that it is certain that Ezra invented a new character, which was still in use ("alias literas reperisse, quibus nunc utimur"), and that up to that time the Hebrews and Samaritans had used the same character (the Phœnician). It must, at any rate, be considered as an inaccuracy, when Jerome, differing herein from Origen, designates Ezra as the inventor of the new character; but he agrees with Origen in thinking that the Hebrews, up to the time of the exile, had employed the Phœnician letters, and that the other character, usual in his time since the exile, viz., since Ezra, had become habitual among them. We can have no doubt that the Fathers found this opinion prevailing among the learned Jews in their time, especially as the statements of the Talmud and Rabbis quite coincide with it. Among them the Quadrate character was usually called, as already remarked, כְּתָב אַשּׁוּרִי. This expression is indeed explained in different ways, sometimes as an appellative designation; and thus Michaelis (*Orient. Bibl.* xxii. 133), Hupfeld (*Theol. Stud. und Krit.*, 1830, ii., p. 292, ff.), and Hävernick (§ 49), would understand it; the two latter consider the probable meaning to be, *guarded, strong, firm*, in reference to the finished, polished style of character. But this explanation is altogether improbable and unnatural, and the right explanation is doubtless the usual one, as it is also in the Talmud, that it is a proper name, *Assyrian*, and that the character is so called because the Jews brought it with them out of Assyria. "Vocatur nomen ejus אַשּׁוּרִית quia ascendit cum iis ex Assyria," *tr. Sanhedr.* fol. 22, 1, where the Assyrian is to be understood in a wider sense for the Babylonian empire, as indeed it often stands in the Bible. In the same passage, we are expressly told, that this re-writing of the law in the Assyrian character was done by Ezra, and that the law remained among the Samaritans in the ancient character; cf. *Talm. Hieros. tr. Megilla*, fol. 71, 2.

There is nothing at all improbable in supposing that in that age a character differing from the Phœnician was prevalent among the Babylonians. We may, then, very well imagine that during the residence of the Jews among the Babylonians and their intercourse with them, they would not only become acquainted both with the language of the latter and also their written characters, but that these would become more familiar to them than their own ancient letters; and that, even after their return to their homes, they would remain in customary use among them. And since it was Ezra who, after the rebuilding of the temple, caused the Jews to be bound over anew to the Mosaic law (Nehemiah viii–x), it is quite conceivable that he also took care that it should be laid before the people in a form of writing which was then familiar to them, and that he prepared copies in this character. It is also very probable, as already remarked (§ 293), that the epithet constantly given to Ezra in the Books of Ezra and Nehemiah—a scribe, סֹפֵר—relates to these labours: it mentions him, indeed, as a scribe skilful in the law of Moses especially (*v.* particularly, Ezra vii. 6, 11, 12, 21). Whether Ezra re-wrote some of the other ancient books in the Babylonian character as well as the Pentateuch cannot be distinctly asserted; yet it is not improbable that this was done in the same age as the preparation of the collection of these books by Nehemiah (according to 2 Macc. ii. 13). The later books after the Captivity, were, however, probably originally written in this Babylonian character. On this point I must remark as follows :

§ 327.—*Partial and temporary Retention of the ancient Phœnician Character.*

(*a*) It must not be assumed that the ancient Phœnician character became after this time completely unknown to the Jews, and forthwith went out of use for Holy Scriptures in every place. There is, especially, no doubt with respect to the Jews who, at the time of the Babylonian Captivity and earlier, lived in *Egypt* and had there no peculiar occasion for adopting the Babylonian character for the Sacred Books in the Hebrew language, that where they wrote Hebrew, they retained the ancient Phœnician character, and that this prevailed among them for a long time.

It may be concluded, from the following circumstances, that, among the Egyptian Jews, the Sacred Books in the Hebrew language were still written in this ancient character in the third century B.C. The Greek translators of the Old Testament appear sometimes, from an anxious timidity, not to have expressed in Greek the name יהוה, but where it occurred in the Hebrew to have written it down in Hebrew letters. Origen met with this in the more accurate manuscripts with the old Hebrew letters (in the Phœnician character), which must be thus explained, —that the translators translated from a Hebrew manuscript with the Phœnician character, and wrote down the word just as they there found it. Among the Egyptian and Hellenistic Jews generally, the Babylonian character for Hebrew would only become customary in the course of time, more particularly through the influence of the Jews of Palestine, especially those who had emigrated from Palestine to Egypt after the exile, partly also by reading the later books of the Old Testament, which existed in the Babylonian character only. Subsequently, therefore, in the manuscripts of the Greek Old Testament, and also of the Pentateuch, where the name Jehovah would be written with Hebrew letters, it would be written in the Babylonian character instead of the Phœnician. The mode of expression of Origen, *ut supra* (*Hexapla*, i. p. 86), leads to this view, when he says that the word occurs in the *more accurate* manuscripts (ἐν ταῖς ἀκριβέσι τῶν ἀντιγραφῶν) written with the *old* letters, therefore that in others, perhaps, it occurred written with those of the Babylonian character; this is also corroborated by the statement of Jerome (*Ep.* 136, *ad Marcellam*), that ignorant transcribers read the word as if they were Greek letters, ΠΙΠΙ, which was only possible with the figures of the Babylonian character, and not with those of the Phœnician.

(*b*) The ancient character remained in constant use among the *Samaritans*, just as it did for some time among the Egyptian Jews.

Before the separation of the kingdom of the ten tribes, the Israelites doubtless used the Phœnician character, and perhaps those of the people who afterwards remained behind in the land and their descendants still retained it. The foreign colonists who were brought into the land used perhaps partly the Babylonian, partly the Phœnician character. We are, however, quite unaware how the case stood in this respect, so little do we know about the art of writing as then practised in that country. We find, however, that in the course of time the Israelitish element in respect to religion and cultus more and more obtained the pre-eminence there, so that at last a strict monotheistic worship of God prevailed among them; and thus the same thing may have happened in reference to the written characters, so that the Israelitish character, which was most in use before the breaking up of the kingdom, viz., the Phœnician, became the ruling one among the whole of the native and foreign inhabitants of the land. The Samaritans adopted the complete Pentateuch as their sole Book of the Law doubtless at the time when they constituted themselves as a separate religious and priestly community, after the Jews who had returned out of exile had refused to admit them to partake in the Cultus at Jerusalem. On this point, we may assume with the greatest probability, from the relation in which, as we shall see, the text of the Samaritan Recension of the Pentateuch stood to that on which the Alexandrine was based, that the Samaritans received their manuscripts of the Pentateuch out of Egypt, and that they were, therefore, in the ancient Hebrew or

Phœnician character. The use, then, of the Book of the Law in this character may have contributed to the latter remaining the prevailing one among them, both for religious writings and also those of other kinds.

(c) Even among the Jews of Palestine, in Judæa and Galilee, after the Captivity and the re-writing of the older books in the Babylonian character, the ancient Phœnician character did not immediately become unknown, and did not also completely go out of use.

Those Jews who were left behind in the land after the destruction of the Jewish State by the Chaldeans, or who very soon after returned thither, and also their descendants, certainly continued to retain the ancient written characters. Although afterwards, through the preponderating influence of the exiles returning from Babylonia with the priests and scribes, the Babylonian character soon became most used among the Jews, still for a long time the Phœnician character was used in writing as well as the other, especially in the intercourse with the neighbouring nations, among whom the Phœnician character continued to prevail, as *e.g.*, with the Phœnicians, Samaritans, &c. Thus, indeed, among the Jews of Palestine, after the Captivity, the ancient Hebrew language remained for a long time in use, as well as the Aramaic dialect. The ancient Hebrew *character*, however, was constantly retained for the inscriptions on coins, and even among the Maccabean princes, the ancient Hebrew language is retained in them. But from this latter circumstance it can hardly be inferred that at that time—after the middle of the second and at the beginning of the first century B.C.—the ancient Hebrew language was that prevailing among the Jews in Judæa (no doubt, the Aramaic was the prevailing one) any more than we are justified in supposing from the former circumstance, against the general Jewish tradition, as many scholars do, such as Ewald (*Hebr. Gr.* § 77 [otherwise in § 10 of the 7th edit.]), Hupfeld (*Theol. Stud. u. Krit.* 1830, ii.) and Kopp, that the Phœnician character was the one prevailing at that time in Judæa, even for the Sacred Books. In the inscriptions on the coins only, they were wont to retain that which was used in the old time, both as regards language and character. In this latter respect, perhaps a consideration for their trade with the Phœnicians, on whose coins the same characters are found, may have been of some influence.

(d) The new Babylonian character, as the Jews adopted it, had indeed essentially the same characteristics as our present quadrate character, but it may be assumed with great probability that the forms of some of the letters became a little modified in course of time, and particularly through the caligraphic care of the Jewish transcribers received more of an analogous and square kind of shape, as uncial letters, having previously had more of a cursive character, with smaller figures.

An expression of Jerome (*Comment. in Ezek.* lib. vii. *proœm.*) points to this; he remarks on the smallness of the Hebrew letters. Probably at an earlier time they were more like the figures in the inscriptions at *Palmyra* [*v.* above § 28, with which are to be compared the inquiries of Beer and Levy given in the *Zeitschrift der D. M. G.*, 1864, pp. 65-117]. This character is essentially allied to the same form as the quadrate, and in many of the shapes appears to bear the same relation to it, as the Italic to the Gothic letter; and it is not improbable that the Babylonian character, previously in use among both the Babylonians themselves and also the Jews, had a shape rather similar to this.

§ 328.—*Origin of the later, or Babylonian Character.*

As regards the general historical relation between the Phœnician writing and the Babylonian, they are both, as already remarked, so mutually allied together that they cannot have been formed independently of one another. But I hold it to be decidedly wrong to consider that one of the two, viz., the Babylonian was formed out of the other —the Phœnician, as we know it—by a gradual transition.

This opinion has been brought forward in modern times by (*a*) Ulr. Fried. Kopp (*Bilder und Schriften der Vorzeit*, vol. ii. Mannheim, 1821, p. 94, ff.; and *Theol. Stud. u. Krit.* 1829), who was followed by Eichhorn (Edit. 4), also by De Wette in the 2nd edit. of the *Hebr.-Jud. Archäologie*, § 278, otherwise in Edit. 3; and (*b*) by Hupfeld (*Theol. Stud. u. Krit.* 1830, ii.). These scholars assume that the Phœnician character, at the time of the Babylonian Captivity and several centuries later, prevailed in the whole of

Anterior Asia as far as the Tigris, and thus also in Babylon. Kopp and those who follow him think, that from this, but not until the first three centuries after Christ, were originated, by a gradual transition into a cursive character, those written forms which are found in the inscriptions at Palmyra, and that therefrom was also formed our quadrate character, but not until the fourth century. Hupfeld also agrees with this in the main, with the modification, however, that he considers the quadrate character to be of Syrian origin, and is of opinion that the Jews derived it from the Syrians, not however all at once, but that the earlier character was gradually developed into this, up to the first or second century after Christ.

But this view is altogether improbable. For (*a*) the characteristics of several of the letters on the Jewish coins and other monuments in the Phœnician writing differ too much, not only from those of the quadrate character but also from those of the writing at Palmyra, to allow of our thinking that the latter could have been developed from the former through any gradual transition. (*b*) If among the Hebrews the one kind of writing had so gradually developed itself into the other, the two kinds of writing employed in the Sacred Books would not subsequently have been so expressly and plainly distinguished. (*c*) It would be difficult to explain how the idea came into vogue among the Jews that they had received the quadrate character (which was alone used for the Sacred Books) from the hated and idolatrous nation of the Assyrians or Babylonians, if this had not been actually agreeable to the truth, and if the re-writing of the Sacred Books in this instead of the old character had not taken place at the prescribed time which they had received by tradition. (*d*) It may be inferred from Matt. v. 18, that, at the time of Christ, *Jod* was the smallest letter in the alphabet, which is the case in the Babylonian character, but certainly not in the Phœnician; from which it is evident that at that time the former was in exclusively prevailing use among the Jews, and that therefore it could not have been formed after this time.

We must, on the contrary, as I think, regard the matter as follows. Both kinds of writing are based upon one and the same Semitic original; where this latter was originally formed, whether in Phœnicia, Babylonia, or some other region of the countries inhabited by the Semitic nations, can no longer be ascertained with any certainty. This Semitic primitive character, from which the names of the Hebrew letters have been as a whole preserved perhaps unaltered, had at an early time been shaped in different places into somewhat various kinds and forms of letters, especially into the Phœnician character in the western, and into the Babylonian character in the eastern district of the Semitic race.

The Phœnician character, as a whole, retained more of the original form of letters, as may be deduced from the fact that in several cases the figures in the Phœnician character correspond more to the shape of that which is indicated by the name than those of the Babylonian do; *e.g.*, *Ajin* = eye, in Phœnician O and the like; *Resch* = head, in Phœnician ᕃ ; *Thau* (cf. Ezek. ix. 4) = a sign, in the form of a cross, in Phœnician ᛏ ; *Jod* = hand, in Phœnician ᚼ. The Babylonian character is but seldom the nearest to the shape of the object indicated by the name; thus, *Kaph* = hollow hand, כ ; in the Phœnician the shape does not much correspond with the object.

Thus, then, these two branches of the Semitic original character existed in various regions of the Semitic districts, at any rate at the time of the Babylonian Captivity, as forms differing considerably from each other and really different kinds of writing—just as at present the German, Gothic, and the Latin—so that to those who know the one, the other might be quite strange ; and this was the case with the Jews as to the Babylonian character when they came to Babylonia. We may, however, very well imagine that, in their long sojourn there among the Babylonians, they adopted their written characters as well as their dialect, and even adhered to them after their return to their homes, and were, therefore, compelled to re-write in this character even their Sacred Books.

§ 329.—*Opinions as to the Antiquity of the Hebrew Vowel-Points and Accents.*

(2) Our investigation has so far related to the consonants only, since at the time of this re-writing of the Sacred Books in the Babylonian character, neither this latter nor the Phœnician was provided with vowel-signs and accents like our present Hebrew points. As to the *origin of*

the *Hebrew vowels and accents*, there has been formerly much controversy, whether they proceeded from the authors of the Old-Testament Books, or whether their writings were furnished with these signs at a later time, and if so, by whom. On this point, it is so far a matter of fact that the Jewish grammarians, since the tenth century, were not only acquainted with our present mode of *pointing*, but that they also appear to presuppose that the Hebrew text was originally provided with it; for they lay no inconsiderable importance on the correctness of the text in this respect, as well as on the investigation of the various readings existing in different manuscripts, or in different regions, and on correcting them according to certain manuscripts considered peculiarly correct. Also, the first of the Jewish grammarians well known to us have composed works in reference to the *pointing*, as R. Saadia Gaon (d. 942), and R. Jehuda Chajjug (d. about 1040; cf. § 46). There are, however, signs that then, and in the centuries next following, the opinion as to the originality of these vowel-signs and accents was not altogether a general one among Jewish scholars.

This is the view of Aben Esra (d. c. 1167); and this very thing may be concluded from the fact, that (*a*) the Book *Sohar* considers it necessary to defend the idea of the antiquity of our vowels with peculiar energy, and (*b*) that several Christian scholars, who had received their knowledge of Hebrew from Rabbis, did not acknowledge the originality and antiquity of these vowels; as Raymund Martini (d. 1284), Perez de Valentia (about 1450: *Introd. ad Exposit. in Psalmos*), and Lyra (*ad Hos.* ix).

These, however, were only isolated expressions of opinion and in general but little noticed. Elias Levita (d. 1549) on the contrary, sought in a more decided way to prove the novelty of the vowels.

Masoreth Hammasoreth, 3rd preface. This appeals particularly to the non-mention of them in the Talmud, and to certain passages in the Talmud where a different pronunciation than that to which our vowels would lead is presupposed as possible, also to the names for the several vowels and accents being Syriac and not Hebrew.

We find this opinion now and then expressed by Christian divines of the time.

Thus by Pellicanus (*Præf. ad Pentat.*); by Zwingli, who (*Præf. in Jes.*) says, that for a long time the vowel-points were not joined to the consonants, and that they were not very skilfully (parum civiliter) invented by the Rabbis; by Calvin (*ad Zach.* ix. 7, ff.), and especially by Luther, *e.g.* *ad Gen.* xlvii. 31, where, according to the LXX and Hebr. xi. 21, he decides for the pointing מַטֵּה instead of מִטָּה, and says as to it : " Tempore Hieronymi nondum sane videtur fuisse usus punctorum, sed absque illis tota Biblia lecta sunt ;" also that he does not accept the "recentiores Hebræos." Thus, he often expresses himself against the points, saying that he does not trouble himself much as to the *supra* and *infra* of the Rabbis, and that it would be better to read the Scriptures according to the *intra*, &c. And, *ad Jes.* ix. 6 (W. A. vi. 292), he designates the points a new invention, which had no right to have more authority than the simple genuine meaning which was strictly conformable to grammar, as he did not care much for their (the Jews) grammatical superstitions.

Among Christian divines in general, especially those of the Protestant Church, the opinion opposed to the above was soon again prevalent, viz., that the Hebrew text came from the hands of the authors of the books exactly in the shape in which we now have it, with all the vowel-marks and accents; this was especially promulgated by those divines who followed the older Rabbis in their treatment of Hebrew; thus especially so by the Buxtorfs and all their school.

Joh. Buxtorf (the father) had already defended the antiquity of the vowel-marks in opposition to Elias Levita (*Tiberias*, 1620). He soon, however, found an opponent on the point in Ludw. Cappellus, in his *Arcanum punctationis revelatum*. Cappellus sent this work to Buxtorf in manuscript, who indeed acknowledged the difficulty of the question ; but still maintained his point that it was a dangerous thing to assume the novelty of vowel-marks ; the work was then printed by Thom. Erpenius (Prof. of Orient. Lang. at Leyden), L. B. 1624, and afterwards enlarged into *Lud. Cappelli Commentarii et Notæ Criticæ in V. T. Accessere Jac. Cappelli Observationes in Eosdem Libros*, &c. Amst. 1689. Joh. Buxtorf (the younger) appeared against him in *Tractatus de Punctorum, vocalium et accentuum in libris Vet. Test. Hebraicis origine, antiquitate et auctoritate*. Basle, 1648.

He throughout maintains the originality of the Hebrew pointing, and even extends to it the same inspiration as to Holy Scripture, an idea which in the Reformed Church of Switzerland received authority as an article of their creed, by the *Formula consensus ecclesiarum Helveticarum* (1675). Can. 2: " Hebraicus V. T. Codex . . . . . . tum quoad consonas tum quoad vocalia, sive puncta ipsa sive punctorum saltem potestatem . . . . . Θεόπνευστος, ut fidei et vitæ nostræ una cum codice N. T. sit Canon unicus et illibatus, &c." Ludw. Cappellus further defended his views against the younger Buxtorf in *Vindiciæ arcani punctationis revelati* (likewise printed in the *Commentarii et Notæ Crit. in Vet. Test.*). Joh. Morinus, among others, concurred in the views of Cappellus in the second part of his *Exercitt. Biblicæ*, &c. Paris, 1669. *Exercitt.* pp. 12–14; thus also Walton, in the preface to his Polyglot, and others. But the antiquity and originality of the vowel-marks were constantly believed in and defended by many, as by Löscher, *de caussis linguæ Hebr.* 1706; Pfeiffer, *Crit. Sacr.* 1680, p. 83, ff; Carpzov, *Crit. Sacr.* 1728, p. 243, ff.

§ 330.—*Various Proofs of the Novelty of the Vowel-Signs and Accents.*

The idea that the ancient Hebrews wrote without our vowel-signs and accents did not become very prevalent until more modern times; but from all the historical facts in question this cannot be doubtful to any impartial critic.[1] In the first place, it may be shown that, at the time of Jerome and the Talmud, the text of the Old Testament possessed none of our vowel-signs and accents.

The surest evidence of this is in Jerome, from whose language it may be deduced most clearly. When he speaks of that which was written in the Hebrew text, he invariably names the consonants only, and often says that these might be expressed in various ways according to the opinion of the reader, or according to the context, or the nature of the passage where they occur, and that therefore they had different significations. *E.g.*, in Jerem. ix. 21

[1] The most modern well-grounded investigation on this point is by Hupfeld: *Crit. examination of some of the obscure and misunderstood passages in the history of the text of the Old Testament. II. Vocalization. Stud. und Krit.* 1830.

Novelty of the Vowel-Signs—Jerome. 379

(דָּבָר) : Verbum Hebraicum quod tribus literis scribitur, Daleth, Beth, Res—vocales enim in medio non habet (*i.e.* no vowel letters)— pro consequentia et legentis arbitrio, si legatur *dabar*, sermonem significat, si *deber*, mortem, si *dabber*, loquere.—*In Habac.* iii. 5: Pro eo quod nos transtulimus mortem, in Hebræo tres literæ positæ sunt, Daleth, Beth, Res, absque ulla vocali; quæ si legantur *dabar*, verbum significat, si *deber*, pestem.—Cf. *in Is.* ix. 7 (likewise in reference to *dabar*); *Ep.* 125, *ad Damasum* (רֵעִים = רָעִים and רֹעִים); *in Is.* ii. 22 (בָּמָה = בְּמָה, in quo, and בָּמָה, excelsitudo). Thus may be explained the very different ways in which various Greek translators have explained this or that word in a passage; *e.g.*, *in Is.* xxvi. 14 (זָכָר) : Nec terrere nos debet, quare LXX masculum, et ceteri interpretes memoriam transtulerunt, cum iisdem tribus literis, Zajin et Caph et Res, utrumque scribatur apud Hebræos. Sed quando memoriale dicimus, legiter *Zecher*, quando masculum *Zachar*. Et hac verbi ambiguitate deceptum arbitrantur Saul, quando pugnavit contra Amalech et interfecit omne masculum eorum. Deo enim præcipiente, ut deleret omnem memoriam Amalech sub cælo, ille pro memoria, non tam errore, quam prædæ seductus cupidine, masculos interpretatus est. (1 Sam. xv.) He certainly at times speaks of *vocalibus litoris in medio*; but from the context it is clear that by this he does not understand anything of the nature of our vowel-signs, but certain other consonants, from which in certain passages the pronunciation of the word may be fixed, and not only the actual vowel letters וּ יֹ' and ה, but also ע. Cf. *Proœm. Comment. in Amos:* Amos propheta non est ipse quem patrem Esaiæ prophetæ legimus. Ille enim scribitur per primam et ultimam nominis sui literam, Aleph et Sade, hic vero per Ajin et Samech; apud nos autem, qui tantam vocalium literarum (therefore א and ע were vocales literæ) et S literæ, quæ apud Hebræos triplex est, differentiam non habemus, hæc et alia nomina videntur esse communia.—Thus he often speaks of the *accentus*. But it is certain, that it is not our accents which are meant, and most probably generally not our written signs, but only a difference partly in the accentuation, and especially in the pronunciation both of whole words in reference to the vowels with which they were to be provided in articulation, and of single consonants according to their various shades. *Vide* the passages in Jahn (*Einl.* i. 343, f., Hupfeld, p. 579, ff., De Wette, *Biblische Archäologie*, 3rd edit. § 279 a, notes c [likewise in the 4th edit. of 1864, p. 430, note 3].

It may likewise be asserted with the greatest probability, that in the *Talmud* where טעמים are mentioned, neither our accents nor written signs generally are meant, but only divisions according to the sense; cf. Hupfeld, p. 565, ff. Still less is there in the Talmud any certain trace of the existence of any vowels like ours; but there is perhaps decided proof of the contrary, as the decision as to the sense of those words which were written with similar consonants, but were expressed with different vowels, is made to depend not on written signs, but on the context. Thus, in *tr. Berachoth*, fin., it was a question, whether in Isaiah liv. 13, בניך should be written: *thy children* (בָּנָיִךְ), or, *thy builders* (בֹּנָיִךְ), &c.

The data of an earlier time, before Jerome and the Talmud, as well as some other points which will come under consideration, all concur with the above results.

That the *Septuagint* was translated from a text without vowels may be perceived from the frequent confusing of words having the same consonants, and likewise from the spelling of the proper names, which often differs so much from our Masoretic placing of the vowels; the very same thing may be observed in the other Greek translators, as Josephus and Origen. Agreeing with all this is the fact, that the writing on the *Jewish coins* and on all the Phœnico-Punic monuments, is altogether without vowel-signs; and also, that the *synagogue-rolls* of the Sacred Books are even now written by the Jews, and indeed are obliged to be written, without vowels and accents; and this certainly is derived from the ancient usage, and could not easily be understood, if these books had been originally written with the vowel-signs and accents; and also, that in the other Semitic dialects, the introduction of vowel-signs into the writing did not take place until a tolerably late date. Among the Arabians it did not take place, at the earliest, until the seventh century, shortly before the Hegira, perhaps not till after it. The Koran at least, was originally written without vowels and diacritical signs, which perhaps were not added until the first century of the Hegira, by the grammarians at Kufa.

§ 331.—*Date and Origin of the Introduction of Vowel-Signs.*

But as to the time when our Hebrew text of the Old Testament was first provided with the present vowel-signs and accents, and by whom it was done, there is altogether a complete deficiency in any historical accounts. All we can do, from the several historical facts which we can get at, is to fix certain limiting points, between which the introduction of them must have taken place. On the one hand, in the tenth and eleventh centuries our system of vowels must have been complete and must have been in use some considerable time.

A comparison of the readings of the Hebrew text in various manuscripts, which was instituted about 1034, by Ben Asher and Ben Naphthali, relates only to the vowels and signs for reading, and shows that considerable importance was attributed to their agreement, and that they were in no way left to the discretion of the transcribers. The Rabbi Jehuda Chajjug, living about this time, and Saadia Gaon, of a still earlier date, wrote grammatical works as to the *pointing* (v. § 46), and the latter's Arabic translation of the Books of the Old Testament, in its comprehension of the sense, completely follows our Masoretic pointing, so that it may be inferred that the Hebrew text had been previously provided with our system of *pointing*. The Masora likewise mentions by name most of the vowels, and speaks of variations in respect to them. The Jewish grammarians after the eleventh century, appear generally to have had no other opinion, than that the vowel-signs had always been united with the text; so that it may be assumed, perhaps with certainty, that a considerable time, perhaps some centuries had elapsed at that time, since their introduction had been completed.

On the other hand, it results from what has gone before that up to the middle of the fifth century, the text had not been provided with vowel-marks and accents such as are now in use. We shall, therefore, be brought approximately to the time between the sixth and eighth centuries. The idea that the introduction could not have taken place earlier, and that it was rather nearer the eighth century than the sixth, is favoured by the relation of the Hebrew vocalization and accentuation connected with it (which were doubtless introduced at the same time), to the vocalization of the other Semitic languages.

For it cannot be doubted that, as regards the introduction of the vowel-signs into their writing, the various Semitic nations exercised some influence on one another. But the present Hebrew vocalization is decidedly the most ingenious and most artificial system among those of the other Semitic languages; from which it may be concluded, that the more simple systems of the other Semitic languages were the first. Thus Joh. Morinus (*Exercitt. Bibl.* p. 565), and R. Simon understand it, and likewise de Sacy, Gesenius, Hupfeld, &c. Among the Semitic nations, the Syrians probably were the first who noticed words and forms which were written with similar consonants, and distinguished them from one another by the means of certain diacritical signs; and this was at first (before the sixth century) done by the use of a point in different positions (cf. Ewald, *Abhandlungen zur orient. bibl. Literatur*, i. 1832, pp. 53–129; *Ueber das Syrische Punktations-System, nach Syrischen Handschriften.* Next followed the more complete system of the Arabians; and somewhat later the Syrians also began to adopt a *more complete* system of vocalization; and later still, the much more ingenious Hebrew system was introduced; as to this cf. Hupfeld, *Theol. Stud. u. Krit.* 1830. (Ewald, in the *Lehrbuch der Hebr. Sprache*, p. 66, Edit. 7, was of a different opinion.) We can, therefore, scarcely fix the date of this introduction before the eighth century, and at the earliest in the seventh. In general, Hupfeld, and formerly Eichhorn, and others, agree as to this.

This introduction, therefore, must have preceded the transplanting of the Jewish scriptural erudition from Babylonia and Palestine into the West, having been effected in the learned schools in Asia, and according to Hupfeld's opinion, at Tiberias. When the Jewish scriptural erudition made its way into the West, this alteration had been effected as much as a century before, and it may thus be easily explained, that in the West its origin was soon forgotten.

It may be assumed, with great probability, that the present ingenious and complex system of pointing in the Hebrew text was not added all at one time, but that it was preceded by a more simple vocalization and accentuation, in which fewer vowels and accents were used, or perhaps

Origin of the Vowel-Signs. 383

certain diacritical signs were added only to some doubtful words, in order to distinguish them from one another.

This latter plan was the case *e.g.*, with the Samaritans, who, in their Hebrew Pentateuch, intimated by a stroke either above or below, when any form from its signification had to be expressed in a different mode than in most cases; thus, *e.g.*, דבר, *dabar*, דֶּבֶר, *deber* = pestilence; אל = אַל, אל = אֵל. Thus it is very probable that the Jewish scholars, now and then, before the introduction of vocalization, affixed to the text similar incomplete intimations of the pronunciation and the sense; and also that when they began to indicate the vowels and accents, they did not all at once make use of our present complex system, but that some more simple methods came first.

I must here remark, that some years ago (1845–46), Pinner in Berlin, and Luzzatto at Padua, communicated certain passages of the Old Testament from manuscripts of the *Karaite Jews* (cf. above § 46), in the East, having a vocalization and accentuation very different from ours, which was called the *Assyrian* (ours is called that of Tiberias); (as to this, cf. Ewald, *Jahrb.* i. 160–172). Ewald is of opinion, that this Assyrian pointing and the other that subsequently came into use are grounded on a more ancient base common to both. [As to Simcha Pinsker's *Einleitung in das Babylonisch-Hebräische Punktations-System* (Vienna, 1863), cf. Ewald in the 7th edit. of the *Lehrbuch der Hebr. Sprache*, p. 7, f., and Nöldeke (Prof. at Kiel), in Zarncke's *Literar. Centralblatt*, 1863, No. 43.]

This much, however, may be decided with certainty, that in Jerome's time the Hebrew text was not provided with any marks like our pointing; and from this it follows that those persons[1] are decidedly wrong who think that the ancient Hebrews had any vowel-signs like ours; the fact being that marks were placed as hints as to some difficult and doubtful words.

From the great sanctity which, since the formation of the Canon, was attributed to the very shape of the text handed down from antiquity, these signs would have been

[1] Thus Michaelis (*Von d. Alter. d. Hebr. Voc.* &c., *Verm. Schriften*, Part ii.; *Orient. Bibl.* ix. 82, ff., 88. f. ; Trendelenburg (in Eichhorn's *Repert.* xviii. 78, ff., Eichhorn, Berthold.

likewise preserved. So long as the language was a living one the Hebrews had absolutely none of these vowel-marks any more than the Phœnicians, the Punic, and other Semitic nations in ancient times. The vowels in the Semitic languages are generally of far less importance compared with the consonants than in the Western, as the essential radical meaning of a word is not usually defined by them, but only the modifications of different forms of a root. Also even in later times, long after the vowel-signs had been introduced into the various Semitic dialects, the text was frequently without them. In the Hebrew, however, while the language was a living one, certain consonants were sometimes used for the general intimation of the vowel with which a word or syllable was to be expressed, namely, ו and י, and also א and ה; as to which we must observe that at a later time these letters were more frequently used in pointing out the vowels than they were previously, as, e.g., the Pentateuch is the most sparingly supplied with them of all the Books of the Old Testament.

Our present vowel-signs and accents do not, therefore, form a part of the real text of the Old-Testament Scriptures, but only serve as evidence to show how the Jewish scribes expressed the Hebrew in the age in which these signs were introduced. They are also of equal use in showing how they understood the text, as the meaning of a passage is frequently settled by the *pointing*, and the consonants by themselves often allow another rendering. Now, it is certain that the Rabbis managed this with great care, and their pointing is derived from an exegetical tradition in general correct; but vowels can never have the same authority for us as the consonants, so that a deviation from the traditional *form* of a word can only, by a misuse of terms, be styled a variation of the *reading*.

§ 332.—*The Division of the Text into Words.*

(3) It may also be assumed with great probability that the Old-Testament authors wrote without any *division of words*. Yet the necessity for marking the division of words in the writing was sooner felt than the need for the vocalization; but even after the beginning and the end of separate words had commenced to be shown by means of points

or small intervals, a long time, perhaps, elapsed before it was done in a constant and regular way. If, therefore, by a division of words varying from that now existing in manuscripts and editions, the interpretation is facilitated or a more natural sense better suited to the context can be attained to, we ought to have no hesitation in following this altered arrangement; for the most ancient translations, particularly the LXX, often divide words differently to the present Masoretic text.

§ 333.—*The Division into Verses.*

(4) As to the division of the text into sections, larger or smaller according to the sense, such as our *verses* and *chapters*, I will briefly remark as follows:—

(a) In the really *poetical* books and passages the custom certainly very early obtained of distinguishing from one another in the writing, both the parallel members of an idea, and also the members themselves, either by a little interval or the beginning of a new line. This sometimes was done, most probably, by the *author* himself; *e.g.*, in alphabetical songs; but how far in other songs cannot be certainly decided. But it is certain that in Jerome's time these divisions were to be seen in the poetical books not only in the Greek and Latin, but also in the Hebrew manuscripts.

Jerome speaks of a *diversa distinctio inter Hebraicum et Septuaginta* (*Ep. ad Cyprian ad Ps.* lxxxix. [Hebr. xc.], 11). In the alphabetical songs, a passage consisting of several members and assigned to a single letter is called *versus* by Jerome. Thus he says (*Ep. ad Paulam*), in reference to Ps. cxix, that 8 *versus* begin with א. Elsewhere, however, he designates by the same expression the single hemistichs, or members, which form a single line in the writing, and are also called στίχοι; thus (*Proœm in L. xvi Comment. in Jes.*), where a small fragment, which in the Vulgate makes now only three verses, is specified as "8 *versus*." These single limbs, or *stichi*, are perhaps those which in the Talmud, in the Psalms, are called פסוקים (*commata, cæsa*), which expression was subsequently in use for our verses; *r. tr. Kidduschim*, fol. 30, 1,[1] according to

[1] Tradunt Rabbini nostri : 5888 al. 8888, as instead of ח ח is read) versus habet Lex, Psalmi habent octo versibus plus, 1 Chron. octo versibus minus.

which the Psalms contain 5896 Pesukim, whilst the number of our verses amounts to 2527.

In our Hebrew editions and manuscripts, in some of the songs in the historical books, the divisions into separate members are indicated by means of intervals, viz., in Exod. xv, Deut. xxxii, Judges v, which is still more frequently the case in the most ancient manuscripts; which usage has perhaps been retained from antiquity downwards.

As regards the *prosaic* books, it is certain that in these the authors themselves did not divide their writings either into small portions resembling our verses or still smaller parts, and make these divisions perceptible in the writing. Yet, at least in the Pentateuch and in the Prophets, these divisions are mentioned in the Mishna (*tr. Megilla*, c. 4, 4) under the name of פסוקים. They corresponded in general to our verses. These divisions were made to assist the reading of the books, first in the Pentateuch—the *Gemara* (*tr. Megilla*, fol. 22, 1) appears to attribute them to Moses himself—next in the Nebiim and the Megilloth, and then in the rest of the books.

According to *tr. Kidduschim, ut supr.*, the Pentateuch had 5888 Pesukim, whilst the number of our verses is 5845; cf. also De Wette, § 80 *a*, Notes *b* [Eichhorn, § 143[1]]. In the same way, also, the number of these divisions in the Chronicles is stated at 5880. Hupfeld (*Stud. u. Krit.*, 1837, p. 852, ff.) is of opinion that these Talmudical verse-divisions were not indicated to the eye, but were only made in the reading by verbal tradition (cf. De Wette, § 80 *b*). But, from what has gone before, this is altogether improbable, as they had been distinctly enumerated at the date of the Mishna.

Perhaps, at the time of the Mishna, the division was made by two points, in the mode of our *Soph-pesuk*, as, at least a little later[2] it must have been to some extent usual, even before our *pointing*. But it was not perhaps until the introduction of pointing that the

[1] According to *tr. Kidduschim*, fol. 30, 1 (*vide* under § 357, Levit. xiii. 33, would be the middle Pesuk in the Pentateuch; according to the present division of verses, the number of the verses preceding this exceeds those following it by about 300,—a proof that the verses were not the same in detail as at present.

[2] According to *tr. Sopherim*, 3, 7: Liber Legis in quo incisum est (שפסוק), et in quo capita incisorum punctata sunt, ne legas in eo.

Division of Verses. 387

verses were definitively settled for the whole of the Books of the Old Testament. Thus, we find them in the manuscripts of the Old Testament (only not in the synagogue-rolls, which are obliged to have no division into verses), and also in the earliest editions of the Old-Testament Books, but without any numbering; they are first numbered in the Sabbionettic Pentateuch, 1557, in which every fifth verse of a chapter is provided with a number. The single verses of the chapters were first numbered in the Hebrew text in the edition of Athias, 1661; this had been previously done in the Vulgate in the 7th edit. of Rob. Stephanus, 1555–58.

§ 334.—*Division into Sections and Chapters.*

(*b*) In any connected works, such as our historical books, &c., *greater divisions*, like our chapters, were not perhaps made by the authors themselves, or at least not made evident in the writing so that they could be retained by transcribers. Yet, in the multifarious religious uses of these books, the need for this kind of division must soon have made itself felt. Jerome often mentions *capitula*, in reference both to the Hebrew and also the Greek and Latin texts, and it is certain that these were not divisions made by himself, but that they then existed, and had been made conspicuous in the text in some external way; for he several times speaks of the end of a chapter and of the variations in this respect which the LXX and the Latin translation present as compared with the Hebrew text.[1] These "capitulæ" in the Hebrew text are most probably the very same divisions which occur in the Talmud and the Mishna under the title *Parashioth* (פָּרָשָׁה, from פָּרַשׁ, *separare, distinguere, dividere*, therefore = *separatio, divisio, sectio*). Divisions under this latter name are now found in manuscripts and editions of the Pentateuch, and of two kinds (1), smaller ones, 669 altogether, and (2) larger ones, or Sabbath-Parashioth, fifty-four in number. These latter, which are probably more modern than the former,

[1] *E.g., in Mich.* vi. 9: In Hebraicis alterius hoc capituli exordium est, apud LXX vero finis superioris. In *Sophon.* iii. 14: Non videatur mirum, aliter Hebraica capitula et aliter LXX Græca videlicet Latinaque finiri. Ubi enim in sensu diversa translatio est, iti necesse est diversa esse vel principia vel fines.

were read out on each Sabbath in the synagogue, so that the reading of the whole Pentateuch would be completed within a year.

The Jewish year, as a lunar year, has, as a rule, twelve months of twenty-nine and thirty days alternately, 354 days altogether, consequently fifty or fifty-one Sabbaths; but after some years, in order to bring it into harmony with the solar year, a month is intercalated; and for this leap-year the number of these Parashioth has been fixed at fifty-four, in the ordinary year *two* Parashioth being read on some Sabbaths.

According to the usual opinion, the Sabbath-Parashioth are the older, and were again divided into the smaller ones; as to which Bertholdt thinks that the smaller divisions were intended to be read out on week-days. But this idea is quite unfounded. But what Hupfeld (*Stud. u. Krit.*, 1837, p. 833, ff.) asserts, and following him De Wette (edits. 5 and 6) also approves, seems altogether more likely: that the shorter Parashioth were the older, and the Sabbath-Parashioth, in which a quantity of the shorter divisions are united in one section for reading out on the Sabbaths, were a subsequent arrangement.

The Parashioth — and the smaller ones are doubtless those meant — are mentioned in the Mishna; in the Gemara (*tr. Berach.* fol. 12, 2), they are derived from Moses himself; a sign, that at that time, they must have been long in use.

In the Talmud[1] (*a*) the *open*, and (*b*) the *closed Parashioth* are distinguished — (*a*) פְּתוּחָה, and (*b*) סְתוּמָה, or סְמוּכָה, *leaning* — and it is insisted that this distinction is to be observed in writing; the *open* Parashah begins with a fresh line, the *closed* only with a small interval in the same line as that which goes before. These Parashioth have been ever since kept up in the Pentateuch, and are distinguished in the manuscripts and editions, the open ones by פ, the closed by ס; in all the editions, however, care is not taken in all cases to begin the *open* ones with a new line. — When the Sabbath-Parashah begins with an *open* Parashah, it is indicated by פפפ; when it begins with a *closed* one, by ססס.

[1] *Tr. Schabbath* fol. 103, 2 (*vide* under § 357).

(c) In the Mishna the name Parashah occurs also in reference to the *Nebiim* (*Megilla*, c. 4, 4), and probably here the same sections are meant as by the *capitula* of Jerome. These are probably in general the same sections which now in the Nebiim and Ketubim are separated from one another in the more correct manuscripts and editions by small interval-spaces, without however being otherwise indicated.

In the Babylonian Gemara (*Berachoth*, fol. 9, 2; 10, 1), the separate Psalms are also pointed out as Parashioth, by being divided from one another by small interval-spaces.

(d) The Haphtharoth in the Nebiim are quite different from the above *capitula* or *Parashioth*. These are *selected* portions—like our ecclesiastical *Pericopæ* (sections)—out of the Scriptures of the second division of the Canon, which were read out on various Sabbaths together with the Sabbath-Parashah.

Elias Levita explains the name הַפְטָרָה, from פָּטַר, *Aphel;* liberum dimittere, dimittere; therefore *dimissio* or *cessatio*, because the Scripture reading on the Sabbath was concluded with the reading of these sections. It must, however, remain uncertain, if this explanation be correct. The Haphtharoth are so selected that the contents correspond to those of the Parashah used at the same time: they were also taken out of the Nebiim and written on separate rolls. There are, however, many variations in this respect between the Spanish and the German Jews.

The Haphtharoth are mentioned in the Mishna (*Megilla*, c. 4, 5). Yet it is questionable how the Haphtharoth of that time are circumstanced as regards those subsequently in use. That at the time of Christ and the Apostles, the prophetical Scriptures, as well as the Law, were permitted to be read out in the synagogue on the Sabbath, may be deduced from Luke iv. 17, Acts xiii. 15; but from the former passage it may be concluded with tolerable certainty that at that time particular Haphtharoth had not yet been prescribed for different Sabbaths, nor doubtless particular sections of the Torah.

(e) Our present *division into chapters* comes considerably later than the present division into verses,—not until the first half of the thirteenth century. It is of Christian origin, and—for the New Testament also—was first introduced into the Vulgate.

Hugo de St. Caro (Hugh de Saint-Cher, Provincial of the Dominicans in France, afterwards Cardinal in Spain, d. 1263), is usually named as the originator of this division; he is said to have made it to assist his Concordance of the Vulgate (according to Gilbert Genebrard, *Chron.* l. 4, p. 644). Another statement (Balæus, *Hist. Eccl. Cent.* xiii. c. 7, 10), gives Stephen Langton (Archbishop of Canterbury, d. 1227) as the author. The Jews subsequently adopted this division from the Vulgate into the Hebrew text; R. Isaak Nathan first used it for his Concordance, made about 1440; he expressly says in the preface, that he had derived the division into chapters from the Vulgate. The first printed edition of the Hebrew Old Testament, which had the division into chapters, was Bomberg's edition of the year 1525. Among the Jews these chapters are usually called פֶּרֶק, also קַפִּיטוּלִי.

These chapters were, from the first, pointed out by consecutive numbers, and thus these divisions became peculiarly convenient for quotations. Previously they were content, in quoting Scripture, to mention only generally the book or the author; if they wished to point out more closely the passage quoted, the section—the Capitulum or Parashah—relating to it was named, with an intimation of its contents; thus, *e.g.*, Philo, *De Agricultura*, § 24: λέγει γὰρ ἐν ταῖς ἀραῖς (Gen. iii. 15); *Rom.* xi. 2: ἐν Ἐλίᾳ τί λέγει ἡ γραφή (1 Kings xix. 10); *Mark* xii. 26: οὐκ ἀνέγνωτε ἐν τῇ βίβλῳ Μωυσέως ἐπὶ τοῦ βάτου (Exod. iii); Raschi, on *Hosea* ix. 9: "this is Gibeon Benjamin in the concubine" (Judg. xix); *id.* on *Ps.* ii: "as is said in Abner" (2 Sam. ii. 8 ff.). Thus among the Rabbis, Parashioth are quoted, as the Parashah *Balaam, red heifer,* &c. Subsequently it became usual to specify the separate Sabbath-Parashioth, by the word which began it, *e.g.*, the Parashah בְּרֵאשִׁית, &c.

B.—INTERNAL HISTORY OF THE TEXT.

§ 335.—*Proofs of Extreme Care in its early Transmission.*

Hitherto we have considered the chief alterations in the external form of the Hebrew text. Now, as regards its *internal history*, as long as it was circulated in manuscript only—up to the fifteenth century—we have, as already remarked (§ 324), every reason for assuming that, since the incorporation of the books into the Canon, the scribes, by whom the text was handed down to us, have used the utmost and even painful care in its being transmitted in an uncorrupted state; so that what Josephus (*c. Apion*, i. 8) says in reference to these scribes, and from the time above-named downwards, may be considered in general as correct: δῆλον δ' ἐστιν ἔργῳ, πῶς ἡμεῖς τοῖς ἰδίοις γράμμασι ͵ ἐπιστεύκαμεν· τοσούτου γὰρ αἰῶνος ἤδη παρῳχηκότος, οὔτε προσθεῖναί τις οὐδὲν οὔτε ἀφελεῖν αὐτῶν οὔτε μεταθεῖναι τετόλμηκεν.

As to the nature and the different classes of the *Hebrew manuscripts* handed down to us, v. De Wette, §§ 108–114, and the works there quoted. As already remarked (§ 324), they are all of a tolerably late date, and furnish us with the text essentially in a similar shape to that in which it was settled in the Middle Ages, after the completion of our present system of *pointing*. Nevertheless in various remarks and peculiar phenomena, in all of which they agree essentially, they contain intimations which point out how carefully pains were taken in earlier times to transmit the actual text in an uninjured state (cf. § 357, f.).

§ 336.—*Comparison of the Hebrew Text with the Samaritan Pentateuch.*

This is likewise pointed out by other documentary evidence and means of proof which we possess as to the state of the Hebrew text in different centuries of an earlier date. Among these are, in the first place, the ancient translations, and for the *Pentateuch*, the *Samaritan Recension* of the same as compared with our Jewish Recension in the Hebrew manuscripts written by the Jews. We have already seen (cf. §§ 139, 305) that, among all the Scriptures of the

Old Testament, the Pentateuch alone obtained canonical authority among the Samaritans. This authority it has constantly maintained among them, and they possess it partly in the Hebrew language, and partly in *translations*, of which there are two:—

(*a*) A translation in the Samaritan dialect (in the Paris and London Polyglot) by an unknown author, and of an unknown age, but, at all events, of a date when the Samaritan was still a living language among this race; at the latest, a few centuries after Christ; according to Winer and Gesenius (*de Pent. Sam.* p. 18, f.), not after the second century after Christ.[1]

(*b*) An Arabic translation composed by the Samaritan Abu Said in the eleventh or twelfth century, which is only partly published;[2] seven codices of which are, however, extant in Europe (*v.* De Wette, § 67).

Here, however, the matter for us to consider is, in what form the Pentateuch was received among the Samaritans in the *Hebrew* language.

It was known to some of the Fathers that the Samaritan often differed from the Jewish text, and Jerome particularly often quotes these variations. It was only from these quotations, particularly Jerome's, that the Samaritan Pentateuch was known in Europe up to the seventeenth century. It was first printed in the Paris Polyglot (Part 6, 1632), according to one Codex, under the superintendence of Joh. Morinus, in the Samaritan character; subsequently also in the London Polyglot. Afterwards Kennicott caused fifteen other manuscripts to be completely or partly collated. A separate edition of this Samaritan Pentateuch —re-written, however, in the Quadrate character—was brought out by Benjamin Blayney (*Pentat. Hebr.-Samaritanus*, &c. Oxford, 1790). Gesenius has, however, furnished

---

[1] *Vide* Winer, *De Versionis Pentat. Samar. indole.* Leipzig, 1817.

[2] Genesis in 3 Codd.; *Libr. Genesis sec. Arab. Pentat. versionem ab Abu Saido conscr.* Edit. Abr. Kuenen (under Juynboll's guidance). L. B. 1851.—*Libr. Exod. et Levit.* by the same, 1854. [In the fragments (cf. Eichhorn's *Introd.* ii. p. 268) of the Triglott of the Pentateuch written in the Samaritan character, the Arabic translation stands in the middle; the columns on the right hand contains the Samaritan text or the Samaritan Recension in the Hebrew language, whilst the Samaritan version is on the left, which alone, therefore, is composed in the Samaritan language.]

an exact collation of the text of this Recension (*De Pentat. Samarit. origine, indole et auctoritate.* Halle, 1815).

As to the nature of the Hebrew text of the Samaritan manuscripts, and its relation to the Hebrew text of the Jewish manuscripts, I remark as follows:—

(a) The various Samaritan manuscripts differ much among themselves, which, however, is only caused by their all being, in general, written much more carelessly than the Jewish manuscripts, and the variations have no particular influence on the sense. In any more important readings they agree, and, among many other variations from the Jewish text, they also present all those which Jerome brings forward, with the exception only of Gen. v. 25–28.

(b) The variations of the Samaritan manuscripts from the Jewish are very numerous, those variations even in which the former completely agree among themselves. In by far the most cases, however, we cannot doubt that the readings in the Jewish Recension are the original ones, and that those in the Samaritan have proceeded from them.

The variations sometimes relate merely to the orthography or grammatical forms, more difficult or less correct forms being altered into easier and more usual ones; sometimes they consist of alterations and additions, the aim of which is unmistakeably to throw light on the sense of a passage, to obviate seeming or actual difficulties in the text, or to remove anything which, in an historical or doctrinal point of view, might bear the appearance of giving offence. The alterations of the chronological statements are of this nature; thus particularly the dates (Gen. v. xi. 10, ff.); the statement of the duration of the sojourn of the Israelites in Egypt (Exodus xii. 40); besides, in the narratives of Divine appearances it is not God Himself—Jehovah—who is mentioned as the Person appearing, even where this is the case in the Jewish text, but always an Angel. The reading (Deut. xxvii. 4) is particularly famous, where, instead of Ebal, as it is in the Hebrew text, Gerizim is named as the mountain on which, according to Moses' command, the stone with the law written upon it was to be set up.

(c) There are only comparatively few variations in which, from internal reasons, probability exists that the reading of the Samaritan Recension is the original one; thus, *e.g.*, Gen. iv. 8; xxii. 2: perhaps also ch. ii. 2, &c.

(*d*) In cases of the latter kind the LXX everywhere agrees with the Samaritan Recension as opposed to the Jewish text; but this is the case not merely in these passages, but also in numerous others, altogether more than a thousand, in which it can in general be assumed that the original reading is that of our Jewish text. This agreement often refers to the merest trifles; *e.g.*, the omission or addition of the prefix ו, but, in other places, to other kinds of alterations, completions, and facilitations of the text. In many passages, however, the LXX agrees with the Jewish text as opposed to the Samaritan, or it presents variations from the Jewish text in which the Samaritan Recension is not in its favour; or both the LXX and the Samaritan Recension differ from the Jewish text, but in different ways.

Thus, *e.g.*, in the statements of the dates (Gen. v. xi. 10, ff.), where the—doubtless original—statements of the Jewish text appear altered in the LXX and in the Samaritan Recension according to some fixed principles, but in different ways. (Cf. Ed. Preuss, *Die Zeitrechnung der Septuaginta vor dem 4. Jahr Salomo's*. Berlin, 1859.)

(*e*) The reasons for these phenomena are variously explained. I have stated my opinion about them in Rosenmüller's *Repert*. i. pp. 62–79; and I still hold that the view there asserted was the correct one, viz., that the peculiar form of the Alexandrino-Samaritan Recension originally arose among the Jews resident in Egypt, perhaps after the beginning of the Babylonian Captivity; that the Samaritans received copies of the Pentateuch from the Egyptian Jews at the time they instituted among themselves a settled worship of Jehovah, after the Babylonian Captivity, and before the composition of the LXX; that this shape of the text afterwards experienced still farther and various alterations at the hands both of the Egyptian Jews and also of the Samaritans.

(*f*) The comparison, however, of the Samaritano-Egyptian Recension of the Pentateuch with the Jewish Recension of the same serves as a proof of the care which has been taken by the Palestine Jews, by whom the Jewish Recension has been transmitted to us, in handing down the text of the

Ancient Translations.

Book of the Law in an unaltered shape; and that this care has continued since the time when Ezra bound over the people to the Law afresh. Even in those few passages in which it may be assumed with reason that the Egypto-Samaritan Recension gives the original reading, it is probable that the corruption did not get into the Jewish text *after* the time of Ezra, but in the time between the discovery of the Book of the Law in the Temple in Josiah's days and the fresh delivery of it to the people by Ezra, perhaps in its re-writing in the Babylonian character instead of the Phœnician, either by or at the time of Ezra.

§ 337.—*The Septuagint—Traditions as to its Origin.*

Among the documentary evidence as to the text of the Old Testament, not only of the Pentateuch, but also of the rest of the books, we have now to consider chiefly

THE ANCIENT TRANSLATIONS.

Of these, firstly, only the *direct* translations will come under consideration; the *indirect*, which have been made from another translation, from the LXX, the Vulgate, or the Peshito, can only serve as documentary evidence for the text of this particular translation itself. The *direct* translations are, so far as is known, all composed by Christians; the *indirect* ones are made partly by Jews, partly by Samaritans (§ 336), partly by Christians, and sometimes, indeed, in the Western, and sometimes in the Eastern, languages.

The most ancient translation of the Old Testament now existing, and probably the most ancient absolutely which has been made of it, is the Greek Alexandrine translation, or—

THE SEPTUAGINT.[1]

This is the only complete translation existing in the Greek language, and stood in the highest estimation among the Jews before Christ and for a long time after Christ, likewise also in the Christian Church. We find much that is fabulous amongst the ancients as to the *origin* of this translation. These stories principally depend on a Greek letter which purports to be written by Aristeas, a Greek

[1] *Vide* Humphry Hody (Archdeacon and Professor of Greek at Oxford, d. 1706), *De Bibliorum textibus originalibus, versionibus Græcis et Latina Vulgata, libri* iv. Oxford, 1705.

living at Alexandria, at the court of Ptolemæus Philadelphus (reg. 284–247), to Philocrates, a brother of the former, in which, as an alleged partaker in the matter, he gives an account as to the motive for the translation.[1]

According to the letter, the well-known Athenian, Demetrius Phalereus, is said to have induced the Egyptian king Ptolemæus Philadelphus to have a Greek translation prepared of the Jewish Book of the Law. After he had previously, by buying the freedom of the whole of the Jewish bondsmen in Egypt to the amount of more than 1000 Talents, assured for himself the favour of the Jews, he requested the then high priest, by means of an embassy in which Aristeas took part, to send him men learned in both languages and suitable for the translation, six out of each tribe. The high priest sent the number of men which was asked for, together with a Hebrew codex written in golden characters. These persons were highly honoured by the king; they completed the translation in seventy-two days, working in common at it in a beautiful building on the shore of the Island of Pharos. Demetrius wrote down the translation as soon as they agreed on any portion of it. Then Demetrius convoked an assemblage of the Jews, and read out the translation in their presence and in that of the translators, and it found general approval. The Jews asked Demetrius to let their principal men have a copy of this translation of the law and to utter an anathema on any who should venture to alter anything in it. The king was highly rejoiced at the success of the work and, commanding Demetrius to take particular care for its preservation, dismissed the translators to their homes with rich presents.

This detailed account by one engaged in the transaction forms the ground-work of all the statements of later writers as to the origin of this translation, even of those of Philo and Josephus.

Philo, *de Vita Mosis*, 1. 2, §§ 5–7 (p. 657, ff. ed. Par.), refers to the way in which this translation was originated as a proof of the great authority the Jewish law possessed even among foreign kings. He does not indeed name Aristeas

---

[1] The letter has often been printed; among others by Hody, pp. i–xxxvi, and by Van Dale, *Dissert. super Aristea de LXX interpretibus*, &c. Amsterdam, 1705.

Origin of the Septuagint. 397

as his source, but agrees so much with his account in essential things, and even in allusions to several special circumstances which Aristeas related more in detail, that it may be assumed with tolerable certainty that he was acquainted with this letter, and considered its contents as undoubtedly historical. Philo has the following special details in his account:—(a) that all the translators, as if by coincident inspiration, made use of expressions best corresponding to the original and always indicating things in the most distinct and clearest way; and (b) that in remembrance of the above event there was a festival every year on the Island of Pharos, to which not only the Jews but others also crossed over, in order to thank God for His blessing experienced in the translation and to enjoy themselves in feasts. Josephus expressly appeals to the letter of Aristeas, and relates the affair circumstantially and almost in exact conformity with the latter, with slight differences which need not be noticed (*Ant.* xii. 2; cf. *Præf. ad Antiqq.* § 3 ; *c. Apion.* ii. 4).

All the writers of the Church who speak of the origin of the LXX equally depend, either directly or indirectly, on Aristeas, only they add certain things which serve to further embellish the narrative and to place the matter in a still more wonderful light.

Thus, in the first place, Justin Martyr, *Cohort. ad Græc.* c. 13. He asserts that Ptolemæus sent for seventy scholars learned in Hebrew and Greek from Jerusalem, to whom were assigned, according to the king's directions, seventy different cells (οἰκισμοί) in the Island of Pharos, where they worked; and that then care was taken that they had no communication with one another, and could not act in concert; nevertheless, that they all translated every passage in the same words, without the slightest difference. Philo doubtless was the origin of this embellishment, although it is not probable that he intended it; it, however, became customary after that time to tell the tale in this way, viz. (cf. Irenæus, iii. 25; Clemens Alex. *Strom.* i. 22; Augustine, *de Civ. Dei*, xviii. 42, *Doctr. Christ.* ii. 22. Cf. also, *tr. Megilla*, fol. 9): that the king collected the seventy-two elders without making his views known to them, that he then shut them up in seventy-two dwellings, and directed that each single one should write out for him the Law of

Moses (in Greek); and that this was done by all of them in an exactly corresponding way. Epiphanius (*de Mens. et Pond.* c. 3, 6, 9–11) only differs from this in making the seventy-two interpreters work in pairs in thirty-six cells. Justin Martyr assures us, that, during his sojourn in Alexandria, he had found traces of these cells in Pharos; which goes to prove that at that time the thing was generally believed in the district, and thus people were readily induced to give this application to certain ruins in Pharos. There have been still further additions made to the story by the Fathers: (*a*) that the Egyptian king in the first place procured from Judæa the books in the original Hebrew, and then, by means of a second embassy, the men fitted to translate them; thus, *e.g.*, Justin M. *Apolog.* i. 31, Epiphanius and others; (*b*) that then, at the king's suggestion, not only the Pentateuch was translated, but also the other Books of the Canon; thus, Justin M. *ut supra* (twice), Clemens Alex., and Epiphanius, who names seventy-two Apocryphal Books, in addition to the twenty-two canonical ones.

Much importance could not be given to these additions to the legend, even if their foundation, the pretended letter of Aristeas, deserved credit. But it is now universally acknowledged that the latter is forged.

Its spuriousness has been so satisfactorily proved by Hody and Van Dale, that there can be no doubt about it; cf. also Rosenmüller, *Handb. für die Lit. der Bibl. Krit. u. Exeg.* ii. p. 377, ff. Its spuriousness is really sufficiently proved by the circumstance pre-supposed in it, viz., that, at the time of Ptolemæus Philadelphus, and indeed when the latter was monarch over Egypt, Demetrius Phalereus managed the Library at Alexandria, and enjoyed the confidence of the king. It can be proved certainly by historical evidence that this Athenian who lived at the court of Ptolemæus Lagus was, after the death of this king, immediately removed from the court by his son and successor (Ptol. Phil.), and soon after died in prison by the bite of a venomous snake. Added to this, there are a quantity of improbabilities in the whole narrative of the event, as it runs in this letter. Generally, it is perfectly evident, that the letter is not, as it claims to be, the work of a Greek, but is by a Jewish author who, however great pains he may have taken, cannot discard his nation. The composition of the letter must have been before the time of Philo and Josephus; but how long before cannot be ascertained with certainty; probably, however, it was not long before Christ. The view of the Jewish composer appears to have been not so much to elevate the authority of this translation, as rather to glorify generally his people and their law in the eyes of the Hellenes, by showing what honour was rendered to the nation by the Egyptian king, and to what great expense the latter had put himself in order to obtain their Sacred Book of the Law in a language which he could understand. The author was perhaps induced to assume the person of Aristeas, because the latter was already well known as the composer of a letter about the Jews, which Alexander Polyhistor (in Euseb. *Præpar. Evang.* ix. 25) mentions; this letter also is, perhaps, referred to when the Pseudo-Aristeas says at the beginning of the letter we are speaking of, that he had previously sent to Philocrates some other letters concerning noteworthy things which he had learned from high priests of the Jewish race.

§ 338.—*Conclusions as to the real Origin of the Septuagint.*

Although this letter may not be genuine, it may well be supposed, that it was not all pure invention on the part of the author, but that he followed the prevalent opinion or tradition which was in circulation in his times as to the prompting cause and origin of this translation. On this point, it certainly will not be easy to make a separation with any certainty, and to distinguish the historical groundwork from the invented matter which surrounds it. Some points, however, may be determined with a certain degree of probability.

(*a*) In the first place, it is probable that the translation of the *Book of the Law* was put in hand by Ptolemæus Philadelphus, and that it was carried on by Demetrius Phalereus in particular; for we have on this point other evidence certainly independent of Pseudo-Aristeas, in the statement of *Aristobulus*, a Jew of Alexandria, living about the middle of the second century before Christ.

This Aristobulus had written Ἐξηγήσεις τῆς Μωϊσέως γραφῆς, and had dedicated it to Ptolemæus Philometor

(181-147, B.C.); in 2 Macc. i. 10, he is called an instructor of the King Ptolemæus (probably Philometor). Various fragments of it have been preserved, particularly by Clemens Alex. and Eusebius, collected by Eichhorn (*Allgem. Bibl. der bibl. Liter.* v. 281-298). Incorrectly, as I believe, R. Simon, Hody, Eichhorn, and others, have disputed the genuineness of the letter from which these fragments are taken, and regarded it as the work of a Christian author; (on the contrary, cf. Valckenaer, *Diatribe de Aristobulo Judæo* (L. B. 1806), p. 22, ff.). This Aristobulus says, in a fragment in Euseb. *Præp. Evang.* xiii. 12 : ἡ δὲ ὅλη ἑρμήνεια τῶν διὰ τοῦ νόμου πάντων (γέγονεν) ἐπὶ τοῦ προσαγορευθέντος Φιλαδέλφου βασιλέως, σοῦ δὲ προγόνου προσενεγκαμένου μείζονα φιλοτιμίαν, Δημητρίου τοῦ Φαληρέως πραγματευσαμένου τὰ περὶ τούτων. I believe that we have no[1] just cause for doubting generally these statements of Aristobulus, whose age falls about one hundred years after that of Ptol. Philad. and for explaining the origin of this translation as being only the necessity of it for the Egyptian Jews for the purpose of Divine worship; on the contrary, we may perhaps assume, that Demetrius Phalereus actually managed the translation of the Book of the Law with peculiar zeal.

There is a difficulty here, caused by the statement that the translation is said to have taken place during the reign of Ptol. Philadelphus, as from certain accounts we cannot doubt that, at the very beginning of the reign of this king, Demetrius was removed from court, and soon after died. There must be, therefore, some inaccuracy here. We may, perhaps, accept the following view of several earlier writers. It is well known that Ptolemæus Lagus, in the last year of his reign, took Ptolemæus Philadelphus as his co-regent. Now, if the translation was instituted or completed during the common reign of these two princes (and it may be that Ptol. Philad. assisted the undertaking in an especial way), it might well be explained, how some persons subsequently have specified the reign of the latter as the date of the production of this translation, and others the reign of Ptolemæus Lagus.[2] It might therefore be most pro-

[1] Otherwise, *e.g.* O. F. Fritzsche in Herzog's *Real-Encycl.* i. p. 227, f.
[2] Thus Irenæus, iii. 21; cf. Clemens Alex. *Strom.* i. 22, § 148, where he says that, according to some, the translation was made at the time of Ptol. Lagus; according to others, of Philadelphus; and especially also

Origin of the Pentateuch in the Septuagint. 401

bable, that the translation of the Book of the Law took place during the end of the lifetime of Ptolemæus Lagus, at the suggestion of Demetrius Phalereus, and that Ptolemæus Philadelphus was especially interested therein, consequently about 285–284 B.C.

There is nothing at all improbable *per se* in the fact that the Egyptian kings generally, either Ptolemæus Lagus or Philadelphus, had, at the suggestion of Demetrius Phalereus, been induced to obtain for their Library the book of the Jewish law in a language which was intelligible to himself and the Jews generally, as it is sufficiently well known what zeal both princes showed for this Library instituted by the first of them, and how various Greek scholars and especially Demetrius Phalereus helped them and excited their energy in its establishment and enlargement. Plutarch (*Apophthegm. Reg.* tom. viii. p. 124, ed. Hutten) expressly relates that Demetrius Phalereus urged Ptolemæus to procure and read books—περὶ βασιλείας καὶ ἡγεμονίας. We may readily believe that the books of the Jewish law are here meant; because so great a multitude of this people dwelt at that time in Egypt, and especially in Alexandria, living then as later, in close intercourse of various kinds with the Hellenes, and sometimes filling no unimportant official positions.

(*b*) We have no ground for assuming that the translation then proposed by the Ptolemies and managed by Demetrius Phalereus embraced any books of the Old Testament besides the Pentateuch, or indeed the whole Old Testament, as Valckenaer and others, and Hävernick (§ 70), suppose.

Aristobulus' words are certainly intended only to apply to the whole of the Book of the Law—the Pentateuch—although the above scholars explain them otherwise; and also by Pseudo-Aristeas, Philo, and Josephus, the law of the Jews only is spoken of, by which we are led to think the Torah is intended, with which the rest of the books had not, perhaps, yet been united in one collection; likewise in the Talmud (*v.* Hody, p. 169; *e.g., tr. Megilla:* "Traditio est, ut dicit R. Judah, quod, quum permiserunt [magistri

the passage by Anatolius, an Alexandrine, Bishop of Laodicea, in the second half of the third century, in Eusebius, *Hist. Eccl.* vii. 32, in which we are told that the Seventy interpreted the Sacred and Divine Scriptures of the Hebrews Πτολέμαιῳ τῷ Φιλαδέλφῳ καὶ τῷ τούτου πατρί.

nostri], Legem in Græcum conscribi, permiserunt id tantum libro Legis ; atque inde ortum est opus Ptolemæi regis "). Jerome also asserts the same in various passages (in Hody, p. 174, f.). Other Fathers, from Justin downwards, make out that the other books of the Old Testament were translated on the same occasion, and Epiphanius adds numerous apocryphal books; but this is certainly an unhistorical addition, which might have been easily suggested to them by the union of these books with the Book of the Law in the Canon.

(*c*) It may be assumed as certain, that the Greek translation of the Pentateuch which was then prepared is generally the earliest which was made of this book in the Greek language.

Aristobulus indeed (in Clemens Alex. *Strom.* i. 22, § 150; Eusebius, *Præp. Evang.* ix. 6 ; xiii. 12) speaks of an earlier Greek translation, which was made before the dominion of Alexander and the Persians, as to the march of the Hebrews out of Egypt, the conquest of Canaan, and the whole giving of the law. But, if we consider the context of what he says, it is tolerably clear that he himself was not acquainted with anything definite about it, and that it was merely a supposition or assertion on his part, which was induced by an endeavour to prove that Plato himself had in part derived his wisdom from the Mosaical Scriptures. As it could not be credibly asserted that Plato had read the latter in Hebrew, and it was sufficiently well known that the Greek translation of that time was not made until long after Plato's days, he might easily have been induced to proceed upon the hypothesis that Plato had read the Jewish law in some older translation made before his time.

(*d*) As regards the Jewish scholars, by means of whom the Egyptian king caused the translation of the Book of the Law to be made, the internal nature of the translation decidedly points out that these scholars belonged to Egypt and not to Palestine, and certainly that they were not those whom the high priest expressly sent to Egypt with a codex of the Books of the Law for this purpose.

The whole nature of the text on which the translation of the Pentateuch is based, is against this latter idea; its text differs very much from *our* Hebrew text, and frequently coincides with that of the Samaritan Recension, as to which we have already remarked (v. § 336 (e)), that it was doubtless formed among the Egyptian Jews. If scribes sent from Palestine by the high priest at Jerusalem had made the translation, we could not doubt that they would have followed the text accepted in Palestine. There is likewise no doubt that in this case they would have translated from a codex in the Babylonian character, which was then in exclusive use in Palestine in copies of the Sacred Books. It appears, however, very probable that the codex from which the Pentateuch was translated was written in the ancient Hebrew or the Phœnician character, which was then in partial use among the Jews out of Palestine, particularly in Egypt; v. my remarks in Rosenmüller's *Repert.* i. 74–79. Added to which, the translation of the Pentateuch often shows a considerable acquaintance with Egypt and the Egyptian institutions, which renders it very probable that it was produced by natives of the country. I will here only mention, what is remarked by Hody (lib. ii. c. 4) that the word תֻּמִּים is rendered by ἀλήθεια, which is doubtless caused by the fact, that (according to Ælian. v. part xiv. 34; Diod. Sic. i. 48) ἀλήθεια was the usual designation in Egypt for a figure which the highest of the Egyptians priests and judges bore on their collar, which therefore bore a great similarity to the Israelitish Urim and Thummim. There is still more on this point in Hody, *ut supra.* Finally, in that age it would be in Egypt rather than in Palestine that we should expect to find scribes who had, besides a knowledge of Hebrew, such cultivation in the Greek language as would be requisite for making this translation, as is attested by the translation of the Pentateuch particularly.

Whether the translation was the work of several scholars or of a single one, cannot be ascertained. But it is probable that in the preparation of it, application was made to the chief men of the body of Egyptian Jews, and that these, although they did not make the translation themselves, yet assisted in and approved of it; thus also can be best explained the reception and approbation which the work must have very early met with from the Jews both in and out of Egypt.

(e) *Nature of the Text.*—We have already seen above

(§ 336), that the text on which this translation is based very often differs from our Hebrew text, and only in comparatively few cases appears to give the original reading, having doubtless received its shape in Egypt itself. This text it follows exactly and gives the sense of it truly and in most cases appropriately, as Jerome (*Quæst. ad Genes.*) remarks, who justly gave the preference to the translation of the Pentateuch over that of all the other books of the Old Testament: " quos (libros Mosis) nos quoque confitemur plus quam ceteros cum Hebraicis consonare." Especial care has unmistakeably been given to the translation of the Pentateuch.

§ 339.—*Completion of the Septuagint—Nature of the Text.*

As regards the translation of the other books of the Old Testament, nothing about its production is known to us through express historical evidence; yet, from its nature and other circumstances the following points may be laid down, some certainly, some only with probability:—

(*a*) That they also were all translated in Egypt; in many of the books we are led to this opinion by peculiar circumstances, and in none of them are we distinctly led to a contrary one.

(*b*) That they were not translated by the same persons as the Pentateuch had been, and that the whole of the Nebiim and Ketubim were not translated by the same men nor at the same time.

A variety of translators may be inferred, both from the different character of the translation in different books, and also from certain perpetually recurring variations. Of the latter I will only quote one example. Thus, *e.g.*, פְּלִשְׁתִּים in the Book of Joshua, as in the Pentateuch, appears as Φυλιστιείμ, and in the other books is rendered by ἀλλόφυλοι: פֶּסַח in the Chronicles is throughout φασέκ, in the other books πάσχα. In Chronicles we find for *Gentilitia* the prevailing form Θηκωί, 'Αναθωθί, Φαραθωνί, for which, in the Books of Samuel and Kings, we have Θεκωίτης, 'Ανωθίτης, Φαραθωνίτης. In the Books of Judges, Ruth, Samuel, and Kings, we find the remarkable use of ἐγώ εἰμι, emphatically for ἐγώ, *e.g.*, Judges v. 3 : ᾄσομαι ἐγώ εἰμι τῷ κυρίῳ. That different translators were employed on Isaiah and the minor prophets appears, according to Gesenius (*Isaiah*, i. 1, p. 57) from a comparison of Isaiah ii. 1–4, with Micah iv. 1, ff., and as regards Isaiah and the Books of Kings, from a comparison of Isaiah xxxvi–xxxix. with 2 Kings xviii. ff. A comparison of Ps. xviii. with 2 Sam. xxii. also points to a difference in translators. There is more on the point in Hody, p. 204, ff. But certainly all differences of this kind do not serve as proofs of different translators, for even the same translator does not everywhere proceed exactly in the same way, even in the same book.

(*c*) In the case of several books, it is probable that the translation of them was made even before the union of Nehemiah's collection with the Pentateuch, and before they had thus received canonical authority in a strict sense; also that it was not made according to that form of the text in which the books were adopted into Nehemiah's collection, but that in which they were circulating singly in Egypt. This is especially the case with *Jeremiah*; as we have previously seen (§ 215, ff.), the Greek translation appears to give this prophet, both as a whole and in details, in a more original shape than our Hebrew text itself, although we have no reason for doubting that the Hebrew text presents the book to us in the shape in which it was received into Nehemiah's collection, and that it has subsequently experienced no essential alterations. Among the other books, *Job*, *Proverbs*, *Daniel*, and *Esther*, must be especially named as those which present important variations from the Hebrew text; in these books, however, we have well-grounded reasons for considering the Hebrew text as the original form.

On this point, however, it cannot always be decided, whether (*a*) the translators had an altered text before them, or whether (*β*) they themselves ventured sometimes to make additions and alterations, or whether (*γ*) the translation subsequently experienced these additions and alterations. The second case is, perhaps, that which has occurred with regard to the *Proverbs*. In many passages the translation of this book is successful, yet it is very often anything but literal, and often when the translator did not agree with, or could not rightly understand, the sense of the Hebrew Maschal, he has not hesitated to place another sentence for it, sometimes also to make additions. The same thing is in general[1] the case with *Job*. The translator of this book appears to have had no very considerable knowledge of Hebrew, and he has very frequently expressed another sense than that which the Hebrew words could bear, but still preserved a sense which was not without judgment and taste. In the poetical portions of the book, —in the speeches—whole sentences are often omitted, very likely because the translator did not understand them; indeed Origen and Jerome complained of these omissions. Much matter, however, which was deficient at the time of Origen has been since supplied (perhaps from the *Hexapla* of Origen). In the Prologue and Epilogue the translation has many additions amplifying the text, as to which there may be a doubt whether they proceed from the translator himself, or whether they were subsequently added; in the Epilogue at least, the latter is certainly partly the case.—The Book of *Esther*, in the Greek translation, has very considerable additions made to it in various sections of the book; these additions Jerome placed at the end of the book, where we still find them in the Vulgate (as ch. x. 4–xvi. 24); in Luther's translation they stand among the Apocrypha, as portions of Esther (*v.* De Wette as to this, § 200) All of these additions are without doubt of Alexandrine origin, and never existed in Hebrew. At the end of the Greek text (Vulg. as xi. 1), there is a remark that the preceding letter as to the Feast of Purim, interpreted by one Lysimachus of Jerusalem, was inserted by Dositheus, a priest, and his son, in the fourth year of the reign of Ptolemæus (Philometor) and Cleopatra; from which it may be concluded that the book was not known in Egypt before this time (177 B.C.). It was, perhaps, translated here before it was admitted in the Canon. The same may be said of the Book of *Daniel*. Bertholdt asserts of this book, without any proof, that it was not translated until a considerable time after Christ. On the contrary, it appears very probable that the Greek translator of the First Book of Maccabees was acquainted with, and made use of, the Greek translation of Daniel; and it is also very probable in itself, that on

---

[1] Cf. Paul de Lagarde, *Anmerk. zur Griech. Uebersetzung der Proverbien*, Leipzig, 1863; and Gust. Bickell, *De indole ac ratione versionis Alexandrinæ in interpretando libro Jobi.* Marburg, 1863.

account of the contents of the book claiming the general interest of the Jews, it made its way into Egypt very soon after its appearance, and was there translated. The translation itself, however, even where it adheres to the Hebrew text, is among the worst of all the books of the Old Testament. There are important apocryphal additions in it; viz., (1) after ch. iii. 23, Azariah's Prayer and the Song of Praise of the three men in the furnace, in the Vulgate ch. iii. 24–90; (2) the history of Susannah, Vulg. ch. xiii; (3) the history of Bel and the Dragon at Babylon, Vulg. ch. xiv; in Luther all these are among the Apocrypha. Besides, ch. i–vii, and ix, have much in them that differs from the Hebrew text, additions, abridgements, and other alterations (cf. De Wette, §§ 258, 259). There is, however, no doubt, that our Hebræo-Chaldee text affords everywhere the original form of the book; the alterations proceed, perhaps, from the translator, the larger additions from some subsequent reviser, and were originally composed in Greek. On account of these great differences from the original text, the ancient Church before Jerome's time rejected this translation of the Book of Daniel, and adopted instead of it that of Theodotion as the orthodox translation, which, therefore, we find in the ordinary editions of the Septuagint.

(d) Of the other books, I will only remark as follows:—The translation of *Ecclesiastes* follows the Hebrew text with peculiar accuracy, and sometimes with excessive literalness, which, e.g., in ch. vii. 29, verges on obscurity.[1] Jerome (*Præf. ad Ez.*) points out the translation of Ezekiel as of great excellence compared with the others. That of Isaiah is, however, very bad, the author frequently giving an incorrect sense, and often translating so as to convey no meaning. The same remark applies to the translation of the Psalms.

(e) We can perceive from the preface to Ecclesiasticus, that, at that time (about 130 B.C.), the Nebiim and Ketubim were translated, as well as the Pentateuch. As the books are not there enumerated singly, it cannot be distinctly shown from the passage that no single book of our Hebrew Canon

---

[1] Πλὴν ἴδε τοῦτο εὗρον, ὃ (אֲשֶׁר = that) ἐποίησεν ὁ θεὸς σὺν τὸν ἄνθρωπον (אֶת־הָאָדָם) εὐθῆ.

—viz., among the Hagiographa—was then untranslated. But still it is probable that they were then all translated.

§ 340.—*The name given to the Greek Translation.*

As regards the designation for this translation, we call it the Alexandrine, or the Septuagint. The latter name is the more ancient, occurring indeed in the Fathers, from the presumed number of the originators of it, the statements relating to the translation of the Pentateuch being transferred to that of the other books. The number is stated by Pseudo-Aristeas and those who follow him, as seventy-two. But the numbers seventy-two and seventy are promiscuously used by Jewish and Christian authors in reference also to other subjects; from whence also is to be explained that in Luke x. 1, 17, the manuscripts waver between ἑβδομήκοντα and ἑβδομήκοντα δύο (cf. Hody, lib. ii. c. 5, § 6). Thus Josephus, when he wishes to designate generally the Jewish scholars sent to the Egyptian king, calls them the ἑβδομήκοντα, and their number is similarly stated by most of the writers of the Church, as Justin Martyr, Irenæus, and others. The translation was therefore called that of the seventy πρεσβύτεροι, or that of the Seventy, or directly Septuagint. Cf. Augustine, *de Civ. D.* xviii. 42, where, after relating that six scholars out of each tribe, seventy-two in all, were sent to Alexandria, he adds: "Quorum interpretatio ut Septuaginta vocetur, jam obtinuit consuetudo." It is usually indicated by the Roman or Greek cyphers (LXX, ο').

§ 341.—*Authority of the Septuagint in the Jewish and Christian Churches.*

From all that has preceded as to the representations and accounts of Jewish authors, it may be inferred what authority this translation must have had among the Jews both before and after Christ, not only among the Jews of Alexandria, but also among those of Palestine. They considered it as an authentic and even inspired version of their Sacred Books, and had no hesitation in reading them in this translation, and even in making use of it for doctrinal purposes, to which use they were led by a deficiency in their knowledge of the original language of the Old Testament. Philo of Alexandria can have had but the poorest knowledge of

Hebrew, and all his interpretations of Scripture are based entirely on the LXX. Josephus of Palestine was not unacquainted with Hebrew and sometimes refers to the Hebrew text. but in general he takes the Greek translation as his ground-work. We find the same prevailing in the New-Testament Scriptures. In quoting passages of the Old Testament, and making use of the Old-Testament history, some of the New-Testament authors keep entirely to the LXX, even in cases where the translation differs more or less from the original text; thus, the author of the Epistle to the Hebrews, Peter, Mark, Luke; others, as Paul, John, Matthew, show a knowledge of the Hebrew text, and sometimes give the Old-Testament passages according to their own translation; but most even of these keep to the LXX, especially Paul. Also in the synagogues of the Alexandrian and Hellenistic Jews generally, the Sacred Books were for a long time almost always read out in this translation, and explained from it. This was still the case in the first century after Christ, as appears from passages of Justin Martyr (*Apolog.* i. 31; *Dial. c. Tryph.* 72, where he speaks of the manuscripts in the Jewish synagogues), and Tertullian (*Apolog.* 18, where he says, in reference to this translation, that the *Judæi palam lectitant*).

Soon after this time, however, the Jews began more and more to renounce their reverential and unhesitating use of the LXX: they were prompted to this not only by the great zeal which was exercised in the Jewish schools in the study of the Sacred Books in the original language, but also by the controversies between the Jewish scholars and Christian divines, in which the Scriptures were appealed to in this translation. We find traces in Justin Martyr (*Dial. c. Tryph.* c. 68, 71) of these controversies, in which the Jewish scholars pronounced the interpretations in the LXX as not everywhere true and correct. Still less did they accept the additions to the Hebrew text contained in it, whilst the Christian divines continually asserted that these passages had been subsequently expunged from the text by the Jews (cf. Justin, *ut supr.* c. 72, &c). Instead of the LXX, the Jews who were not well acquainted with Hebrew began to use the translation of Aquila, which follows the Hebrew text so closely (according to Origen, *Ep. ad Afric.*; Philastrius, *Hæres.* 90; *v.* Hody, p. 236). Later, however, the Greek translations generally of the Old Testament were offensive to them. A law of Justinian's of the year 551 A.D. (*Novell.* 146) shows that controversies existed on this point among the Jews themselves: some wishing to continue to use a Greek translation, others, however, being opposed to it. The passage proves that it was free to the Jews, if they wished, to make use, even in the Synagogue, of a translation of the Scripture in the language of the country whatever it might be, and in the Greek of the LXX and Aquila's translation. From their aversion to the LXX have proceeded all the invidious additions made by the later Jews to the legend as to its origin, that at the time it was being made a three days' darkness came over the earth, &c. (cf. De Wette, § 43, note f, and the works there quoted).

In the *Christian* Church, however, the LXX appears to have retained a higher and more continuous authority. By most of the writers of the Church it seems to have been held as equally inspired with the Hebrew text; as, *e.g.*, by Irenæus (iii. 25: "unus et idem Spiritus Dei, qui in Prophetis præconavit, in senioribus autem interpretatus est quæ prophetata fuerant"); Clemens Alex. (*Strom.* i. 22, § 149), and Augustine (*De Civ. Dei*, xviii. 43: "Spiritus enim, qui in Prophetis erat, quando illa dixerunt, idem ipse erat etiam in Septuaginta viris, quando illa interpretati sunt"), and others. This translation, therefore, was considered—even in its variations from, and additions to, the Hebrew text— as a complete authorized interpretation of the sense of the Old-Testament Scriptures as intended by the Holy Spirit (thus, *e.g.*, Augustine, *ut supra*). Some teachers in the Church were indeed more circumspect in their judgment in this respect, and in the case of variations gave the preference in general to the Hebrew text; thus, especially Origen, and still more Jerome. But in the *Greek* Church, the authority of the LXX as an authentic translation became more and more settled, and it retains this authority to the present day. This authority of the LXX in the Church, joined to a deficiency in the knowledge of the Hebrew language, has had this effect;—that when a need arose for a translation of the Holy Scripture into the vulgar tongue of the Christian Churches in those countries in which Greek was not sufficiently known, especially where the Christian communities had taken rise from the Greek Church, the Old Testament was translated from the LXX, and this re-translation received and retained ecclesiastical authority. This was the case especially (a) with the *Æthiopian* translation; (b) with the *Egyptian* translation, both the *Coptic*, or Lower-Egyptian, and also the *Sahidic*; (c) with the *Armenian*; (d) with the *Georgian*; (e) probably also with the *Slavic*. The Old Testament was translated into these languages at the same time as the New Testament, and for further details as to the history of these translations, v. " Introduction to the New Testament." The Old-Testament Scriptures have been often translated into the Arabic language by Christian scholars in behalf of Christian communities, and these were partly made from the LXX, as the translations of the *Prophets*, the *Psalms*, *Solomon's Books*, and the Book of *Ezra*, printed in the Paris and London Polyglot; as to these and others, v. De Wette, § 55, Eichhorn, §§ 295–301.—The *Syrian* Church, indeed, possessed from an early date a translation made directly from the Hebrew, the *Peshito* (§ 351); yet, subsequently, the authority of the LXX in the neighbouring Greek Churches was the cause of translations being made of the LXX into Syriac, which, however, did not attain to ecclesiastical use (of these translations I shall speak later).

In the Latin Church, up to the end of the fourth century, the only Latin translations of the Old Testament which existed had been made from the LXX, and possessed ecclesiastical authority as well as the latter (I shall speak of their history when treating of the Vulgate). When Jerome made a fresh Latin translation immediately from the Hebrew text, it excited great offence at first on account of its manifold variations from the translation hitherto considered authentic. But this translation in the course of time gradually found more and more favour in the Western Church, and at last attained to general ecclesiastical authority, in connection with which the LXX quite lost its former consequence. In later days, in the Protestant Church, Isaac Vossius, in two works, 1661 and 1663, has sought to assert the authority of the LXX as an authentic and inspired interpretation which merited greater authority than the Hebrew text; as to these works and the contro versies by them, v. Rosenmüller, *Handbuch*, ii. 401, ff.

§ 342.—*The Greek Translations of Aquila, Theodotion, Symmachus, and others.*

Towards the conclusion of the second century after Christ, there were various other Greek translations of the Old Testament, in addition to the LXX, some made by Jews, others by Christians; they were suggested by the endeavour to give the Old Testament in the Greek language in a shape more corresponding to the Hebrew text. These, indeed—with the exception of one book, *Daniel*—never attained ecclesiastical authority, but were made use of by many Fathers together with the LXX, and exercised an influence on its text, particularly after the undertaking of Origen, who placed them with the LXX in his *Tetrapla* and *Hexapla*. They have not been preserved complete, but exist only in fragments in these works of Origen, and in quotations by the Fathers; this is mostly the case in the translations of Aquila, Symmachus, and Theodotion, in which we at least know the names of the authors, although we know little else about them that is authentic.

(1) *Aquila*. He is first mentioned by Irenæus, iii. 24.[1] It has been sometimes thought that Justin M. (*Dial. c. Tryph.* 71), had this man in view;[2] but Justin's words do not point to a written translation; and it is at least probable that Aquila's translation may not have been meant by him; as to which point, *v*. Credner, *Beiträge zur Einl. ins N. T.* ii. 197, ff. Irenæus designates him as a Jewish proselyte (*i.e.*, born of heathen parents, and converted to Judaism) of Pontus. This is doubtless correct, and most of the later ecclesiastical authors agree therein. Thus also the *Talmud* of Jerusalem (*tr. Kiddusch.* fol. 59, 1) calls him a proselyte. Epiphanius (*De Mens. et Pond.* c. 15) relates some fabulous matters about him—that he was first converted from heathenism to Christianity, and subsequently, being expelled from the Christian Church, went over to Judaism. Before Epiphanius, no one knew anything about his ever having been a Christian, and it is therefore altogether im-

[1] 'Αλλ' οὐκ ὡς ἔνιοί φασὶ τῶν νῦν μεθερμηνεύειν τολμώντων τὴν γραφήν· ἰδοὺ ἡ νεᾶνις ἐν γαστρὶ ἕξεται υἱόν, ὡς Θεοδοτίων ἡρμήνευσεν ὁ Ἐφέσιος καὶ Ἀκύλας ὁ Ποντικὸς, ἀμφότεροι Ἰουδαῖοι προσήλυτοι, οἷς κατακολουθήσαντες οἱ Ἐβιωναῖοι, ἐξ Ἰωσὴφ αὐτὸν γεγενῆσθαι φάσκουσιν. (The LXX has, Isaiah vii. 14, παρθένος).

[2] Περὶ τῆς λέξεως τῆς, ἰδοὺ ἡ παρθένος ἐν γαστρὶ λήψεται, ἀντειπατε, λεγοντες εἰρῆσθαι, ἰδοὺ ἡ νεᾶνις ἐν γαστρὶ λήψεται.

Aquila's Greek Translation. 413

probable. Since Irenæus (*ut supr.*) seems to speak of him as a contemporary, his translation must probably have been made after the middle of the second century. In his translation he shows much etymological knowledge, but is literal to an excess, expressing every Hebrew word and every particle by a separate Greek word as exactly as possible, to an extent that makes him often quite unintelligible to those who are not well acquainted with the original text; as, *e.g.*, Gen. i. 1 : ἐν κεφαλαίῳ ἔκτισεν ὁ θεὸς σὺν τὸν οὐρανὸν καὶ τὴν γῆν. Gen. v. 5 : καὶ ἔζησεν Ἀδὰμ τριάκοντα ἔτος καὶ ἐννακόσια ἔτος. (Cf. Origen, *Ep. ad African.*,[1] and Jerome's opinion as to him in De Wette, § 44, note *e.*)

It is quite evident that he produced his translation in opposition to the LXX, which was independent in its character, and differed so frequently from the Hebrew text. It cannot, however, be proved that he had in view in his translation that which was often laid to his charge by the Fathers, viz., from hostility to the Christians, to remove in every way any possible allusions to Christ. Jerome often absolves him of this, and acknowledges that he had found in his translation much matter, "quæ ad nostram fidem pertineant roborandam," *Ep.* 74, ad *Marcell.*; cf. *in Habac.* iii. 13, where he says that Aquila has translated the passage: "egressus es in salutem cum Christo tuo," according to the Christian sense.[2] We see from various passages of Jerome that there was a two-fold edition of Aquila's translation, which the Fathers distinguish as *Editio prima et secunda* (*v.* Eichhorn, § 188); he often quotes both when they vary, in other cases only either the one or the other. The second edition appears to be distinguished from the first by a still more strictly literal character; therefore Jerome, *in Ezek.* iii., says, that the Hebrews name it κατ' ἀκρίβειαν. Aquila's translation met with great approval from the Jews; they preferred it to the other translations

[1] Οὕτω γὰρ Ἀκύλας δουλεύων τῇ Ἑβραικῇ λέξει ἐκδέδωκεν εἰπών. φιλοτιμότερον πεπιστευμένος παρὰ Ἰουδαίοις ἡρμηνευκέναι τὴν γραφήν, ᾧ μάλιστα εἰώθασιν οἱ ἀγνοοῦντες τὴν Ἑβραίων διάλεκτον χρῆσθαι, ὡς πάντων μᾶλλον ἐπιτετευγμένῳ.

[2] Theodotio quasi pauper et Hebionita, sed et Symmachus ejusdem dogmatis, pauperem sensum secuti Judaice transtulerunt. Isti semi-Christiani Judaice transtulerunt; et Judæus Aquila interpretatus est ut Christianus.

(Augustine, *De Civ. Dei*, xv. 23; Origen, *ut supra*). In the Talmud of Jerus., we are told that he translated with such great approval, that the words of the Psalm were used as to him, יפיפית מבני אדם (Psalm xlv. 3). This translation was also read out in some synagogues, although in others the LXX was retained for this use (*v.* above, § 341).

(2) *Theodotion.* He also is first mentioned by Irenæus, who speaks of him as a contemporary, just as he speaks of Aquila, so that we can perhaps assume it as certain that he also translated after the middle of the second century. Irenæus calls him an Ephesian, and styles both him and Aquila Jewish proselytes. The former remark, relating to his native country, we have no reason to doubt. Epiphanius (*De Mens. et Pond.* c. 17), indeed calls him Ποντικόν, but not much weight is to be placed on this, or on his further statement, that he was a follower of Marcion, and was after this converted to Judaism. But, as I believe, it is open to doubt whether he was a Jewish proselyte and belonged generally to the Jewish Church, notwithstanding the weighty evidence of Irenæus, who lived so shortly after his time. Jerome, indeed, also calls him a Jew,[1] but mostly speaks of him as a Judaizing heretic, as a semi-Christian, and an Ebionite.[2] It seems very probable to me that he belonged to the Christian Church, and for the following reasons in particular: (*a*) We find no traces that Jews ever made use of his translation, still less that it ever stood in authority among them; this was far more the case in the Christian Church, which accepted his translation of the Book of Daniel for ecclesiastical use. (*b*) In Isaiah xxv. 8, Theodotion has rendered the words בִּלַּע הַמָּוֶת לָנֶצַח κατεπόθη ὁ θάνατος εἰς νῖκος, exactly as in 1 Corinth. xv. 54, quite differently, however, from the LXX, which has κατέπιεν ὁ θάνατος ἰσχύσας, and had it also at the time of Irenæus. This coincidence is probably not purely accidental, but is to be explained by the assumption that Theodotion appropriated Paul's translation of the passage; but this makes it highly probable that he was a Christian at the time of his making the translation. He was, perhaps,

[1] *Ep.* 89 *ad August.*: Ex Theodotionis editione ab Origene additum est . . . . præsertim cum ea, quæ audita sunt, ex hominis Judæi atque blasphemi editione transtulerit.
[2] Cf. above, p. 413, note 2, and De Wette, § 44, note *g*.

born of heathen parents, and, as a Christian, was not allied to the Judaizing party.

Jerome remarks as to the character of his translation,[1] that he very much follows the LXX, and takes a middle course between that translation and Aquila's. He decidedly deviates from the LXX only where it presents omissions and wider deviations from the Hebrew text; in these he often agrees with Aquila, only that he avoids being so slavishly literal. He does not appear to have had a comprehensive knowledge of Hebrew. It does not seem improbable to me that Theodotion made his translation in reference to that made by Aquila for his brethren in faith, as a version for the purpose of the Christian Church, and as a fresh revision of the LXX, following more exactly the Hebrew text. The Book of Daniel in his translation has been preserved complete in the ordinary editions of the LXX, as this translation—perhaps between the age of Origen and that of Jerome—received ecclesiastical authority, and was adopted into the Codices of the LXX. According to Jerome, *in Jerem.* xxix. 17,[2] a second edition was made of his translation also, unless it is Aquila's second edition that is here meant; except in this passage no such *secunda edito* of Theodotion is mentioned.

(3) The translation of Symmachus took place later than the two just spoken of. We may pretty certainly conclude that Irenæus was not yet acquainted with it, because, in reference to Isaiah vii. 14, where all three translators give νεᾶνις for the Hebrew הָעַלְמָה, he finds fault with this only in Aquila and Theodotion. Jerome also presupposes this relation of date between Symmachus and Theodotion, *e.g.*, in Is. lviii. 9 : "Symmachus in Theodotionis scita concedens." Finally, we may conclude from Eusebius, *Hist. Eccl.* vi. 17, that Symmachus' translation was little known before the time of Origen, that the latter received it from one Julian, who got it from Symmachus himself. Eusebius and Jerome style him an Ebionite.[3] Nothing further is known to us about him, as no notice is to be taken of the

[1] *In Eccles.* ii : LXX et Theodotio, sicut in pluribus locis, ita et hoc quoque concordant.—*Præf. in Evangg.*: inter novos (Aq. et Symm.) et veteres (LXX) medius incedit.

[2] Theodotio interpretatus est *sudrinas* ; secunda *pessima* ; Symmachus *novissimas*.

[3] Euseb. *Hist. Eccl.* vi. 17; *Demonstr.* vii. 1; Hieron. *in Habac. ut supr.*

statements of Epiphanius (*De Mens. et Pond.* c. 17), which are fabulous on this point also. As regards the character of his translation, it is of a freer nature than that of Aquila and Theodotion. Symmachus expresses more the ideas than the exact words of the Hebrew text, and he is clear and intelligible, for which he is praised by the ancients, especially and repeatedly Jerome (*vide* Hody, p. 588). Jerome in two passages (*in Jerem.* c. 32; *in Nah.* c. 3) expressly distinguishes two different editions of this translation also, as *prima* and *secunda editio*.

These three translations are besides often quoted as οἱ τρεῖς. "*tres* (alii, reliqui) interpretes" (*v.* Hody, p. 589).

(4.) Besides these Greek translations which we have just considered, Origen was acquainted with three others by unknown authors, which from the position which they assume in his *Hexapla*, are styled *Quinta, Sexta, Septima* (ε', ς', ζ'). Little that is authentic is known about them. They did not embrace the whole Old Testament; thus much we know, however, that all three contained the Psalms and the Minor Prophets, the two first the Pentateuch and Solomon's Song also; and the Quinta, perhaps also the Septima, gave the Books of Kings as well.

§ 343.—*Origen's Hexapla and Tetrapla—Their Aim and Nature.*

Through the existence of these other Greek translations, and the disputations with the Jews, the Christian Church became increasingly conscious that the LXX, as accepted by the Church, differed much from the Hebrew text, even in those books and sections which in general were to be found in the Hebrew Codex. A necessity, therefore, arose for members of the Christian Church, even divines who were not able to read the Hebrew text itself, that they should possess means so that, without any adequate knowledge of Hebrew, they might know—particularly in disputations with the Jews—where and how far the orthodox translation either agreed with or differed from the Hebrew text. This necessity, therefore, Origen sought to satisfy by the pains he took to supply editions of the LXX, in which he endeavoured to make the latter convenient and fitted to be used by Christians in their controversies with the Jews; so that the former might easily and readily know when the latter were justified in rejecting the LXX as incorrect

The Hexapla of Origen. 417

and not agreeing with the Hebrew text; at the same time he sought to provide them with means for making the former correspond more with the latter. For this purpose, Origen prepared two different editions,—which Eusebius (*Hist. Eccl.* vi. 16)[1] appears expressly to distinguish,—the *Hexapla* and the *Tetrapla*. It is, however, doubtful what relation these two bore to one another.

The arrangement and the aim of the *Hexapla* is the best known, as to which Origen himself speaks in *Ep. ad African*. It was not his idea to publish a new text of the LXX—one differing from the text which prevailed in the Church—but by a kind of synoptical arrangement, to place the LXX side by side with the other Greek translations and with the Hebrew text; also, by intimations and diacritical signs in the text of the LXX, sometimes to assist the comprehension of the latter, and sometimes to point out its relation to the Hebrew text, so as to prevent Christians when disputing with the Jews from bringing forward matter which did not exist in the Hebrew text, or rejecting, as a matter of course, passages brought forward out of the original text, because they could not find them in the LXX. Origen worked many years both in collecting materials for this work and also in its preparation; he was assisted with money for this purpose, especially by his friend Ambrosius.

The external arrangements of the work were these:[2] he placed the Hebrew text and the different Greek translations by one another in columns, in the following order: (1) The Hebrew text in the Hebrew character; (2) the same in Greek letters; (3) the translation of Aquila;— perhaps as that which the closest follows the Hebrew text—

---

[1] Ταύτας δὲ ἁπάσας ἐπὶ ταὐτὸν συναγαγὼν διελών τε πρὸς κῶλον καὶ ἀντιπαραθεὶς ἀλλήλαις μετὰ καὶ αὐτῆς τῆς Ἑβραίων σημειώσεως, τὰ τῶν λεγομένων ἑξαπλῶν ἡμῖν ἀντίγραφα καταλέλοιπεν, ἰδίως τὴν Ἀκύλα καὶ Συμμάχου καὶ Θεοδοτίωνος ἔκδοσιν ἅμα τῇ τῶν ὅ ἐν τοῖς τετραπλοῖς ἐπικατασκευάσας.

[2] Rufin, *H. E.* vi. 13; Hieron. in *Ep. ad Tit.* 3: Unde nobis curæ fuit, omnes veteris legis libros, quos vir Adamantius in Hexapla digesserat, de Cæsariensi Bibliotheca descriptos, ex ipsis authenticis emendare, in quibus ipsa Hebræa propriis sunt characteribus verba descripta, et Græcis literis tramite expressa vicino. Aquila etiam et Symmachus, Septuaginta et Theodotio suum ordinem tenent. Nonnulli vero libri, et maxime hi, qui apud Hebræos versu compositi sunt, tres alias editiones additas habent. quam Quintam et Sextam et Septimam translationem vocant, auctoritatem sine nominibus interpretum consequutus.

VOL. II. 2 E

(4) that of Symmachus; (5) the LXX, the text of which he probably gave according to the collation of several manuscripts, and perhaps, where there were several readings, he selected that which came the nearest to the Hebrew text; (6) the translation of Theodotion, as that which often exactly followed the expressions of the LXX. The work was thus shaped as regards the greater part of it, and to these six columns refers the usual name for the whole of it,—Hexapla, ἑξαπλᾶ. In some books, the *Quinta* and *Sexta* (translations) are added—in which case there were eight columns, for which Epiphanius, *De Mensur. et Pond.* c. 19, intimates that the name ὀκτάπλα would be more suitable, though it is not exactly to be inferred from his words, that this was then a customary designation for it. In later Scholia ὀκτασέλιδον occurs. Where the *Septima* (translation) is added, there are actually nine columns; but this was comparatively but seldom added, and had no influence on the name of the work. In the column of the LXX, Origen not only copied the simple text, but also at the same time showed how and where it differed from the Hebrew text. Matter that stood in the LXX, without being in the Hebrew text, he allowed indeed to remain, but placed before the additional matter an *obelus* (or, according to Jerome, *Ep. ad Suniam et Fretelam*), a *virgula jacens* (a straight or somewhat twisted line, — or ⸝, according to Epiphanius),[1] and after it two points ⁚, for which in some manuscripts other signs are found, *e.g.* ⸔. When, on the contrary, the Hebrew text contained anything which was not expressed in the LXX, Origen mostly supplied this from Theodotion, sometimes from Aquila (perhaps where Theodotion also had not expressed it), sometimes also from Symmachus; before these inserted passages he placed an asterisk, with the initial letter of the passage from which it was taken, and after it two points, *e.g.* ✻ Θ. ΑΥΤΟϹ ⁚. In hexaplar manuscripts there also occur *Lemnisci* ÷ and *Hypolemnisci* ⟋, which, however, are not mentioned by Origen and Jerome, but first by Epiphanius and Isidorus Hispal. *Origg.* i. c. 20. According to the latter, the *Lemniscus* was intended to intimate that the various translators express the same sense in different words; the *Hypolem-*

[1] *De Mensur. et Pond.* c. 3 (of the *obelus*): παραπλησίως γράφεται τῇ καλουμένῃ γράμμῃ.

niscus, which he calls *antigraphus*, that they differ from one another in the sense. It is, however, very questionable if these latter marks proceeded from Origen. From Augustine, *de Civ. Dei*, xviii. 43, it may be concluded pretty certainly, that he was not aware of these marks in the hexaplar manuscripts, but only recognized the obeli and the asterisks. Origen also wrote for this work a history of the translations and Prolegomena on the several books of the Old Testament, as well as marginal notes of an exegetical and critical character, many of which have been preserved.

Fifty years after Origen's death—at the beginning of the fourth century—this comprehensive work was brought out of its obscurity (probably at Tyre) by Eusebius and Pamphilus, and placed in the library of Pamphilus (d. as martyr 309) at Cæsarea. Here Jerome found it and made use of it, as he himself says (in *Ep. ad Tit.* 3). After this time it is not further mentioned; it is supposed (Jahn) that it was destroyed in 653, at the capture and destruction of Cæsarea by the Arabians. It is not probable that the whole work, consisting of many volumes, was ever completely copied out, and we find no trace of this. But certain matter was perhaps selected from it for critical and exegetical use. Thus, from Jerome, *Præf. in Paralip. ad Chromatium*,[1] we may perceive that Eusebius and Pamphilus copied out of the work and issued the columns of the LXX with the critical signs. These manuscripts, which Jerome (*ut supr.*) calls *Palæstinos Codices*, are the hexaplar manuscripts of the LXX; they contain the translation in the shape in which it stood in the Hexapla of Origen, with the obeli and the asterisk, and the added portions out of the other Greek translations. There were very many of these manuscripts of the LXX in use at the time of Jerome, not only in the Churches of Palestine

[1] Alexandria et Ægyptus in LXX suis Hesychium laudat auctorem. Constantinopolis usque Antiochiam Luciani martyris exemplaria probat. Mediæ inter has provinciæ Palæstinos codices legunt, quos ab Origine elaboratos Eusebius et Pamphilus vulgaverunt. Totusque orbis hac inter se trifaria varietate compugnat. Et certe Origenes non solum exemplaria composuit quatuor editionum, e regione singula verba describens, ut unus dissenticus statim ceteris inter se consentientibus arguatur; sed, quod majoris audaciæ est, in editione LXX Theodotionis editionem miscuit: astericis designans, quæ minus ante fuerant, et virgulis, quæ ex superfluo videbantur apposita.

but in those of other countries also. *V. Hieron. Ep.* 89, *ad Augustin.*: "Vis amator esse verus LXX interpretum? non legas ea, quæ sub astericis sunt; imo rade de voluminibus, ut veterum te fautorem probes. Quod si feceris, *omnes ecclesiarum bibliothecas* damnare cogeris; vix enim unus aut alter invenietur liber, qui ista non habeat."—*Proœm. Comment. in Dan.*: "Cumque omnes Christi ecclesiæ, tam Græcorum quam Latinorum, Syrorumque et Ægyptiorum hanc sub astericis et obelis editionem legant," &c.—Augustine, *de Civ. Dei*, xviii. 43.—In Scholia on Greek manuscripts, these editions are also mentioned often as those of Eusebius and Pamphilus, or as those of Eusebius (*v.* Hody, p. 620).

In the same Scholia, however, the *Tetrapla* (or τετρασέλιδον) is mentioned, as well as the above editions. But it is very questionable what the relation of the Tetrapla was to the Hexapla. Many scholars, as Eichhorn and Augusti, are decidedly wrong in considering it merely as a different name for the same work; the statements of the above scholiasts clearly point out a difference between the two,[1] as the *Scholia* of Eusebius, *ut supra*, Epiphanius, *De Mens. et Pond.* c. 19. According to the statements of these Fathers, the Tetrapla contained, as its name would imply, only four columns, with the four chief translations,—the LXX, Aquila, Theodotion, and Symmachus; and, indeed, Origen himself (according to Eusebius, *ut supra;* cf. Jerome, *Præf. in Paralip.*) produced this as a separate work, as a synoptical edition of the four translations. That it was constantly in use in the Church, we may well conclude; because the Fathers so often quote these translations, that we are induced to assume that they must have had them written out before them in a form convenient for comparison. As in the scholiasts, the text of the LXX in the Tetrapla is often pointed out as differing from the text of the Hexapla in the editions of Eusebius and Pamphilus, it is scarcely admissible that Origen himself can have composed the Tetrapla as an abstract of the Hexapla, the LXX with the critical marks, &c.; for then the subsequent labour of Eusebius and Pamphilus would have been quite unnecessary. It is, on the contrary, much more pro-

[1] *E.g.*, ad *Psalm.* lxxxvi: τὸ (ῥῶ) κατὰ προσθήκην ἔκειτο εἰς τὴν τῶν ἑβδομήκοντα ἐν τῷ Τετραπέλιδῳ, ἐν δὲ τῷ Ὀκτασελίδῳ μήτηρ Σιών.

bable, as Montfaucon assumes, (a) that Origen composed the Tetrapla *before* the Hexapla; which may also be inferred from the words of Eusebius; and (b) that the Tetrapla was merely a combination of the above four translations, containing the LXX in the usual text, without the critical marks and the additions taken out of the other translations. [What can be recovered of the Hexapla is in course of publication at the Clarendon Press, under the care of the Rev. F. Field.]

§ 344.—*Other Recensions of the LXX—Variations in Manuscripts.*

At the end of the third century, two other men attempted, in a somewhat different way from Origen, to render service to the text of the LXX: (a) *Lucianus*, Presbyter at Antioch, d. at the end of the third century as a martyr in Diocletian's persecution (Euseb. *Hist. Eccl.* viii. 13, ix. 6); and (b) Hesychius, an Egyptian Bishop, who (according to Euseb. viii. 13) perished in the same persecution. They each prepared a separate Recension of the text of the LXX, which was circulated in their respective countries.

According to Jerome, *Præf. in Paralip.* (*ut supra*), Hesychius' edition was, in his time, chiefly prevailing in Alexandria and Egypt; and that of Lucian from Constantinople to Antioch. We know little or nothing else of Hesychius' Recension; Jerome, *in Is.* lviii. 11, quotes it as *exemplaria Alexandrina.* That of Lucian is more often mentioned, and is spoken of by later authors of the Greek Church as almost a new translation from the Hebrew—which is decidedly wrong—also as a correction of the LXX from the Hebrew text. Jerome (*Ep. ad. Suniam et Fretelam*[1]), however, ranks it with the κοινή, *i.e.* ordinary pre-hexaplar text.

Both, doubtless, endeavoured to purify the text of the LXX which was in use in their district, by the collation of

[1] Sciatis aliam esse editionem, quam Origenes et Cæsariensis Eusebius omnesque Græciæ tractatores κοινήν. *i.e.*, communem appellant atque vulgatam et a plerisque nunc Λουκιανός dicitur; aliam LXX interpretum, quæ in ἑξαπλοῖς codicibus reperitur . . . κοινή autem ista, h. e. communis editio, ipsa est quæ et LXX. Sed hoc interest inter utramque, quod κοινή pro locis et temporibus et voluntate Scriptorum veterum [al. leg. vetus] *corrupta* editio est; ea autem, qua habetur in ἑξαπλοῖς et quam nos vertimus, ipsa est, quæ in eruditorum libris incorrupta et immaculata LXX interpretum translatio reservatur.

various manuscripts; how far this was done by recourse to other means of assistance, can now hardly be ascertained with any certainty. So, also, we cannot determine with certainty what influence these two editions exercised on the further shaping of the text of the LXX. We see from the expressions of Jerome, that, in his time the κοινή, or *editio vulgata*, i.e., the text in the non-hexaplar manuscripts—among which he reckoned Lucian's revision—was shaped in many different ways according to the various countries.[1] The manuscripts of the hexaplar editions were, however, often employed for religious uses, first especially in Palestine, and subsequently in other regions.[2] Sometimes, also, the LXX was translated into other languages from these hexaplar editions, and with the critical marks, or the translations of the Books of the Old Testament already existing in these languages were emended from these manuscripts of the LXX, and in the hexaplar mode; this took place especially in the Latin and Syrian Churches (v. §§ 348 b, 352). Both for private use, and also for public religious service, they were wont to read the Greek text as it was in these hexaplar manuscripts, without noticing the critical signs; they therefore read the passages marked with obeli as well as those marked with asterisks, and they likewise read the hexaplar editions of the old Latin translation of the several Books of the Old Testament.[3] Thus they were accustomed in the Church to consider the hexaplar additions as belonging to the text of the LXX, and these additions have frequently made their way into other manuscripts of the LXX which were not provided with Origen's critical marks. Thus, e.g., we find in our Greek manuscripts of Job much that corresponds with the Hebrew text, which was wanting in them in the time of Origen.[4] The LXX might thus become more fitted for public religious use, so far at least, that nothing was omitted in it

[1] *Proœm in L.* xvi. *Comment. in Jes.*: in editione vulgata, quæ Græce κοινή dicitur et in toto urbe diversa est.—*Ep. ad Sun. et Fret.* (*vide* above).

[2] *Vide* the passages of Jerome, above v. p. 418, f.

[3] Jerome's language shows this (*Ep.* 89, *ad Augustin.*), above p. 418, f., and Augustine (*de Civ. D.* xviii. 43).

[4] According to Jahn, i. 169, Jerome complains: "error exoritur, quod astericis subtractis distinctio confunditur." But he does not point out the passage, and I doubt if this can be found in Jerome.

which was afforded by the Hebrew text. But this necessarily caused that the text of the LXX often became settled in a way which more widely differed from its original shape, than in the manuscripts before Origen. That which the LXX had beyond the Hebrew text was indeed suffered to remain, but the hexaplar additions to supply the deficiencies of the former became firmly settled in the text, as if they had originally belonged to it. Yet the manuscripts of the LXX present numerous variations from one another, and many of them are not directly connected with the influence of the hexaplar text. A text differing much from each other, is often presented by the two manuscripts which are the most ancient and most celebrated—at least among those which contain the whole Greek Old Testament (together with the New Testament): (a) the *Codex Alexandrinus*, and (b) the *Codex Vaticanus*, the former of which has been, since 1628, in the British Museum, the latter in the Vatican Library at Rome; both belong to a date between the fourth and fifth centuries.[1]

For further details as to these, v. "Introduction to the New Testament," p. 700, ff. A copy of the Greek Old

---

[1] In 1859, Tischendorf found in a room in a monastery on Mount Sinai a manuscript [known now as the *Codex Sinaiticus*, and marked ℵ], which, in his opinion, belongs to the fourth century (Hilgenfeld, in his *Zeitschrift für wissensch. Theologie*, 1864, Part i. places it in the sixth century; cf. *ibid.* Part ii. Tischendorf's vindication and Hilgenfeld's answer, who considers his opinion strengthened by the self-evidence of the Codex), and is to be considered as the most ancient and the most valuable of all the manuscripts extant of the Greek Bible; unfortunately it only contains about twenty books of the Old Testament. *Vide Wissensch. Beilage der Leipzig. Zeitg.* 1859, No. 31, 17th April; Gelzer's *Protest. Monatsblätter*, vol. xvii. pp. 310-322, and the *Notitia editionis Cod. Bibl. Sinait.* &c. Leipzig, 1860. Tischendorf rightly considers the *Codex Friderico-Augustanus*, found by him in 1844, and published at Leipzig in 1846, a fragment of the same manuscript. This contains, besides Nehemiah and Esther, the Book of Jeremiah from ch. x. 25, as well as portions of Chronicles, Ezra, Lamentations, and Tobit. As to the value of the Sinaitic Bible-manuscript, cf. K. Wieseler in the *Theol. Stud. und Krit.* 1864, pp. 399-438, and H. Ewald in the *Gött. Gel. Anz.* 1863, pp. 1379-92. This manuscript has been printed in fac-simile, 4 vols. fol. (*Bibliorum Codex Sinaiticus edid. Tischendorf.* Petropoli. 1862). [In 1863 the New Testament was published at Leipzig, 4to, in columns as in the original. Scrivener has also printed its readings in a small volume, 1863, and Hansell has added them to his edition of the New Testament, 1864.—Tr.]

Testament according to the Cod. Alex.—with type expressly cast for it in the character of the original—was published in London, at the royal expense, by H. Hervey Baber: *V. Test. Græc. e Cod. MS. Alex. . . . . typis ad similitudinem ipsius Cod. Scripturæ fideliter descriptum,* 1812–26. The Cod. Vatic. has two great deficiencies—almost the whole of Genesis (ch. i–xlvii), and Psalms cv–cxxxviii, and the Books of Maccabees being wanting; from this Cardinal Mai (d. 1854) had a copy prepared of the Old and New Testaments, the printing of which was completed in 1837; its publication, however, was not permitted by the Roman Curia until 1857: *V. et N. Test. ex antiquissimo Cod. Vat. ed. Angelus Maius,* 5 vols. But this edition afforded no kind of certainty as to the nature of the text of this codex, the omissions in it being supplied out of other manuscripts. Even in other portions Mai went to work with such great carelessness, that they found themselves compelled to print afresh a great number of leaves before publication. Even after this, much that is very faulty has been allowed to remain.[1]

It is very doubtful what relation these two manuscripts stand in, in their variations, to the different forms of the text existing in Jerome's time. The hypotheses on this point are directly opposed to one another. I believe, however, that the two forms of the text presented by these manuscripts go back to a date before the time of Origen, to the apostolic age, and that there were at that time various forms of the text in various manuscripts of the LXX, one of which forms we find preponderating in the Cod. Vat., another in the Cod. Alex.[2] Very difficult is it, however, in numerous cases, to decide whether the readings in the one or other codex, and generally, which of the varying readings in the different manuscripts are the most ancient and original; for the criticism of the text of the LXX is in general a very difficult task, and if we attempt to deal with it, so as to restore it everywhere to its original shape, it is a matter perhaps altogether not to be solved, notwithstanding all the material gathered in modern times.

[1] [A fac-simile edition of the *Codex Vaticanus* is in course of publication at Rome, by Vercellone and Cozza. The New Testament appeared in 1868.]
[2] *Vide* my "Epistle to the Hebrews," i. pp. 369-375.

§ 345.—*The four chief printed Editions of the LXX.*

Of the *editions* of the LXX up to this time, four must be considered in reference to the text as chief or fundamental editions, on which the others are dependent:

I.—The *Complutensian*, in the Complutensian (*v.* § 364) Polyglot (1514 to 1517).—It is based upon several manuscripts, which, however, are not named. It has been sometimes suspected that the text of the LXX was altered according to the Hebrew; but this, by closer investigation, has been shown to be unfounded, for the suspected readings actually exist in manuscripts of the LXX. This text is also printed in the Antwerp and Paris Polyglots, and others.

II.—The *Editio Veneta* or *Aldina*, published in 1518 at Venice, in the office of Aldus Manutius, two years after his death, by his father-in-law, Andreas Asulanus, who declared that the edition had been prepared from *multis vetustissimis exemplaribus*, and that the advice of learned men had been made use of; yet the accusation has been made that the text has been occasionally interpolated out of other Greek translations, and even out of the New Testament. But in this case also, the suspected passages have been actually found among the readings brought to light in manuscripts in modern times. This edition is rare, but several versions in Germany have been based upon it: (1) Strasburg, 1526; (2) Basle, 1545; (3) *Ibid.* 1550; (4) Frankfort, 1597.

III.—The *Roman Edition, Vaticana s. Sixtina*, 1587.—This appeared, under the authority of Pope Sixtus V., as the joint work of several scholars, among others, of Petrus Morinus; their work extended over nine years. It is based on the Cod. Vat.; its deficient passages are supplied out of two other manuscripts, not, however, so ancient as the Cod. Vat. The text of the Cod. Vat. is, however, by no means everywhere retained; not only is the orthography of the codex altered into that usual in Greek, but the editors have also sought to emend that which they considered faulty in the manuscript, without always indicating the alteration. Besides the text, the most note-worthy readings are quoted from many other manuscripts, especially from the Medicean Library at Florence, also fragments out of other Greek translations, which Petrus Morinus had collected out of the *Catenæ*.

By far the greater part of the later editions are based upon the text of the above. Of these editions I will only mention here: (*a*) The "London Polyglot," 1657, with readings of the Cod. Alex., and, in the 6th vol., a collection of readings from other manuscripts and earlier editions. (*b*) That of Lambert Bos, Francker, 1709; with Prolegomena as to the history and criticism of the LXX; under the text stand Greek *Scholia* from the Roman edition, and readings from the "London Polyglot." The text of the LXX is not everywhere exactly that of the Roman edition, although Bos protests that it is so. The text of Bos has been repeated by David Mill in a portable edition (Amsterdam, 1725); readings of two manuscripts are appended. (*c*) That of Joh. Reineccius, Leipzig, 1730; 2nd edit., 1757; the Roman text, with the most important deviations from the Alex. and other manuscripts. (*d*) That of Leander von Ess, Leipzig, 1824. Reprint of the Roman text. (*e*) That of Const. Tischendorf, 2 vols. Leipzig, 1850; edit. 2, 1856 (edit. 3, 1860). Likewise a reprint of the text of the Vat. with the readings of the Cod. Alex.; also of the Ephraemus and Friderico-Augustanus.

IV.—The *Edition of Grabe*, Oxford, 1707–20, 4 vols., by Joh. Ernst Grabe (born at Königsberg, lived as a private teacher in England, d. 1711); he himself edited only vols. 1 and 4; the two middle ones did not appear until after his death; the 2nd was arranged by Francis Lee, the 3rd by some one not named, from materials, however, from amongst Grabe's papers. This edition bears the same relation to the Cod. Alex., as concerns the text, as the Sixtina to the Cod. Vat. It was intended, except as to orthography, to give in general the text of the Cod. Alex.; but the editors have not only often adopted the readings of other manuscripts of the LXX instead of those of the Cod. Alex., where they considered the former to be more correct, but have also supplied from other translations the omissions of the LXX, after Origen's plan. These deviations from the Cod. Alex., however, have been distinguished by being printed in smaller characters, and the reading belonging to the Cod. Alex. is placed in the margin in the usual character; but the requisite care has not been everywhere taken as to this, and sometimes a reading deviating from the Cod. Alex. has been adopted, without its being specially

Alexandrine Translation of Daniel. 427

indicated. Prolegomena of critical and historical purport are prefixed to the several volumes. Grabe had also the idea of editing a separate volume with critical remarks; the notes on Gen. xlix. were fully prepared by him, and published by Bruns. in Eichhorn's *Repert.* iv. pp. 1-40.

The edition of Joh. Jak. Breitinger (Prof. at Zürich, d. 1776), 1730-32, 4 vols., contains a reprint of Grabe's text; only that the typographical errors are corrected, and the alterations are adopted, which were considered necessary by Grabe in his Prolegomena. Under the text stand the varying readings of the Roman edition, and this edition is, therefore, very valuable. The editor promised a 5th vol., with critical discussions and readings from the Basle, Augsburg, and Zürich manuscripts, which, however, has not appeared.[1]

In all these editions, the translation of the Canonical Book of Daniel is given from *Theodotion* (only the larger Apocryphal additions are given from the LXX). Of the Alexandrine translation of the book, only one codex is known, in the library of Cardinal Chigi at Rome; and from this it was first published, Rome, 1772, probably arranged by Simon de Magistris, from a not very correct copy of the Codex. The Codex is hexaplar, being provided with the additions and critical signs of Origen, which also are adopted in the edition, as well as other things contained in the Codex, together with some additions by the editor himself. J. D. Michaelis superintended a twofold reprint of this edition: (*a*) Göttingen, 1773, which contains only the Greek text; and (*b*), 1774, with the most important additions of the Roman edition. From Michaelis' edition, that of Segaar (Utrecht, 1775) was prepared. Lately another separate edition of this Alexandrine translation of Daniel has been edited by H. A. Hahn (d. 1861), with collation of a Syrian translation obtained from the hexaplar text of the LXX, which had been edited by Cajetan Bugati from a Milan codex (Milan, 1788), with critical and philological notes, Leipzig, 1845.

By far the most editions of the LXX contain the Apo-

[1] Appeared at Oxford, 1859: Vet. Test. Græce juxta LXX interpretes. Recensionem Grabianam ad fidem codicis Alex. aliorumque denuo recognovit, Græca secundum ordinem textus Hebraici reformavit, libros apocryphos a canonicis segregavit Fridericus Field.

crypha, according to this translation, as well as the Canonical Books of the Old Testament. These, however, have often been published separately, by Augusti among others, Leipzig, 1804, from the text of Reineccius' second edition, but with many alterations [and by Henricus Edwardus Apel, Leipzig, 1837].

A vast fund for criticism of the text of the LXX is furnished by a large edition of it which appeared in England, in 5 vols., in separate parts, from 1798-1827 (the last volume contained the Apocrypha). It was undertaken by Robert Holmes (Professor of Divinity at Oxford), with the literary and pecuniary assistance of others. He himself, as he died in 1805, edited only the first volume, containing the Pentateuch, and besides, the Book of Daniel separately (from Theodotion and the LXX). The remaining portion was edited after his death by J. Parsons. The text of this work is throughout that of the *Sixtina*. But under the text stand the readings from the manuscripts collated, the principal editions, the ancient authors, and the ancient translations of the LXX. The number of manuscripts collated amounts to twelve Uncial-Codices (which are indicated by Roman numerals) and 261 Minusculi (numbered with Arabic cyphers). The whole contains rich material for a revision of the LXX; the editors themselves, however, have done nothing towards it. It must be considered as a deficiency in it, that the quotations from the Fathers are everywhere only noticed where their readings differ from the Sixtine text, but not where they agree.

G. L. Spohn (Pro-Rector at Dortmund, d. 1794) has made an attempt to restore the Græco-hexaplar text of *Jeremiah*, with peculiar reference to Grabe's edition of the LXX: *Jerem. Vates e versione Judæorum Alex. ac reliquorum interpr. Gr. emend. notisque crit. illustr.* Leipz. 1794. Vol. ii. ed. F. R. Guil. Spohn, 1824.

Various scholars have endeavoured to render service in the collection and revision of the actual fragments which have been preserved of the ancient Greek translations—with the exception of the LXX—sometimes in the quotations of the Fathers, sometimes in the ancient manuscripts of the LXX, and in those that have resulted from the hexaplar text of the same, especially in Syrian translations of certain books. We must mention particularly Bern.

Concordances, &c., of the Greek Translations. 429

de Montfaucon (Benedictine at Paris, d. 1741), *Hexaplorum Origenis quæ supersunt*, &c., 2 vols., Paris, 1713; an abstract of this was given by K. F. Bahrdt (2 vols., Leipzig, 1769–70), in which the Greek fragments given by Montfaucon were printed, but the Hebrew words written with Greek letters and Montfaucon's notes were omitted. Several other scholars have since furnished additions and emendations to the Hexapla, cf. De Wette, § 45, *fin.*, and Eichhorn, § 174. [In Tischendorf's *Monumenta Sacra, nova collectio*, vol. 3, Leipzig, 1860, there are fragments of Origen's Octateuch.]

There are various *Concordances* and *lexicographical works* to these Greek translations. The most ancient is that by Conr. Kircher (Minister at Jaxthausen : *Concordantiæ V. Test. Græcæ Hebræis vocibus respondentes,* πολύχρηστοι, Frankfort, 1607), and is really an Hebræo-Greek Concordance; the Hebrew words are alphabetically arranged, and under each the various Greek words are placed, which are used for the above Hebrew word in the LXX, with a reprint of the several passages in which the same are found. This arrangement is useful, in an exegetical point of view, for the explanation of the Hebrew of the Old Testament out of the LXX. At the end, however, an alphabetical Greek index is added, and in it also the passages are printed in which the several Greek words occur in the Apocrypha. On the other hand, real concordances and lexicons to the LXX and the other Greek translations, following the alphabetical order of the Greek words, have been furnished by (*a*) Abr. Tromm (Minister at Gröningen, d. 1719), *Concord. Græcæ versionis LXX*, &c., Utrecht, 1718; (*b*) Joh. Chr. Biel (Pastor at Brunswick, d. 1745), *Nov. Thesaur. philol. sive lexicon in LXX et alios interpr. et scriptores apoc. Vet. Test.*, Hague, 1779–80, edited by Mützenbrecher (d. 1801, as General Superint. at Oldenburg); (*c*) Joh. Fried. Schleusner (d. 1831, at Wittenberg), *Nov. Thesaur. philol.-crit. sive lexicon in LXX,* &c., Leipzig, 1820. The latter work, however, has very great deficiencies, and is in no way correspondent to the just claims of our time in such an undertaking. A new lexicographical work on these translations was begun by Böckel (Gen. Sup. at Oldenburg), who died a few years ago : *Novæ clavis in Græcos V. Test. interpretes . . . atque editionis LXX interpretum hexaplaris specimina*, Leipzig, 1820.

§ 346.—*Ancient Greek Translations.*

Besides the Greek translations which we have hitherto considered, on the margins of manuscripts of the LXX, and in the Fathers, some other ancient Greek translations and readings are quoted under different names, viz. as follows:—

(*a*) ὁ Ἑβραῖος.— The matter that is cited under this name consists of certain emendations of the LXX out of the Hebrew text, and are mostly derived from Jerome's exegetical works on the Old Testament. Eichhorn, § 206, correctly thinks this. It is, however, very probable that some one collected these in a separate form, and made them known under the above title, whence it is explained why they are always quoted under this name.

(*b*) ὁ Σύρος.—The work which after the fifth century is quoted under this title is, most probably, as Semler (*Vorbereitung zur theol. Hermeneutik*, p. 421) supposes, and Döderlein (*Quis sit* ὁ Σύρος *V. Test. Græcus interpr.* Altdorf, 1772) in particular has shown, the Greek translation of the Books of the Old Testament made by Sophronius, Patriarch of Byzantium, from Jerome's Latin translation (*v.* Hieron. *de viris illustr.*, and *Ep.* 134, *ad Sophr.*). As to the name ὁ Σύρος, we must compare the fact that Theodorus of Mopsuestia (in Photius' *Bibl. Cod.* 227) calls Jerome Ἀράμ: probably in reference to his long sojourn in Palestine. ὁ Σύρος and ὁ Ἑβραῖος are often quoted as quite in accordance.

(*c*) τὸ Σαμαρειτικὸν is the name for readings of the Samaritan Recension of the Pentateuch translated into Greek; they may have been collected from the readings differing from the LXX, which were found in this recension, either in the Hebrew language or in the Samaritan translation. They could hardly have been a complete Greek translation of this recension; cf. Eichhorn, § 208.

(*d*) ὁ Ἑλληνικός. — Under this name a Greek translation is often quoted, together with the Ἑβραῖος (Eichhorn, § 209); but no details are known about it.

The *Versio Veneta s. St. Marci* belongs to a much later date; it now exists in one codex only in the library of St. Mark at Venice.

Cf. De Wette, § 56; Eichhorn, § 211. It contains the Pentateuch (ed. Ammon, Erl. 1790–91, in 3 parts), also the three Books of Solomon, Ruth, Lamentations, and Daniel (ed. Villoison, Strasb., 1784). This codex is of about the fourteenth century, the composition of the translation is some centuries earlier; it presupposes our pointed text, and follows it exactly. The language shows an attempt at Attic elegance, but there are many barbarisms and solecisms mixed up in it. The translator was probably a Christian scholar, who obtained his knowledge of Hebrew from Jewish Rabbis.

§ 347.—*The Vulgate—Ancient Latin Translations.*

Just as in the Greek Church, the LXX has constantly been held in authority as the authentic translation of the Old Testament; so also in the Latin and the entire Roman Catholic Church generally, the Latin translation, or the VULGATE,[1] has held the same rank.

This translation is also in general made directly from the Hebrew text, but not every portion of it, and not in an absolutely independent way. This is shown by the history of this translation, for which we must go back to that of the *earlier* Latin translations. As in the other districts of the Church, so also in the West, the Old Testament was at first read in Greek from the LXX, and when the need was felt of possessing the former in the Latin language, it was translated from the LXX. How early, by whom, and in what part of the West this was first done we have no accounts to tell us, just the same as regards the Latin translation of the New Testament. But it may be assumed that the Scriptures of the Old Testament in general were translated into Latin at the same time as those of the New Testament, and that at the time of Tertullian there was such a Latin translation of the Bible, which was in common use, at least in his district.[2] Subsequently, after the middle of the fourth, and about the beginning of the fifth century,

[1] Cf. O. F. Fritzsche's article " *Vulgata* " in Herzog's *Encyclop.*, and the first volume of Car. Vercellone's *Variæ Lectiones Vulgatæ Latinæ Bibliorum editionis.* Rome, 1860.

[2] As regards the New Testament, this follows from Tertull. *De Monogamia*, c. 11 : Sciamus, plane non sic esse in *Græco authentico*, quomodo in usum exiit per duarum syllabarum aut callidam aut simplicem *eversionem* (*i.e.* wrong translation): " si autem dormierit vir ejus ' (1 Cor. vii. 39), quasi de futuro sonet.

several such Latin translations are spoken of, both of the New and also of the Old Testament, in distinct statements of Hilarius Pictaviensis[1] and of Augustine particularly. The latter goes so far as to speak decidedly of a plurality of Latin translations;[2] and the same may be inferred from the language of Jerome.[3] We may, therefore, of course, assume that when Jerome elsewhere (*Præf. in Jos. et Præf. in Evangg.*) says, that in the Latin there were "*tot exemplaria, quot codices,*" he, by the term *exemplaria*, does not intend merely various forms of one and the same translation arising from corruption, but (also) various translations, and that Augustine's meaning is the same in the term *codices*, when he (*Ep.* 71, *ad Hieron.*) speaks of the multiplicity of the Latin text "*in diversis codicibus.*" But, on the other hand, we see from a comparison of the portions that have been preserved of these ancient Latin translations, that they were not actually different translations, entirely independent of one another, but only different forms of one and the same translation, which probably had been originally made in proconsular Africa, in Latin of a rude and barbarous character, but subsequently in other countries experienced various revisions which prevailed in their respective regions,[4]

[1] *E.g.* in Ps. liv: Hymnos *aliqui translatores nostri* carmina nuncuparunt, *plerique* autem Hymnos ex ipsa Græcitatis usurpatione posuerunt.

[2] *De doctr. Christiana*, ii. 11: Qui enim scripturas ex Hebræa lingua in Græcum verterunt, numerari possunt, Latini autem interpretes nullo modo; ut enim cuique primis fidei temporibus in manus venit codex Græcus et aliquantulum facultatis sibi utriusque linguæ habere videbatur, ausus est interpretari.—*Ib.* at the beginning of the chapter: ut ad exemplaria præcedentia recurratur (viz. to the Hebrew and Greek original text), si quam dubitationem attulerit *Latinorum interpretum infinita varietas.*—*Ib.* c. 12: nonnullas obscuriores sententias plurium codicum sæpe manifestavit inspectio, sicut illud Isaiæ prophetæ (ch. lviii. 7) *unus* interpres ait . . . *alius* autem ait . . . uterque sibimet invicem adtestantur . . . nunc collato *interpretum* sensu, &c. . . . Difficile est enim, ita diversos a se interpretes fieri, ut non se aliqua vicinitate contingant.—*Ib.* c. 13. c. 14: Plurimum hic quoque *juvat interpretum numerositas* collatis codicibus inspecta atque discussa, &c.—*Ep.* 71, *ad Hieron.*, ed Ben.

[3] Particularly, *Ep.* 140, *ad Principiam* (on Ps. xlv. 9): Pro eo, quod nos transtulimus "domibus eburneis," . . . *quidam Latinorum* ob verbi ambiguitatem "a gravibus" interpretati sunt.

[4] Augustin. *c. Faust.* xi. 2: Itaque si de fide exemplarium quæstio verteretur, sicut in nonnullis, quæ et paucæ sunt et sacrarum literarum studiosis notissimæ sententiarum varietates: vel ex aliarum regionum

and would be perhaps looked upon as different translations.[1]

Among these ancient Latin translations there is one which Augustine calls the *Itala*, and peculiarly recommends as the most faithful, the most literal, and at the same time the clearest.[2] The name *Itala* refers perhaps to the fact that this translation was common in Italy, especially in Upper Italy, where probably it was formed.

In this the language was polished and made more elegant than in the original African shape, and the translation was also perhaps emended by collation with Greek manuscripts. Augustine doubtless became acquainted with this Italian form of the Latin Bible, as compared with the African, during his stay in Rome and Milan, and learnt to appreciate its superiority, and perhaps also brought it to the attention of other Latin Christians in his home in Africa.

All that has been preserved of the ancient ante-Hieronymian Latin translations of the LXX is very often embraced under the name *Itala*. This is inaccurate if we look at the use of the word by Augustine; and besides this, the name does not occur in the ancients. It cannot, however, be decided as regards what has been preserved of the ante-Hieronymian translations, what portion belongs to the Itala, and what portion to the other forms of the translation.

The fragments of these translations have been most completely collected by the Benedictine, Peter Sabatier, from the quotations of ancient Latin Church-authors: *Bibliorum s. Latinæ versiones antiquæ, seu vetus Italica et ceteræ quæcunque in codd. MSS. et antiquorum libris reperiri potuerunt, &c.*,

---

codicibus, unde ipsa doctrina commeavit, nostra dubitatio dijudicaretur, vel si ibi quoque codices variarent, plures paucioribus aut vetustiores recentioribus præferrentur, et si adhuc esset incerta varietas, præcedens lingua, unde illud interpretatum est, consuleretur.

[1] For details as to this doubtful point, *vide* "Introduction to the New Testament," p. 739, ff. Cf. *Theol. Stud. und Krit.* 1858, iii. p. 560.

[2] *De Doctr. Christ.* ii. 15: "In ipsis autem interpretationibus Itala ceteris præferatur, nam est verborum tenacior cum perspicuitate sententiæ." Without any adequate reason the text here has been considered incorrect, and various conjectures have been made about it. Reuss' *Geschichte d. N. T.* § 452) supposition that Augustine intended to refer to Jerome's improved translation from the Hexapla can hardly be regarded as correct.

Rheims, 1743, 3 vols. fol. ed. Auct. 1749–51. The two first volumes contain the fragments of the Old-Testament Books. But in a critical point of view there is much left to be wished for in this collection. Thus there are many passages quoted from Jerome's works, which most probably in this shape did not form a part of the ancient translation, but had been emended by Jerome in citing them (v. Ranke, in the work quoted below, i. p. 9, ff.). On the other hand, there is much that may be added from works of ancient Latin authors which were subsequently published, viz. by Mai (v. Ranke, p. 5). A very valuable contribution to the knowledge of these ancient translations has been made by Ernst Ranke (in Marburg): *Fragmenta versionis s. Script. ante-Hieronymianæ e codice Mscr. Fuldensi eruit atque adnotatt. criticis instruxit.* Marburg, 1860 (from Hosea, Amos, Micah, &c.; v. *Theol. Stud. u. Krit.* 1856, ii. 1858).

All the various forms of this ancient Latin translation appear throughout to have been made from the ante-hexaplar text, and follow it pretty closely; they are therefore a useful assistance in the criticism of the LXX for the restoration of the above ante-hexaplar text.

§ 348.—*Jerome's Latin Translation.*

The Western Church could hardly fail to become more and more conscious of the defectiveness of this ancient translation, and of the need for an improvement of it; this need Jerome sought in several ways to supply.

(a) Firstly, in his sojourn at Rome about 382 A.D., where he also prepared a new Latin translation of the New Testament, he revised—perhaps prompted by the Romish Bishop Damasus—the Latin translation of the Psalms, doubtless the one which was in use in Rome, therefore perhaps the Itala of Augustine. This he revised from the LXX, but, as he himself says (*Præf. ad edit. poster. Pss.*), only *cursim*. This edition is called *Psalterium Romanum*, as it came into use in the Church at Rome, and retained its authority there down to the time of Pope Pius V. (c. 1566).

(b) This emended edition, however, very soon after its appearance, again became corrupted in transcribing, especially by the re-admission of the old readings. But some years afterwards, when Jerome, after the death of Damasus (384 A.D.), was staying at Bethlehem, he undertook with still increased care, a new revision of the Latin Psalter. This he did in the hexaplar manner, revising the Latin translation from the hexaplar edition of the LXX. sometimes also making it afresh, and adopting the critical signs of Origen, so that he showed the relations of the Latin translation to the original Hebrew text. This edition is called the *Psalterium Gallicanum*, as it found acceptance in the Gallican Church. He then, in a similar way, revised the other Books of the Old Testament. From an intimation in *Ep.* 94, *ad Augustin.*, much of this work appears to have been lost by faithlessness (*fraude*); and besides the *Psalter*, none of it except *Job*, the *three Books of Solomon*, and the Chronicles, came into the hands of the public.

Of this work, only the Psalter and Job have been printed. Both together with the *Psalterium Romanum* are included with other things in the first volume of Jerome's works by Martianay. As a whole, this revision met with much approval. Rufinus, indeed, among other accusations, charged Jerome with preferring the hexaplar to the usual text. But Augustine so much valued this edition, that from it he made his Commentary on Job, and about 403 A.D. he expressed the wish that Jerome would, in a similar way, revise the other books as well.

(c) Of more abiding influence in future times was Jerome's own translation of the Books of the Old Testament,[1] which he made direct from the Hebrew. To this he was prompted by various friends, such as the Bishop Chromatius, Sophronius, and others, who, in their disputations with the Jews, were often embarrassed by not knowing what the Hebrew text of these books contained, and what it did not contain.

Cf. *Præff. in Pent.*, *in Paralip. ad Chromat.*, *in Esdr. et Neem.*, *in Tobiam*, *in Jes.*, *Ep.* 134, *ad Sophron.*, &c.

He did not translate the whole of the Old Testament in successive order, but took the several books as he was

---

[1] A critical edition of it does not up to the present time exist; as to the most important manuscript, the *Codex Amiatinus*, from which the Old Testament is not yet made public, cf. my communications in the second appendix to the Explanation of Deuteronomy xxxii. p. 371, ff.

specially prompted by the request of this or that friend; first the four Books of Kings; next the Greater and Lesser Prophets; then—at the request of Sophronius—the Psalms; then the three Books of Solomon; after these Ezra and Nehemiah; Job, 393 A.D.; the Pentateuch about 405 A.D.; and immediately afterwards, Joshua, Ruth, Judges, Chronicles, besides Tobit and Judith from the Chaldee. In doing the latter he caused the Book of Tobit to be read out to him into Hebrew by learned Hebrews, whose help he made use of, and then translated this into Latin and dictated it to a transcriber, all in one day. Judith, however, he translated himself; lastly Daniel, Esther, and Jeremiah.

As Jerome received his instruction in Hebrew from Jewish scribes of Palestine, and often made use of their advice in his interpretations of the Old Testament, his comprehension of the original and his translation of it, as already remarked (p. 112), naturally very much follow the interpretations accepted in the schools of these Jewish scholars, and therefore often agree both in general and in detail with the explanations of the later Rabbis, as also with our Masoretic text in respect to the placing of vowels, the interpunctuation, and the divisions. Added to this, neither is it too free and paraphrastic, and too much addicted to arbitrary renderings; nor, on the other hand, is it too slavishly literal, like that of Aquila; so that it was in general well fitted to be made use of as an ecclesiastical translation. But in some of the books he has worked with too great haste, as, *e.g.*, according to his own avowal he dismissed the three Books of Solomon in three days.[1] Added to this, where the LXX does not differ too decidedly from the sense of the Hebrew text, he often follows this translation, or one of the other Greek versions, "ne novitate nimia lectoris studium deterrerem."[2] It might thus happen, that his translation did not permanently satisfy even himself, and he subsequently often speaks of it in his Commentary as incorrect, and emends it.[3]

[1] *Præf. in libros Salomon.* Cf. *Proœm. in L.* iii. *Comm. in Amos*: post gravissimam corporis ægrotationem dictandi celeritate ostendi temeritatem meam, &c.
[2] *Præf. Comm. in Eccles.*
[3] Cf. Hody, p. 361, f.; L. v. Ess, *Gesch. d. Vulg.* 1824, p. 130, f.

The Vulgate. 437

349.—*Acceptance of Jerome's Translation as the Vulgate.*

In the Western Church, however, this new translation at first experienced considerable opposition, as an innovation. Rufinus assailed it the most vehemently; among other things, the name Barhanina, that of Jerome's Jewish teacher, was perverted by him into Barabbas; also, because Jerome had allowed himself to be guided by this teacher (in opposition to the LXX), he was compared to the the Jews, who preferred Barabbas to Christ. Cf. de Wette, § 69, note *d*; § 70, note *a*; v. Ess, *Gesch. d. Vulg.* p. 114, ff. Even Augustine himself blamed him at first, because by his labours he had brought perplexity into the Church where they were accustomed to the LXX and the Latin translations corresponding to it, and wished that Jerome had in preference completed his revision of the Latin translation, according to the hexaplar text.[1] Subsequently, however, Augustine repeatedly acknowledged the superiority of Jerome's translation, and often made use of it.[2] It found still greater approval from some learned friends of Jerome, *e.g.*, from Sophronius, who therefrom translated the Psalms and Prophets into Greek (*v.* above § 346 (*b*)).

Not until later, and by a gradual progress, did it meet with more general publicity, and application to ecclesiastical use.

At the end of the fifth century, in the Roman Church, it was used similarly to the ancient translations which had been made from the LXX. Gregory the Great (d. 604) testifies to this (*Præff. Moral. in Jobum*), in which he even says that he himself had learned it (*novam translationem* he still calls it) by heart, and made use of it together with the ancient one, sometimes the one, sometimes the other, "ut comprobationis causa exigit." Somewhat later (about 630), Isidorus Hispalensis (*De Offic. Eccl.* i. 12) assures us, that "omnes ecclesiæ usquequaque" availed themselves of

---

[1] Aug. *Epp. ad Hieron.* 28, 71, 82 (ed. Bened.); cf. *de Civ. D.* xviii. 43. Hieron. *ad Aug. Ep.* 89.
[2] *Ep.* 261, *ad Audacem.—De Doctr. Christ.* iv. 7 (Opp. iii. 92, B).— *Quæst. in Deut.* xx. 54; *in Jos.* vii. 15, 19, 24, 25; *in Jud.* xvi. 37, 47, 55.

this translation, as it was both more correct and clearer. After the seventh century, the Western Councils as a rule follow this translation; a few only still gave the preference to the LXX. The distinction between the two was more especially shown in the Biblical chronology. As the Church had previously been accustomed to reckon dates according to the LXX, in this respect the preference was still given to it by Julianus of Toledo (seventh century) (Hody, p. 405). But after this time some began to reckon according to the statements of Jerome's translation, which coincided with the Hebrew text, *e.g.*, the Venerable Bede, in his *De sex ætatibus mundi*, and in other works, calling this translation *nostra editio*.

From the seventh century downwards, this translation—the *Vulgate*—was and has since remained the one acknowledged by the Church of the West. An exception was, however, made as regards (*a*) the *Psalter*, and (*b*) *some of the Apocrypha*.

For the *Psalter*, the *Psalterium Gallicanum* (v. p. 435) remained in ecclesiastical use, and when the other portions of Jerome's new translation were adopted as the Vulgate, was accepted into the latter (doubtless because the Psalter was so much in every-day use among the people, that a new edition of this could not have been introduced for ecclesiastical purposes without giving great offence). Those books of the Apocrypha which Jerome had not translated from the Hebrew or Chaldee, were also retained in the form of the old translation.

Thus the Vulgate still contains: (*a*) the Books of Baruch, Sirach, Wisdom, the 1st and 2nd Maccabees, all according to the ante-Hieronymian translation; (*b*) the Psalms according to the *Psalterium Gallicanum*; (*c*) the remainder of the Books of the Old Testament according to Jerome's own translation. But in the Middle Ages the various elements of this translation experienced many kinds of alterations, sometimes by the negligence of transcribers, sometimes intentionally. This was particularly the case with the new portions by Jerome, by their becoming mixed up and blended with the old translation in those passages which had been employed for liturgical uses, and were still found in the liturgies in the old form. This, therefore, gave rise to many attempts at critical emendation in the Middle Ages. As to these, and also as to the history of the printed text of the Vulgate, in which both the Old and New Testaments had the same fortune, *v.* " Introduction to the New Testament," p. 745, ff. As to the various old translations which were made from the Vulgate into the native languages of those countries of the Roman Catholic Church where they were not learned in the Latin language, viz., into the *Anglo-Saxon, Arabic,* and *Persian, v.* De Wette, §§ 73, 74. [Cf. Smith's *Dict. of the Bible,* Art. " *Vulgate.*"]

§ 350.—*Chaldee Paraphrases or Targums.*

Both before and after Christ, among the Hellenistic Jews, and sometimes even among those of Palestine, the LXX was in general use. Among the Jews subsequently the same position was filled by the *Chaldee* translations[1] or *paraphrases* of the Old Testament, principally called Targums (תַּרְגּוּמִים), *i.e.,* interpretations, from תִּרְגֵּם. These are translations or transcriptions of the Books of the Old Testament from the ancient original Hebrew into the language which, both before and after the birth of Christ, was the actual vulgar tongue of the country, among the Jews in Palestine and Babylon. We possess Targumim of this sort on all the Books of the Old Testament, with the exception of Daniel, Ezra, and Nehemiah; there are two or three different ones on the Pentateuch and the Book of Esther. By the later Jews they were applied to ecclesiastical use. The historical accounts as to the *origin* of these Targumim are, for the most part, very uncertain.

The later Jews entertain to some extent similar ideas about them as about the origin of the Talmud, that these interpretations were revealed to Moses on Mount Sinai, and were then orally handed down to the time of their record in writing. The written composition of these Targumim has been often placed at the time of the Babylonian Captivity, or just afterwards, and it is sometimes assumed that they had then already been used publicly, and had received ecclesiastical authority. But this is hardly correct. It may be, of course, assumed that, a considerable period before

---

[1] Cf. Volck's article " *Thargumim* " in *Herzog's Encyclop.,* and Abr. Geiger, *Urschrift und Uebersetzungen der Bibel in ihrer Abhängigkeit von der inneren Entwickelung des Judenthums.* Breslau, 1857.

Christ, it was not unusual in Palestine, and especially in Babylonia, to explain the Sacred Books in the synagogue in the Chaldee language of the country. But we must make an absolute distinction between this procedure and the production and reading out of written translations in this language. Such translations may have been prepared as a private work without attaining to public use and authority, which, even in the first century after Christ, had probably not been the case with any of them; for otherwise it would be difficult to conceive how the LXX at that time, even in Palestine, could have attained such authority and circulation among the Jews as we have seen to have been the case; and, also, how it happens that we find absolutely no mention or trace of these Targumim either in Josephus, the Church-authors, or even in the Mishna. Hävernick (§ 79) is of opinion that the Mishna, in tr. *Jadaim*, c. 4, § 5, quotes written Targumim : but this is a mistaken view of the passage.

The first express mention of written Targumim—and they are partly, indeed, those now extant—is found in the Babylonian Gemara. The accounts given here are sometimes quite contradictory, or of a very fabulous nature, and show that the Talmudists themselves were not acquainted with anything authentic as to their origin and as to the historical circumstances of their authors; but, on the other hand, they also show that the date of their composition must have preceded the age of the Talmudists by some considerable period.

At all events, the most ancient of the Targumim now extant are that of *Onkelos* on the Pentateuch, and that of *Jonathan, Son of Uziel*, on the *Prophetæ Priores et Posteriores*. These two enjoyed the highest authority among the later Jews, particularly the former, on which there is a Masora peculiar to itself, as on the Hebrew Bible = *Masoreth hat-targum*. Both are first mentioned expressly in the Babylonian Talmud, therefore not before the fifth to sixth century after Christ. Firstly, now, as regards *Onkelos*, from the nature of the language relating to him, the only thing that can be decided about him is, that the Babylonian Talmudists were not acquainted with anything at all definite as to his personality from authentic tradition, which proves that his Targum had then been extant for a long time, but for how long, even from the contents of the Targum, cannot be ascertained with any degree of certainty and accuracy.

In the Babylonian Talmud the same things or something quite similar are told of Onkelos, who is called the son of Kalonymus, as previously the Jerusalem Talmud had stated of Aquila (עקילס), viz., that he was a proselyte, a nephew of Titus, and had translated under the direction of Eliezer and Joshua (v. in De Wette, § 58, note a); so that we may easily perceive that, owing to the similarity in name, there has been a confusion between Onkelos and the above Greek translator. Thus, therefore, the accounts relating to him in the Talmud naturally lose all their significance, and other statements also both of the Talmud and some later Jewish authors are not very authentic.

Gfrörer (*Das Jahrhundert des Heils*, i. [1838], p. 55, f.), and following him Ebrard (*Kritik der Evang. Gesch.* p. 855, f.; 2nd ed. p. 659, f.), conclude from the paraphrase of Gen. xlix. 27; Num. xxiv. 9; Deut. xxxiii. 18, f., that Onkelos' Targum must have been written before the destruction of Jerusalem by the Romans. It is, perhaps, possible that it may be thus proved from these passages, but I think not (cf. under p. 442). At all events, however, it did not attain ecclesiastical authority until a considerably later time.

Compared with the other Targums, Onkelos is distinguished by his great fidelity and simplicity, although he does not always confine himself strictly to the translation of the Hebrew text, but often acts as a paraphraser and interpreter.

As to his character in a critical and exegetical point of view, v. Winer (*De Onkeloso ejusque paraphrasi Chaldaica*. Leipzig, 1820).

His language also is comparatively pretty pure, and very little mixed up with foreign non-Semitic words. He is usually considered to have been a Babylonian, but Winer, on the contrary, takes him to have been an inhabitant of Palestine. No decisive reasons can be brought forward for either opinion.

The Targum of *Jonathan, the Son of Uziel*, is mentioned in the Babylonian Talmud (*Megilla*, fol. iii. 1) with the highest respect, so that we can perceive that it must then have attained to considerable authority; and Jonathan himself, son of Uziel, is named (*Baba Bathra*, fol. 134, 1) as the most eminent scholar of Hillel the elder (grandfather of Gamaliel). This may be correct. By several passages—such as, particularly, 1 Sam. ii; Jer. ii. 3; Ezek. xxxvi. 38; Hab. iii. 17—we are led to a date before the destruction of Jerusalem by the Romans, by the latter passage to a time when the Jews were compelled to pay tribute (*censum*) to the Romans, when, therefore, Judæa was a Roman province; but by Is. xxxii. 14; liii. 4, not improbably to a time after the Temple was destroyed. Thus Jonathan, if the Targum on all the Nebiim belongs to him, which there is no reason to doubt,[1] must have lived both shortly before and shortly after the destruction of Jerusalem; therefore, in the latter passage, something must have been subsequently interpolated into the text, if the composition of the whole Targum took place before the above catastrophe.

Joh. Morinus (*Exercit. Bibl.* p. 321) and Is. Vossius (*de LXX interpr.* c. 28) are decidedly wrong in placing him in the seventh to eighth century after Christ. It is also certainly wrong to place him, with others, in the second to fourth century. Gfrörer (*ut supra*, p. 39, ff.) has endeavoured to prove that he flourished in the first part of the reign of Herod the Great, before the destruction of the Temple. This is probably too early a date.

All this also serves to point out the age of *Onkelos*, for in several passages[2] Jonathan agrees so much with Onkelos that the dependence of one on the other cannot be doubted, and there is indeed preponderating probability that Jonathan, and not Onkelos, as Hävernick thinks, is the dependent one: in which case, then, the age of Onkelos must be fixed a little earlier, which also *per se* is the most probable.

In the historical books Jonathan acts more as a paraphrastic interpreter than Onkelos does, and in the really prophetical books this is the case to a still greater extent.

This same Jonathan is also named—only, however, by later authors (*v.* in De Wette, § 60, note *a*)—as the composer of a Targum on the *Pentateuch* still extant. But this

[1] As to this, *vide* Gesenius, *Isaiah*, i. 69, ff., Hävernick, *Einl.* § 80.
[2] Cf. Targ. Deut. xxii. 5 with Judges v. 26; Deut. xxiv. 16 with 2 Kings xiv. 6; Num. xxi. 28 with Jer. xlviii. 45, f.

can neither have been written by him nor in his age. It cannot well have been composed before the seventh century after Christ, and is distinctively only of value as affording a source of knowledge as to the ideas of Jewish scholars at that time.

In this the Mishna, Constantinople, Lombardy, and the Turks are mentioned; and the language is intersprinkled with Latin, Greek, and Persian words. It cannot be looked upon at all as a translation of the Hebrew text, but is an interpretation of it according to the acceptation of later Judaism, joined with most fanciful legends and other additions.

Together with this, there is in the Bombergo-rabbinical Bible, and also in the London Polyglot, another Targum— that, *of Jerusalem,* יְרוּשַׁלְמִי; but it only exists in fragmentary interpretation of single passages of the Pentateuch; these often agree literally with the Pseudo-Jonathan Targum, and modern investigations[1] have shown that the two are really identical, only in a somewhat different Recension; the above later Targum ascribed to Jonathan being entitled by the elders the *Targum of Jerusalem.*

As to the various Targumim of most of the *Hagiographa, v.* De Wette, § 62. [Volck, *ut supra,* p 682, f.]

I will only remark that the Targum on *Solomon's Proverbs* not only presents a great affinity to the old Syriac translation and appears to have made use of it, but also the language in it in a grammatical point of view has many peculiarities of the Syriac. [Cf. Smith's *Dict. of the Bible,* Art. "*Targum.*"]

§ 351.—*The Peshito—Its Origin and Character.*

This *Syriac translation* embracing both the Old and New Testament, bears the name of THE PESHITO,[2] *i.e. simplex, simple, literal, faithful.* It did not, perhaps, receive the name until a later time. It refers to its character, inasmuch as it simply gives the text of the Sacred Books in Syriac, without paraphrastic or allegorical interpretations. There are no authentic historical accounts as

[1] Zunz, *Gottesdienstl. Vortr. d. Juden.* 1832, pp. 66–72.
[2] Cf. Arnold's article on the "*Peschittho.*" in Herzog's *Encyclop.* xv. pp. 398–404. [Smith's *Dict. of the Bible,* "*Ancient Versions* (Syriac)."

to its origin. We find it first used by Ephraem Syrus (d. 378), who calls it *our* translation; in whose time, also, as it appears, it was already generally received as an ecclesiastical translation among the Syriac Christians.

Later Syrian authors make out that it was produced in the Apostolic age at the instigation of the Apostle Addai (Thaddeus), and King Abgarus of Edessa, and others state that a part of it was translated in the time of Solomon, for Hiram King of Tyre. Both statements, however, must be considered as unhistorical legends.

In ascertaining its origin we must chiefly have recourse to conjectures, arising from its internal nature. But it may be assumed with the greatest probability, that it is entirely the work of Syrian Christians, and not of Jewish scribes,[1] and was produced in behalf of the Syrian Christians at Edessa and its neighbourhood, generally at the same time as the Syriac translation of the New Testament; and, as regards the Old Testament, immediately from the Hebrew.

Its Christian origin is evident from its Messianic interpretation of many passages, as well as from other circumstances (cf. Gesenius, *Isaiah*, i. 85, f.; Hävernick, *Einl.* § 83), and also from its early and general use in the Syrian Church. The conclusion that the translation resulted directly from the Hebrew, as presupposed by Ephraem Syrus (*on Josh.* xv. 28), is favoured by the circumstance that it only embraces the elements of the Hebrew Canon. The Syriac translation of the Apocrypha is of later origin, and the apocryphal additions in the LXX to the Book of Daniel were also wanting in the Peshito at the time of Ephraem Syrus and Polychronius (about 410 after Christ). Added to this, the whole nature of the translation itself, and the faithful way in which, as a whole, it follows the original text, leave no room for doubt that it was prepared immediately from the latter.

But however faithfully the Peshito has in general followed the Hebrew text, still, in the form in which we know it, it presents certain points of agreement with the LXX in not a few passages; this agreement is doubtless to be ascribed to the influence of the latter, and, from the great authority

---

[1] Thus R. Simon and many moderns, as Frankel, Rapoport, Grätz, lastly Jos. Perles, *Meletemata Peschitthoniana*. Breslau, 1859.

Origin of the Peshito.

which the LXX possessed in the Christian Church—even the Syrian—is very easy to be understood. It is, indeed, not improbable, that much matter of this kind has got in by means of later interpolations; but I do not believe that all of it can be referred to this cause, and think that the LXX assisted in the first preparation of the Syriac translation. Gesenius endeavours (*Isaiah*, i. p. 83, f.), to show that, as regards the Nebiim, a use has also been made of the Targum of Jonathan, which is not improbable, as this Targum was, no doubt, extant before the Peshito, and there is a great affinity between the two idioms,—the Chaldee and the Syriac; but this use of the Targum can only have been of influence in the comprehension and rendering of single passages, and not on the character of the whole work.

Whether the translation of the Old Testament is the work of *one* or of *several* translators, is not yet settled.

Ephraem Syrus, *ut supr.*, appears to presuppose the latter, and it may be assumed as very possible that the translation was not prepared piecemeal at different times, but in general at one time as a common work among the Syrian Christian community; in the same way with the translation of the New Testament. For at a very early date it received ecclesiastical authority in the Syrian Church, which it also maintained in the various parties into which this Church was subsequently divided.

It was printed first in the Paris and then in the London Polyglot, not, however, in a very reliable way. It was emended from the manuscripts in a more critical mode, and was limited to its original extent—the canonical elements of the Old Testament—in the edition edited by S. Lee, London, 1823, at the suggestion of the London Bible Society.

In consequence of the supplanting of the Syriac language by the *Arabic*, translations from the Peshito of the Biblical Books were subsequently made into the latter language.

Of this class are, among others, the Arabic translations in the Paris and London Polyglots, comprising Job, Chronicles, and as Rödiger (*de orig. et indole Arabicæ Librr. V. T. hist. interpr.* Halle, 1829) has asserted, the books also of Judges, Ruth, Samuel, 1 Kings i–xi; 2 Kings xii. 17–xxv, and Neh. ix. 28–xiii; cf. de Wette, § 65.

§ 352.—*Other Syriac Versions.*

But in consequence of its wide-spread circulation, and the great authority which the LXX continued to possess in the Greek and almost the entire Eastern Church, subsequently, as already remarked (§ 341), Syriac translations of the Books of the Old Testament were made from the former version: these translations never attained to actual ecclesiastical authority among the Syrian Christians, but still were sometimes made use of in addition to the Peshito.[1] About *one* only of these are we acquainted with any details; this also was perhaps the only one which—together with the Peshito—met with any publicity in the Syrian Church. It is made from the hexaplar text of the LXX, and follows it in a servilely literal way, committing grievous offences against Syriac grammar and linguistic usages; it has the critical marks of Origen, without however mentioning in the text the names of those from whom the various additions have been adopted, and is provided on the margin with readings, fragments from other Greek translations, and exegetical Scholia. It is the work of the Bishop Paul of Tela, who made it in 617 A.D., at the suggestion of Athanasius, a monophysite bishop. This, at least, is the account given of it in the postscript of a codex of this translation, existing at Paris, containing, however, only the fourth Book of Kings. Another manuscript, in the Ambrosian Library at Milan, contains the prophetical and poetical books. From this, Norberg has published Jeremiah and Ezekiel (Lund. 1787), and Cajetan Bugati, Daniel (Milan, 1788), and the Psalms (1820); the remaining contents of both codices have been published by H. Middeldorpf (d. 1861); *Codex Syriaco-Hexaplaris, Lib.* 4, *Regum e cod. Paris, Isaiah,* 12 *Proph. Minor., Prov., Job, Cant., Threni, Eccles. e cod. Mediolano.* Berlin, 1834–35, 2 vols., the first of which contains the text, the second Middeldorpf's Commentary. This translation is of very great importance in the criticism of the hexaplar text of the LXX. Besides these two manuscripts, there was formerly a *third,* possessed by Andr. Masius, which contained most of the historical books, viz.:—Judges, Kings, Chronicles, Ezra, Esther, Judith, and part of Tobit and Deuteronomy; *v.* Masius' *Josuæ imperat.*

[1] Cf. de Wette, § 49; Eichhorn, §§ 259–274; Hävernick, § 76.

hist. illustr. atque explic. Antw. 1574, fol. *Ep. dedic.* p. 6. Masius has from this given the Book of Joshua in a Latin translation; but the manuscript itself has disappeared.[1]

This Syriac hexaplar translation is most probably the same which is spoken of by the Syrian author *Abulfaradsch* or *Bar Hebräus* (in the thirteenth century), when he says, that the Western Syrians were in possession of another Syriac translation besides the Peshito, and that this had been made from the LXX. *V.* De Wette, § 49, note *a*. Pococke has so translated the passage, that this translation is designated as *figurata*, in contrast to the Peshito as *simplex*, and this name *figurata* has become customary with us. Bertholdt renders it *bene formata, egregie condita*, in contrast to a merely simple, faithful translation. But according to a conjecture of De Sacy, which has been subsequently confirmed by documentary evidence, this translation is simply styled by Bar Hebräus *the one named from the LXX.*

In two manuscripts in the Paris Library, there are Græco-Syriac translations, in the one of the *Pentateuch*, in the other (the same which contains the fourth Book of Kings from Paul of Tela's translation) of the Book of *Daniel;* according to similar statements in the postscripts, Jacob, Bishop of Edessa, is pointed out as the person who (703 and 704 after Christ) arranged them from the two translations,—from that of the Greeks (LXX), and that of the Syrians (Peshito). What relation this bore to the translation of Paul of Tela, is not with certainty ascertained, but most probably it is only a new Recension of it, in which the latter is emended from the Peshito.

V. de Wette, § 49, 2, and the works quoted there, note *h*, and particularly Herbst, *Introd.* i. 203, f.

§ 353.—*Arabic Translations from the Hebrew Text.*

We have already briefly touched upon several *Arabic translations*, one of the Pentateuch composed by a Samaritan

[1] Lately Thomas Skat Rordam has made public of Paul of Tela's translation: *Libri Judicum et Ruth sec. vers. Syr. = Hex. &c. editi, Græce translati [restituti] notisque illustrati.* Fasc. i. Copenh. 1859. Fasc. ii. 1861; from a manuscript from the Nitrian desert, which has been for some time in the British Museum. There are in the British Museum the Books of Exodus, Numbers, Deuteronomy, 1 Samuel, and a part of Genesis.

(§ 336), others composed by Christians (§§ 341, 349, 351), but these were only *indirect* translations. There are, however, *direct* Arabic translations composed by Jews, in the age when, in consequence of the rule of the Mahometans, the Arabic language spread over the countries in which Jewish erudition had its seat, and was adopted by the Jewish scholars as their written language, to the exclusion of the Chaldee. The Arabic translations made by these Jewish scholars were produced immediately from the Hebrew text, at a time when the latter was completely provided with vowels and accents, and the interpretation intimated by the latter is followed, not, however, in a perfectly strict and timid way.

Among these Jewish translators into Arabic, the only one known by name is Saadia Gaon, d. 942 (cf. § 46, A). From statements in manuscripts, he probably translated the entire Old Testament, only a part of which is preserved and printed. His translation manifests considerable linguistic knowledge, and is very useful in the interpretation of the Scriptures it refers to. It is indeed often not strictly literal, and often paraphrastic and explanatory, after the manner of the Targums; but to a less extent than most of the latter.

For further detail as to its character, *vide* in Gesenius, *Isaiah*, i. pp. 88–96.

There has been printed of it: (*a*) The *Pentateuch*, first at Constantinople, in Hebrew writing (1516), then with Arabic characters in the Paris and London Polyglot. There is a codex of the Pentateuch in the Bibliotheca at Wolfenbüttel, in the Arabic character, the text of which differs very much from that of the London Polyglot. (*b*) *Isaiah*, in a manuscript at the Bodleian Library, written 1244 after Christ, in Hebrew characters. Isaiah has up to the present time been published by Paulus only (2 vols. Jena, 1790–91); he has re-written the Hebrew character in Arabic, but frequently incorrectly, especially at the beginning, so that a new edition is much to be desired. Another codex of Isaiah came into the possession of the Jewish scholar, Rapoport.

There are, besides, existing in manuscript, (*c*) *Job*, in a codex in the Bodleian Library, which Gesenius copied and often made use of in his *Thesaurus* [Ewald has given extracts in the first volume of his *Beiträge*]. (*d*) The *Minor Prophets*, likewise at Oxford. (*e*) *The Psalms*, in two manuscripts at Oxford, and in one at Munich; some portions of the latter have been published by Schnurrer, and subsequently by Ewald.

The following direct translations from the Hebrew, have also been printed:

(1) A translation of the Pentateuch, edited by Van Erpen (L. B. 1622), *Arabs Erpenii*, from a codex at Leyden, written in the Rabbinical character, which Erpenius converted into the Arabic writing. The translation appears to have been made by some African Jew of a late date; it keeps strictly to the Masoretic text, and is on the whole very literal.

(2) The translation of the Book of Joshua, printed in the Paris and London Polyglot, which is made by a Jew immediately from the Hebrew text. The same thing is said by Em. Rödiger (*De origine et indole Arabicæ librorum Vet. Test. historicorum interpretationis*. Halle, 1829), to have been the case with a portion of the translations in the Polyglot: (*a*) The Books of Kings (1 Kings ch. xii-2 Kings ch. xii. 16, according to Rödiger, translated by a Jew of the eleventh century), and (*b*) Nehemiah (ch. i-ix. 27), this latter, however, in his opinion was altered from the Peshito by some Christian of a later date.

§ 354.—*Persian Translations from the Hebrew Text.*

As to the direct *Persian translation* of the Pentateuch, printed in the London Polyglot, made by Jacob, a Jew, son of Joseph Tawus, according to others of Joseph of (the Persian city) Tus, at the earliest in the ninth century, *v.* De Wette, § 68; Rosenmüller, *De vers. Pentat. Pers.* Leipzig, 1813 [and Munk, *Notice sur Saadia Gaon*, pp. 62-87, according to which Jacob Tawus made use of Kimchi]. The translator keeps strictly to the Masoretic text, and expresses it with pretty literal exactness. In earlier times, however, there appears to have been a Persian translation of the Pentateuch, or of the Old Testament generally; we gather this from intimations of Chrysostom, Theodoret, the Talmud, and Moses Maimonides (*v.* Hävernick, § 86); we do not, however, know anything further about it.

450   *History of the Text of the Canon.*

§ 355.—*Our Hebrew Text the Basis of the Ancient Translations.*

I have considered it desirable, in this summary consideration of the ancient translations, to refer to their exegetical character, and their authority both in the Jewish and Christian Church. But as regards their importance as documentary evidences for the Hebrew text, certainly this is very much diminished by the nature even of the direct translations. In some cases, in consequence of the arbitrary and unliteral character of the version, in others through the uncertainty of their own texts, and through the occasionally important alterations, often scarcely to be discerned in details, which in the course of time they have experienced. These alterations have been chiefly made in the ecclesiastical translations. If due attention be paid to these circumstances, we shall not be justified in assuming that these translators, with the sole exception, and that but partial of the LXX, had before them as their basis any Hebrew text essentially different from that which we now possess in our manuscripts and editions; only that the more ancient of those translators read from a still unpointed text.

§ 356.—*Ancient Quotations from the Hebrew Text.*

The same result may likewise be derived from a consideration of the *quotations of ancient authors*, both Christian and Jewish, among whom naturally those only will claim our attention, who quote the Scriptures of the Old Testament from the Hebrew text itself, and not in the words of some other old translation. But on this point we must not fail to notice, that the most ancient authors who come under our attention, viz., the *authors of the New Testament*, although they may quote from the Hebrew text itself, yet most frequently quote it in an arbitrary way, and often pay more regard to the general sense than to the mere words. If we pay due attention to the above consideration, we are not compelled to infer from the quotations in the New Testament, those even in which the authors follow the Hebrew text in sense and differ from it only in words, that the text of the manuscripts of that time differed from those we now possess; from the nature of the quotations, and from the character of the deviations

Ancient Quotations.

from our present text, in no single case should we be justified in any such supposition. In later times, when the Jewish scribes began to attach an increasing importance even to the single words and letters of the Holy Scriptures, they became more accurate in their quotations and kept more strictly to the very words of it. This is, *e.g.* the case in the quotations in the *Mishna* and the *Talmud*. The Biblical quotations in these present, as compared with our text, so few variations, and these so unimportant in signification (cf. Eichhorn, §§ 339 *b*, 340), that they need, in fact, hardly be noticed; but, on the contrary, these quotations serve as a proof that the text of the Books of the Old Testament was at that time a settled and accepted one, and—with exception of the subsequently added pointing—almost entirely coincident with our present text.

§ 357.—*Proofs from the Talmud of the Care devoted to the Hebrew Text.*

We find, however, in the Talmud, and also in the text itself of the Old-Testament Books, data of various kinds which go clearly to prove with what anxious and even painful solicitude, care was taken to preserve and circulate the Hebrew text in an uncorrupted shape.

The Talmud gives express directions for writing manuscripts of the Bible. It permits indeed that manuscripts should be accepted which have been made by those who were not Jews, but requires that they must be made according to the prescribed rule (*tr. Gittim*, fol. 45, 2), and directs that peculiar care shall be taken in the writing, that one letter should not be confounded with another, that א should not be written instead of ע, and the reverse; that ב and כ, ג and צ, ר and ד, ה and ח, ו and י, ט and פ should not be confounded, or ן with נ, or ם with ס; that crooked letters should not be written instead of straight; that the *Mem* finale should not be placed instead of the customary letter, and the reverse; that an *open* Parashah should not be put for a *closed* one, and the reverse (*tr. Schabbath*, fol. 103, 2). Still more conclusive in favour of our assertion is the fact, that it was a practice to count not only the number of verses, but also that of the words, and even of the letters of the various books, in order to ascertain the middle verse, the middle word, and the middle letter of each book; cf. *tr. Kidduschim*, fol. 30, 1.[1] Investigations of this sort could not have been possible, unless the text be supposed to have been, as regards the consonants, fully and firmly settled.

These arduous investigations were indicated in the text by distinguishing certain letters in a peculiar way, by writing them in a peculiar mode, which has been handed down to our time in the manuscripts and editions. Cf. Buxtorf, *Tiberias*, i. c. 14–16. Thus in Levit. xi. 42, the ו is written and printed peculiarly large (and under the text " great Vau, this is the middle letter in the Pentateuch "). In Ps. lxxx. 14, however, the ע is removed away over the line, as a *litera suspensa* (under the text is " Ajin suspensum"). There are still in our manuscripts and editions several letters written in a similarly unusual way; thus there are perhaps some thirty *literæ majusculæ* (רַבָּתִי), and about as many *literæ minusculæ* (זְעֵירָא) ; twice a *litera suspensa* (תְּלוּיָה), viz., twice a ע and once a נ; and twice the *Nun inversum* (נוּן הֲפוּכָה). Some of these letters are expressly mentioned in the Talmud, *e.g.*, the *Nun suspensum*, Judg. xviii. 30, in *Baba Bathra*, fol. 109, 2 (De Wette, § 89, *fin.*) ; others in the Talmudical tract *Sopherim*, others in the Masora. In many cases we can no longer ascertain their original signification, which is differently stated by the later Jews; sometimes they serve to indicate certain cabalistic or allegorical ideas, to which attention was desired to be called ; *e.g.*, the ה, *minusculum*, Gen. ii. 4, is intended most probably to call attention to the idea, that, by means of the same letters the transposition of this ה with the א would produce the word בְּאַבְרָהָם, as an intimation that the world was created for the sake of Abraham the Father of the Faithful. By the *Nun inversum*, Num. x. 35, according to the opinion of the Jews, the wish is meant to be signified, which Moses had likewise expressed in his prayer, that the enemy might be driven back. It is certain that these exceptionally written letters did not proceed

---

[1] Idcirco vocati sunt prisci סופרים, quia numerarunt omnes literas Legis, dicentes; litera Vav vocis גחון (Levit. xi. 42), est media litera legis; דרש דרש, media vox legis; והתנלח (Levit. xiii. 33), medius versus in lege; יכרסמנה חזיר מיער (Ps. lxxx. 14), litera ע vocis יער, est media litera in Psalmis; רחום יכפר עון (Ps. lxxviii. 38), est medius versus in Psalmis.

from the authors of the Sacred Books, but from various scribes,—some of them before, and some after the date of the Talmud. They were afterwards retained by the copyists with the most careful conscientiousness, and circulated with the rest of the text of the book. It may sometimes have been the case, that this unusual mode of writing a letter may have arisen in a manuscript originally (from caligraphic reasons, or) by mere accident; but being retained by subsequent copyists, an attempt has afterwards been made to find out some peculiar signification for it.

The so-called *Puncta extraordinaria* took their rise, at least in part, in ancient times, before the Talmud. We find them in our manuscripts and editions, sometimes over whole words, *e.g.*, Ps. xxvii. 13, over (לולא), sometimes over single letters, *e.g.*, over the ו, in בקומה, Gen. xix. 33 (under the text: "A point over the Vau"). There are several notices of them not only in the Talmud,[1] but at least of one (Num. ix. 10) in the Mishna also (*tr. Pesach.* c. 9, § 2), and of one also in Jerome.[2] We find them now in the manuscripts and editions, as in the Masora, in fifteen passages, ten of which are in the Pentateuch, four in the Nebiim, and one in the above Psalm (*v.* Buxtorf, *Tiberias*, i. c. 17; Vogel, *ad Cappelli Crit. Sacra*, i. p. 455, ff.). Opinions differ as to their origin and real signification. The Jewish scribes find in them intimations of some mysterious references, to which they are intended to draw the attention of the reader, but they are very uncertain, and at variance with one another in the more detailed accounts of these references in the several passages, as *e.g.*, Jerome and the Talmud (*ut supra*) interpret this reference in the passage, Gen. xix. 33, in different ways. Most probably, however, they had—at least in most passages originally—a critical signification [cf. Ewald's *Lehrbuch*, § 19 *d*, Edit. 7], and were intended to intimate that the letters and words provided with these points would be more suitably omitted. Less probable is the opinion of Hüpeden (*Neue wahrsch. Muthmassung v. d. wahren Ursache u. Bedeut.*

[1] *E.g., tr. Nasir*, fol. 23, 1: Quare est punctatum supra literam ו in ובקומה de primogenita (Gen. xix. 33)? Ad indicandam, quod, cum decumberet, non cognoverit, et dum surgeret, noverit.

[2] *Quæst. ad Gen.* xix. 33: Appungunt desuper, quasi incredibile et quod rerum natura non capiat, coire quempiam nescientem.

d. ausserord. Punkte, &c., Hann. 1751), Vögel and others, who intimate that these letters and words were actually wanting in many manuscripts. This much can be gathered from the expressions of Jerome, the Mishna, and the Talmud,—that they must have met with these points, or at least several of them, as being in use from antiquity downwards; and if our opinion as to their original signification be correct, they serve as a clear proof of the anxious solicitude which must have been exercised in preceding centuries to hand down the text of the Sacred Books, especially of the Torah, in an uncorrupted state, as it was not considered right to erase even those letters and words which it was thought it would be more suitable to omit.

§ 358.—*The Keri and Ketib.*

We are led to the same conclusion by a consideration of the so-called *Keri*, in relation to the *Ketibs*, with which the writers of the Talmud were acquainted, at least in part. כְּתִיב, *i.e.*, *the written*, is the reading in the text, where there is in reference to it a marginal reading, which is called קְרִי, *i.e.*, *the read*. These names show that they are not to be considered as two different readings standing in the same line, which were, perhaps, met with in different manuscripts, and were both adopted, one in the text, the other in the margin. In later times, of course this may often have been done; when two readings of similar import were met with, between which a doubt might lie, *e.g.*, עיי״ם and עניים, they would place one of them in the margin, and might, perhaps, call it *Keri*. But originally, and in most cases, the matter stood in a decidedly different way, viz., that in cases where the actual reading in the text presented matter that was incorrect or of a peculiarly difficult nature, or something in the mode of expression that was held to be unbecoming or inelegant, by means of the marginal reading of the *Keri*, that phraseology was suggested in its stead which was considered more suitable to be read and uttered in reading; but, at the same time, the liberty was never taken of adopting it into the text itself by the erasure of the original reading. It is, therefore, easily to be understood, that in the subsequent pointing of the text the vowels were indeed placed under the reading in the text, but not so as to be suitable to it, but

The Keri and Ketib. 455

rather to the Keri, which, according to the views of the Jewish scribes, was to be read and uttered instead; whilst we, if we wish to read the actual text-reading, are compelled to shape our vocalization of it in a way corresponding to the construction of the word, for it is purely accidental if the vowels belonging to, and calculated for the Keri alone, are also suitable for the Ketib, as *e.g.*, in לֹא and לוֹ, and in similar cases.

The Keri, in its external relation to the Ketib, is of three kinds: (*a*) where it was desired that a word in the text should be omitted, because it was considered superfluous or unfit; this word was, therefore, provided with a circle above it, which refers to the marginal note: כְּתִיב וְלֹא קְרִי, or כְּ" וְלֹא ק". In pointed manuscripts and editions, a word of this kind is wanting in vocalization. Thus, *e.g.*, Ezek. xlviii. 16.

(*b*) In cases where it was desired that one or more words which were not in the text, should be read with it; there is then a small space left in the text, with the circle referring to the margin, in which the word or words are placed with the remark קְרִי וְלֹא כְתִיב, or ק" וְלֹא כ"; in the present pointed text the vowels belonging to the added words are placed in the vacant space in the text itself, and, although the addition should exercise influence on the vocalization of the surrounding words, this is made to correspond to it, but not in the way that would be requisite if the mere matter in the text were read; *e.g.*, 2 Sam. viii. 3, בִּנְהַר ; in the margin פרת קרי ולא כתיב. The reading of the text would have to be pointed, בַּנָּהָר. There is another example, Judg. xx. 13.

(*c*) In cases, where, in reading, a different word is to be spoken, instead of one existing in the text. This word is also provided with a circle over it referring to the margin, in which the substituted word is placed with קרי. In pointing the text, as before remarked, the vowels referring to the marginal reading are given to the word in the text. Keris of this kind are often placed instead of Ketibs: (*a*) where the text-reading presents something incorrect or abnormal in a grammatical point of view; the regular and habitual linguistic form being substituted for it. *E.g.*, Jer. xlii. 6, we find the construction אָנוּ = *we*; which occurs nowhere else, but is found in the Rabbinical language. For this, the Keri has substituted the usual form אֲנַחְנוּ, and those who subsequently added the points have applied the vowels belonging to the latter word to the text-reading, although they do not belong, and are in no way suitable, to it (אֲנוּ). Thus, in the twenty-two passages in the Pentateuch in which נַעַר stands for *puella*, the form which was afterwards in use for the feminine has been added as Keri (נַעֲרָה), and the former word is pointed in the text נַעֲרָ; *e.g.*, Gen. xxiv. 14. (β) In cases where the text-reading appeared to be somewhat unseemly or indelicate, some phrase considered more decent was annexed as Keri, and uttered in reading out. Thus, in the four passages where the verb שָׁגַל occurs, שָׁכַב is placed as Keri. Thus, also in Is. xxxvi. 12, and 2 Kings xviii. 27, for חֲרֵי, human excrement, the more general term צוֹאָה was placed as Keri, and for שַׁיִן, urine, the euphemistic paraphrase, מֵימֵי רַגְלַיִם, water of the feet, and it is to these words that the pointing belongs which is noways suitable to the words in the text.

The later Jews almost entirely followed these readings of the Keri. But, if what we have put forward on the point be correct, we must look upon the Ketib as being in almost every case the original reading, and the Keri as being only an exegetical, grammatical, or critical gloss, but not really a varying reading. It is of course often the case that the Keri is applied in passages where the text-reading—the Ketib—affords no natural sense, so that one would be induced to suppose that some ancient corruption exists; and the Keri then supplies sometimes a suitable sense. But even in these cases, as a rule it is not to be considered as a different reading, but only as a kind of critical conjecture; and in almost every case, in the interpretation of the Sacred Books, we must take the Ketib as our base and starting-point, and not the Keri. The Rabbis, however, are certainly wrong in tracing back some of the Keris to Moses and other Old-Testament authors. They can hardly have proceeded, as others think, from Ezra or the compilers of the Canon generally, but more probably from later scribes, in some cases before, and in some cases after, the date of the Talmud. The number of the Keris and Ketibs in the course of time greatly increased, and that at an early date, on which account their numbers differ

The Keri and Ketib. 457

in various manuscripts. These Keris, however, serve as another proof of the anxious timidity with which the Jewish scribes, through whom the Hebrew text was handed down, evinced their care at the time when the Keris originated in transmitting it in an uncorrupted state; for, even when they believed that some other expression should be substituted in reading, they did not consider it right, as the author of the Samaritan Recension has so often done, to insert this in the text, or to make any alteration.

I also notice that in several words for which, in every place where they occur, the Jewish scribes have desired to have something else read or expressed, they have subsequently in every case omitted to expressly annex the Keri, and those who added the points have only applied to these words the vowels adapted to the supposed Keri; this is the case: (a) in יהוֹה, the vowels of which are not appropriate to this name, but usually to אֲדֹנָי, and where it is in immediate connection with this word, to אֱלֹהִים (יְהֹוִה), as the later Jews always utter these words instead of that name. (b) In the name Jerusalem, when, as is usual in the earlier books, it is written with the Jod before the Mem. The pointing in this case, יְרוּשָׁלַם, is adapted to the form with Jod before the Mem, which is usual in the later books, the more ancient form itself is יְרוּשָׁלֵם or ם֫. (c) In numerous cases in the Pentateuch, where הוא stands for the feminine. It is then pointed הִוא, in reference to the form הִיא, which was afterwards always used for the feminine, whilst the former construction, הוּא, is certainly to be regarded as feminine. (d) In the name Isaschar, which is always written and pointed יִשָּׂשכָר, in reference to a Keri with a single שׂ.

§ 359.—Ancient Alterations by the Scribes.

Of course we find traces in the Talmud, that in earlier times there were various readings in Hebrew manuscripts, that these were compared, and the preference given to that reading which had the greater number of manuscripts in its favour; thus, *Hieros. tr. Taanith*, fol. 68, 1,[1] and almost to the same effect, *tr. Sopherim*, c. 6, § 4. But this clearly

---

[1] Tres libros invenerunt in atrio, librum מְעוֹנִי, librum עֲטוֹטִי, et librum הִיא: in uno invenerunt scriptum (Deut. xxxiii. 27) מְעוֹן, in

relates to very early times when the Temple still existed, and to manuscripts which must have been met with in the fore-court of it. Likewise to the earliest times belong certain alterations, which, from intimations in the Talmud and in the Masora, appear to have been made in the text of the books, and are styled *Ittur Sopherim* and *Tikkun Sopherim*.

Ittur Sopherim (עִטּוּר, from עָטַר, *recedere, abire = ablatio scribarum*), where the writer or scribe had omitted something which previously stood in the text; this designation occurs once in the Talmud (*tr. Nedarim*, fol. 37, col. 2). Five of this kind are named, three in the Pentateuch and two in the Psalms, all indeed merely relating to the omission of a ו copulativum, in four passages before אַחַר. In our editions the Vau is also wanting in these passages, with the exception of Num. xii. 14. (This exception rests upon the erroneous opinion of Buxtorf in the *Lex. Chald. Talm.*, &c., col. 1597, f. The mention in the Talmud of one passage, where the *ablatio scribarum* occurs, much rather points to Num. xxxi. 2; cf. Riehm in *Theol. Stud. und Kritik*, 1862, p. 421).

Of greater significance are the *Tikkun Sopherim*—not mentioned in the Talmud—(תִּיקּוּן, from תָּקַן, *aptare, disponere = correctio scribarum*); according to the statement of the Masora there are said to have been eighteen of these, sixteen of which are expressly stated, with a notice of another reading, which was altered or emended by means of the Sopherim. (Cf. S. Frensdorff, *Das Buch Ochlah W'Ochlah (Masora)*, Hanover, 1864, p. 113, No. 168, and Geiger, *Urschrift*, &c., p. 308, ff.). It is usually assumed that the notes called *Tikkun Sopherim* were merely alterations of incorrect readings in many manuscripts, according to others which were more exact, and it is supposed, unquestionably, that the readings brought forward by the Sopherim, which are just those of our present manuscripts and editions, were the genuine and original ones. But in

---

duobus מעונה, et approbantes duos, rejecerunt unum. In uno invenerunt (Exod. xxiv. 5) scriptum ועטוטי, in duobus נערי, et approbantes duos, rejecerunt unum. In uno invenerunt scriptum (Gen. xxxii. 23) אחר עשרה היא (ed. Fr.—הוא אחד עשר), in duobus היא תשע (ed. Fr.—היא עשר אחד , et approbantes duos, rejecerunt unum.

what we find stated there is nothing to the effect that they were emendations from other manuscripts; thus then the question would arise how the readings set aside by the corrections of the Sopherim were introduced into the manuscripts; as from the nature of many of the readings, they could not have got in by mere accident. Partly from the statements of the Masorites, and partly from the nature of many of the readings set aside by the *Tikkun Sopherim* as compared with those introduced by the latter and now existing in the text, we are led to look upon the matter in the following way:—that in these passages there actually existed generally, or at least in most of the manuscripts in use, other readings which, because in some points of view they presented certain offensive or doubtful expressions, the Sopherim considered themselves justified in altering. Thus in a critical point of view, these earlier readings which are specified as being altered always deserve much attention, and, at least in many cases, it may be really assumed with great probability that they are the original ones. Thus, *e.g.*, the words, Gen. xviii. 22, "Abraham stood yet before Jehovah," are a *correctio scribarum* for "Jehovah stood yet before Abraham." I consider that it is very probable (but compare Gen. xix. 27), that the latter is the original reading; for this mode of expression is better suited to the context. They were induced to make the alteration, because it was considered unseemly to say that Jehovah stood before Abraham, this phraseology often being made use of to point out a relation of dependence. There is another example in Hab. i. 12: "Jehovah my God, mine Holy One? *we* shall not die," לֹא נָמוּת. This also is marked as a *correctio scribarum*, instead of לֹא תָמוּת, "*thou* diest not;*" and from the context it is very probable, as Ewald also thinks, that the latter is the genuine reading, which, on account of the expression seeming offensive, they thought they ought to alter. It may, however, be assumed with probability, that these *correctiones scribarum* existed in ancient times, indeed before the date of the Talmud, and that it is only by accident that they are not expressly mentioned in the latter. But the fact that the knowledge of them was afterwards preserved serves as a direct proof of the anxiety that was shown as to the form of the text.

460   *History of the Text of the Canon.*

§ 360.—*The Masora and Masoretic Notes.*

Remarks of the same kind as and similar to those just considered make up the contents of the *Masora*. It contains statements as to the *Keri*, the *Puncta extraordinaria*, the exceptionally written consonants, the *Ittur* and *Tikkun Sopherim;* as to the number of letters in each book, and which of them is the middle letter; as to the number of verses in each book, and how many verses begin or end with any particular word; how many verses there are which contain exactly a certain number of letters, or in which the self-same word occurs so many times repeated; also in what verses a word is construed in a somewhat unusual way or is used in a meaning which is not quite common,[1] and many of the like observations often very paltry and useless, but always painstaking.

Cf. Buxtorf, *Tiberias s. Commentarius Masorethicus*, Basle, 1620; Elias Levita, *Masoreth Hammasoreth* (translated into German under the care of and with notes by J. S. Semler, Halle, 1772). [*V.* the edition of the Masora by Frensdorff, quoted in p. 458, and Arnold's article "*Masorah,*" in Herzog's *Encyclop.*, in which annotations by Hupfeld are made use of.]

The real *signification of the name* Masora is doubtful. The form of the word is also not always alike. We find for it the forms מְסוֹרָה, מָסֹרֶת, and מָסוֹרֶת. The latter forms with the ת, are, as it appears, those used in ancient times, and in the Talmud and Mishna. The usual derivation is from מָסַר, *tradere*, thus often in the Rabbis: *to hand down* (to others, some doctrine one has received); thence the noun = *traditio, tradition;* its contents being looked upon as handed down from ancestors, just as the Talmud. Another interpretation, however, derives the word from אָסַר, *to bind*, from which in Ezek. xx. 37, מָסֹרֶת (contracted from מַאֲסֹרֶת) occurs in the signification of *bond, vinculum.* (Bond of the Covenant); the name refers to the idea that the Masora was, as it were, a bond, to hold together the law and the Holy Scriptures generally, and that with it the people were bound to circumscribe the text of the Sacred Books as with a bond or bridle. Cf. the Mishna, *Pirke*

[1] Remarks of the latter kind in De Wette, § 91, note *g*.

Masoretic Notes. 461

Aboth, c. 3, § 13: "the Masoreth is a bridle for the law," (מסורת סייג לתורה). To me it seems most probable that the name came originally from the first derivation (as מָסֹרֶת), but that a wider idea, that of the entire traditional interpretation of the law and the Sacred Books was combined with it, and that subsequently, the Jewish scholars, having decidedly transferred the name to the collection of notes of the kind in question, joined with it, at least frequently, the other meaning of a bond, *vinculum*, induced perhaps by the above passage in the Mishna.

The Masoretic notes are found chiefly in the margin of the manuscripts of the Hebrew Old Testament. There are, indeed, some manuscripts, but only a few, which contain merely a collection of Masoretic notes; thus a Codex Palatinus (in the Heidelberg Library, which afterwards was incorporated with the Vatican Library); Bruns had another of the kind in his private library. But it is most probable that these were not originally written in separate books, and thence transferred to the margin of Biblical manuscripts, as many have assumed (even De Wette, § 90); but just the reverse. The manuscripts give these Masoretic notes with many variations, sometimes to a greater, sometimes to a less extent; the notes, having originated very gradually from the inquiries and conclusions of different scribes, were continually being added to. The Masora is published in several of the large editions of the Rabbinical Bible, especially in the Rabbinical editions of Bomberg and Buxtorf (at the beginning of the sixteenth and of the seventeenth centuries). In these editions of the Bible, the Masora is divided into the *greater* and *lesser*. The *greater* contains all the Masoretic notes of the kind in question, and is placed in these Bibles, sometimes on the lower and upper margin (above and under the Hebrew text = *textualis*), sometimes at the end of the several Biblical Books (*finalis*). The *lesser* Masora is an epitome of this, chiefly relating to the Keri, and is placed in these Bibles on the inner margin (between the Hebrew text and the Targum, in the Rabbinical character); the latter is adopted in most of our small editions of the Hebrew Old Testament, either under or at the side of the text.

The Notes of the Masora, or of the Masorites (בַּעֲלֵי הַמָּסוֹרֶת) relate, however, not only, as those hitherto spoken of, to the actual text of the Sacred Books, but also in numerous cases to the subsequent additions to it,—the vowels, diacritical signs and accents.[1] The observations and notes of the former kind were made in great part, as may be inferred from what has gone before, at a time anterior to the introduction of the present system of pointing, those of the latter kind would naturally follow the introduction and establishment of the same.

§ 361.—*The Western and Eastern Readings.*

To this former time, probably, belong a collection of readings which is known under the name of the *Western and Eastern Readings*. They were first published (1526) by R. Jacob Ben Chajim, in Bomberg's second Rabbinical Bible, without any intimation whence he derived them, as variations between the Orientalists and Occidentalists, which by a use of the language, which does not occur elsewhere, is most probably intended to refer to the Babylonian and Palestine Jews.

The collection contains 220 readings, which, with the exception of two referring to the *He mappicatum*, all relate to consonants; but they are of very slight importance and refer almost entirely to differences in orthography, the adding or omission of vowel-letters, and their change one for the other, or to the Keri and Ketib, and, with very little exception, are without any influence over the sense. There are no varying readings brought forward out of the Pentateuch, perhaps, because, owing to the superior care which was exercised pre-eminently in the copying of the law, the manuscripts of the latter did not present even the trivial variations which are cited in the above collection, out of the other books. As to these readings themselves, *v.* Cappellus, *Crit. Sacr.* lib. iii. c. 17.

This collection also affords a proof of the anxious care which at the time of its compilation (probably before the introduction of our system of vowels, as no notice is taken of them in it) was exercised in maintaining the purity of the text of the Sacred Books, and of the almost entire identity of its form in the different seats then existing of Jewish scriptural erudition.

[1] There are instances in De Wette, § 91, note *g*, and Buxtorf, c. ix.

§ 362.—*Early Readings and Manuscripts.*

But the same conscientious and almost painful care, which long previously had been devoted to the actual text, was, after the addition of the present vowels and accents, extended to these also. The invention, formation, and perfecting of the present system of pointing was in general the work of the same learned Jewish schools—in Babylonia and Palestine, in the latter most probably at Tiberias—from which the more ancient Masoretic observations and notes took their rise. This system, when it was once begun, quickly found, as it appears, general approval, and a few centuries after it was perfected, began to be looked upon as actually belonging to the text, and even as having been originally combined with it; thus great care and attention were paid to it, both as a whole and in details. This is vouched for by the later Masoretic observations and notes relating to the vowels and accents, and carefully setting forth where there is anything peculiar in this respect, or differing from the usual procedure. This care is also testified to by the statements of the various readings in which two Jewish scholars of the first half of the eleventh century differed from one another—Ben Asher, who is said to have been a teacher at Tiberias, and Ben Naphthali, perhaps of Babylonia (cf. above § 331).

The later Jews often mention these readings. They are collected in Bomberg's and Buxtorf's Rabbinical Bibles, in which their number amounts to 864, further increased in the London Polyglot from an ancient manuscript. With the exception of one variation relating to the word-division (Sol. Song viii. 6, שַׁלְהֶבֶתְיָה, B. Naphthali, יָהּ שַׁלְהֶבֶת), they all refer to the vowels and accents only, and as Elias Levita remarks, to the choice of the smaller accents, the short or the long vowels, the *Milel* and *Milra*. They also afford a proof of the great value which was then attached to these additions to the real text, and what care was taken to arrange it in an uniform way in this respect, and to keep it so.

Where there was any want of uniformity in the manuscripts, an endeavour was made to assimilate them by means of careful revision from manuscripts enjoying peculiar authority.

The manuscript revised by Ben Asher appears to have been specially used for this purpose. Moses Maimonides says (*v.* Kennicott, *Dissert. Gen.* § 54), that he copied the Pentateuch from this celebrated manuscript, which was then in Egypt, previously having been in Jerusalem, and from the expressions which he uses as to it, must have been held in high authority for the purposes of revision. Another manuscript holding a like authority was (*a*) the so-called *Codex Hillelis*, which Kimchi often made use of; from this the Spanish manuscripts especially were revised. From the name given to this codex one would be induced to attribute it to the older Hillel, or to Hillel Hannasi, yet, as it was pointed, it could not have come from either of these, but must have belonged to a much later time. (*b*) The manuscript of Sinai, and (*c*) that of Jericho; both of these contained the Pentateuch only, and are celebrated on account of their correctness, the former in placing the accents, the latter in placing the *matres lectionis*.

Where the variations of the text are spoken of in this age, they relate only to the pointing and the *matres lectionis*.

This may be clearly inferred from the expressions of R. Meir Hallevi (Haramah, d. 1244) of Toledo (he is called Todrosius by De Rossi, from his father Todros). He remarked to his sorrow the numerous variations of the manuscripts, especially as compared with the Masora, and sought to purify the Pentateuch from these faults by means of his work: *Liber Masoræ sepis legis* (ספר מסורת סייג לתורה; printed at Florence, 1750, and at Berlin, 1761). But he, in the preface, laments the variations only in reference to the *matres lectionis;* and by far the greater part of his statements in the work itself, relate to the *scriptio plena* and *defectiva*. He also remarks that the most ancient manuscripts agree the closest with the Masora.

§ 363.—*The Masoretic Text.*

From the great and constantly advancing authority of the Masora, it was, perhaps, often the case that the text of manuscripts would be revised from the Masora, and that an endeavour would be made to reconcile with the latter any variations that were found. This could only have the same effect as revising them according to the ancient manuscripts which the Masorites must have had under their view. Our present manuscripts agree, not indeed in every point, but still generally, with what is laid down in the Masora.

The present text, both in reference to the original elements, the consonants, and also to the subsequent additions, vowels, accents, &c. is called the *Masoretic*. This designation is not altogether unsuitable, inasmuch as, on the one hand, the settling of the text and its pointing were brought about by the same learned Jewish schools from which the earlier Masoretic observations and notes proceeded; and, on the other hand, the regard paid to these Masoretic notes has much contributed to bring the text to a high degree of uniformity, both in reference to the consonants, and subsequently to pointing. But it would be incorrect if, viewing the matter in a very usual way, we were to imagine that the Masorites themselves arranged special recensions of the text of the Old Testament, by means of which it obtained any shape essentially different from that in which it had been handed down from the date when the Biblical Books received canonical authority. It might, however, sometimes have been the case, that the Keri was adopted into the text instead of the Ketib, the latter being placed in the margin; we find sundry traces of this, but not to say frequently.

§ 364.—*Editions of the Hebrew Old Testament—Polyglots.*

After the Old Testament was printed in the original language, the text of the *Editions* corresponded generally to that of the manuscripts.

As regards the history of the printed text, the following observations may be made. The first portion of the Hebrew Old Testament which was printed was the *Psalter*, 1477 (without points, with Kimchi's Commentary); next the *Pentateuch*, Bologna, 1482 (pointed, with the Targum of Onkelos and Raschi's Commentary); the *Prophetæ Priores et Posteriores*, in two parts, Soncino, 1486 (unpointed, with Kimchi's Commentary); then the whole of the *Hagiographa*, Naples, 1487, in three volumes (with vowels, but without accents, with various Rabbinical Commentaries).

A complete edition of the entire Old Testament followed soon after, at Soncino (a small town in the Duchy of Milan),

1488; it was pointed. The text, as it appears, is based on that of the editions of the separate portions of the Old Testament which we have just quoted. This edition is very scarce; there are only nine copies of it known in Europe, one of which is at Vienna, and one at Carlsruhe.

The *Brescian* edition (Brescia, 1494), had, in part, a specific text of its own, with many readings peculiar to itself; by the printer it was also called the Gersonian. This edition, also, is very rare. The exceptionally written letters are wanting in it, and also the notifications of the Keri and Ketib, the Keri being for the most part adopted into the text; it is, also, full of typographical errors. It has, however, a peculiar interest for us, because from it Luther translated the Old Testament; *v.* B. W. D. Schulze (Tutor at the Joachimsthal Gymnasium of Berlin), "Complete Criticism on the ordinary editions of the Hebrew Bible which Luther made use of in his translation." Berlin, 1766.

It was not until the beginning of the sixteenth century that Christian scholars rendered any service in the preparation of editions of the Hebrew Old Testament, and after this time only was any great care taken as to its text; this was first done in the *Complutensian Polyglot*, and Bomberg's Bible. In the former, which comprised the Old and New Testaments, the Old Testament appeared under the title: *Biblia sacra, V. T. multiplici lingua nunc primo impressum.* Complutum (*i.e.*, Alcala, in New Castile), 4 vols. 1514-17 (a separate volume contained a Hebrew and Chaldee vocabulary of the Old Testament), at the expense of Francis Ximenes de Cisneros, Cardinal Archbishop of Toledo, who, at great cost (4000 golden florins), acquired for his purpose seven Hebrew manuscripts from different countries. Besides the Hebrew text—which is translated into Latin, and is provided with vowels but not with accents—the work contains: (1) The LXX, with an interlineary version in Latin; (2) The Vulgate; (3) In the Pentateuch, the Targum of Onkelos with a Latin translation.

About this time, Daniel Bomberg, of Antwerp, established a printing-press at Venice, which was exclusively devoted to Hebrew and Rabbinical literature; from this office appeared various larger and smaller editions of the Old Testament, viz., five editions of the Hebrew text (1518-1545, in 4to), and three large Rabbinical Bibles in folio. The first of these large editions, Venice, 1518, was edited by Felix Pratensis, a Jew converted to Christianity, and comprises the great Masora (then first printed), the Targums and Rabbinical Commentaries of Raschi, Kimchi, and others (it also contained Kimchi's Psalms, which appeared in a Latin translation by Janvier, Paris, 1666). Its text is based chiefly on that of the Gersonian or Brescian editions. Great authority, especially among the Jews, was attained by the second edition, Venice, 1526, edited by the Jewish scholar, Jacob Ben Chajim. The text of this is grounded on that of the first edition; but it is altered in many ways by the editor, from data derived from the Masora particularly, but also from manuscripts; he has recourse to Spanish manuscripts especially; some further Rabbinical Commentaries are also adopted. A more correct impression of this edition appeared 1547–1549, in which some of the Rabbinical Commentaries printed in the previous edition were omitted, and some other fresh ones added in their place.

Bomberg's text forms the groundwork of most of the later editions, others, however, followed more the Complutensian text or that of the edition of Soncino.

Of the small editions which appeared about the middle of the sixteenth century, I will mention the following:

(a) That of Seb. Münster, or—according to the printer—the edition of Frobenius, Basle, 1536. The text is, on the whole, that of the Brescian or Bomberg's first edition, but still deviates much from it; this very rare edition is valuable, on account of a collection of various readings, partly derived from manuscripts.

(b) Two editions by Robert Stephanus (Etienne), both in sundry parts, containing single books: (1) In large 4to, Paris, 1539–1544, in thirteen parts; the text (according to Opitz) is that of Bomberg's second edition (not that of the Brescian edition, as De Wette and Keil think), and is not very correct. (2) In ten volumes, in large 16mo, 1544–46; the text of this is more correct, and has a greater individuality. Both of these editions are distinguished by the beauty of their typography, and are rare.

(c) Several Plantine editions, from the press of Christopher Plantin, at Antwerp, the first of which is especially valued on account of the correctness of its printing, but it is scarce (1566); the second, 1580; the third, 1590.

From this same office of Plantin's appeared a new, comprehensive, Biblical, polyglot work—the *Antwerp Polyglot*, 1569–1572, 8 vols. fol., the four first of which contain the Old Testament, the fifth the New Testament, and the three others a fund of Biblical appliances of critical, philological, and antiquarian purport, among these, in the eighth volume, is a Latin translation of the entire Bible, by Santes Pagninus (improved by Arias Montanus); the work was produced at the expense of Philip II. of Spain, under the superintendence of Benedict Arias Montanus, a Spanish scholar, sent to Antwerp by the king for this purpose; he was assisted by several other scholars, some of Antwerp, and some foreigners. As regards the Old Testament, this edition contains the Chaldee Paraphrases, the LXX, and the Vulgate, as well as the Hebrew text. The latter is based on the text of the Complutensian edition, which, however, has been collated with one of Bomberg's Bibles, so that the text is a mixed one. Of the 500 copies which were printed of this edition, a part, which was sent to Spain by sea, is said to have been lost in a storm. This edition was accepted with approbation by Gregory XIII., Pope at that time, but it also met with much opposition, it being made a ground of accusation against the editor that he had a leaning to Judaism, because he had allowed the Targums to be printed complete, and, among his materials, had made so industrious a use of Jewish works; he was, on this account, compelled more than once to vindicate himself at Rome, and had some trouble to get acquitted.

The text of this Antwerp Polyglot is repeated in two other large Polyglots, those of *Paris* and *London*, which appeared about the middle of the seventeenth century.

1.—The "Paris Polyglot": *Biblia* (1) Hebraica, (2) Samaritana, (3) Chaldaica, (4) Græca, (5) Syriaca, (6) Latina, (7) Arabica, &c. Paris, 1629–1645. Nine parts, in 10 vols. large fol. This work was undertaken by the Parliamentary Advocate, Guy (Guido) Michel Le Jay; a share in the labour was also taken by Johann Morin (in the Samaritan Recension, and Samaritan translation of the Pentateuch), and the Maronite, Gabriel Sionita (in the Syriac and Arabic translation), and when Le Jay disagreed with the latter, for a time Abraham Echellensis also. The four first parts contain the Old Testament, printed from the

Antwerp Polyglot, the Hebrew text with the Targums, the LXX, and the Vulgate; the Hebrew text in it is very incorrect; the fifth part contains the New Testament, the sixth, the Pentateuch from the Samaritan Recension (then printed for the first time), also the Samaritan translation of it, as well as the Arabic and Syriac translation of the Pentateuch, with a Latin translation of these versions; Parts 7-9 contained the Arabic and Syriac translations of the Old Testament. Le Jay sacrificed the whole of his property in the preparation of this work, and made it a point of honour that it should be named after him, so that he refused leave to Cardinal Richelieu to prefix his name to the work, although the latter offered him very large sums of money to grant his request. The work, however, found but few purchasers, and Le Jay found himself compelled to sell it as waste paper, and soon after fell into bitter poverty.

II.—The " London Polyglot": *Biblia Sacra Polyglotta*, &c. London, 1657. 6 vols. large fol., edited by Brian Walton, who undertook the work at the time of the English Revolution, during which, on account of his adherence to the Royal family and the Episcopal Church, he was deprived of his preferment (in St. Paul's Cathedral, in London); after the Restoration, he was nominated Bishop of Chester. The work was dedicated to King Charles II. Edmund Castle (Castellus), Sam. Clarke, Thomas Hyde, and others, were co-workers with him. Besides the Hebrew text, the work contains all the ancient translations comprised in the "Paris Polyglot," and also an Æthiopic translation of the Psalms and Solomon's Song, and a Persian translation of the Pentateuch. The three first volumes contain—besides very learned prefaces prefixed to the first part—the Canonical Books of the Old Testament, so arranged that, on the two pages, the Hebrew text (with the interlineary Latin translation of Santes Pagninus, as improved by Arius Montanus) and the different ancient translations (the Oriental versions being provided with Latin translations, as literal as possible) stand together, or by the side of one another; the fourth volume contains the Apocrypha, and also the Persian translation of the Pentateuch, which had not been printed in the first volume, and the Targums of Pseudo-Jonathan and Jerusalem; the fifth volume, the New Testament; vol. 6 contains an appendix with critical notes, and a collection of various readings of the Hebrew text of the Old, and the Greek of the New Testament, also of the various ancient translations. The editor had intended to give in a seventh volume various hitherto unprinted ancient translations (especially Eastern) of the separate Biblical Books; but this was left undone, as Walton died in 1661. There appeared, as a supplement to the work, Edm. Castellus' (Prof. of Arabic) *Lexicon Heptaglotton*, 2 vols. fol. 1669. Up to the present time Walton's Polyglot is still the most complete, and continues to be much valued, although, in a critical view, it leaves much to be desired. Some considerable time back there was a talk in England about preparing a new edition, but the idea is fallen into the background. This work, moreover, has not failed to meet with attacks from a theological point of view, some thinking that the Bible in so many languages could only bring about perplexity, and that there was much in the preface and appendix which was doubtful in its bearing both on the Reformation and also on Christianity itself. By Pope Alexander VII., the Polyglot was placed in the class of prohibited books soon after its appearance.

We find this same Antwerp text in the edition of Christian Reineccius (Rector and Prof. at the Gymnasium at Weissenfels, d. 1752), both in the Polyglot of the Old Testament edited by him (*Biblia Sacra quadrilinguia V. T.*, viz., (1) Hebrew, (2) LXX, (3) Seb. Schmidt's Latin translation, (4) Luther's German translation, Leipzig, 1750–51), and also in his previous much used small editions in 8vo; the first of these appeared Leipzig, 1725; from the statements of the preface and title he appears to have collated manuscripts in their preparation, but he does not expressly say so; the fourth edition, 1793, 8vo (and with broad margin in 4to), edited by Joh. Christoph Döderlein, and, after his death, by Heinrich Meisner, with a judicious selection of various readings from Kennicott and De Rossi, but printed in a type injurious to the eyes; this edition was revised 1819, when published by the Halle Orphan Asylum, and was provided with a new title and a preface by Knapp.

§ 365.—*Various Editions of the Hebrew Old Testament.*

Before these last named editions, at the end of the sixteenth and the beginning of the seventeenth century, two other editions appeared with Recensions of the text of an individual character, viz., those of Hütter and Buxtorf.

(a) The edition of Elias Hütter (Prof. at Leipzig, afterwards living at Nuremberg), Hamburg, 1587, and furnished with new title 1588, 1596, 1603; the text is a mixture of those of Bomberg, Stephanus, and Münster. This edition, which came out through the assistance of some wealthy inhabitants of Hamburg, appears to have been entirely prepared for the use of beginners in Hebrew; the primary and radical letter in each word being printed in a darker and more conspicuous character than the rest of the letters, and where the primary letter is omitted in a word, this is always placed in a smaller character, over the text, in the place to which it belongs.

(b) The edition of Joh. Buxtorf, the father. A small edition first appeared at Basle, 1611, 8vo; it contained a Recension of the Hebrew text peculiar to itself, which Buxtorf made with great care from the Masora. The same text, only again revised from the Masora, is used in the large Rabbinical Bible, edited by him. Basle, 1618, 1619, 4 vols. large folio, with the Commentaries of Raschi, Aben Esra, D. Kimchi, R. Levi Ben Gerson, and others; comprising also the Targums, the great and small Masora, the readings of Ben Asher, and Ben Naphthali, those of the Eastern and Western Jews, and others. In this edition, especial care is exercised in the pointing, both of the Hebrew text and also of the Targums, in the latter, however, the manuscripts are not followed, but amendments are introduced according to the mode of pointing used in the Chaldee fragments of the Books of Daniel and Ezra. Buxtorf's small edition was again printed: Amsterdam, 1639, 8vo., edited by Menasse Ben Israel. This Jewish scholar had previously edited a special Recension of the text, in two editions,—one unpointed, Amsterdam, 1630 and one pointed, *ibid.* 1635; he often, as he himself confesses, altered the text, not only following the Masora, but also according to the rules of grammar. This text has not been again printed.

The case has been very different with the text of the editions of Joseph Athias, a Jewish scholar and printer at Amsterdam. The first edition appeared at Amsterdam, 1661, large 8vo., with a preface, by Joh. Leusden (Professor at Utrecht); Athias revised and corrected the text by means of data derived from manuscripts; from two ancient manuscripts especially. The second edition of 1667, was revised afresh. Both editions, especially the first, are much valued on account of their correctness and the beauty of their typography. On this text, that of most of the later editions is based, either directly or indirectly; of these, in the seventeenth and the first half of the eighteenth century, I will mention the following:

(a) The edition of David Clodius (Prof. of Orient. Languages at Giessen, d. 1687), Frankfort, 1677. This edition was again brought out twice after his death; in 1692 (edited by Joh. Heinrich Mai of Giessen, revised, and with a preface, by Joh. Leusden, inferior in correctness to the first edition); and 1716 (edited by Georg Christ. Bürklin, Tutor at the Gymnasium at Giessen, collated with some other editions and manuscripts, printed in clear and sharp type, although not quite correct in respect to the accents).

(b) The edition of Dan. Ernst Jablonski (First Court-Chaplain at Berlin, d. 1741), Berlin, 1699. The text is made up from Athias' second edition, collated with several other editions and also some manuscripts; very great care has been exercised in the pointing and accentuation; and the edition is reputed to be one of the most correct. He was assisted in the correction of it by a Jewish scholar. Another edition, Berlin, 1712, is very inferior to the former one in correctness and clearness of type.

(c) The edition of Everard van der Hooght (Minister in Holland), Amsterdam and Utrecht, 1705, a copy of Athias' second edition, surpasses those which preceded it in beauty, sharpness, and clearness of type, and is also tolerably correct; a copious list of various readings is annexed.

(d) The edition of Heinrich Opitz (Prof. at Kiel), Kiel, 1709. The text of Athias' edition is amended by the collation of seventeen other editions and some manuscripts, and is printed with large and clear type. Unusual care was taken in the correctness of the printing, the editor going over every sheet for correction at least six times; this edition is therefore the most correct of all.

(e) The edition of Johann Heinrich Michaelis (Prof. at Halle, d. 1738), Halle, 1720. The text is grounded on that of Jablonski's (first) edition; this was collated with twenty-four other editions and five Erfurt manuscripts, and the most important variations, both as to the consonants and vowels, are specified in the margin. This collation was made rather cursorily, but still the edition is very valuable on account of the parallel passages and philological notes with which the text is surrounded, both on the margin and underneath.

(ƒ) The edition of Joh. Simonis (d. 1768, as Prof. of Eccles. Hist. and Christ. Antiq. at Halle), Halle, 1752; 2nd edit. 1767. This edition was intended to be a more correct and cheaper copy of Van der Hooght's edition ; but the first edition is much less correct than the second, which is also more fairly and sharply printed. Appended to it are, (a) a vocabulary, and (b) a really useful explanation of the Masoretic signs and notes occurring in manuscripts of the Old Testament: these can also be procured separately. Subsequently, this edition again appeared in two impressions; 3rd edit. Halle, 1822; 4th edit. 1828; in both, however, the printing is inferior to that of the second edition.

On account of its critical appliances, we must notice the *Mantuan Bible*. Four Parts, large 4to. Mantua, 1742-44, edited by the Jewish Physician, Raphael Chajim Italia, at his own expense; the text is printed from that of Bomberg's last, or Van der Hooght's edition. Under the text of it, however, we find—in the Rabbinical character— printed for the first time, the Critical Commentary of Jedidja Salomo Norzi, a Rabbi at Mantua, at the beginning of the seventeenth century. This Commentary here bears the title מִנְחַת שַׁי, *Offering of a gift*. For this work, numerous editions and manuscripts of the Hebrew Old-Testament were collated, also manuscripts of the Masora and Talmud, and the most esteemed writings of Jewish interpreters. Special care is taken in the correctness of the vowels, accents, and the *matres lectionis*, ו and י, as regards their placing or omission; sometimes also, critical reflections are made as to entire words of the text. Bruns has called special attention to this critical commentary [v. Tychsen, *Befreyetes Tentamen*, p. 78, ff.] Norzi's Commentary is printed (*complete*, cf. the Appendix to the D.M.G.Z. 1862, p. xxxi.) in an edition of the Old Testament, Vienna, 1813-16, from the printing-office of G. Holzinger.

To the same age as Norzi belonged R. Menahem de Lonzano, who undertook a personal journey for the purpose of collating manuscripts of the Pentateuch. The various readings collected by him are found in אוֹר תּוֹרָה, *Light of the Law*, in the first section of the work, שְׁתֵּי יָדוֹת, *The Two Hands*, Venice, 1618; the *Or thorah* is printed separately, Amsterdam, 1659. It is based on Bomberg's small edition of the year 1544 ; the text of which he carefully examines, comparing it with manuscripts, also making use of the Masora and critical works by the Rabbis; he gives an especial preference to the Spanish manuscripts.

Not long after the Mantuan Bible appeared, the already (§ 323) mentioned edition of Houbigant, Paris, 1753, 4 vols. folio, splendidly printed. The text is copied from Van der Hooght's edition, but without points; with critical notes and a Latin translation of the Books of the Old Testament following his own critical conjectures. These critical notes and Houbigant's preface were also printed separately, Frankf. 1777.

We have already (§ 323) spoken of the collection of readings by Kennicott and De Rossi, and also of Kennicott's edition of the Hebrew Old Testament, containing his collection of readings, Oxford, 1776–80; the text is that of Van der Hooght's edition, but without points.

Besides the selection of Kennicott's and De Rossi's readings in Reineccius' fourth edition, edited by Döderlein and Meisner, a similar one is contained in that of Joh. Jahn, Vienna, 1806, 4 vols. The text is based on that of Van der Hooght, but the edition has this peculiarity, that many of the later Masoretic notes are omitted, and that only the greater accents are inserted.

In modern times, various new and beautiful editions have appeared, which are also based on Van der Hooght's text ; among them, two impressions of this edition, brought out by the English Bible Society: (*a*) Edited by Judah d'Allemand, London, 1825, in which the various readings of Van der Hooght's edition are added under the text. (*b*) Basle, 1827; very correct. Also, (*c*), edited by A. Hahn, stereotyp. Leipz. 1831 ; 4th edit. 1839. In the 4th edition, Van der Hooght's text is revised in many ways by Hahn, and Norzi's Commentary is especially used for this purpose. (*d*) A very beautiful and correct edition, by Karl Gottf. Wilh. Thiele (Prof. at Leipz. d. 1854), Leipzig, 1849.

Stereotyp. Of this edition are printed separately: *Genesis, The Psalms, Isaiah, The Lesser Prophets,* and *Job.*

As a work both useful and deserving of commendation, I must also mention the *Polyglotten-Bibel zum praktischen Handgebrauch,* edited by R. Stier and G. W. Thiele. The New Testament first appeared as vol. iv. Bielefeld, 1846; 3rd edition, 1853; then the Old Testament in 3 vols. (vols. 2 and 3 each containing two divisions, 1847–1855; 2nd edit. in stereotyp. 1854. The Old Testament contains: (*a*) The Hebrew text; (*b*) the LXX, edited by Böckel,[1] and from vol. 2 by Landschreiber, with various readings; (*c*) The Vulgate, according to the Clementine text, with the variations of the Sixtine edition, and some other various readings; (*d*) Luther's translation with the most important variations of the other most celebrated German translations (*v.* Meyer, De Wette,[2] Allioli, Von Ess, the Berleburg Bible).

[1] Supplement to this: Landschreiber, *Quellen zu Text und Noten der LXX.—Uebers. in Bd. I. und Bd. II. I. der Polyglotten-Bibel,* 1856.

[2] As De Wette's translation (*vide* p. 138) has the highest scientific value of those collated, a further supplement to the Polyglot Bible might be desired which, to its purchasers, would render it unnecessary to procure the third or fourth edition of De Wette's translation. Stier appears not to have been acquainted with the third, *much improved* edition of De Wette's Bible, which appeared seven years before the beginning of the Polyglot, for even in the concluding part of the Polyglot, which was published sixteen years after De Wette's work, De Wette's second edition continues to be made use of. In this way an injustice is done to De Wette (the reader of the Polyglot finds, for instance, in 1 Cor. i. 10, a mistaken expression of De Wette's, whilst De Wette's third edition gives the same as Stier in his translation of 1856); and as regards others the Polyglot is rendered of less service. [In the "carefully revised and improved edition," issued since 1862, it is to be hoped that this fault is removed from the Polyglot.] I will also remark that De Wette's fourth edition is not much superior to the third, at least as regards the Old Testament; if it was collated throughout with the original text, errors would be removed such as those censured by Thenius, in 1 Kings iv. 11, xviii. 10; 2 Kings vi. 25. The improvement on the third edition over the second is much greater, which is to De Wette's honour.

THE END.

INDEX.

A.

Abarbanel, i. 115.
Aben Esra, i. 115, 193; ii. 44, 376.
Abulfaradsch, i. 60.
Abulwalid, i. 111, 113.
Accents, v. Pointing.
Adam, Book of, i. 62.
Æthiopic Language, i. 45, f.
Ahasuerus (Achaschverosch), i. 420, 428.
A Lapide (Von Stein), i. 128, 141.
Alcuin, ii. 334.
Alting, i. 136, f.
Amharic (Dialect), i. 46.
Amos, Book of, ii. 137, ff., cf. 132, f.
Antoninus, Archbishop of Florence, ii. 335.
Apocryphal Books, ii. 301, ff., 315-357, 438, f.
Apocrypha, meaning of the term, ii. 303, f.
Appropriation of supposititious names as authors of books, with a hortatory aim, ii. 201, 209.
Aquila, ii. 412, ff., 441.
Arabic Language, i. 42, ff., 105; cf. 135.
—— Pointing, ii. 380, 382.
—— Translations of the Bible, ii. 445.
Aramaic Language, i. 46, 103.
Artachschasta (Artaxerxes Longimanus), i. 421, f., 428.
Asaph's Psalms, ii. 234.
Assemani, i. 59, f.
Assyrians, their language, i. 48, ff.
Astruc, i. 257.
Athanasius, ii. 321, 325.
Athbasch, The, ii. 92.
Augusti, i. 21, 151, 199.
Augustine, i. 6, f., 121; ii. 331, 410.

B.

Babylonians, The, their language, i. 47, f., 51; their writing character, ii. 366.
Barhebräus v. Abulfaradsch.
Barnabas, Epistle of, ii. 316.
Baruch, i. 408; ii. 96, 98.
Baruch, Book of, ii. 320, ff., 339.
Bauer, G. L., i. 18, 137, 150, 199.
Baumgarten, Mich., i. 160, 263, 451.
Baur, Gust., ii. 1.
Baur, v. Von Baur.
Beersheba, i. 298, f.
Bellermann, i. 94.
Ben Asher and Ben Naphthali, ii. 381, 463.
Bertheau, i. 158, 176, 181, 205, 388, 392, 436; ii. 256.
Bertholdt, i. 21, f., 202; ii. 199.
Bethel, i. 298, ff.
Bochart, i. 136, 141.
Bogomili, The, as to the Pentateuch, i.193.
Bohle, i. 138.
Bohlen, v. Von Bohlen.
Böttcher, i. 157.
Brandis, Joh., i. 50, f.
Brentano, i. 151.
Brenz, i. 131.
Bunsen, i. 161; ii. 1, 189, 287.
Buxtorf, Joh. (The Father), i. 10, 133; cf. 61, 106, 134, 141; ii. 377.
Buxtorf, Joh. (The Son), i. 10; ii. 361, 377.

C.

Cajetan, ii. 335.
Calasio, Marius de, i. 134.
Calmet, i. 128, f.
Calov, i. 140.
Calvin, i. 129, ff.; ii. 377.

Canon of the Old Testament, History of, ii. 289.
Canones Apostolorum, ii. 323.
Cappellus, Jac., i. 142.
Cappellus, Ludw., i. 8, 10, 142, f.; ii. 360, 377.
Carpzov, i. 15, f., 197, 264, 449; ii. 285, 361.
Carthage, Synod of, ii. 331.
Caspari, i. 26, 160.
Cassiodorus, i. 7; ii. 333.
Castellio, i. 141; ii. 260.
Castellus, i. 61, 135; ii. 470.
Catenæ, The, i. 120.
Catholic Church, Opinions of, as to Apocrypha, ii. 340, ff.
Celsus, i. 5.
Chaldeans, The, i. 47, f.
Chaldee Language, i. 51, f., 57, f., 148; employed in the Old Testament, i. 38, 103, 427, ff.; ii. 200.
Chronicles, Books of, i. 176, ff., 328, 433; ii. 297.
Clarius, Isidor, i. 141.
Clement. Alex., ii. 316, 410.
Clementine Homilies, i. 193.
Clericus, i. 13, 142, 196, 256.
Coccejus, i. 139.
Commentaries on the Old Testament, i. 114–124, 127–132, 139–151, 157–161.
Concordances to the Old Testament, i. 129, 134, f., 138, 148; ii. 429, f.
Constantinople, Synod of, ii. 343.
Cornelius a Lapide, i. 128, 141.
Corrodi, i. 198; ii. 198.
Credner, i. 158.
Critici Sacri, i. 140, f.
Criticism on the Old Testament, its justification, i. 26, f.
Cuneiform Character, i. 49.
Cureton, i. 60.
Cyprian, ii. 316.
Cyril, of Alexandria, i. 119.
Cyril, of Jerusalem, ii. 324.
Cyrillus Lukaris, ii. 343.

D.

Daniel, Book of, ii. 190, 299, 301, 354, 405, ff.; additions to it in the LXX, ii. 339, 341, f.; person of, 225, f.

Danz, i. 107, notes; 137, f.
Darius, the Median, ii. 217.
Darjavesch (Darius), i. 420, 432.
Dathe, i. 137, 149, f.
David's Psalms, ii. 234.
Davidson, i. 24; ii. 199.
De Dieu, i. 136.
De Lagarde, i. 60.
Delitzsch, i. 160, f., 259, 263; ii. 199, 207, 261, f.
Dereser, i. 151.
De Rossi, i. 54; ii. 362.
Deuteronomist, The, i. 323–344, 347, 352, 357–359, 364, 375.
Deuteronomy, Book of, i. 190, 193, 233, ff., 237, 244, 319–342, 442.
De Wette, i. 22, ff., 85, ff., 151, 199, 203, 206, 259, 435, f.; ii. 88, 163, 245.
Dialects of the Hebrew, i. 98.
Dietrich, i. 152, 158.
Division of the Old Testament, i. 32, f.
—— into Chapters, ii. 387–389.
—— into Verses, ii. 385, f.
Dositheus (*Confessio Dos.*), ii. 343.
Drechsler, i. 26, 160, 205; ii. 45.
Drusius, i. 132, 141.
Du Pin, i. 13.

E.

'Εβραῖος, ὁ, ii. 430.
Ecclesiastes, Book of, ii. 263–267, 298, 301, 310, 353; in the LXX, 407.
Eckermann on the Pentateuch, i. 198.
Editions of the Hebrew Old Testament, ii. 465, ff.
Edomites, The, i. 300, 331; ii. 141, f.
Egypto-Aramaic Inscriptions, i. 64.
Egyptian Jews, their writing characters, ii. 370.
Eichhorn, i. 17, f., 148, 199, 202, f., 257, 435; ii. 23, 198.
Elkosh, ii. 148.
'Ελληνικὸς, ὁ, ii. 430.
Elohist, The, i. 268–281, 285–296, 304, 311, 316, 319, 326, 328, 354, 359, f., 362, 375, 381, f.
Englisches Bibelwerk, i. 149.
Enumeration of the Books of the Old Testament, i. 37.
Ephodacus, i. 112.

Index. 479

Ephraem Syrus, i. 59, 117.
Epiphanius, ii. 321, 326.
Essenes, Canon of the, ii. 311.
Esther, Book of, i. 445–454; ii. 297, f., 302, 305, 310, 338, 352.
——— Apocryphal Additions, ii. 339, 341, 405, f.
Ethan the Ezrahite, ii. 236.
Ethico-religious spirit of the Old Testament, ii. 245, 350.
Eusebius, i. 118; ii. 317.
Ewald, i. 24, 89, 154, ff., 206, f, 260, ff., 285, ff., 341, 386, 436; ii. 88, 131, 238.
Exodus, i. 187, 222, f., 232, 238, ff., 244–248, 301–308.
Ezekiel, i. 331; ii. 105–119; LXX, 407.
Ezra, ii. 291, f., 294, f., 312, 368, f.
Ezra, Book of, i. 413–417, 422–432; ii. 297.
———, Third Book of, ii. 292, 312.
———, Third and Fourth Book of, ii. 337.

F.

Faber Stapulensis, ii. 335.
Florence, Council of, ii. 335.
Förster, Joh., i. 134.
Fulda, on the Pentateuch, i. 197, f.
Fürst, Jul., i. 110, 134, 138, 156.

G.

Geier, i. 141.
Gelasius I., ii. 332.
Gemara, The, i. 108, f.
Genesis, Book of, i. 186, 211, f., 229, ff., 255–301.
George, on the Pentateuch, i. 204.
Gesenius, i. 69, 101, 138, 152.
Glass, i. 137, 141.
Gnostics, The, i. 5, 193.
God, Name of, among the Hebrews, i. 268, ff., 273, 279, ff.; ii. 248, notes.
Gousset, i. 143.
Graf, K. H., i. 158; ii. 88, notes.
Gramberg, i. 24; 436.
Grammars, Hebrew, i. 110, ff., 125, f., 128, 133, 135–137, 145–147, 152–159.

Greek Church, The, ii. 321, 336, 342.
Gregory, the Great, ii. 333.
Gregory Nazianzen, ii. 321, 324, ff.
Grotius, i. 127, 139, f.; ii. 265.

H.

Habakkuk, Book of, ii. 151, ff.
Hadrian (εἰσαγωγή), i. 6.
Haggai, Book of, ii. 157, f.
Hagiographa, The, i. 34, f.
Hahn, i. 160; ii. 256, 260, 265, 282.
Haphtharoth, The, ii. 389.
Hartmann, A. Th., i. 24, 203, f., 259.
Hartmann, Joh. Melch., i. 149.
Hasse, J. G., i. 197.
Hävernick, i. 25, f., 160, f., 205, 450; ii. 182, 199.
Hebrew, as the designation for Aramaic at the time of Christ, i. 54.
Hebrew Language, i. 53, f., 64, ff., 105, ff.
Hebrews, their Name, i. 76, f.
Hebrew Writing, ii. 365–375.
Hebrew and Hellenist Jews, i. 104, f.; ii. 302, f., 370, 409.
Heidegger, i. 8.
Heiligstedt, i. 159.
Hellenistic Canon, The, ii. 302, 309.
Hengstenberg, i. 25, 160, 205, 229, 243, 367; ii. 14, 38, 162, 199.
Herbst, i. 19, f., 201; ii. 199.
Herder, i. 16, 85; ii. 185, 260.
Hexapla, The, ii. 417.
Hilarius Pictavensis, ii. 327, 333.
Hilkiah, ii. 65.
Hillel Hannasi, i. 106.
Hippo Regius, The Council of, ii. 331.
Hirzel, i. 159.
Historical Books of the Old Testament. i. 171–173; references in them to the Pentateuch, 373, 396; their Canonical dignity, ii. 353.
Historical Books, Lost, i. 175, 396, 406, 409, ff., 438.
Historical Writing among the Hebrews, i. 253, f., 263, f., 441, f.
Hitzig, i. 24, 158, f.; ii. 88, 162, 180 188, 231, 238, 255.
Hizkiah, ii. 154.
Hobbes, i. 10, 194.
Hody, ii. 395, ff.

Hosea, Book of, ii. 121-128.
Hottinger, i. 9, 136.
Houbigant, ii. 361, f.
Hug, i. 201; ii. 260.
Hugo Carensis, ii. 335.
Hugo, of St. Victor, ii. 334.
Hupfeld, i. 55, 156, 262, f.; ii. 378.

I.

Iambi ad Seleucum, ii. 321, 327.
Ilgen, on Genesis, i. 258, f.
Innocent I., ii. 332.
Inspiration, i. 264; ii. 352, f.
Irenæus, ii. 316.
Isaak ben Jasos, i. 193.
Isaiah, as a Historian, i. 180, f.; ii. 44, 59.
Isaiah, Book of, ii. 41-63; LXX, 404.
Itala, The, i. 122; ii. 333, 433.
Ittur Sopherim, The, ii. 458.

J.

Jahn, i. 19, 149, 201, 259; ii. 342.
Japhet ben Heli, i. 114.
Jehoahaz, ii. 67.
Jehoiachin, ii. 73.
Jehoiakim, ii. 67.
Jehovist, The, i. 266-275, 281-285, 294-301, 302, 312, 317, 319, 340, 343, 363, 375, 381-383.
Jchuda Chajjug, i. 111; ii. 381.
Jeremiah, Book of, i. 331; ii. 64-100; LXX, ii. 84, f., 405.
———, Epistle of, ii. 319, 329, 341.
Jerome, i. 6, 121, ff.; ii. 329, 358, 378, 413, 430, f., 434, ff.
Jerusalem, Synod of, ii. 343.
Jewish Canon, i. 5; ii. 290-315.
Jewish Scripture Researches, i. 7, 105-116, 193; ii. 44.
Job, if an historical personage? ii. 272-274.
Job, Book of, ii. 268-288, 297, 353; LXX, 405, f.
Joel, Book of, ii. 128-136.
John Chrysostom, i. 118.
John Damascenus, ii. 336.
John of Salisbury, ii. 335.
Jonah, Book of, ii. 179-189, 352.
Josephus, Flavius, ii. 307, f.

Joshua, Book of, i. 287, ff., 343, ff., 362, ff., 372; ii. 291, 294.
Joshua, Samaritan Book of, ii. 312.
Josiah, i. 332, 369; ii. 66.
Jubilee Year, The, i. 309, f.
Juda, The Holy, i. 105, 107.
Juda ben Karisch, i. 113.
Judges, Book of, i. 377-389; ii. 294.
Judge, Office of, i. 377, f.
Judith, Book of, ii. 339.
Junilius, i. 6.

K.

Karaite Punctuation, ii. 383.
Karlstadt, i. 8, 194; ii. 337.
Keil, i. 25, f., 160, 263, 436; ii. 259.
Kennicott, ii. 362.
Keri and Ketib, The, ii. 454, ff.
Ketubim, The, i. 32, f.; their reception into the Canon, ii. 295, 298.
Kimchi, David, i. 112, ff.
Kimchi, Joseph, i. 112.
Kimchi, Moscheh, i. 112.
Kings, Books of, i. 328, 386, ff.; 394-399, 406-412; their relation to the Chronicles, i. 438-442.
Kleinert, i. 26.
Knobel, i. 158, 259; ii. 162.
Korahite Psalms, ii. 235, f.
Koster, i. 95; ii. 162, 239.
Kurtz, i. 26, 209, 263.

L.

Lamentations, Book of, i. 34; ii. 101-104, 295, 300, 309, 318.
Lanckish, i. 129, 148.
Laodicea, Council of, ii. 321, ff., 327.
Latin Church, The, ii. 327, ff., 411.
Law of Moses, its Canonical Authority among the Jews, ii. 290, ff.
———, its significance to Christians, ii. 349-352.
Laws in the Pentateuch, i. 211-226.
Lengerke, v. Von Lengerke.
Leusden, i. 9.
Levi ben Gerson, i. 115.
Levita, Elias, i. 112, 133.
Levites, The, i. 243, ff., 314, f., 323-325.
Leviticus, Book of, i. 187, f., 213, ff., 238, 248, 308-312.

Index. 481

Lexicography, Hebrew, i. 112, ff., 128, 133–139, 147–157.
Literary Art, among the Hebrews, i. 82, f., 221, 253, f., 263, 361, f.
Literæ majusculæ, minusculæ, suspensæ, ii. 452.
Löscher, i. 144.
Lowth, i. 85.
Luther, i. 8, 126, 129, 135, 296, 449; ii. 337, 359, 377, 466.

M.

Maccabees, Books of, ii. 302, 306, 338.
——, First Book of, ii. 355.
——, times of the, ii. 206–209, 219–221, 355.
Maimonides, i. 109, 116.
Malachi, Book of, ii. 175–179.
Maldonatus, i. 128.
Manasseh, Prayer of, ii. 342.
μάντις, ii. 7, 13.
Manuscripts of the Old Testament, ii. 362–365, 391, f.
Mardochai ben Nathan, i. 134.
Maronites, The, i. 58.
Masius, i. 8, 141, 194.
Masora, The, ii. 460, f.
Maurer, i. 158.
Megilloth, The, i. 32.
Meier, Ernst, i. 157; ii. 131.
Melito, of Sardis, ii. 317.
Menhahem ben Saruk, i. 113.
Mercerus, i. 128, 131.
Messianic Prophecies, ii. 30–36, 350; in the various prophets: Isaiah, ii. 61–63; Jeremiah, ii. 100; Hosea, ii. 127, f.; Joel, ii. 136; Amos, ii. 140; Nahum, ii. 150; Zephaniah, ii. 156; Zechariah, ii. 171; Malachi, ii. 179; Daniel, ii. 228, f.; in the Psalms, ii. 244, ff.
Metrophanes Kritopulus, ii. 342, f.
Micah, Book of, ii. 144.
Micaiah, the son of Imlah, ii. 144.
Michaelis, J.D., i. 17 f., 147, 197, 259.
——, J. H. i. 146; ii. 473.
——, Chr. B., i. 146.
Mishna, The, i. 107.
Morinus, Joh., i. 10; ii. 359.
Mosaical Laws, i. 211–226, 304, f., 307—311, 361.

VOL. II.

Mosaical Songs, i. 226–228, 303; ii. 234.
—— History—Writing, i. 253–256
Moser, Phil. Ul., i. 148.
Movers, i. 20, 205, 333, 436; ii. 88.
Münster, Seb., i. 125, 133, 141.
Music as an accompaniment of the Prophetical Discourses, ii. 16, f.

N.

Nachtigall, on the Pentateuch, i. 198.
Nahum, Book of, ii. 148, ff.
Nathan Bar Jechiel, i. 109.
Nazarenes, The, on the Pentateuch, i. 192.
Nebiim, The, i. 33; ii. 300.
Nehemiah, Book of, i. 413, 417–432; ii. 297, ff.
Nehemiah's Collection of Books, ii. 291–293.
Neumann, Casp., i. 143.
New Testament, Quotations in it of the Old Testament, ii. 305, ff., 409, 450.
——, its relation to the Old Testament, 347, ff.
Nicephorus (Chronography), ii. 336.
Nicolas de Lyra, i. 7, 124, f.; ii. 335, 376.
Nitzsch, ii. 35.
Nold, i. 138.
Notker, Abbott of St. Gall, ii. 334.
Numbers, Book of, i. 188, f., 224, f., 227, f., 236, f., 240, 244, 248–251, 253–255, 312, f.
Nun inversum, ii. 452.

O.

Obadiah, ii. 141, ff.
Œcolampadius, i. 131.
Olshausen, Justus, i. 156, 159; ii. 238, f.
Olympiodorus, i. 120.
Order of Succession in the Old-Testament Books, i. 32, ff.; ii. 299.
Origen, i. 117; ii. 318, 358, 409, 416.

P.

Palmyrene Language, i. 63; its characters, ii. 373.
Parallelism of Members (Hebrew Poetry), i. 84, ff.

2 I

Parashioth (Sections), ii. 387.
Pastor of Hermas, ii. 329, 335.
Pellicanus, i. 125; ii. 377.
Pentateuch, The, i. 184–344, 351–376; ii. 290.
———, The Samaritan, i. 366, ff.; ii. 311, f., 391, 430; in the LXX, ii. 394, 399, f.
Peshito, The, i. 117; ii. 443.
Pesukim (Verses), ii. 386.
Peter of Cluny, i. 334.
Peyrerius, i. 10, 194.
Pfeiffer, Aug., i. 9, f., 136, f.
Philistines, The, i. 271.
Philo, i. 105; ii. 6, 305, 408.
Phœnico-Punic Language, i. 66, ff., 104.
——— Literature, i. 73, f.
——— Writing, ii. 366, ff.
Pico of Mirandola, i. 124; ii. 335.
Piscator, i. 132, 141.
Pococke, i. 136.
Poetical Language, i. 84, ff., 96, ff.
——— Books of the Old Testament, ii. 230, f.
Polus (*Synopsis Crit.*), i. 141.
Polyglot Bibles, i. 8; ii. 465, ff, 475.
Porphyrius, i. 5; ii. 198.
Prescriptive Authority of the Old Testament, ii. 346–352.
Priests, Relation of, to the Levites, i. 325, 346.
Procopius, of Gaza, i. 119.
Prophet, name and idea of, ii. 4, ff.
Prophets, Greater and Lesser, i. 33; ii. 120.
———, Priores, Posteriores, i. 33.
———, as Historians, i. 176–183; ii. 1, f.
———, Schools of, ii. 9, f.
———, Christian, ii, 11, 13, 27.
Prophetical Books of the Old Testament, i. 373, f.; ii. 41.
———, Their Compilation, ii. 120, 294.
———, Their Canonical Dignity, ii. 352; f.
Prophecy among the Hebrews, ii. 1 ff.; ii. 350.
Protestant Church, The, i. 7, 126, ff.; ii. 336, 344.
Proverbs, Book of, ii. 252, ff., 295, 297, f., 405.
Psalms, The, i. 86, ff., 373; ii. 230, ff., 293, f., 351, 353; in the LXX, ii., 407; in the Vulgate, ii. 434, f.

Pseudepigrapha of the Old Testament, ii. 304, f., 316, f.
Ptolemæus (Scholar of Valentinus), i. 192.
Puncta Extraordinaria, ii. 453.
Punctuation, Hebrew, i. 109; ii. 375, ff., 463, f.
———, in the other Semitic Languages, ii. 382.
Pustkuchen, i. 201.

Q.

Quadrate Character, The, ii. 366.
Quinta, The (translation), ii. 416.

R.

Rabbinical Dialect, The, i. 106, 134, f.
Rabbis, i. 105, f.
Rambach, f. f., i. 146.
Ranke, F. H., i. 26, 205, 263.
Ruschi, i. 109, 112, 114.
Rau, Sebaldus, ii. 362.
Raymundus Martini, i. 123; ii. 376.
Reading-books, ii. 322, 328, 334.
Reuchlin, i. 125.
Reusch, i. 20.
Rhyme in Hebrew Poetry? i. 88, ff.
Richard, of St. Victor, ii. 334.
Riehm, i. 322.
Rivetus, i. 8.
Rödiger, i. 152, 156.
Rosenmüller, i. 150, 201.
Rufinus, ii. 329, 333.
Rupert of Deutz, ii. 334.
Ruth, Book of, i. 35, 386, f., 390, ff.; ii. 295, 300, 309, 318.

S.

Saadia Gaon, i. 111, f., 114; ii. 381.
Sabians, The, their language, i. 62.
Sack, K. H., i. 201, 263; ii. 182, 199.
Sadducees, The, Canon of the, ii. 310, f.
Σαμαρειτικὸν, τὸ, ii. 430.
Salomo ben Melech, i. 115.
Salomo Parchon, i. 113.
Samaritans, The, i. 366; their language, i. 61; their writings, ii. 371, f.; their punctuation, ii. 383; their Canon, i. 367; ii. 311, f., 391, ff.
Samuel, as a prophet, ii. 9.
Samuel, Books of, i. 386, 394–406; ii. 294; their relations to the Chronicles, i. 438–442.

Sanchoniathon, i. 74.
Santes Pagninus, i. 8, 127 ; ii. 335.
Schindler, i. 135.
Schleiermacher, ii. 348.
Schlottmann, i. 158 ; ii. 277, 281.
Schmidt, Seb. i. 141.
Schoder, i. 150.
Scholz, i. 19, 151.
Schröder, N. W., i. 144.
Schultens, i. 144.
Schultz, J. C. F., i. 139, 150.
Scriptio plena et defectiva, i. 102, 440.
Scythians, The, in Jeremiah, ii. 66, f.
Semitic Language-stem, The, i. 39.
Semler, i. 16, f., 449.
Sens, The Synod of, ii. 341.
Septima, The (translation), ii. 416.
Septuagint, The, i. 105, 117, 120; ii. 120, 302, 380, 395, ff., 416 ; in relation to the Book of Jeremiah, ii. 84, ff., 405; to the Pentateuch, ii. 394, 399 ; to the rest of the Books, 404, ff.
Servant of God, The, ii. 62.
Sexta, The (translation), ii. 416.
Shallum, ii. 67, 169.
Shiloh, i. 284, 304, 327.
Sibylline Oracles, The, ii. 209.
Simonis, i. 148.
Sirach, Book of (or Ecclesiasticus), ii. 301, 339, 355.
Sixtus Senensis, i. 8, 449 ; ii. 342.
Solomon's Song, ii. 257–263, 298, 310.
Solomon's Writings, ii. 234, 252, ff.
Sommer, i. 90, 94.
Spinoza, i. 10, 195, f.
Stähelin, i. 24, 206, 322.
Stier, R., i. 26, 155 ; ii. 347, f., 475.
Strophes in Hebrew Poetry, i. 95.
Studer, i. 385.
Symmachus, ii. 415.
Synagogue, The Great, ii. 313
Syriac Language, The, i. 55, f.
―――― Literature, i. 59, f.
―――― Punctuation, ii. 382.
―――― Translation of the Bible, ii. 443, ff.
Σύρος, ὁ, ii. 430.

T.

Talmud, i. 107, 192, 380, 408, 422, 448; ii. 273, 309, 380.

Tanchum, i. 115.
Targums, i. 55 ; ii. 439, ff.
Tertullian, ii. 316.
Testament, Origin of the Name, i. 30, f.
Tetrapla, i. 117 ; ii. 420.
Thenius, i. 159.
Theodore of Mopsuestia, i. 119 ; ii. 231, 260.
Theodoret, i. 76, 119.
Theodotion, ii. 414, f.
Theophylact, i. 120.
Therapeutæ, Their Canon, ii. 311.
Tikkun Sopherim, ii. 152, 458.
Titles of the Old-Testament Books, i. 184.
Tobit, The Book of, ii. 339.
Translations of the Old Testament: Arabic, ii. 445, f. ; Chaldee, ii. 439 ; German, i. 129, f., 132, 148, 152, f, 160 ; Greek, i. 117–120; ii. 395; Latin, i. 127, 132, 149; ii. 431 ; Persian, ii. 449 ; Syriac, ii. 443 ; indirect translations, ii. 411, 438, 446.
Tridentine Council, ii. 341.
Tuch, Fried., i. 158, 205, 259, f.

U.

Umbreit, i. 161 ; ii. 162.

V.

Van Dale, on the Pentateuch, i. 196.
Vatablus, i. 127, f., 141.
Vater, i. 138, 148, 199, 259.
Vatke, on the Pentateuch, i. 204.
Venema, i. 146.
Venerable Bede, The, ii. 334, 438.
Veneta, Versio, i. 120 ; ii. 430.
Verse-Measures (Hebrew), i. 94.
Vienna, Council of, i. 124.
Visions of the Prophets, ii. 15, 39.
Vitringa, i. 139.
Von Baur, ii. 188.
Von Bohlen, i. 24, 204, 259.
Von Lengerke, i. 208 ; ii. 238.
Vossius, i. 12 ; ii. 360, 411.
Vulgate, The, i. 117, 122 ; ii. 341, 431, ff.

W.

Walther, Mich., i. 8.
Walton, i. 8 ; ii. 470.

Welte, i. 20, 263, 436.
Wessel, i. 124.
Western and Eastern Readings, ii. 462.
Whiston, i. 15; ii, 361.
Winer, i. 148, 153, 161.
Wisdom, the Book of, ii. 306, 341, 355.
Worship in High Places, i. 327, f., 383, 395, f.

X.

Ximenes, Cardinal, ii. 335, 466.

Y.

Year of Sabbath, i. 309.

Z.

Zechariah, Book of, ii. 159–175.
Zedekiah, ii. 73, ff.
Zephaniah, Book of, ii. 154, ff.; apocryphal Book of, ii. 157.

www.ingramcontent.com/pod-product-compliance
Lightning Source LLC
Chambersburg PA
CBHW021415300426
44114CB00010B/494